LAW, RELIGION, HEALTH AND HEALING IN AFRICA

Editors

M. Christian Green
Faith Kabata
Fortune Sibanda

Associate Editors

Abiola Akiyode-Afolabi
Mahfoud Ali Zoui
Loreen Maseno
Kenosi Molato

Law, Religion, Health and Healing in Africa

Published by African Sun Media under the SUN PReSS imprint
Place of publication: Stellenbosch, South Africa

All rights reserved

Copyright © 2022 ACLARS

Abstracts of conference papers published in this volume were peer reviewed and approved by the editorial board of the conference before the conference took place. Papers submitted for publication were subject to a further round of single-blind peer review by two reviewers, resulting in further revision of the papers for publication.

No part of this book may be reproduced or transmitted in any form or by any electronic, photographic or mechanical means, including photocopying and recording on record, tape or laser disk, on microfilm, via the Internet, by e-mail, or by any other information storage and retrieval system, without prior written permission by the publisher.

Views reflected in this publication are not necessarily those of the publisher.

First edition 2022

ISBN 978-1-991201-90-4
ISBN 978-1-991201-91-1 (e-book)
https://doi.org/10.52779/9781991201911

Set in Palatino Linotype 10/13

Cover design, typesetting and production by African Sun Media

SUN PReSS is an imprint of African Sun Media. Scholarly, professional and reference works are published under this imprint in print and electronic formats.

This publication can be ordered from:
orders@africansunmedia.co.za
Takealot: bit.ly/2monsfl
Google Books: bit.ly/2k1Uilm
africansunmedia.store.it.si *(e-books)*
Amazon Kindle: amzn.to/2ktL.pkL
JSTOR: https://bit.ly/3udc057

Visit africansunmedia.co.za for more information.

Contents

INTRODUCTION i
   M. Christian Green, Faith Kabata & Fortune Sibanda

I. LEGAL REGULATION OF RELIGION IN THE COVID-19 PANDEMIC

1   Covid-19, religious liberty and state overreach: Experiences from Zimbabwe 3
   Fortune Sibanda & Bernard Pindukai Humbe

2   "Seeking the face of God in trying times": Law, religion and the Covid-19 crisis in secular Ghana 15
   Seth Tweneboah

3   Religious freedom and responses to Covid-19 management in Masvingo District, Zimbabwe 33
   Excellent Chireshe

4   Covid-19, curtailment of religious liberty and religion-state relations in West Africa: Nigeria and Ghana in focus 53
   Idowu A. Akinloye

5   The Covid-19 pandemic, the AU Agenda 2063 and the relationship between law and religion in Nigeria 71
   Azizat Omoloyosi Amoloye-Adebayo & Barakat Adebisi Raji

II. RELIGION-STATE RELATIONS AND RELIGIOUS AUTHORITY IN THE COVID-19 PANDEMIC

6   Covid-19, power imbalance and the reshaping of state-religion relations in North Africa: The Algerian context 87
   Mahfoud Ali Zoui

7   The role of religious leaders in the Covid-19 crisis in Niger 99
   Seyni Moumouni

8   Religious responses to the Covid-19 pandemic: A comparative analysis of the spiritual methods of Christians and Muslims in Nigeria 111
   Francis O. Falako & Adam A. Sirajudeen

9   Government responses, religious authorities and justice innovations in the Covid-19 pandemic in Nigeria 127
   Hajara Ahmad Shuaib

III. COVID-19 CULTS, COMMUNICATIONS AND CONSPIRACIES

10   Digitalised cults in the time of the Covid-19 lockdown in Abidjan: Theological foundations of liturgical resilience 141
     Célestin Gnonzion†

11   The conflict between faith-based and science-based messages in public health pandemics in Africa 151
     Brian Muyunga

12   The role of legal and religious responses in debunking Covid-19 conspiracy theories in Africa 167
     Flora Alohan Onorerhinor

13   The socio-cultural foundations of the Waaba reluctance to vaccinate against Covid-19 in Benin 187
     *Tchokomi Sabine Toungakouagou Sama &
     N'Koué Emmanuel Sambiéni*

IV. SEX, GENDER AND VULNERABILITY IN THE COVID-19 PANDEMIC

14   Tamar's voice in the context of Covid-19: Re-reading 2 Samuel 13 for the dignity of women's sexuality 201
     Dorcas Chebet Juma

15   The Kenyan Covid-19 prevention protocols: An unexpected boost in the observance of the female *hijab* 217
     Moza Ally Jadeed

16   The impact of the Covid-19 lockdown on the informal sector in Zimbabwe: A legal perspective 237
     Lillian Mhuru

17   Pushed to the margin: The rights of women living with HIV and AIDS during lockdown in Zimbabwe 249
     Priccilar Vengesai

18   The effects of the Covid-19 pandemic on women in the United Church of Zambia 269
     Upendo Mwakasenga

19   Religious responses to domestic violence and mental health issues during the Covid-19 pandemic 287
     Opeyemi Oyewunmi Ekundayo

20   The impact of Covid-19 on infertility and assisted reproductive technology in Nigeria: Legal challenges and prospects 303
     Zaynab Omotoyosi Shittu-Adenuga

V. AFRICAN TRADITIONAL HEALING AND AFRICAN INITIATED CHURCHES

21   African Christianity, healing and Covid-19 in Zimbabwe: Re-thinking the efficacy of African Traditional Medicine 317
Molly Manyonganise, Clemence Makamure & Vengesai Chimininge

22   The syncretism healing atonement motif and African traditional healing in African Independent Churches in Botswana: A response to Covid-19 335
Kenosi Molato

23   Healing and deliverance in the context of the Covid-19 pandemic in Nomiya Church, Eastleigh, Kenya 349
Fancy Cheronoh & Telesia Kathini Musili

24   The African value of communality in virtual space amidst Covid-19: The case of WhatsApp welfare communities in Nomiya Church, Eastleigh 365
Telesia Kathini Musili & Fancy Cheronoh

25   Digital ethnography and networked theology: New forms of religious space and solidarity in Covid-19 at CITAM Ngong, Kenya 379
Loreen Maseno

VI. THEOLOGIES, SOLIDARITY AND SPACES IN COVID-19

26   "Behold, the end of all things in near": African theologies and beliefs about sin and death in times of Covid-19 395
Milda Alberto Bernardo Come & Marlino Eugénio Mubai

27   Towards healing our broken food system: A social and theological response to food insecurity in South Africa 413
Linda Naicker

28   The roles of law, religion and the Covid-19 pandemic in the rise and decline of South African church architecture 427
Yolanda van der Vyver

INDEX 443

INTRODUCTION

The Covid-19 pandemic was global in its spread and reach, as well as in its medical, social and economic effects. In many respects, the global effort to "flatten the curve" produced a flattening of experience around the world and a striking coincidence of similar experiences in countries the world over. In their original form, many of the chapters in this volume began with a nearly identical sentence: "In December 2019 and January 2020, a new virus emerged in China. On 11 March 2020, the World Health Organization declared Covid-19 to be a pandemic." Nearly every chapter followed this announcement with recitations of remarkably standard facts: the identification of the first Covid-19 case in each country, the implementation of a national lockdown, the extensions of lockdowns, the resort to face masks and social distancing, the development and distribution of the Covid-19 vaccine and a range of social, political and legal responses to all of the above. This was an editorial challenge – clearly, each chapter could not have the same beginning!

The identity, simultaneity and uniformity of experience were also manifest in common concerns at the intersection of law and religion in many nations around the world, including Africa. The lockdowns and closure of religious worship centres – churches, mosques and religious organisations of all sorts – raised questions of freedom of religion and the related concern for freedom of assembly, along with concerns about the relation of religion to science and public health, religious channels of communication and religious provision of social services. After all, health, communications and social services are all areas in which African religious organisations play key roles. Potential tensions around these issues raised further considerations about the nature of religion-state relations, the status of religious authority and whether religious and state actors would work together or at odds in addressing the Covid-19 pandemic.

Religion was also both implicated in – but also a potential antidote to – conspiracy theories about the coronavirus that were widely circulated in communities and particularly on social media. These conspiracy theories played a role in fuelling resistance to anti-Covid-19 public health measures and the Covid-19 vaccine, but they also became opportunities for religion to work with the state and with science to allay fears and distribute vaccines and other resources. In Africa, the common knowledge goes, people often prefer to get information and resources from religious leaders, rather than the state.

Amidst all of these commonalities, there were also differences that emerged – not only between countries but also within them – as the Covid-19 pandemic had disproportionate effects on already vulnerable or marginalised groups. Women and girls experienced greater exposure to sexual and domestic violence, often because they were locked down at home with their aggressors. Workers in the informal economic sector that dominates many African economies experienced particular economic hardships from restrictions on movement. Other vulnerabilities involved

HIV status, mental illness and other sources of marginalisation, often in ways that intersected with gender, poverty and other factors. There were new challenges for people seeking non-Covid-19-related forms of health care, such as treatment for infertility. Even so, some previously marginalised groups, such as *hijabi* women in Africa's Muslim communities, reported feeling greater freedom in wearing their chosen garb in a context in which most in society were wearing face masks.

There were also distinctively African methods of coping that emerged in the Covid-19 pandemic. Some groups resorted to African traditional methods and healing, including a wide variety of plants and herbs, to address Covid-19 symptoms and restore vigour. African Initiated Churches drew on norms of community and *Ubuntu*, particularly where technology allowed them to develop new forms of virtual space and online community. The Covid-19 pandemic even affected basic understandings and uses of physical space, pushing people into private homes and away from schools, marketplaces and worship sites, but in ways that also illustrated the value of congregate worship in religious spaces. In the pandemic, Africans formed groups of mutual aid and support, while also being pushed in new ways to deal with long-standing issues of food insecurity and move forward on projects such as the African Union's Agenda 2063 and creating "The Africa We Want".

Overall, even though deficits of tracking and tracing may obscure some of the full-scale effects of Covid-19 in Africa, there is the sense that Africa came out better than expected by sceptics in parts of the world considered to be more advanced.[1] This has been attributed to various factors, including a younger population, more of life lived outdoors in warmer climates and the overarching value of *Ubuntu* and care for community.[2] There is a sense that the world may have much to learn from Africa not only about Covid-19,[3] but about health and healing more broadly, in ways that implicate both law and religion. While not immune from religious freedom controversies, conspiracy theories and vaccine hesitancy that hindered the Covid-19 response in other countries, Africa came through the pandemic in a way that took some more affluent and developed parts of the world quite by surprise. The contents of this volume may provide some indications as to how and why.

The first part of this book, on "Legal Regulation of Religion in the Covid-19 Pandemic", addresses concerns about the particular effects that anti-Covid-19 measures

---

1 Soy A. 2020. "Coronavirus in Africa: Five Reasons Why Covid-19 Has Been Less Deadly than Elsewhere", *BBC*, 8 October; Campbell J. "COVID Less Deadly in Africa", *Africa in Transition* / Council on Foreign Relations, 29 September.
2 Nolen S. 2022. "Trying to Solve a Mystery: Africa's Low Death Rates", *New York Times*, 23 March; Ezeh A, Silverman M and Stranges S. 2021. "Why has Covid had less of an impact in Africa", *Quartz*, 23 August; Fauzia M. 2020. "Fact Check: Coronavirus deaths across the continent of Africa are far less than in U.S.", *USA Today*, 9 December; Munyati C, Dana G, De Bruin C. 2021. "Africa's Covid-19 response: It's all about people on the ground", World Economic Forum, 12 November. But see Taylor A. 2022. "Africa may have been hit harder by Covid-19 than anyone knew", *Washington Post*, 18 February.
3 Spinney L. 2021. "What can we learn from Africa's experience of Covid?", *The Guardian*, 28 February; Pilling D. 2020. "How Africa fought the pandemic – and what coronavirus has taught the world", *Financial Times*, 20 February.

introduced by the state had on religion, particularly freedoms of religion, assembly, and worship practices. In their chapter on religious liberty and state overreach in Zimbabwe, Fortune Sibanda and Bernard Pindukai Humbe lay out the case made by many groups – not only in Zimbabwe but around Africa and the rest of the world – that state measures taken against Covid-19 infringed upon the freedom of religion of religious groups. In their study of resistance by African Initiated Churches of the Apostolic and Zionist traditions to state regulations, Sibanda and Humbe focus on how the regulations, operating as "carrots and sticks" were unevenly applied, such that the law functioned as a "spider's web" in which only the "little insects" were caught.

A more positive interaction of religion and the state is evident in Seth Tweneboah's chapter on the interaction of law and religion in Ghana, even in the context of Ghana's constitutional separation of church and state. While religion played a "dual role" in limiting and promoting public health measures against the Covid-19 pandemic, the Ghanaian state was able to marshal religious actors in the anti-Covid-19 push in a way that Tweneboah argues raises questions about Ghanaian secularism. Covid-19 proved to be an environment in which the Ghanaian president, media and other sectors affirmed the public's need to "seek the face of God in trying times" and the necessity of religion and state working together to address the pandemic.

Excellent Chireshe gives a sense of how these religion-state relations played out on the ground in her chapter on Protestant, Pentecostal and African Initiated Churches (AICs) in Zimbabwe and their responses to the effects of Covid-19 regulations. Each of the Christian traditions surveyed in Chireshe's chapter differs from the others in its relationship to biomedical versus spiritual approaches to health and healing, with Protestants embracing the biomedical model as an important legacy of their connection to missionary health centres, Pentecostals giving primacy to spiritual healing and the AICs largely rejecting Western medicine for spiritual healing approaches. These various orientations between biomedical and spiritual approaches to health and healing significantly conditioned their responses to government-imposed regulations.

A comparison of Nigerian and Ghanaian approaches to the pandemic is the focus on Idowu Akinloye's chapter. Akinloye examines constitutional protections of freedom of religion as well as laws in each country on religious preaching, and how these were necessarily modified or limited in the pandemic context. While both Nigeria and Ghana take largely secular state approaches to the state-religion relation, Akinloye chronicles how a separationist paradigm of state and religion gave rise in Covid-19 to a more cordial model of state-religion relations, as religion in Nigeria and Ghana largely supported state lockdown, bans on religious gathering, and other measures in order to stem the pandemic.

Rounding out the first section, Azizat Amoloye-Adebayo and Barakat Raji's chapter examines the religion-state relation in Nigeria through the lens of the African Union's aspirations expressed in the document "Agenda 2063: The Africa We Want". Challenging the idea of religion as a purveyor of conflict and violence,

Amoloye-Adebayo and Raji emphasise the positive role that religion can play – with law – towards the promotion of human flourishing. This positive use of religion is one that they see operating in the Agenda 2063 aspirations in a way that can be especially important in conflict-torn societies like Nigeria and in confronting challenges like the Covid-19 pandemic.

Building upon this prospect of the positive uses of religion in addressing threats to health and healing and in promoting good governance, chapters in the book's second part, "Religion-State Relations and Religious Authority in the Covid-19 Pandemic", examine the role of religious authority in the Covid-19 pandemic. In his chapter on Algeria, Mahfoud Ali Zoui, describes how contestation over religious authority in Covid-19, took place against the backdrop of a popular movement against authoritarianism, the Hirak, which was significantly disrupted by the pandemic itself. Increased state surveillance of and intervention in religion by a government that already had a monopoly on religious life with Islam as the state religion raised particular challenges for Algeria's imams, mosques and religious and charitable institutions, as well as for non-Muslim groups. The use of emergency decrees and provisions by the state became controversial, in some cases giving rise to competing fatwas between the government and Muslim leaders, as religious leaders sought to maintain authority within the confines of their official religious establishment.

The situation was somewhat similar in Niger, though as Seyni Moumouni recounts in his chapter, the backdrop was not a popular resistance movement, but the decade-long persistence of terrorist-driven, armed conflict. As a result of this conflict, Niger's social, health and education sectors were already weak before the Covid-19 pandemic. In light of this, the Nigerian government took immediate measures to seek to control the pandemic's spread, while also recommending national prayer and inviting the participation of religious leaders in the anti-Covid-19 effort. Muslim and Christian religious leaders marshalled scriptural and theological resources in support of the government's pandemic measures. Even so, abuses of government authority are said to have occurred with "securitisation" of the pandemic, resulting in threats to freedom of religion and other human rights.

The social and psychological role of religion in Covid-19 and its implications for religious authority is the focus of Francis Falako's and Adam Sirajudeen's chapter, which examines strategies for coping with the pandemic among Muslim and Christian groups in Nigeria. Falako and Sirajudeen describe responses by some Nigerian Muslims that either discounted the pandemic as not real or not serious or spiritualised the pandemic as punishment from God – both of which discouraged adherence to government measures. Some Islamic scholars did grapple theologically with the merits and demerits of some of the measures, but Falako and Sirajudeen report considerably less subscription to anti-Covid-19 measures among the Muslim communities in Nigeria's northern states. Some Nigerian Christians viewed Covid-19 through lenses of sin or "end times" theologies in ways that led to resistance to government measures; while others, especially in more urban areas, adapted readily to online worship and prayer. Thus, both Muslims and Christians resorted to "spiritual metrics" to cope with Covid-19, but the particular ways in which they did so had different implications for the collaboration of religious and government authorities.

Also writing from the Nigerian context, Hajara Ahmad Shuaib, focuses on the role of religious leaders in Bauchi and Plateau states in Nigeria's northern and central regions. By Shuaib's account, illiteracy and religious beliefs were factors that impeded adherence to the government's anti-Covid-19 regulations by both Muslims and Christians there. As in other African nations, there were concerns about the Nigerian government's adherence during the course of the pandemic to constitutional and international commitments to freedom of religion and the "*forum internum*" of believers. Even so, some religious groups did end up supporting government regulations. In its enforcement of the pandemic regulations, the Nigerian government and justice system also innovated through new judicial mechanisms of mobile and virtual courts.

One thing that became apparent in the Covid-19 pandemic, globally, was the key role played by new means of communication – particularly digitised communications and social media – for good and for ill. These responses are taken up in the book's third section on "Covid-19 Cults, Communications and Conspiracies". On the side of good, Célestin Gnonzion, chronicles how "digitalised cults" and worship practice developed in the Catholic Church in Côte d'Ivoire. The shift to digital cultic practices became necessary during Holy Week 2020, the first occurrence of the pinnacle of the Christian year in the Covid-19 pandemic. These digitalised cultic practices proved not only to be justified within the Catholic Church by papal pronouncements but also to be key methods of resilience during crisis for Ivorian Catholics under Covid-19, offering "'real' possibility through the 'virtual' to meet God". With great sadness, we publish this chapter posthumously, as Gnonzion passed away suddenly after surgery, just one week after submitting his chapter for publication. We reflect further on Gnonzion's passing below.

Where Gnonzion focused on the theological justifications for new methods of worship and community, Brian Muyunga focuses on the content of the communications themselves, specifically the contrast between faith-based and science-based methods of communication when it comes to matters of public health, such as Covid-19. Though both faith-based and science-based messages were resorted to by Africans in the Covid-19 pandemic, Muyunga argues for the need to promote harmony, instead of conflict, between faith and science. Through interviews with religious and public health leaders in Uganda, Muyunga lifts up three strategies for harmonising faith and science messages and argues for their inclusion in training programs for both religious and public health professionals.

When it comes to questionable Covid-19 communications, Africa seems to have been a locus for the proliferation of conspiracy theories of all kinds. Flora Alohan Onomrerhinor examines the conspiracies around Covid-19 that arose in Nigeria. As the abundant literature from scholars around Africa recounts, many of these theories circulated not only around Africa but also the world – and yet they seem to have had particular cogency and breadth of communication in Nigeria. Onomrerhinor identifies particular roles that religion and media could and did play in debunking Covid-19 conspiracy theories, while also noting the way in which the law was confounded by and ill-equipped to deal with conspiracies and their technologies of transmission.

Among the Waaba people of Benin, conspiracy theories were just one of several social and cultural factors leading to vaccine hesitancy, as Sabine Toungakouagou Sama and Emmanuel Sambiéni describe in their chapter. In Benin, divergent opinions about the existence of Covid-19, certain vocabularies and cultural referents that developed around the disease and the availability of alternative treatments prompted many Waaba to discount the novelty and severity of the disease. Alongside these factors were religious understandings of pandemics as reflective of discontent against humans by a Supreme Being. These factors conspired to keep vaccine rates low among the Waaba people.

The fourth part of the book, on "Sex, Gender and Vulnerability in the Covid-19 Pandemic", builds on our ongoing interest at ACLARS in the distinctive experiences of African women. It also explores how sex, gender and other factors produced distinctive vulnerabilities in the Covid-19 pandemic. Dorcas Juma's chapter on re-reading 2 Samuel 13 towards the dignity of women's sexuality examines reconsiders an oft-read and reinterpreted passage of the rape of Tamar in the context of Covid-19, thereby bringing biblical wisdom to the problem of sexual and gender-based violence that worsened for women in Kenya under Covid-19.

Moza Jadeed examines another aspect of the Kenyan experience of the pandemic, namely the relief that Kenyan Muslim women who wear the *hijab* experienced under anti-Covid-19 regulations requiring face masks and other coverings and various forms of social distancing. *Hijabi* women who had experienced marginalisation and discrimination for wearing the *hijab* prior to Covid-19 in many cases found the same practices validated and normalised under the Covid-19 regulatory regime. This aspect of the pandemic had important liberatory effects – a "silver lining" – for *hijabi* women, both personally and in educational and professional settings, while also illustrating the unnecessity and illegality of discrimination against *hijabi* women pre-Covid-19.

Writing from Zimbabwe, Lillian Mhuru examines another vulnerability created by the Covid-19 pandemic that affected women not exclusively, but disproportionately. This was the dramatic economic effect of the various lockdowns and shutdowns particularly on workers in the informal sectors that dominate many African economies. Mhuru focuses on the informal trade sector, dominated by women, and the informal transportation sector, dominated by men. The lockdowns and closure of borders made it difficult, if not impossible, for transporters to procure goods for traders to sell, particularly the imported goods that predominate in many African markets, forcing many informal workers in the transport and trade fields to seek new strategies for survival.

In another chapter from Zimbabwe, Priccilar Vengesai examines the new vulnerabilities that Covid-19 introduced into the lives of Zimbabwean women living with HIV and AIDS. Much as with Mhuru's chapter on the informal economic sector, these were effects that impacted both men and women living with HIV. But while HIV and AIDS affects both men and women, Vengesai argues that women suffered disproportionately under lockdowns that not only prevented them from accessing life-preserving antiretroviral treatments, but also did so in ways that violated a range of their human rights. These included the rights to health, water, food, privacy and even freedom of religion.

The pandemic experience of women in the United Church of Zambia (UCZ), the largest Protestant church in Zambia and one whose membership is 60% women, is the focus of a chapter by Upendo Mwakasenga. Focusing on two UCZ congregations, Mwakasenga exposes how women were often frontline theological workers for the church, given their significant role in weddings, funerals and other aspects of church life, in ways that made them especially vulnerable to Covid-19 infection. Their vulnerability was exacerbated by caregiving inequalities between spouses and by women's lesser access than men to cellphones and other technologies to enable virtual communication and community.

The particular vulnerabilities of women from mental illness and domestic violence in Nigeria are the subject of Opeyemi Ekundayo's chapter. Ekundayo describes a cultural climate in which mental illness continues to be stigmatised and domestic violence is often a religious problem. The chapter draws significantly on Ekundayo's interviews with a Muslim imam, a Pentecostal pastor and a chief priest from the Obatala traditional religion to uncover each religious tradition's ways of addressing mental illness and domestic violence in the home. Both of these problems were exacerbated by the Covid-19 lockdowns in ways that made it both difficult and imperative for spouses and other family members to access help outside the home.

Zaynab Shittu-Adenuga examines the impact of Covid-19 on access to assisted reproductive technologies by couples experiencing infertility in Nigeria's robust infertility treatment industry. Infertility has a gendered dimension in Nigeria, as it is often culturally ascribed to women, sometimes in religiously inflected ways, even though both men and women can experience a range of conditions leading to difficulty conceiving and infertility. Shittu-Adenuga uncovers, in part through survey data, the difficulties that those experiencing infertility had in accessing treatment, a problem made worse by weaknesses in Nigeria's legal framework surrounding assisted reproductive technologies.

The fifth part of the book, on "African Traditional Healing and African Initiated Churches", contains chapters examining the resources that distinctively African institutions brought to bear in addressing the Covid-19 pandemic. In their chapter from Zimbabwe, Molly Manyonganise, Clemence Makamure and Vengesai

Chimininge examine the implications of Covid-19 for African traditional medicine (ATM). It was a context in which Zimbabweans, with many across Africa, found new utility and efficacy in ATM in treating Covid-19 symptoms, even as both faith healing and scientific medicine seemed ineffective against the disease. Manyonganise and her colleagues examine this resurgence of ATM through the lens of decolonial theory.

The particular value of syncretism of Western and traditional medicine is the focus of Kenosi Molato's examination of the responses of African Initiated Churches in Botswana, in what he describes as a "syncretism healing atonement motif". Molato provides an account of the suppression of African traditional healing methods by Western missionaries as part of the reason that AICs were established in the first place. The AICs became key institutions for the syncretism of cultural and religious concepts into methods of healing. This syncretism opened the door to blending theologies of water and plant-based healing into the range of treatments deployed against Covid-19.

Reflecting the location of this year's ACLARS conference in Kenya, the next three chapters involve close studies of particular African Initiated Church congregations and how they grappled with the challenge of Covid-19. Research collaborators Fancy Cheronoh and Telesia Musili both focus on the Nomiya Church, Eastleigh, in Nairobi and how its members coped with Covid-19. Nomiya Church was the first independent church to be established in Kenya. The chapter led by Cheronoh gives an overview of Nomiya Church, health and healing in African independent churches, and the challenges of the lockdown on community life. The chapter led by Musili takes up the particular challenges associated with death and grief in Covid-19 and how Nomiya Church members turned to WhatsApp groups as a means of sharing grief, support and material aid to those experiencing illness and death.

Loreen Maseno's chapter explores the world of the CITAM Ngong Church in Kajiado, Kenya, and how the resort to online worship and community under the Covid-19 lockdown produced new forms of religious space that were novel and challenging both for congregants and the scholars who study them. Maseno examines the rise of a "networked theology" at CITAM Ngong that necessitated "digital ethnography" as a method of study. It was one in which CITAM Ngong members experienced "divine action, transcendent presence and supernatural reality in the virtual world" and an "amplification of transcendent presence and intimacies in the virtual space" in a way that had distinctly impacted both member and scholarly participant observers.

The final section of the book, on "Theologies, Security and Spaces in Covid-19", collects chapters that probe theological approaches to security and space under themes of *kairos, ecclesia* and *koinonia* and the implications of these for health and healing. Milda Come's and Marlino Mubai's chapter surveys Catholic, Protestant and Islamic responses in Mozambique to Covid-19 and to the lengthy list of regulations enacted by the Mozambican government to secure the population from the pandemic. The survey includes studies of the scriptural and theological resources regarding sin and death to which members of the various religious denominations resorted to cope with the pandemic and bolster compliance with the government's many anti-Covid-19 measures.

Linda Naicker's chapter examines a different problem of security that grew worse during the Covid-19 pandemic – namely, the persistent problem of food insecurity, with which so many African nations struggle. As Naicker observes, through an apt quote by Arundhati Roy, even though many around the world wanted a return to "normality" amidst the "new normal" of the pandemic, the problem of food security in Africa illustrates how a return to the pre-existing normal would be an injustice. Instead, Naicker calls upon churches and governments, including the government of her native South Africa, to use the crisis of Covid-19 as an opportunity "*re-envision* a more healthy and inclusive society, where poverty is holistically addressed and measured to eradicate food insecurity and food related health disparities are decisively challenged and confronted".

In the book's final chapter, Yolanda van der Vyver examines the role of church architecture as a source of both *ecclesia* and *koinonia*. As Van der Vyver notes, "Christianity is a congregational religion, not built around the individual, but rather focused on the sense of community through worship or *koinonia*." While much has been made of the transfer of ecclesial functions to new spaces – particularly virtual spaces – Van der Vyver argues that there are certain functions of *ecclesia* and *koinonia* that require a physical architecture. Within the security and shelter of the ecclesial walls, the architecture of the church becomes both a site, source and symbol of "assembly and community, liturgy and ritual, sacred space, spiritual healing and pastoral care".

One thing that became apparent in the editing of this volume was the profusion of description. Whereas many essays in ACLARS's past have parsed texts and traditions and elaborated and expounded upon theories within legal, religious studies, it seemed that the shock and novelty of the Covid-19 pandemic, required much description just to articulate the basic facts of what was occurring, along with all of the concepts of "lockdown", "flattening the curve", "personal protective equipment", "social distancing" and more that made their way into the lexicon of the "new normal". There is a reason for the many surveys, interviews and ethnographies in the present volume. Just figuring out what was going on became a global challenge in Covid-19 amidst scientific unknowns, rampant conspiracies and other forces that challenged notions of facts and authority. And even though the stories began in the same way with the emergence of the Covid-19 pandemic, there were many distinct facets and effects of Covid-19 to chronicle.

As the world began to emerge from Covid-19 in the summer of 2022, we at ACLARS suffered our own loss of Célestin Gnonzion, a contributor to this volume and the leading light behind our planning for the next ACLARS conference on "Law, Religion and Reconciliation in Africa" to take place in his home country of Côte d'Ivoire. The loss of Célestin was not a loss due to Covid-19, but it was an especially sad and tragic event for our ACLARS organisation in a trying time for the entire world. Célestin saw the Covid-19 as a crisis containing the seeds of possible resilience. We look forward to honouring his life and contributions to ACLARS at our 2023 conference in Abidjan, modelling resilience in the face of tragedy.

M. Christian Green
Senior Fellow, Centre for the Study of Law and Religion, Emory University, USA
Editor, Journal of Law and Religion and Canopy Forum
Publications Manager, African Consortium for Law and Religion Studies

Faith Kabata
Lecturer in Law, Kenyatta University School of Law, Kenya
Board Member, African Consortium for Law and Religion Studies

Fortune Sibanda
Professor of Religious Studies, Department of Philosophy and Religious Studies, Great Zimbabwe University
Professor of Religious Studies, Department of Theology and Religious Studies, University of Eswatini
Academic Associate/Research Fellow, Research Institute for Theology and Religion, College of Human Sciences, University of South Africa
Board Member, African Consortium for Law and Religion Studies

I. Legal regulation of religion in the Covid-19 pandemic

1 Covid-19, Religious Liberty and State Overreach: Experiences from Zimbabwe

Fortune Sibanda[1]
Bernard Pindukai Humbe[2]

The law is a spider's web; only the little insects get caught in it.
– African Proverb[3]

INTRODUCTION

The coronavirus (Covid-19) pandemic is the largest public health crisis that has ever manifested in contemporary times.[4] As the pandemic took its toll, both rich and poor nations were affected, as many were underprepared for the disease. Indeed, the pandemic worsened fragile public health care systems, the situation of religious liberty and shook the levels of rule of law in Africa and beyond. Radical measures, backed by regulations, were introduced by different governments to reduce the spread of the Covid-19 pandemic and the impact and deaths incurred from the disease. State regulatory systems evoked to curb the spread of Covid-19 were either justified or invited criticism, the latter often in the form of lawsuits that sought to defend constitutionally guaranteed rights to freedom of religion.[5] In Zimbabwe, the legal basis for measures adopted in response to Covid-19 include the Civil Protection Act, 1989, the Public Health Act, 2018, and the Public Health (Covid-19 Prevention, Containment and Treatment) (National Lockdown) Order, 2020. These

---

1 Professor of Religious Studies, Department of Philosophy and Religious Studies, Great Zimbabwe University and Professor of Religious Studies, Department of Theology and Religious Studies, University of Eswatini. Academic Associate/Research Fellow, Research Institute for Theology and Religion, College of Human Sciences, University of South Africa. This chapter emerged as part of the end products from a broader research project titled "African Spirituality, Health and Well-being in the Face of the Covid-19 Pandemic in Zimbabwe", where Professor Fortune Sibanda was the Project Leader/Principal Investigator to a five-member Team at Great Zimbabwe University. The research project was generously supported by the Nagel Institute for the Study of World Christianity at Calvin College, USA, under the theme "Engaging African Realities".

2 Lecturer, Department of Philosophy and Religious Studies, Great Zimbabwe University. Academic Associate/Research Fellow, Research Institute for Theology and Religion, College of Human Sciences, University of South Africa.

3 African proverb that depicts the unequal impact that the law has in some African societies including Zimbabwe. It shows the selective application of the law by the government among its citizens thereby resulting in legal inconsistencies.

4 See, for example, Sibanda F, Muyambo T and Chitando E. 2022. *Religion and the Covid-19 Pandemic in Southern Africa*. London and New York: Routledge.

5 Van Coller H and Akinloye IA. 2022. "Religion, Law and Covid-19 in South Africa", in Sibanda F, Muyambo T and Chitando E (eds). 2022. *Religion and the Covid-19 Pandemic in Southern Africa*. London and New York: Routledge, 89.

statutes effected lockdowns and travel restrictions and prohibited gatherings for worship services. Such regulatory measures affected the flourishing of religious liberty in Zimbabwe, which beckons for a closer interrogation.

This chapter seeks to examine religious liberty and state overreach in the context of Covid-19 pandemic using the experiences from Zimbabwe. Despite the government's noble cause to curb the pandemic by any means necessary, we argue that some Apostolic and Zionist church groups defied government policies regarding public health safety measures meant to treat and reduce the spread of Covid-19 in a way brought them under justifiable scrutiny in Zimbabwe.[6] We further argue that there was a selective application of the law by the government among the Apostolic and Zionist churches. In other words, when the state selectively applied the law in favour of some Apostolic and Zionist groups, it created a legal "comedy of errors". This confirms the assertion by the English writer Charles Dickens that "the law is an ass".[7] The paradox of effecting exceptions to some regulatory measures, such as the ban on religious gatherings, puts the African proverb in the above epigraph to the fore. Thus, like a spider's web, the Zimbabwean law tended to trap only "the little insects"– namely, certain African Initiated Churches.

In the context of the present study, we concur with the observations by Helena van Coller and Idowu Akinloye, accomplished scholars of law and religion in South Africa and Nigeria, respectively, that the lockdown regulations restricted "the constitutionally guaranteed human rights, including the rights to freedom of movement, freedom of association, freedom of religion and the right to human dignity, among others."[8] Therefore, one of the key research questions with which this the study grappled was: does a health emergency such as Covid-19 pandemic allow the government to violate human rights and freedom of religion? The present study established that there was an ambivalent approach by the government towards religious liberty in the process of controlling the spread of Covid-19 pandemic in Zimbabwe. While the Constitution of Zimbabwe, 2013,[9]

---

6 The Apostolic and Zionist church groups are churches known by the acronym "AICs", which translate to various labels such as African Initiated Churches, African Independent Churches, African Indigenous Churches, African International Churches and African Instituted Churches. These churches were established and led by Africans as offshoots from the Western mainline missionary Christianity. In this study, the Apostolic and Zionist churches are not Pentecostal. They lay emphasis on the fusion of African Indigenous Religion and Christian beliefs in their modes of worship, theology and practice, in varied proportions. See, for example, Sibanda F and Maposa RS. 2014. "The Ethic of Economic Engagement in AICs", in Chitando E, Gunda MR and Kugler J (eds). *Multiplying in the Spirit: African Initiated Churches in Zimbabwe*, Bible in Africa Studies, No. 15. Bamberg: University of Bamberg Press, 217-226.

7 Charles Dickens meant that there are times when the law is useless to society, thereby it is like a stupid ass. See Sibanda F. 2018. "The Legality of Witchcraft Allegations in Colonial and Postcolonial Zimbabwe", in Green MC, Gunn TJ and Hill M (eds). *Law and Security in Africa*. Stellenbosch: African Sun Media, 313.

8 Van Coller and Akinyole, "Religion, Law and Covid-19 in South Africa", 89.

9 Constitution of Zimbabwe Amendment (No. 20) Act, 2013.

protects certain fundamental rights and freedoms, such as rights to life, health care, worship and to food and water, some of these rights were violated by the state, thereby resulting in legal inconsistencies. Before delving into the details of the legal restrictions and related inconsistencies, we turn to the conceptual framework and research methodology.

CARROTS AND STICKS:
A RESEARCH FRAMEWORK AND METHODOLOGY

This qualitative study was guided by the "carrot and stick"[10] conceptual framework. In the "carrot and stick" approach, the carrot stands for incentive that promises pleasure, and the stick stands for pressure to punish.[11] In other words, carrot refers to the rewards, which are given or promised to individuals in order for them to act in a desired way, while the stick refers to punishments that are to be inflicted on individuals for not acting in the desired way. This entails power dynamics whereby power is the ability to *affect the behaviour of others either through coercion, payment, and or attraction*.[12] The carrot and stick approach emanates from an analogy of "a cart driver who seeks to both induce his mule to move forward by dangling a carrot in front of it as well as goad/force it into moving forward by wielding the stick from behind".[13] Thus, an individual is given carrot, that is, a reward when they perform efficiently and is jabbed with a stick or is given a punishment in case of non-performance. This fable is applicable in determining a range of relations, such as religion and state, gender dynamics and international relations.

Carrots and sticks can be applied either concurrently or serially, that is, one after another. The relationship is determined by the particular context prevailing in a certain historical epoch as well as the worldview of the decision-maker concerned. Therefore, the carrot and stick are instruments employed to make the other party

---

10 The "carrot and stick" approach of motivation is based on the principles of reinforcement traceable to Jeremy Bentham, an English philosopher, who developed his ideas during the Industrial Revolution. Thereafter, "carrot and stick" concept has been used in many contexts. For instance, the concept has been deployed in the sphere of politics and management of health care where reference is made to "soft power" (incentives/rewards) and "hard power" (coercion/punishment). In US political theory circles, Professor Joseph Nye, a political scientist at Harvard, is associated with the use of "soft power". See Nye JS. 2009. "Get Smart: Combining Hard and Soft Power", *Foreign Affairs* 88(4):160-163. In the African context, the concept has also been applied in peace and conflict situations, such as in 2018, when East African leaders were expected to use both carrots and sticks to force the warring sides to compromise in South Sudan. See Yusuf M. 2018. "South Sudan: Only Incentives, Pressure Can Achieve South Sudan Peace – Analysts", *Voice of America*, 14 May. Further use of the "carrot and stick" approach can be found in the management of Covid-19 vaccine hesitancy in Africa. See, for example, Elks S. 2021. "Africa: Carrot or Sticks? How Countries are Tackling Covid-19 Vaccine Hesitancy". Thomson Reuters Foundation, 1.

11 Nye, JS. 2009. "Get Smart: Combining Hard and Soft Power", *Foreign Affairs* 88(4):160-163.

12 Nye, "Get Smart: Combining Hard and Soft Power", 160.

13 Lemu AA. 2020. "Carrots and Sticks for Ethiopia's Election", *Aiga Forum*, 21 March.

change their policy on a particular issue in tune with what one desires. However, there is no guarantee of success, whether carrots or sticks are employed either serially or together. For example, the Johanne Marange Apostolic Church defied the government order for its members to be vaccinated and to observe the bans on church gatherings at the height of the Covid-19 pandemic in Zimbabwe.[14] In addition, despite the shortcomings of the approach, it remains useful to employ it to evaluate the case of the Zimbabwe government's relations with the African Initiated Churches. As such, it can be argued that the state's use of carrots and sticks worked only up to a certain extent in enforcing Covid-19 regulations. This implies that the other party, that is, the AICs, had their own interests and, moreover, practically did not consider the carrots sweet enough or the stick painful enough.

The present study utilised documentary analysis of print and electronic media of newspapers and social media, ethnographical observations of religious and social practices of participants and in-depth interviews with AIC leaders, adherents and legal experts to gather data. The study utilised purposive sampling in in-depth interviews encompassing 15 participants from five AICs, consisting of three Apostolic churches and two Zionist churches in Masvingo and Bikita Districts.[15] Out of ethical considerations, the research observed voluntary informed consent, anonymity and confidentiality. There was no reference to actual names of participants in the study, except for those who are in the public domain through electronic and print media.

In addition, the study used a public theological approach (PTA) and interpretive phenomenological analysis (IPA). As for PTA, David Bromell, a systematic theologian, identifies public theology as a branch of Christian theology that "reflects critically on the ethical and political implications, here and now, of claims expressed or implied in religious faith and witness, and does so in the public sphere, in publicly accessible ways".[16] In other words, public theology is a form of applied theology, which provides the meaning and truth of Christian faith and witness. According to Frits de Lange, a professor of systematic theology and ecclesiology at Stellenbosch University, historically, health care is one of the key domains where the Christian Church started its public engagement.[17] This is summarised in the biblical scripture John 3:16, which says, "God so loved the world that he gave his only Son, so that everyone who believes in him may not perish but may have eternal life." Lange further states that theological reflection on health care needs to start with the experience of the love of God and Jesus's promise of an abundant life for those

---

14 See, for example, Moyo J. 2020. "Zimbabwe's Open-Air Churches Fueling the Spread of Covid-19", *Anadolu Agency*, 27 August.

15 Purposive sampling is a qualitative research technique mainly used in for the identification and selection of information-rich cases knowledgeable about or experienced with a phenomenon of interest. See Cresswell JW. and Plano Clark VL. 2011. *Designing and Conducting Mixed Method Research* (2nd ed.). Thousand Oaks, CA: Sage.

16 Bromell D. 2011. "What is Public Theology?", *ResearchGate*, January.

17 De Lange F. 2017. "Public Theology and Health Care", in Kim S and Day K (eds). *A Companion to Public Theology*. Leiden: Brill, 235.

who share in it, as the heart of Christian faith (cf. John 10:10).[18] Christians, in other words, believe in and experience a God who cares. In the context of the majority of AICs, *Mweya Mutsvene* (the Holy Spirit) and the love of God can protect them from diseases, including the Covid-19 pandemic. Therefore, PTA is helpful to provide a hermeneutical tool for understanding the experiences and responses of the AICs to the Covid-19 restrictions and guidelines.

The PTA was corroborated by the use of interpretive phenomenological analysis. IPA is a method designed to understand people's lived experiences and how they make sense of it in the context of their personal and social worlds.[19] With IPA, the main thrust of the method is to get as close as possible to the lived experience of participants, in order to examine them in detail. Through this approach, the researchers were in a position to get insider perspectives from participants and to elicit thick descriptions that captured their emotions and experiences. The personal meanings associated with the lived experiences of participants were regarded as vital in IPA.[20] IPA was useful for this chapter to address a variety of research questions in health-related experiences, such as receiving a medical diagnosis and the popular reception of Covid-19 tests and vaccinations in Zimbabwe.

AFRICAN INDIGENOUS CHURCHES IN ZIMBABWE: AN OVERVIEW

African Initiated Churches are variegated spirit-type churches, which include Apostolic and Zionist groups.[21] They have a strong sense of patriarchy in their outlook. These church groups meet at *masowe* (open sacred spaces) mostly in the periphery of residential areas, forests and on hills.[22] Though they put on garments of different colours, depending on a prescription given by their prophets, but largely Apostolic church adherents use white garments, which has earned them a descriptor *venguwo chena*, meaning those of white garments. In the context of the Zionist churches sampled for this study, the members use different colours such as green, red, blue, white and yellow for their regalia. The AICs are mainly faith healing institutions.[23] The faith healing in AICs has attracted a large following in rural and urban spaces. Since they strongly believe that healing is provided by the Holy

---

18 De Lange, "Public Theology and Health Care", 235.
19 Smith JA and Nizza IE. 2022. *Essentials of Interpretive Phenomenological Analysis.* Washington, DC: American Psychological Association, 3.
20 Smith and Nizza, *Essentials of Interpretive Phenomenological Analysis*, 4.
21 Sibanda F and Maposa RS. 2013. "Behind the Smokescreen: African Instituted Churches and Political Processes in Zimbabwe", in Chitando E (ed). *Prayers and Players: Religion and Politics in Zimbabwe.* Harare: SAPES Books.
22 Mukonyora I. 1997. *Wandering a Gendered Wilderness: Suffering and Healing in an African Initiated Church.* New York: Peter Lang.
23 Chitando E, Gunda MR and Kuegler J. 2014. "Multiplying in the Spirit: African Initiated Churches in Zimbabwe", in Chitando E, Gunda MR and Kuegler J (eds). *Multiplying in the Spirit African Initiated Churches in Zimbabwe.* Bamberg: University of Bamberg Press.

Spirit, they shun hospitalisation and Western biomedicine, including the Covid-19 vaccination. They argue that pandemics such as Covid-19 are understood to be caused by neo-colonial forces and evil spirits, which require a practical and spiritual remedy. Adherents of these churches have economic lives centred on informal self-help jobs, in which they move around selling their wares. This dovetails with the ZANU-PF ideology of indigenisation.[24] AICs have been entangled in Zimbabwe politics. They are well known for conflating with ruling ZANU-PF party. The religion-politics relations tended to be complementary, through a marriage traced back to the colonial epoch when both were used to forcibly dislodge colonialism.[25] The strong relationship continued to flourish in post-colonial Zimbabwe. In election times, some of the AIC gatherings were patronised by ZANU-PF leaders, such as the former President Robert Mugabe and the current President Emmerson Dambudzo Mnangagwa. During the ZANU-PF leaders' visits, AIC leaders often pledge their unwavering support for the ruling party. Endorsements from religious leaders are decisive in the country's general elections.[26] This is because AICs have a large group of congregants who are likely to tow their leaders' political positions. We now turn to the experiences of selected AICs in Zimbabwe in the context of Covid-19 pandemic.

COVID-19, RELIGIOUS LIBERTY AND STATE OVERREACH: EXPERIENCES FROM ZIMBABWE

Zimbabwe had unique experiences between the state and select AICs under the shadow of Covid-19 pandemic. Being a multi-party democracy that boasts of upholding human rights of all, Zimbabwe has had church-state relations that were often cordial and seemingly in tandem with the Constitution of Zimbabwe, when in fact they were on a collision path. It is important to note that the perspectives and experiences of the AICs towards the government efforts to curb the spread of the pandemic were not homogeneous. In other words, some supported the government rules and regulations, while others resisted them by any means necessary. There are three themes that emerged from our study pertaining to the experiences of AICs against the backdrop of state overreach in Zimbabwe, namely (1) responses of AICs to lockdown measures, (2) dynamics surrounding worship services in AICs, and (3) responses to "command vaccination" in AICs.[27]

---

24 See ZANU-PF. 2018. "The People's Manifesto 2018", 11. (The theme of the 2018 manifesto was "Unite, Fight Corruption, Develop, Re-engage and Create Jobs". See particularly the discussion of "Indigenisation and Economic Empowerment" at the indicated page.)

25 The AICs, being African-initiated institutions, easily found inclination to support anti-colonial initiatives such as ZANU-PF liberation forces in Zimbabwe. Both regarded the colonial system of government as foes.

26 Chitando et al, "Multiplying in Spirit", 9; Sibanda and Maposa, "Behind the Smokescreen"; See also Tarusarira J and Humbe BP. 2022. "The Ambivalence of African Independent/Initiated Churches in Colonial and Post-colonial Politics", in Goldstein WS and Reed JP (eds). *Religion in Rebellions, Revolutions, and Social Movements*. London: Routledge.

27 This is a Zimbabwean term for "vaccine mandates".

Responses of AICs to lockdown measures

In its response to the Covid-19 pandemic as a "national disaster", the government pronounced the lockdowns and travel restrictions, and it also prohibited church gatherings. The legal bases for the measures adopted include the Civil Protection Act, 1989; and Public Health Act, 2018; The Public Health (Covid-19 Prevention, Containment and Treatment) (National Lockdown), Order, 2020.[28] Some AICs responded positively to the government's lockdown measures to mitigate against the spread of Covid-19 pandemic. For example, Bishop Nehemiah Mutendi, leader of Zion Christian Church (ZCC) became one of the first indigenous faith leaders to publicly mobilise people to observe the government Covid-19 rules and regulations, which included sanitisation, masking up, social distancing and a ban on gatherings for church services at his ZCC Mbungo shrine in Bikita District. Accordingly, some of his Covid-19-related messages trended on social media, complementing the government's efforts to harness the deadly pandemic.

The study also established that Bishop Mutendi reached out to his congregants virtually as a way of ensuring persistence of worship services while adhering to lockdown rules and regulations. His livestreamed sermons were accessed on various media platforms, including WhatsApp, YouTube and Facebook. One participant stated, "Though the bishop informed us that cancellation of traditional church gatherings was in favour of virtual services, Jesus Christ was always present in our homes each time the bishop delivered his sermons." Therefore, this was a point of compliance to government rules despite the initial scepticism about the spiritual efficacy of online services as compared to the traditional physical services.

However, through observation and interviews, some Apostolic churches defied the lockdown rules on the basis of venturing in their informal businesses to make ends meet. One participant remarked that the lockdown rules were more dangerous than the Covid-19 pandemic itself, because they exposed people to extreme poverty and hunger. This particular concern confirms the AIC ethic of economic engagement, whereby they took the production of wares such as tinkered pots, buckets, dishes, kettles, candle stands, baking sheets and handcrafted items like door mats and pillows, as well as baskets, mops and brooms, as forms of self-reliance and survival.[29] Put differently, some Apostolic groups risked both contracting the virus and being arrested for breaching Covid-19 rules. They did this not only because of informal "hustling" or the "*kukiya-kiya* economy"[30] (what the youth called

---

28 See Ministry of Health and Child Care 2020. Statutory Instrument 2020-083 Public Health (Covid-19 Prevention, Containment and Treatment) (National Lockdown) Order, 2020.

29 Sibanda F and Maposa RS. 2014. "The Ethic of Economic Engagement in AICs", in Chitando E, Gunda MR and Kuegler J (eds). *Multiplying in the Spirit African Initiated Churches in Zimbabwe*. Bamberg: University of Bamberg Press, 220.

30 See, for example, Jones JL. 2010. "Nothing is Straight in Zimbabwe: The Rise of Kukiya-kiya Economy 2000-2008", *Journal of Southern African Studies* 36(2):285-299. See also Nyota S and Sibanda F. 2012. "Digging for Diamonds, Wielding New Words: A Linguistic Perspective on Zimbabwe's 'Blood Diamonds'", *Journal of Southern African Studies* 38(1):134.

"*kungwavha-ngwavha*" or trying to make ends meet) was a source of their livelihoods, but also because it was a form of resilience inspired by the need to get liberation and spiritual fulfilment. It is useful here to cite a case that falls outside the Masvingo and Bikita Districts concerning some Johanne Masowe Church leaders in Harare, who were arrested in July 2021 for breaching lockdown rules.[31] What is interesting by contrast is that thousands of Johanne Marange Apostolic Church members gathered at Mafararikwa shrine in Bocha, Marange, in the same period without any interference from law enforcement agents. One explanation for treating the two churches differently is that members of the Johanne Marange Apostolic Church are among the "sacred cows" who are readily milked for political expediency by the ruling elite and are protected by any means necessary. This is very critical to understanding the context under which regulations were flouted by the churches and individuals. Hence, there were successes and failures in implementing the regulations to curb the spread of Covid-19.

Dynamics surrounding worship services in AICs

During Level 4 lockdown rules of Covid-19 pandemic, the government initially banned all religious gatherings and instituted curfews throughout the country. Under the lockdown, no one was expected to visit worship places physically. The curfews meant that night vigils associated with AICs were banned. In response to these measures, some defiant AICs skirted the lockdown rules and chose to stick to their normal worship services.[32] The majority of AIC respondents in Bikita and Masvingo Districts argued that there was no risk in continuing with congregate worship services because most of the churches congregated in open spaces which were safer than the indoor worship services of some AIC, mainline and Pentecostal churches. In addition, some respondents also pointed out that they were fully guided by the Holy Spirit, which was more powerful than the "demonic pandemic" of Covid-19. This was confirmed through documentary analysis, whereby Tongai Muhacha of Masvingo, an AIC leader, had more than a hundred followers at his shrine at a time when no church gatherings were allowed.[33] Though Muhacha's Covid-19 status was not confirmed through PCR testing, he had symptoms of the novel coronavirus, such as coughing, enduring chest pains, runny nose and general body weakness.[34] On this note, some AICs were accused of being epicentres of the virus, with the majority becoming presumptive cases of Covid-19 because no testing was done or available.

In addition, reports from the electronic versions of journalistic publications of local newspapers noted that in July 2020, over 5 000 members of the Johanne Marange Apostolic Church were also dispersed by the police for illegally gathering on the

---

31 Murwira S. 2021. "Zimbabwe: Johane Masowe Leaders Arrested for Breaching Covid-19 Regulations", AllAfrica.com, 27 July.
32 Moyo "Zimbabwe's Open-Air Churches Fueling the Spread of Covid-19".
33 Moyo "Zimbabwe's Open-Air Churches Fueling the Spread of Covid-19".
34 Moyo "Zimbabwe's Open-Air Churches Fueling the Spread of Covid-19".

outskirts of Masvingo for their annual Passover ceremony. As one of the leaders of the church put it: "While we are not against what the authorities want us to do, we are just requesting to have our Holy Communion as per the tradition of our church, then we can go back home."[35] In this case, they violated rules that forbad groups of more than 50 people to congregate. Though they did not refer to any legal instrument to defend themselves, these AICs were consciously evoking tradition, which tallied with their right to freedom of worship and association as stated in the Constitution of Zimbabwe. It is instructive to cite another case that does not fall under the main thrust of the study but illustrates the state overreach under Covid-19 in the same period. In April 2020, ZimLive.com reported that in Bulawayo, police arrested 48 congregants of Christ Apostolic Church Worldwide Revelation in Tshabalala for holding a church service in breach of coronavirus lockdown regulations. The congregants were ordered to pay fines of ZWD400 each, while those failing to pay faced jail of up to two months.[36] This shows that government would go after congregants who breached the lockdown statutes.

In contrast to the foregoing example of government action against those who breached the Covid-19 regulations at worship places, some AIC members defied the lockdown regulations with impunity. A typical case was where the state law enforcement agents turned a blind eye to the AIC members who gathered at Mafararikwa shrine in Bocha, Marange, in July 2021 without interference as already cited above. Notably, besides the worship gatherings that repeatedly happened at Marange in Bocha (Johanne Marange Apostolic Church), other AICs were reportedly found gathering at Defe in Gokwe (Zion Christian Church of Bishop Mutendi) and Ndarikuri near Chaka Business Centre (African Apostolic Church of Paul Mwazha), even under Covid-19 restriction measures. The case of Bishop Mutendi appears as a contrast to what he once preached and implemented concerning lockdown rules by adopting online churches services. Because churches are a battleground for politicians seeking to entice voters in Zimbabwe,[37] during the height of the Covid-19 pandemic, there was government amnesty in the enforcement of Covid-19 rules and regulations towards the AICs. This was a lackadaisical enforcement of set guidelines, whereby the congregants from Johanne Marange Apostolic Church, Zion Christian Church of Bishop Mutendi and African Apostolic Church of Paul Mwazha were left unscathed, arguably on the basis of patronage.

Responses to "command vaccination" in AICs

In response to the compulsory vaccination driven by the government, Bishop Mutendi was among the pioneering AIC leaders to receive their first doses of Sinopharm vaccine at Wilkins Hospital in Harare on the 19 March 2021. After the jab,

---

35 Maponga G. 2020. "Police Disperse 5000 Sect Members", *The Herald*, 20 July.
36 Mabuza S. 2020. "48 congregants fined for holding Sunday service during lockdown", ZimLive.com, April.
37 Matiashe FS. 2022. "Zimbabwe: Churches are a battleground for politicians seeking to entice voters", *The Africa Report*, 4 May.

Bishop Mutendi said the following words: "I urge Zimbabweans to take the vaccine which is offered for free by the government. Prevention is better than cure."[38] This shows that he was in full support of the government programme to vaccinate its people as a strategy to reduce the spread of the disease. The government gradually allowed congregants who were fully vaccinated to attend church services. In a post-cabinet media briefing, the Zimbabwe Information Minister, stated: "Only congregants who have received two doses of the vaccine are allowed to attend ... all Ministry of Health and Child Care and WHO protocols are adhered to and all those found in breach will be arrested, including leaders of the churches."[39] Hence, the government position was meant to get a herd immunity among the Zimbabweans. Their hope was to ride on numbers from the church organisations.

Despite the positive uptake of vaccination campaigns by some AIC religious leaders, the study also established that some Apostolic church members shunned the vaccination programme. One participant in Bikita District from Johanne Marange Apostolic Church vowed that she would not accept a voluntary jab because it was against their beliefs and the teaching of the founder, Johanne Marange, who preached anti-Western biomedical options. Therefore, in effect the opposition to "command vaccination" against Covid-19 was a perpetuation of their resistance to the government programmes for immunisation. As such, the vaccination campaign was against the Constitution of Zimbabwe, 2013, provision on "Freedom of Conscience", which states: "Every person has the right to freedom of conscience, which includes freedom of thought, opinion, religion or belief."[40] Therefore, the position of Johanne Marange Apostolic Church was a theological standpoint that they could not compromise by any means.

RELIGIOUS CONTROVERSIES AND LEGAL (IN)CONSISTENCIES: CRITICAL REFLECTIONS

Based on the findings of the present study, there are a few reflections that come to the fore. Firstly, there was an ambivalent approach by the government towards religious liberty in the process of controlling the spread of Covid-19 pandemic in Zimbabwe. For instance, the gatherings for worship by some AICs in Masvingo were reprimanded for breaching lockdown rules, in contrast to thousands of Johanne Marange Apostolic Church members who gathered at Mafararikwa shrine in Bocha, Marange, in the same period. The law enforcement agents did not interfere in the latter case. In this manner, the state agents dangled a carrot towards some Apostolic churches for political expediency. One can further argue that the AICs, particularly the Johanne Marange Apostolic Church, were more susceptible to state entreaties probably because of their malleability and numerical advantage on the basis of *quid*

---

38 Zinyuke R. 2021. "Covid-19: More Church Leaders Take Vaccine", *The Herald*, 27 March.

39 Dauramanzi F. 2021. "Churches Reopen for Fully Vaccinated Congregants", *The Herald*, 12 August; See also "Zimbabwe Reopens Churches for Fully Vaccinated Congregants", *Channel Africa*, 12 August 2021.

40 Constitution of Zimbabwe, 2013, s 60(1)(a).

pro quo.⁴¹ The congregants in Masvingo were few and far between, yet they were either arrested or dispersed from their worship places. One could suspect that they were dispersed because numbers count on the Zimbabwean political and religious landscape. This was a selective application of the law, a typical legal "comedy of errors", and it arguably violated Section 60 (1)(b) of the Constitution of Zimbabwe, 2013, on "freedom to practice and propagate and give expression to their thought, opinion, religion or belief, whether in public or in private and whether alone or together with others".⁴² Therefore, church gatherings to a certain extent were justified. In addition, there was resistance towards "command vaccination", which was perceived as a stick approach and a legal error against the freedom of conscience for some AICs. On this basis, it is informative to concur with Iain T. Benson, a professor of law at the University of the Free State, who argues that "Law and politics must not unduly interfere with religious associations and should, ideally, co-operate with them. Seeking some kind of homogeneity or convergence in which religious communities are bleached out is inconsistent with constitutional freedoms properly understood."⁴³

Secondly, in the interest of protecting all the citizens of Zimbabwe, the state overreach was justified where it reprimanded violators of Covid-19 regulations on the basis of the Constitution of Zimbabwe's Section 86(1) provision that: "The fundamental rights and freedoms … must be exercised reasonably and with due regards for the rights and freedoms of other persons."⁴⁴ This limiting clause shows that religious liberty is not absolute in the context of public interests and benefits for all, particularly in the context of the uncertainty associated with pandemics. In the context of the pandemic, it was a form of stick employed to whip citizens into line and to justify the constitutionality of restrictions imposed by government on the freedom of movement and association. A paradox was that, while the churches were barred from normal gatherings, the ruling party went on to hold voting processes – even splashy birthday parties –, oblivious to the statutory instruments that they instituted against which they now acted with impunity.⁴⁵ It also emerged that some statutory instruments had controversial origins and were intended to cripple opposition politics and subversive church institutions through selective applications of the law. Through the various statutory instruments, the dominance of the executive arm of government was apparent in the decision-making associated with Covid-19 pandemic, at the expense of the parliament and the judiciary.

---

41 Johanne Marange Apostolic Church members are known for traditionally dodging the child immunisation programmes by the government. In the context of Covid-19 vaccination and lockdown rules, the government appeared to reciprocate by exonerating AICs from inoculation for the potential of getting political votes even at the expense of a health emergency.

42 Constitution of Zimbabwe, 2013, s 60(1)(b).

43 Benson IT. 2013. "The attack on Western Religions by Western Law: Re-framing Pluralism, Liberalism and Diversity", *International Journal for Religious Freedom* 6(1/2):117.

44 Constitution of Zimbabwe, 2013, s 86.

45 "Mutsvangwa Defends Flouting Covid-19 Restrictions after throwing Bash", *New Zimbabwe*, 2 December 2020.

Thirdly, whereas the Zimbabwe Ministry of Public Service, Labour and Social Welfare was expected to cater for vulnerable people under lockdown conditions, this did not materialise on a large scale. As such, some AIC members were in danger of an economic and humanitarian crisis, with high levels of unemployment and poverty that created an unstable lifestyle. This forced them to breach Covid-19 regulations in order to survive, as stipulated in Section 48(1) of the Constitution of Zimbabwe, which says "every person has the right to life".[46] Thus, the government's failure to effectively respond to the humanitarian crises under the Covid-19 pandemic was a violation of basic human rights. This became a legal error in light of Section 66, which upholds the right to freedom of movement, which was crucial in order to ensure the right to life and survival as they moved around selling their wares. Paradoxically, there is an extent to which some AICs were complicit in curtailing their own freedom liberties by blindly operating in cahoots with the ruling party. Hence, the state overreach was a carrot dangled in front of the AICs.

CONCLUSION

The Covid-19 pandemic was a health emergency that caught the government of Zimbabwe unprepared. One of the key research questions this chapter has grappled with was: does a health emergency such as Covid-19 pandemic allow the government to violate human rights and the freedom of religion? The Covid-19 pandemic put the rule of law to the test and the violation of religious freedom in Zimbabwe. While the Constitution of Zimbabwe, 2013, protects certain fundamental rights and freedoms, such as the rights to life, health care, worship, food and water, some of these rights were violated by the state, thereby resulting in legal inconsistencies. Through the various regulatory instruments, the dominance of the executive arm of government was apparent in the decision-making associated with Covid-19 pandemic at the expense of parliament and the judiciary. Therefore, we further conclude with Kenyan legal scholar Faith Kabata, that "Zimbabwe has more politicisation of religion and religionisation of politics than any other country in Africa."[47]

On that basis, the chapter illustrated that the Zimbabwean state and AICs had the potential to promote or impede the public good in the context of the Covid-19 pandemic. This brought the carrot and stick approach to the fore, because in the midst of a health crisis the state was justified in taking exceptional measures to ensure health and safety, even at the expense of religious freedom. Notably, freedom of religion is not absolute in the context of public interests and public benefits. There was an extent to which AICs were complicit in curtailing their own freedom liberties and at the same time where the state and its law was like a spider's web that only caught the "little insects".

---

46   Constitution of Zimbabwe, 2013, s 48(1).
47   Interview with Faith Kabata by F Sibanda. Nairobi, Kenya, 16 May 2022.

2 "SEEKING THE FACE OF GOD IN TRYING TIMES": LAW, RELIGION AND THE COVID-19 CRISIS IN SECULAR GHANA

Seth Tweneboah[1]

INTRODUCTION

Prior to March 2020, a pertinent topic at the nexus of religion, law and politics in the Ghanaian public arena was the dispute over the ruling government's decision to construct a Ghana National Cathedral.[2] This controversial project was in fulfilment of President Nana Addo Dankwa Akufo-Addo's promise as part of his supplication to God to win the 2016 presidential election.[3] The political decision to construct a national house of prayer attracted critical public debate and ultimately ended up in the Supreme Court for determination on its suitability and constitutionality.[4] The emergence of the novel coronavirus SARS-CoV-2, which causes the disease Covid-19, however, imposed itself upon the life and faith of Ghanaians, changing the public narrative on the intricate relationship between religion, law and politics in Ghana. Indeed, the deadly virus is believed to have altered the course of nations and the world at large.[5] On 30 January 2020, during a press briefing, the World Health Organization (WHO) declared the coronavirus outbreak a public health emergency of international concern.[6] According to the WHO, further international spread of cases across the globe was expected. The WHO therefore urged all countries to put preparedness plan in place for containment, including active surveillance, early detection, isolation, case management, contact tracing and prevention of onward spread of the disease.

Like most of Africa and elsewhere, Ghana was unprepared for the coronavirus when it recorded its first two cases on 12 March 2020. The government was confronted with the challenge of protecting its citizens in an emergency situation, while at the

---

1   Lecturer, Centre for Africa Studies, University of Education, Winneba, Ghana.
2   Tweneboah S. 2019. "Religion, Law, and the Politics of Building a National Cathedral in 'Secular' Ghana", *Issues in Conflict, Human Rights and Peace* 1(1):19-34.
3   "I Promised God a National Cathedral; I'm Redeeming My Pledge – Akufo-Addo", *GhanaWeb*, 29 December 2018.
4   *James Kwabena Bomfeh Jnr vrs Attorney General* (J1 14 of 2017) [2019] GHASC 2 (23 January 2019).
5   Flood CM et al. 2020. "Introduction: Overview of Covid-19: Old and New Vulnerabilities", in Flood CM et al (eds). *Vulnerable: The Law, Policy and Ethics of Covid-19*. Ottawa: University of Ottawa Press, 1-27.
6   World Health Organization (WHO). 2020. "Covid-19 Public Health Emergency of International Concern (PHEIC) Global research and innovation forum Towards a research roadmap", *WHO.int*, 12 February.

same time making sure it did not unreasonably infringe on their rights, including the rights to corporate worship, freedom of movement and public gathering. To achieve effective public health goals, however, a number of pandemic-related measures were put in place. Notable among these were quarantine of victims and mandatory lockdown for all citizens. By 15 March 2020, Ghana had recorded six cases.[7] That night, President Akufo-Addo, in his second nationwide address on measures taken by the government to combat the coronavirus, outlined a series of pandemic-related restrictions to be implemented, including the suspension of all public gatherings, including conferences, workshops, funerals, festivals, political rallies, sporting events and religious activities, such as services in churches and mosques.[8] Universities and schools were also closed a day after the president's announcement. The country's borders were also shut until 27 March 2022.[9] On 30 March 2020, President Akufo-Addo issued an executive instrument, the Imposition of Restrictions (Coronavirus Disease (Covid-19) Pandemic) (No. 2) Instrument, 2020, thereby ordering the total lockdown of some major cities of the country as a measure to contain the spread of the coronavirus. These measures, to be sure, were some of the many collective mechanisms to contain this public health menace. A section of the population found wisdom in the Covid-19 safety protocols and relief programme, hailing it as the surest way to curb the menace.[10] Yet these barely achieved the intended effect. For one reason, the majority of the population found these measures to be unbearable, since their livelihood depended on freedom of movement on a daily basis in search of their daily bread. Others, however, were unwilling to abide by them. As a result, the state deployed its coercive powers, using both the police and the military to seek compliance.[11]

In its 27 March 2020 edition, the editorial of the major national newspaper, the *Daily Graphic*, was titled "Seeking the Face of God in Trying Times".[12] This editorial echoed the president's earlier call on Ghanaians to seek divine intervention in mitigating the effects of the global pandemic. In the context of Covid-19 in Ghana, religious leaders, beliefs and ritual practices have played a decisive role, necessitating a proper interrogation.

---

7   "Coronavirus: Ghana confirm four new cases of Covid-19, total cases rise catch six", *BBC*, 15 March 2020.

8   Ghana Ministry of Health (MoH). 2020 "President Akufo-Addo Addresses Nation On Measures Taken By Gov't To Combat The Coronavirus Pandemic", *MoH.gov.gh*, 15 March.

9   Mensah K. 2022. "Ghana Reopens Borders to Bolster Economy", *VOA News*, 28 March. For details of the president's speech, see, for example, Akufo-Addo NAD. 2020. "Address to the Nation by President of the Republic, Nana Addo Dankwa Akufo-Addo, on Updates to Ghana's Enhanced Response to the Coronavirus Pandemic", German Embassy of Accra, 27 March.

10 "Traders in Cape Coast Hail Directive on Enforcement of Covid-19 Protocols", *Ghana News Agency (GNA)*, 18 January 2021.

11 "Military descends on man for flouting lockdown directive", *GhanaWeb*, 30 March 2020; "Coronavirus lockdown: Woman cries after police officer hits her with a stick at CMB", *GhanaWeb*, 31 March 2020.

12 "Seeking the face of God in trying times", *Daily Graphic*, 27 March 2020.

In this chapter, I examine the coronavirus pandemic as an arena of religious and legal entanglement. In spite of the constitutional insistence on the separation of law and religion, I contend, religion played a dual role as both a limiter and promoter of public health and safety. I present the state's deployment of law and the activities and operations of religious actors of society as a cardinal mode of managing the coronavirus crisis in Ghana. In doing so, I demonstrate the ambivalent nature of Ghanaian secularism, paying attention to the role of law and religion in sustaining public health and safety in Ghana. The chapter demonstrates the extent to which religious resources have forged a significant constellation of the management of the pandemic in Ghana.

RELIGION, LAW AND HEALTH CARE IN GHANA

Contemporary Ghana offers an interesting account of a state that is secular by edict but a profoundly religious society in fact.[13] Its Constitution of Ghana 1992, which derives its authority from the sovereign will of the people, is held to be the supreme law of the land and any other law found to be inconsistent with any provision of it is void to the extent of the inconsistency. The Constitution does not give primacy to any particular religion. Even so, owing to its highly religious population, religion occupies a special place in private and public life in contemporary Ghana. In spite of the constitutional insistence of its secularity, in Ghana, as in most of Africa, a remarkable interrelationship exists between the religious, political and legal realms. Thus, the Supreme Court of Ghana affirmed the ambivalence of this interrelation in *Bomfeh vs Attorney General*, when it held that the Constitution of Ghana 1992, "while secular in nature, affirms and maintains the historical, cultural, and religious or atheist character of Ghanaian society" and argued that "secularism in the context of the Ghana Constitution must be understood to allow, and even encourage State recognition and accommodation of religion and religious identity".[14]

The Ghanaian Constitution gives the population a wide range of rights of universal significance. Eminently, the right to freely practice one's faith is a protected category. As a deeply religious society, matters of physical health, spiritual wholeness and healing are equally of prime concern. Given its decisive role in the political and legal maturation of society, Ghana's health care delivery is regulated by a number of constitutional, legal, policy and human rights frameworks. While the Constitution of 1992 does not expressly mention health or health care, the right to health care is guaranteed in Ghana. In truth, the state's responsibility for the health of its citizens is based on affirmative responsibility, and this is regulated by a number of legal enactments.[15] Prominent among these are the Public Health Act, 2012 (Act 851), the

---

13   Tweneboah S. 2020. *Religion, Law, Politics and the State in Africa: Applying Legal Pluralism in Ghana*. Abingdon and New York: Routledge.

14   *James Kwabena Bomfeh Jnr vrs Attorney General* (J1 14 of 2017) [2019] GHASC 2 (23 January 2019), 18.

15   Atuguba RA. 2013. "The right to health in Ghana: Healthcare, human rights, and politics", in Zuniga JM, Marks SP and Gostin LO (eds). *Advancing the Human Rights to Health*.

Ghana Health Service and Teaching Hospitals Act, 1996 (Act 525), the Pharmacy Act, 1994 (Act 489), and the National Health Insurance Act, 2012 (Act 852). There is also the Health Institutions and Facilities Act, 2011 (Act 829), which aims to ensure the licensing and regulation of facilities. This Act also sets up the Health Facilities Regulatory Agency to supervise the activities and functioning of public and private institutions and monitor the quality of service rendered by them.

Policy interventions in the health sector via the expansion of health infrastructure, introduction of health insurance schemes, provision of free maternal health care services and other measures have been remarkable means of achieving national health goals and objectives in Ghana. Outstanding policy frameworks include the Private Health Sector Development Policy (2003), which has a fourfold objective of improving the investment climate for private health sector growth, supporting the transformation of the private health businesses to meet industry expectations, building the capacity of private health care providers and increasing opportunity for the poor to access private health care services. There is also the National Health Policy (2007) and the Health Sector Medium Term Development Plan (2010-2013), reflecting the health development agenda for the medium term, and the National Environmental Sanitation Policy (2010), which seeks to give priority to increased access to enough sanitation facilities, among others. Within the human rights framework, as noted above, Chapter Five of the Constitution of 1992 provides for a range of fundamental human rights and freedoms. In particular, Article 21 of the Constitution provides for the right to freedom of speech and expression and to freedom of thought, conscience and belief, as well as the freedom to practise any religion and to manifest such practice and the freedoms of assembly, association, information, movement, among others. In the event of an imminent emergency, however, as we shall see later, the state as a duty-bearer (an entity with the obligations or duties to uphold rights) reserves the right to temporary curtail the enjoyment of this right.[16]

Health care is, therefore, a key political issue in Ghana. As a matter of fact, health-related issues, particularly the sustainability of the National Health Insurance Scheme, have been high on the political electioneering campaign agenda.[17] In the last two decades, Ghana has demonstrated its commitment to the betterment of its health care delivery. Evidence of this is seen not only in the construction of health facilities, but also through increased public spending on health care.[18]

Oxford: Oxford University Press, 101-112.

16 Article 21(4) of the Constitution of Ghana provides for conditions under which the rights of citizens can be restricted including "in the interest of defence, public safety, public health or the running of essential services, on the movement or residence within Ghana of any person or persons generally". See also Section 4(1) of the Public Order Act, 1994 (Act 491).

17 Mubarik A. 2016. "NHIS has collapsed under Mahama-Akufo-Addo", *Pulse*, 4 September; "Stop registering your supporters on NHIS if it's collapsed – Mahama tells NPP", *GhanaWeb*, 26 October 2016.

18 Adua E, Frimpong K, Li X and Wang W. 2017. "Emerging issues in public health: a perspective on Ghana's healthcare expenditure, policies and outcomes", *The EPMA*

Despite the state's effort, crucial challenges continue to persist. These challenges are largely a problem of financing, access and the quality of health care services, which give rise to the existence of substantial equity gaps when it comes to access to the provision of health care.[19] Inadequate medical officers, a high patient-doctor ratio and inadequate health facilities are also part of the challenges in the health sector, and funding inadequacies in health services remain a foremost challenge to health care delivery. Some studies have tried to privilege Ghana's performance in terms of its commitment to health delivery as against neighbouring countries.[20] The introduction of the NHIS in 2003-2004 has been found to have resulted in "high general healthcare spending and a reduced share of private and out-of-pocket spending, known as the cash-and-carry system".[21] Among other goals, the NHIS aims to provide equity in health care coverage and promote access by the poor and vulnerable against financial risk. The proportion of the population who have access to quality health care has, therefore, improved comparatively. The 2021 census results, for example, show that 68.6% of the citizenry is covered by either the NHIS or private health care schemes. Despite these frameworks, crucial gaps continue to exist when it comes to the demand for health and the state ability to supply.

In the face of the many philosophical and conceptual challenges in the health sector, most people depend on religiosity for their daily health care needs. It is imperative that Ghana operates a pluralistic health sector, recognising allopathic, traditional and alternative providers, both private and public. Despite the claims of secularity, there is a vital link between religiosity and health-seeking belief outcomes in Ghana.[22] For years, most Ghanaians have relied on traditional health care delivery systems. At the state level, attempts to promote traditional medicine practices as alternative medicine are gaining prominence. Efforts to train personnel at the Kwame Nkrumah University of Science and Technology, leading to the setting up of numerous herbal outfits especially in the cities, provide a tangible fledging alternative to orthodox medicine. Even so, the orthodox medical system has been largely privileged and encouraged by the government and the elite. As the sociologist Robert W. Wyllie has noted, the relative lack of attention to indigenous etiological theory of healing appears to emanate largely from the supposition that, "while the healers may well possess a stock of potentially useful herbal cures, their explanations of illness are hopelessly embedded in a magic-religious theory of causation which is not amenable to testing in laboratory or clinic".[23] Besides this, the continuing Pentecostal-charismatic Christian propensity to demonise the

---

Journal 8(3):197-206.

19 Atuguba, "The right to health in Ghana", 103; Adua et al, "Emerging issues in public health", 197.

20 Atuguba, "The right to health in Ghana", 198.

21 Atuguba, "The right to health in Ghana", 198.

22 Okyerefo MPK and Fiave DY. 2017. "Prayer and health-seeking beliefs in Ghana: understanding the 'religious space' of the urban forest", *Health Sociology Review* 26(3):308-320.

23 Wyllie RW. 1983. "Ghanaian Spiritual and Traditional Healers' Explanations of Illness: A Preliminary Survey", *Journal of Religion in Africa* 14(1):46-57.

indigenous religious fields as channels of demonic influences has cast traditional medical systems in a bad light.[24] In spite of this, since independence, the state has harnessed the noteworthy contribution of traditional religious medicine and its practitioners. The state has also forged a closer partnership with imported religious institutions, especially Christian and Muslim ones, in order to provide quality and accessible health care outcomes.

RELIGION AND PUBLIC HEALTH

In the public health history of Ghana, religion and politics play a major role in the healing processes of the people. In particular, the pandemic periods of the 1920s and the 1930s, which were followed by the economic recession, spurred meaningful religious interventions of interest. These periods also politicised public health care in ways that have continued to play out in recent times. This was a period when the colonial state in the Gold Coast (independent Ghana) experienced major health care challenges, such as the cerebrospinal meningitis, influenza, trypanosomiasis and onchocerciasis.[25] Funding inadequacies and resource constraints owing to the Great Depression, as well as certain colonial decisions, rendered many health facilities ineffective.

Despite these challenges, the positive health care outcomes of religious institutions, especially those of the missionaries, have been well documented. The historian Sean Hawkins explains that these major illnesses were treated almost exclusively as issues of public health in the Northern Territories, which were isolated from colonial policies.[26] That is to say, they were handled in terms of "the economic health and social stability of the Northern Territories". In this sense, colonial interventionist policies were geared toward the colonialists' economic interest, as the colonialists sought to limit the spread of outbreak of infectious diseases by isolating the sick. Hawkins writes: "Little or no effect was made to protect the Northern Territories from the pandemic even though their cattle which were the main economic mainstay were inoculated."[27]

It is within this context that the role of the missionaries can be interrogated. The success story of the missionaries during pandemic periods largely depended on their ability to recognise the convergence of spiritual and physical well-being as

---

24 For a discussion on the demonisation of the indigenous religious spaces, see, for example, Hackett RIJ. 2003. "Discourse of Demonization in Africa and Beyond", *Diogenes* 50(3):61-75. See also Meyer B. 1998. "'Make a Complete Break with the Past': Memory and Post-Colonial Modernity in Ghanaian Pentecostalist Discourse", *Journal of Religion in Africa* 28(3):316-348.

25 Patterson KD. 1983. "The Influenza Epidemic of 1918-19 in the Gold Coast", *The Journal of African History* 24(4):485-502.

26 Hawkins S. 2014. *Writing and Colonialism in Northern Ghana*. Toronto: University of Toronto Press.

27 Hawkins, *Writing and Colonialism*, 199. See also Kimble D. 1963. *A Political History of Ghana, 1850-1928*. Oxford: The Clarendon Press, 533-536.

a coherent whole. As Remigius F. McCoy, a premier missionary to northwestern Ghana, has recounted: "The daily routine of the clinic would begin with a prayer aimed at reminding our patients that the curative powers of medicines and the care dispensed was a result of God's great love for them and his children."[28]

Post-independence health care delivery continues to follow the pattern of religionisation and politicisation, details of which I provide in the ensuing sections. It is not uncommon to find health professionals engaging in morning devotions, seeking divine mercy and interventions as they start their day.[29] Religious organisations have complemented and even rivaled governments efforts of health care delivery in some parts of Ghana. The existence of prayer and healing centres across the country also exemplifies the extent to which religion is interspersed with issues of health care delivery. Over the years, the operations and activities of prophetic healers and healing centres have raised compelling human rights concerns.[30] Yet their services continue to be patronised by a section of the population exemplifying the intricate relationship between religion, healing and health. It is within this context that the coronavirus crisis must be examined.

CORONAVIRUS AND THE LAW: ACT 1012 AND MORE

In a 15 March 2020 national address on measures taken by Ghana's government to combat the coronavirus pandemic, President Akufo-Addo hinted that he had directed the attorney general to introduce "emergency legislation" to mitigate the spread of the coronavirus, relevant portion of which I cite below.

> I have directed the Attorney General to submit, immediately, to Parliament emergency legislation, in accordance with Article 21 (4) (c) & (d) of the Constitution of the Republic, to embody these measures, and I have further directed the Minister for Health to exercise his powers, under section 169 of the Public Health Act, 2012 (Act 851), by the immediate issuance of an Executive Instrument, to govern the relevant measures. I call upon Parliament to support the Executive in this national endeavour.[31]

The result of this directive was the enactment of the Imposition of Restrictions Act, 2020 (Act 1012) by Parliament within five days. The president assented to the bill, and the day after, the Act 1012 was published in the gazette and entered into force. Act 1012, thus, became the government of Ghana's main legal instrument in the fight against the coronavirus pandemic. It provides for powers to impose

---

28 McCoy RF. 1988. *Great Things Happen: A Personal Memoir of the First Christian Missionary among the Dagaabas and Sissalas of Northwest Ghana*. Montreal: Society of the Missionaries of Africa, 58.

29 Adugbire BA and Aziato L. 2020. "Surgical Patients' Perception of Spirituality on the Outcome of Surgery in Northern Ghana", *Journal of Holistic Nursing* (1):19-29.

30 Tweneboah S. 2015. "Pentecostalism, Witchdemonic Accusations, and Symbolic Violence in Ghana: Some Human Rights Concerns", *Pneuma* 37(3):375-393.

31 The Presidency, Republic of Ghana. 2020. "President Akufo-Addo Addresses Nation on Measures Taken by Gov't to Combat the Coronavirus Pandemic", 15 March.

restrictions on persons, to give effect to paragraphs (c), (d) and (e) of clause (4) of Article 21 of the Constitution of Ghana 1992 in the event or imminence of an emergency, disaster or similar circumstance to ensure public safety, public health and protection. Crucially, it recommends sanctions for violating any provisions therein. Section 6 especially recommends that: "A person who fails to comply with a restriction imposed under the Executive Instrument issued under subsection (1) of section 2 commits an offence and is liable on summary conviction to a fine of not less than one thousand penalty units and not more than five thousand penalty units or to a term of imprisonment of not less than four years and not more than ten years or to both."

Act 1012 received mixed reactions from Ghanaians. Some commended the president for being proactive, hailing him for taking bold steps to control the situation.[32] For example, to help further alleviate the implications of the lockdown, the government introduced a number of interventions including free water and electricity programmes.[33] Under the Coronavirus Alleviation Programme (CAP), the government also provided cash donations to specific beneficiaries and also collaborated with some faith-based organisations to distribute food items to poorest and vulnerable families and households affected by the lockdown.[34] Even so, there were also severe criticisms from the population, particularly from minority Members of Parliament, legal experts and interested Ghanaians, regarding its procedures, nature, form and content.[35] These criticisms, to be sure, were a combination of facts, emotion and political calculation. Procedurally, Act 1012 has been accused of being a product of rushed procedure, raising issues over its constitutionality and expressly regarding "the procedural propriety of using a voice vote in Parliament".[36] Principally, the minority in Parliament challenged the legal reasoning of using a voice count to decide on a crucial bill of that nature and indicated their resolve to file an action in the Supreme Court to seek an interpretation of Article 104 of the Constitution which specifies the conduct of votes in the Parliament.[37]

Experts have also suggested that Act 1012 was not necessary, since there were already specific national and international laws that limited governments potential excesses

---

32 "Pentecostal and Charismatic Council Commends Directive to Ban Church Activities over Coronavirus", Sendwestafrica.org, 3 April; "Traders in Cape Coast hail directive on enforcement of Covid-19 protocols", *Ghana News Agency (GNA)*, 18 January 2021.

33 Asare K and Donkor J. 2020. "Ghanaians to Enjoy Free Water, Electricity for 3 More Months", *The Ghanaian Times*, 24 July.

34 Lartey NI. 2020. "Covid-19 Lockdown: Government Announces Free Food for over 400 000 Ghanaians", *Citi Newsroom*, 6 April.

35 Addadzi-Koom ME. 2022. "Quasi-state of emergency: assessing the constitutionality of Ghana's legislative response to Covid-19", *The Theory and Practice of Legislation* 8(3):311-327.

36 Addadzi-Koom, "Quasi-state of emergency", 313.

37 Mordy JT. 2020. "Minority Signals Supreme Court action after rushed Restriction Bill Approval", *MyJoyonline*, 20 March.

and violations of human rights.[38] The minority in Parliament saw Act 1012 as out of touch with the realities that the coronavirus crisis presented. They contended that the specific concerns about Covid-19 could have been dealt with using the Constitution and Public Health Act, 1994 (Act 851), which makes provisions for quarantine and restriction of movement. Besides, they described Act 1012 as too broad in scope. While it sought to specifically address the coronavirus crisis, according to the minority, there was no mention of coronavirus.[39] For other critics, the Act hardly did justice to ordinary Ghanaians, whose plights had already been exacerbated by the pandemic. Because many people's sustenance depended on daily hustles, the lockdown was seen as a limitation to their livelihood. Some, therefore, described it as draconian and a recipe for other abuses.[40] The punishment for violating this law was, moreover, deemed by some as unduly harsh. Given the social and economic situation of the majority of the people, the measures put in place by the state to achieve public health goals were seen as draconian to some citizens. As a result, such people largely came into conflict with law enforcement agencies, particularly the police and the military. There were reports of these security agencies exceeding their mandate and abusing the rights of innocent citizens.[41]

Some critics also complained that Act 1012 did not have any expiry date on when its provisions would be lifted. Besides, the Act was seen as too general and also as giving the president broad powers to restrict constitutionally guaranteed rights without recourse to parliamentary oversight. Specifically, while Section 7 provides for a definition of "disaster", as noted, the Act did not, in any way, mention Covid-19 as its reference point. This suggests that any president could invoke this under different situations. Furthermore, the critics argued, Ghana already has laws that can be used to address the issue at hand. For example, the Emergency Powers Act, 1994 (Act 472), provides for the declaration of emergency under certain circumstances. Section 5(2)(b) of this Act provides that in periods of an emergency affecting the whole or a part of the country, the president may order the: (1) detention of persons or the restriction of movement of persons, (2) deportation and expulsion from the Republic of a person who is not a citizen, (3) taking possession or control of a property on behalf of the Republic, (4) acquisition of property, (5) searching of premises without a warrant, (6) payment of compensation to a person affected by an action taken under the emergency, (7) arrest, trial and punishment of a person for breach of an instrument, order or a declaration related to the state of emergency and (8) suspension of the operation of law. Similarly, the Constitution of 1992 also makes provisions for emergencies, including public health

---

38 See, for example, Appiagyei-Atua K. 2020. "Emergency without a State of Emergency: Effect of Imposition of Restrictions Act, 2020 on rights of Ghanaians", *MyJoyOnline*, 2 April.

39 Gakpo JO. 2020. "Imposition of Restriction Bill 2020 worse than State of Emergency – Muntaka", *MyJoyOnline*, 19 March.

40 Gakpo JO. 2020. "Imposition of Restriction Bill 2020".

41 "Military descends on man for flouting lockdown directive", *GhanaWeb*, 30 March 2020; "Woman cries after police officer hits her with a stick", *GhanaWeb*, 31 March 2020.

emergencies. In view of these provisions, some have interpreted the attempt to enact a new law to invoke a quarantine or isolation order as a trump card to justify restricting people's movement.[42]

Another significant legal instrument related to the Covid-19 pandemic is the introduction of the Electronic Communications System Instrument, 2020 (EI 63). EI 63 sought to establish an emergency communications system with the distinct aim of contact-tracing all persons who may be potentially infected through contact with an infected person. This instrument has equally been criticised as a trump card for possible mass surveillance by the ruling government. There are, of course, considerable challenges associated with the implementation and enforcement of this instrument. EI 63 precisely breaches Article 18(2) of the Constitution. That article provides that no person shall be subjected to intrusion with the privacy of their home, property, correspondence or communication except in accordance with law and as may be necessary in a free and democratic society for public safety or the economic well-being of the country, for the protection of health or morals, for the prevention of disorder or crime or for the protection of the rights or freedoms of others. Cognisance of the fact that the courts have previously ruled against violation of privacy of communication in Ghana, some have described the EI 63 as "a step backward" as far as the right to privacy in Ghana is concerned.[43]

Like Act 1012, the legal validity of EI 63 has, thus, been effectively questioned. It has been criticised as having no basis in law. Some have dubbed it as *ultra vires*, an illegality.[44] In the view of critics, the EI 63 was framed on legally non-existent grounds. It is argued that the Act's attempt to impose order in society did not satisfy the exception contemplated under Article 21(4). It was seen as an attempt to compromise the privacy of the citizenry.

LAW AND RELIGIOUS AMBIVALENCE:
"SEEKING THE FACE OF GOD IN TRYING TIMES"

Recent analysis of the coronavirus crisis has shown the relationship between the pandemic and conspiracy thinking. Indeed, a cardinal outcome of the pandemic has been the rise of various types of conspiracy beliefs.[45] In a pervasively religious society, the pandemic pandered to a series of coronavirus conspiracy beliefs and reliance on religiosity. On 19 March 2020, President Akufo-Addo convened a breakfast prayer session at the seat of government with representatives of the

---

42 Appiagyei-Atua, "Emergency without a State of Emergency".
43 Appiagyei-Atua, "Emergency without a State of Emergency".
44 Asare J. 2020. "Establishment of Emergency Communications Instrument, 2020 (E.I. 63); A Dangerous Illegality", *Ghana Law Hub*, 26 May.
45 Stephens M. 2020. "A geospatial infodemic: Mapping Twitter conspiracy theories of Covid-19", *Dialogues in Human Geography* 10(2):276-281; Łowicki P et al. 2022. "Does religion predict coronavirus conspiracy beliefs? Centrality of religiosity, religious fundamentalism, and Covid-19 conspiracy beliefs", *Personality and Individual Differences* 187:1-9.

major Christian groups in Ghana.[46] The goal of this meeting was to implore divine mercy and intervention in the face of the spread of the coronavirus pandemic. The president explained that the call for prayer for the nation was motivated by his strong conviction in divine healing power and the saving grace of the maker of heaven and earth. Furthermore, the president's address relied on biblical passages to paint a picture of profound hope owing to the faith the Ghanaian people have in the Almighty, that the country will be better able to mitigate the pandemic for, as he said, "this too will pass."[47] This meeting was followed by another one hosted for Muslim clerics led by the Vice President, Mahamudu Bawumia, who is himself a Muslim. A national day of fasting and prayer was also set for 25 March 2020 to seek divine intervention against the coronavirus pandemic.

On 22 March 2020, President Akufo-Addo, as part of his usual update on the coronavirus pandemic, declared 25 March 2020 as a national day of fasting and prayer to God to protect the nation and save it from the coronavirus crisis.[48] This was followed by another national prayer on 27 March 2020 organised by Muslims and attended by the vice president. The president reiterated the popular Ghanaian belief in the links between the spiritual and physical dimensions of healing. He entreated all Ghanaians to pray "to God to protect our nation and save us from this pandemic".[49] This episode reaffirms the general notion that healing and health are interspersed with divine intervention – *Onyame ne oyaresafoɔ* (God is the healer).

On 27 March 2020, the *Daily Graphic* in its editorial, "Seeking the Face of God in Trying Times", implored Ghanaians to turn to God's mercy and intervention to avert the dangers of the pandemic. The editorial reminded readers of the president's earlier call on 22 March 2020, and it indicated the newspaper's deep support for this call. Given the crucial role that belief in prayer plays in health and healing, the editorial called on the need to hold national prayer days biannually instead of it being a once-off event.[50] Framing the virus as divine design presupposes that divine surgery must to be applied. Thus, the editorial reminded Ghanaians that the antidote to the disease was a complete knowledge of the wisdom of God. Citing the biblical passage of Joel 2:12, it beseeched Ghanaians to return to God with all their heart, with fasting and weeping and mourning. Again, it referred to Proverbs 1:7 to remind Ghanaians that "the fear of the Lord is the beginning of knowledge, but fools despise wisdom and instruction." What this means is that the coronavirus crisis was seen as a divine design and a consequence of human evil deeds. The crisis was, hence, interpreted as an inescapable divine sanction. The editorial, therefore,

---

46 Dapatem DA and Nunoo C. 2020. "These aren't normal times: Seek God's face for restoration – President tells Christians over Covid-19", *Daily Graphic*, 20 March.
47 Dapatem and Nunoo, "These aren't normal times".
48 Yeboah I. 2020. "Coronavirus: Ghana to observe national day of fasting and prayer", *Daily Graphic*, 22 March.
49 Dapatem and Nunoo, "These aren't normal times".
50 "Seeking the face of God in trying times", *Daily Graphic*, 27 March 2020.

threw its decisive support behind the idea that the disease was a symptom of people's sinful ways.

Like the old Israel, Ghana has variously been labelled as God's favourite society.[51] Yet as the society flourishes, complacency and false security continue to set in, leading to trust in institutions instead of divine will. This leads to evil deeds, abomination, dishonesty, social injustice, and other ills becoming rife in society. In this sense, the virus was deemed to be unmistakable evidence of the evils of a once blessed society that has been estranged from God. In such a trying epoch of national and global history, the answer to the divine epidemiology lies not primarily in strengthening the political and economic base, but rather in returning to God and seeking his face. The pandemic, then, was seen as an opportunity given to mankind for the reformation and reorientation of their lives and relationships with one another. As the editorial noted, "we should be honest, forgiving and show love, care and compassion for one another. As a nation, it seems we have all sinned and come short of the glory of God. The church and the Mosque, as a body, cannot escape blame in this whole enterprise of abomination. It is time to do away with injustice."[52]

Significantly, however, the outbreak of the pandemic also led to public discourse on the role of religion, especially Pentecostal-charismatic Christianity in the Ghanaian public arena. It is important to remember that over the years, pastor-prophets have been particularly active in the public domain and the actions and forms in which their activities and operations take have become a matter of concern. Prophetic healers are prominent in Ghana's public arena, owing to their claims to protect people from contracting certain diseases and their claims of power to heal those who already have specified diseases. This, indeed, is a key reason for the attraction of prayer and healing centres, despite reports of grave human rights concerns.[53] Over the years, it has been a tradition for prophetic actors to predict impending catastrophes of the year, especially during their New Year Eve's watchnight service. In this sense, for pastor-prophets to miss this global pandemic was quite ironic to some observers. The emergence of the virus, therefore, renewed the public anxiety over the supposed relevance of prophetic men and women of God. Many ridiculed them for their inability to predict the disease. Others also accused them of falling short of healing victims of the virus or offering protection. For example, as J. Kwabena Asamoah-Gyadu, a Ghanaian scholar of African Pentecostalism, has noted regarding the coronavirus pandemic, "The fact that most of the personalities

---

51 Asamoah-Gyadu JK. 2013. "'God Bless our Homeland Ghana': Religion and Politics in a Post-Colonial African State", in Omenyo CN and Anum EB (eds). *Trajectories of Religion in Africa Essays in Honour of John S. Pobee.* Leiden: Brill, 163-185.

52 "Seeking the face of God in trying times".

53 Human Rights Watch. 2012. "'Like a Death Sentence': Abuses against Persons with Mental Disabilities in Ghana", *Human Rights Watch*, October.

to face misfortune tend to be high profile public figures has led to suspicion that these so-called prophetic utterances are nothing but prophetic blackmailing for material gain."[54]

RELIGIOUS ACTORS AND THE FIGHT AGAINST CORONAVIRUS

In his 15 March 2020 nationwide address, President Akufo-Addo directed the suspension of public gatherings, including gatherings for religious purposes. He further declared that establishments, such as supermarkets, shopping malls, restaurants, night clubs, hotels and drinking spots, should observe enhanced hygiene procedures by providing, among other things, hand sanitisers, running water and soap for washing of hands.[55] This directive initially did not go well with many Ghanaians, especially those in the charismatic churches.[56]

A key legal function of religious institutions that is largely ignored in the religion-state discussion is that they are useful in explaining vital state decisions to members and advising congregants to adhere to the coronavirus pandemic safety protocols. To demonstrate their commitment, religious institutions all over the country, apart from isolated incidents, complied with the ban on public gatherings. Most religious organisations resorted to livestreaming, radio and television services to reach out to their members. Through the use of social media, religious groups supported the government's safety measures and urged their congregation to strictly adhere to the president's directive and other public health regulations. Most religious groups enacted a "No mask, No entry" policy. These measures, to be sure, went a long way towards limiting the spread of the virus emanating from close contact infection. The office of the National Chief Imam supported the president's directive and further urged Muslims to use two days to pray and fast for the nation.

In fact, when on 31 May 2020 the ban limiting public gathering to twenty-five people was lifted, to demonstrate its full effort to contain the spread of the virus, some religious organisations decided not to congregate for religious services and continued to monitor the situation.[57] The Christian Council of Ghana, for example, admonished its congregants to exercise restraint in the reopening of churches, as they needed time for proper preparation and strategising. It stressed on the need to plan, train and educate members before opening the churches for services.

To alleviate the situation, in April 2020, the government passed the Covid-19 National Trust Fund Act, 2020 (Act 1013) to establish a coronavirus fund. The aim of this

---

54 Asamoah-Gyadu JK. 2020. "Dealing with a spiritual virus: whitter the prophet?", *Religious Matters*, 13 April.

55 The Presidency, "President Akufo-Addo Addresses Nation".

56 "Coronavirus: Pastor Arrested for Contravening Ban on Social Gatherings", *Daily Graphic*, 18 March 2020; Donkor KD. 2020. "Coronavirus: Pastor Arrested Again for Flouting Ban on Social Gatherings", *Daily Graphic*, 22 March.

57 Kuatsinu JE. 2020. "Easing of restrictions on religious activities: Churches reluctant to congregate for worship", *Ghanaian Times*, 4 June.

trust fund was to marshal the necessary funds to complement the government's efforts to address the coronavirus crisis in Ghana. Religious organisations, as part of their commitment towards addressing the pandemic, contributed towards this fund. For example, the Ghana Catholic Bishops' Conference donated an amount of GH₵700 000 (about USD12 200) into the fund.[58] Similar cash and other donations were made by other religious organisations. In his mid-year budget review presented to parliament on 23 July 2020, the finance minister noted the contribution of religious organisations in Ghana thus:

> Mr. Speaker, the Church of Pentecost, as a humanitarian gesture, and in keeping with recent social partnership arrangements, offered the Pentecost Convention Centre at Gomoa Fetteh as an isolation centre for infected persons. Similarly, the Catholic Church released a host of its facilities located across the country to house and treat infected persons. The 140-bed capacity Ghanaman Soccer Centre in Prampram, owned by the Ghana Football Association, also served as an isolation centre. The work of the traditional churches, Charismatic, Pentecostal churches and our Islamic leaders continue to uphold our people.[59]

The above statement, to be sure, exemplifies the contribution of religious organisations and how they impact policy and decision-making in society.

As previously mentioned, Ghana's initial level of preparedness towards the coronavirus crisis was weak. A key accusation against the government was that frontline healthcare workers lacked priority medical devices and other pandemic medical supplies. For example, doctors at the Department of Accident and Emergency Unit of the Korle Bu Teaching Hospital on 2 April 2020 expressed their dissatisfaction and threatened to go on strike over poor level of readiness to combat the coronavirus pandemic.[60] In a memo to the Head of Department of the Unit, the aggrieved doctors lamented that management has "woefully failed" to provide the necessary protection they required to work including the provision of protective personal equipment.

To ameliorate the situation, religious institutions assisted the government by leveraging their resources. For instance, the National Catholic Secretariat, in collaboration with Caritas Ghana, which is an important Relief and Humanitarian Agency of Ghana Catholic Bishops' Conference, instituted a nine-month National Response Plan for Covid-19. The aim was to appeal to its members, Catholic organisations, and businesses to donate protective equipment and other medical supplies to support Catholic frontline healthcare workers in the Church's 46 hospitals and the 83 clinics

---

58 Mayaki B. 2020. "Bishops in Ghana donate to National Covid-19 Fund", *Vatican News*, 4 May.

59 Ofori-Atta K. 2020. "Mid-Year Review of the Budget Statement and Economic Policy of the Government of Ghana & Supplementary Estimate for the 2020 Financial Year". Presentation to Parliament of Ghana, 23 July.

60 "Korle-Bu doctors threaten to strike over poor coronavirus preparedness", *GhanaWeb*, 2 April.

across the country.⁶¹ Similarly, on 30 April 2020, the Church of Jesus Christ of Latter-day Saints, in partnership with Project Hope, a health and humanitarian relief organisation of global repute, donated to the Ghana Health Service relief items that included 400 000 surgical nose masks and 30 000 isolation gowns.⁶² Significantly, as seen in the finance minister's statement on the 2020 Mid-Year Budget Review, religious institutions devoted their facilities to serve as isolation centres.

Religion contributed essentially to the fight against the coronavirus pandemic. While the disease was seen as a mundane affair in many respects, in the fight against its spiritual effects, spiritual intervention became cardinal. Traditional religious functionaries sought spiritual intervention through the performance of certain rituals. In May 2020, it was reported that authorities of the Aflao Traditional Council, in the Volta region of Ghana, performed rituals to ward off the virus from entering their communities. According to media reportage, led by the traditional priest in Aflao, a town on Ghana's border with Togo, the authorities offered a black goat as a sacrifice to the deities who were believed to be the causal agents of the coronavirus crisis. The goal of this ritual was to prevent the virus from entering through any of the three entry and exit points in the area. Like the prophetic actors of Christianity, the traditional authorities believed that the virus was a plague visited on the population by the deities as a result of the ban on libation and other traditional rituals along with other Ghanaian public events.⁶³ Some traditional priests also predicted the disappearance of the virus following the performance of some rituals to the deities. For instance, on 28 March 2020, the media reported that an elder at the Zakadza shrine, popularly known in Ghana as the Nogokpo shrine, predicted that the pandemic would vanish from the shores of Ghana and, indeed, Africa on 19 April 2020 after they had invoked the mystical powers of the shrine to cleanse the land of the pandemic.⁶⁴ Some traditional authorities connected to the shrine, however, issued a disclaimer arguing that the prediction was a self-opinion of the elder.⁶⁵

Notwithstanding the positive contributions of religious organisations, beliefs, imaginations, rituals and practices were also used to frustrate state efforts to manage the pandemic. Unsurprisingly, in defiance of the executive order and advice and warning of public healthcare workers, some churches continued to organise

---

61 "Church in Ghana Appeals for Protective Gear to Aid Catholic Hospitals Battling Covid-19", *Aciafrica.org*, 31 March.

62 "The Church of Jesus Christ of Latter-day Saints in partnership with Project Hope, donate Covid-19 protective gear to the Ghana Health Service", *The Church of Jesus Christ of Latter-day Saints News*, 12 May 2020.

63 Bless P. 2020. "Aflao Traditional Council offers sacrifices to stop Coronavirus", *Celebritiesbuzz.com*, 30 March.

64 "Coronavirus will disappear April 19 – Nogokpo Shrine", *Ghana News Agency (GNA)*, 28 March 2020.

65 Kpodo E. 2020. "Somey reacts to 'Coronavirus will disappear on April 19' Comment", *Ghana News Agency (GNA)*, 16 April.

services, leading to conflict between the churches and law enforcement agents.[66] Of particular interest to the tension between religion, law and public health safety was the violation of the pandemic-related measures by the members of the Christ Embassy Church.

On 30 April 2021, a video circulated and trending in social media depicted the gathering of the youth of Christ Embassy Church. In the said video the non-masked youth of the church were seen in an ecstatic mood, screaming, chanting and dancing as part of their youth evangelism event dubbed the "Pneumatic Night."[67] This attracted substantial public disapproval and agitation. In a statement, Occupy Ghana, a pressure group, questioned why the event was allowed to go on in the first place given the position of the church's leader, Pastor Chris Oyakhilome, regarding the coronavirus pandemic.[68] Oyakhilome had been accused of holding a fundamentalist and coronavirus conspiracy theory, asserting that the coronavirus crisis was "planned" by a power wielding cartel. On 31 March 2021, the UK government imposed a fine of £125 000 on LoveWorld Television Ministry, a television network owned by Oyakhilome's church for airing inaccurate and potentially harmful positions regarding the coronavirus pandemic, a claim which was seen as a breach of UK's broadcasting code.[69] Oyakhilome had also previously been accused of encouraging his members to ignore the Covid-19 protocol. Following public agitation, on 2 May 2021, the Ghana Police Service, through Director of Public Affairs Sheilla Kessie Abayie-Buckman, issued a press release hinting that it was investigating the said act because it was worrying and "putting the entire country at risk of spreading Covid-19".[70] Four members of the church were subsequently held responsible and arraigned before court.[71]

Thus, in spite of religious resources serving as coping mechanism in the management of the coronavirus pandemic, they also contributed to frustrating the scientific measures put in place to mitigate the pandemic. For example, given that the closure of the churches had an impact on freedoms of religion, expression, and association, some leaders threatened that continued closure would lead to the visitation of God's wrath. Reverend Christian Kwabena Andrews, popularly known as Osofo Kyiri Abosom, is noted to have sent strong warning to Ghana's president regarding the closure of Churches. According to the Osofo Kyiri Abosom, God had told him

---

66 "Coronavirus: Pastor Arrested"; Donkor, "Coronavirus: Pastor Arrested Again".
67 "Police investigate Christ Embassy for flouting Covid-19 protocols", *Daily Graphic*, 3 May 2021.
68 "Deal with Christ Embassy Church leaders over COVID-spreader event – Occupy Ghana", *GhanaWeb*, 2 May 2021.
69 Sweney M. 2021. "Christian TV channel fined by Ofcom over Covid conspiracy theories", *The Guardian*, 6 October.
70 Ghana Police Service. 2021. "Christ Embassy Youth Church's 'Pneumatic Night'", *Facebook*, 2 May. [https://www.facebook.com/GhPoliceService/photos/a.525861720942535/1622039361324760/?type=3&source=57]
71 Ullo SD. 2021. "Four granted bail after arrest over Covid-19 breaches at Christ Embassy's event", *Citinewsroom.com*, 7 May.

that perilous consequences awaited the leaders of the country should they fail to open the churches within a week's time.[72] Such attitudes, surely, frustrated efforts at containing the coronavirus crisis.

CONCLUSION

While a secular state, the Republic of Ghana has demonstrated a noteworthy amount of what might be called "strategic secularism." Despite being a professed secular state, religious resources in the form of actors, beliefs and ritual practices function decisively in the public domain. Religion has in diverse ways been used to direct, detect and influence many of the public decisions of legal and political importance, sometimes undercutting the political and legal maturation of the state. As a pervasively religious society, Ghana is a nation where religion plays a vital role in the healing and health delivery processes of the people. Due to its political and legal value, religion has been decisive in the management of the ongoing coronavirus crisis.

This chapter has brought to light the ways in which religious resources and law forged a vital constellation of the management of the pandemic in Ghana. The chapter has also shown how in its quest to contain the coronavirus pandemic, the state of Ghana put in place a wide range of public health safety measures including a ban on public gatherings and social intervention policies. To further mitigate the spread of the virus, these measures were supplemented with legislative instruments, significant among which is the enactment of the Imposition of Restrictions (Coronavirus Disease (Covid-19) Pandemic) (No. 2) Instrument, 2020. This law, which mandates a partial lockdown in some parts of the country, had certain consequential effects, as it restricted movement in the affected areas. This situation brought some citizens into direct confrontation with law enforcement agencies. Despite this, the law and other measures put in place collectively contributed to the successful management of the Covid-19 crisis.

In particular, this chapter has noted precise challenges associated with these measures, especially when it comes to restrictions on religious gathering, focusing on the degree to which religious institutions in Ghana have played an ambivalent role in mitigating the coronavirus pandemic. Importantly, they have been useful in combatting the pandemic largely through: (1) their cooperation with and adherence to the Covid-19 preventive measures, (2) assisting state agencies in educating their members on the pandemic safety measure and (3) the provisioning of humanitarian services including cash donations and logistics. These measures have made their own unique contribution towards the management of the disease. Yet, despite these contributions, religious resources also frustrated the efforts to mitigate the crisis presented by the coronavirus.

---

72 Bantie R. 2020. "Generational curse will befall on Ghana if Akufo Addo fails to open churches by Sunday", *BBC Ghana*, 8 May.

3 Religious freedom and responses to Covid-19 management in Masvingo District, Zimbabwe

Excellent Chireshe[1]

INTRODUCTION

In a bid to enhance the prevention, containment, and treatment of Covid-19, and hence promote public health and well-being, the government of Zimbabwe put in place measures in the form of statutory instruments. The instruments show the government's commitment to fulfil its constitutional mandate to take preventive measures against the spread of disease.[2] Measures put in place in Zimbabwe included the following statutory instruments, among others. These are the decrees most relevant to the study in terms of content and time frame.

Table 3.1: Statutory instruments put in place in Zimbabwe due to Covid-19

Decree no.	Content	Impact on religious activities
SI 76/2020 of 23 March	The President declares a State of Disaster due to an infectious disease and declared a pandemic by the WHO on 11 March 2020.	The alertness of religious organisations on disaster preparedness.
SI 77/2020 of 23 March	The Minister of Health and Child Care declares Covid-19 a Formidable Epidemic Disease.	The instrument allows for the implementation of lockdown regulations including the suspension of religious gatherings.
SI 83/2020 (the principal order) of 28 March	Establishes measures to contain the spread of the Covid-19 pandemic, while the State of Disaster is in force.	Suspension of religious gatherings for an initial 21 days from 30 March 2020 to 19 April 2020. The stay-at-home policy takes effect.
SI 93/2020 of 19 April	Reviews the measures to contain the spread of the Covid-19 pandemic, while the State of Disaster continues.	Extension of the national lockdown and continued suspension of social, including religious gatherings, by two weeks, from 19 April to 3 May 2020.

---

1 Associate Professor of Religion, Faculty of Arts, Culture and Heritage Studies, Department of Philosophy and Religious Studies, Great Zimbabwe University/ Research Fellow, Faculty of Theology and Religion, Department of Religion Studies, University of the Free State.
2 Constitution of Zimbabwe, 2013, s 29.3.

Decree no.	Content	Impact on religious activities
SI 136/2020 of 12 June	Reviews the measures to contain the spread of the Covid-19 pandemic, while the State of Disaster continues.	Extension of the national lockdown. Religious gatherings are permitted on condition that no more than 50 adult individuals are gathered at a place of worship. Those gathered are to wear face masks, observe the social distancing rule, have their hands sanitised and their temperatures taken upon admission to the space. Buildings for worship to be disinfected.
SI 234/2021 of 17 September	Reviews the measures to contain the spread of the Covid-19 pandemic, while the State of Disaster continues.	Only fully vaccinated individuals or those with negative PCR tests taken not more than 48 hours, are to be admitted at places of worship. The number of worshippers must not exceed 50% of the maximum capacity of each place.

However, some of the measures promulgated in these instruments, particularly SI 83 of 2020, which entailed curtailing mobility and a temporary ban on social gatherings, were considered drastic, as they infringed on human rights.[3] These rights, enshrined in the Constitution of Zimbabwe, 2013, include freedoms of assembly and association, freedom of religion or belief, and freedom to practise and propagate and give expression to one's religion, whether in public or in private and whether alone or together with others.[4] This chapter analyses the effects of these measures from the perspective of three churches in Zimbabwe.

EFFECTS OF COVID-19 REGULATIONS ON CHURCHES IN ZIMBABWE

In the interest of promoting public health in the face of Covid-19 and in accordance with the Public Health Act, the president of Zimbabwe proclaimed a national lockdown which commenced on 30 March 2020. The lockdown, aimed at containing the Covid-19 pandemic, entailed prohibition or limits of social gatherings, requirements of social distancing and restriction of movement. The measures on restriction of movement included the closure of national borders to restrict immigration. This is because Covid-19 cases were associated with inbound travellers from abroad.[5]

Due to social distancing interventions during phases 4 and 5 of the Covid-19 lockdown in Zimbabwe, people were no longer attending school, no longer left

---

3   Chirisa I et al. 2021. "The Impact and Implications of Covid-19: Reflections on the Zimbabwean Society", *Social Sciences and Humanities Open* 4(1):100181, 21.
4   These are contained in the Constitution of Zimbabwe, 2013, s 58, s 60.1a, and s 60.1b, respectively.
5   Chirisa et al, "The Impact and Implications of Covid-19", 2.

their homes to spend time with friends and relatives and no longer attended church, funerals or other social gatherings. Given that social interactions are a basic human need, social distancing is disruptive, as it can lead to social rejection, broken relationships, loneliness, individualism and poor mental health, among other effects.[6] Thus, Covid-19 disrupted the observance of rituals that enhance social solidarity. In the religious sphere, there was a shift from public to private worship, from live face-to-face interactions to online engagement. Although adequate social contact is critical for mental health, social distancing policies disrupted this, thereby compromising freedoms of assembly, association and conscience.[7] In view of the foregoing, the present study sought to find out how these government directives conflicted with the constitutional guarantee of freedom of religion and how religious people from three selected churches in Masvingo District, Zimbabwe, responded to the government regulations.

Participating churches

The three churches represent different forms of Christianity, namely mainstream Protestant, Pentecostal, and African Initiated Churches. At this point, a brief description of each of the three churches is in order.

The Protestant church

The Protestant church that participated in the study was the Reformed Church in Zimbabwe (RCZ). It is a missionary church that was planted by the Dutch Reformed Church of South Africa,[8] whose origin is the Netherlands. The mission approach used by the Dutch Reformed Church in the implantation of the church in Zimbabwe combined the proclamation of the gospel with education, medical, agricultural and industrial activities.[9] The Reformed Church in Zimbabwe's approach to disease is biomedical, given its history and missionary thrust, which includes setting up and operating conventional health care centres.

The Pentecostal church

The Pentecostal church that participated in the study is the Apostolic Faith Mission in Zimbabwe (AFMZ). Lovemore Togarasei, a biblical scholar, says the church is the mother of Pentecostal movements in Zimbabwe.[10] The church was born in South

---

6   Eddy CM. 2021. "The Social Impact of Covid-19 as Perceived by the Employees of a UK Mental Health Service", *International Journal of Mental Health Nursing* 30(Suppl. 1): 1366-1375.
7   Eddy, "The Social Impact of Covid-19 as Perceived by the Employees of a UK Mental Health Service", 2.
8   Munikwa C and Hendriks HJ. 2013. "The Binga Outreach: A Critical Reflection on the Reformed Church in Zimbabwe's Cross-cultural Ministry", *Missionalia* 41(3):291.
9   Munikwa and Hendriks, "The Binga Outreach", 291.
10 Togarasei L. 2016. "Historicising Pentecostal Christianity in Zimbabwe", *Studia Historiae Ecclesiasticae* 42(2):1.

Africa and came to Zimbabwe through transnational movement of people.[11] Like other Pentecostal churches, the church places emphasis on the centrality of the Holy Spirit as the driving force behind the church and its members, including practices of speaking in tongues, faith healing, miracles (especially those of healing) and the gospel of prosperity. Biomedical and spiritual causes of and remedies for disease are acknowledged, but primacy is given to spiritual explanations, given the place accorded to the Holy Spirit.

The African Initiated Church

The African Initiated Church (AIC) that was involved in the study is the Johanne Marange Apostolic Church (JMAC). The church is the oldest and one of the largest AICs in Zimbabwe.[12] The church incorporates elements of African traditional religion by accommodating polygamy and exorcising evil spirits. Belief in the power of the Holy Spirit to enable the performance of healing miracles, speaking in tongues and exorcising evil spirits is a central feature of the church. So strong is the church's belief in the healing power of the Holy Spirit that it is opposed to the secular biomedical health system, which it labels as evil. The church believes that the Holy Spirit guarantees good health for those who tenaciously follow church teachings and regulations.[13] The church also believes that only God can heal provided there is faith on the part of the healed. Members are therefore barred from seeking modern biomedical health care services.[14] Those who do so are considered as lacking faith and so are penalised. The origin of pandemics is spiritualised – demons or spiritual powers are perceived as the cause.

Rationale for selection and method of the study

The motive for selection was to diversify the sample to get divergent views on the conceptualisation, experiences and responses to both the Covid-19 pandemic and to mitigation measures decreed by the government of Zimbabwe in order to contain the pandemic. The selection of religious people was based on the fact that religious beliefs, as indicated in the literature, influence understanding and responses to public health issues.[15] In the African worldview, religion, disease, healing and

---

11   Togarasei, "Historicising Pentecostal Christianity in Zimbabwe", 2.

12   Musevenzi J. 2017. "The African Independent Apostolic Church's Doctrine under Threat: The Emerging Power of Faith-based Organisations' Interventions and the Johanne Marange Apostolic Church in Zimbabwe", *Journal for the Study of Religion* 30(2):186.

13   Musevenzi, "The African Independent Apostolic Church's Doctrine under Threat", 184.

14   Masvaure S. 2021. "Liberalising Health-seeking Behaviour of the Johanne Marange Apostolic Sect", *Journal of Health Management*, 7 December.

15   See, for example, Chatters LM. 2000. "Religion and Health: Public Health Research and Practice", *Annual Review of Public Health* 21:335; Sibanda F, Muyambo T and Chitando E (eds). 2022. *Religion and the Covid-19 Pandemic in Southern Africa*. London and New York: Routledge, 5; Mwale N and Chita J. 2022. "Standing Together in the Time of Covid-19: The Responses of Church Umbrella Bodies in Zambia", in Sibanda et al (eds). *Religion and the Covid-19 Pandemic in Southern Africa*, 155.

health are closely linked.[16] Given this close link, religious responses have come to the forefront of explanation, analysis and responses to Covid-19, hence the thrust of the study.[17] While several studies have been conducted in Zimbabwe and beyond on the impact of Covid-19 and its associated containment measures,[18] not much has been documented on the interface between the Covid-19 control measures, concern about religious freedom and religious responses of the three churches under consideration. Hence, the current study fills in this geographical and conceptual gap.

The study was qualitative, as it sought to establish people's perceptions and experiences in relation to the Covid-19 pandemic and government-instituted regulations to contain the pandemic. It involved participants from three churches with branches or congregations in both urban and peri-urban Masvingo, Zimbabwe,[19] namely the Reformed Church in Zimbabwe, the Apostolic Faith Mission in Zimbabwe and the Johanne Marange Apostolic Church. The churches represent mainstream Protestant, Pentecostal and African Initiated Church groupings, respectively, within the Christian tradition. Data were collected, by means of in-depth, semi-structured interviews, from a purposefully selected sample of six clergy members (two from each of the three churches) and twelve laypersons (four from each church).[20] There was a balance of urban and peri-urban participation in the study.

Participation was voluntary, as informed consent was sought from prospective participants before they got involved in the study. All participants were above 18 years of age and so gave their own consent as adults. Anonymity and confidentiality were observed by means of using descriptions in lieu of names for participants. Interviews were conducted from 16 January to 4 February 2022. Interview questions related to the participants' conceptualisation of the pandemic, government directives, protection of human rights and their lived experiences.

It should be noted that participants, though belonging to particular churches, were not speaking on behalf of their churches as spokespersons, but rather as members who voluntarily participated in their individual capacities. Thus, their views may

---

16 Ukah AFK. 2020. "Prosperity, prophecy and the Covid-19 Pandemic: The Healing Economy of African Pentecostalism", *Pneuma* 42(3/4):430-439.
17 Ukah, "Prosperity, prophecy and the Covid-19 Pandemic", 431.
18 See, for example, Sibanda et al (eds). *Religion and the Covid-19 Pandemic in Southern Africa;* Van Coller H and Akinloye IA. 2022. "Religion, Law and Covid-19 in South Africa", in Sibanda F et al (eds). *Religion and the Covid-19 Pandemic in Southern Africa*, 89-102; Gathogo J. 2022. "Covid-19 Containment Measures and 'Prophecies' in Kenya", in Sibanda et al (eds). *Religion and the Covid-19 Pandemic in Southern Africa*, 126-140; Chukwuma OG. 2021. "The Impact of the Covid-19 Outbreak on Religious Practices of Churches in Nigeria", *HTS/Teologiese Studies/Theological Studies* 74(4):6377; Mahiya IT and Murisi R. 2022. "Reconfiguration and Adaptation of a Church in Times of Covid-19 Pandemic: A Focus on Selected Churches in Harare and Marondera", *Cogent Arts and Humanities* 9(1):art 2024338.
19 Peri-urban means around the urban area; on the outskirts.
20 It is worth noting that participants from the same church did not come from the same assembly or congregation.

not necessarily represent the official positions of the churches with which they are affiliated. What emerged was that participants from the three churches did not respond uniformly to the Covid-19 pandemic, notwithstanding some similarities among them.

CHURCHES CONFRONT COVID-19: PROTESTANT, PENTECOSTAL, AND AFRICAN INITIATED CHURCH VIEWS

The Reformed Church in Zimbabwe (RCZ)

Responses by participants from the RCZ exhibited a more cooperative stance with regard to the observance of government-instituted Covid-19 regulations. The two clergy members who were interviewed revealed that, as a church, they were duty-bound to observe government rules, since in Romans 13, God commands Christians to obey authorities. They conceptualised Covid-19 as a pandemic God allowed to happen and for which he had a purpose.

RCZ clergy responses

One of the two RCZ clergymen interviewed said: "Everything that God allows to happen has a purpose and this applies to Covid-19. Those who are meant to die as a result of the pandemic will die, while those who have not been predestined for such will not. However, as human beings, we need to do what is in our capacity to prevent the spread of the virus that causes the disease."[21] Regarding compliance with government-instituted regulations pertaining to Covid-19, the same clergyman said: "The orders given by the Government do not contradict the word of God, so there is no reason why as a church we would go against them. We encourage our members to always put on face masks in public places, sanitise or wash their hands regularly and exercise social distancing as much as possible. To avoid overcrowding in our church buildings, we have phased worship sessions so that all worshippers do not attend church service at the same time but in batches."[22]

Responding to a question on the church's response to the temporary prohibition of religious gatherings, which has since been lifted, the RCZ clergyman had this to say:

> I advised members of my congregation to use online platforms. As a church, we adopted online platforms such as Zoom, WhatsApp, Facebook and the radio to preach and share the word of God. Of course, this application of technology has its challenges, as some congregants did not have the gadgets, data or even network, to fellowship with others online. Others lacked technological competence, that is, they could not apply technology to access sermons or words of encouragement from their pastors or fellow worshippers, especially the elderly. However, notwithstanding these

---

21 Interview with Rev A by E Chireshe. Masvingo, Zimbabwe, 16 January 2022. The clergyman led an urban congregation while his counterpart led a peri-urban congregation.
22 Interview with Rev A, 16 January 2022.

challenges, online engagements were better than no contact at all. I had a list of the elderly from my congregation. During the time of a complete ban on gatherings, I occasionally contacted these elderly people through phone calls, encouraging them in their faith and assuring them that though distant I had them in prayer.[23]

On the question of possible violations of the constitutional right to assemble and practice religion under these regulations, the reverend indicated that Covid-19 control measures were meant to safeguard people's health, and he considered this as more important than insisting on freedom of assembly at that moment when Covid-19 was a real danger. The clergyman's responses showed the church's support for government initiatives to contain the pandemic.

The church's official Covid-19 response was compliance with government regulations, and its conceptualisation of Covid-19 was in terms of scientific causes and biomedical solutions; hence, the second RCZ clergyman, leading a peri-urban congregation, reiterated many of the same points as the first. On the duty to obey civil authorities, the second RCZ clergyman said: "As a law-abiding church, when the president announced a national lockdown that entailed a temporary ban on social gatherings, we did not try to resist. Our church is 100% behind all health protocols in a bid to contain the spread of Covid-19."[24] On alternative means of worship during the period of a temporary ban on social gatherings, the RCZ reverend had this to say:

> We considered other ways of reaching out to our congregants so that they do not backslide. It was really a trying time, but we had to operate within the confines of government stipulations. I have to point out that the pandemic and the attendant order to stop in-person church gatherings caught us off guard. Rather than lamenting, however, we decided to be proactive by turning to technology to provide pastoral services, although this is by no means a perfect substitute for face-to-face fellowship meetings. There are many challenges associated with the use of technology, but we had to make do with what was there.

On vaccination, the second RCZ clergyman said:

> We encouraged, and still encourage, our members to get vaccinated to protect themselves and others. Vaccines, especially those preventing child-killer diseases like polio and measles, have been effective, and so there is no reason for one to doubt the effectiveness of the Covid-19 vaccine. On the issue of conspiracy theories suggesting that vaccines are a programme meant to wipe out Africans by some from the West and East, I do not believe that God would allow such a thing to happen. If those people wanted to destroy us (Africans) they would have done so long back, as we have been using vaccines from the international community. God is in control.[25]

---

23 Interview with Rev A, 16 January 2022.
24 Interview with Rev B by E Chireshe. Masvingo, Zimbabwe, 24 January 2022.
25 Interview with Rev B, 24 January 2022.

Pertaining to the period when Covid-19 control measures were eased to allow people to gather in restricted numbers, the second RCZ clergyman said:

> When the ban on social gatherings was lifted, but still with restrictions on numbers, we ensured that there is no overcrowding in our churches by controlling the number of attendees per Sunday service session. At the entrance of the church building, there is someone who sanitises people and checks their temperature on entering the building. All worshippers are required to put on face masks. We explained to our members that the Covid-19 control measures were meant to protect all of us and therefore there was no need to resist them.[26]

What was clear from the two Protestant clergymen was that the church's official position was to support government initiatives aimed at containing Covid-19, notwithstanding their belief in the power of God as the controller of everything. Throughout the interviews, the religious leaders were wearing face masks. They indicated that they were fully vaccinated, which was an indication that they practised what they preached with regard to the observance of Covid-19 control measures decreed by the Zimbabwean government. The church's support for government initiatives can be explained in terms of its biomedical orientation when it comes to sickness and health-seeking. The church combines gospel proclamation with medical activities. including establishing hospitals and clinics.[27] This suggests that religion and science are not contradictory in its worldview.

RCZ laity responses

Interviews with RCZ congregants showed consistency between the official position of the church and the practices of members, although it did emerge that in some cases there was laxity, especially pertaining to the proper wearing of face masks, social distancing and sanitisation. On Covid-19 control measures in general, including the temporary ban on social gatherings, the first RCZ layman interviewed said: "Our church supports Government initiatives to halt the spread of the pandemic. The Covid-19 control measures put in place are for the protection of all. When a temporary ban on church gatherings was announced, we readily stopped meeting face-to-face for services and resorted to online means. Although this has its challenges, it was a practical substitute for in-person gatherings."[28] Regarding wearing face masks, sanitisation and social distancing, the first RCZ laywoman said: "As for safety measures, such as wearing face masks and sanitisation, we observe as we meet for worship. The challenge I see in our church is that of social distancing. Sometimes it is not strictly observed, although the church at the policy level has tried to group members and stagger services so that we don't attend church service

---

26 Interview with Rev B, 24 January 2022.

27 Munikwa and Hendriks, "The Binga Outreach: A Critical Reflection on the Reformed Church in Zimbabwe's Cross-cultural Ministry", 292.

28 Interview with RCZ layman no. 1 by E Chireshe. Masvingo, Zimbabwe, 19 January 2022.

at the same time."²⁹ Still, of Covid-19 the control measures generally, the second RCZ layman had this to say:

> I personally try to observe Covid-19 rules, but sometimes I fail to do so when some members do not observe the same, especially social distancing during worship, temperature checks and sanitisation at gatherings. I move around with my bottle of sanitiser for my safety. I should, however, point out that if God does not protect a city, those who watch over it are doing so in vain. In the same way, observance of safety measures alone is not enough unless God protects you. So, while as human beings we need to do what we can, it is ultimately God who provides the protection.³⁰

What is clear from the responses of the RCZ laypersons is that their leaders encouraged them to follow Covid-19 regulations, but they did not always do so. It appears that apart from getting Covid-19 information from their ministers of religion, they also got it from other sources, including the communities in which they lived, and some of these other sources of information may have caused laxity. The preached word is not always the lived word, and in some cases the laity may move in a different direction from that of their ordained leaders, as revealed by the interviews with RCZ participants.

Concerning vaccination, the second of two RCZ male laypersons said, "Our leaders encouraged us to get vaccinated for our safety, and some of us are fully vaccinated."³¹ Further to the issue of vaccination, echoing the words of her male counterpart said, the second RCZ female layperson said: "When vaccines became available, our reverend encouraged us to get vaccinated. When it was announced that only vaccinated congregants should be allowed to attend church service, many members in our church, including myself, got vaccinated."³² Responses by both RCZ clergy and laity thus showed vaccine acceptance. Vaccine acceptance could have been influenced by the theology and ideology of the church, which sees no contradiction between the medical and the spiritual.

Regarding the constitutional provisions on freedom of religion and worship in relation to the government restrictions, the second of two RCZ laywomen said: "Although freedom of religion is contained in the constitution, to me the temporary ban on gatherings and therefore the suspension of the right to association, as well as the right to express one's religiosity, was necessary. There is no use observing rights while grossly undermining other rights, such as the right to health."³³ It can be inferred that the participant understood Covid-19 as a biomedical health challenge that required biomedical solutions, hence the support for measures contained in

---

29 Interview with RCZ laywoman no. 1 by E Chireshe. Masvingo, Zimbabwe, 27 January 2022.
30 Interview with RCZ layman no. 2 by E Chireshe. Masvingo, Zimbabwe, 22 January 2022.
31 Interview with RCZ layman no. 2, 22 January 2022.
32 Interview with RCZ laywoman no. 2 by E Chireshe. Masvingo, Zimbabwe, 1 February 2022.
33 Interview with RCZ laywoman no. 2, 1 February 2022.

statutory instruments on Covid-19 prevention, containment and treatment. In her estimation:

> Covid-19 is a pandemic that came to us unprepared. When I first heard about it, little did I know that it shall alter our lives, including church life. When the president announced the national lockdown on 30 March 2020, and the ban on social gatherings, as well as the stay-at-home decree, I felt uneasy, but these measures had to be taken to contain the spread of the pandemic and to ensure public safety. Although the temporary ban on gatherings was disruptive, it was necessary for the health benefit of society.[34]

Likewise, responding to the question of whether the government-instituted measures to control Covid-19, violated religious freedom, as provided for in the Zimbabwe Constitution, the second RCZ layman also replied, "Although the ban constituted an infringement of the right to religious expression, it was justifiable on health grounds. Our reverend advised us to adhere to government orders and at the same time continue to worship, though in new ways. We used technology to continue to fellowship."[35] Worth noting from the responses by members of the Reformed Church in Zimbabwe is that they supported government initiatives to control the pandemic, although there were some challenges in implementing this. The sentiment that emerged was that it was better to forego religious freedom in order to safeguard human health. This also shows subscription to the scientific causation and control of Covid-19, which is an antithesis of the spiritualisation of the pandemic.

The Apostolic Faith Mission in Zimbabwe (AFMZ)

AFMZ clergy responses

Responses from participants belonging to the Apostolic Faith Mission in Zimbabwe exhibited a somewhat different perspective of the pandemic, that is a spiritual one alongside a biomedical one, as compared to the largely biomedical one that the Reformed Church in Zimbabwe reflected. As presented above, the church places importance on the Holy Spirit as a healing agent. The two AFMZ pastors who participated in the study, one leading an urban assembly and the other a peri-urban one, shared similar sentiments on the genesis, impact and control of the pandemic. The spiritualisation of the pandemic is evident from the responses given to questions posed.

Concerning the government's ban on social gatherings, the first AFMZ pastor, leading an urban assembly, had this to say:

> Coming together physically to worship is an expectation of God as expressed in Hebrews 10:25 where believers are exhorted not to abandon the custom of congregating for worship. This was temporarily undermined

---

34 Interview with RCZ laywoman no. 2, 1 February 2022.
35 Interview with RCZ layman no. 2, 22 January 2022.

when a ban on social gatherings was pronounced in order to curtail the spread of Covid-19. The ban not only offset normal church practices, but also seriously undermined the freedom of religion provided for in the Constitution of the country. We acknowledge the presence of Covid-19 as a threat to human health, but we believe that God provides the cure. While we don't believe that the banning of church gatherings is the solution, we had no choice but to refrain from meeting physically to avoid clashes with authorities. We had to obey the government directive on the ban on religious gatherings when this was announced, but we believe that prayer is the key to fighting the pandemic. We believe that the blood of Jesus can heal those infected and immunise those not yet infected. Banning church gatherings is not the solution.[36]

On alternative means of worship during the lockdown, the AFMZ pastor said: "To continue ministering to our members amidst the suspension of face-to-face meetings, we have been using online engagements with our members. We used platforms such as WhatsApp, Facebook, the radio, phone calls, especially when communicating with the sick and elderly, as well as text messages, although the use of this mode was minimal."[37] Thus the church, like the RCZ, continued to have fellowship but in a non-physical form.

On the question of vaccination against Covid-19, the AFMZ pastor (A) said:

> We accept vaccination, being fully aware that the real solution to the pandemic lies with God. When the government announced that church gatherings would be permitted, but only on the condition that only the fully vaccinated are supposed to attend physically, we laughed at the idea. It is not our duty as the church or religious leaders to screen people who have come to church in terms of their vaccination status. We knew the believers well before Covid-19 and the vaccination programme. We will not bar anyone who has come to worship with us. We are glad the government has lifted the ban on church gatherings. This is a cause of joy for us. They have opened the church and that is good news for us. Let those who want to fellowship with others do so, without being asked questions about vaccination. On limits to numbers, this is not feasible. How can one ask someone to go back home because the church has reached the prescribed limit in terms of numbers?[38]

A number of issues emerge from the pastor's responses. The pastor was opposed to the ban on church services as a Covid-19 control measure, believing that God is the controller and healer of Covid-19 and that the blood of Jesus is both a cure and a vaccine. There was vaccine acceptance, but also resistance to coercive measures instituted by the government. Compliance with the ban on church gatherings was meant to ensure peace with authorities and not as a conviction that the cessation of gatherings was helpful. Defiance of government directives was notable on

---

36 Interview with AFM Pastor A by E Chireshe. Masvingo, Zimbabwe, 20 January 2022.
37 Interview with AFM Pastor A, 20 January 2022.
38 Interview with AFM Pastor A, 20 January 2022.

some points. However, the official position of the church was one of compliance with government regulations. The church has been actively involved in educating members on Covid-19 regulations and safety precautions.[39]

The second AFMZ pastor, from a different assembly, a peri-urban one, shared similar sentiments in observing:

> Covid-19 came as a challenge, but not one that is beyond God's control. The emergence of the pandemic and the subsequent suspension of church gatherings has seriously undermined the right to freely express religion. We understand where the government is coming from but we believe that church service is an essential service that should not have been banned because it is through our relationship with Covid-19 pandemic in this case.[40]

On the subject of vaccination, the second AFMZ pastor further observed:

> While as a church we are not against vaccination, we are against the idea of forced vaccination as when the government said those who have not been fully vaccinated should not attend church services. As a church, we cannot bar people from attending church because they are not vaccinated. We resolved to allow everyone who wanted to attend church to do so. Fortunately, no law-enforcement agents came to our church demanding the presentation of vaccination certificates by worshippers.[41]

Finally, on social distancing and wearing of face masks, the second AFMZ pastor said: "Social distancing is not practical during communal worship. We encourage the wearing of masks, as is mandated by government, but we find that some of our members do not take this seriously as they do not cover the mouth and nose. We only encourage but do not enforce, bearing in mind that the ultimate healer and protector against any form of disease is God."[42]

The second pastor's responses thus indicate some compliance with government rules in some respects, such as acceptance of vaccination and encouraging the wearing of masks, though without enforcement within the congregation. The second pastor did see the ban on religious gatherings as an unnecessary violation of freedom of worship, given the necessity of access to God in dealing with the pandemic. The second pastor also showed noncompliance with anti-Covid regulations in failing to bar the unvaccinated and limit the number of church attendees.

AFMZ congregants' responses

The sentiments of the pastors were reiterated by congregants, who expressed the belief that to get sick or die of Covid-19 is in accordance with God's master plan for everyone and that Covid-19 protocol observance was not the real solution, but

---

39 Pavari N. 2020. "The Role of Apostolic Faith Mission in Zimbabwe in the Fight Against Coronavirus", *Journal of Public Administration and Governance* 10(3):306-320.
40 Interview with AFM Pastor B by E Chireshe. Masvingo, Zimbabwe, 26 January 2022.
41 Interview with AFM Pastor B, 26 January 2022.
42 Interview with AFM Pastor B, 26 January 2022.

rather that the solution lies in the blood of Jesus. For the pastors and congregants, spirituality was the ultimate mitigation against Covid-19. The first AFMZ layman interviewed on the ban on church gatherings said: "Yes, the Covid-19 disease is there but the solution lies in God. Whether one survives or dies as a result of Covid-19 is all up to God. Initially, when the president announced a ban on social gatherings, including church gatherings, we tried to resist by secretly meeting in our houses, but we later realised that we might be in trouble with authorities, so we stopped."[43] This suggests opposition to the ban on church gatherings and belief in spiritual solutions to the pandemic.

The second of two AFMZ laywomen interviewed echoed similar sentiments, suggesting that Covid-19 is spiritual in origin and therefore demands spiritual solutions. She expressed this in remarks which suggested a certain trivialisation of the government's Covid-19 measures, replying: "We have been healed by his [Jesus's] wounds and therefore we need not live in fear of the pandemic. God is in control. No amount of sanitisation and degree of wearing face masks can prevent the pandemic from attacking us if God has not protected us. I do wear face masks and sanitise as regularly as I can. In addition, I have been vaccinated as a matter of choice, without considering the vaccination as the ultimate protector."[44] The first AFMZ laywoman interviewed in the study said that she believed the pandemic was a real threat to health and a cause of death. However, she said that the focus should not be on the dreadful nature of the pandemic, but rather on the healer Jesus Christ.

When it came to specific, government-recommended measures against Covid-19, the second AFMZ laywoman said of vaccination, "When it was announced that people can now gather for worship services but that they should be vaccinated, some of us were glad that we were going back to our normal way of worship. We did not consider vaccination important as no one monitored this at the assembly. However, our pastor encouraged us to get vaccinated but indicated that it was up to an individual to decide to get vaccinated or not."[45] The picture that emerges from the female congregant's response is that everything happens according to God's plan, and so there is no need to fear the pandemic. She combined spirituality with science by getting vaccinated and observing Covid-19 protocols, yet also believed in God as protector and healer. The response shows some trivialisation, but not opposition, to vaccination.

On sanitisation measures, the response was mixed, but it indicated a general laxity in implementation. The first AFMZ layman said:

> As for sanitisation and temperature checks, there was and still is no consistency on this at our assembly. We wear face masks so that we are not in trouble with authorities, but often when we are worshipping inside, we normally don't put on face masks as directed, but we will be having them

---

43 Interview with AFMZ layman no. 1 by E Chireshe. Masvingo, Zimbabwe, 18 January 2022.
44 Interview with AFMZ laywoman no. 2 by E Chireshe. Masvingo, Zimbabwe, 30 January 2022.
45 Interview with AFMZ laywoman no. 2, 30 January 2022.

by the neck, so that when the police happen to pass by, we will not be in trouble. However, there are some of our members who take face masks seriously and would always put them on during service. As for our pastor, he does not explicitly insist on Covid-19 protocols, but he has not told us not to adhere to them.[46]

There were, thus, mixed reactions to Covid-19 control measures. What is clear is that the Covid-19 control protocols were not strictly observed, which could suggest more reliance on spirituality than on biomedical measures.

What can be noted from responses from members of the Pentecostal-charismatic church is that Covid-19 has been spiritualised. It is conceived in terms of a force that God can overcome when invoked to do so through prayers. The members generally exhibited an attitude of laxity when it comes to observance of Covid-19 prevention, containment and treatment measures, especially social distancing, sanitisation and proper wearing of masks. While accepting modern medication as a remedy for Covid-19-related sickness, including the vaccine and other preventive measures, members of the church insisted that God was the divine healer, who can completely put Covid-19 under control. As such, spirituality took precedence over seeking biomedical remedies when it came to Covid-19. Thus, while the church officially supported WHO and government-instituted Covid-19 control measures, the implementation of the measures by members was compromised.[47]

The Johanne Marange Apostolic Church (JMAC)

As already indicated, the church believes in the Holy Spirit and faith healing and considers the biomedical health system as evil.[48] Pandemics are understood as the results of demonic or spiritual forces. As such, the church undermines the role of modern medical services, which could be detrimental in the context of Covid-19. Participants from JMAC revealed that although they were aware of Covid-19, they were not afraid of it, as they believed they were protected by God because of their faith. They did not believe in biomedical remedies to the pandemic, as they have a negative attitude towards Western medication and hospitalisation. There was also a sense in which they insinuated that Covid-19 did not exist among them, as they were protected by God. So, in terms of conceptualisation of Covid-19, there appears to be both an affirmation of the existence of the pandemic as well as denial – it was a threat elsewhere and not among them.

JMAC clergy responses

For the purpose of present analysis, the leader of a church assembly or congregation is referred to as an "apostle". However, in conventional usage in African Initiated Churches, the term "apostle" (*mupositori* in Shona language) refers to a member of

---

46 Interview with AFMZ layman no. 1, 18 January 2022.
47 Pavari, "The Role of the Apostolic Faith Mission in Zimbabwe", 306.
48 Musevenzi, "The African Independent Apostolic Church's Doctrine under Threat", 184.

the church, whether in leadership or not. There is no formal training for leaders in the church, since leadership is based on a special calling by God, evidenced by "signs", such as miracle performances: to prove the calling.

The following quotation from the first church apostle interviewed for the study reflects some of the perceptions and attitudes of the church in relation to Covid-19. Regarding the conceptualisation of Covid-19, the ban on church gatherings and vaccination, the apostle had this to say:

> I have heard about Covid-19, but this is not a danger to us who are protected by God. When the government banned church gatherings, we were disturbed, because we did not see a good reason for that. Covid-19 does not do anything to us. We survive by faith in God, so no one can tell us to get vaccinated in order to be safe. We are safe already. Even if we were to die of the disease, it will be part of God's plan, so we discourage our members from taking the vaccine against Covid-19.[49]

On measures like social distancing, wearing face masks, sanitisation and temperature checks, the apostle said: "We respect the government leaders and understand that we have to observe them as instructed by God, but we do not believe the Covid-19 control measures will help us. How can someone I used to be close to make me sick? Masks are not important. We wear them in public to avoid clashing with the police, but often we do not put them on. We don't use sanitisers and thermometers at our assembly."[50] What is evident is that the apostle downplayed the threat of Covid-19 and believed in spiritual protection against the pandemic. The second apostle interviewed had similar views. He said: "As children of Johanne, we are not afraid of Covid-19. We are protected. We don't believe in those preventive measures like face masks, social distancing and sanitisation and vaccination. We are protected by the Holy Spirit. I will not get vaccinated, in spite of the government's pressure to get everyone vaccinated."[51] Like apostle A, apostle B also trivialised Covid-19, based on the belief in the protective power of God. The responses confirm what is documented about the church in relation to diseas or illness and health care seeking.[52]

JMAC laypersons' responses

Members of the JMAC affirmed what their leaders said in relation to Covid-19 control measures. They did not believe Covid-19 posed a threat to them, as their relationship with God was enough protection. They were not vaccinated and affirmed that members of their church were not vaccinated against Covid-19 or

---

49 Interview with apostle A by E Chireshe. Masvingo, Zimbabwe, 21 January 2022.
50 Interview with apostle A, 21 January 2022.
51 Interview with apostle B by E Chireshe. Masvingo, Zimbabwe, 4 February 2022.
52 See Musevenzi, "The African Independent Apostolic Church's Doctrine under Threat", 184; Masvaure, "Liberalising Health-seeking Behaviour of the Johanne Marange Apostolic Sect", 1; UNICEF. 2011. *Apostolic Religion, Health and Utilization of Maternal and Child health Services in Zimbabwe*. Collaborating Centre for Operational Research and Education.

any other diseases for which people have historically been vaccinated. They did not deem Covid-19 safety measures ordered by government to have the capacity to protect them. What is notable from the JMAC responses is that the church was not supportive of government initiatives to prevent, contain and treat Covid-19. The church has alternative ways of dealing with diseases including pandemics. Examples of responses given are provided below. The following statements illustrate the views and experiences of congregants:

> I know that Covid-19 is there and some people are dying as a result of infection. However, I believe that God is the only one with power to protect and heal. This is what I have been taught since childhood. So, I don't see the need for taking measures like sanitisation, wearing face masks, social distancing or vaccination. Our church has taught us against taking medicines. Since birth, I have not visited a clinic or hospital for treatment. Prayers and holy water are important for treatment of any type of disease. I am not vaccinated and will not get vaccinated. Even if I am to die of Covid-19, it will be God's will.[53]

The above response shows the negation of modern health systems and belief in faith healing. Death is interpreted as God's will. Similar beliefs were expressed by a female congregant who said: "Covid-19 is a disease like others. It is a flu that requires to be treated in the manner other flus are treated – that is, the use of holy water and prayer. We don't go to the hospital for treatment. Our church does not allow that. When we fall sick, prophets in our church pray for us. We believe in God as the true healer, so faith in him, in the face of Covid-19, is important. Government requirements like sanitisation, wearing of face masks and vaccination are not important. Our church does not allow us to get vaccinated." On the ban on church gatherings, the second JMAC layman indicated that this should not have been done, since worshipping together is necessary for physical and spiritual health.

The JMAC church responses seem to show that some beliefs and practices of the church in relation to Covid-19 do not help in containing the pandemic. The negation of biomedical explanations and solutions shows that some religious doctrinal responses may be counterproductive and therefore promote the spread of the virus that causes Covid-19.

CHURCH RESPONSES IN CONTEXT

The responses from the three churches reflect their (churches) histories and contexts. As Bernard Pindukai Humbe has stated, religion influences all areas of life including the way individuals and groups conduct themselves and interpret certain phenomena, Covid-19 in this case.[54]

---

53 Interview with JMAC layman no.1 by E Chireshe. Masvingo, Zimbabwe, 17 January 2022.
54 Humbe BP. 2022. "Living with Covid-19 in Zimbabwe: A Religious and Scientific Healing Response", in Sibanda et al (eds). *Religion and the Covid-19 Pandemic in Southern Africa*, 73.

The Protestant church

The mainline Protestant church represented in this study, the Reformed Church in Zimbabwe (RCZ), is a product of missionary activity, having been set up as a Western-oriented church in terms of the conceptualisation of the relationship between religion, health and healing. When missionaries brought the church, they built churches to cater to spiritual needs and hospitals to physiological needs.[55] For the Western missionary, the church was the sphere of the spiritual and moral, hence the setting up of hospitals to cater for physical ailments. Disease and healing were conceived of in biomedical terms. This seems to explain why the RCZ in the present study was supportive of biomedical and scientific control measures announced by the government against Covid-19. It should, however, be noted that they saw God as ultimately responsible for all that happens, including the emergency of Covid-19, who gets infected and sick, and who recovers and who dies. They saw science and spirituality as harmonious. Thus, the belief was that although God is ultimately in charge, human beings have been given the capacity to take action to make things happen or prevent them, hence the support for initiatives to put Covid-19 under control. The RCZ responses in this study confirm the findings of other scholars of religion, such as Fortune Sibanda, Tenson Muyambo and Ezra Chitando, that most mainstream Christian leaders were forthcoming in promoting public health measures aimed at containing Covid-19.[56] They encouraged members to pray as they observed Covid-19 regulations.

The Pentecostal church

Pentecostalism represents a shift from mainline Protestant theology in its emphasis on the manifestation of the Holy Spirit as an agent of healing. It emerged in the present study of the Apostolic Faith Mission of Zimbabwe (AFMZ) that some Pentecostal Christians believed that the Holy Spirit was protecting them, a finding that confirms Bernard Pindukai Humbe's similar observations.[57] This seems to explain the appeal to spiritual interventions to control Covid-19, the centring of God in the healing narratives and laxity in implementation of government-instituted Covid-19 regulations. As religion scholar Asonzeh Ukah notes, "African Pentecostalism, especially the prosperity variant, has been at the forefront of promising to make its members healthy and wealthy through divine means."[58] The promise of healing is one of the attractions of Pentecostal churches. Healing is, therefore, one of "the most important sacred goods on sale in the African Pentecostal marketplace".[59] Although Pentecostals subscribe to the doctrine of faith healing, they also accept biomedical

---

55 See Munikwa and Hendriks, "The Binga Outreach", 292.
56 See Sibanda et al (eds). 2022. *Religion and the Covid-19 Pandemic in Southern Africa*; see, specifically, Van Coller and Akinloye, "Religion, Law and Covid-19 in South Africa", in Sibanda et al (eds), *Religion and the Covid-19 Pandemic in Southern Africa*, 90.
57 Humbe, "Living with Covid-19 in Zimbabwe", 76.
58 Ukah, "Prosperity, prophecy and the Covid-19 Pandemic", 430.
59 Ukah, "Prosperity, prophecy and the Covid-19 Pandemic", 446.

solutions to the pandemic, hence their acceptance of vaccination, although they believe that true healing is the work of God through the Holy Spirit.

The AFMZ responses in this study suggest mixed reactions concerning the virus and the pandemic. While they believed in spiritual healing, they saw no harm in observing some of the Covid-19 control protocols. While they saw no harm in vaccination, they were against the idea of mandatory vaccination and barring entry into the place of worship on the ground that one has not been fully vaccinated. The adherence to stipulated gathering sizes emerged as particularly difficult for the Pentecostal church under consideration. In this regard, the believers conflicted with government regulations. This finding confirms medical communications scholar Olivia Kowalczyk and her fellow researchers' findings pertaining to believers' conflict with authorities warning that gatherings must be limited to combat the spread of the coronavirus.[60]

The African Initiated Church (JMAC)

The Johanne Marange Apostolic Church's responses suggest counterproductive attitudes. The responses generally showed that the church was not cooperative with the state when it came to measures to control the pandemic. However, the magnitude of infection and deaths among members as a result of noncompliance, in comparison with churches that were more compliant, has not yet been empirically established, to my knowledge. The church has historically not supported government initiatives when it comes to health matters, because it insists on faith healing and the demonisation of biomedical or scientific remedies. As has already been highlighted, the church does not allow its members to seek treatment from public health institutions.[61] However, in defiance of the rule, some members clandestinely get medical treatment from conventional medical health institutions.[62]

The church was against the immunisation programme, hence infant mortality rate is high in JMAC communities because of preventable child-killer diseases, such as polio, measles, and whooping cough, among others. There have been clashes between members of the church and government authorities due to the former's evasion of child immunisation.[63] The resistance to the Covid-19 vaccine needs to be understood against this background. As the government insisted on following science-based solutions,[64] JMAC church leaders discouraged members from getting vaccinated. The spiritualisation of the pandemic, as well as the doctrine of repelling biomedical interventions, explains why the church was not supportive of

---

60 Kowalczyk O et al. 2020. "Religion and Faith Perception in a Pandemic of Covid-19", *Journal of Religion and Health* 59:2671-2677.

61 Musevenzi, "The African Independent Apostolic Church's Doctrine under Threat", 184.

62 Sibanda F and Marevesa T. 2013. "March or Die?: Theological Reflections on the Violation of Children's Rights in African Initiated Churches, Zimbabwe", *Asian Academic Research Journal of Multidisciplinary* 1(7):170.

63 Sibanda and Marevesa, "March or Die?", 175.

64 Humbe, "Living with Covid-19 in Zimbabwe", 77.

government initiatives to combat Covid-19. While members put on face masks and sanitised when they had no option, such as when it was required to enter shops, they did not consider this important as protection against the virus, since their "vaccine" and healer is God through the Holy Spirit.

A note on technology

It emerged from both the Protestant church and the Pentecostal church in this study that technology was used to share the word of God. This helped to break the distance between congregants, thereby maintaining contact. However, not all people had access to technology, suggesting that the digital have-nots were left out of the communication network. They were isolated, a scenario that could have compromised their faith. Social distancing was not so easy for congregants, as the study indicates. The natural inclination to stay in close contact clashed with public health officials' advice to stay away from each other by social distancing. As Kowalczyk and colleagues note, pandemics are a challenging test, as they demand people to act in unusual ways, violating social norms.[65]

COVID-19 REGULATIONS, FREEDOM OF RELIGION AND HUMAN RIGHTS

Participants acknowledged that the emergence of the pandemic and the attendant promulgation of statutory instruments to keep the pandemic in check resulted in violation of human rights, particularly the right to religious expression; "the right to manifest one's belief in community with others."[66] However, for some Christians, particularly from the Reformed Church in Zimbabwe, the violation was a necessary one, as it was propelled by the need to safeguard public health. The violation was justifiable under certain emergency circumstances. Section 86.2 of the Zimbabwe Constitution states that fundamental human rights set out in the constitution may be limited to the extent that the limitation is fair, reasonable, necessary and justifiable in a democratic society, taking into consideration whether it is necessary in the interests of public safety, public health or the general public interest.

It appears that the Zimbabwe government put in place measures that violated some fundamental human rights after weighing the costs and benefits of protecting those rights in the face of the pandemic. The Public Health Act, in particular, demanded that every person must do what is in their capacity to control a public health risk.[67] The Act authorised the minister of health to respond to a formidable epidemic by making regulations relating to, among other things, the regulation and restriction of public traffic and of the movements of persons, the closing of churches and Sunday schools and the restriction of gatherings or meetings for the purpose of public worship.

---

65 Kowalczyk et al, "Religion and Faith Perception in a Pandemic of Covid-19", 2671-2677.
66 See also Van Coller and Akinloye, "Religion, Law and Covid-19 in South Africa", 91.
67 Public Health Act (Chapter 15:17), No. 11, s 68 a, c.

In view of this, it can be noted that the statutory instruments containing various measures to prevent, contain and treat Covid-19, were reasonable under the Zimbabwe Constitution, given that the purpose was public health protection. The limiting of human rights for the public good is in line with the principle of *Salus Populi Suprema Lex* ("Let the welfare of the people be the supreme law").[68] In cases of extreme emergency, such as Covid-19, it was justifiable to consider what is in the best interest of society as a whole, and this appears to have inspired Zimbabwe authorities to come up with Covid-19 control measures that might otherwise be deemed to be violative of human rights set forth in the Constitution.

While it is beyond doubt that some human rights were infringed upon by measures contained in statutory instruments on Covid-19 prevention, containment and treatment, the infringement was, arguably, for a good cause – namely public health. At the time of this writing, the lockdown rules in Zimbabwe have been relaxed and worshippers are allowed to congregate while observing Covid-19 health protocols. It can be extrapolated that religion can inhibit or accelerate the transmission of coronavirus, depending on the religious grouping one is considering. However, no systematic study, to my knowledge, has been conducted to determine whether non-compliance to the Covid-19 regulations harmed some religious communities more than others.

CONCLUSION

The study revealed that religion is ambivalent when it came to the control of Covid-19. It contains both attitudes that are health-promoting and others that are health-endangering when it comes to dealing with a public health crisis such as Covid-19. Sometimes what congregants did was at variance with the official positions of the churches to which they belonged. It is apparent from this study that the official positions of the RCZ and the AFMZ were supporting the government-initiated Covid-19 control measures, yet members sometimes behaved on the contrary, for example, by trivialising vaccination, not putting on masks in public spaces, not practising social distancing and not sanitising.

It also emerged that Covid-19 was conceived of in spiritual terms by some participants in terms of causation and treatment. This spiritualisation of Covid-19 seemed to engender attitudes of laxity when it came to observance of Covid-19 safety protocols. Although this study did not explore the extent to which laxity in Covid-19 management influenced infection and death, one could conclude that failure to take precautionary measures has the potential to spread the virus, based on studies conducted elsewhere. If the Zimbabwe government could set up organisations to work with churches with a view to soliciting their cooperation in its programmes, this could go a long way towards fostering a cooperative spirit and a reconsideration of some of the beliefs and practices, so that there is a blending of spiritual and biomedical solutions to dealing with pandemics now and in the future.

---

68 Chirisa, "The Impact and Implications of Covid-19", 2.

4 COVID-19, CURTAILMENT OF RELIGIOUS LIBERTY AND RELIGION-STATE RELATIONS IN WEST AFRICA: NIGERIA AND GHANA IN FOCUS

Idowu A. Akinloye[1]

INTRODUCTION

The coronavirus known as Covid-19 is the largest public health crisis in contemporary times. At the outbreak of the pandemic, and in light of its threat and on the advice of health specialists, most states in West Africa, as in other regions of the world, adopted radical measures to contain the rate of transmission, impact and deaths resulting from the virus and to ensure effective contact tracing. Some of the measures were backed by legal regulations,[2] with fines and imprisonment as the attendant effect of their violation in some instances.[3]

The effect of the lockdown regulations was to restrict constitutionally guaranteed human rights, including the rights to freedom of movement, freedom of association, freedom of religion and the right to human dignity, among others. In light of the nature of African religiosity and religious practice,[4] the aspects of the regulations that imposed restrictions on religious gatherings elicited much public debate and ultimately affected religion-state relations.[5] While some members of the public welcomed the regulations and legal restrictions, others rejected and flouted the regulatory measures, particularly the provisions of the lockdown regulations that banned religious gatherings in an attempt to stem the spread and the numbers of death arising from the virus.

---

1 Senior Lecturer, College of Law, Osun State University (Ifetedo Campus), Nigeria.
2 In Liberia, for instance, see "Covid-19 Declaration of National Health Emergency" made pursuant to the Public Health Law of Title 33, Chapter 14 of the Liberian Code of Laws Revised. In Sierra Leone, see the Declaration of a State of Public Emergency by His Excellency, Dr Julius Maada Bio, President of the Republic of Sierra Leone in terms of Section 29(1) of the Constitution of Sierra Leone, 1991, Act 6 of 1991.
3 Sun N, Christie E, Cabal L and Amon JJ. 2022. "Human Rights in Pandemics: Criminal and Punitive Approaches to Covid-19", *BMJ Global Health* 7(2).
4 Quashigah K. 2010. "Religion and the Secular State in Ghana", in Martinez-Torrón J, Durham WC (Jr) and Thayer D (eds). *Religion and Secular State: National Reports*. Madrid: Servicio de Publicaciones de la Facultad de Derecho de la Universidad Complutense de Madrid, 331-338.
5 "Senegal: Covid-19 Response Violates Rights", Article19.org, 28 June 2021; Mat NFC, Edinur HA, Razab MKAA and Safuan S. 2020. "A single mass gathering resulted in massive transmission of Covid-19 infections in Malaysia with further international spread", *Journal of Travel Medicine* 27(3):taaa059; Singh DE. 2020 "Role of Religions in the Spread of Covid-19", *Journal of Ecumenical Studies* 55(2):289-310.

Against this backdrop, the goal of this chapter is to analyse and reflect upon the literature, statutes, electronic and media reports and case examples in order to evaluate the state regulatory response in containing the spread of coronavirus disease. The analysis proceeds in light of the constitutionally guaranteed right to freedom of religion in two West African nations – Nigeria and Ghana. It appraises the response of the religious constituents in the two countries in terms of how they rejected or became complicit in curtailing religious liberties through the lockdown regulations. It reflects on how these responses impact on religion-state relationship during the outbreak of the pandemic. It further reflects upon the nature and quality of judicial oversight, if any, of the government action in these restrictions. This analysis is relevant, given the tensions that often attend religion-state relations in African states, and it can help to understand and aid religion-state relationships in African contexts in navigating future pandemics.

Jurisprudentially, Nigeria and Ghana have a number of things in common. For instance, both are commonwealth countries, and their national constitutions were enacted in the same decade,[6] providing for constitutional democracies that guarantee religious liberty[7] and give recognition to state neutrality in religious matters.[8] Christianity, Islam and African traditional religions are the main religions practised in both countries. A key difference between the countries is that Nigeria operates a federal system of government,[9] while Ghana practices a unitary system with some features of federalism.[10]

This chapter, first, outlines the legal framework for the protection of the right to freedom of religion in Nigeria and Ghana. It then examines the provisions of the lockdown regulations and their impact on freedom of religion. The legal section is followed by an examination of the responses of religious groups to the regulations. In this section, I analyse the opinions of scholars and public commentators to determine the justification of the regulatory measures in light of the constitutional limitation to human rights. Thereafter, I reflect on how these responses impacted the religion-state relationship during the pandemic. Overall, the conclusion is that religious constituencies in both Nigeria and Ghana largely endorsed the lockdown regulations, partnering with the state to stem the spread of the virus. Although the parts of the regulations that provide for the total or partial ban on religious gatherings in the wake of the outbreak of Covid-19 may have increased the suffering and violated the rights of most religious adherents, they were justifiable and permissible limitations of religious freedom under the circumstances.

---

6   See Constitution of the Federal Republic of Nigeria, 1999 (hereinafter CFRN) and the Constitution of the Republic of Ghana, 1992 (hereinafter CRG).
7   CFRN, s 38 and CRG, art 21(1)(c).
8   See CFRN, s 10 and CRG, art 56; Quashigah EK. 1999. "Legislating Religious Liberty: The Ghanaian Experience", *BYU Law Review* 2:596.
9   Nigeria is a Federal Republic with 36 federating states and a Federal Capital Territory.
10 Penu DAK. 2022. "Explaining Defederalization in Ghana", *Publius: The Journal of Federalism* 52(1):26-54.

LEGAL FRAMEWORK FOR FREEDOM OF RELIGION IN NIGERIA AND GHANA

"Freedom of religion" is a recognised human right that means different things to different people. The scope of what it entails varies between states, religions, individuals and legal instruments.[11] What appears to gain a consensus, however, is that freedom of religion implies a state's duty to refrain from interfering with an individual or community's pursuit of a chosen religious belief. It includes the right to choose and change one's religion without force and coercion, including the freedom to manifest and practise the religion individually or in fellowship with other believers. The importance of the protection of freedom of religion as a fundamental human right has been widely acknowledged as crucial for the development of an individual's self-definition and the promotion of democratic pluralism within a society. In fact, it is regarded by some as "the most sacred of all freedoms".[12]

This acknowledgment underscores the protection of the right in multiple international treaties and conventions, including the Universal Declaration of Human Rights (UDHR),[13] the International Covenant on Civil and Political Rights (ICCPR),[14] the African Charter on Human and Peoples' Rights,[15] the Declaration on the Elimination of All Forms of Intolerance and of Discrimination Based on Religion or Belief,[16] and the European Convention for the Protection of Human Rights and Fundamental Freedoms.[17] Although the wording of these international instruments varies, they convey fundamentally similar meanings. Nigeria and Ghana are signatories to these instruments.

Nigeria has a longer constitutional history of the protection of the right to freedom of religion than Ghana. At the time of Nigeria's independence in 1960, some minority ethnic and religious groups had expressed the fear of domination by the majority

---

11 Evans C. 2001. *Freedom of Religion under the European Convention on Human Rights*. Oxford: Oxford University Press, 18; See also Sullivan WF, Hurd ES, Mahmood S and Danchin P (eds). 2015. *Politics of Religious Freedom*. Chicago: University of Chicago Press, 5.

12 Robertson M (ed). 1991. *Human Rights for South Africans*. Oxford: Oxford University Press, 124; See also *Wisconsin v Yoder* 406 US 205 (1972).

13 Universal Declaration of Human Rights (hereinafter UDHR), G.A. res. 217A (III), U.N. Doc A/810 at 71 (1948).

14 International Covenant on Civil and Political Rights, G.A. res. 2200A (XXI), 21 U.N. GAOR Supp. (No. 16) at 52, U.N. Doc. A/6316 (1966), 999 U.N.T.S. 171, *entered into force* Mar. 23, 1976.

15 African [Banjul] Charter on Human and Peoples' Rights, adopted June 27, 1981, OAU Doc. CAB/LEG/67/3 rev. 5, 21 I.L.M. 58 (1982), *entered into force* Oct. 21, 1986.

16 Declaration on the Elimination of All Forms of Intolerance and of Discrimination Based on Religion or Belief, G.A. res. 36/55, 25 November 1981.

17 European] Convention for the Protection of Human Rights and Fundamental Freedoms, ETS 5, 213 U.N.T.S. 222, *entered into force* Sept. 3, 1953, as amended by Protocols Nos 3, 5, and 8 which *entered into force* on 21 September 1970, 20 December 1971 and 1 January 1990 respectively.

groups. This prompted the British colonial government of Nigeria to set up the Willink Commission to look into the agitation. The Willink Commission found that the fear was genuine and suggested that provisions on fundamental rights be entrenched in the Independence Constitution of Nigeria of 1960. This suggestion was accepted, and the provisions on fundamental rights, including the right to freedom of religion were included in the Constitution of the Federation of Nigeria, 1960.[18] These provisions were later entrenched in the country's 1979 Constitution and are include in the Constitution of the Federal Republic of Nigeria, 1999 (hereinafter 1999 Constitution or CFRN). Section 38 of the 1999 Constitution guarantees the right to freedom of religion.

A vital point to make is that, in Nigeria, there is a double guarantee for freedom of religion by virtue of the provisions of both Nigerian Constitution and the African Charter on Human and Peoples' Rights (Ratification and Enforcement) Act.[19] The latter was enacted in terms of Section 12(1) of the 1999 Constitution to domesticate the provisions of the African Charter.[20] Thus, in *Abacha v Fawehinmi*,[21] the Nigerian Supreme Court held that the African Charter on Human and Peoples' Rights (Ratification and Enforcement) Act, being a statute with an international component, was superior to any other Nigerian statute except the Constitution. It follows, therefore, that no statute enacted by the Nigerian legislature can take away the rights guaranteed by the African Charter, which includes the right to freedom of religion for Nigerians, except as may be permitted in the 1999 Constitution.

In the current Nigerian Constitution, Section 38 protects the right to freedom of religion by adopting Article 18 of the Universal Declaration of Human Rights, which provides that: "Every person shall be entitled to freedom of thought, conscience, and religion, *including* freedom to change his religion or belief, and freedom (either alone or in community with others, and in public or in private) to manifest and propagate his religion or belief in worship, teaching, practice and observance."[22] The use of the non-exclusive term "including" in the above provision, arguably, presupposes that the scope of the rights that are listed in the provision is not exclusive. Furthermore, the Nigerian Constitution contains a number of other secondary rights that reinforce the enjoyment of the freedom of religion to ensure that the entitlement to this right is meaningful. These sections include Section 42, providing that no person shall be discriminated against on the basis of religion; Section 40, protecting freedom of association; and Section 39, protecting freedom of

---

18 Abuza AZ. 2017. "Derogation from Fundamental Rights in Nigeria: A Contemporary Discourse", *East African Journal of Science and Technology* 7(1):108.
19 African Charter on Human and Peoples' Rights (Ratification and Enforcement), Act 2 of 1983.
20 CFRN, s 12(1).
21 *Abacha v Fawehinmi* (2000) 6 (NWLR) (Part 660) 228. See also *Inspector General of Police v All Nigeria Peoples Party* (2007) LPELR-8217(CA) 1, 43.
22 UDHR, art 18 (emphasis added).

expression.[23] There are four basic aspects to the constitutional right to freedom of religion in terms of Section 38 that are worthy of examination. These are the rights to belong to any religion, the right to change one's religion, the right to *manifest and propagate* one's religion either in public or in private, and the right to *manifest one's belief* either alone or in community with others.

Ghana has also given constitutional effect to the protection of the right to freedom of religion. The Constitution of Ghana, ever since the 1969 Constitution, has protected freedom of religion.[24] Within the Ghanaian context, Article 21(1)(c) of the Ghanaian Republican Constitution of 1992 also protects the right.[25] It states: "All persons shall have the right to freedom to practise any religion and to manifest such practice." Article 17(2) further prohibits discrimination on the grounds of religion, and Article 17(3) describes discrimination to include a situation where some are granted privileges or advantages which are not granted to persons of another description.[26]

A detailed analysis of the legal frameworks for the protection of religious liberty in Nigeria and Ghana reveals the protection of individual and group religious autonomy, equality of all religions and nondiscrimination on the basis of religion. In Nigeria, the courts have on a few occasions been called to determine the efficacy of the right to freedom of religion.[27] This includes the recent case of *Lagos State Govt and Ors v Asiyat AbdulKareem*.[28] In that case, the Supreme Court affirmed the right of a Muslim pupil to wear *hijab* in public school. However, in Ghana, it seems that cases contesting religious liberty violations hardly ever come to court.[29] A handful of relevant cases have come before Ghana's Commission on Human Rights and Administrative Justice (CHRAJ), an administrative quasi-judicial body.[30] The case of *Tyron Iras Marhguy v Board of Governors Achimota Senior High School & Anor*,[31] decided in 2021, is a very recent and novel court decision giving judicial approval to the constitutional protection of religious liberty in Ghana. The applicant in that case

---

23 CFRN, ss 42, 40 and 39.
24 Quashigah, "Legislating Religious Liberty: The Ghanaian Experience", 596.
25 CRG, art 21(1)(c).
26 CRG, art 17(2-3).
27 Thus, in *Medical and Dental Practitioners Disciplinary Tribunal v Okonkwo* (2001) 10 WRN 1 SC.; *Agbai v Okagbue* (1991) 7 NWLR (Pt 204) 391. See also, *Nkpa v Nkume* (2001) 6 NWLR (Pt 710) 543.
28 *Lagos State Govt and Ors v Asiyat Abdul Kareem*, Suit Number SC/910/16 (2022).
29 See Quashigah, "Religion and the Secular State in Ghana", 333. Quashigah, a Ghanaian, says: "There is not any case law that directly asserts the right to religious freedom." See also Nyinevi CY and Amasah EN. 2015. "The Separation of Church and State under Ghana's Fourth Republic", *Journal of Politics and Law* 8(4):283, 286.
30 *Alhasuna Muslim Faith v Regional Police Commander, Bolgatanga* [1994-2000] CHRAJ 191.
31 *Tyron Iras Marhguy v Board of Governors Achimota Senior High School & Anor* (2021) JELR 107192 (HC).

successfully challenged the decision of the management of the Achimota Senior High School denying him admission on the ground that he keeps long hair. Long hair and dreadlock braids are a practice of members of the Rastafarian religion, a minority religious group in Ghana.

The right to manifest one's religion is, however, not absolute. Section 45 of the Nigerian Constitution and Articles 21(4)(c) and (e), and 12(2) of the Ghanaian Constitution allow a law to derogate from the right when it is in the public interest and benefit.[32] Accordingly, a state may be obliged in certain cases to limit the right to freedom of religion. The aspect of the right to religious liberty that was violated by the lockdown regulations is the right to *manifest one's belief* in community with others – the right to a religious gathering. This right is at the heart of the freedom of religion, because it underscores the collective group or institutional right to freedom of religion. Israeli international law scholar Yoram Dinstein rightly argues, "Freedom of religion, as an individual right, may be nullified unless complemented by a collective human right of the religious group to construct the infrastructure making possible the full enjoyment of that freedom by individuals."[33] Relevant to the collective group right of freedom of religion, Asonzeh Ukah, a Nigerian scholar of religion, submits that "collective face-to-face ritual performances and mechanisms not only build, maintain, and sustain social dynamics and solidarity; they are also the foundations of religion, social systems, and community domains."[34]

THE LOCKDOWN PROVISIONS AND FREEDOM OF RELIGION

Both Nigeria and Ghana enacted lockdown regulations that limited the right to freedom of religion. After Covid-19 hit the shores of Nigeria on 19 February 2020 and following the fear of its escalation and the number of deaths that it might cause, President Muhammadu Buhari on 20 March 2020 and under the terms of Sections 2, 3 and 4 of the Quarantine Act enacted Covid-19 Regulations of 2020 (hereinafter, the Nigerian Regulations).[35] The Nigerian Regulations were enacted through an executive order that did not pass through the usual legislative route, but was based on the advice of the Federal Ministry of Health and Nigeria Centre for Disease

---

32 Section 45(1) states: "Nothing in sections 37, 38, 39, 40 and 41 of this Constitution shall invalidate any law that is reasonably justifiable in a democratic society (a) in the interest of defence, public safety, public order, public morality or public health; or (b) for the purpose of protecting the rights and freedom or other persons."

33 Dinstein Y. 1992. "Freedom of Religion and Religious Minorities", in Dinstein Y (ed). *The Protection of Minorities and Human Rights.* Netherlands: Springer, 18; Govindjee A. 2016. "Freedom of Religion, Belief and Opinion", in Govindjee A (ed). *Introduction to Human Rights Law.* Second Edition. Durban: LexisNexis, 15. See also, the Nigerian case of *Ajayi v The Registered Trustees of Ona Iwa Mimo Cherubim and Seraphim* (1998) 7 NWLR (Pt. 556) 156.

34 Ukah A. 2020. "Prosperity, Prophecy and the Covid-19 Pandemic: The Healing Economy of African Pentecostalism", *Pneuma* 42:430, 431.

35 See Quarantine Act, Cap Q2, LFN, 2004; Covid-19 Regulations 2020 [hereinafter Nigerian Regulations].

Control (NCDC).³⁶ The NCDC is a government agency that promotes, coordinates and facilitates the prevention, detection and control of communicable diseases in the country.³⁷

Rule 1(1) of the Nigerian Regulations did not impose lockdown in all parts of the country; it only did so for two weeks in the first instance in the Federal Capital Territory, Abuja, and in the two federating states of Lagos and Ogun. The Nigerian Regulations restricted all movements and gatherings during the period.³⁸ As the rate of the virus spread was escalating, the lockdowns were later extended beyond the initial two weeks. Exceptions to the restrictions were allowed for those in essential and commercial services under the terms of Rule 1(5) and (6) of the regulations. Security agencies were directed to enforce and did enforce compliance with the regulations, and there is scanty evidence that security agents were selective in their enforcement approach.³⁹

As the rate of the virus spread increased, other federating states in Nigeria came up with their lockdown regulations to complement the Federal Government regulations.⁴⁰ There were, however, variations in the degree of strictness in the restrictions imposed by the regulations of the federating states. What was common to them was that they all imposed night curfews and restrictions on freedom of movement and assembly, including religious gatherings. Some states, such as Lagos, Osun and Kaduna, imposed total restrictions against religious gathering, while others, such as Oyo State, allowed religious gathering, but limit attendance to fifty or fewer people.⁴¹

In Ghana, the first two cases of Covid-19 were reported and confirmed on 13 March 2020. Ghana's Minister for Health, in exercise of the powers conferred on him by Sections 169 and 170 of the Public Health Act, 2012 (Act 851) declared a public health emergency, pursuant to the Declaration of Public Health Emergency (Coronavirus Covid-19 Pandemic) Instrument, 2020.⁴² Similarly, Ghanaian President Nana Akufo-Addo enacted the Imposition of Restrictions (Coronavirus Disease (Covid-19)

---

36 Nigerian Regulations, rule 1(1).
37 See the Nigeria Centre for Disease Control and Prevention Establishment Act, 2018.
38 Nigerian Regulations, rule 1(1) and (2).
39 Nigerian Regulations, rule 1(3). See also Abdulrauf L. 2020. "Nigeria's Emergency (Legal) Response to Covid-19: A Worthy Sacrifice for Public Health?", *Verfassungsblog on Matters Constitutional*, 18 May; Omogbolagun T. 2020. "From Worship Centres to Courtrooms: Tales of Pastors, Imams who Flouted Lockdowns", *Punch*, 23 May.
40 For instance, the Ekiti State Corona Diseases (Prevention of Infection) Regulations, 2020; Lagos State infectious Disease (Emergency Prevention) Regulations, 2020.
41 "Covid-19: Oyo Gov Imposes Curfew, Bans Inter-State Movement from Sunday", *Nigerian Tribune*, 28 March 2020.
42 Public Health Act, 2012 (Act 851), Sections 169 and 170; Declaration of Public Health Emergency (Coronavirus Covid-19 Pandemic) Instrument, 2020.

Pandemic) Instrument, 2020 (hereinafter Ghana Regulations) on 23 March 2020.[43] The Ghana Regulations "imposed restrictions on public gatherings, including religious activities in churches, mosques, shrines and at crusades, conventions, pilgrimages and other religious gatherings".[44] They further suspended all public gatherings and also limited attendance in burial to a maximum of twenty-five people.[45] The Ghana Regulations provided exemptions to the above restrictive rules exempting a service, manufacturing or industrial workplace; a market, supermarket, shopping mall, restaurant, hotel, or drinking spot; and security and other essential services.[46] These organisations that enjoyed exemptions were to maintain social distancing and comply with enhanced hygiene procedures.[47] Unlike Nigeria, the restrictions were made for an initial period of three weeks and applied to the entire territory of Ghana.[48] This was understandable because Ghana operates a unitary government.

The aspects of the provisions of these regulations banning movement and gathering in Nigeria and Ghana meant that worship places, such as churches, synagogues and mosques, were closed for worship during the day and at night. In other instances, religious bodies were forced to reduce attendance to as low as ten members per service. This further meant that in some locations individuals were not allowed to invite other people to their home for prayer, worship or cell group meetings or to anoint the sick with oil or pray for healing with them. This point is very critical to Nigeria and Ghana, given that they are home to worship centres with large physical structures that ordinarily seat thousands of congregants. Although some religious organisations with large congregations were savvy in information and communications technology and easily moved their services online, those without these resources had to close their places of worship for the entire period of the ban.

RELIGIOUS RESPONSES TO THE REGULATIONS

Immediately after the various regulations that introduced "lockdowns" were announced in Nigeria, religious organisations, mostly mainstream Christian churches and the Nigerian Supreme Council for Islamic Affairs (NSCIA), largely supported the regulations as a worthy move by the government to protect the inhabitants of the country against the virus.[49] Interestingly, but not unexpectedly,[50]

---

43 Imposition of Restrictions (Coronavirus Disease (Covid-19) Pandemic) Instrument, 2020, 23 March 2020.
44 Ghana Regulations, rule 1(1)(a)(ix).
45 Ghana Regulations, sub-rule (2) and sub-rule (3).
46 Ghana Regulations, rule 4(1).
47 Ghanaian Regulations, rule 4(2).
48 Ghanaian Regulations, rules 2 and 3.
49 Okoye AC and Obulor I. 2021. "Religious Organisations and Fight against the Spread of Covid-19 in Nigeria", *Journal of Sustainable Development in Africa* 23(1):65, 70.
50 Akinloye IA. "Human flourishing, church leadership and legal disputes in Nigerian churches", in Green MC (ed). 2019. *Law, Religion and Human Flourishing in Africa.*

some religious organisations went to the extent of aiding the efforts of the government in containing the spread and caring for those infected with the virus.[51] Some examples are worthy of mention. The Catholic Church donated 425 health facilities as isolation centres to fight coronavirus.[52] Dunamis International Gospel Centre, a charismatic Pentecostal church located in Abuja, donated medical equipment worth millions of naira to the government to combat the pandemic outbreak.[53] Further, some faith-based organisations, including Islamic organisations, assisted in mobilising and conveying health precautionary notices needed to safeguard spreading the virus[54] and even vaccination campaigns to their adherents.[55]

A few religious organisations and religious leaders reportedly rejected the ban on social and religious gatherings. The group of those who rejected or violated the regulations can be grouped into three categories. The first is those who publicly rejected the ban because they did not believe in the true existence of the virus. Accordingly, they tagged the lockdown as "satanic manoeuvre targeted at preventing people from worshipping God."[56] An example is Chris Oyakhilome, the senior pastor of the Christ Embassy, who strongly argued in support of a "conspiracy theory" that associated the Covid-19 pandemic with the development and launching of 5G networks.[57] The second group accepted the existence of the virus, but claimed possession of spiritual powers to cure the virus; hence, there was no need to pronounce lockdowns. For instance, T.B. Joshua predicted that Covid-19 would disappear after heavy rainfall on 27 March 2020,[58] and Elijah Ayodele claimed he possessed holy water and oil that could cure the virus.[59] In addition, on 13 April, Goodheart Val Aloysius of Father's House International Church in Calabar asked the government to gather all those who tested positive for Covid-19 in an isolation

---

Stellenbosch: African Sun Media, 25-41.

51 "How Faith Based Organizations Support the Containment of Covid-19 in Nigeria", *Proshare* 4 April 2020.

52 Adebowale-Tambe N. 2020. "Covid-19: Catholic Church Donates 425 Health Facilities as Isolation Centres – Official", 12 May.

53 Ewepu G. 2020. "Covid-19: Dunamis Church Donates Medical Equipment to FCTA", *Vanguard*, 26 March.

54 "Covid-19: Enugu Religious Leaders Urge Residents to Obey NCDC's Regulations", *Vanguard* 6 May 2020.

55 Okafor C. 2021. "Covid-19: Pastor Adeboye Joins Vaccination Campaign", *Premium Times*, 3 October.

56 Okoye and Obulor, "Religious Organisations and Fight against the Spread of Covid-19 in Nigeria", 70.

57 Ibrahim J. 2020. "Covid-19 in Nigeria: Once Again, Religion Stands in the Way", Friedrich-Ebert Stiftung, 29 June.

58 Dube C. 2020. "TB Joshua Covid-19 Prophecy: It Will Disappear on 27 March", *Savanna News*, 29 July.

59 Ashaolu O. 2020. "My Anointing Oil, Holy Water Can Cure Covid-19 – Primate Ayodele", *News Break*, n.d.

centre for him to heal.⁶⁰ The third group did not publicly reject the regulations but nevertheless defied government policies regarding public health safety measures meant to curb the spread of the virus. This group of religious leaders continued to hold religious activities without adhering to the precautionary rules. Some of these people were arrested and prosecuted.⁶¹ A handful of Pentecostal churches and radical Islamic clerics dominated this group. It can be argued that the public utterances of the first and second groups catalysed those in the third category.

In the same vein, Ghanaian religious actors largely accommodated the regulations restricting religious assembly and public gathering. Only a very few religious organisations reportedly flouted the lockdown regulations.⁶² Religious institutions in Ghana could best be described as visible symbols of communities to stem the tide against the virus. Besides providing support services and making donations,⁶³ they effectively participated and cooperated with the government to fight the virus. On 19 March 2020, the president of the country, a professed Christian who said he believed in the healing powers of Jesus Christ against Covid-19,⁶⁴ invited Christian leaders to government house to invoke prayers against the virus. The following day, on 20 March 2020, the vice president of the country, Dr Mahamadu Bawumiah, a Muslim, also invited Islamic leaders and clerics to government house in Accra to offer prayers against the spread of the virus. African traditional religions were also not left out to intervene in stopping the spread of the virus.⁶⁵ Currently, religious leaders are still effectively involved in educating, sensitising, mobilising and creating awareness to encourage people to get vaccinated against the virus.⁶⁶

Surprisingly, in both Nigeria and Ghana, none of the critics of the regulations or those who flouted the regulations and were later prosecuted ever predicated their criticism or basis of their violation on illegality or unconstitutionality of the regulations. Also, unlike some other countries on the continent, mostly from countries

---

60 Asuquo B. 2020. "Gather all Covid-19 Patients in Nigeria Let me Heal Them – Pastor Tells FG", *The Paradise*, 10 April.

61 "From Worship Centres to Courtrooms: Tales of Pastors, Imams who Flouted Lockdowns".

62 2021. "Covid-19: Ghana Police Arrest Christ Embassy Youth Pastor, Church Members for Flouting Safety Protocols", *Sahara Reporters*, 3 May.

63 Dapatem DA. 2020. "Covid-19: Methodist Church Ghana Supports Govt with Cash, Other Items", *Graphic Online*, 1 April; "Covid-19: Pentecost Church Donates PPES Worth GHS45,000 to Ministry of Health", *SEND West Africa*, 3 April 2020.

64 "Ghana's President Says He Believes in Healing Powers of Christ against Covid-19", *Vanguard*, 20 March 2020.

65 Ntewusu SA and Nkumbaan SN. 2020. "Fighting Covid-19: Interventions from Ghana's Traditional Priests", *Religious Matters*, 13 May.

66 Ajiambo D, Avevor D and Silimina D. 2022. "Sisters in Africa Debunk Myths and Educate People to get the Covid-19 Vaccine", *Global Sister Report*, 17 February.

in Eastern and Southern Africa, such as Kenya,[67] Namibia,[68] Malawi[69] and South Africa,[70] which contested the constitutionality and legitimacy of the lockdown regulations banning religious gatherings via lawsuits, I am not aware of any reported lawsuit challenging the government action restricting religious gatherings at the outbreak of the virus in Nigeria and Ghana. This makes it not so easy to assess the judicial perspective on the constitutionality of the restriction of religious liberty in the region. I consider the basis for not challenging the restriction from three perspectives. First, it can be argued that, as already observed, challenging violations of religious liberty in law court is not very common in West Africa, particularly in Ghana. Secondly, most of the courts that should adjudicate on the cases were also shut down during this period.[71] The courts were attending to only urgent cases, and of limitation of religious liberty during the pandemic and likely did not fall within the urgent and important cases from the view of judicial officials. Thirdly, the members of the judiciary, possibly not sure of how severe the spread of the virus could be, were themselves cautious of contracting the virus and therefore refrained from attending to litigants. Meanwhile, most of the African courts were not technologically advanced and prepared to easily migrate to online court proceedings at the inception of the outbreak of the virus.

The above responses of the religious actors suggest that most religious organisations substantially tolerated and endorsed the restrictions at the outset of the outbreak of the pandemic. They did this for both principled and pragmatic reasons. On the principled side, the religious actors acknowledged the restrictive measures as steps in the right direction since they know that the medical structures, facilities and personnel of virtually every African state were inadequate, fragile and poor.[72] It is widely known that most of the trained medical personnel in Africa migrate in deluge to other continents for greener pastures,[73] leaving limited numbers of

---

67 *Law Society of Kenya v Mutyambai* Petition 120 of 2020 (Covid 025).

68 *NEF & Ors v President of the Republic of Namibia & Ors.* (HC-MD-CIV-MOT-GEN-2020/00136) [2020] NAHCMD 198 (23 July 2020).

69 *HRDC and Others v President of Malawi and Others* (Judicial Review Case Number 33 of 2020) [2020] MWHC 26 (27 August 2020). See also *Kathumba v President of Malawi* [2020] MWHC 29 (3 September 2020); *The State and the President of the Republic of Malawi and others v Steven Mponda and others* (Judicial Review No. 13 of 2020).

70 See *Mohamed v The President of the Republic of South Africa* (Case No: 2140/20) (30 April 2020); *Khosa v Minister of Defence and Military Veterans and of Police* (Case No. 21512/2020) [2020] ZAGPPHC 147 (15 May 2020); *De Beer N.O. and Others v Minister of Cooperative Governance and Traditional Affairs* (21542/2020) [2021] ZAGPPHC 67 (19 February 2021).

71 Nigerian Regulations, rule 1(1); See also Chief Justice of Nigeria's Circular No. NJC/CIR/HOC/11631 of 23 March 2020.

72 Ntewusu and Nkumbaan, "Fighting Covid-19: Interventions from Ghana's Traditional Priests"; Oleribe OO et al. 2019. "Identifying Key Challenges Facing Healthcare Systems in Africa and Potential Solutions", *International Journal of General Medicine* 12:395-403.

73 Poppe A et al. 2014. "Why Sub-Saharan African Health Workers Migrate to European Countries That Do Not Actively Recruit: A Qualitative Study Post-migration", *Global Health Action* 7.

personnel on the continent. For instance, the General Medical Council of Britain recently revealed that 805 Nigerian medical doctors were licensed in the United Kingdom between July and December 2021. The body further revealed that 15 049 Nigeria-trained nurses obtained licences to practise in the United Kingdom between March 2017 and March 2021.[74] The ban on religious gatherings was thus to allow the states to build up an extensive public health response for the anticipated surge of infections. They were convinced that every state has the constitutional duty to protect the life and health of citizens, and every citizen and religious institution has a duty to support the government to achieve this.

On the more pragmatic side, the religious leaders accepted that the restrictions were short-term and finite, not permanent. They were temporary measures meant to achieve a greater good of saving lives. Accordingly, some of the religious institutions quickly extended their frontiers, framed new means of religious participation, and embraced modern virtual technology as a temporary means of conducting worship.[75] Moreover, since some of the federating states in Nigeria allowed limited attendance in religious gatherings during the pandemic, some religious organisations devised meeting several times for their corporate worship. The religious leaders also accepted that their religious liberty is not absolute; hence, the states were acting within their constitutional powers in limiting religious liberty for public benefit.

Furthermore, some religious leaders complied with the government directives and explained away the restrictions because they could easily deploy scriptural passages to back the need for compliance with the lockdown regulations. For instance, Eric Kwabena Nyamekye, the chairman of the Church of the Pentecost in Ghana enjoined his church members to obey the directive of the government to stay at home. He emphasised that during biblical times, when there were tough plagues, what people did was to stay in lockdown. Nyamekye referenced the narrative about Noah and the Ark. He said God locked Noah and the people in the Ark to prevent them from being drowned. He further gave an instance about the lockdown of the Israelites when the angel of death struck in Egypt. He concluded by quoting from the book of Isaiah 26:20-21, which reads in part: "Go, my people, enter your room and shut the doors behind you; hide yourselves for a little while until his wrath has passed by."[76] In the same vein, the president-general of the Nigerian Supreme Council for Islamic Affairs (NSCIA), Sultan of Sokoto Muhammad Sa'ad Abubakar, reminded the Muslim community in Nigeria that Prophet Mohammed himself called for social distancing in times of disease, thus "leaving the town and hiding on mountains and in caves, [suspending] congregational prayers and Jumu'ah (Friday) prayers, temporarily." Further, the Sultan noted that Muslims have a religious duty to

---

74 Deji-Folutile O. 2021. "Feasting on Nigeria's Stupidity", *The Cable*, 31 December.
75 Nwaka JC. 2020. "Between Religious Freedom and the Public Good: Reactions to Religious Restrictions to Prevent the Spread of Covid-19 in Nigeria", *Kujenga Amani*, 20 May.
76 Adu V. 2020. "Comply with Lockdown Directive – Apostle Eric Nyamekye to Ghanaians", *Atinka Online*, March 30.

prevent the spread of the virus.[77] Akin to this is the interpretation that the pandemic was a way of God in punishing human for disobedience to divine directives.[78]

However, as the trajectory of the pandemic became clearer but restrictions persisted beyond the time anticipated, more religious actors, even ones who originally endorsed the ban of religious gathering, became more suspicious of the government restrictions. They began to express their displeasure in the media – though not through lawsuits – against the prolonged ban on religious gatherings.[79] Their grounds were mainly premised on the fact that people would become depressed without the opportunity to manifest their religiosity in gatherings with others and that religion is an avenue to give succour in a time of pandemic. Further, some felt that religious institutions were treated less favourably than similar institutions, such as retail stores, markets and workplaces which were allowed to engage in minimal operations under certain precautions.[80] Some religious actors also felt threatened and had a sense of distrust, perceiving that the prolonged ban on gatherings was an attempt by secular powers to regulate their religion.[81]

Another interesting and ironic situation played out during this pandemic, particularly in Nigeria. There were instances where some political actors, such as the elected governors of federating states, seeking and clamouring for the reopening of worship places during the peak of the pandemic,[82] attempted to make offers that religious leaders rejected.[83] The only possible formulation for this religious overture by the political leaders is what I describe as "the politicization of religion and the religionisation of politics" in Africa.[84] Some African political actors, like the aforementioned, get entangled in religious affairs and try to use religion as a tool to score political points and to woo religious adherents to legitimise their political advances.

---

77 Nigeria Working Group on Peace Building and Governance. 2020. "Nigeria: The Response to Coronavirus is an Opportunity for Reform", 12 May.

78 Ukpabio H. 2020. "Corona Virus Plague Reveals God's Anger", *Facebook*, 23 February. Online at: https://www.facebook.com/ladyapostlehelenukpabio/videos/533021300734044; Ukah A. 2020. "Prosperity, Prophecy and the Covid-19 Pandemic: The Healing Economy of African Pentecostalism", *Pneuma* 42:453.

79 "Covid-19: Reopen Churches, Mosques Now, CAN Tells Nigerian Government", *Sahara Reporters*, 20 May 2020; Krippahl C. 2020. "Nigerian Religious Leaders Demand Lifting of Covid-19 Lockdown", *Deutsche Welle*, 19 May.

80 "Covid-19: Reopen Churches, Mosques Now, CAN Tells Nigerian Government", *Sahara Reporters*, 20 May 2020.

81 Krippahl, "Nigerian Religious Leaders Demand Lifting of Covid-19 Lockdown".

82 Sabiu M. 2020. "Despite Hike In Covid-19 Cases, Six Northern Govs Open Mosques, Churches", *Nigerian Tribune*, 16 May.

83 Odunsi W. 2020. "Covid-19: 'Thank You Gov Wike, We'll Stay at Home' – Catholic Church Rejects Lockdown Ease in Rivers", *Daily Post*, 10 April; Opejobi S. 2020. "Church Opening in Nigeria: Primate Ayodele Blasts TB Joshua, Pastor Sam Adeyemi", *Daily Post*, 3 June.

84 Akinloye IA. 2021. "The Right to Freedom of Religion or Belief: African Perspectives", in Ferrari S, Hill M, Jamal AA and Bottoni (eds). *Routledge Handbook of Freedom of Religion or Belief*. Abingdon and New York: Routledge, 200.

RELIGION-STATE RELATIONS DURING THE PANDEMIC

The extant constitutions of Nigeria and Ghana both exemplify a secular state approach in which there is strict separation between all religious activities and the state.[85] Their constitutions expressly give a commitment to religious neutrality. For instance, Section 10 of the Nigerian Constitution *prima facie* adopts the approach of an absolute separation of the state from religion. The provision states: "The Government of the Federation or of a State shall not adopt any religion as State Religion." Generally, this presupposes a state of secularism or neutrality between religion and the state.[86] Accordingly, some scholars and public commentators argue that Section 10 makes Nigeria a secular state in which there is no interference from the state in any religious affairs. Commenting on this view, one legal scholar posits, "In the absence of the adoption of a state religion, a nation is most accurately described as secular. Thus, Nigeria's prohibition of a national or state religion automatically qualifies the country as a secular nation."[87] In the same vein, Article 56 of Ghanaian Constitution states: "Parliament shall have no power to enact a law to establish or authorise the establishment of a body or movement with the right or power to impose on the people of Ghana a common programme or a set of objectives of a religious or political nature."; commenting on this constitutional provision, Kofi Quashigah, a Ghanaian professor of law and religion affirms that "Ghana is constitutionally a secular state" … "The Constitution depicts Ghana as a secular state …"[88] Quashigah further observes that "religious autonomy is guaranteed in Ghana".[89]

However, it must be noted that although the constitutions of Nigeria and Ghana claim to operate under religious neutrality, there is evidence that their governments do not in fact practice a strict separation approach. Rather, they have both adopted in practice a religious pluralism approach that requires the state to maintain a fair and nondiscriminatory relationship with all religions or worldviews.[90] This point

---

85 See, for instance, Devenish GE. 2005. *The South African Constitution*. Durban: Lexisnexis Butterworths, 88; Nsereko DD. 1986. "Religion, the State and the Law in Africa", *Journal of Church and State* 28(2):269. Both Nigeria and Ghana fall into the second of three religion-state approaches that Devenish identifies.

86 For different perspectives to secularism, see Ben-Yunusa M. 1995. "Secularism and Religion", in Mitri T (ed). 1995. *Religion, Law and Society: A Christian-Muslim Discussion*. Geneva: World Council of Churches, 81-82. See, further, Ansari AM. 2000. *Iran, Islam and Democracy: The Politics of Managing Change*, 15.

87 Tyus J. 2004. "Note: Going Too Far, Extending Shari'a Law from Personal to Public Law", *Washington University Global Studies Law Review* 3(1):205 See also Nwabueze BO. 1992. *Military Rule and Constitutionalism* Ibadan: Spectrum Books, 282; Iwobi AU. 2004. "Tiptoeing through a Constitutional Minefield: The Great Shari'a Controversy in Nigeria", *Journal of African Law* 48:133-135.

88 Quashigah, "Religion and the Secular State in Ghana", 331-332.; Quashigah, "Legislating Religious Liberty: The Ghanaian Experience", 596.

89 Quashigah, "Religion and the Secular State in Ghana", 333.

90 Quashigah, "Religion and the Secular State in Ghana", 333; See also Nyinevi CY and Amasah EN. 2015. "The Separation of Church and State under Ghana's Fourth Republic",

may underlie the observations of Rosalind Hackett and W. Cole Durham that Africa may be closer to Europe and Scandinavia than to the United States in its approach to religion–state relationships.[91] In this approach, there is a "far greater acceptance of state involvement with religious affairs as long as this is done in a fair and transparent way".[92]

Notwithstanding the close cooperation between the state and religions in Nigeria and Ghana, what is clear is that religious organisations have always had the history of vehement rejection of any attempt by the state to interfere in their doctrinal and internal affairs. In the Nigerian context, two recent experiences come to mind. In October 2016, the religious community rejected the attempt by the Financial Reporting Council of Nigeria, a body charged with the responsibility of ensuring good corporate governance practices in the public and private sectors of the economy to regulate the tenure of religious leaders.[93] The Council issued a Code of Governance for Not-for-Profit Entities, including religious organisations, in 2016. Section 9 of the Code touched on leadership tenure in nonprofit organisations, including that of religious leaders. The religious community rejected the Code. Musa Asake, the General Secretary of the Christian Association of Nigeria, said that "the code was ill machinery targeted at the church. Government has no business interfering in a church's affairs because it is a no-go-area".[94] The heated public outcry prompted President Muhammadu Buhari's government to sack Jim Obazee, the Council's boss and also to suspend the implementation of the Code "until after further reviews".[95]

In the same vein, in 2016, the democratically elected governor of Kaduna State, Nasir El-Rufai, sought to repeal the existing Kaduna State Regulation of Preaching Law of Kaduna State[96] through an executive bill for the Kaduna State Religious Preaching (Regulation) Law, 2016.[97] The Bill sought to establish regulatory committees of the two predominant religious bodies in the state, that is, the Committee of Jama'atu Nasir Islam (CJNI) for the Muslims and the Committee of Christian Association of Nigeria (CCAN) for the Christians,[98] as well as a third body referred to as "the Inter-faith Ministerial Council", to be appointed by the governor which

---

Journal of Politics and Law 8(4):283, 286-287.

91 Hackett RIJ. 2011. "Regulating Religious Freedom in Africa", *Emory International Law Review* 25:853 (quoting Durham WC. 1996. "Perspectives on Religious Liberty: A Comparative Framework", in Van der Vyver JD and Witte J (Jr) (eds). *Religious Human Rights in Global Perspective: Legal Perspectives*. Leiden: Martinus Nijhoff Publishers, 1).

92 Hackett, "Regulating Religious Freedom in Africa", 860.

93 Federal Reporting Council of Nigeria Act, No. 6 of 2011, ss 7 and 8.

94 Asake M. 2017. "Government has no Business Deciding who Runs a Church", *Punch*, 14 January.

95 Oguntola S. 2017. "Churches Challenge Nigeria Forcing Pastors to Retire", *Christianity Today* 13 January. See Adebulu A. 2021. "CAN sues FG over CAMA", *The Cable*, 15 March.

96 Kaduna State Regulation of Preaching Law, 1984.

97 A Bill for the Kaduna State Religious Preaching (Regulation) Law, 2016 [Religious Preaching Regulation Bill]. Online at: https://kdsg.gov.ng/documents-library/.

98 Religious Preaching Regulation Bill, s 6.

shall execute oversight control over the CJNI and CCAN.[99] According to the Bill, CJNI and CCAN are empowered to screen preachers and applications for preaching licences, and making recommendations to the Local Government Inter-Faith Regulatory Committee[100] to issue licences to accredited preachers,[101] which licences shall be valid for a period of two years.[102] A preacher who is not based in the state, but who is visiting the state would be issued a permit for the period of the event that brings the preacher to the state. The Inter-faith Regulatory Committee is further to regulate the activities of religious preachers.[103] More recently, on 19 June 2019 in a lawsuit instituted by the Pentecostal Fellowship of Nigeria challenging regulation of its activities by Kaduna State, a Kaduna High Court held that the state government can regulate religious activities, but that it has no right to license religious preachers and that licensing religious preachers by the state would violate the constitutional right of religious organisations.[104]

In Ghana, religious organisations have always resisted state's attempts to interfere in the internal affairs of religious organisations. For instance, before the Constitution of Ghana of 1992 was enacted, the then military government passed the Religious Bodies (Registration) Law, 1989. The rationale of the law was "to check the activities of some religious bodies that in the view of the government, constitute a nuisance to the general public, and militate against public order, public interest or morality, or acceptable standards of decency."[105] The law was in reaction partly to public outcry against the activities of some churches that verged on fraud, debauchery and corruption of public morals. The effect of the law was therefore to force the registration of all religious organisations in Ghana.

It is, however, surprising that in the wake of coronavirus and despite the blanket ban on religious activities, most religious organisations endorsed the ban. Most of them willingly accepted for their religious liberty to be restricted. This is an illustration of separationist approach of religion-state relations for which Nigeria and Ghana are known. This thus suggests that religion and state relation is fluid and relative phenomenon. It has the capacity to metamorphose, depending on the demands of time. In the present circumstance, the Covid-19 pandemic is a common enemy facing both religious organisations and the state. Both institutions

---

99 Religious Preaching Regulation Bill, s 4.

100 The Local Government Inter-Faith Regulatory Committee is to be established by Section 7 of the Bill.

101 Religious Preaching Regulation Bill, ss 6(2)(a) and 8(1)(a).

102 Religious Preaching Regulation Bill, 2016, s 6(2)(a) and 8(1)(b).

103 Religious Preaching Regulation Bill, s 6(2)(a).

104 *Pentecostal Fellowship of Nigeria v Governor Kaduna State* (Unreported, Suit No. KDA/HC/ 2016). Isenyo G. 2019. "You Have No Right to License Preachers, Court Tells Kaduna Govt", *Punch*, 20 June.

105 A Message from the Christian Council of Ghana and the Ghana Catholic Bishops' Conference to their Faithful and Congregation, 14 November 1989.

are collaborating to fight their common enemy without consideration of interfering with or controlling each other's affairs.

CONCLUSION

Like other continents, Africa was not immune to coronavirus, and Nigeria and Ghana were no exception. The responses of the government, religious organisations and citizens to the outbreak of the pandemic in Nigeria and Ghana were largely similar. To reduce the spread of the virus, Nigerian and Ghanaian governments came up with measures and regulations that imposed lockdowns and bans on large gatherings and movements and closure of religious places, with attendant consequences for their infractions. A common feature of the regulations is that they were enacted in haste. Accordingly, many of them did not meet the minimum normative standards of legitimate legislation, since they did not have input of parliament. Further, some of the measures infringed on rights, such as the freedom to assemble and to worship in public. This is of particular importance to Africans, who are widely known to be very religious.

There was evidence that political actors were cajoling the religious communities to play a role to invoke their spiritual abilities to stem the tide of the virus both in prayers and to support the lockdown regulations. And indeed, religious organisations largely supported and mobilised their constituencies to support the regulations. This is illustrative of collaborative and cordial relations between religious and state actors in fighting a common enemy. In this wise, no institution sees the other as superior, but as collaborators and partners in achieving a common goal. This is suggestive of a possible cordial model of state-religion relationship in a time of pandemic. This further reveals that religious actors are well positioned to help the state governments to popularise and communicate their advances to their religious constituents. It further reinforces the view that religious institutions are forces to reckon with in state governance in most African countries.[106]

The complicity of religious leaders in the restriction of religious liberty appears to limit lawsuits challenging the legality, legitimacy and constitutionality of the restriction of religious liberty. Arguably, the restriction placed on religious gathering may be deemed to be legitimate and constitutionally permissible given the circumstances of the pandemic and the imminent risk large gatherings may pose. The pandemic presented a "deep and uncertain health crisis", and the efforts to curtail it were legitimate. Although some of the governments' approaches in dealing with the pandemic might have been at the expense of the livelihood of the people, arguably, they were based on saving lives and preserving livelihoods.

---

[106] See Agbiji OM and Swart I. 2015. "Religion and Social Transformation in Africa: A Critical and Appreciative Perspective", *Scriptura* 114(1); Mbiti JS. 1990. *African Religious and Philosophy*. Heinemann, 1.

5 THE COVID-19 PANDEMIC, AU AGENDA 2063 AND RELATIONSHIP BETWEEN LAW AND RELIGION IN NIGERIA

**Azizat Omotoyosi Amoloye-Adebayo[1]
& Barakat Adebisi Raji[2]**

INTRODUCTION

Religion has been useful, but also much misused, in Nigeria.[3] Nigerian religion scholar Utensati Apyewen correctly notes that religious leaders and actors have employed religious language, historically and continually to encourage community engagement for "inter-religious peace and action for social justice", religion, particularly Christianity and Islam, has been exploited as an "engine for spreading violence, deceit and encouraging the destruction of lives and properties".[4] Unfortunately, Nigerian media coverage of issues related to religion mostly misrepresents situations involving religion and cases of misuse and abuse of religion.[5] This is

---

1 Faculty of Law, University of Ilorin, Ilorin, Nigeria.
2 Faculty of Law, University of Ilorin, Ilorin, Nigeria.
3 For academic analysis on this twin perspective by Nigerian scholars of religions studies, see the following works: Apyewen UA. 2020. "The Use and Abuse of Religion", *Ilorin Journal of Religious Studies* 10(1):65; Aluko OP. 2017. "Tolerance in Multi-religious Society for national Security: The Nigerian Experience", *Ogirisi: A New Journal of African Studies* 13:291; Oloyede IO. 2014. "Theologising the Mundane, Politicising the Divine: The Crosscurrents of Law, Religion and Politics in Nigeria", *African Human Rights Law Journal* 14:178; Ajah M. 2015. "Religious Education and Nation-Building in Nigeria", *Stellenbosch Theological Journal* 1(2):263; Nwauche ES. 2008. "Law, Religion and Human Rights in Nigeria", *African Human Rights Law Journal* 8:568; Amoloye-Adebayo AO 2019. "The Nigerian Constitution and the *Sharī'ah* question in Southwestern Nigeria", in Opeloye MO, Bidmos MA, Oladosu AO and Musa Ismail (eds). *Islam in Yorubaland: History, Education and Culture*. Lagos: University of Lagos Press and Bookshop Ltd, 259; Amoloye-Adebayo AO. 2020. "'Freedom of Religion': Nigerian Constitutional Provision for Religious Peace and National Stability'", in Imam OY et al (eds). *Religion, Peace and Nation Building in Nigeria*. Ile-Ife: Department of Religious Studies, Faculty of Arts, Obafemi Awolowo University, Nigeria, 175; and Kukah MH. 1993. *Religion, Power, and Politics in Northern Nigeria*. Ibadan: Spectrum Books Ltd. For some non-Nigerian perspective, see Nolte I, Danjibo N and Oladeji A. 2009. "Religion, Politics and Governance in Nigeria", University of Birmingham, Religions and Development Working Paper 39.
4 Apyewen, "The Use and Abuse of Religion", 66.
5 For example, the effect of negative media reporting on religion and citizens' religious rights in educational institutions in Nigeria is discernible from the somewhat lopsided 2021 report on Nigeria by the U.S. Office of International Religious Freedom. The report, which expressed its perspectives on the religious rights in educational institutions to be based on media accounts, incorrectly asserts that religion is employed in Nigeria to compel Christian-affiliated public schools to accommodate the wearing of *hijab* by Muslim

despite the availability of scholarly works that have demonstrated the positive effects and inroads that religion can make in areas such as legal development, social justice and nation-building in Nigeria.[6]

This chapter is a contribution to understanding the positive influence of religion to human flourishing through law. It argues that religion, for the most part, has contributed to health and healing, both during and in the aftermath of the Covid-19 pandemic.[7] This is particularly the case where religious actors and rhetoric contributed to large-scale compliance with lockdown restrictions and non-congregation orders in most states in Nigeria.[8] Cases of noncompliance occurred in few areas, such as in Kano, Yola and Ugheli,[9] where religious clerics called for continued congregation that led to a spread of the contagion and high mortality rates in some affected areas were examples of the misuse and instrumentalisation of religion, and not for the sake of religious observance. Such instrumentalisation of religion has a long history in Nigeria, resulting in current mixed feelings as to the precise role of religion in public administration and legal development. In this

---

female students while allowing Muslim-affiliated public schools to compel all female students regardless of faith to wear the *hijab*. See United States Department of State, Office of International Religious Freedom. 2022. "International Religious Freedom Report 2021: Nigeria", 2 June. This assertion in the report is contrary to the unambiguous position of the law in Nigeria as contained in the following decision of the Nigerian Supreme Court that Muslim female students in all public educational institutions who freely chooses to appear in *hijab* may not be compelled to appear otherwise. See *Lagos State Government & 3 Ors v Miss Asiyat Abdul Kareem & 2 Ors* (SC.910/2016) delivered on 17 June 2022. It is important to note that even though the date of this decision of the Supreme Court came after the date of the report of the U.S. Department of State, the decision of the Supreme Court merely affirmed what had been the existing position of the law in the decision of the Court of Appeal in the following cases: *Abdulkareem v Lagos State Government* (2016) 13 NWLR (Pt 1535) 177; *Incorp. Trustees, CAN v Kwara State Govt* ((2020) 13 NWLR (Pt.1740) 99); *Provost Kwara State College of Education Ilorin & 2 Ors v Bashirat Saliu & 2 Ors* (Unreported) Appeal No. CA/IL/49/2006 decided on 18 June 2009).

6   See again cited works in note 3 above.

7   The index case of Covid-19 in Nigeria was reported on 27 February 2020. See World Health Organization (WHO). 2020. "Listings of WHO's response to Covid-19", *WHO News*, 29 June (updated 29 January 2021).

8   Ayeni T. 2020. "Religion in Nigeria despite coronavirus measures", *The Africa Report*, 3 April. In this article, part of the series "Corona Chronicles: 30 March–3 April 2020", Ayeni reports, "Around Nigeria, religious and social gatherings have been restricted to 20 people, in an effort to stop the spread of the coronavirus. This is having a big impact on the country's churches and mosques." There is also a further description in this article of specific measures adopted by various places of worship ranging from following the number restriction strictly or moving from in person to virtual religious meetings. For other editorials in the online version of the national dailies. See Alabi CT and Ramoni R. 2020. "Covid-19: How Worshippers Are Coping With 'New Normal' In Lagos", *The Daily Trust*, 16 August; "Eld-Fitri: Pray In Your Homes – Sultan Tells Muslims", *Africa Daily News*, 20 May 2020; Adeshida A. "Sallah: Adhere strictly to health, safety regulations during celebration, Oyeyemi urges Nigerians", *Vanguard*, 30 July.

9   Yusuf U, Brisibe P and Bello B. 2020. "Covid-19: Muslim faithful ignore social distancing in Kano, Yola, Ughelli, observe Jum'at prayers", *Vanguard*, 4 April.

chapter, we contend that the present complex situation of ambivalence towards religion is aided by an unclear constitutional direction of the utility of religion in the construction of the Nigerian identity and the emergence of Nigeria itself as a body politic.

It is in this context that the continent-wide developmental and aspirational document, the African Union's "Agenda 2063: The Africa We Want",[10] appears to be highly instructive and relevant in its positive and hopeful perspective on the use of religion. What follows in the sections below is an analysis of the Nigerian situation through an Agenda 2063 perspective with a view to demonstrating that even though some of the history of law and religion co-development in Nigeria may be problematic and result in present conflict situations, religion continues to be useful in coping with unforeseeable challenges, such as the Covid-19 pandemic. In that regard, the Constitution of the Federal Republic of Nigeria, 1999 requires revision in relation to the utility of religion and the aspirations and objectives of Agenda 2063.

THE EFFECT OF THE COVID-19 PANDEMIC ON THE LAW AND RELIGION RELATIONSHIP IN NIGERIA

The role of religion and religious actors in the responses to the pandemic in Nigeria cannot be overemphasised. One of the major ways in which religion and religious actors helped in public administration was in ensuring compliance with the government's implementation of social restrictions and lockdown orders.[11] As one observer correctly notes, "lack of trust in the political class means that many people are more likely to listen to and believe the words of their religious and traditional rulers".[12] The closure of places of worship was essential to achieve compliance with non-aggregation requirements for social events. Another way that religious institutions and religious actors also proved extremely useful was in the provision of food and other necessities and where governmental provisions were either non-existent or highly insufficient.[13] Thus, during the pandemic, religion constituted, to a considerable extent, an informal measure of maintaining a stable, peaceful and responsive citizenry, which is a core objective of the law. The period of the pandemic witnessed two important religious festivals – the Easter celebrations at the end of the Christian Lent and the Eid-al Fitr festival to mark the end of Muslim fasting in Ramadan.[14] During these periods and at other times when religious

---

10 African Union. 2015. "Agenda 2063: The Africa We Want". Addis Ababa: African Union Commission. Tagged "The Africa We Want", Agenda 2063 is a 50-year "blueprint and master plan for transforming Africa into the global powerhouse of the future", and it was adopted by the African Union in 2013.

11 See again Ayeni, "Religion in Nigeria despite coronavirus measures", and accompanying texts.

12 Ayeni, "Religion in Nigeria despite coronavirus measures".

13 For some accounts of this, see Ayandele O, Okafor CT and Oyedele O. 2021. "The role of Nigeria's faith-based organisations in tackling health crises like Covid-19", *Africa Portal*, 27 January.

14 See again Ayeni, "Religion in Nigeria despite coronavirus measures" above.

congregation might have occurred, media outlets overflowed with messages from religious leaders to obey lockdown measures and other restrictions as a matter of religious duty, not merely patriotic responsibility.[15] Although there were situations of noncompliance based on religion or instrumentalisation of religion in some states, such cases constituted the exception rather than the norm.[16]

Furthermore, scholars of religious studies would readily agree that religion is an important source of mental stability, internal peace and emotional strength to cope with the complex and enigmatic nature of natural phenomena, such as a contagion or structural asymmetries in human relations.[17] The added uncertainties of how to appropriately contain the Covid-19 pandemic, even for developed societies,[18] increased the allure of religion in developing and transitioning societies, such as Nigeria, as an appropriate response protocol in the face of challenges of insufficient material resources for medical and alimentary needs.[19] The utility of religion in this regard has been stated, correctly in our view, in the following words of international religious freedom advocate Thomas Farr that:

> Religion is, first and foremost, the human search for a greater-than-human source of being and ultimate meaning. Religion is the effort of individuals and communities to understand, to express, and to seek harmony with a transcendent reality of such importance that they feel compelled to organize their lives around their understanding of it … Most people by their nature seek answers to questions that seem to be in our DNA. For example, is there something or someone to which or to whom I owe my being? If so, how should I order my life in light of that discovery? Why is there suffering? Is there life after death? If so, does my behavior in this life affect my fate after death?[20]

Thus, aside from obeying religious instructions not to congregate, the inner propensity of religion helped Nigerians to cope mentally with enforced isolation that occurred without much preparedness in terms of emotional and material resources.

---

15 Ayeni, "Religion in Nigeria despite coronavirus measures".

16 See Yusuf et al, "Covid-19: Muslim faithful ignore social distancing".

17 For instance, see Jordan J. 2016. "Religion and Inequality: The Lasting Impact of Religious Traditions and Institutions on Welfare State Development", *European Political Science Review* 8(1):25.

18 For examples of preliminary assessments as the world was battling with the pandemic, see Tisdell CA. 2020. "Economic, Social and Political Issues Raised by the Covid-19 Pandemic", *Economic Analysis and Policy* 68:17-28; Belhassine O and Karamti C. 2021. "Contagion and Portfolio Management in Times of Covid-19", *Economic Analysis and Policy* 72:73-85; Padhan R and Prabheesh KP. 2021. "The Economics of Covid-19 Pandemic: A Survey", *Economic Analysis and Policy* 70:220-237.

19 As shall be discussed in the next section, it will be observed that in the case of Nigeria, religion has always been an important component of individual and collective responses to social challenges or legal and political development.

20 Farr T. 2019. "What in the World is Religious Freedom", *Religious Freedom Institute*, 1 November.

HISTORY OF LAW IN NIGERIA: THE ROLE OF RELIGION

Religion always been an important component of individual and collective responses to social challenges, as its use in the response to the pandemic indicates, but religion has also been part and parcel of legal development in Nigeria. Religion is connected to the development of law in Nigeria in a way that predates the emergence of Nigeria as a modern nation-state.[21] This is because the indigenous societies that that were amalgamated in the colonial era into Nigeria had various systems of law connected to their belief systems.[22] African traditional religion and customary law, as well as Islamic law, were in existence in Nigeria before the advent of British colonialism in Nigeria. Then, with colonialism, came the received English law, elements of which persist in Nigerian today. Thus, the discussion below of religion in terms of both Nigeria's historical heritage and the objectives of Agenda 2063 is highly relevant in the Nigerian context. To understand this heritage in Nigeria, it is helpful to know something about each component of Nigeria's tripartite legal system.[23] This discussion is important to demonstrate how religion contributed to health and healing during the Covid-19 pandemic.

Customary law

In most of the indigenous societies that constitute the territories of the South-South, South-East and South-West geopolitical zones of Nigeria, along with a few communities in northern Nigeria, the applicable law before the advent of colonial administration was "unwritten customary law".[24] This law was essentially based on traditional systems of belief and administered through indigenous courts invested with the traditional authority exercised by the kings. By the time of colonialism, the indigenous courts were replaced by the "native courts" through the Native Court Proclamations of 1900 and 1901, respectively. The former established the native courts while the latter provided that "the civil and criminal jurisdiction of a statutory native court in a district was to be exclusive of any jurisdiction by any traditional authority".[25] The implication of these proclamations was that even

---

21 See Sampson IT. 2014. "Religion and the Nigerian State: Situating the De facto and De Jure Frontiers of State-Religion Relations and Its Implications for National Security", *Oxford Journal of Law and Religion* 2(3):311-339, wherein the author presents a brilliant analysis of the paradoxical relationship that has historically existed between religion and politics, on the one hand, and between religion and law, on the other, which has continued influence over citizens' perceptions to date. However, the author's recommendation of a "moderate secular regime", which seemingly indicates to a reductionist attempt to legislate religion in the current authors' opinion, is a bit romantic and unrealistic as the analysis of Agenda 2063 seeks to demonstrate.

22 Sampson, "Religion and the Nigerian State", 320.

23 For more detailed discussion, see Elias TO. 1963. *The Nigerian Legal System*. Second Edition. London: Routledge and Paul; Obilade AO. 1979. *The Nigerian Legal System*. Ibadan: Spectrum Books Ltd.

24 Obilade, *The Nigerian Legal System*, 17.

25 Native Court Proclamation No. 25, 1901, s 12.

though the native courts that replaced indigenous courts were to apply customary law, the authority of the courts came not from the local custom or traditional authority but from "English-type law".[26] This is the origin of the customary legal system that evolved over time into an appeal system as is now contained in the Constitution of the Federal Republic of Nigeria, 1999.[27] The current practice is that the native courts are now called customary courts, which are courts of first instance, and appeals from these courts are to the customary court of appeal, which has appellate and supervisory powers over application of customary law.[28]

Islamic law

In most parts of the indigenous societies that constitute the territories of northern Nigeria, the applicable law was Islamic law.[29] This is also true of some communities in southern Nigeria, as the historical record shows.[30] During colonialism, the northern protectorate was administered through a regime of indirect rule and a complicated system of appeal was created to act as a watchdog on the workings of the existing Islamic legal system.[31] Also, the jurisdiction of the existing Islamic law courts was curtailed in areas such as criminal law, commercial law, tort and other areas, and it was relegated to Muslim personal law to keep the very large Muslim population cooperative.[32] Some scholars have described this as the "systematic abrogation of Islamic law in arears incompatible with the interest and agenda of the colonial authority".[33] This process was made easy through the machinery of the repugnancy and incompatibility tests. For example, the Native Courts Proclamation of 1906 declared Islamic law to be part of native law and custom. Therefore, any aspect of native law and custom that was in the view of the colonialist repugnant to natural justice, equity and good conscience or that was incompatible with the colonial laws was deemed to be void to the extent of such repugnancy or incompatibility. This situation continued until 1960, when Nigeria became independent and its court system underwent further development up to its current state under the 1999 Constitution.[34] It is important to emphasise here

---

26 Obilade, *The Nigerian Legal System*, 23.
27 See CFRN, ss 265-269 and 280-284.
28 See CFRN, ss 265-269 and 280-284.
29 Obilade, *The Nigerian Legal System*, 17. See also Sodiq Y. 2017. *A History of the Application of Islamic Law in Nigeria*. Switzerland: Palgrave Macmillan, 27.
30 Gbadamosi TGO. 1978. *The Growth of Islam among the Yoruba 1841-1908*. London: Longman, 4
31 For a full description of the workings of this system and the types of courts established under it in the words of an officer of the colonial authority then in Nigeria, see Orr C. 1965, *The Making of Northern Nigeria*. Second Edition. London: Frank Cass & Co Ltd, 230-243.
32 Clarke PB. 1981. *West Africa and Islam*. London: Edward Arnold, 191.
33 See, for example, the observations of Coulson NJ. 1964. *A History of Islamic Law*. Edinburgh: Edinburgh University Press, 9-61.
34 For constitutional provisions on the Islamic court system, see CFRN, ss 260-264, 275-279.

that the constitutional status of the Islamic legal system continues to be a source of conflict and tension for the non-adherents of the Islamic faith in Nigeria.[35]

Received English law

The term "received English law" is used in the Nigerian context to refer to the colonial legal heritage of the common law of England, the doctrines of equity and English statutes of general application. According to Section 45(1) of the Interpretation Act, 1964, laws that were enforced in England as of 1 January 1900 were made applicable in the colony of Lagos as the seat of the central authority of the colonial government. By the same provision, where any matter is connected to the exclusive legislative competence of the federal legislature, the legal sources were also made applicable throughout Nigeria. Some of the English statutes were eventually repealed and replaced by Nigerian legislation. In terms of religious influence on the law, the Christian origin of the common law and doctrines of equity made applicable throughout Nigeria is evident from the old decision of Lord Sumner that: "Ours is, and always has been, a Christian State. The English family is built on Christian ideas, and if the national religion is not Christian there is none. English law may well be called a Christian law."[36] The Christian origin of the received English law was problematic in terms of application in the areas of Nigeria where there was little or no connection with the Christian faith, such as in Northern Nigeria and some areas in Southern Nigeria. From the time of colonialism up to the present date, this has continued to be a source of tension and conflict.[37]

At this juncture, it is important to observe two points. In the first place, religion is clearly connected to the development of the law in Nigeria, regardless of the mix or nature of the citizenry's religious adherence. To understand this, it is pertinent to consider the following remarks in 1909 by one colonial official, W.L. Grant, following his assessment of the demography of the areas that later came to be known as Nigeria, to the effect that "Every native tribe is bound together by laws and customs resting originally on a religious basis, i.e., resting on certain ideas as to man's nature, his relations to his fellows, and to the other world. On the basis of these ideas different tribes have built up very complex systems of laws and observances, resting on, and bearing witness to, certain habits of mind."[38]

---

35 See, for example, the critical remarks of Ordu GE. 2015. "Sharia Law In Nigeria: Can A Selective Imposition of Islamic Law Work in The Nation?", *Journal of Islamic Studies and Culture* 3(2):70, for the proposition that constitutional provisions on the Islamic law ought to be expunged from the 1999 Constitution.

36 *Bowman v Secular Societies* (1917) A.C. 465.

37 For an academic presentation of one such view, see Oloyede IO. 2014. "Theologising the Mundane, Politicising the Divine: The Cross-currents of Law, Religion and Politics in Nigeria", *African Human Rights Law Journal* 14:178.

38 Grant WL 1909. *Revue Economique Internationale* (cited in Orr C. 1965, *The Making of Northern Nigeria*. Second Edition. London: Frank Cass & Co Ltd, 230).

This colonial commentary demonstrates the age-old connection of law and religion in Nigeria and leads to a second point to be observed. This second observation has to do with the great diversity and complexity of Nigerian religious adherence and observance. It is this complexity that sometimes result in conflicts and misuse of religion – so much so that there are calls in some quarters for reducing the religious normative space.[39] Misrepresentations and misuses of religion continue to abound for purposes other than religious. It is understandable that when such instrumentalisation and misrepresentations result in the breakdown of law and order or loss of lives and properties, such reductionist calls may appear persuasive. However, we contend that the experience of the authority exercised by religion in the response to the pandemic, in the face of a citizen's lack of trust of governmental and public administration directives, was strengthened in most cases and ignored only a few, demonstrating clearly that the era of "carpet sweeping" on matters of religion is over. Put another way, there is a need to engage with religion instead of simply consigning religious matters to the realm of private observance. Unfortunately, however, despite the long association of law and religion, when it comes to religious responses to challenges such as Covid-19 pandemic, there is no clear legal or constitutional directive regarding the relationship between law and religion or what normative role should be accorded religion in the public space.

THE THEORY OF LAW AND RELIGION RELATIONSHIP IN NIGERIA: A CONSTITUTIONAL ANALYSIS

The Constitution of the Federal Republic of Nigeria, 1999, contains eleven references to religion. The first is Section 10, wherein it is provided that neither the Federal government nor any of its federation units as States "shall adopt any religion as State Religion". Section 15(1) states the motto of the Nigerian Federation as "Unity and Faith, Peace and Progress." Arguably, the word "faith" is another derivative for religion and perhaps constitutes the twelfth reference to religion in the Constitution. More particularly in Subsection 2 of the same Section 15, it is stated that national integration should be actively encouraged. This is to be achieved by prohibiting discrimination on the "grounds of place of origin, sex, religion, status, ethnic or linguistic association or ties". Further, under Chapter IV of the Constitution on "Fundamental Rights", expresses in Section 38 the fundamental right of all Nigerians to "freedom of thought, conscience, and religion". This right includes the freedom to change one's religion or belief as well as the freedom "(either alone or in community with others, and in public or in private) to manifest and propagate' one's religion or belief in matters of 'worship, teaching, practice and observance". On the one hand, Subsection 2 of Section 38 protects all Nigerians at all levels of education against religious instructions and observance contrary to those of the individual concerned. Further, Subsection 3 gives the right to religious communities or denominations to give religious instruction to pupils "in any place of education maintained wholly by that community or denomination".

---

39 See again Ordu, "Sharia Law In Nigeria", 70; Sampson, "Religion and the Nigerian State".

Religion is recognised in Section 42 as one of the grounds upon which a person may neither be subjected to "disabilities or restrictions" (Subsection 1(a)) nor become the recipient of "any privilege or advantage" (Subsection 1(b)) simply because they belong to such religion. This is regardless of whether the disability or restriction or the privilege or advantage is as a result of express or practical operation of any law in force in Nigeria or any executive or administrative action. The other grounds stated in this section, alongside religion, are connection to a particular community, ethnic group, place of origin, sex or political opinion. The final reference to religion in the Constitution is contained in Part III, which is the segment on Supplemental Provisions. The provision concerned is Section 222 under Segment (D) on Political Parties. The section provides in its Subsections (a) and (b) that:

> No association by whatever name called shall function as a party, unless –
>
> (a) the names and addresses of its national officers are registered with the Independent National Electoral Commission;
>
> (b) the membership of the association is open to every citizen of Nigeria irrespective of his (sic) place of origin, circumstance of birth, sex, religion or ethnic grouping.

The above constitutional analysis does not disclose clearly any theory of law and religion relationship. In light of this uncertainty, both historically and at present, politicians, national and religious leaders as well as ordinary citizens have differed and continue to differ in their approach to the question as to whether Nigeria is a secular country.

Several examples illustrate the point. One of the foremost Nigerian nationalists in the struggle for independence from colonialism, Chief Obafemi Awolowo, commented in 1966, "Nigeria should be a secular state. The existing association between the State and the Church should be completely severed. It is an old British custom which is apish, unreflecting, and discriminatory for us to preserve. ... as far as possible, there should be separation of activities of the state on the one hand, and religious bodies on the other."[40] In the same vein, Alhaji Shehu Shagari, the first executive president of Nigeria, was quoted in 1981 as saying that "though ours is a secular state with diverse religious creeds we do, in fact, live in harmony among ourselves, respect each other's religious beliefs".[41] As a final example, after the tumultuous aftermath of the annulment of the 12 June 1993 elections in Nigeria,[42] then-military President, General Sani Abacha, inaugurated a National Constitutional Conference Commission in 1994 by remarking, "Nigeria is a secular state. We have acknowledged this in all our previous constitutions, and it is not advisable that we deviate from this course. Religion is an instrument for building

---

40 Awolowo O. 1966. *Thoughts on Nigerian Constitution* Ibadan: Oxford University Press, 150-151.

41 Ojigbo AO. 1981. *Shehu Shagari: The Biography of Nigeria's First Executive President.* Yugoslavia: Mladinska knijiga, 387-388.

42 Now celebrated as "Democracy Day" in Nigeria as an official public holiday.

moral bricks in our society and it should remain within the realms of personal faith and group choice. It must never be allowed to interfere with our collective desire to build a unified and indivisible nation."[43]

Upon a dispassionate consideration of the commentaries just cited, it is evident that even though the national leaders employ the word "secular" in reference to the nature of the Nigerian polity, they do not intend that the issue of religion is generally irrelevant. For Awolowo, it appears that there was concern to keep the integrity of religion intact and ensuring its insulation from political instrumentalisation. On Shagari's and Abacha's part, their concerns were seemingly for the respect and protection of various forms of religious beliefs under one nation. To the current authors, they all appear to intend the same consequences in their various contentions for "secularism", namely, that religion should exist solely for the sake of religion and politics for the sake of politics. That this stance may be unrealistic and ludicrous is evident in the following opposition to the theory of secularism supported by the quoted political leaders. In the foreword to a book published in 1993, John Olorunfemi Onaiyekan, now the retired Archbishop of the Diocese of Abuja, stated:

> The strident call for a separation of politics from religion often becomes a slogan used according to the convenience of the moment. The reality is that both are tied together, by the very nature of things- and this for at least two reasons: First, there is something inherently sacred about political power. History has shown that it can only be properly exercised when handled with sacred attention. In religious jargon, we say, "all powers belong to God." Secondly, it is the same concrete human person who assumes both political and religious identity, and one necessarily affects the other. No wonder, even nations which make much of separation of religion and politics find many ways in practice to act against this principle. It seems to me that this is why our prolonged debate over the "secular" nature of the Nigerian state has remained inconclusive. "Secular state" means different things to different people. It is surely more useful to tackle concrete issues of interaction of politics and religion and from there evolve just and fair solutions to our problems of peaceful co-operation.[44]

Onaiyekan is certainly correct that there are different conceptions of secularism and that even though in the ordinary conception secularism incorporates the notion of separating the spiritual and religious realms from the temporal or political, the reality is often the opposite. It is important to be clear what the goals of defining Nigeria one way or the other should be in relation to the law-religion relationship. This is where consideration of the Agenda 2063 objectives can be instructive.

---

43 Umar AM (ed). 1995. *Constitutional Conference 1994/95 Official Handbook and WHO IS WHO*. Abuja: Heritage Press, 48.

44 Kukah MH. 1993. *Religion, Politics and Power in Northern Nigeria*. Ibadan: Spectrum Books Ltd.

AGENDA 2063 AND THE "USE" OF RELIGION

"Agenda 2063: The Africa We Want" is a document that was adopted by the African Union (AU) in 2013 to serve as "masterplan" and "blueprint" for the overall transformation and development of Africa.[45] The main objective of the document was to refocus the activities of the AU and its member states from away from the initial focus of its precursor organisation, the Organisation of African Unity (OAU).[46] The initial agenda of the OAU was struggle against the apartheid regime in South Africa and the attainment of political independence from all forms of colonialism for all societies on the African continent. Agenda 2063 is a long-term 50-year development plan from 2013 with seven aspirations ranging from inclusive social and economic development, continental and regional integration to peace, security and good governance. Key activities are delineated to be undertaken in 10-year development plans across the 50-year period from 2013-2063.[47] Two reports of the implementation plans have been published to date. The first continental implementation report was published in February 2020,[48] while the second continental report was published in February 2022.[49] The first report assessed progress made across the continent on all seven aspirations, with the highest percentage score of 48% recorded for Aspiration 4 (a peaceful and secure Africa) and the lowest percentage score of 12% for Aspiration 5 (Africa with a strong cultural identity, common heritage, value and beliefs).[50] There is no mention of the pandemic and the attendant socio-economic effects on African societies, since the report was published just as the pandemic was spreading to the African continent.

Unsurprisingly, the second report, published in February 2022, contain copious references to the pandemic and its attendant effect on African countries. In fact, in the foreword section of the report, the effect of the pandemic in terms of fiscal deficit and setbacks on developmental gains in relation to Agenda 2063 was underscored as a front-burner issue. However, the issue of religion or religious actors was not mentioned in the report in connection to the pandemic in terms of "use" or "misuse". This is surprising given the nature of reference that the issue of religion receives generally in Agenda 2063.

---

45 See African Union, "Agenda 2063: The Africa We Want". For academic analysis by non-Africans of the implication of the contents of Agenda 2063 for the aspiration of transformation of Africa by the African Union, see Ziebell de Oliveira G and Otavio A. 2021. "Strategies of Development and International Insertion: The Hybridity of Agenda 2063", *Contexto Internacional* 43(2):331. For African perspective on the aspirational nature of Agenda 2063, see Ndizera V and Muzee H. 2018. "A Critical Review of Agenda 2063: Business as Usual?", *African Journal of Political Science and International Relations* 12(8):142.

46 Ziebell de Oliveira and Otavio, "Strategies of Development and International Insertion".

47 Ziebell de Oliveira and Otavio, "Strategies of Development and International Insertion".

48 African Union. 2020. "First Continental Report on the Implementation of Agenda 2063", *AU.intl*, 8 February.

49 AU, "First Continental Report on the Implementation of Agenda 2063".

50 AU, "First Continental Report on the Implementation of Agenda 2063", 7.

In fact, the word "religion" occurs eleven times in the popular version of Agenda 2063. The first mention underscores the need for "transformative leadership" in all fields – notably including religion – -in order to entrench such ideals as good governance, democratic values, gender equality, respect for human rights, justice and the rule of law.[51] The second mention notes the need to eschew all forms of terrorism and religious extremism in the process of attaining "a peaceful and secure Africa".[52] A third mention emphasises the need for respect for religious diversity among other pan-African ideals to be entrenched by 2063.[53] Such diversity on the basis of religion and other stated factors should constitute "a source of strength",[54] and by 2063 pan-Africanism should be fully embedded in school curricula in such a manner that cultural assets, such as religion and spirituality, will be enhanced.[55] In addition, while the agenda recognises that "religious and spiritual beliefs" play significant role in the "construction of the African identity and social interaction", the agenda nevertheless aspires that the continent will "continue to vehemently oppose all forms of politicisation of religion and religious extremism".[56] Finally, Agenda 2063 aspires to a people-driven development, which necessitates the inclusivity of all citizens in all aspects of decision-making with no consideration for their affiliations on any basis, including religion.[57]

From the above discussion, it is clear that Agenda 2063 is very cognisant that in most African societies, including Nigeria, religion is a vital component of African heritage and of the definition of the citizen's identity. It is tightly knitted into the fibre of the social web and relations. The fact that such an important document on the African continent as Agenda 2063 contains unequivocal references to religion signifies its perception that rather than pushing religion to the background, it is better to engage it fruitfully in the public domain. Put differently, Agenda 2063 acknowledges the fact that there must be conversations about religion in the public space, mediated appropriately by government, to avoid degeneration to conflict, while not stifling fringe opinions. Otherwise, as entrenched as religion is in the community life of most African societies, religion will continue to be instrumentalised for less desirable purposes if religious conversations are consigned only to private spheres. While the exploration and acknowledgment of the role of religion underscored by Agenda 2063 is vital, one must also not lose sight of the possible exploitation of religion, with its attendant negative effect, if conversation about religion is not appropriately mediated. Appropriate mediation of religion in the Nigerian case is a dire necessity given existing narratives and historical facts concerning the relationship of law and religion.

---

51 African Union. 2020 "Aspirations for the Africa We Want:", *AU.intl*, Aspiration 3, para 31.
52 AU, "Aspirations", Aspiration 4, para 38.
53 AU, "Aspirations", Aspiration 5, para 40.
54 AU, "Aspirations", Aspiration 5, para 41.
55 AU, "Aspirations", Aspiration 5, para 42
56 AU, "Aspirations", Aspiration 5, para 46
57 AU, "Aspirations", Aspiration 6, para 47.

MISCONCEPTIONS ON THE ROLE OF RELIGIOUSLY INSPIRED LAW AND LEGAL SYSTEM IN NIGERIA

As can be surmised from the discussion so far, the development and application of law in Nigeria has been inexorably linked to religion. Not only does Agenda 2063 make copious references to religion, but the 1999 Constitution also contains provisions on religion. However, the issue of religion continues to occasion much competition, complexity and conflict among adherents of Nigeria's different religions. This chapter argues that erroneous perceptions that lack a historical basis are a major source of these challenges. The influence of religion in the emergence of the customary law, Islamic law and the received English law is a historical fact. However, it is also a historical fact that none of these legal systems emerged and developed in the post-colonial Nigeria according to the aspirations of religious adherents. Put another way, it is historically incorrect to argue, as some observers do, that the system of law derived from these three sources protects religious rights.

As analysis has shown, the development Nigerian law, including religious and customary law sources, was a result of colonial policies for ease of administration and for the convenient exploitation of Nigeria's human and material resources. As British historian of religion Peter Clarke rightly notes, local laws were not interfered with where they served the interest of the colonial masters in keeping the citizen cooperative, as was the case in the indirect rule of the then northern Nigeria where Islamic personal law was left alone.[58] However, existing modes of legal administration were modified in commercial transactions and land transactions and other areas to facilitate the interests of the colonial authority. Thus, the constitutional references to religion and religiously inspired legal systems are, in the perspective of this chapter, no more than "colonial relics". The time is ripe for Nigerians to be responsive enough to this rather than engaging in unnecessary and unhealthy competition and mutual rivalry. Nigerians must appreciate the fact that religion has a place in terms of definition of the African identity and communal coexistence, a fact recognised in Agenda 2063. The hypocrisy in the use to which religion is put in our laws cannot justifiably be blamed on any religion or any of its adherents. It is better to have a conversation about what religious worldviews and resources contribute to development and human flourishing, particularly in the context of health and healing and the particular challenges brought about by the Covid-19 pandemic.[59]

---

58 Clarke, *West Africa and Islam*, 17.

59 This kind of conversation is ongoing in the Western context with the publication of a 2018 report. See International Panel on Social Progress (IPSP). 2018. *Rethinking Society for the 21st Century*: Report of the International Panel on Social Progress. Cambridge: Cambridge University Press, 1 and 4. Chapter 16 of this report is titled "Religion and Social Progress", wherein it is acknowledged in the introduction that "religion is in itself a cultural good" and that "economic wellbeing, education, and healthcare are goals shared by religious groups and are often woven into religious worldviews".

OBSERVATIONS AND PROGNOSIS FOR FUTURE DEVELOPMENT

References in Agenda 2063 to religion are responsive to the dual and ambivalent nature of religion as a unifying factor in the process of identity formation and as well as an index for divisiveness when instrumentalised for political, self-serving or extremist purposes. Aspirations towards transformational leadership and inculcating the spirit of service to fellow citizens in public administration require readjustment and realignment in the African value system. Religion can constitute an important tool in the realisation of these aspirations in Africa, particularly in Nigeria, because it teaches the value of living beyond self-interest, among other values. This positivity is certainly required in Nigeria to overcome vices such as corruption, greed and nepotism that are the product of a single world outlook: self-interest. A sense of service, however, encourages patriotism and religion is a powerful tool in inculcating this value. In this connection, the positive religious responses to the Covid-19 pandemic were a significant indication to the appropriate use of religion and this possibility should be further fruitfully engaged.

An informal colloquial expression in Nigeria is that Nigerians are probably the "most religious people on earth", with places of worship perhaps outnumbering schools and educational institutions. This perspective may seemingly underscore a counterargument that religion has little to offer in terms of human and material development in Nigeria. However, the experience of the Covid-19 pandemic has proven to some extent that what is required is a reorientation of the appropriate use of religion. However, due to the long history of mutual fear and distrust among the adherents of the various religions because of the complex past, much negativity has been erroneously attached to religion. The brief history of the emergence of the religiously inspired laws has demonstrated that there is need for correct assessment of the role of religion in terms of development of laws that are "homegrown" and in tune with the values of the citizenry as expressed by their religious followership.

CONCLUSION

Religion is part and parcel of the history and heritage of the African people. This is why Agenda 2063, with its inspiring and rightly ambitious aspirations, references religion and its capacity for positive engagement. Such bold references in an era when people in other Western societies are engaged in "secularism" debates, as regards whether there can be too much, too little or no religion at all, is, a pan-African way of standing for the future. Religion is a constitutive element of individual identities that adds up to a collective national identity. Rather than avoiding the issue of religion in Nigeria, even though religion has too often been a negative force, it is better to face head-on the factors that prevent religion from playing a positive role. Because religion is embedded deeply in the fibre of the existence of the nation's people, the engagement of religions in combatting the Covid-19 pandemic in Nigeria shows the powerful role it can play. Facing both the negative and positive dimensions of religion in relation to law and governance would entail creating robust atmosphere for exchange of ideas and histories across the different religions to uncover a common a homegrown "Nigerian" response to the relationship between law and religion.

II. Religion-state relations and religious authority in the Covid-19 pandemic

6 COVID-19, POWER IMBALANCE AND THE RESHAPING OF STATE-RELIGION RELATIONS IN NORTH AFRICA: THE ALGERIAN CONTEXT

Mahfoud Ali Zoui[1]

INTRODUCTION

In an attempt to contain the dangers resulting from the deadly pandemic of Covid-19, governments in democratic and autocratic countries alike have imposed lockdowns and adopted special measures, including emergency provisions that restricted freedom of movement, gathering and freedom of religious practice. The impact of the lockdown measures has been profound, leading to a resurgence of authoritarianism and a reshaping of state-religion relations, even in leading world democracies with long-established traditions in respecting freedoms and the rule of law. Due to the pandemic, "towns, cities and entire countries [were] placed into lockdown and places of worship closed, with the active concurrence, or passive acceptance, of faith leaders".[2]

The implementation of emergency provisions in the so-called young democracies of North Africa has had immense implications for the free practice of religious activities and for the role of the state in the religious sphere. The restrictions on religious freedoms in countries like Algeria have been severe, and authorities increased their surveillance and control of mosques and religious associations leading to a visible expansion of state powers. Hence, one consequence of the pandemic is that it made the practice of religious activities more open to state intervention.

In this chapter, I argue, through the Algerian example, that this increase in state intervention has been more visible in countries where the state enjoys monopoly on religious life and those already characterised by strict restrictions on civil liberties and basic freedoms. Due to the nature of the state-religion relation and the way that religion is administered in Algeria, the pandemic has reshaped the state-religion relationship creating a power imbalance as it allowed the state to increase its surveillance powers and to strengthen its monopoly of the country's religious sphere.

While the special emergency lockdown measures were justifiable to some extent, their implementation caused alterations in the state-religion relations and triggered controversies – legal and socio-political – on the protection of religious freedoms and

---

1 Associate Professor of Civilisation, Department of English, 8 May 1945 Guelma University, Algeria.
2 Hill M. 2021. "Locating the right to freedom of religion or belief across time and territory", in Ferrari S, Hill M, Jamal A and Bottoni R (eds). *Handbook of Freedom of Religion or Belief*. London: Routledge.

rights during public health emergencies and the tension between basic freedoms and constitutional rights, on the one hand, and public safety and order, on the other. These developments, too, are the subject of the analysis in this chapter. Through qualitative analysis of relevant texts, documents, laws and views of state and non-state actors, I argue that the pandemic provided an appropriate pretext for the state to impose its narrative through official religious institutions and to consolidate its control of the country's religious affairs.

THE MANAGEMENT OF RELIGIOUS AFFAIRS IN ALGERIA

The impact of the Covid-19 pandemic in Algeria and other North African countries has been different from its impact in Europe, mainly because of the different nature of state-religion relationship. The state in North African countries plays a major role in religious life through official religious institutions. These institutions have become important tools for the state to monitor religious activities, increase its control of religious ideology and enforce official interpretations of religious texts and laws.

The Constitution of Algeria provides for freedom of worship, freedom of conscience and freedom of assembly in accordance with the law, and it states that freedom of conscience and freedom of opinion are inviolable. Article 42 states: "The freedom of conscience and the freedom of opinion shall be inviolable and the free exercise of worship shall be guaranteed under the respect of law."[3] However, the way the religious sphere and the practice of religious freedoms are organised in Algeria differs completely from the Western state-church relation, where the two institutions are separate and the religious and political powers in society are clearly distinct. As in the other countries of the Maghreb region, the state in Algeria administers and dominates the religious sphere. It is due to state monopoly on religion that the impact that Covid-19 had on the power balance between state and religion in North African countries, such as Algeria, differs largely from its influence in Western countries.

With the independence of Algeria in 1962 from the French colonial rule, which lasted 132 years, Islam became the official religion in the country. In fact, even before independence, the first founding text of the modern Algerian nation, which declared the revolution against the brutal French colonialism, set the goal of the fight for national liberation as: "the establishment of the sovereign democratic social Algerian state within the framework of Islamic principles".[4] Article 2 of the first constitution of the independent Algerian state in 1963 made Islam the "religion of the state".[5] The subsequent constitutions of 1976, 1989, 1996 and 2020, kept the

---

3   Constitution of the People's Democratic Republic of Algeria, Official Gazette No. 76 of 8 December 1996.
4   The National Liberation Front, Algeria, General Secretariat. 1954. "The Declaration of the First of November 1954".
5   Constitution of the People's Democratic Republic of Algeria.

second article as it is. The state has always sought to organise the religious sphere and to control the religious doctrine and discourse in the country. Consequently, the state enjoys an almost complete control over the country's religious sphere. The executive branch of the state is responsible for the management of religious affairs and mosque activity in the country.

The state constructs and licenses mosques and *waqfs* (which are also known as *habus*). The Ministry of Religious Affairs along with other state institutions regulates and controls the management of mosques and other religious and charitable institutions. It oversees mosques and clerical staff, administers *hadj* (pilgrimage), *umra* and *zakat* (almsgiving).[6] The state also appoints imams and other civil servants (inspectors, teachers of Quran, female spiritual guides (*murshidat diniyyat*) and pays their salaries. Only state-sanctioned mosques can lead Islamic services, and only government-authorised imams, hired and trained by the state, can lead prayers in mosques.

Besides the Ministry of Religious Affairs, the High Islamic Council (HIC) is the other important institution set by the state to help organise and control religion in the country. It was first established in January 1966 as part of the Ministry of Religious Affairs by Decree 66-4, with the purpose of "affirming the real face of Islam and eradicating every falsification and fiction introduced in the Islamic faith".[7] Later, in 1989, a constitutional amendment separated the HIC from the Ministry of Religious Affairs and promoted it to a "constitutional institution". The significance of the HIC lies in the fact that it is responsible for issuing official *fatwas*, which can be promoted by different tools owned by the state. According to Article 161 of the 1989 Constitution, the High Islamic Council is established directly by the president of the Republic, who chooses a president for the council from among its 15 members.[8]

As far as the practice of religions other than Islam, besides the constitutional guarantee of religious freedom, Algeria was the first Maghrebi country to have adopted a specific law guaranteeing the freedom and regulating the practice of non-Muslim belief through Ordinance 06-03 of 2006 Establishing the Conditions and Rules for the Practice of Beliefs other than Islam.[9] Prior to the enactment of this law, there had been only a few scattered provisions dealing with religious freedoms of non-Muslims in the country. Ordinance 06-03 was adopted with the aim of implementing the constitutional proclamations of religious freedom for non-Muslims. The ordinance is seen as the most important legal reform in the area of religious freedom and the first specific law adopted to guarantee freedom

---

6   Ghanem D. 2018."State-Owned Islam in Algeria Faces Stiff Competition", *Carnegie Middle East Center*, 13 March.

7   Bousadia M. 2021. من هيئة تنظيمية إلى مؤسسة دستورية [From an organisational body to a constitutional institution], *Elwassat*, 14 January.

8   Tamburini F. 2019."The 'Islam of the Government': The Islamic High Councils in Algeria, Morocco, Mauritania and Tunisia", *Journal of Asian and African Studies* 55(4):1-17.

9   People's Democratic Republic of Algeria, General Secretariat of Government. 2006. *Joradp* (Official Journal of the People's Democratic Republic of Algeria), 25.

of religion in Algeria. Ordinance 06-03 was designed to apply to non-Muslims the same constraints imposed on Muslims, including stipulating that religious rites must comply with the law and respect public order, morality and the rights and basic freedoms of others, also established also the National Commission for Non-Muslim Religious Groups, a new government entity, responsible for facilitating the registration process for all non-Muslim groups.[10]

While government officials argued that Ordinance 06-03 came to enforce the constitutional guarantee of freedom of religion, and to extend state protection to all the religious groups and their houses of worship, some argued that with its many limitations, it came in fact to tighten up state control of religious associations and their religious activities.[11] As a matter of fact, the assumption of the Algerian authorities that the 1990s Algerian Civil War had its roots in the rise of an imported type of extremist religious ideology pushed the state to seek more control of the religious sphere and doctrine, to increase its surveillance over mosques and to tighten its control of religious discourse. Hence, since the 1990s, "relations between Islam and the state have evolved toward greater government control of the religion".[12] The state has also promoted and elevated religious streams and ideologies that are deemed moderate and represent the real Algerian values and identity, including Sufi orders.[13]

Nevertheless, state monopoly of the religious doctrine and the organisation of religion have never been taken for granted. The state has always found itself in contest with a diverse array of religious actors, particularly Islamic parties and Salafist movements.[14] The religious discourse and ideology of the latter, which have always been significant and influential, did not appeal to the state, which used different tools to weaken them and succeeded to promote and co-opt other ideologies. The association of some religious groups and ideologies with extremism and security during the 1990s led the state increasingly to seek to control the country's religious sphere. Hence, because of this sensitivity towards religion and the way religion is administered in Algeria, the state of emergency during Covid-19 led to an immense expansion of state power at the expense of religious freedoms.

---

10 People's Democratic Republic of Algeria, General Secretariat of Government. 2006. "Ordinance 06-03, s 2, art 9", *Joradp* (Official Journal of the People's Democratic Republic of Algeria), 26.

11 Ferchiche N. 2013. "Religious Freedom in the Constitutions of the Maghreb", in Durham WC, Ferrari S, Ciannitto C and Thayer D (eds). *Law, Religion, Constitution*. London: Routledge, 196.

12 Ferchiche, "Religious Freedom in the Constitutions of the Maghreb", 186.

13 Boukhars A. 2021."Algeria's Sufis Balance State Patronage and Political Entanglement", *Carnegie Endowment for International Peace*, 7 June.

14 Sakthivel V. 2018. "Algeria's Religious Landscape: A Balancing Act", *Foreign Policy Research Institute*, 1 September.

THE PANDEMIC AND THE SOCIO-POLITICAL CONTEXT

When Covid-19 hit the region in 2019, Algeria had already been grappling with the consequences of previous crises that shaped the decade of the 2010s. It was a very tense decade, as a series of successive crises hit the region and caused economic and social instability. These included the 2014-2016 oil price decline and the 2019 resurgence of large-scale popular protests known in Algeria as the Hirak (Arabic for "movement"). During this mass protest movement, there was a sense of distrust between the state and the general public. Hence, the pandemic intensified the social and political problems, and the new measures adopted by the state to slow down its spread led to the expansion of its powers at the expense of civil society and religion.

The resurgence of large-scale popular protests in Algeria, initially in outrage at then-president Abdelaziz Bouteflika's bid for a fifth term in office, created a tense climate. The demonstrations started on 22 February 2019 in most Algerian cities, and they turned into the largest and longest protests in the country's history within a short time.[15] The Hirak forced Bouteflika to step down weeks later. Yet, the weekly Friday rallies did not stop, as Algerians were determined to accompany the political transition taking place. Over many weeks, the mosque was the hub of the Hirak mass protest movement. The weekly marches took place every Friday and started from mosques after Friday Prayer, benefitting from the huge gatherings of congregants to perform the Islamic Jumu'ah prayer.[16] The Hirak, however, was interrupted by the outbreak of the coronavirus pandemic.

Algeria confirmed the first case of Covid-19 within its borders in late February 2020 and subsequently suspended domestic and international air and maritime travel and closed universities, schools and mosques. The closure of mosques and the suspension of Friday Prayer would subsequently weaken the Hirak. The authorities formally banned the demonstrations held each Friday in March 2020 after 57 weeks of mass demonstrations in major Algerian cities. As a matter of fact, even if the demonstrations had not been formally banned, the mere suspension of Friday Prayer would have made it difficult for the demonstrators to mobilise as big a number of people as had been the case when the prayers were allowed. The government also implemented partial lockdowns and curfew measures in critical areas, such as Algiers, Blida, Batna, Oran, TiziOuzou, Setif and other cities with high numbers of Covid-19 cases.[17]

Since its beginning, the pandemic has paved the way for the regime to deal with the demonstrations and to halt the Hirak. After the government's decree prohibiting the protest movement, nominally to prevent the spread of the pandemic, some key

---

15 Ghebouli ZL. 2020. "Algeria, One Year into the Hirak: Successes and Setbacks", *Fikra Forum/Washington Institute for Middle East Policy*, 21 February.

16 Blidi S. 2020. "New wave of Algeria protests raise questions about future of Hirak", *The Arab Weekly*, 17 June.

17 Mestek YML. 2020. "Algeria: Politics and Protests in Coronavirus Times", in Kempe F et al (eds). *The politics of pandemic: Evolving regime-opposition dynamics in the MENA region*. Washington, DC: The Atlantic Council.

figures in the protest saw the move as a convenient attempt to restrict the demonstrations.[18] Opposition parties and Hirak activists accused the government of exploiting the pandemic to crack down on religious and political rights and using it as an excuse to weaken the Hirak, especially because of the interplay between religious and political freedoms. Suspending Friday Prayer (a religious right) led to the halting of the demonstrations of the Hirak movement (a political freedom). The suspension of Friday Prayer was the key measure that facilitated the suspension of the Hirak movement. Hence, the pandemic was "a perfect public health pretext to ban gatherings and demonstrations."[19]

The president of the Islamist Justice and Development Party, Abdelah Jaballah, described the decision of the Ministry of Religious Affairs to suspend daily congregational prayers and the Jumu'ah Prayer in mosques as incorrect. He maintained that the *fatwa* was not based on any religious basis and argued that if the real purpose behind the decision was to prevent the spread of the virus, then the ban would also have included markets and public administrations where people gather in large numbers.[20] The authorities defended the validity of the emergency measures, arguing that the restrictions they imposed on some constitutionally guaranteed political and religious rights, including suspension of religious gatherings, become legitimate in such emergency times – not least because health experts worldwide advised that the lockdowns and certain restrictions were legitimate and indeed could be the most effective option to face the exceptional emergency. President Abdelmajid Teboune assured Algerians that "the state is determined to protect freedoms and rights as much as it is responsible for protecting persons and property".[21]

Despite the formal suspension of the protests, thousands of protestors had previously defied lockdown measures and challenged the state on many occasions. There was wide opposition to the banning of congregational prayers in general and the suspension of Friday Prayer in particular. Many of protestors who violated the lockdown were arrested and jailed.[22] In fact, even before the pandemic, there had been complaints about the regulations organising the right to gather and demonstrate in Algeria.[23] During the pandemic, religious rights overlapped with political freedoms. Hence, the impact of the pandemic on the religious life in Algeria was multidimensional and rapidly transformed socio-religious life of millions of

---

18 Mestek, "Algeria: Politics and Protests in Coronavirus Times".
19 Abdelhadi M. 2021. "Viewpoint: Algerian blame games expose deep political crisis", *BBC*, 2 September.
20 "Algeria, President of an Islamist Party Considers Closing Mosques because of Covid Illegal", *Al-Quds Al-Arabi*, 18 March 2020.
21 "Algeria Fights Corona", *Al-Arabiya*, 18 March 2020.
22 "Thousands defy Algeria's Covid-19 curfew in pro-democracy protests", *Al-Arabiya*, 3 March 2021.
23 The International Human Rights Framework on the Right of Peaceful Assembly, Algeria. Online at: https://www.rightofassembly.info/country/algeria# [Accessed 8 December 2022].

Muslims who used to organise their life and activity around the five congregational daily prayers. The ensuing restrictions impacted their right to freedom of religion, restricted their collective religious activities, changed notions about the spiritual and the physical and severely altered state-religion relations.

EMERGENCY PROVISIONS AND THEIR IMPACT

The official religious institutions in the country came to prominence during the fight against the pandemic. Their religious authority has been used to explain and justify the emergency measures, including the closure of mosques and the suspension of congregational prayers. The government found these institutions a useful tool to help it manage the exceptional situation during the pandemic.

In the beginning of the pandemic, the Algerian government responded to the threat of the virus by issuing a set of decrees and executive orders to impose social distancing and lockdown limiting some constitutional rights and liberties.[24] Under emergency decree legislation, the state, which had already been in control of the religious sphere, gradually gained excess powers, which allowed it to impose further restrictions on religious freedoms. Later on, with the spread of the pandemic and the increase in human losses, there was a need to amend some articles in the criminal law. In particular, the Algerian authorities adopted amendments to the Penal Code. Article 459 of the Penal Code, relating to noncompliance with decrees and administrative orders, was amended, and a new article was introduced to criminalise "endangering the lives and physical integrity of others" with the aim of enforcing the respect of social distancing and other lockdown measures.[25] Article 290 bis of the Penal Code punishes with up to two years imprisonment anyone who "exposes the life of another human being or his physical integrity by not following a rule or a law. The sentence is of up to five years if the events happen during sanitary lockdown, a catastrophe or another calamity."[26] This law imposed further restrictions on freedom of expression and of association by punishing with prison sentences any act that may be considered a threat to the safety of others.[27]

There were complaints that the emergency provisions led to tightening the lockdown measures on mosques in a discriminatory way. Authorities were not as severe with other sectors where large gatherings of people were allowed to take place. Gatherings of people in markets, transportation system and post offices did not cause much concern for authorities. People questioned the real purpose behind

---

24 Khelfi H and Khelfi A. 2020. "Legal Characterization of Violations Recorded after the Covid-19 Legal Prevention Measures: A dissertation on the light of law N.2220-06 of April 28, 2020, Amending the Criminal Law", *Annales de l'université d'Alger* 34 (Special Edition).

25 Khelfi and Khelfi, "Legal Characterization of Violations Recorded after the Covid-19 Legal Prevention Measures".

26 People's Democratic Republic of Algeria, General Secretariat of Government. 2020. *Joradp* (Official Journal of the People's Democratic Republic of Algeria), (29 April):13.

27 Khelfi and Khelfi, "Legal Characterization of Violations Recorded after the Covid-19 Legal Prevention Measures".

this discrimination, with some wondering whether Covid-19 was "a religious virus", which infects gatherings in worship houses but not the long lines of post at offices, public transportation and other workplaces.[28] There were also complaints that houses of worship were being discriminated against particularly. This gave the impression that the state had implicitly decided that the practice of religious duties was less essential compared to other activities of economic nature. Tightening the lockdown on mosques, in particular, created a feeling that the state was being less considerate of religious communities, compared to other communities of economic value.

The exceptional measures adopted by the government in a bid to contain the pandemic led to increased surveillance and ramped up the state's control over houses of worship, associations and citizens. The result was an increased intervention of the state in the religious life of people and limitation of their right to gather for their congregational religious practices. The organisation of religion by the executive branch of government through the Ministry of Religious Affairs made it easier for the Algerian state to tighten its control of religious activity in the country. Hence, the Covid-19 crisis created further disequilibrium in the balance of power between state authorities and religious associations and mosques. The implications of the new imbalances have been more visible in countries like Algeria, because democracy and the rule of law are not yet well established. The exceptional measures and the strict lockdown allowed for a huge expansion in state powers on the expense of the freedom to gather and worship.

One of the clear consequences of the Covid-19 pandemic was the discrimination by the state between houses of worship and other institutions, which might be an outcome of considering religious activity less essential and less important due to valuing the physical over the spiritual.[29] Also, the way authorities implemented the lockdown measures raised doubts about the declared objectives and increased distrust of the government actions at a time when trust in government measures and the cooperation of the civil society and other associations – including religious ones, which have a significant weight in North African Muslim-majority countries – were crucial for an effective management of such emergency crisis.

This lack of trust in the emergency provisions taken by the state led to discontent and resistance to some measures. Suspending Friday Prayer, closure of ablution areas in mosques, limiting the Friday sermon to fifteen minutes and imposing distancing during prayers after the reopening of mosques caused wide discontent. People wondered, once again, whether Covid-19 infects people only in houses of worship rather than in workspaces and other crowded places.[30]

---

28 Elgendi Y. 2020. "Impact of Covid-19 on Religious Freedom: State-Religion Relations in the Time of a Pandemic", *Dialogue Institute*. SUSI Scholars Virtual Conference. Online at: https://dialogue institute.org/2020-susi-scholars-virtual-conference

29 Elgendi, "Impact of Covid-19 on Religious Freedom".

30 Boukebba A. 2020. بعد إجراءات رفع الحجر تدريجياً.. استياء شعبي متّزايد من تمديد غلق المساجد [After the partial lifting of the lockdown, popular dissatisfaction for the extension of the

The state's bid to exploit the Covid-19 emergency to consolidate its monopoly on religious doctrine and the *fatwa* was resisted by religious actors who had traditionally challenged the state's monopoly of religious sphere and competed with the official religious doctrine, particularly scholars of the Salafist movement and some Islamic parties. Other religious associations, imams and independent religious scholars also criticised particular measures and tried to push back against harsher government restrictions on mosques. This led to the termination of the service of some imams and their final dismissal, due to their violation of its decision to close mosques or criticising the discrimination against houses of worship.[31]

In one famous case, the most influential Salafi scholar contested an official *fatwa* issued by the Ministry of Religious Affairs, causing a big controversy. After the pandemic eased down and the number of infections decreased, the ministry allowed congregational prayers to be resumed under new conditions, including observing safe distancing between the congregants Professor Cheikh Mohamed Ali Ferkous, the most prominent Salafi scholar and spiritual leader in Algeria, issued a *fatwa* stating that distancing during prayer is not justified and that for the prayer to be accepted congregants need to pray side by side, shoulder by shoulder.[32] This scholar and his *fatwas* enjoy a huge popularity in Algeria, but his *fatwa* regarding observing safe distancing between the congregants could not be implemented in mosques as the Ministry of Religious Affairs enforced its own official *fatwa*.

This triggered a heated debate on the religious validity of distanced prayers. Performing the five daily prayers is the second of the five pillars of Islam and one of the distinguishing features of this religion. According to the *sunnah* (traditions regarding Prophet Muhammad), in normal circumstances, congregants are to stand abreast, shoulder-to-shoulder. Given the Covid-19 pandemic's exceptional circumstances, the Ministry of Religious Affairs issued a *fatwa* advising that congregants in mosques should stand at a distance from each other during prayers.

It is well-established in Islamic juristic tradition that due to the sanctity of human life, Muslims may be exempted from fulfilling some of the duties during exceptional circumstances such as wars or plagues. Islam, for instance, prescribes limiting movement, gathering, and traveling during plagues. Prophet Muhammad (PBUH) also encouraged quarantine to keep the plagues from spreading. The Prophet says: "If you hear that there is a plague in a land, do not enter it; and if it (plague) visits a land while you are therein, do not go out of it"[33]

Hence, the *fatwa* council of Ministry of Religious Affairs based its *fatwa* regarding the closure of mosques and social distancing during congregational prayers on the

---

closure of mosques], *Ultrasawt*, 15 June 2020. Online at: https://ultraalgeria.ultrasawt.com

31 Mustapha K. 2021. قطبار حقوق الإنسان تطالب بالعدول عن قرار توقيف الشيخ ياسين لراري. [Human Rights League demands reconsideration of the decision to suspend cheikh Yacine Lerari], *Elhiwar*, 16 April. Online at: https://elhiwar.dz/featured/199789/

32 Ferkous MA. Fatwa No. 1280 (in Arabic). Online at: https://ferkous.com/home/?q=fatwa-1280

33 *Sahih al-Bukhari* 5728, bk, 76: ch 30: "What has been mentioned about the plague".

Islamic principle of *hifz al-nafs* (protection of life), which is one of the main *maqasid al-sharia* (objectives of sharia).[34] However, those who supported Farkous's *fatwa* believed that maintaining social distance during congregational prayer makes the prayer *batila* (incorrect). The *fatwa* that social distancing during congregational prayers is not permissible is based on the assumption that the harm that can be inflicted on the congregants if they prayed in the normal manner is only a perceived harm not a real one, and a *Fard* (religious duty) cannot be dismissed because of perceived harm.[35]

Disagreement between the state's official *fatwa* and some imams and independent scholars caused controversy and even disorder in some mosques, as in the same mosque one could find some congregants abiding by the ministry's instructions in some lines and others violating the instructions refusing to maintain social distance while praying. Numbers of congregants visibly decreased after the reopening of mosques, as many decided they would rather pray at home than forego praying shoulder to shoulder, in the traditional fashion.[36]

CONCLUSION

Under emergency decree legislation, the state exploited the pandemic to tighten its control of the country's religious sphere. Two factors allowed the state to use the pandemic to consolidate its domination of the religious sphere and to mute the religious voices that have traditionally challenged its monopoly of religious ideology and doctrine. The first factor relates to the power imbalance between official religion and the other religious actors. The second factor is related to the fact that the country is a young democracy where the rule of law is not yet well-established and there exists a wide gap between the promise of the existing laws and their application.

One dangerous consequence of the sometimes unjustified limitations imposed by the state on religious freedom in the time of the Covid-19 pandemic is that it led to widening the gap between the general public and the state. As the state gained excess powers within the fear-dominated climate resulting from the pandemic, it imposed further restrictions on religious freedoms and increased the measures of surveillance and control over mosques and religious associations, which further increased distrust of government measures.

In this chapter, I have examined the discrimination against mosques in implementing the lockdown measures, which led many to believe that the state is less considerate of the practice of religious and spiritual duties and the views and *fatwas* of religious scholars and imams, especially if they are not in favour of its plans and policies.

---

34 See Padela AI. 2018. "The Essential Dimensions of Health According to the Maqasid al-Shari'ah Frameworks", *International Medical Journal Malaysia* 17(1)

35 Ferkous, Fatwa No.1280.

36 قباقب الأئمة تحذر من فتاوى تحريضية على المساجد [Imams' Union warns of Agitative Fatwas against Mosques], *Echourouk Newspaper*. 4 November 2020.

I have also explained how the organisation of religious affairs in the country led to a visible expansion of the state monopoly of the country's religious sphere during the time of pandemic. The political role of the mosque and the interplay between religion and politics can account for the impact of the pandemic on the practice of freedoms in general and religious freedoms in particular. The state has been accused of exploiting the pandemic for political gains. Tightening control and imposing surveillance over mosques, in addition to suspending Friday Prayer, led to the weakening of Algeria's 2019 mass protest movement.

7 THE ROLE OF RELIGIOUS LEADERS IN NIGER'S COVID-19 CRISIS

Seyni Moumouni[1]

INTRODUCTION

Around the world, the Covid-19 crisis has totally changed our habits and our daily way of life, depriving us of many basic rights, including freedom of movement to come and go, both within and across borders. It put more than half of humanity into lockdown and brought much of the global economy to a standstill, depriving many people of their daily resources. It was necessary to hermetically seal borders between neighbouring countries. With regard to the Sahel countries, and Niger in particular, the existing security crisis was compounded by the health crisis.[2]

Indeed, for the past ten years, Niger has been facing a plurality of security threats. The presence of numerous armed and terrorist groups on the borders with Mali, Nigeria, Burkina Faso and Libya has exposed Niger to significant violence.[3] In addition, there has recently been an increase in communal conflicts, an intensification of the migratory phenomenon[4] and a still precarious political stability, all of which accentuate the recurrence of episodes of violence.[5] This context creates an environment conducive to the infiltration of organised crime and violent extremism, which further fuels the spiral of violence and creates a climate of fear.[6] The violence

---

1   Director of Research in Civilization and History of Islamic Ideas, Institute of Research in Human Sciences, Abdou University Moumonui of Niamey, Niger.

2   Niger is one of the vast countries west Africa with an area of 1.267.000 km. With an estimated population of about 24.2 million, of which 50.1% are women and 70% are young people under 25 (INS projection). The vastness of the territory and population growth are major challenges for the country's socio-economic development in view of the scarcity of natural resources accentuated by climate change.

3   On religion and security in the region, see Moumouni S. 2018. "Religious radicalism and security threats in the Sahel", in Green MC, Gunn JT and Hill M (eds). *Religion, Law, and Security in Africa*. Stellenbosch: African Sun Media, 21-30.

4   Boyer F and Mounkaila H. 2018. "La fabrique de la politique migratoire au Niger: les approches sécuritaires et humanitaires au service de la fermeture d'une route migratoire [The making of migration policy in Niger: security and humanitarian approaches in the service of closing a migration route]", in Boyer F and Lestage F (eds). *Routes et pauses des parcours migratoires: Afrique-Amérique* [Routes and pauses in migratory journeys: Africa-America]. Paris: Cahiers du CEMCA, Série Anthropologie 3:33-40.

5   On the migration crisis, in particular, see Sourou JB. 2021. "The tragedy of Amina: Migration as told by the wives of migrants", in Green MC and Kabata F (eds). *Law, Religion and the Family in Africa*. Stellenbosch: African Sun Media, 325-331.

6   On the problem of religious radicalism and fear, see Moumouni S. 2017. "Prévention à la radicalisation au Niger: Etude réalisée auprès des détenus présumés Jihadistes [Prevention

has also particularly affected women and children.[7] When Covid-19 emerged in Niger, religious leaders were already mobilised on security issues, particularly on the prevention of religious extremism and on religious and traditional mechanisms of community conflict resolution. It is in this context that the Covid-19 pandemic appeared.

The climate of insecurity greatly affected the health and education sectors, even before the Covid-19 pandemic. Indeed, according to the UN Office for the Coordination of Humanitarian Actions OCHA,[8] more than six hundred schools were closed and 62 610 students are out of school in the Tillabéri region because of insecurity.[9] Other regions of Niger were also affected, such as the Diffa region.[10] It also affected the socio-economic activities of civilians, increased the number of internally displaced persons and contributed to mistrust of the state and its representatives.[11] These enormous security challenges cost the state 15% of its budgetary resources in 2017, thus reducing its investment capacity in the productive and development sectors.

The Nigerien authorities have taken measures to contain the spread of the epidemic. This analysis here seeks to examine the role of religious leaders in the crisis of Covid-19. It addresses the following questions: What were the attitudes of the authorities in the face of the Covid-19 epidemic in Niger? What measures were taken by the authorities against the pandemic? How did religious leaders

---

of radicalisation in Niger: A study of carried out among presumed jihadist detainees]". Niamey: Etudes de l'IRSH, February.

7   Moumouni S. 2017. "Rapport d'étude sur la prévention à la radicalisation au Niger: Études sur les détenus présumés djihadistes [Study report on the prevention of radicalization in Niger: Studies on presumed jihadist detainees]", IRSH-Niamey.

8   Chahed N. 2022. "Niger: 672 écoles fermées dans la région de Tillabéri à cause de l'insécurité (OCHA) [Niger: 672 schools closed in the Tillabéri region due to insecurity (OCHA)]", *Andolu Agency*, 27 January.

9   Lamizana A. 2022. "Gestion des conflits locaux et communautaires au Sahel: cas de la zone frontalière du Liptako-Gurma [Management of local and community conflicts in the Sahel: case of the Liptako-Gurma border area]". End of study dissertation G5 Sahel Defence College, under the direction of S Moumouni, Nouakchott, Mauritanie.

10 Moumouni S. 2016. "Boko Haram: origine, doctrine et implication dans l'instabilité régionale Boko Haram: origin, doctrine and involvement in regional instability]", *Editions mélange en hommage à Djouldé Laya, Hamidou A. Sidikou, Boubé Gado, les Sciences Humaines et le défi du développement en Afrique de l'ouest: Adaptations, Résiliences et Perspectives* [The human sciences and the challenge of development in West Africa: adaptations, resilience and perspectives: mixed edition in tribute to Dioulde Laya, Hamidou Arouna Sidikou and Boubé Gado]. Niamey: Editions Gashingo, 307-317.

11 Abdourrahim H. 2022. "Terrorisme et migration forcée: le Zarmaganda dans la tourmente des djihadistes, actes colloque sur le terrorisme et la criminalité transfrontalière organisés: Adaptation et évolution du droit pénal organisé par l'Association Nigérienne de Droit Pénal [Terrorism and forced migration: Zarmaganda in the turmoil of jihadists, conference proceedings on terrorism and organised cross-border crime: Adaptation and evolution of criminal law organised by the Nigerien Criminal Law Association]", *Revue béninoise des sciences juridiques et administratives*, 119-134.

become involved in the fight against Covid-19? What religious foundations were marshaled to sensitise the population to the need to respect the measures taken in the fight against the coronavirus? How could religious leaders convince people that closing places of worship is the right thing to do when they don't believe the pandemic exists?

MEASURES TAKEN BY THE AUTHORITIES AGAINST THE PANDEMIC

After the appearance of the first case of Covid-19 in Niger on 17 March 2020, in the absence of treatment and vaccine, the Nigerien authorities recommended prevention and treatment as a means for people to protect themselves from the pandemic. The authorities took several measures to control the chain of contamination and to establish communication. The government made a formal denial of the information given by a Dr Zourkaleyni Alzouma Maïga veterinarian about the coronavirus on the private television station Ténéré. In the interview, the veterinarian returned to the origin and history of the raging coronavirus. According to him, this virus, discovered for the first time in animals, could not survive the high Sahelian heat. This prompted him call upon the inhabitants of the Sahel countries not to give in to panic.[12] After this interview the Ministry of Public Health would henceforth be the only authority authorised to communicate about the pandemic. As the Nigerian government stated:

> The Government wishes to formally deny the erroneous information given by Veterinarian Dr. Zourkaleyni Alzouma Maïga regarding the epidemic, which was broadcast by a local television station and widely circulated on social networks. The Government wishes to specify that only the Ministry of Public Health is authorised to communicate on the management of the coronavirus epidemic. The administrative, customary and religious authorities are responsible for the application of these measures as well as for the work of sensitisation necessary for the observance of all these measures which are imposed on all.[13]

As for the citizens, they were invited to implore God to protect Niger, to refrain from shaking hands and to wash their hands regularly with soap.

In general, the initial measures against Covid-19 were aimed at limiting the risk of importing cases from outside and limiting the transmission of the virus within national borders. The first wave of measures took place at the Council of Ministers on 20 March 2020, after the first case appeared in Niger the day before. The measures included the closure of the international airports of Niamey and Zinder, as well as land borders, schools, universities, drinking establishments and other places of leisure. The closure of the borders to medical tourism countries favoured by the

---

12 "Dr vétérinaire nigérien Zourkaleyni Aloizouma Maïga: 'Le Coronavirus est un virus qui ne peut pas résister à plus de 20°C'", *Bamako.com*, 16 March 2020.

13 The Minister of Public Health Dr Iliassou Mainassara by communique of the extraordinary council of ministers of Tuesday 17 March 2020.

country's elite forced leaders to seek treatment within Nigeria and in a defective health system they did not trust.[14] The number of people allowed at gatherings was reduced to fifty people throughout the country. The government instituted mandatory hygiene measures in public places, a social distancing requirement of one metre between people and free diagnosis and management of confirmed cases. It also announced consultations with religious leaders to determine measures relating to access to places of worship. In order to convince Nigeriens to stay at home, the country's authorities did not hesitate to rely on religion, using historical religious arguments that evoke the life and behaviour of the Prophet Muhammad in epidemic situations. They recalled that confinement was already practiced at the time of the Prophet.

The second wave of measures came on 27 March 2020, at a time when the pandemic was already established in Niger. It involved asking the people to pray for divine protection against the pandemic, a proclamation of the state of emergency throughout the territory, the sanitary isolation of the city of Niamey and the establishment of the curfew in the capital from 7 pm to 6 am. There was also free care for confirmed patients of Covid-19 according to officially adopted protocols, which included screening tests and enhanced protections of health personnel. Citizens and religious leaders were invited to implore God to protect Niger. In his message to the nation of 27 March 2020, then former president of the Republic of Niger Mahamadou Issoufou noted particularly his consultation with religious leaders to determine the measures relating to access to places of worship.[15]

CONSULTATION BETWEEN THE AUTHORITIES AND RELIGIOUS LEADERS

The former prime minister, Brigi Rafini, was instructed to organise the consultation with religious leaders that the president had mentioned that very day. During this meeting, the prime minister asked the leaders of the different religious denominations of Niger to help face Covid-19. The Minister of the Interior called on religious leaders and their communities to pray for Niger to be preserved from this scourge.[16] Religious leaders demonstrated their readiness to accompany the authorities in the prevention and response against Covid-19. Among these measures was the closure of places of worship.[17] The Niger Islamic Council, the Catholic mission of Niger, the

---

14 Niger has recorded deaths from Covid-19 of sitting and former ministers.

15 "Message à la Nation du Président de la République du 27 mars 2020 [Message to the Nation from the President of the Republic of 27 March 2020]", *Sahel*, 30 March 2020.

16 Yahaya S. 2020. "Mobilisation contre le covid 19: le premier minister rencontre les leaders religieux [Mobilisation against covid 19: the Prime Minister meets with religious leaders]", *Sahel*, 17 March 2020.

17 It should be noted that in Niger, as elsewhere, the place of worship is also the place where the ceremonies of everyday social life are celebrated (weddings, births, deaths), where family conflicts are settled (inheritance, divorce, etc.), and where religious education is provided (schools, Quranic, biblical). Quranic school students were particularly affected

alliances of evangelical missions of Niger and the Association of Zima and Bori of Niger, the last being an association of traditional religions, all decided to close the places of worship.

Following this consultation, both Islamic Council and the Christian churches decided to suspend collective prayers and other religious events to be held in places of worship and invited the faithful to pray at home, individually or with their families. In addition, the Islamic Council and other Islamic associations issued an invitation to the *ulema* (Islamic scholars) to play a leading role in organising awareness campaigns and asked the government for substantial means to carry out this mission of general interest. Christian churches in Niger invited their faithful to observe a week of fasting and prayers at home, so that God might extend his mercy on Niger and its people.

In their statements, the religious leaders were keen to highlight the religious prescriptions of their faiths that were perfectly in line with the measures already taken by the authorities. They invited the faithful to comply with the preventive measures taken by the government and religious leaders so that Niger might be spared from the worst of the pandemic. In a statement held on 20 March 2020, the Roman Catholic Archbishop of Niamey, Monsignor Djalwana Laurent Lompo, commended the efforts that the services were making in the churches to raise awareness among the Christian faithful.[18] He drew particular attention to the efforts of religious leaders and the authorities to strengthen sanitary hygiene measures.

RELIGIOUS ARGUMENTS SUPPORTING CLOSURE OF PLACES OF WORSHIP

In his message to the nation on 30 March 2020, the president of the Republic Mahamadou Issoufou put in place further strategies to fight the pandemic.[19] These strategies included: (1) the strengthening of prayers throughout the territory; (2) the proclamation of the state of emergency throughout the national territory; and (3) the curfew established in Niamey from 29 March at midnight.

These measures were to be respected, because any other behaviour would amount to suicide, and suicide is condemned by all religions. "Thou shalt not kill", say Christians, who consider suicide to be murder. Likewise, the Quran says: "And don't kill yourself. Allah in reality is merciful to you. And whoever commits this, out of excess and iniquity, we throw him into the fire, that is what is easy for Allah."[20] Protecting one's life and those of others is therefore a sacred duty. According to

---

  by the confinement and closure of the mosque. Indeed, the Koranic students called "Almajirai" beg and live on the food donations that they collect from one house to another.
18 Yahaya S. 2020. "Declaration des leaders religieux du Niger [Declaration of religious leaders of Niger]", *Sahel*, 20 March.
19 "Message à la Nation du Président de la République du 27 mars 2020 [Message to the Nation from the President of the Republic of March 27, 2020]", *Sahel*, 30.
20 Quran 4:29-30.

former Nigerien president: "All the measures taken are in accordance with our religious traditions. Let's respect them."[21]

Archbishop Lompo of Niamey stressed in a message addressed to all communities on the occasion of the Feast of Passover, that the holiday was to be celebrated that year without noise or fuss, because the pandemic spares no country, no race, no religion.[22] The archbishop declared Passover to be a Christian holiday. "The resurrection of Christ thus founds our faith. Christ is risen to illuminate and save the world that cries out for its desolation", Archbishop Lompo continued for as St. Paul said, "If Christ is not risen, our proclamation is without content, your faith too is without content."[23] The archbishop expressed hope that this Easter feast, celebrated in the spiritual family of the Church, would be an opportunity for the faithful to place their trust in God who, alone, can save us from the evil of the century that is Covid-19.[24]

In Niger, Christian and Islamic religious holidays are officially declared national holidays and celebrated by the respective religious communities. On this occasion, religious leaders send a message of peace and solidarity to all communities. In 2020, the main difference was that the coronavirus invited itself to the holidays and changed habits and observance. The Islamic Council urged the faithful to observe the preventive measures issued by the authorities, during the blessed month of Ramadan. The Council called on the population to show endurance and protect others in accordance with the *hadith* set out by Abdourahamane ben Aouf in which he advised Umar bin Al-Khattab not to return to the confined holy city of Quddus,[25] saying, "I heard the Prophet say, 'If a deadly contagious epidemic breaks out in a city, those who are inside there do not go out and those who are outside do not go in'."[26] Thus, the *ulema* emphasised the coherence of the measures taken by the Nigerien authorities with the principles of Islamic law. The authorities also broadcast a message from the Council of Scholars, Saudi Arabia's highest religious body. The message called on Muslims around the world to pray at home during Ramadan if their country recommended social distancing. Muslims were also to avoid gatherings because they were the main cause of the spread of the virus and should remember that "preserving people's lives is a great act that brings them closer to God".[27]

---

21 See "Message à la Nation du Président de la République du 27 mars 2020".
22 Yahaya, "Declaration des leaders religieux du Niger".
23 Bible. Corinthians 15:14.
24 Moctar A. 2020. "Célébration de la fête de pâques 2020: un fête marquée par la peur de la propagation du Covid-19", *Sahel*, 14 April.
25 Caliph Omar Ibn al-Khattab was born in Mecca in 584 and died in Medina in 644. He became Caliph when he succeeded Abu Bakr in 634 and led the Islamic community for ten years.
26 See *Sahih al-Bukhari*, 5396.
27 "Coronavirus/Ramadan: L'Arabie Saoudite adresse un message important aux musulmans du monde entier", *Le canard déchaîné*, 21 April 2020.

RELIGIOUS HOLIDAYS IN THE COVID-19 PERIOD

The fight against the pandemic coincided with the major Christian and Muslim religious holidays of Easter and Ramadan. The celebrations of this important moment of collective religious practice, encompassing both Christianity and Islam, fueled the fear of the authorities.[28] As the month of Ramadan 2020 approached, the government feared an increase in violence related to the closure of mosques. The prime minister, Brigi Rafini, then chose to prolong the restrictions and remobilised the Islamic Council. In his press briefing of 19 April 2020, the representative of the Islamic Council made three arguments in response to those calls.[29] The first was the duty of obedience of Muslims to the political, religious and scientific authorities of their country. He explained that healthcare workers, as holders of knowledge, were entitled to respect and obedience. In his view, such obedience was a submission to God, whereas disobedience was rebellion against God. For God said, "O you who believe! Obey Allah, His Prophet and those of you who hold authority."[30] The second argument concerned the reality of the pandemic, which was widely questioned by the population.[31] On this point, the Islamic Council representative replied to all those who did not believe:

> Our health specialists, who are also Muslims, have confirmed the existence of the virus, which a person can carry for two weeks without symptoms. The grouping of mosques, weddings or baptisms is an opportunity for its spread. Since it is invisible and a bearer is indistinguishable from a non-bearer, Islam recommends avoiding any gathering. The suspension of mosque attendance thus becomes an obligation accepted by all schools of Islamic jurisprudence and in the light of Islamic history.[32]

Finally, the third argument concerned the merit of night prayers in the month of Ramadan, which was put forward as a pretext for calls to reopen mosques. The Islamic Council representative explained that these prayers had a supererogatory character and had more merit when they were made at home rather than at the mosque. Muslims were asked to avoid mosques during this month of Ramadan and to preserve their health and serenity.

---

28 Moumouni S. 2017. "Ramadan et espace public au Niger: entre pratique, religiosité et discorde [Ramadan and public space in Niger: between practice, religiosity and discord]", *Nous: Revue scientifique du CERPHIS Université Félix Houphouët-Boigny d'Abidjan-Cocody*, 18(7721):85-96.

29 "Mahamadou Diallo, le premier Ministre sur les sites de prise en charge des malades du covid 19 [Mahamadou Diallo, the Prime Minister on the care sites for covid 19 patients]", *Sahel*, 20 Avril 2020, 6-7.

30 Sheikh Ousmane Malan Garba, Member, Niger Islamic Council.

31 "Le Ramadan s'accommode mal du confinement [Ramadan does not adapt well to confinement]", *MondAfrique.com*, 28 April 2020.

32 Toudjani AA. "Déclaration du Conseil Islamique du Niger relativement à la lutte contre le Covid-19: Le Conseil exhorte les fidèles à observer, pendant le mois béni du Ramadan, les mesures préventives édictées par les autorités [Declaration of the Islamic Council of Niger on the fight against Covid-19]", *Sahel*, 20 April 2020.

The expected serenity finally returned on 13 May 2020 with the announcement of the reopening of mosques and the lifting of the curfew. This reopening was subject to conditions: respect for barrier measures (wearing masks, hand washing, physical distancing between the faithful, individual carpets, and similar measures), ventilation of the mosque, periodic disinfection of the mosque and closure of the mosque immediately after prayer. A committee was set up to ensure the effectiveness of these measures.[33] However, the government reserved the right to close mosques in the event of a deterioration in the epidemiological situation.

In the announcement communiqué of 19 March 2020, the Secretary General of the Islamic Council justified the closing of mosques upon notification on 19 March 2020 of the first case of Covid-19 in Niger, by the fact that the Nigerien population is 99% Muslim,[34] such that there was risk of expansion of the disease because of the free access to mosques and following confirmation by the specialists of the dangerousness of the coronavirus and the powerlessness of the countries in front of the pandemic. The Secretary General pointed out that Islam recommends the culture of prevention. He then emphasised the decision of the World Union of Ulema to suspend Friday Prayer and daily prayers in Muslim countries affected by the pandemic in accordance with what Islam recommends regarding the culture of prevention.

ACCEPTANCE AND REJECTION OF PANDEMIC MEASURES IN NIGER

It is normally the case that when there is a pandemic, people adhere to the recommendations of healthcare workers in order to avoid aggravating the disease. In the field of disease control, healthcare workers are the competent ones, and the *ulema* (Islamic scholar) has absolutely nothing to say. It is important to follow the prescriptions of healthcare workers and also to place trust in God. For some worshippers, the closure of mosques was a good and necessary action to prevent the disease. Medicine is a system of knowledge that has both a curative and preventive dimension. For some, this fact generated unwavering adherence to the measures recommended by the health services.

In Niger, the environments most affected by the pandemic were the spheres of politics and the Abdou Moumouni University of Niamey. Both of these areas allow for travel privileges and contact with other people. These are also the spheres in which people went abroad for medical treatment, leaving the rest of the national population to treat their diseases in an under-equipped and defective health system.

Some complied with the measures did so out of fear of illness, others out of fear of the authorities. Those who adhered to the measures out of fear often feared

---

33 The committee was not set up, because day after day the tension fell and the political and religious authorities, apart from showing what is happening in Europe, had no more arguments of local reality to convince the population.

34 In Niger, there are no official statistics on the religious beliefs of the population. Percentages vary from one religion to another and do not reflect reality.

sanctions and counter-terrorism measures more than the disease itself. They did not trust the words of the authorities and thought that they were doing the usual "sanitary theater", imposing measures on populations to restrict their public freedoms under the guise of public health and sanitation. Police brigades, sometimes accompanied by the governor of Niamey, crisscrossed the city in search of offenders. The governor warned the people of Niamey against any attempt to violate the curfew. "Those who dare to transgress these measures will be struck down at supersonic speed", the governor said.[35]

The brief arrest of the recalcitrant imams, who were members of the Sunni groups "*ahlu al-sunna*" and "*Izala*"[36] of the popular districts, did not deter the other worshippers, who went to mosques in large numbers for their daily collective prayers. In highly visible places, the strategy was to pray in small groups on mats spread out in the open air in front of the mosques, which were kept closed. The instruction to avoid gatherings at the mosque was thus reinterpreted in a new sense to mean avoiding praying inside the mosque. They urged the faithful to pray collectively at the mosque, but not in it, such that "when a believer hears the call to prayer, he is not allowed to pray at home, but he must hasten to participate in the collective prayer at the mosque".[37]

Regarding Friday Prayer, the authorities showed firmness and the population was stubborn, which made riots inevitable. Several riots were declared in the major cities of Niger. In Niamey, public and private infrastructure was ransacked in some neighbourhoods for several consecutive days. According to the police, 108 demonstrators were arrested. Anti-measures riots regularly targeted symbols of the state. When they were unable to celebrate prayer in their neighbourhoods, worshippers went in search of open mosques in other neighbourhoods. People were very attached to their religion. In their view, the mosque was the house of God and needed to remain open to pray to God. As one imam put it, "a collective prayer performed at the mosque is equivalent to 25 or even 27 rewards for a single prayer performed alone at home."[38] The collective Friday Prayer was the right moment for imams to justify the rejection of measures to close places of worship, according to the imam of the mosque of the small market of Niamey. In the history of the Muslim world and Niger in particular, when there is a disaster like the Covid-19 pandemic, places of worship are opened and religious people are gathered in these places to implore God. As the Niamey imam put it in a sermon, "When the faithful make his ablutions and take the direction of the mosque, God erases a sin for him

---

35 Issaka Hassan Karanta, the former Governor of Niamey, died a few months later, on 23 December 2020.
36 These are the fundamentalist Islamist groups known as Jama'at Izalat al-Bid'a wa-Iqamat al Sunna (Movement for the Rejection of Innovation and the Establishment of the Sunna).
37 It just talks about the obligation to pray collectively, whether it is inside or outside the mosque.
38 *Sahih Al-Bukhari*, 645 and *Sahih Muslim*, 650.

by step made, writes him a reward and raises him by one degree. When he sits in the mosque after his prayer, angels invoke God on his behalf until he comes out."[39]

For the Muslim, the mosque is therefore not a gathering space conducive to the spread of the pandemic, but rather "the obligatory passage for access to divine grace".[40] For the believer, this grace is the guarantee of well-being here on earth and salvation in the hereafter. To fully understand the rejection of the measure, it is necessary to identify the representations associated with mosques in Islam. The mosque is the epicentre of community life. In addition to gatherings after prayer, weddings or baptisms are commonly celebrated. It is also a space for religious learning for young people and adults, and thus for the transmission of spiritual values. By closing places of worship, the authorities were touching the spiritual interests of the faithful and shattering their dreams of earthly and heavenly happiness. When a social group loses its right to dream, it has no alternative but revolt. It is in this context that we must understand the riots related to the closure of places of worship.

Beyond spiritual considerations, we should also note the popular understandings of the pandemic. For some, Covid-19 did not exist – it was a plot by the West to consolidate its hegemony on the planet. For others, it was a divine punishment in response to the depravity of morals. Still others thought it was an invention of the political elites to capture foreign aid and restrict public freedoms. It should be noted that reasons for opposing the anti-Covid measures the motivations were not only religious or political, but also economic. Many people in Niger live from day to day, and the night-time closures of small business with the imposition of the curfew from 7:00 pm to 6:00 am seriously affected their profits and savings.

As for the security situation, the measures related to Covid-19 had a windfall effect for the Nigerien authorities, who took the opportunity to tighten their control of the populations by highlighting security and health restrictions in connection with Covid-19. Covid-19 was a pandemic of exceptional severity, but in West Africa and Niger, in particular, the population was much less affected than in other countries. Even so, the authorities considered it useful to take "security theater" type measures in the form of closing borders, prohibiting travel and confining the population. Part of the population thought that these prohibitions were unfounded and unjustified by the number of cases recorded. Some believed that these measures were undertaken in an instrumental way to silence all opposition party protests. There was perceived to be pretext and not a legitimate motive for a hardening against public freedoms that was desired by the authorities and occasioned by the crisis. In Niger, the health crisis allowed the authorities to further restrict freedom of expression and strengthen censorship and carry out arbitrary arrests. Civil society actors, such as journalist and internet users, were arrested for violating

---

39 Friday sermon of the Imam of the mosque of the small market of Niamey, 24 April 2020.
40 Friday sermon of the Imam of the mosque of the small market of Niamey.

Covid-19 restrictions. Covid-19 made it possible to ban civil society protests against corruption and misappropriation of public funds.[41]

CONCLUSION

The Covid-19 pandemic upset our concept of the world and solidarity between nations. Africa, and nations like Niger, had been seen as prime places for the development of pandemics, such as HIV and AIDS and Ebola. Pandemics were thought to be limited to places like Africa. They were matters affecting the poor, underdeveloped countries with slums and precarious populations, along with poor hygiene and poor sanitation. For once, Africa was not responsible for the birth or development of a pandemic. The management of Covid-19 imposed new and unexpected challenges on states. In Niger, this management was made possible by the fact that the surrounding region in Africa was much less affected by the pandemic. Nevertheless, the Nigerien authorities followed the rest of the world in order in taking measures against the coronavirus.

The appearance of Covid-19 in Niger, at a time of security crisis, allowed us to analyse the authorities' crisis management capacities. Indeed, it is remarkable that the authorities spontaneously and quickly took all the measures recommended to prevent the spread of the coronavirus with a communication and awareness campaigns well organised through the media and advertising posters. Throughout the preceding ten years of security crises, the authorities have put forward what was mostly a security approach in the fight against terrorism. Still, there was not enough communication to sensitise and warn the population about the danger of terrorism and the security measures to be taken locally to prevent jihadist attacks. And yet, terrorism has claimed many more victims than the Covid-19 pandemic.

Religious leaders, too, were involved in the fight against Covid-19. The role played by religious organisations began with consultation and statements to the faithful. The state authorities found themselves in a situation of appealing to and negotiating with religious leaders to bear responsibility for the decisions taken by the authorities. The measures were ultimately more respected by Christians than

---

41 "Niger: le journaliste arrêté après un post sur facebook portant sur un cas suspect de coronavirus doit être libéré [Niger: Journalist arrested after Facebook post about suspected coronavirus case must be released]", *Amnesty International*, 9 March 2020. This is the biggest financial scandal in the history of Niger. The funds intended to equip the army were misappropriated under the presidency of Mahamadou Issoufou in a context of war, more than 70 billion were misappropriated by the political-military network that runs the country, with disastrous consequences for the civilian and military populations, victims of terrorism. See Aksar M. "Niger – Malversations au Ministère de la Défense: 71.8 milliards de fcfa captés par des seigneurs du faux [Niger – Malpractices at the Ministry of Defense: 71.8 billion CFA francs captured by lords of forgery]", *L'Événement Niger*, 21 September 2020. Also, funds collected to fight the pandemic were diverted to fancy purchases made by the Minister of Public Health. According to the report of the Court of Accounts there are discrepancies at the level of realisations of resources and expenditures. "Cour de Compte du Niger", *Rapport Général Public*, 2021, 94.

by Muslims. When Islamic associations are poorly structured and often copied by politicians, their words and speeches are mixed with those of the politicians, which influences their credibility with the faithful.

8 Religious Responses to the Covid-19 Pandemic: A Comparative Analysis of the Spiritual Methods of Christians and Muslims in Nigeria

Francis O. Falako[1]
Adam A. Sirajudeen[2]

INTRODUCTION

The Covid-19 pandemic paralysed many human activities in 2020. It changed the global orientation of nearly all human endeavours. Attempts were made to contain the pandemic by individuals, groups and governments. Apart from the medical approach to the Covid-19, there were also religious responses from the adherents of both Christianity and Islam in Nigeria. It is instructive to mention that this religious response was not without the knowledge of the Nigerian government, who specifically sought the recourse of the religious leadership during the period. This moral support was sought by the government to ensure absolute compliance to the necessary restrictions in the Covid-19 pandemic.

Nigeria is a pluralistic society, with over 250 ethnic groups roughly divided between the Muslim-dominated North and the Christian-dominated South. Unarguably, the nation is culturally and politically diverse. Christianity and Islam are the two dominant religions, each with a range of denominations. Though perceptions about the pandemics differ and are not constant,[3] the contribution of religion in the fight against the virus and the attendant disruptions was never in doubt.[4] The present study employs a functional theory to understand the social and psychological role of religion in Nigeria in the Covid-19 crisis. The functional theory views religion as performing certain functions for society.[5] Sociologist Victor Lidz, appraising the works of contributors to the functionalist theory has concluded that the theory focuses on associations between religion and other social institutions in both

---

[1] Associate Professor of Church History & Religious Education, Department of Religious Studies, Faculty of Arts, University of Lagos, Nigeria.
[2] Professor of Afro-Arabic Literary Criticism & Historiography, Department of Arabic Studies, Faculty of Arts, Federal University of Lafia, Nigeria.
[3] Oyero K. 2021. "Covid-19: Adeboye, Ighodalo, other clerics differ on jabs for church members", *Punch Nigeria*, 3 October.
[4] Musa IA. 2021. "Contrasting Muslim Perspectives on Covid-19 Containment in Nigeria", *JRCI: Journal of Religions and Contemporary Issues* (Department of Religious Studies, Faculty of Arts, University of Lagos) 1:301.
[5] Christiano KJ, Swatos WH and Kivisto P. 2008. *Sociology of Religion: Contemporary Developments*. Second Edition. Maryland: Rowman & Littlefield.

"synchronic and diachronic perspectives", thereby emphasising the reciprocity of the relationship.[6]

Two months after the initial outbreak in China, the Covid-19 index case in Nigeria, an Italian, was diagnosed on 14 February 2020.[7] As the virus spread in Nigeria, it turned out that most of the Covid-19 cases in Nigeria were imported from Europe and America, rather than China, where the virus originated.[8] This was an indictment of the sloppy nation's travel ban and other containment procedures. According to a religion scholar, Ismail Musa,[9] the nation attained a critical stage of community transmission of the virus with the index case, at which juncture the effectiveness of containment depended on the level of receptivity of preventive strategies, which itself depended on understandings, attitudes and behaviour towards the pandemic. In March 2020, the World Health Organization (WHO) listed Nigeria among other 13 African countries identified as high-risk for the spread of the virus.[10] The Nigerian government swung into action by closing air and land borders and reactivating all medical bodies. Some of the emergency measures put in place included the 9 March 2020 establishment of a National Coordination Team, tagged the Presidential Task Force (PTF) on Covid-19, the reactivation of the Nigeria Centre for Disease Control and Prevention (NCDC) and the passing of the Control of Infectious Disease Act. Other measures included a phased lockdown in Lagos and Ogun States as well as the Federal Capital Territory (FCT) effective from 4 May 2020, mandatory use of face masks, social distancing, a ban on religious and social gatherings, flight restrictions, and mandatory provision of hand washing facilities, sanitisers and temperature check in all public places.[11] By October 2021, the nation had recorded over 200 000 cases of infections and more than 2 700 associated deaths.[12]

Expectedly, the religious community reacted to the outbreak and government's efforts at containing the spread. Perceptions were shaped by the diversity of doctrinal views ideological orientations and levels of knowledge about the pandemic within each religion. Three main, but fluid, camps could be deciphered. First, there was the antagonist camp led by conspiracy theorists, which viewed and interpreted the pandemic as hoaxes. The Muslim Rights Concern (MURIC), an Islamic human

---

6   Lidz V. 2010. "The Functional Theory of Religion", in Turner BS (ed). *The New Blackwell Companion to the Sociology of Religion*. Chichester, West Sussex: John Wiley & Sons, 76-102.
7   Musa, "Contrasting Muslim Perspectives on Covid-19 Containment in Nigeria", 301.
8   Maclean R. 2020. "African braces for Coronavirus, but slowly", *The New York Times*, 17 March.
9   Musa, "Contrasting Muslim Perspectives on Covid-19", 301.
10 Falaye TA. 2020. "Impact of Covid-19 on the Church of God in Nigeria", *Kampala International University Journal of Humanities* 5(2):319-330.
11 See the Nigeria Centre for Disease Control and Prevention NCDC publications, such as "Case Definitions for Coronavirus Disease", "Covid-19 Guidelines on Re-Opening Places of Worship", "Guidelines on Social Distancing", and many more. Online at: https://ncdc.gov.ng
12 Oyero, "Covid-19: Adeboye, Ighodalo, other clerics differ".

rights organisation, alleged that Covid-19 and the restrictive policies in its wake were intended to decimate the *Ummah* (the Muslim faithful), with some Christians also accusing the government of systematic destruction of the church.[13] The second category included the protagonists who readily complied with all directives. The last camp was composed of those who adopted a "wait-and-see" approach. Among the factors that worsened the spread of the pandemic and its attendant socioeconomic crisis are illiteracy, poverty, distrust of government, misinformation and corrupt practices, especially during the distribution of relief packages.[14]

ASSESSING RELIGIOUS COPING STRATEGIES FOR COVID-19

Nigerian Christians and Muslims tried to devise means of containing the situation. These methods are deployed within the confines of their socio-religious practices. Impacts on both Christian and Muslim groups included, but were not limited to, restrictions of number of public worshippers that snowballed into a total ban, compulsory use of face masks, enforcement of social distancing of two metres in a way that conflicts with the practice of rubbing of shoulders encouraged by *sharia*, mandatory washing of hands and frequent use of sanitisers, suspension of handshakes among members, home communion pastoral visitations among Christians and *dawah* proselytisation by Muslims, deferment of marriage and other public religious rituals.[15]

The present study adopts the model that religion influences both physical health and mental well-being, that physical health and mental well-being affect each other and that both physical health and mental well-being impact religiosity. This model emphasises the bidirectional and interactional quality of the relationship between religion, physical health and mental well-being.[16] Relatedly, this study probes into the nature and quality of the spiritual methods employed by Nigerian Christians and Muslims in coping with the stress and trauma of the pandemic. The focus is particularly on the adoption of "religious coping strategies", defined as the "use of cognitive or behavioural techniques, in the face of stressful life events, that arise out of one's religion or spirituality".[17]

---

13 Musa, "Contrasting Muslim Perspectives on Covid-19", 302.

14 Okoye UO and Nwatu UL. 2022. "Covid-19 Pandemic in Nigeria: A Story worth telling from the Eyes of Social Workers", in Gonçalves MC et al (eds). *The Coronavirus Crisis and Challenges to Social Development*. Cham: Springer, 281-293.

15 Shibambu N and Egunjobi JP. 2020. "The Impact of Covid-19 Pandemic Lockdown on the Community Life of Religious Men and Women in Southern Africa", *ResearchGate* [Accessed 28 April 2022].

16 Erwin-Cox B, Hoffman L, Grimes CSM and Fehl S. 2007. "Spirituality, health, and mental health: A holistic model", in Rockefeller K (ed). *Psychology, spirituality and healthcare*. Westport, CT: Praeger Books.

17 Tix AP and Frazier PA. 1998. "The use of religious coping during stressful life events: Main effects, moderation, and mediation", *Journal of Consulting and Clinical Psychology* 66:411-422.

Religious coping mechanisms are direct offshoots of the individuals' and communities' religio-spiritual beliefs and practices. The mechanisms and strategies help individuals to construct meaning and form interpretations, both positive and negative, of difficult situations and events.[18] Religious mechanisms however have been found to be a distinct form of coping strategies separate from secular forms of coping like cognitive restructuring.[19] Drawing extensively on empirical work, scholars have reached three fundamental conclusions about religious coping.[20]

First, during existential crises, many religious faithful turn to their faith for comfort, succour, support and a sense of meaning and control. Second, people use prayer, worship and social support from a faith community as a coping mechanism during times of major life stress or trauma. Finally, gender, religious affiliation, level of education and ethnicity tend to be the most important determining factors, overall, in the use of religion to contain the pandemic.[21] In another study by the present author Francis Falako, it was found that Nigerians in particular and Africans in general take a holistic approach to life and healing.[22] Religion indisputably plays a leading role in the coping and healing processes, which often may be more implicit than explicit. Yet, reliance on religious matrices, especially prayer, as the sole weapon against the pandemic sometimes resulted in a carefree attitude towards and disregard for other safety measures.[23]

SURVEYING RELIGIOUS RESPONSES TO THE COVID-19 PANDEMIC

The study underlying this chapter employed a qualitative research method. Primary data for the study were retrieved from 40 participants (clergy, intellectuals and religious congregation members) selected through a purposive sampling method. Data collection was through in-depth interviews involving a preset, structured interview guide and recorded using a tape recorder. Interviews were conducted mainly in English, Yoruba and Hausa, with a few communications in Nigerian Pidgin (NP), which were translated by the researchers. Most of the interviews did not go beyond twenty-five minutes, and the majority of the interviews conducted were face-to-face. The study was conducted within a period of four months between

---

18 Tarakeshwar N and Pargament KI. 2001. "Religious coping in families of children with autism", *Focus on Autism and other developmental disabilities* 16:247-260.

19 Gall TL and Cornblat MW. 2002. "Breast Cancer Survivors give voice: A Qualitative Analysis of Spiritual factors in long-term Adjustment", *Psycho-Oncology* 11:524-535.

20 Denney RM. and Aten JD. 2010. "Religious Coping", in Leeming DA, Madden K and Marlan S (eds). *Encyclopedia of Psychology and Religion*. Cham: Springer, 771-773.

21 Habib MA, Dayyab FM, Iliyasu GN and Habib AG. 2021. "Knowledge, attitude and practice survey of Covid-19 pandemic in Northern Nigeria", *PLoSONE* 16(1):e0245176.

22 Falako FO. 2011. "The perceived interplay of spirituality, religion and quality of life: A Study of the University of Lagos", *Lagos Education Review: A Journal of Studies in Education* 12:129-144.

23 Olapegba PO et al. 2020. "A preliminary assessment of novel coronavirus (Covid-19) knowledge and perceptions in Nigeria", *medRxiv.org* [Accessed 10 July 2022].

January and April 2022. Out of the participants, twenty-five were male, while the remaining fifteen were females. It is instructive to add that considering the spatial distribution of Nigerian demography and difficulty of access to Muslim women across both northern and southern regions of Nigeria accounts for the discrepancies in the number of male and female respondents. This is because of the practice of *purdah*, which keeps women indoors, that is prevalent among the Muslims.

The survey straddles both the Muslim-dominated northern parts and the Christian-populated southern parts of Nigeria. The participants were generally practising Christians from the Southern part of the country and Muslims from the North. It is equally interesting to note that while the study tended to focus on Muslims in the north and Christians in the south, this does not in any way indicate that there are not members of both religions in both halves of Nigeria. Put differently, just as we have a significant number of Muslims in the south, especially the southwestern part of Nigeria, the northern part of the country is also replete with considerable number of Christian faithful.

Due to the large size of the nation and the need for representation, interviews were conducted over the phone with respondents who resided in locations very far from the reach of the researchers. Two trained research assistants helped in data collection, which was later transcribed. All the participants were duly informed of the purpose of the research and granted their consent. The researchers ensured the confidentiality, anonymity, justice, privacy and respect for persons during the research and beyond. The identities of participants were treated with anonymity as pseudonyms were used.

As noted above, scholars have confirmed the role of religion in healing and coping strategies in the face of both personal or corporate existential crises. With this in mind, the present study focuses on the following questions: (1) In what specific ways did the virus impact Nigerian Christians and Muslims? (2) In what ways did the leaders of the two religions cooperate with the government in the fight against the scourge of the virus? (3) How far did Nigerian Muslims and Christians avail themselves of the religious and spiritual methods inherent in each religion? (4) To what extent did these practices help in coping and healing during the pandemic? Due to overlapping responses between the Muslim North and the Christian South, the next section overlooks the geographical divides and concentrates on religious leanings.

SOCIO-RELIGIOUS APPROACHES TO COVID-19 BY NIGERIAN MUSLIMS

Islam has provisions for nearly every human endeavour, the issue of Covid-19 not being an exception.[24] The pandemic was perceived by Nigerian Muslim clerics as a

---

24 For example, in one of the prophetic traditions, an *hadith* was quoted to have said: "الطاعون آية الرجز ابتلى الله عز وجل به ناسا من عباده، فإن سمعتم به في أرض فلا تدخلوا عليه وإن وقع (صحيح مسلم) "صحيح" ("أهم اورفت الف امب متنأو ضرأب ["Epidemic is but a filth Allah inflicts on people from among His servants. Whenever you hear about it (in a place anytime) do

punishment by Allah on humanity that was consequent upon the perpetuating of immoralities.[25] Verses of the Quran, *hadiths* of the Prophet Muhammad (PBUH) and laws adapted from these sources in the writings of the Muslim scholars buttress this point. Besides, the outbreak of the pandemic was also believed by most Muslim scholars to be a Western conspiracy. This has been expressed in their writings in response to the pandemic.[26] It is important to mention that this belief, which is mostly common among the northern Muslims, suggested to them that the pandemic did not require any serious attention.

It is from these two premises that Nigerian Muslims responded to the pandemic in the first instance, with particular reference to their socio-religious life. Nigerian Muslim clerics did believe and enjoin members that the commandments of the government at all levels must be obeyed in order to contain the epidemic. However, this was to be done within the limits of their belief in the efficacy of the pandemic, especially as it affects the practice and conduct of their religious rituals, such as *salaat* (the daily prayers) and the performance of Hajj rites in Saudi Arabia.[27]

Despite these admonitions to obey the government, Muslim-dominated northern Nigeria ignored most of the directives by the government aimed at minimising the spread of the pandemic. For example, the compulsory use of face masks, especially during ritual prayers, was found to be difficult to practise. Some of these measures recommended to combat Covid-19 were ones seen by these clerics as being part of Islamic rituals, such as compulsory washing of hands and face in the performance of ablution and the use of veil by Muslim women. Other preventive measures prescribed by the government, such as the enforcement of social distancing of two metres to avoid the rubbing of shoulders, was viewed as contrary to the *sharia*.

In fact, the permissibility of this new form of social distancing design, especially during the daily prayer and the Hajj rites, generated controversies among the Muslim scholars globally. It also opened new vistas in Islamic. Globally, Muslim jurists debated the legality and application of social distancing during the Muslim prayers to prevent the spread of the pandemic and whether this would render the prayer null and void according to Islamic legal maxims. The frequent use of sanitisers was also an issue that generated attention global Islamic jurisprudence, given the religious prohibition or use of anything alcoholic. The controversy

---

not enter unto it, and if it befalls the land where you are, do not run away from it." *Sahih Muslim*, Hadith no. 2218.

25 For more information on the belief of Muslim clerics that Covid-19 is divine punishment by Allah, see the ode (unpublished) composed by Abdul Ghaniy Bello Folohunsho Abu Zahra in March 2020 on the topic of Covid-19, titled *La Misaasa* (Do Not Touch), as well as poetry composed by Abdulrahman Abdulazeez (popularly known as al-Zakawy) on Covid-19 in 2020.

26 For more information on the belief of Muslim clerics that Covid-19 is a Western conspiracy, see Abu Zahra, *La Misaasa*.

27 Isah MB et al. 2020. "Coronavirus Disease 2019 (Covid-19): Knowledge, attitudes, practices (KAP) and misconceptions in the general population of Katsina State, Nigeria", *UMYU Journal of Microbiology Research* 6(1):24-37.

emerged as a topic of debate when scholars differ on the permissible alcoholic contents of the sanitisers prescribed for use to prevent the spread of the Covid-19. While some scholars of Islam saw nothing forbidden, according to the *sharia*, in the use of the sanitisers as prescribed, others consider it to be completely *haram* (forbidden) according to Islamic law. There was also a third view among some scholars who were of the opinion that the quantity of the sanitisers used could be overlooked under the *sharia*.[28]

It is important to note that, despite these concerns, some Muslim clerics and communities collaborated significantly with the federal and respective state governments in creating awareness. Following the "unexplained deaths" of 640 people in the Kano metropolis within two weeks in April 2020, the state government instituted a lockdown and intensified awareness campaigns in mosques on the necessity of the preventive measures.[29] However, because the pandemic was seen by many as a farce, little attention was accorded its spread among the populace. It was mostly from this theological sense of being punishment from Allah requiring divine intervention that Covid-19 was considered by Muslims to be an epidemic.

There was more belief in spirituality of the epidemic than there was in the physiological aspect, hence the need for a spiritual approach in curbing its scourge. Muslim poets lifted up the spiritual orientation of the epidemic and referred it as the outcome of sins committed by members of the society. It is the belief in Islam that whenever people sin against Allah, the consequence is to be befallen by epidemic as punishment for the unprecedented sins, and that in the case of Covid-19, this is what was happening, as had earlier been the case in the spread of AIDS, which was believed to be the consequence of immoral sexual relations.

Specified prayer formulas were dedicated for the eradication of the epidemic. Important to mention here is the phrase 'ساسم ال' (Do not touch).[30] As part of a verse from the Quran,[31] this phrase is believed in some quarters to be efficacious in preventing any form of epidemic, whether spiritual or not.[32] In some cases, designated fasting was recommended for members to ward off evil. This was an indication that the Muslim people of Nigeria, like their counterparts in other climes, believe very much in the spiritual background of pandemics. Fasting as a means of appeasing God, especially in such a situation, was employed as succour. Members of the congregation were implored to fast to ward off the evil befalling humanity. Prophetic medication was recommended, some of which simultaneously served as both preventive and cure. Natural and organic extracts, such as black seed oil (*Habbat al Sawdaa'*), olive oil, pure honey and apple juice, all in hot water, were

---

28 Utebor S. 2022. "Why we asked Muslims to avoid alcohol-based sanitisers – Imams", *Punch Nigeria*, 5 April.

29 Habib et al, "Knowledge, attitude and practice survey of Covid-19 pandemic in Northern Nigeria".

30 For more information on this, see Abu Zahra, *La Misaasa*.

31 Quran 20:97.

32 See Abu Zahra, *La Misaasa*.

administered as a preventive measure. This was derived from healing methods prescribed by the Prophet Muhammad for ailments that may befall a Muslim.[33]

SOCIO-RELIGIOUS APPROACHES TO COVID-19 BY NIGERIAN CHRISTIANS

The pandemic hit the nation through the southern states of Lagos and Ogun in February 2020. This changed the initial attitude towards the virus from being a distance "white man's infirmity" to being a "big man's disease" afflicting the rich and influential when some of the social elite succumbed to it.[34] Church leaders were divided on their opinions about the menace, and the pandemic became a catalyst for heated diatribes from the pulpit and the social media.[35] Of the three camps of rejoinders mentioned earlier, the antagonists were the loudest and most critical. They put up fierce objections to nearly all the containment efforts, especially the lockdown and vaccination.[36] Factors that aided the antagonists included the region being largely Christian and a centre of charismatics, who had vast print and electronic media and a more literate populace.[37] Some Christians interpreted the virus not only as a punishment for sin, but as an "end time sign".[38] In 2020, churches and mosques that flouted orders were forcefully closed. The Covid-19 Task Force arrested and prosecuted some pastors and imams in Lagos,[39] Ebonyi,[40] Abuja[41] and Kano.[42]

---

33 Ibn Qay'em El-Jozeyah. 2003. *The Prophetic Medicine*. (Translated by ABD El-Qader). Directives on the use of olive oil, pure honey and apple juice are found in different pages of the book. See Maideen NMP. 2020. "Prophetic Medicine – Nigella Sativa (Black cumin seeds) – Potential herb for Covid-19?", *Journal of Pharmacopuncture* 23(2):62-70. But see Maideen NMP. "Correction: Prophetic Medicine – Nigella Sativa (Black cumin seeds) – Potential herb for Covid-19?", *Journal of Pharmacopuncture* 23(3):179.

34 Okoye and Nwatu, "Covid-19 Pandemic in Nigeria: A Story worth telling from the Eyes of Social Workers".

35 Ntoka G. 2020. "Shutting down Churches over Covid-19 not Acceptable – Bishop", *Newsbreak Nigeria*.

36 Campbell J. 2020. "Principal Nigerian Religious Leaders Largely in Lockstep with Government on Lockdowns", Council on Foreign Relations, 14 April.

37 Christianity penetrated modern-day Nigeria through the coastal towns of Lagos, Badagry and Onitsha beginning in 1842. Today, the southern region boasts more educational institutions, large media outlets and a well-read public than its northern counterpart.

38 Aluko OP. 2020. "Covid-19 Pandemic in Nigeria: The Response of the Christian Church", *African Journal of Biology and Medical Research* 3(2):111-125.

39 "Three pastors arrested for violating over 50 gatherings in Lagos", *plusTVafrica*, 23 March.

40 Agwu C. 2020. "Covid-19: 5 pastors arrested, others flee as Ebonyi lockdown task force storm churches", *SunNewsOnline*, 2 April.

41 Adegbite AA. 2020. "Court shuts church indefinitely in Abuja over lockdown violation, as pastor, others evade arrest", *Nigerian Tribune*, 3.

42 Bello B. 2020. "Total lockdown: Kano Imam arrested for conducting Jumaat congregational prayer", *Vanguard*, 18 April.

Being more advanced technologically, many city dwellers in state capitals and urban centres switched to online worship services with relative ease.[43] Churches in the rural areas, particularly those whose parishes could not afford internet connectivity, joined their parent bodies or headquarters for joint services.[44] Social and interactive media, such as Zoom, Facebook, Instagram, Twitter, WhatsApp, SnapChat, TikTok and others became sources of connectivity between priests and parishioners.[45] Churches used thermometers and provided face masks, wash basins and hand sanitiser for worshippers. In enforcing social and physical distancing, members were encouraged to sit metres apart and wave at one another instead of the normal shaking of hands and hugging. "No Face Mask, No Entry" and other Covid-19 signage was conspicuously displayed.

In addition, various Christian centres collaborated significantly with the federal and respective state governments in creating awareness. Being the citadel of print and news media in Nigeria, the South West in particular is replete with church-owned radio and television stations. These became channels for generating awareness among church members, in addition to being platforms for worship and spiritual uplift during the restrictions. Churches also created helplines, through which they prayed for, counseled and donated to callers. Furthermore, many churches subscribed to government and private-owned radio and television stations to air messages and create awareness.[46] There was also provision of relief packages, including material and financial assistance for the vulnerable. Justifying this gesture, one Pentecostal pastor from Onitsha made references to Jesus's feeding of the multitudes in Matthew 14:13-21 and Mark 8:1-9. He claimed that church-branded buses were used to send alleviation packages during the lockdown and regretted that his parish could not reach non-members due to paucity of funds.

Finally, special fasting and prayer sessions became veritable tool in the fight against the pandemic and its attendant loss of jobs, loneliness and sickness. Findings showed an upsurge in poverty, distress, violence and suicide during the period.[47] The many prayer mountains and camps that serve as religious resource centres

---

43 Oyero E. 2020. "Coronavirus: Nigerian church suspends physical services, moves online", *Vanguard*, 18 April.

44 Sunday services, mid-week bible study and vigils were centrally conducted in many denominations. Churches like the Deeper Christian Life Ministry (DCLM) leveraged on an existing platform for collective worship while others hurriedly put the internet structures in place.

45 Churches employed different patterns to communicate. The Anglican Communion News Service provided information, prayer guides, and recorded sermons. It opened up opportunities for joint worship throughout. See http://www.anglicannews.org/

46 Television, radio, Facebook and WhatsApp had the strongest reach according to the Communication Survey carried out by Charney Research for NCDC in March 2020. See NCDC, 2020. "Risk Communication and Community Engagement Strategy Covid-19 Prevention and Control in Nigeria", Office of the Secretary to the President, 20.

47 See Olaseni AO, Akinsola OS, Agberotimi SF and Oguntayo R. 2020. "Psychological distress experiences of Nigerians during Covid-19 pandemic; the gender difference", *Social Sciences & Humanities* 2(1):100052.

by individuals and churches were deserted during the lockdown.[48] This created a spiritual vacuum that was filled through other means. An Anglican priest in one of the dioceses in Rivers State shared his experience of how the parish used the prayers of litany.[49] During the lockdown, members were encouraged to say this special prayer in their respective homes from every day at noon. One Methodist bishop sent out recorded prayers through WhatsApp. This trend became the norm among pastors, as many created WhatsApp group platforms to reach out to their members. This led to a surge in the production of daily meditation platforms for prayer mandates and declarations that were posted and reposted to members and non-members. Pastors also used the opportunity to bless and anoint people's water, oil and other effects for use. All these proved helpful in eliciting hope and healing during the pandemic.

COMPARATIVE ANALYSIS OF MUSLIM AND CHRISTIAN RESPONSES

Religious leaders, faith-based organisations and faith communities can play a major role in saving lives and reducing illness related to Covid-19. They are a primary source of information, support, comfort, guidance, direct health care and social services in their respective communities. Religious leaders of faith-based organisations and communities of faith can share health information to protect their own members and wider communities, which may be more likely to be accepted than from other sources. As the World Health Organization (WHO) has observed, religious organisations can provide pastoral and spiritual support during public health emergencies and other health challenges and can advocate for the needs of vulnerable populations.[50]

As the WHO has envisaged and as our study corroborates, Nigerian Christians and Muslims turned to religion to find succour and healing during the pandemics. The directive from the Nigerian Presidential Task Force (PTF) to close down religious centres from 20 March 2020 was one of the specific ways the virus affected Nigerian Christians and Muslims. The ban on public worship "was one directive that in a number of ways has reshaped the outlook of the Church in its entirety; and for a couple of weeks has redefined the faith, worship life and financial commitments of the Church".[51] On the impact of the ban, Ismail Musa observes: "(T)he government

---

48 Religious camps and enclaves like the Redemption Camp of the Redeemed Christian Church of God (RCCG) and the Prayer City of the Mountain of Fire and Miracles Ministry (MFM) along the Lagos-Ibadan Express way are common features in Yorubaland, South West Nigeria.

49 The litany is a lengthy prayer consisting of a series of invocations and supplications by the leader with alternate responses by the congregation.

50 World Health Organization (WHO). 2020. "Practical considerations and recommendations for religious leaders and faith-based communities in the context of Covid-19", *WHO.int*, Interim Guidance, 7 April.

51 Fape MO. 2020. "Covid-19: A Test for Faith, Worship and Prudence: The Post Covid-19 Church". Paper presented at the 13th General Synod of the Church of Nigeria, Anglican

policy that people found most disconcerting is that the lockdown that confined people to their homes and ensured the closure of worship centres, including churches and mosques. Muslims were allowed to summon people through *adhan* (Muslim Call to prayer) but were required to confine religious activities to houses including the five daily prayers. The *tarāwih*, (Ramadan supererogatory prayer) *tafsīr* (Quranic Exegesis) sessions and sundry mosque activities were encouraged to be carried out online where feasible."[52]

All Christian and Muslim clerics submitted that the six-week ban on public worship affected the finances of each congregation.[53] A pastor in Lagos confessed that while Sunday income dropped drastically, sundry expenses, such as the daily fuelling of buses and generators, were also reduced considerably. Questioned about how he managed financially, the Lagos pastor confessed:

> We resorted to paying half salaries monthly to avoid layoff. The balance was paid when things picked up. We encouraged members to make online transfers in paying necessary dues. Yet, much of what came in went into the provision of palliatives for indigent members. The parish also spent enormous amount on online worship, sanitisers, face masks, hand washing basins and printing of "No face mask, No entry" signs that we conspicuously displayed as directed by the Government.

This was the trend in most churches as priests and parishioners battled for survival. The finances of individuals and groups nosedived and cutting costs became necessary to avoid bankruptcy and layoff.

On how religious leaders worked and collaborated with the government during the struggle against the virus, respondents spoke of the inclusion of religious and community leaders. Membership of the monitoring committee set up at the federal, state and local government levels included community and religious leaders.[54] They assisted in the awareness campaign, monitored compliance with restrictions on public gatherings, aided the distribution of relief packages and encouraged quarantine and vaccination. Each congregation leveraged existing welfare boards or set up new ones to cater both to members and the general public.[55] Mosques and churches became platforms for creating awareness of the need to maintain social distance, wash hands, use sanitisers, wear face masks and to take other measures.

   Communion, Abuja, Nigeria, 21 September.
52 Musa, "Contrasting Muslim Perspectives on Covid-19 Containment in Nigeria".
53 This was one of global effects of the pandemic. See Meyer H and Hadero H. 2022. "At many churches, pandemic hits collection plates, budgets", *Amarillo Globe-News*, 22 January.
54 Members of the Multi-Sectoral Multi-Hazard Social Mobilisation Committee of the NCDC included royal fathers and religious leaders. See NCDC, "Risk Communication and Community Engagement Strategy Covid-19 Prevention and Control in Nigeria".
55 Most Anglican churches already have various welfare committees like Elderly Helpline, Prison Welfare Committee, Social Welfare Unit, Care Ministry/Women of Grace (widows), etc. See Fafowora OO. 2008. *The Cathedral Church of Christ, Marina Lagos, 1867-2007: A Venture of Faith*. Lagos: CSS, 104-106.

Those who gave daily messages on Covid-19 matters through state-sponsored radio and televisions channels in the Nigerian South included chief imams, state chairmen of the Christian Association of Nigeria (CAN), clerics and prominent royal fathers. In addition, churches all over the nation cooperated by making huge financial donations to augment federal, state and local government initiatives.[56] They donated medical facilities, distributed relief packages and provided face masks, sanitisers and other personal protective equipment.[57] In May 2020, the Nigerian Catholic Bishops' Conference (NCBC) volunteered 425 hospitals and clinics nationwide for adaptation and use as isolation centres.[58] Unfortunately, none was utilised by the government.[59] According to a journalist, Olufemi Adediran, the League of Imams and Alfas in Ogun State also donated the sum of N2.5 million to the state government towards the fight against the pandemic.[60]

The comparative analysis of the present study reveals that many Nigerians found succour, elicited hope and were able to sustain life against the odds of the pandemic. All participants, at one time or the other in their comments, identified religious behaviours and attitudes such as fasting, prayer, meditation, charity and online worship as essential coping mechanisms. A clergyman of a prominent Pentecostal church in the South observed thus:

> When the government announced a total ban on public worship, we resorted to the social media and organised fasting and prayer chains. Our strong belief is that God is omnipresent and that prayer avails. Through that, we were able to raise an army of (prayer) warriors. As pastor, I used social media applications like WhatsApp, Facebook and Zoom to send messages of comfort and prayers to all my contacts. This made me relevant during the lockdown. Daily testimonies from my contacts encouraged me as a person to cope. I used the period of the lockdown to engage in extensive bible study and meditation. The threats of extinction were real as

---

56 Okoye AC and Obulor I. 2021. "Religious Organisations and Fight against the Spread of Covid-19 in Nigeria", *Journal of Sustainable Development in Africa* 23(1):65-78.

57 The Redeemed Christian Church of God (RCCG) donations included 8 000 hand sanitisers, 8 000 surgical face masks and 200 000 hand gloves. Also, the Church of Jesus Christ of Latter-day Saints donated N95 masks, disposable facemasks, surgical gowns, protective eye shields, disposable hand gloves, hand sanitisers, antiseptic liquid soaps, disposable shoe covers, veronica buckets and tissue papers. See Eyoboka S. 2020. "Covid-19: Adeboye, Oyedepo donate medical supplies to Lagos, Ogun", *Vanguard*, 1 April; Church Supports Covid-19 Response Efforts in Nigeria", The Church of Jesus Christ of Latter-day Saints in Nigeria, 30 April 2020; Adebayo O. "The Impact of Covid-19 on Churches in Nigeria", Baptist World Alliance.

58 Omeiza A. 2020. "Catholic Church donates 425 hospitals, clinics nationwide as isolation centres", *Vanguard*, 11 May.

59 Jannamike L. 2021. "Catholic Church laments FG's failure to use 425 hospitals offered for treatment of Covid-19 patients", *Vanguard*, 15 February.

60 Adediran O. 2020. "Covid-19: Islamic leaders donate N2.5m to Ogun govt", *Blueprint Nigeria*, 9 April.

> daily figures of infections and deaths were announced. I was terrified but put my trust in God. It was indeed a harrowing experience.[61]

The imams and pastors sampled seem to follow this general trend with minor variations. The confession above confirms the fears that engulfed the land and shows how religious leaders made themselves relevant during the tumult.

These crises, to say the least, put religious leaders and their faith communities under much stress. Due to their positions of influence, religious leaders received an increased amount of attention and criticism, even as many expected them to provide guidance, comfort, hope and accurate information.[62] Unfortunately, many of the religious leaders were themselves ill-informed about the pandemics. A few even championed the conspiracy theories and condemned the lockdown and vaccination. A Christian respondent confessed that he was able to gather information for his parish from the internet, while the publications and the daily briefings by the Presidential Task Force cleared his ignorance about the pandemics.[63] Another respondent, who is an information communication technology expert, described how the church had to switch to online worship with some urgency.[64] She observed that a few members, particularly the elderly, were initially sceptcal of the approach, while the youths followed along with ease. After the lockdown, her team was highly commended for the innovation. On the prospect of online worship, she said that the church now streams every service online, and that the model has become part of the "new normal".

One of our respondents, an elderly Catholic woman,[65] became emotional as she narrated her fears and coping mechanisms.

> I was terribly shaken for two reasons: my health has been worsening and my children abroad. My blood pressure rose each time my daughter in Europe narrates the horror of deaths, loss of jobs and lockdown created by the pandemics. I contacted our parish priest on phone. He prayed for me and my children though he couldn't administer the sacrament to me. I missed that a lot (laughs). I couldn't fast due to old age, yet I prayed fervently with the aid of my rosary. I stayed glued daily to the television, and my radio (she showed a small transistor of dual model, rechargeable and battery) proved very helpful.

As described by Baptist clergyman Oladeji Adebayo:

> Big churches with private television stations have little or no problem, as their leaders preached directly to their members in their homes, and they also joined others in making use of online services thanks to social media.

---

61   Interview with Pastor Johnson by F Falako. Abeokuta, Nigeria, 13 June 2022.
62   Łagowska U, Sobral F and Furtado LMGP. 2020. "Leadership under Crises: A Research Agenda for the Post-Covid-19 Era", *BAR – Brazilian Administration Review* 17(2):e200062.
63   Interview with Benjamin Onyejiaka, by F Falako. Enugu, Nigeria, 12 June 2022.
64   Interview with Ope Banjo by F Falako. Lagos, Nigeria, 13 June 2022.
65   Interview with Madam Victoria Ofuafo by F Falako. Onitsha, Nigeria, 15 June 2022.

> Members were asked to buy data and watch online services, and offerings and tithes were collected through e-banking. But as a result of the level of illiteracy, many Christians were disfranchised from worship due to unreliable power supply and ignorance of information technology. Others could not afford the cost of weekly data.[66]

Faith-based organisations (FBOs) also provided a sense of belonging in times of individual or corporate stress, upheaval and suffering.[67] Clinical psychologist, Christopher Grimes notes, "Religion also provides a systematized faith and value system that helps the believer organize and makes sense out of his/her existence and relationships with fellow humans and the natural world."[68] Doctrinal differences on use of medicine, differing knowledge or education levels, perception and awareness of Covid-19, also affected the spiritual and religious approaches by the two leading faiths.[69]

In addition to daily rituals of prayer, fasting and meditation, the study focused on other practical steps common to both Muslims and Christians. Churches and mosques created support lines where adherents could reach out for emotional recharge and financial and material supplies.[70] Due to the lockdown, religious leaders reached out to the emotionally troubled ones through house fellowship leaders, where available, as well as through telephone contacts. According to a pastor of the Living Faith Church, the church practice of house-cell fellowship centres all over the federation proved helpful, as the leaders of each unit attended to distress calls from the immediate environment.[71] The organisational structures of each church and mosque also became avenues for distribution of relief packages conveyed in designated church or mosque vehicles. The restriction laws permitted special services, such as the use of ambulances, couriers and relief distributions, throughout the period. People postponed occasional services, such as wedding, birthday and other anniversaries, until the restrictions were lifted. Burials, however, took place under strict surveillance because mortuary facilities in the cities were overstretched, creating a situation in which quick disposition of the remains of the dead became necessary. An Anglican priest in Lagos confirmed that they conducted

---

66 Adebayo O. 2021. "The Church's response in Times of Crisis: The Impact of Covid-19 on Churches in Nigeria", Baptist World Alliance.

67 Falako, "The perceived interplay of spirituality, religion and quality of life: A Study of the University of Lagos".

68 Grimes CSM. 2010. "Religion and Mental and Physical Health", in Leeming DA, Madden K and Marlan S (eds). *Encyclopedia of Psychology and Religion*, 776-768.

69 Ilesanmi O and Afolabi A. 2020. "Perception and practices during the Covid-19 pandemic in an urban community in Nigeria: a cross-sectional study", *PeerJ Computer Science* 8:e10038.

70 Anglican churches in Lagos reached out to the elders through the existing Elderly Helpline Unit in each parish. The Coordinator of the Lagos Mainland Diocese said the Unit catered for those from 65 years and above.

71 It was reported in 2021 that the church has over 17 000 home cells in Lagos and Ota alone. See "We Have Established 17,124 New Home Cells (Lagos and Ota) This Year – Bishop David Oyedepo", *Sportafriq*, 13 September 2021.

burials according to the pandemic protocols.[72] A priest and a few family members witnessed the rite at the cemetery, without church service, fanfare or celebratory gatherings. Other family, relatives and friends joined through Zoom or other online means.

It is important to note here that despite the commonalities in the responses of Christianity and Islam, the two major religions in Nigeria, to the Covid-19 pandemic, elements of differences can be identified. For example, while the Muslims resorted to ablutions of ritual washing, which included the prescribed hand washing; their Christian counterpart did not have or share a similar approach. Muslim scholars differed in their juristic understanding of whether the use of hand sanitisers was permissible for Muslims.

CONCLUSION

Both Nigerian Muslim and Christian religious communities responded to the Covid-19 pandemic in ways that complemented and supported the global effort. Doctrinal differences, education and awareness levels affected the socio-religious response to the pandemic. However, prayers, fasting and prophetic medication were the primary religious methods for prevention and cure. It was believed that a spiritual problem required a spiritual solution. The present study analysed the positive coping mechanisms that were available and utilised by Nigerian Muslims and Christians during the Covid-19 pandemic. It confirmed the importance of organised religion in socio-political and cultural initiatives, and it showed that members of religious groups themselves benefited from the social support and psychosocial resources made available. The study further explored the rituals of personal hygiene, charity, fasting and prayer as veritable means of containing Covid-19 in addition to carrying out government directives on preventive measures in the pandemic.

Recommendations from our study are twofold. First, the Nigerian government should improve on the collaborations with religious leaders through training and retraining towards the utilisation of spiritual and religious capital in tackling local and global challenges. This is because religious leaders are influencers of socio-cultural forces in their communities. Besides, religious leaders should regularly update their medical, organisational knowledge and leadership skills to overcome dangers and harness opportunities posed by any crises. A former president of the United States, John F. Kennedy, once observed that "When written in Chinese, the word 'crisis' is composed of two characters – one represents danger and one represents opportunity. ... Along with danger, crisis is represented by opportunity."[73]

---

72 Interview with Venerable Femi Fatile by F Falako. Yaba, Lagos, 10 June 2022.
73 Kennedy JF. 1959 "Remarks of Senator John F. Kennedy, Convocation of The United Negro College Fund, Indianapolis, Indiana, April 12, 1959".

9 GOVERNMENT RESPONSES, RELIGIOUS AUTHORITIES AND JUSTICE INNOVATIONS IN THE COVID-19 PANDEMIC IN NIGERIA

Hajara Ahmad Shuaib[1]

INTRODUCTION

The promulgation of measures by the Federal Government of Nigeria as a response to fight the outbreak of the Covid-19 pandemic received a mixture of reactions by the religious bodies in the northern region of the country, particularly because of the restrictions imposed through the lockdown policy, which limited the fundamental human rights to freedom of religion or belief dealing with the *forum externum*. In support of this thesis, one may cite reports and research publications on the attitude of religious leaders in Plateau and Bauchi States, particularly the use of their capacity and influence to manipulate the perceptions of followers and to flout the lockdown policy that restricted their freedom to practise their religion. The outbreak of coronavirus known as Covid-19, which began in Wuhan, China, late 2019,[2] became a global nightmare in 2020. The underlying illiteracy and religious beliefs of the vast majority of Muslim and Christian inhabitants of the states resulted in a backlash against the efforts to stop the spread of the virus. Many Nigerian citizens continue to doubt the existence of the deadly virus in the country, even after the recorded incidence of deaths. However, upon detection and confirmation of the Covid-19 pandemic, the Nigerian government promulgated and implemented several public policies and measures to contain the spread of the virus.

Public policy has been defined as a "purposive direction or course of action undertaken by governmental institutions and officials to address a specific social problem or issue in society."[3] Among the measures put in place by the Nigerian government,[4] some aimed at fighting the virus and its expansion and others were meant to mitigate the pandemic's consequences for economy and public health.[5] The containment period under the lockdown was enacted to identify, trace and isolate all individuals who came in contact with confirmed cases of Covid-19.[6] Other

---

1 Department of Public Law, Faculty of Law, Bauchi State University, Nigeria
2 Hengbo Z et al. 2020. "The novel coronavirus outbreak in Wuhan, China", *Global Health Research and Policy* 5 (art 6).
3 Ogbeidu UE. 2007. *Public Policy Making and Evaluation in Nigeria: theories, strategies and Techniques*. Lagos: Amfitop Books Company.
4 Quarantine Act (CAP Q2 LFN 2004) (cited as Covid-19 Regulations 2020).
5 Martinez-Torrón J. 2021. "Covid-19 and Religious Freedom: Some Comparative Perspectives", *Laws MDPI* 10(2):39.
6 Okoisabor JO. 2021. "Public Policies Against Covid-19 Pandemic in Nigeria: Challenges, Effects and Perception", *Journal of Public Administration and Social Welfare Research* 6(1):17-30.

measures included physical and social distancing, restrictions on large gatherings and hand washing, among others, based on the recommendations of World Health Organization (WHO) safety principles and guidelines to curb the spread of the virus. The restrictions crippled Nigeria's economy, which was already battling a ravaging recession at the moment Covid-19 was detected.

The measures put in place also affected religious practice, affecting not the right to freedom or religion *per se*, but the way the right was exercised.[7] According to a "nationally representative" survey by NOI Polls, 30% of the Nigerian population believed that they were genetically immune to the disease because the disease did not originate from either Nigeria or Africa.[8] Some religious leaders in the country debunked the existence of the virus, while others prophesied to their willing congregations that Covid-19 could not affect them, since they were afforded additional protection from being covered by the special blood of Jesus.[9] The confusion perceived, and in some cases caused, by the citizens led to both legal uncertainty and an increasing sceptcism on the part of a large part of the population, who were not convinced that the measures were appropriate and proportionate.[10] Some were of the view that politicians generally discounted the importance of religion while believing strongly in a pandemic which itself was questionable.[11] In the same vein, widespread perceptions of Nigerian politicians as self-interested and corrupt fuelled suspicions, as many Nigerians perceived the virus to be an attempt by political elites to create an emergency and siphon public money.[12]

The persistent noncompliance with Covid-19 safety protocols by some unbelieving Nigerians, due to their lackadaisical attitude towards containing the pandemic, became a hindrance to "flattening the curve" of the disease's transmission and spread.[13] Despite this apparent opposition, religious organisations played crucial roles in the fight to limit the spread and community transmission of the virus. The study in this chapter examines the impact of the measures against the Covid-19 pandemic on freedom of religion in northern Nigeria amidst the fight to stop the spread of the Covid-19, along with the particular role of the Nigerian judiciary in implementation of the policies by ensuring strict adherence to the policies promulgated, trial and punishment in an event of a flout.

---

7   Milcarek P. 2012 "Glosa. Uwagi do doktryny Dignitatis humanae" [Gloss: Notes to the doctrine Dignitatis humanae], cited in Mazurkiewicz P. 2021. "Religious Freedom in the Time of the Pandemic", *Religions MDPI* 1(2):103.

8   Onapajo H et al. 2021. "Covid-19 is a Big scam: Citizens' Distrust and the Challenge of Combating Corona virus in Nigeria", *The Republic*, 30 March.

9   Okoye AC and Olubor I. 2021 "Religious Organizations and Fight against the Spread of Covid-19 in Nigeria", *Journal of Sustainable Development in Africa* 23(1).

10 Mazurkiewicz, "Religious Freedom in the Time of the Pandemic", 13.

11 Mazurkiewicz, "Religious Freedom in the Time of the Pandemic", 1.

12 Okoisabor, "Public Policies Against Covid-19 Pandemic in Nigeria", 24.

13 Ajayi O. 2020. "Federal Government to Nigerians: we would have flattened Covid-19 curve but for your nonchalance", *Vanguard*, 21 August.

GOVERNMENT RESPONSES TO THE COVID-19 PANDEMIC IN NIGERIA

The far north of Nigeria is home to numerous ethnic and religious communities. With a predominantly Muslim population and a significant Christian minority, there is a strong sense of belief, perception and solidarity among religious organisations. The neighbouring Bauchi and Plateau States share the same boundary from each other, but they have completely different social, cultural and religious perspectives.[14] The region has challenges with its educational system, and most of the population does not receive good formal or Western education.[15] With insecurity threatening peaceful livelihood, inter-tribal and religious conflicts continue to loom within most of the states in this region. This is a product of several complex and interlocking factors, including a mix of historical grievances, political manipulation and ethnic and religious rivalries.[16] Racing against the clock in a complex, politicised, multilingual, multi-ethnic and uncertain environment with widespread poverty and a lack of access to good healthcare facilities, among other problems, Nigerian responses to the fast-spreading Covid-19 crisis needed to address the well-being perspective in a holistic and integrated manner, especially where laws and policies were promulgated to curtail the further spread of the virus.[17] Failure to do so risked deepening inequalities, creating new divides and undermining the resilience of societies.[18]

Several measures were instituted by the Federal Government through the Presidential Task Force on Covid-19 and the Ministry of Health to reduce the spread of the disease and protect the health of Nigerians.[19] Governmental measures against

---

14 Bauchi State is located in the North-East political zone in Nigeria with an estimated population of about 7.3 million habitants, which comprises Muslims, a Christian minority, and religious traditionalist, all of whom come from a range multiple ethnic and cultural backgrounds. Health Policy Plus (HP+). 2017. "Nigeria Population and Development: Bauchi State Fact Sheet". Abuja: HP+, September. Online at: http://www.healthpolicyplus.com/ns/pubs/7149-7284_BauchiRAPIDFactSheet.pdf. Plateau State, located in the North Central political zone of Nigeria has a population of about 3.5 million habitants, with over 40 ethno-linguistic groups, including Muslim minority and a Christian majority. See Government of Plateau State Nigeria. 2021. "Plateau State: At a Glance". Jos: Plateau State ICT Development Agency. Online at: https://www.plateaustate.gov.ng/plateau/at-a-glance

15 Almu B, Adesina M and Kanmodi KK. 2019. "Northern Nigeria: An Overview", in Kanmodi KK and Merrick J. *The Traditional Sakkiya Practice: A Public Health Issue in Northern Nigeria*. Happauge, NY: Nova Science Publishers, 3-16.

16 International Crisis Group. 2010. "Northern Nigeria: Background to Conflict. International Crisis Group", Africa Report No. 168, 20 December.

17 OECD. 2020. "Covid-19: Protecting People and Societies", *OECD.org*, 31 March; OECD. 2020. "Tackling Coronavirus (Covid-19) Contributing to a Global Effect", *OECD.org*, 9 April.

18 OECD, "Covid-19: Protecting People and Societies" and "Tackling Coronavirus (Covid-19) Contributing to a Global Effect".

19 NCDC. "Covid-19 Nigeria". Online at: https://covid19.ncdc.gov.ng

Covid-19 across the globe can be subdivided into two broad categories: measures aimed at fighting the virus and its expansion and measures that are put in place to mitigate the pandemic's consequences for the economy and public health.[20] Before the arrival of the index case in Nigeria, an advisory was issued by the Nigeria Centre for Disease Control (NCDC) to the public on the new coronavirus, which provided factual information on the cause, symptoms, routes of transmission and preventive measures.[21] There was rapid deployment of surveillance and temperature screening at airports from equipment purchased during the Ebola pandemic, and passengers arriving from Covid-19 hotspots were interviewed and their contact was collected for further investigation.[22] A 14-day isolation period was advised for returnees from countries with active cases; however, Nigeria did not isolate the visitors and returnees as had earlier been recommended. Instead, self-quarantine on arrival was recommended without check by the government to confirm adherence.[23] Subsequent to the official confirmation of the first case on February 27, the process of contact tracing was initiated by the Federal Government.[24] Despite experiences gained during the Ebola epidemic, contact tracing in Nigeria still had its challenges. The director of Nigeria's Centre for Disease Control reported that people avoided testing and isolation at various centres out of fear of stigmatisation, hampering the NCDC's response and control efforts.[25]

THE LOCKDOWN AND ITS IMPLICATIONS FOR RELIGIOUS FREEDOM

The lockdown policy was introduced in Nigeria following a regulation, signed by the president on 30 March 2020 under the Quarantine Act, which included stay-at-home orders and the closure of schools, religious worship centres and markets. The regulation was imposed in Abuja, Lagos and Ogun States between 30 March and 14 April 2020.[26] The order was later extended for two more weeks to 28 April 2020. On 27 April 2020, the president announced a gradual opening of the lockdown in the states, effective from 4 May 2020. State governments later implemented similar lockdown policies, with varying degrees of restrictions. On 23 April 2020, the state governors from all 36 states agreed to implement a complete ban on interstate travel

---

20 Krippahl C. 2020. "Nigerian religious leaders demand lifting of Covid-19 lockdown", *Deutsche Welle*, 19 May.
21 NCDC, "Covid-19 Nigeria".
22 Ebenso B. 2020. "Can Nigeria contain the Covid-19 outbreak using lessons from recent Epidemics?", *The Lancet Global Health*. 8(6):e770.
23 Dixit S et al. 2020. "Nigeria's Policy Response to Covid-19", *The Center for Policy Impact in Global Health Policy Report*, June.
24 Momoh M. 2020. "Nigeria starts tracing contacts of first coronavirus patient", *The East African*, 28 February.
25 Adebowale-Tambe N. 2020. "Stigma against Covid-19 patients affecting our efforts – NCDC", *Premium Times*, 16 April.
26 Quarantine Act (CAP Q2 LFN 2004) (cited as Covid-19 Regulations 2020).

for two weeks.[27] Many of the states had imposed a similar interstate lockdown policy, with Bauchi State being the first state to implement it. Only essential service providers were allowed to travel during this period. A number of industries were exempt from the travel ban, such as hospitals and related medical establishments, health care-related manufacturers and distributors, food processing, petroleum distribution and retail stations, power generation and transmission companies, and print and electronic media staff who could prove they were unable to work from home.[28]

The imposed lockdown was not without unintended consequences, as socio-economic activities were restricted to the lowest level. To contain the spread of the virus, the lockdown was enforced to restrict the movement of people and social events.[29] While the lockdown has been helpful in flattening the curve, commercial activities were limited across the country, and this largely affected the fabric of the informal sector, which dominates the Nigerian economy. A "hunger virus" due to inadequate food supply and low flow of income is alleged to have been caused by the lingering of the lockdown amidst constraints on resources, threatening the general well-being of the people. The government's palliative measures, which included foodstuffs and cash transfers to cushion the effects of the lockdown, were grossly inadequate and ineffectively distributed. Much of it did not get to the actual vulnerable people and households in the society. The meagre palliatives distribution was not properly organised and subsequently coordinated, since the social register contained a limited number of most vulnerable households.[30] There was also increase in the incidence of domestic abuse, human rights violations and even extra-judicial killings by security personnel, and this further exacerbated the insecurity situation of the country.[31]

The introduction of the policies did not go without the public outcry, particularly considering the fact that Nigeria was struggling under a crippled economy. UNICEF warned that the impact of the policy of lockdown and school closure has farther reaching consequences than just the loss of education.[32] What became a threat to public health in northern Nigeria under the lockdown were the kids roaming around the street in the name of "Almajirai" with no tentative home or place to stay and having to go from house to house begging for food under the teaching and care of their *malams*.[33] The state governments relocated the interstate *almajirai* by bus to their states of origin, and those from within the state were left with their

---

27 Dixit S, "Nigeria's Policy Response to Covid-19".
28 The Quarantine Act (CAP Q2 LFN 2004) (cited as Covid-19 Regulations 2020).
29 Okoisabor, "Public Policies Against Covid-19 Pandemic in Nigeria", 26.
30 Okoisabor, "Public Policies Against Covid-19 Pandemic in Nigeria", 26.
31 Okoisabor, "Public Policies Against Covid-19 Pandemic in Nigeria", 21.
32 Armitage R and Nellums LB. 2020. "Considering inequalities in the school closure response to Covid-19", *The Lancet Global Health* 8(5):e644.
33 An *almajirai* is a person who migrates from one place, seeking for Islamic knowledge under the guidance of a *malam*, or teacher.

malams, with only temperature checks as a screening tool.[34] There are reports that some *almajirai* tested positive for Covid-19 following the relocation exercise.[35] Freedom of religion and belief has been internationally recognised, and Nigeria is a signatory to the International Covenant on Civil and Political Rights (ICCPR).[36] This international law obligation was coupled with the provisions of the Constitution of the Federal Republic of Nigeria, 1999, declaring Nigeria a non-secular state and allowing everyone to practise their religion.[37] The government's measures against Covid-19 have raised, in virtually all contemporary democracies, important issues regarding the proportionality of limitations on fundamental rights, including freedom of religion or belief.[38] Article 18 of the ICCPR states: "Everyone shall have the right to freedom of thought, conscience, and religion. This right shall include freedom to have or to adopt a religion or belief of his choice, and freedom, either individually or in community with others and in public or private, to manifest his religion of belief in worship, observance, practice, and teaching."[39] It is important to understand that in the context of the ICCPR, the lockdown policy and other restrictive measures imposed to flatten the curve of the disease does not deal with the *forum internum* (the right to have, change and adopt a religion or belief of choice), but rather with the *forum externum* (the freedom to manifest a religion or belief in worship, observance, practice and teaching).[40] The rights of the *forum externum* can be exercised individually or "collectively", as well as in private or in public, but that is not absolute and can be limited if prescribed by law or where it is necessary to "protect public safety, order, health, or morals or the fundamental rights and freedoms of others".[41]

Nigeria is a deeply religious country. The people take religious matters very judiciously and sensitively, especially when it comes to the *forum externum*. Politicians often use religion as a tool to govern, and this contributed to the spread of Covid-19 when religious extremists saw the lockdown policy as a politicised tool to deter them from free and open practice of their religion.[42] It is evident that many people in predominantly Muslim northern Nigeria were swayed by the idea that the

---

34 "Nigeria's Almajiri Children Sent Home as Covid-19 Threat Looms", *InFocus, AllAfrica.com*, 2020.

35 UNICEF. 2020. "Nigeria: Covid-19 Situation Report No. 10 (Reporting Period 23-30 May 2020)", *ReliefWeb.com*, 1 June.

36 International Covenant on Civil and Political Rights, G.A. res. 2200A (XXI), 21 U.N. GAOR Supp. (No. 16) at 52, U.N. Doc. A/6316 (1966), 999 U.N.T.S. 171, *entered into force* Mar. 23, 1976.

37 Constitution of the Federal Republic of Nigeria (CFRN), 1999, ss 10 and 38.

38 Martinez-Torrón, "Covid-19 and Religious Freedom: Some Comparative Perspectives", 39.

39 ICCPR, art 18.

40 General Comment 22: The Right to Freedom of Thought, Conscience and Religion (Art. 18): 30/7/93 CCPR/C/21/Rev.1/Add.4, para 3.

41 General Comment 22, para 4.

42 Anyanwu MU et al. 2020. "A perspective on Nigeria's Preparedness, Response and Challenges to Mitigating the Spread of Covid-19", *Challenges MDPI* 11(2):22.

coronavirus pandemic was merely "fake news" and that its magnitude was being overemphasised on social media. There is a history of sceptcism in the region towards global public health measures. Interventions seen to originate from the West frequently spark suspicion in northern Nigeria, and in the case of Covid-19 they triggered questions about the motivations and intentions of the Western leaders.[43] This particularly cast Nigerian people's minds back to the era of British colonial rule and treatment up to present day, along with the undeniably horrible experiences of Muslims across the globe.[44]

This is what led a renowned Islamic preacher in Jos, Plateau State, in an incendiary sermon, to denounce the coronavirus pandemic as yet another Western plot to stymie the practice of Islam.[45] A member of the political elite in Bauchi State argued that it was the nature of Nigeria's traditional society that led Muslims to feel threatened by perceived attempts to regulate their religion and to see it as conspiracy to prevent Muslims from praying.[46] The argument of Sheikh Sani Yahaya Jingir, an Islamic cleric and scholar in Plateau State, was that it was unbelievable and unacceptable that states across Nigeria suspended congregational prayers in an effort to stem the spread of the virus and that traveling to Saudi Arabia for the Islamic pilgrimage in Mecca (*umrah*) had been stopped. Recognising the possible negative effect of such messages, the Jama'atul Nasril Islam, an umbrella group of Muslim organisations, issued a statement cautioning Islamic preachers and their disciples against misleading their followers over the coronavirus.[47] Another significant cause of disbelief over the coronavirus was the public mistrust and perception of Nigerian politicians as self-interested and corrupt, and the fact that the early detected cases were commonly among the rich, elites and politicians.[48] The governors of Bauchi and Kaduna States, as well as the son of the former vice president Atiku Abubakar, were the earliest detected victims, and most deaths occurred among the rich, prompting rumours to spread that the virus was a hoax. This was largely due to the fact that at the beginning of the pandemic, the travel and international mobility of elites and rich politicians, as well as their privileged access to testing facilities, led to the detection of the virus within their circle.[49] It was also reported that several religious leaders were suspended for flouting the Covid-19 state imposed measures.[50]

---

43 Particularly the white people of the British Empire that colonised Nigeria. Northern Nigeria was not seriously penetrated by the British colonial masters and Islam had been in circulation in the religion dating back to thousands of years.

44 Hann H. 2020. "In Northern Nigeria, distrust jeopardizes the response to coronavirus", *The Conversation*, 15 April.

45 Adamu J. 2021. "The Impact of Labeling Covid-19 As a Scam", *Daily Trust*, 23 September.

46 Krippahl, "Nigerian religious leaders demand lifting of Covid-19 lockdown".

47 Hanna, "In Northern Nigeria, distrust jeopardises the response to coronavirus".

48 Hanna, "In Northern Nigeria, distrust jeopardises the response to coronavirus".

49 Hanna, "In Northern Nigeria, distrust jeopardises the response to coronavirus".

50 Krippahl, "Nigerian religious leaders demand lifting of Covid-19 lockdown".

Consultations, cooperation and reflection could all be ways that the Federal Government might involve religious bodies and other organisations before imposing restrictive policies that hinder the practice or exercise of religious beliefs. However, there is no record of any religious body, individual or organisation in Nigeria mounting legal challenges in court to regulations that they believed to have contravened their religious beliefs or practices, even though such challenges were witnessed in other countries.[51] Health centres, religious leaders and faith-based and social care organisations are among the most trusted in Nigerian communities, especially when it comes to dissemination of factual information.[52] People in Nigeria see to trust and follow guidance about Covid-19 from the religious leaders, even if the knowledge and understanding of the religious leaders is contrary to the belief of the governments and health authorities. In most rural and marginalised communities, where there is little access to healthcare facilities, people resort to social services of faith-based organisations. The menace of misinformation, hate speech, misleading teachings and illogical rumours, which can spread rapidly and cause great damage, can be addressed by trusted religious leaders from the various religions. Sermons and messages can build on factual information provided by the WHO and national or local public health authorities in ways that are in line with doctrines, teaching and practices of their respective faith traditions.[53]

There were numerous cases in Nigeria during the Covid-19 pandemic where religious leaders taking political positions tended to overlook the already instated measures and defied the instructions of the Federal Government. For instance, the founder of Living Faith Church described the policy as an attempt to cripple Christianity and agitated through his online sermons for reopening of churches.[54] On the other hand Pastor Tunde Bakare, the head of Latter Rain Assembly Church disagreed with this assertion and advised collaboration between the government and the religious authorities.[55] Akwa Ibom, Rivers and Katsina States in Nigeria approved mass gatherings for religious activities on Easter weekend and did not consider the transmissibility of Covid-19 when a large crowd gathered for a large congregation during a church service.[56] The people's sentiments were manipulated by religious leaders, who influenced the reasoning of their followers threatened to reverse the gains of the lockdown.[57]

---

51 Martinez-Torrón, "Covid-19 and Religious Freedom: Some Comparative Perspectives".

52 Ayandele O, Okafor CT and Oyedele O. 2021. "The role of Nigeria's faith based organisations in tackling health crises like Covid-19", *The Africa Portal*, 27 January.

53 World Health Organization. 2020. "Practical Considerations for Religious Leaders and Faith Based Communities in the Context of Covid-19", *WHO.int*, Interim Guidance, 7 April.

54 Krippahl, "Nigerian religious leaders demand lifting of Covid-19 lockdown".

55 Krippahl, "Nigerian religious leaders demand lifting of Covid-19 lockdown".

56 Anyanwu et al, "A perspective on Nigeria's Preparedness, Response and Challenges to Mitigating the Spread of Covid-19", 9.

57 Wahab B. 2020. "Wike, 3 other Governors Relax Restriction on Religious Gatherings Because of Easter", *Pulse Nigeria*, 9 April.

THE ROLE OF THE JUDICIARY AND THE IMPLEMENTATION OF THE POLICIES

Dispute resolution and the administration of justice has been an integral aspect of every society. In an attempt to enforce the directives of the president of Nigeria, the Chief Justice of Nigeria issued a circular on 23 March 2020 further directing all heads of courts in Nigeria to suspend court sittings for the initial lockdown, except for matters that were urgent, essential or time-bound, according to the existing laws of Nigeria.[58] On 7 May 2020, the CJN issued another circular following the National Judicial Council on Covid-19, which adopted the guidelines for court sittings and related matters in the Covid-19 period guidelines, directing all heads of court to be guided by the guidelines in adopting or formulating rules, directives and further guidelines as appropriate to the legal and material circumstances of their courts, with the main aim of achieving justice and safety while delivering judgments.[59] The Constitution of the Federal Republic of Nigeria assigns judicial powers to courts other than the ones expressly provided for by the Constitution,[60] and these courts are the creation of various enabling laws, which are specifically created to adjudicate only within a particular jurisdiction,[61] on a particular matter. The mobile court is constituted by the Chief Judge of every state and the Federal Capital Territory, designated to be presided over by a magistrate for the purpose of dispensing justice on particular legal business,[62] Even before the outbreak of the Covid-19, mobile courts were created in respect of traffic offences in violation of the Federal Road Safety Act, 2007, and other violations on which the mobile court is constituted to adjudicate. The mobile courts were created for summary trials in respect of adjudicating matters of flouting the Covid-19 measures and policies regarding social distancing, wearing of face masks, lockdown, hand washing and other recommendations.[63] The mobile courts were a special arrangement of the court system, and the court moves from one place to another.[64] For the dispensation of justice in Nigeria under Covid, virtual court proceedings were also introduced as a means of decongesting the already congested caseloads before the courts of

---

58 National Judicial Council. 2020. "Re: Preventive Measures on the Spread of Corona Virus (Covid-19) and the Protection of Justices, Judges and Staff of Courts", NJC/CIR/HOC/II/631, 23 March.

59 National Judicial Council. 2020. "Re: National Judicial Council Covid-19 Policy Report: Guidelines for Court Sittings and Related Matters in the Covid-19 Period", NJC/CIR/HOC/II/660, 7 May.

60 CFRN 1999, s 6.

61 *APC vs Eng. Suleiman Aliyu Lere* (2020)1 NWLR (PT 1705)254.

62 Ezonfade D. 2022. "Mobile Courts Legality in Nigeria", *Nigerian Law Forum*, 29 September.

63 Obankwa D. 2020. "Why mobile Courts are illegal", *The Nation*, 3 November.

64 Ewulum BE. 2019. "The Mobile Court in the administration of Criminal Justice in Nigeria", *International Journal of Comparative Law and Legal Philosophy* 1(2):27-32. For an account of how mobile courts have been used in another country, see also Hosen GD and Ferdous SR. 2011. "The Role of Mobile Courts in the Enforcement of Laws in Bangladesh", *The Northern University Journal of Law* 1:82-95.

competent jurisdiction. These proceedings were not largely utilised in the northern region, however, due to the background illiteracy and the passive nature of the people in the remotest areas that have difficulties accepting innovations and advancements.

CONCLUSION

Nigeria's quick and aggressive response to Covid-19 is a testament to its experience from previous epidemics and pandemics and provides lessons on how other developed countries manhandled the further spread and transmission of the virus. The initial introduction of the emergency operation centres at the Nigeria Centre for Disease Control and the establishment of the Presidential Task Force on Covid-19 to monitor and contain the spread of the virus, as well as other logical decisions to ban international travel and advising on 14-day isolation and contact-tracing, were significant in the fight against the pandemic. Government policies and measures, as well as restrictions of movement, executed against the Covid-19 pandemic also contributed to the protection of public health in Nigeria.

The right to religious freedom is included in all the basic international human rights documents, the provisions under the Universal Declaration of Human Rights (UDHR), the International Covenant on Civil and Political Rights (ICCPR) and the Nigeria's *grundnorm* that allows free practice of one's faith without actually adopting a state religion in the multi-religious country.[65] In the strict sense, it was not the right to religious freedom that was subjected to restrictions by the policies imposed to fight the spread of Covid-19, but rather the way the right was exercised, since experts argued quite unanimously that its spread could only be limited by reducing direct contacts between people. Exercising religious freedom in the *forum externum*, however, is naturally associated with people leaving their homes, gathering in the sacred space and even shaking hands as a sign of greetings. The wide majority of the religious leaders in Bauchi and Plateau States collaborated with Federal Government agencies to flatten the curve of the disease, and also resorted to virtual communication for delivering religious sermons.

It was understood that the inclusion of religious leaders in policymaking was important, due to the nature of religious inclination of Nigerians. In situations of crisis, such as a pandemic, dialogue with religious leaders in the determination of decisions and policymaking is essential especially for policies concerning multiple religious communities that place limitations on the freedom of religion should be employed. Religious leaders should be integrated into the communities through service and compassionate networks and should be able to reach the most vulnerable with assistance and health information and to identify those most in

---

[65] See Universal Declaration of Human Rights, G.A. res. 217A (III), U.N. Doc A/810 at 71 (1948), art 18; International Covenant on Civil and Political Rights, G.A. res. 2200A (XXI), 21 U.N. GAOR Supp. (No. 16) at 52, U.N. Doc. A/6316 (1966), 999 U.N.T.S. 171, *entered into force* Mar. 23, 1976, art 18.

need. Religious leaders are a critical link in the safety net for vulnerable people within their faith community and wider communities.

For the adequate dispensation of justice, the establishment of the mobile courts to punish the flouting of public health measures by imposing sanctions should be extended to the rural areas to enable easier access to justice. It has so far been operational in state capitals. The setting up of virtual court to battle the congestion of cases was also a significant response to the new reality, though it faced backlash due to the nature of the archaic laws of the land, which hindered the establishment and creation of courts outside the ones stipulated by the Constitution, given the difficulty in amending the laws to welcome and adopt the new normal and technological advancements. During the Covid-19 period, Nigeria moved into a virtual age, with more use of computer and mobile devices to communicate and engage in businesses. This led to innovations in mobile courts and virtual justice, along with the introductions of storage systems for documentation and information to be accessed by the parties and the judicial staff at the court of record. Sustenance of these innovations has invariably contributed to the development of justice system in Nigeria and would continue to create lasting solutions of importance to the administration of justice in Nigeria.

Knowledge is the greatest tool for combatting so many societal social issues, and it is certainly advised that information be disseminated through the most popular means to the remotest parts of the country. Education and information influence people's perceptions, even the perceptions of people who disagree over the very existence of these contemporary problems. Religious leaders should advise and educate their people without any political or evil motive – particularly when their health and livelihoods are at risk.

III. Covid-19 cults, communications and conspiracies

10 Digitalised cults in the time of the Covid-19 lockdown in Abidjan: theological foundations of liturgical resilience

Célestin Gnonzion†[1]

INTRODUCTION

Côte d'Ivoire is a French-speaking West African country of nearly 23 million inhabitants and sixty ethnic groups. It is a secular and multi-confessional state.[2] Several religious institutions rub shoulders and compete with ardour in their strategies to increase their number of faithful and retain them.[3] The concept of "religious institution" is taken here in the broad sense of the term and refers to religious groups and sects active in the territory of Côte d'Ivoire. Figures from the 2014 General Population and Housing Census (RGPH) show the presence of several religions and sects in Côte d'Ivoire.[4] Out of a resident population of 22 671 331, Islam is the religion with the most followers, making up 42% of the population. Christianity is the next largest group, comprising 34% of the population.[5] Animists and members of other religions are, respectively 4% and 1% of the population. Those "Without Religion" account for 19% of the population.[6] The data on religion in Côte d'Ivoire also specify that among the foreign population, Muslims represent 72% and Christians represent 18% of the population. Among the native Ivorian population, however, Christians comprise 39% and Muslims 30% of the population.[7]

---

1 Research Professor at Félix Houphouët-Boigny University, UFR Information, Communication and Arts. It is with great sadness that ACLARS reports that Professor Célestin Gnonzion passed away suddenly on 31 August 2022, just one week after submitting this essay. We remember and honour his life and many contributions to ACLARS.

2 Gadou MD. 2011. Gadou Dakouri, "Muslims and Christians of Côte d'Ivoire: How religions triggered the Ivorian crisis!", *Our Way*, No. 3966, 22 October. See also Mathias Dacouri Gadou's earlier remarks on religion as Côte d'Ivoire was approaching another crisis, that of civil war, in 2002, in Hartill L. 2002. "In time of crisis, Ivorians turn their eyes to heaven", *The Christian Science Monitor*, 25 November.

3 Gadou, "Muslims and Christians of Côte d'Ivoire: How religions triggered the Ivorian crisis".

4 Institut National de Statistique. 2014. General Population and Housing Census [hereinafter RGPH]. Online at: https://www.ins.ci/RGPH2014.pdf

5 Christianity includes in order of the number of followers, Catholics, Protestants and other Christian religions.

6 Those "Without Religion" include agnostics, atheists and deists.

7 Institut National de la Statistique (INS) de Côte d'Ivoire. 2014 Recensement Général de la Population et de l'Habitat (RGPH) 2014 [General Population and Housing Census 2014].

All of these religious groups make use, to varying degrees, of the means of media for the communication of faith, whether traditional broadcast media in the sense of television and radio or new media in the sense of digital social networks. It is also notable that among non-Catholic churches, especially the Pentecostal churches, new information and communication technologies and media are "used in a competitive logic by prophetic pastors to give a gain of 'marketability' to revelations".[8] In this competitive religious media environment, "Divine revelations become 'media products' and a marketing space facilitating the meeting of supply and demand."[9]

Unlike in the Protestant churches, in the time before Covid-19, there was rather timid use of new media within the Catholic Church in Côte d'Ivoire. But the advent of Covid disrupted the communication and media practices of Catholic Christians, prompting them to move from the communication of faith through in-person and face-to-face interactions and to an intensive use of social media networks in a time of health crisis. This is why this use of new media and information and communication technology imposed upon the Catholic Church in Côte d'Ivoire by Covid deserves attention and is the subject of this study.

The present study examines, from a communications and media perspective, the forms of resilience implemented during the Covid lockdown period and their theological justifications in the founding texts of the theology and the magisterium of the Church. The study was based on a qualitative approach to data collection, using both individual interviews and group and focus group interviews, as well as virtual observation of religious practices on Facebook during the lockdown that took place during Holy Week 2020. The target population of the study comprised Catholic Christians from a dozen parishes in the city of Abidjan, as well as leaders of Christian movements and religious leaders of the parishes.

CONCEPTS FOR UNDERSTANDING DIGITAL RELIGIOSITY AND RESILIENCE

Before presenting the results of the research, it is important to define some key concepts of the study. These are the concepts of Lent, worship, digitalised worship and digitalised religiosity, crisis, and resilience. These provide context for the Catholic Church's shift to new media and communication methods during Holy Week 2020 in Côte d'Ivoire.

Lent

The time of Lent among Catholics is a key moment in the liturgy and expression of the religiosity of the Christian. In Côte d'Ivoire, this religiosity is often popular, expressive and syncretic, but also spiritual. Lent can be defined as "a time of

---

[8] Guiblehon B. 2014. "Le marche des revelations divines dans le contexte de crise politique en Côte d'Ivoire [The market in divine revelations in the context of political crisis in Côte d'Ivoire]", *Journal of the Anthropological Society of Oxford Online* 6(1):79-98.

[9] Guiblehon, "Le marche des revelations divines".

preparation of forty days for the feast of Easter, the heart of the Christian faith, which celebrates the resurrection of Christ".[10] Of Lent, it is said: "These forty days … make it possible to relive with Christ in the desert the forty years of the Hebrews' march to the promised land. It is the same experience of intimacy with God that the whole community of believers, baptised or candidates for baptism, wishes to relive as it sets out towards Easter."[11] In 2020, the other key moments in this spiritual journey were: Palm Sunday (5 April 2020), Holy Thursday (9 April 2020), Good Friday (10 April 2020), Holy Saturday (11 April 2020) and Easter Sunday (12 April 2020). It should also be noted that the last three days of Lent, called the Paschal triduum, have a special importance in that they mark the passion, death and resurrection of Christ.[12] In 2020, all of these holy days fell within the Covid lockdown period.

Worship

The notion of worship alludes to a moment of celebration or worship during which the followers of a religion pay homage to their divinity. Among Catholics, the most used term for worship is that of the Mass. When the Mass is celebrated remotely through the internet through means of communication, such as digital social networks, we speak of digitalised worship.

Digitalised worship

The expression "digitalised religiosity" refers to the manifestation of religious faith, beliefs, convictions and piety through the resources offered by the internet. In the expression "digitalised cults" we mean the religion celebrated through digital social networks.

Crisis

The notion of crisis can be understood well through the work of Ivoirian communications scholar Jules Evariste Agnini Toa. Toa quotes French communications theorist Thierry Libaert in defining crisis as "a passage between order and disorder … perceived as an unexpected event jeopardizing the reputation and functioning of an organisation".[13] Libaert further describes crisis as a "sudden and brutal change

---

10 Église Catholique en France. n.d. "Carême [Lent]". Online at: https://eglise.catholique.fr/approfondir-sa-foi/la-celebration-de-la-foi/les-grandes-fetes-chretiennes/careme-et-paques/careme/

11 ECF, "Carême".

12 Église Catholique en Yvelines. n.d. "Pâques et la Semaine sainte [Easter and Holy Week]. Online at: https://www.catholique78.fr/priercelebrer/liturgie/les-fetes-catholiques/triduum-pascal/

13 Toa JEA. 2017. "Les technologies médiatiques dans le traitement de la crise de Grand-Bassam en Côte d'Ivoire [Media technologies in the treatment of the Grand-Bassam crisis in Côte d'Ivoire]", *Communication, technology and développement* [Communication,

between two states, which causes a rupture of equilibrium ... a serious phenomenon, but nevertheless normal, disrupting the functioning of an organisation, and altering its course".[14]

Resilience

As for the notion of resilience, there is the definition provided given by Beninese-Ivorian sociologist Francis Akindès, who has written, "Resilience is to faith, in the face of a crisis, the ability to resist, to adapt, to respond, to bounce back, to rebuild, to self-organise, to return to its state of equilibrium, to absorb a shock, to load structurally, to perpetuate."[15]

COVID IN CÔTE D'IVOIRE: FINDINGS, PROBLEMS AND QUESTIONS

Having defined the concepts of the study, it is important now to specify the context, findings, problem and questions underlying this research pertaining to Covid-19. The reality and context of Covid in Côte d'Ivoire can be perceived, initially, through a number of observations about government measures, including restrictions and constraints on individual and religious freedoms. Côte d'Ivoire recorded its first Covid case on 11 March 2020. The balance sheet from the health point of view reported 81 959 cases and 799 deaths, as of the time of this writing in 7 May 2022; yet, just days after the first case, from 16 March 2020 forward, the Ivorian authorities had already taken measures against the disease.[16] These included the closure of schools and places of worship, the isolation of greater Abidjan, the curfew, the closure of land borders, the mandatory wearing of masks, the imposition of barrier measures, the closure of leisure areas, such as bars and discotheques, a ban on gatherings of more than 50 people and prohibitions on shaking hands. The last of these had direct religious and liturgical consequence in the manifestation of the peace sign during Mass, which was now to be signified by the gesture of nodding one's head in acknowledgment from a distance instead of the customary handshake.

These measures presented some problems at the level of religious practices, especially for the Catholic Church. In the middle of Lent, it was impossible to physically visit the churches to celebrate worship in assembly, to participate in the Stations of the Cross, to receive the Eucharist and to celebrate the Paschal triduum, a key moment in the Catholic faith. These problems aroused great fear among Christians and religious leaders, as well as an economic shortage in parishes.

---

    technology and development] 4, 3 para 10 (citing Libaert T. 2001. *La Communication de crise*. Paris: Dunod, Les Topos, 9).

14 Thierry Libaert, *La Communication de crise*, 9.

15 Akindès F. 2011. *Côte d'Ivoire: La reinvention de soi dans la violence*. Dakar: CODESRIA, n.p.

16 Coronavirus disease: Côte d'Ivoire. Google. [Accessed 7 May 2022].

The Covid pandemic also raised a number of other questions: What kind of resilience did Christians in Abidjan implement in the face of the restrictive measures caused by Covid? How did they experience their religiosity in times of confinement? What were the media preferred by the parishioners of Abidjan during the period of confinement in Holy Week? What are the theological foundations of and justifications for these remote liturgical celebrations?

Finding answers to these questions was the focus of the present study. The presentation of the results of the study below is structured around five key points: (1) the perception of Covid-19 by Catholic Christians, (2) liturgical and spiritual resilience through digitalised religiosity though the use of media and social networks, (3) the formation of new forms of communities and virtual practices, (4) the theological foundations of the use of the media for the communication of faith and, finally, (5) the role of digital culture and digital social networks in the popular religious expression of crisis.

PERCEPTIONS OF COVID-19 BY CATHOLIC CHRISTIANS: AN ATTACK BY THE DEVIL IN WHICH BELIEVERS WIN

The measure banning gatherings of more than fifty people was initiated on 16 March 2020 by the government during the extraordinary meeting of the National Security Council (NSC), chaired by the president of the Republic. This measure was taken 18 days after the beginning of Lent, which had begun with the celebration of Ash Wednesday on 26 February 2020 and which marked the beginning of the spiritual and liturgical journey towards the Feast of Easter. But how was Covid perceived by Catholic Christians in Côte d'Ivoire? The answer obtained from listening to the focus group for the present study was that "Covid is an attack from the devil".

According to some of the Catholic Christians whose words were collected during the focus group, Covid and the lockdown that followed were perceived by parishioners as "a personal and spiritual fight", "an attack of the devil", "a spiritual attack that began in the middle of Lent and ending the liturgical celebrations" and "a ruse of the devil to weaken the faith of the Catholic Christian that because the Church was closed without celebration."[17] Moreover, if Covid was perceived as an attack from the devil, for some Christians, it was also perceived that believers would emerge victorious from this attack. The following quotes from the focus group attest to this idea of the victory of the believer over the pandemic: "The devil thought to weaken the faith of Christians, but he allowed us to find other ways to praise God", "The Church came out of this matter grown", "During the lockdown I thanked GOD, because he used the stupidity of the devil to awaken the faith of Christians."[18]

---

17 Interview with focus group participants by C Gnonzion. Abidjan, Côte d'Ivoire. c. April 2020–May 2022.

18 Interview with focus group participants.

LITURGICAL AND SPIRITUAL RESILIENCE OF BELIEVERS THROUGH A DIGITALISED RELIGIOSITY

Beyond the perception of Christians of the challenges of the Covid-19 lockdown, it is also important to account for liturgical and spiritual resilience through digitalised religiosity and the use of media and digital social networks. From the point of view of liturgical resilience, there were adaptations at two levels. First, there was rationing and limitation of the participants in the Mass, and then there was the transition from the church of assembled faithful to the church of connected faithful.

One of the structural responses to the ban on gatherings of more than fifty people was rationing and limitation of participation in the Mass. This was accomplished through ration tickets, which had to be secured from the parish every week. Each Christian had to take an individual number, choosing the time of the Mass in which they wished to participate. Once the number of fifty people was reached, it was necessary to choose another time of passage.

Apart from the rationing of places in churches, resilience in times of Covid mainly manifested itself in forms of religiosity that were no longer face-to-face and involving physical interaction. There was a shift from assemblies of the faithful to building connections among the faithful, and there was a change in the order of community interactions through the use of the media. The new order of interaction was no longer face-to-face. But it was a new order of interactions centred on virtual distance via the media, especially digital social networks, namely Facebook and then WhatsApp, during the Pascal triduum, as well as WhatsApp forums, web-based radio stations, the television station KTO, and the Ivorian Catholic radio station Radio Espoir. The celebration of Holy Thursday was the one for which the media were most used, followed by Good Friday and then Holy Saturday. The most used social network was Facebook, followed by WhatsApp.

These efforts at digital and communicated resilience were initiated in the face of the great fear that parish leaders had of losing ardour, piety, faith and, ultimately, Christians. If it was impossible to see Christians, greet them physically and talk to them, what could be done to keep them in the faith? These efforts prompted many reflections from leaders of Christian movements in Abidjan parishes who participated in focus groups conducted for the present study. One participant observed, "Christians began to ask questions of the various parish priests who raised the problem, it was at this moment that the Vatican gave the order to the various leaders of the communities to use the means of communication through the Internet to keep Catholic Christians always in the faith."[19] Another religious leader observed, "As the leader of a prayer group when the problem arose, the clergy sent us notes asking us to do everything possible to be able to keep Christians but also our members in the bath of the spiritual. This is how we set up a web radio that works 24 hours a day and that has helped to maintain the flame of the members of our group."[20] Still another religious leader participating in the study observed, "The

---

19 Interview with focus group participants.
20 Interview with focus group participants.

various leaders have made efforts to keep their members in prayer, either through WhatsApp forums or online publications. But it is difficult to maintain this flame if the Christian is not previously in a group on the parish."[21] This last participant raised a possible limit of social networks, in that they can only be useful if the Christian belonged to a face-to-face community.

FORMATION OF NEW FORMS OF VIRTUAL EUCHARISTIC COMMUNITIES AND PRACTICES

Covid has led to the formation of virtual Christian communities. Though the formation of these virtual communities was imposed during the period of lockdown, it is notable that many Christians remained at home during the time when the churches were opened, forgetting that virtual religiosity is an exceptional case. The advent of the pandemic also gave rise to the concept of virtual communion. This expression and the practice to which it alludes emerged during the focus group.

Virtual communion can be defined as: "Communion with Christ present in the Eucharist, not by receiving him sacramentally, but by the sole desire stemming from a faith animated by charity." Focus group participants also added, "The value of spiritual communion rests on faith in the presence of Christ in the Eucharist as a source of life, love and unity. It is a privileged way of uniting with Christ for those who cannot receive communion bodily." It was also noted that the lockdown period during Holy Week 2020 was also marked by the exhibition of the Blessed Sacrament in the Archdiocese of Abidjan and it was said to be "a comfort for Christians to worship the Eucharist".

THEOLOGICAL FOUNDATIONS OF THE USE OF THE MEDIA FOR THE COMMUNICATION OF THE FAITH

It is important to understand the theological foundations of this use of the media for the communication of the faith. Following the fracturing and fears aroused in Christian communities by Covid-related restrictions, the concern of clergy and community leaders was the maintenance of the flame of belief. Therefore, there was need to communicate the faith.

To understand the concept of communication supporting these efforts at communication of faith, one can look the definition of communication offered by French philosopher and political theorist Francis Balle, to the effect that communication is "the action consisting, for humans, of exchanging messages, face-to-face or at a distance, with or without the help of a media, and whatever the form or purpose of this exchange". As Balle describes it, "Communication therefore refers to both an action and the result of that action: *communicare* et *communitas*."[22] From this definition, we can adapt the idea of the purpose of communication to consider the

---

21 Interview with focus group participants.
22 Balle F (ed). 2006. *Lexique d'information communication* [Lexicon of communications information]. Paris: Dalloz, 82.

purpose of the communication of faith. And in the communication of faith, there is an insistence on media and mass media. Several studies and publications have indeed highlighted the importance of the media in the communication of the faith.

The pastoral instruction *Aetatis novae* on social communications for the twentieth anniversary of the papal encyclical *Communio et progressio* notes that: "The means of communication can and must be instruments at the service of the programme of re-evangelisation and new evangelisation of the Church in the contemporary world."[23] But long before that, the *Commuunio et progressio* had shown the importance of the media in proclaiming the Gospel. As the encyclical stated, "The media are rightly among the most effective resources and possibilities that man can use to strengthen charity, itself a source of communion."[24]

In the context of the Covid pandemic, as Cameroonian priest and social scientist Noël Sofack points out, "The health crisis has therefore been an opportunity to strengthen the link that the Catholic Church has forged with the media since the Second Vatican Council."[25] The Covid pandemic crisis enabled the Church to "equip itself with electronic culture to transmit the message of Jesus to the men of audiovisual, digital and Internet civilisation".[26] Much as Pope John Paul II had seen in the Internet "a new forum for proclaiming the Gospel",[27] Pope Benedict XVI had considered social networks to be "doors of truth and faith" and "new spaces for evangelisation".[28] This is because they were not a pure virtual space or disconnected from a "real" life but, on the contrary, an element of social life that was increasingly important in interpersonal relationships. During the Covid pandemic, these digital media offered a "real" possibility, through the "virtual", to meet God.

It can therefore be said that the "rise in power of the spiritual uses of the media … which has made it possible to give the faithful the opportunity to follow religious services through radio, television, Facebook live, and other digital media" finds its foundation and follows several writings of the magisterium of the Church.[29] It is also important to highlight "double religiosity" of the virtual and the real that prevailed in the face of Covid-19 during the 2020 lockdown in Côte d'Ivoire.

---

23 Vatican, Pontifical Council for Social Communications. 1992. Pastoral Instruction *Aetatis novae* on Social Communications for the 20th anniversary of *Communio and Progressio*. Vatican City: Libreria Editrice Vaticana, para 11.

24 Second Vatican Council. 1971. Pastoral Instruction *Commuunio and Progressio* (On the Means of Social Communication), 23 May, para 12.

25 Sofack N. 2021. "Catholicisme et Covid-19 au cameroun: contraintes et resilience [Catholicism and Covid-19 in Cameroon]", *Revues de l'ACAREF*.

26 Sofack, "Catholicisme et Covid-19 au cameroun".

27 Pope John Paul II. 2002. "Internet: A New Forum for Proclaiming the Gospel", Message for the 36th World Communications Day, Vatican City, 12 May.

28 Pope Benedict XVI. 2013. "Social Networks: portals of truth and faith; new spaces for evangelisation", Message of His Holiness Pope Benedict XVI for the 47th World Communications Day", Vatican City, 24 January (quoted in Sofack, "Catholicisme et Covid-19 au cameroun", 493).

29 Sofack, "Catholicisme et Covid-19 au cameroun".

DIGITAL CULTURE, DIGITAL SOCIAL NETWORKS AND THE EXPRESSION OF POPULAR CRISIS RELIGIOSITY

Studies have highlighted the use of new media by evangelical and Pentecostal pastors and preachers. The latter, in particular, make extensive use of the new media for the communication of the faith and to expand their ministries. They have websites and are present on digital social networks. These means are an integral part of the communication of the faith and the expansion of these religious leaders. They thus make Marshall McLuhan's expression that "the real message is the medium itself" a reality, because the medium determines and conditions the message. For the faithful who use them, the media are not just means of communicating the faith through ministries, but constituent objects of the message of faith to be communicated.[30] These preachers make structured, elaborate and professional use of social networks in their vocation and profession of ministry.

But this professional use is not the main focus of the present study, which has focused mainly on the perspectives of laypeople in the church and their perspective on media use in the context of a crisis. We consider these "popular" laypeople to be amateurs, because their communications, mostly through Facebook and WhatsApp, are not part of a constructed and well-elaborated pastoral process. The study focused on the use of mobile phones and digital social networks by these amateurs, not only to disseminate messages with religious connotations, but also to keep in touch with fellow believers and to maintain their religiosity in times of Covid and confinement.

It is in this sense, that we note that the advent of Covid has given rise to the manifestation of a "double religiosity". The first religiosity, popular and profane, sees in Covid an attack of the devil. This perception does not seem far from those who think in terms of a conspiracy. There is, in this an attempt to atone for the violence of the pandemic, something of a theory of the scapegoat, "because we need a culprit" as theologian René Girard points out.[31]

But we also have the manifestation of a form of a second and non-secular religiosity that one could even describe as "intellectual". The latter can be seen through the hierarchy of the church, which apprehends the need for communication strategies in a context of crisis with much more intellectual and theological hindsight, the heart of which demands information and uninterrupted contact between the cardinals, princes and leaders at the top of the summit and the flock of the Christian faithful in the grassy fields below. It therefore appears that in the context of the Covid-19 pandemic in Côte d'Ivoire and especially during the lockdown period, digital social

---

30 See Asamoah-Gyadu JK. 2009. "'We Are on the Internet': Contemporary Pentecostalism in Africa and the New Culture of Online Religion", in Hackett RIJ, Soares B et al (eds). *New Media and Religious Transformations in Africa*. Bloomington: Indiana University Press, 157-170.

31 Girard R. "Le 'bouc émissaire' [The "Scapegoat"]. Online at: https://www.les-crises.fr/wp-content/uploads/2015/02/le-bouc-emissaire.pdf

networks served as a space for the expression of a popular religiosity that may be framed by leaders, but which also often erupts in a spontaneity dictated by digital culture and context.

CONCLUSION

Côte d'Ivoire is a secular republic in which freedom of expression and religious freedom are recognised freedoms guaranteed by the fundamental law of the Constitution of the Republic of Côte d'Ivoire, 2016. The advent of the Covid pandemic has put these constitutional freedoms to the test, inviting the state to intrude upon the field of religion by imposing measures of restrictions and constraints on these freedoms. The state has certainly not questioned the "freedom of worship", but it has imposed limitations on "freedom of participation in worship" that have caused much frustration among believers, especially Catholics.

The present study showed the type of resilience developed by parishioners as a response to government restrictions and bans. The use of the media, especially of social media networks, in a crisis context and in an unstructured way, can sometimes entail inaccuracies and amateurism that fall short of crisis solutions that are structured, elaborate and professional. Despite these limitations, the present study has also shown that the use of social media by Christians in Abidjan in the time of Covid was justified and is based on writings of the magisterium of the Catholic Church from the documents of Vatican II, Pope John Paul II to Pope Benedict XVI and beyond. We can learn from this magisterium that social media networks offer a "real" possibility through the "virtual" to meet God.

11 THE CONFLICT BETWEEN FAITH-BASED AND SCIENCE-BASED MESSAGES ON PUBLIC HEALTH PANDEMICS IN AFRICA

Brian Muyunga[1]

INTRODUCTION

In the face of a pandemic or any other occurrence that is destructive to people's health and well-being, it is vital that people are provided with appropriate advice and the information they need to ensure their safety.[2] HIV/AIDS and Covid-19 are examples of major pandemics that threatened every aspect of human life in sub-Saharan Africa,[3] and both necessitated formulation and dissemination of public health messages.[4] Public health messaging is a crucial part of responding to public health pandemics, such as HIV/AIDS and Covid-19.[5] Faith and science have served as the main sources of information and messages consumed by people in Africa, and both have influenced their responses to the pandemics.[6]

The messages on the HIV/AIDS and Covid-19 can, therefore, be categorised into faith-based and science-based. Much as both kinds of messages are formulated and disseminated with an intention of aiding people in triumphing over the pandemics, there exists a conflict between faith-based and science-based messages on these pandemics that poses a serious challenge to their management. The negative consequences of this conflict on public health management in sub-Saharan Africa present a dire need to affirm the mutual relationship between faith and science as "tools" that must work inclusively for public health management and to create harmony between faith-based and science-based messages on pandemics whenever they arise.

This chapter examines the conflict between faith-based and science-based messages on two public health pandemics in sub-Saharan Africa. HIV/AIDS and Covid-19,

---

1   Student, Faculty of Theology, St. Paul's University – Kenya; Founding Chairperson, The Game Changers Ecumenical Youth Network (GC-EYN), Uganda.
2   See Gill PT and Boylan S. 2012. "Public health messages: Why Are They Ineffective and What Can be Done?", *Current Obesity Reports* 1:50-88.
3   See Aborode AT et al. 2021. "HIV/AIDS Epidemic and Covid-19 Pandemic in Africa", *Frontiers in Genetics* 12:670511.
4   See Newman T, Brossard D and Howell E. 2021. "Covid-19 public health messages have been all over the place – but researchers know how to do better", *The Conversation*, 14 April.
5   See Nan X, Iles IA, Yang B and Ma Z. 2022. "Public Health Messaging during the Covid-19 Pandemic and Beyond: Lessons from Communication Science", *Health Communication* 37(1):1-19.
6   Phillips H. 2020. "'17, '18, '19: Religion and science in three pandemics, 1817, 1918, and 2019", *Journal of Global History* 15(3):434-443.

highlighting its impact on the management of the two pandemics. The chapter also presents strategies through which this conflict can be addressed from the perspective of two theologians and two public health specialists involved in the Ecumenical HIV and AIDs Initiatives and Advocacy (EHAIA) programmes of the World Council of Churches on HIV/AIDS and Covid-19 in Eastern Africa.[7]

STUDYING FAITH- AND SCIENCE-BASED MESSAGES: A METHODOLOGICAL NOTE

Developing this chapter entailed a literature review on the role of faith and science in the management of HIV/AIDS and Covid-19. The literature review examined sources on faith-based and science-based messages on HIV/AIDS and Covid-19, religious leaders' perspectives on HIV/AIDS and Covid-19, scientific discoveries regarding HIV and Covid-19, and analysis of the relationship between faith and science in these sources. In addition to these sources, a set of interviews was conducted with two theologians and two public health personnel involved in programmes responding to HIV/AIDS and Covid-19 organised by the Ecumenical HIV and AIDs Initiatives and Advocacy programme. The four participants were obtained with the support of the staff at the EHAIA Eastern Africa regional office in Nairobi Kenya. The interviews were conducted as part of a pilot study for qualitative research on the conflict between faith-based and science-based messages in public health management. Verbal voluntary consent was obtained from each participant before engaging them in the interviews. To facilitate the interviews, the present researcher shared with the participants a concept paper explaining the subject, aim and nature of the interview. It was agreed that rather than the interviewees' actual names, pseudonyms would be adopted in reporting the results.

Among those interviews for this study, Peter is a Ugandan Anglican, who has worked with EHAIA for 14 years. He has worked as a consultant on theology, ethics and spirituality for ending AIDS faster. For over 30 years, he has championed faith-based responses to pandemics at national, regional and international levels. He has offered technical support to various national and regional initiatives empowering religious leaders to respond to the Covid-19 pandemic. John is a public health scientist affiliated with the Moravian Church in Tanzania and has worked with EHAIA for 5 years. He is a community health officer with over ten years of experience in sexual and reproductive health care and education and has participated in developing resources for promoting sexual and reproductive health and rights. Mary is a Kenyan theologian in the Friends Church who has worked with EHAIA for 14 years. She has been a university lecturer in a school of theology for over 20 years and is an expert in theological education by extension. Mark is a member of a Ugandan Pentecostal church and has worked with EHAIA for 8 years. He is a retired medical doctor and public health consultant with over twenty-five years of experience in HIV/AIDS advocacy. The interviews were held between

---

7 Ecumenical HIV and AIDS Initiatives and Advocacy (EHAIA). Online at: https://www.oikoumene.org/what-we-do/ehaia

1 February and 15 March 2022: Peter was interviewed on 5 February 2022. Mary was interviewed on 9 February 2022. Mark was interviewed on 11 February 2022. John was interviewed on 12 March 2022. These four experts brought a deep and diverse range of perspectives to the study.

FAITH AND SCIENCE IN THE MANAGEMENT OF PANDEMICS: HIV/AIDS AND COVID-19

The outbreak and negative effects of pandemics such as HIV/AIDS and Covid-19 raise many complex questions among African people. HIV is an infectious virus, which can only be transmitted through infected body fluids, such as semen, vaginal fluids, blood or blood products and breast milk. For infection to occur, body fluids from an already infected person must introduce a sufficient quantity of the virus into the body of another person to make an infectious dose. The virus enters the body where the skin is damaged or more delicate, such as the mucous membranes of the anus, vagina, or foreskin of the uncircumcised penis, especially if these are impaired due to a sexually transmitted infection (STI). If not treated, the HIV infection progresses into AIDS, a condition whereby the infected person's immune system is too weak to resist any form of opportunistic infection.[8] Africa remains the region most affected by the HIV/AIDS pandemic, and the biggest proportion of new HIV cases occurs in sub-Saharan Africa.[9]

Covid-19 is an acute respiratory infection caused by the severe acute respiratory syndrome coronavirus 2 (SARSCoV-2). The virus spreads through respiratory droplets produced when a Covid-19 positive person sneezes or coughs. The most common clinical presentation of Covid-19 is that of a respiratory infection with a symptom severity ranging from a mild common cold-like illness to a severe viral pneumonia, leading to an acute respiratory distress syndrome that is potentially fatal. The World Health Organization first declared Covid-19 to be a public health emergency of international concern on 30 January 2020, and it subsequently declared it a pandemic on 11 March 2020. The WHO recommended a number of safety measures and precautions that could be put in place to control the spread of the pandemic, including mandatory national lockdowns in countries where the coronavirus had begun spreading. A lockdown meant that people would be encouraged to stay at home and limit their movements and physical interactions with people, especially those who were not members of their households.[10]

Responses to HIV/AIDS and Covid-19 involve formulation and dissemination of public health messages aimed at creating awareness of their causes, implications, prevention and treatment, as well as attending to the fear and anxiety that pandemics

---

8   "How HIV Is Transmitted?", *HIV.gov*, 16 June 2022.
9   Nweze JA, Eke IE and Nweze EI. 2017. "HIV/AIDS in sub-Saharan Africa: current status, challenges and prospects", *Asian Pacific Journal of Tropical Diseases* 7(4):239-256.
10 Dein S, Loewenthal K, Lewis CA and Pargament KI. 2020. "Covid-19, mental health and religion: an agenda for future research", *Mental Health, Religion & Culture* 23:1.

generate. Faith and science have always been two of the main sources of public health information and messages consumed by people in Africa, and they are major sources of responses to the complicated questions people have in the face of diseases such as HIV/AIDS and Covid-19. "Defined from an ontological and dynamic perspective, faith refers to the supernatural means to achieve union of the understanding with God, enabling this power to participate in Divinity", says one definition of faith.[11] It implies a complete trust and firm belief in something that cannot be proven. Faith is the underpinning of every major religion and spiritual belief system, whether it is faith in the existence of a higher power, faith in the truth or divinity of a doctrine or a specific religious text or faith in the rewards of an afterlife.[12] On the other hand, "Science is a human activity aimed at acquiring a reliable knowledge of the causes and principles of things", as reads a definition of science. Science results from the attempt by human beings to understand the natural world and to comprehend the universe to which they belong, and thus to explain to themselves their longing for transcendence.[13] The relationship between faith and science has been one of the most prominent and visible discourses over the years, and the two sources of understanding have provided people across geographies and cultures with a framework for conceptualising the world, as well as advice on the way to live within it.[14] In Africa, faith and science are both significant determinants of public health.

The biggest proportion of Africa's population are people of faith, and the majority of them reserve a high level of respect and belief in their faith leaders. Christianity and Islam stand out as the two most predominant religions in sub-Saharan Africa, and they not only shape the values, beliefs and practices of their followers, but also influence conceptions of diseases, such as HIV/AIDS and Covid-19.[15] However, it is also true that the people in Africa believe in science and attach significant value to scientific research, discoveries, innovation and advancements. When confronted by a pandemic, a significant number of people in Africa, including people of faith, hope in nothing else but that scientific theories and studies will provide answers to the questions that arise and solutions to the challenges encountered. A significant number of others place their complete hope in their faith exclusively and task their faith leaders to provide answers and solutions. There are also others who equally depend on both faith and science for answers and solutions.

---

11 Cortés ME, Del Río JP, Vigil P. 2015. "The harmonious relationship between faith and science from the perspective of some great saints: A brief comment", *Linacre Quarterly* 82(1):3-7.

12 Pugh SA. 2010. "Examining the Interface between HIV/AIDS, Religion and Gender in Sub-Saharan Africa", *Canadian Journal of African Studies* 44(3):624-643.

13 Cortés et al, "The harmonious relationship between faith and science from the perspective of some great saints".

14 McCaffrey P. 2013. *And Yet, It Moves: The Conflict Between Faith and Science*. Ipswich, MA: H.W. Wilson Publishers.

15 Sloane S. 2012. "Comparing the Impact of Religious Discourse on HIV/AIDS in Islam and Christianity in Africa", *Vanderbilt Undergraduate Research Journal* 8(Spring).

As far as public health messaging is concerned, faith-based messages are those messages that are developed on the basis of beliefs in the existence of God and God's involvement in the affairs of creation, while science-based messages are the messages developed on the basis of scientific research, discoveries, theories and knowledge. Despite these differences, when it comes to public health pandemics, both faith-based messaging and science-based messaging share the same goal: to help humanity emerge victorious over the pandemics. However, there are also certain contradictions between faith-based and science-based messages on HIV/AIDS and Covid-19 in Africa, as will be discussed below.

CONFLICT BETWEEN FAITH-BASED AND SCIENCE-BASED MESSAGES ON HIV/AIDS IN AFRICA

On 5 June 2021, the world marked 40 years since the first five cases of what later became known as HIV/AIDS were officially reported.[16] Since the onset of the HIV infections in the 1980s, the majority of the faith-based messages in Africa have viewed the disease as God's punishment of the sinful, especially the sexually immoral.[17] On the other hand, science-based messages have insisted that the infection was caused by a virus that had originated from monkeys.[18] When it came to prevention, science-based messages presented condoms as a protective tool, capable of preventing the transmission of HIV from one person to another through sexual intercourse. Faith-based messages, on the other hand, admonished against the use of condoms and instead insisted on abstinence and marital faithfulness alone. They claimed that condoms promoted promiscuity and encouraged extra- and pre-marital sex. Condom promotion, therefore, faced tremendous obstacles from religious leaders, who often reached a deadlock with other stakeholders over condom use. The opposition from faith leaders to campaigns in favour of the use of condoms on the grounds that they would encourage promiscuity was met with hostility by medical professionals and other public health professionals.[19]

Since the beginning of the HIV pandemic, there have been faith-based messages promoting faith healing and miraculous cures of HIV/AIDS.[20] Such messages from Christian circles emphasise that Jesus Christ is an answer to all challenges and that with enough faith, every illness can be cured by prayers said in the name of

---

16 Harold JP. 2021. "Special Commentary: The White House Forty Years of Questions and Answers: What Will It Take to End the HIV Epidemic", *Journal of Healthcare, Science and the Humanities* 9(1):13-16.

17 Hess RF and McKinney D. 2007. "Fatalism and HIV/AIDS beliefs in rural Mali, West Africa", *Journal of Nursing Scholarship* 39(2):113-118.

18 Jeffries WL, Sutton MY and Eke AN. 2017. "On the Battlefield: The Black church, public health, and the fight against HIV among African American gay and bisexual men", *Journal of Urban Health* 94:384-398.

19 Pugh, "Examining the Interface between HIV/AIDS, Religion and Gender in Sub-Saharan Africa".

20 Jeffries et al, "On the Battlefield".

Jesus Christ. Others rely on religious objects, such as sanctified water, anointing oil and others, to cure HIV. During the early years of the HIV infection, there was no scientifically approved medication for its treatment, and science-based messages preached that HIV/AIDS had no cure. Towards the end of the twentieth century, scientists invented antiretroviral treatment (ART) and presented it as an intervention capable of treating HIV/AIDS symptoms, prolonging the lives of people living with HIV, helping them live healthy lives and reducing the risk of transmission.[21] In some Christian circles, taking ART was described as a lack of faith and belief in the healing and curative power of God and Jesus Christ. Under the leadership of T.B. Joshua, The Synagogue, Church of All Nations (SCOAN), an evangelical Christian church based in Lagos, Nigeria, has come under particular criticism in recent years for advising their congregations to stop taking HIV medication.[22] The church's website claimed to offer special prayer and "HIV/AIDS healing" as a service, as well as selling "Anointing Water" to help with the healing process.[23] The website also boasts photos and testimonials from members who have been "cured" of HIV.[24] In December 2010, a former pastor with the Evangelical Lutheran Church in Tanzania, Rev Ambilikile Mwasapile, announced that God revealed to him in dreams the cure for HIV/AIDS. His cure was a mixture of natural herbs and the roots of a special tree which he discovered in 1991.[25] Medical officials intervened by encouraging all patients on antiretroviral treatment to continue to comply with their recommended treatment regimen.[26]

CONFLICT BETWEEN FAITH-BASED AND SCIENCE-BASED MESSAGES ON COVID-19 IN AFRICA

The Covid-19 pandemic was confirmed to have spread to Africa on 14 February 2020, with the first confirmed case announced in Egypt.[27] The first confirmed case in sub-Saharan Africa was announced in Nigeria at the end of February 2020,[28] and within three months, the virus had spread throughout the continent. Lesotho, the

---

21 Palmisano L and Vella S. 2011. "A brief history of antiretroviral therapy of HIV infection: success and challenges", *Annali dell'Istituto superiore di sanita* 47(1):44-48.
22 "Tb Joshua Again! Church HIV Prayer Cure Claims 'cause Three Deaths", *Nairaland Forum*, 18 October 2011.
23 SCOAN International "The SCOAN: About". Online at: https://www.scoan.org
24 "Healed From HIV/AIDS At The SCOAN!!!", *Emmanuel TV*, 21 February 2019. Online at: https://emmanuel.tv/testimonies/healed-from-hiv-at-the-scoan
25 "Cleric Discovers HIV/AIDS `Cure` In Tanzania". Online at: http://showbizxklusivs.blogspot.com/2011/03/cleric-discovers-hivaids-cure-in.html
26 Speakman S. 2012. "Comparing the Impact of Religious Discourse on HIV/AIDS in Islam and Christianity in Africa. Vanderbilt University Board of Trust?", *Vanderbilt Undergraduate Research Journal* 8(Spring 2012).
27 "Covid-19: Egypt confirms first coronavirus case in Africa". Online at: https://www.africanews.com/2020/02/14/Covid-19-egypt-confirms-first-coronavirus-case-in-africa/
28 Jacobs ED and Okeke MI. 2022 "A critical evaluation of Nigeria's response to the first wave of Covid-19", *Bulletin of the National Research Centre* 46(1):44.

last African sovereign state to have remained free of the virus, reported a case on 13 May 2020.[29] Science-based messages on Covid-19 asserted that the infection was caused by a SARS virus that had muted into an infectious form, spreading from Wuhan, China. The virus was reported to be highly infectious and spread through direct and indirect human contacts.[30] In the early months of the pandemic, the internet was filled with faith-based messages quoting pastors who alleged a direct relationship between sin and the development of Covid-19.[31] Messages from some church leaders argued that the Covid-19 pandemic was caused by human sin, igniting God's anger upon humanity. To emphasise this claim, a number of accounts accused Europeans of being guilty of perpetuating evils, such as homosexuality and idolatry, while others charged China of trying to imitate God's power by trying to create an artificial moon. The increasing prevalence of Covid-19 in Africa was attributed to an increasing number of people in Africa who have forsaken God, engaged in corruption and amassed ill-gotten wealth. These faith-based messages affirmed that Covid-19 was sent by God and that when the wicked were consumed, it would disappear.[33] Apostle Dr Joseph Serwadda, a Ugandan-based pastor and president of the Inter-Religious Council of Uganda (IRCU) argued that the Covid-19 pandemic was not a disease, but rather an instance of chemical or biological warfare between China and America. Serwadda argued that the faithful should direct their prayers not against the disease, but against a war between the two countries in which Uganda would be an unintended casualty. Other people of faith reported that Covid-19 was part of the "new world order" project championed by China to overtake and outcompete America in trade, politics, science and technology and that it was intended to take people away from God, so that science could take over the world.[32]

When it came to Covid-19 prevention, science-based messages emphasised the need to limit physical contact through avoiding public gatherings and circulation, among other measures.[33] When the Covid-19 vaccines were invented and rolled out, public health scientists advocated their uptake and use across the world, so as to boost people's immunity against the pandemic.[34] A number of faith-based messages,

---

29 Meyer D. 2020. "Lesotho confirm first Covid-19 case with all African countries now infected", *The South African*, 13 May.

30 Cevik M, Kuppalli K, Kindrachuk J and Peiris M. 2020. "Virology, transmission, and pathogenesis of SARS-CoV-2", *British Medical Journal* 371:m3862.

31 Valerio R and Heugh G. 2020. "Decoding coronavirus: Sin, judgement and (not) the end of the world", Tearfund.org, 1 April.

33 Isiko AP. 2020. "Religious construction of disease: An exploratory appraisal of religious responses to the Covid-19 pandemic in Uganda", *Journal of African Studies and Development* 12(3):77-96.

32 Isiko, "Religious construction of disease".

33 Güner R, Hasanoğlu I and Aktaş F. 2020. "Covid-19: Prevention and control measures in community", *Turkish Journal of Medical Sciences* 50(SI-1):571-577.

34 World Health Organization (WHO). 2022. "Advice for the public: Coronavirus disease (Covid-19)", WHO.int, 10 May.

however, stood in opposition to these efforts of the scientific community. In Tanzania, the late President John Magufuli, a staunch Catholic and lay faith leader, didn't believe in people staying at home. He wanted them to get into the churches and worship God with a belief that coronavirus is "satanic" and cannot survive in "the body of Christ."[35] Magufuli questioned the efficacy of the Covid-19 testing procedures,[36] and he also warned Tanzania's health ministry against rushing into embracing the Covid-19 vaccines promoted by foreign companies and countries.[37] In Jamaica, a Popular Santa called Ramgeet, also known by some as "Black Jesus East Kingston" or "Black Jesus", was quoted alleging that Covid-19 vaccines cannot help the people. He revealed that would not take the vaccine himself, because God would see him through the pandemic. He prophesied that a time would come where one could travel or conduct business without the vaccine, but he noted that this would not affect him and that he would not fret, as the Bible instructed, because the vaccine was not the solution.[38] In a sermon on 9 May 2021, Bishop David Oyedepo a Nigerian pastor, claimed that the Covid-19 vaccine in circulation is "a deadly thing" and that the Nigerian government must approach him for a long-lasting solution to the Covid-19 pandemic. The pastor also condemned vaccinators for going to churches to get people vaccinated, describing this as an insult to the church.[39]

To treat Covid-19 infections, there were a number of medications recommended by scientists for the different categories of patients. These include ritonavir-boosted nirmatrelvir, sotrovimad, remdesivir, molnupiravir, dexamethasone and others.[40] In some faith-based messages, miraculous faith curing of Covid-19 was advocated as a better alternative to Covid-19 biomedical treatments. In Ghana, a Pentecostal pastor launched and sold "Coronavirus Oil", telling a packed church that it was effective against Covid-19.[41] On 28 June 2021, a South African news and information website popularly known as IOL, reported that a Ghanaian preacher, Archbishop Nicholas Duncan-Williams, had cursed the Delta Covid-19 variant that was then gripping the African continent with the curse of Adonai, and he said prayers to insulate the organs of the people in Africa by the blood of Jesus such that the variant

---

35 Ng'ang'a G. 2020. "President Magufuli says coronavirus cannot survive in churches", *The Standard*, n.d.

36 Kendo O. 2020. "Magufuli queries Tanzania coronavirus kits after goat test", *The Standard*, 5 May.

37 Oduor M. 2021 "President Magufuli warns Tanzanians against Covid-19 vaccines", *Africa News*, 27 January.

38 Morgan-Lindo S. 2021 "Jamaican Santa refuses to take Covid-19 vaccine", *The Star*, 3 December.

39 Inyang I. 2021. "Covid-19 vaccine is a 'deadly thing' – Oyedepo", *Daily Post*, 10 May.

40 US Centers for Disease Control and Prevention (CDC). 2022. "Covid-19 Treatments and Medications", CDC.gov, 19 October.

41 African News Agency (ANA). 2020. "Ghanaian pastor sells 'holy oil', claiming it protects against coronavirus", *The South African*, 7 February.

would have no impact on them.[42] Another African pastor, Nyame Somafo Yaw, the leader, founder and head pastor of Asomdwoe Ntonton Som Ministry claimed to be in possession of the ability to cure the infection within a twinkle of an eye. He reported that when he laid his hands on anyone infected with coronavirus, all their lost energy, blood, water and breath returned to normalcy. According to Nyame Somafo Yaw, coronavirus is not an earthly disease and it cannot be cured with medicine or herbal concoctions but through words.[43]

This sort of conflict between faith-based and science-based messages regarding pandemics has significant implications for public health management in Africa. It perpetuates stigma towards specific categories of people affected by the pandemics.[44] It results in misguided epidemiological understandings about the pandemics, which undermine efforts at mitigation.[45] The conflict also negatively affects the acceptability and uptake of prevention and treatment strategies that can aid in overcoming the pandemic. Given this, there is a dire need to create harmony between faith-based and science-based messages on public health for more effective and efficient management of public health pandemics in Africa, as well as to affirm the mutual relationship between faith and science as "tools" that must work inclusively for public health management.

HARMONISING FAITH-BASED AND SCIENCE-BASED MESSAGES ON PUBLIC HEALTH IN AFRICA: THREE STRATEGIES

From the interviews, three major themes emerged as strategies through which the conflict between faith-based and science-based messages on public health in Africa can be solved: (1) holding dialogues on the relationship between faith and science, (2) providing spaces for cooperative work between scientists and religious leaders, and (3) transforming the training of public health scientists and theologians. Each of these approaches is discussed below.

Strategy 1: Holding dialogues on the relationship between faith and science

In this strategy, leaders in public health institutions, faith communities, civil society organisations and academic institutions, as well as individuals interested the subject, can organise informative dialogues on the role of faith and science in public health management through workshops, conferences, public lectures and seminars.

---

42 Chad W. 2021. "Ghanaian preacher 'curses' Covid-19 Delta variant", *Independent Online* (IOL), 28 June.

43 Qwame B. 2020. "Nyame Somafo Yaw brags about having the ability to cure all diseases", *Ghana Page*, June 12.

44 Pingel ES and Bauermeister JA. 2018. "'Church hurt can be the worst hurt': Community stakeholder perceptions of the role of Black churches in HIV prevention among young Black gay and bisexual men", *Culture, Health & Sexuality* 20(2):218-231.

45 Speakman, "Comparing the Impact of Religious Discourse on HIV/AIDS in Islam and Christianity in Africa".

John argued that these dialogues "should aim at helping people understand and agree that: God is one and that God is the power behind both science and religion". In his view, people coming to dialogue from both faith-based and science-based perspectives should have the "common goal" to "improve the quality of life for everyone". At the same time, John noted that "differences must be recognised and respected but in a manner that affirms life and people's wellbeing". Mark supported the idea that "dialogues can help people to understand that both science and faith play significant roles in public health management and should be used tools to that supplement each other." He also observed, "Science does not have all the answers required to solve public health questions just as the case is for faith" and that Researchers in each of these fields are in a continuous search for understanding."

Indeed, the dialogue between faith and science should focus on finding ways and means by which the members involved might learn from each other. It is important to acknowledge that neither science nor faith can claim to give a total account of reality. Faith does not provide answers to every question that exists about the world and neither does science. However, when taken together, faith and science can offer a stereoscopic view of reality that cannot be obtained when reality is viewed from only one perspective. In addition to offering opportunities to people of faith and scientists to appreciate the distinct strengths, limitations and identities of the other's field, dialogues on faith and science also have the potential to facilitate a deeper understanding of things than that which can be offered by either faith or science on its own.[46] Religion scholar Whitney Bauman argues that when both science and religion "are recognised as valid interpretations of reality and are seen as being embedded in a specific context, the ends of the dialogue are made explicit and religion and science become instruments toward creative solutions to a given problem in a given context."[47]

Mary proposed that "dialogues on the role of both faith and science in addressing pandemics should aim at transforming people's perspectives on the overall relationship between the two fields: faith and science." She argues, persuasively, that dialogues can transform people's minds and perspectives, but for this to be achieved, the dialogues must be organised and facilitated in a way that ensures honesty and adequate time for the participants to share their feelings and listen to one another with due respected. Commenting on who should participate in the dialogues, Mary proposed that the dialogues should be organised and held at different levels of social organisation and for different categories of people. "Dialogues at school level can target primary school pupils, secondary school students, and university students", she said. "We can also have the dialogues happen between religious leaders, public health scientists and politicians", she continued. This idea of involving politicians in dialogues aimed at addressing the

---

[46] Byrne PH. 2005. *The Dialogue Between Science and Religion: What We Have Learned From One Another*. Scranton, PA: University of Scranton Press.

[47] Bauman W. 2004. "Contextual Methodology in the Science and Religion Dialogue (A Talking Paper)". Online at: https://www.metanexus.net/archive/conference2004/pdf/bauman.pdf

conflict between faith and science in public health management is very strategic. Politicians not only influence the formulation and implementation of policies that affect how different health programmes are run, but they also influence public opinion, given that they command a great level of audience in their spheres of influence.

Peter argued, "When the public health scientists and religious leaders meet to deliberate on the public health challenges a formulate public health messages and discuss other important subjects, the scientists should take time to make the religious leaders understand their scientific speculations on the public health threat being addressed. As they do this, they should be careful to also listen to the religious leaders and to respect and value their opinions." Peter's argument is similar to that made by American astronomer Jennifer Wiseman at a recent online symposium on science, religion and ethics hosted by the American Association for the Advancement of Science.[48] Wiseman noted that the dialogues between faith and science should be "two-way", in the sense that both the faith communities and scientists benefit from engaging with each other. For example, when scientists and religious leaders meet for dialogue, the scientists need to take this as an opportunity to learn how their work impacts various aspects of people's lives. Similarly, the religious leaders can learn how scientific knowledge and discoveries "can improve their ministries."[49]

Strategy 2: Promoting collaborative work between scientists and religious leaders

At the onset of a public health threat, public health entities, governments and civil society organisations should create platforms where public health scientists and popular religious leaders can meet, deliberate over challenges, and decide on the messages to disseminate. Peter noted that "in the face of a pandemic, public health scientists and religious leaders need to convene and agree on the nature of messages to formulate and disseminate." According to Mary, "Public health scientists and theologians should be together when making official communications on public health issues."

This strategy can build on the fact that both faith and science offer powerful avenues of communication on matters that are of interest to human beings.[50] History has recorded scenarios where religious leaders and scientists have come together to agree on how to address certain changes and to come up with joint actions to take moving forward. One such scenario occurred in 1991, when "a group of eminent scientists and religious leaders" met in New York to deliberate on

---

[48] Wiseman J. Remarks to American Association for the Advancement of Science online symposium "Forward Together: Where Science, Ethics, and Religion Intersect in a Changing World", AAAS.org, 15 June 2021.

[49] Roewe B. 2021. "Dialogue demonstrates connections across faith and science", *National Catholic Reporter*, 23 June.

[50] Barnosky AD et al. 2016. "Chapter 9. Establishing Common Ground: Finding Better Ways to Communicate About Climate Disruption", *Collabra* 2(1):23.

ecological concerns. The meeting resulted into religious leaders signing a statement of affirmation that argued that people of faith should prioritise the cause of environmental integrity and justice.[51] Similarly, in 2021, global religious leaders and scientists worked together developed to join a statement, titled "Faith and Science: An Appeal for COP26", calling upon the international community to enhance their action against the climate crisis ahead of COP26.[52] Such initiatives go a long way in convincing people that the fields of faith and science complement one another, and this has the potential to changing people's perspectives on the relationship between the two fields. Therefore, individuals and organisations working towards ensuring that faith and science are partners in Africa's public health managements should be very intentional in ensuring that faith leaders and scientists in Africa can take joint actions towards addressing pandemics.

Strategy 3: Transforming the training of public health scientists and theologians

There is also need to ensure that theological institutions, medical schools and public health institutions train and produce professionals who can appreciate the role of both science and faith in promoting people's health and well-being. Mary emphasised that "many theological institutions in Africa need to review their curricular and integrate it into modules on HIV/AIDS and Covid-19." Peter advised, "Theology lecturers should invite scientists who are also practicing people of faith to share their knowledge and at times deliver lectures on those theological topics that bear a scientific view." He mentioned topics such as gender and sexuality, counselling and psychology, and environmental issues. John advised that medical and public health schools should incorporate programmes on the spirituality of health matters. He argued, "Public health specialists who graduate with a lot of scientific knowledge but blind to the religiosity of the African continent and how it interfaces with public health issues are a big challenge to public health messaging in the continent." Mark added, "Public health specialists who graduate with a lot of scientific knowledge but blind to the religiosity of the African continent and how it interfaces with public health issues are a big challenge to public health messaging in the continent."

Education has always been perceived as a means through which behaviour can be shaped.[53] Both theological education aiming at equipping religious leaders for their ministry and the education that equips public health scientists for work are key processes that contribute to the conflict between faith-based and science-based messages on public health. It is, therefore, important to ensure that these processes are transformed in such a manner that they can facilitate the process of

---

51 "Religious Leaders Join Scientists in Ecological Concerns", *Christianity Today*, 19 August 1991.
52 United Nations Climate Change. 2021. "World Religious Leaders and Scientists Make pre-COP26 Appeal", *UNFCC.int*, 5 October.
53 Bello TT. 2019. "Theological Education as a Tool for Reformation of Church and Society", *International Journal of Research-Granthaalayah* 7(3):346-353.

addressing this conflict. Theological education needs to ensure that the agency of the Church can complement the effort of scientists and government in solving societal challenges.[54] This is an observation that seems to have been realised by the Circle of Concerned African Women Theologians (CCAWT) at the beginning of the twenty-first century, when they began taking practical actions towards making theological education in Africa sensitive to the realities of the HIV/AIDS pandemic. CCAWT's efforts towards achieving this have included engaging in research on HIV/AIDS, gender and religion to contribute to the production of knowledge that could facilitate the integration of course modules on HIV/AIDS in theological curricula. They have laboured to provide reflections "on the role played by sacred texts, faith communities, and African culture in both the spread and prevention of HIV as it affects African women" and to demonstrate how the different disciplines of theology, including biblical theology, systematic theology, practical theology and others, could be taught in a manner that empowers theology students and religious leaders to engage relevantly with and respond to HIV/AIDS.[55] Nevertheless, there was a conflict between faith-based and science-based messages on Covid-19 even after the integration of HIV/AIDS modules into theological curriculum, which equipped theologians to engage with and relevantly respond to the HIV/AIDS pandemic. This is indicative of the fact that the earlier efforts to integrate HIV/AIDS in theological education were not adequate enough to ensure that theologians could apply similar skills and competences acquired from modules on HIV/AIDS to address similar pandemics such as Covid-19.

Does this mean that every time a new pandemic emerges we need to review the theological curriculum, so as to equip religious leaders with skills to address the pandemic? This may seem impossible, given that the process of reviewing curricula is expensive and time-intensive. In agreement with Peter, however, I think that the basics of public health management, disaster preparedness and response and the role of science in God's revelation should be integrated into all aspects of theological education. This means that instead of incorporating module on only HIV/AIDS and Covid-19 in theological curricula, the whole concept of public health management should incorporate it in manner that enables religious leaders respond to any pandemic that they encounter in ways that complement the efforts of scientists and other stakeholders, including the government.

We do not need to review and change our curriculum every time a new pandemic emerges, but we can ensure that its framework is flexible and also shift the approaches of theological education from a rigid curriculum to one that engages the real challenges faced by people in the contemporary world. As Mary argued, "In most cases, the religious leaders who pass on faith-based messages that conflict with science-based messages on pandemics are religious leaders that run churches

---

54 Ottaway AKC. 2011. *Education and Society: An Introduction to Sociology of Education*. London: Routledge and Kegan Paul.

55 Nadar S and Apawo IP. 2013 "HIV Research, Gender and Religion Studies", in Apawo IP and Werner D (ed). *Handbook of Theological Education in Africa*. Oxford: Regnum, 632-638.

and faith communities yet they have never received any formal theological education." She noted that some of them "even lack the minimum requirements to obtain admission into theological institutions for certificate, diploma or degree programmes". Peter advised that theological institutions should initiate educational programmes like theological education by extension, through which such people can be equipped with theological knowledge that enables them to supplement the work of other theologians and scientists in addressing pandemics.

As John and Mark suggested, it is also important that the training of Africa's public health scientists is sensitive to the spiritual realities of the African people. Mary emphasised that for the scientists and doctors to value the opinions of religious leaders on pandemics, they need to be educated on the spirituality of diseases, healing, and health from the different religious worldviews in Africa. There are a number of studies that have been conducted in the past that had affirmed that spirituality is positively associated with quality of life.[56] Additionally, thousands of studies have shown that the biological model alone is not enough for treating people, but public health scientists are usually not trained to address spiritual beliefs around diseases and pandemics.[57] Several instruments have been developed to aid the incorporation of spirituality in various aspects of public health management, such as in clinical practice. Some of these instruments include tools used to obtain the spiritual history of patients, so as to assess their spiritual needs and resources.[58] The use of these tools faces many barriers, however, one of them being the lack of training knowledge among clinicians and the "fear that it's wrong to ask doctor spiritual questions".[59] These barriers can be broken when modules on the spirituality of infections and how faith influences people's health and well-being are integrated into the curricula of the medical and public health schools.

CONCLUSION

Public health messaging is a crucial part of responding to public health pandemics. In the face HIV/AIDS and Covid-19, both faith and science serve as the main sources of information and messages that are consumed by people in Africa and influence their responses to the pandemics. However, the conflict between faith-based and science-based messages on these pandemics poses a serious challenge to their management. The conflict perpetuates stigma towards people affected by the pandemics, results in misguided epidemiological understandings about the pandemics and also negatively affects the acceptability and uptake of prevention

---

56 Miller WR, Thoresen CE. 2003. "Spirituality, religion, and health: An emerging research field", *The American Psychologist* 58(1):24-35.

57 Mariotti L et al. 2011. "Spirituality and medicine: views and opinions of teachers in a Brazilian medical school", *Medical Teacher* 33(4):339-340.

58 Anandarajah G and Hight E. 2001. "Spirituality and medical practice: using the HOPE questions as a practical tool for spiritual assessment", *American Family Physician* 63(1):81-92.

59 Ellis MR, Vinson DC and Ewigman B. 1999. "Addressing spiritual concerns of patients: family physicians' attitudes and practices", *The Journal of Family Practice* 48(2):105-109.

and treatment strategies that can aid in overcoming the pandemic. This presents a dire need to create harmony between faith-based and science-based messages on public health pandemics for the good of people's health and well-being in Africa. The interviews conducted for the present study with two African theologians and two African public health scientists engaged in EHAIA's programmes on HIV and Covid-19 yielded three main strategies through which this need can be addressed. These include holding dialogues on the relationship between faith and science, providing spaces for cooperative work between scientists and religious leaders and transforming the training of public health scientists and theologians. It will be particularly valuable if these insights are included in curricula to train African religious and public health professionals, especially in the context of pandemics.

12 THE ROLE OF LEGAL AND RELIGIOUS RESPONSES IN DEBUNKING COVID-19 CONSPIRACY THEORIES IN AFRICA

Flora Alohan Onomrerhinor[1]

INTRODUCTION

Nigeria was among the first countries in sub-Saharan Africa to identify Covid-19 cases.[2] The first index case was reported on 27 February 2020.[3] In an attempt to contain the spread and transmission of the virus to other parts of the country that were deemed safe at the time, the Federal Government issued stay-at-home orders on 30 March 2020. There was a total lockdown during much of the pandemic that was limited to some states in the beginning but eventually extended to others.[4] The lockdown led to mass unemployment and other inconveniences that incurred social criticism. All social activities were prohibited. As of 21 November 2022, Nigeria had registered 266 283 cases across all the states of the Federation, with 259 643 Covid patients recovered and discharged and 3 155 confirmed dead.[5]

Most states not only adopted the Federal Government's lockdown measures, but also added to it based on their peculiar conditions.[6] While the majority agreed with the need to maintain safety measures, some who believed in conspiracy theories challenged their necessity and imposition. The situation did not improve when vaccinations for the virus began in December 2020, as some believed the vaccine was a conspiracy to depopulate the globe.[7] In fact, both globally and in Nigeria, the Covid-19 pandemic saw a number of conspiracy theories and misconceptions, which significantly influenced the survival mechanisms that people adopted to cope with the pandemic.

According to the Secretary-General of the United Nations António Guterres, a major challenge presented by the pandemic was the related pandemic of misinformation.

---

1 LLB, LLM, PhD, BL, Lecturer, Department of Jurisprudence and International Law, Faculty of Law, University of Benin, Benin City, Nigeria.
2 Siwatu GO et al. 2021. "Impact of Covid-19 on Nigerian households: 10th Round Results (English)", *WorldBank.org* Group, 12 April.
3 Nigeria Centre for Disease Control. 2020. "First Case of Corona Virus Confirmed in Nigeria", *NCDC*, 28 February.
4 UNDP Nigeria. 2020. "The Covid-19 Pandemic in Nigeria-Potential Impact of Lockdown Policies on Poverty and Well Being, Brief 3: *UNDP*, 21.
5 Nigeria Centre for Disease Control. 2022. "Covid-19 Nigeria", NCDC, 21 November.
6 Okoye AC and Obulor I. 2021. "Religious organizations and fight against the spread of Covid-19 in Nigeria", *Journal of Sustainable Development in Africa* 23(1):70.
7 Okoye and Obulor, "Religious organizations and fight against the spread of Covid-19 in Nigeria", 769.

Misinformation and belief in conspiracy theories constituted obstacles to solutions geared towards the prevention and eradication of the disease. Aceme Nyika and fellow researchers in South Africa, in a key article on the topic, have chronicled well some of the conspiracy theories that were popular in Africa.[8] Some of these theories also gained a foothold in Nigeria. For example, the religious conspiracy theory that associated the Covid-19 pandemic with the apocalyptic plague and the Mark of the Beast (666) in the Book of Revelations in the Bible led to antagonism towards the Covid-19 vaccine by some Christian communities in Nigeria. Commenting on the dangers of conspiracy theories, the Director-General of the World Health Organization (WHO) Tedros Adhanom Ghebreyesus stated: "We're not just fighting an epidemic; we're fighting an infodemic. Fake news spreads faster and more easily than this virus and is just as dangerous."[9] In light of these challenges presented by conspiracy theories, this chapter discusses the nature of the conspiracy theories and measures adopted to debunk them, with particular attention to the role of legal and religious actors. Building on the work of Nyika and colleagues, as well as others who have chronicled the rise of Covid-19 conspiracies in Africa, this chapter analyses those conspiracy theories that were prevalent in Nigeria and which had religious origins, amplifications and implications. In many ways, Nigeria was a microcosm of the spread of Covid-19 conspiracies in Africa, but in ways that intersected uniquely with its religious culture and proved difficult for the law to contain.

COVID-19 CONSPIRACY THEORIES

Conspiracy theories are founded upon disinformation or propaganda, which erodes public trust and confidence.[10] They tend to flourish in times of crisis and uncertainty, and the pandemic provided a perfect opportunity for this.[11] Misinformation about Covid-19, and the resultant anxiety and depression, created vulnerabilities that predisposed people to belief in conspiracy theories.[12] Conspiracy theories about the

---

8   Nyika A et al. 2021. "Covid-19 Pandemic: Questioning Conspiracy Theories, Beliefs or Claims that Have Potential Negative Impact on Public Health Interventions and Proposal for Integrated Communication and Information Dissemination Strategies (ICIDS)", *Journal of Development and Communication Studies* 8(10): January-June", 3. See also Sherwin BD. 2021. "Anatomy of a Conspiracy Theory: Law, Politics, and Science Denialism in the Era of Covid-19", *Texas A & M Law Review* 8.

9   World Health Organization (WHO), "Coronavirus disease 2019 (Covid-19) Situation Report – 86", Geneva: WHO, 2020:1; Imhoff R and Lamberty P. 2020. "A Bioweapon or a Hoax? The Link between Distinct Conspiracy Beliefs about the Coronavirus Disease (Covid-19) Outbreak and Pandemic Behavior", *Social Psychological and Personality Science* 11(8):1110-1118.

10 WHO, "Coronavirus disease 2019 (Covid-19) Situation Report – 86".

11 Peitz L et al. 2021. "Covid-19 conspiracy theories and compliance with governmental restrictions: The mediating roles of anger, anxiety, and hope", *Journal of Pacific Rim Psychology* 15:1-13.

12 De Coninck D. 2021. "Beliefs in Conspiracy Theories and Misinformation About Covid-19: Comparative Perspectives on the Role of Anxiety, Depression and Exposure to and Trust in Information Sources", *Frontiers in Psychology* 12:1-13.

pandemic were often made up of rumours of secret cures and other pieces of forbidden knowledge that, when shared, provided feelings of certainty and control amidst the crisis.[13] These rumours and wildly unbelievable claims were spread by everyday people who were often overwhelmed by feelings of confusion and helplessness.[14] In some cases, high-level government officials also promoted conspiracy theories to hide failures or seek political benefits.[15]

The danger of belief in conspiracy theories is that they have serious consequences for how the public responds to Covid-19.[16] In particular, they can undermine public health instructions. This is a cause for concern, since adherence to government policies and public health advice is considered crucial in efforts to control the spread of Covid-19.[17] A growing body of research has identified links between conspiracy beliefs and lower compliance with governmental restrictions, such as the lockdown rules.[18] Research has also shown that most people who believed in conspiracy theories tended to have a lesser adherence to public health recommendations, such as the wearing of face masks, social distancing, hand washing, and the need to get vaccinated.[19] Conspiracy theories in the Covid-19 pandemic accounted for the decrease in trust in the government, health authorities and known science.[20]

A number of theories have been advanced to explain the Covid-19 pandemic and vaccines. While some were misinformation arising from information scarcity and overreliance on social media, others were disinformation and outright propaganda.

---

13 Peitz, "Covid-19 Conspiracy Theories and Compliance", 1.

14 For example, Franks, Bangerter and Bauer have stated that conspiracy theories allow laypersons to interpret such events by relating them to common sense in a bid to defusing some of the anxiety that those events generate. See Franks B, Bangerter A and Bauer MW. 2013. "Conspiracy Theories as Quasi-Religious Mentality: An Integrated Account from Cognitive Science, Social Representations Theory and Frame Theory", *Frontiers in Psychology* 4:1-15.

15 Peitz, "Covid-19 Conspiracy Theories and Compliance", 1.

16 Peitz, "Covid-19 Conspiracy Theories and Compliance", 2.

17 Peitz, "Covid-19 Conspiracy Theories and Compliance", 2.

18 See Marinthe G, Brown G, Delouvée S and Jolley D. 2020. "Looking Out for Myself: Exploring the Relationship between Conspiracy Mentality, Perceived Personal Risk, and COVID-19 Prevention Measures", *British Journal of Health Psychology* 25(4):957-980; Oleksy T, Wnuk A, Maison D and Łyś A. 2021. "Content matters: Different Predictors and Social Consequences of General and Government-related Conspiracy Theories on Covid-19", *Personality and Individual Differences* 1:1-15.

19 Allington D et al. 2021. "Health-Protective Behaviour, Social Media Usage and Conspiracy Belief during the Covid-19 Public Health Emergency", *Psychological Medicine* 51(10): 1763-1769; Biddlestone M, Green R and Douglas KM. 2020. "Cultural Orientation, Power, Belief in Conspiracy Theories, and Intentions to Reduce the Spread of Covid-19", *British Journal of Social Psychology* 59(3):663-673, and Bierwiaczonek K, Kunst JR and Pich O. "Belief in Covid-19 Conspiracy Theories Reduces Social Distancing Over Time", *Applied Psychology: Health and Well-Being* 12(4):1270-1285.

20 Plohl N and Musil B. 2021. "Modeling Compliance with Covid-19 Prevention Guidelines: The Critical Role of Trust in Science", *Psychology Health and Medicine* 26(1):1-12.

Social media platforms, such as WhatsApp, Facebook, Twitter and YouTube, were used to spread this information.[21] Sometimes, however, conspiracy theories were also covered by mainstream news.[22] Many of the common Covid-19 conspiracy theories traded in misinformation, beliefs and claims that were based in religion in some way and had the effect of reducing compliance with legal regulations and government recommendations.

Biblical Mark of the Beast conspiracy [23]

As noted by Nyika and fellow researchers, one conspiracy theory that arose associated the Covid-19 pandemic with the mark of the beast mentioned in the last book of the Bible.[24] This was the Book of Revelation, which contains the visions of the Apostle John on the Island of Patmos.[25] According to the Bible, in the thirteenth chapter of the book of Revelation, John saw two beasts. The first beast was like a leopard and the second beast had two horns like a lamb.[26] This second beast forced people from diverse backgrounds around the world to receive a mark on their right hand or on their forehead, without which no one could buy or sell. The number 666 was stated as representing the beast.[27] Proponents of this theory believed that the Covid-19 pandemic was the effect of this Mark of the Beast. The theory claimed that the mark of the beast, the number 666, would be introduced into people through injections, disguised as either treatment for the illness or vaccination to prevent it.[28]

For adherents of the Christian faith with little understanding of the Book of Revelation, it was not surprising that the uncertainty and vulnerability occasioned by the pandemic led to rationalising implausible ideas, such as the above. Nyika and fellow researchers have pointed out a number of reasons why this theory is implausible. For one thing, the supposed Mark of the Beast and the number 666 had been linked with modern technology in general, rather than to any particular disease or event

---

21 Allington et al, "Health-Protective Behavior", 1763.
22 Spring M. 2020. "The Casualties of This Year's Viral Conspiracy Theories", *BBC News*, 26 December.
23 This theory and others such as the Covid-19 vaccine conspiracies, radiation from 5G transmission, staged health crisis propagated by the media, a disease for them, not us, traditional herbs or alternative traditional medicines cure Covid-19, beliefs in supernatural powers and Covid-19 prophesies which are presented in the succeeding subheads, have been discussed in remarkable detail by Nyika et al in "Covid-19 Pandemic: Questioning Conspiracy Theories". As indicated earlier, they are presented here to show the perception of these theories or misinformation in the Nigerian society.
24 Nyika et al, "Covid-19 Pandemic: Questioning Conspiracy Theories", 5.
25 Watchtower Bible and Tract Society. 1984. *Revelation – Its Grand Climax at Hand*. Brooklyn: Watchtower Society, New York, 303.
26 Group Bible Study. n.d. "15, The Mark of the Beast". Online at: https://www.groupbiblestudy.com/engrevelation/15.-the-mark-of-the-beast? [Accessed 21 November 2022].
27 Group Bible Study, "15 The Mark of the Beast".
28 Nyika et al, "Covid-19 Pandemic: Questioning Conspiracy Theories", 3.

that existed before the pandemic.[29] For another, the conspiracy did not show why people who did not receive the vaccine died of the virus infection. It also did not give any answers to the valid questions about Covid-19 that baffled many.[30]

Covid-19 vaccine conspiracies

Another conspiracy theory floating in connection with the Covid-19 vaccine concerned the alleged implantation of micro-chip tracking devices. This theory claimed that a tracking chip would be inserted into people's bodies simultaneously with and through a vaccine without people's knowledge or consent for the purpose of tracking them.[31] It further claimed that the chip, which is in the form of a nano-tattoo, would be implanted in people's skin upon vaccination, supposedly for precision medicine purposes, but with the real objective being tracking and surveillance.[32] Some in Nigeria who believed in this theory claimed that Dr Anthony Fauci in the United States and global elites, such as Bill Gates and George Soros, had planned the Covid-19 pandemic so that they could accomplish a sinister plot of depopulation under the guise of vaccination.[33]

From the outset of the Covid-19 pandemic in Nigeria, local conspiracy theories connected Bill Gates to the pandemic. This did not change when it was time for vaccination. In fact, the Coalition for United People's Party (CUPP) stated that Bill Gates bribed the Nigerian government with the sum of ten million dollars to pass a law to test vaccines on children. This false claim was given credence by the fact that there is a high level of mistrust for authorities in Nigeria.[34] As a result of the yawning gap in trust between Nigerians and the government, many members of the public saw Covid-19 as another conspiracy by the ruling elite to receive foreign financial aid and embezzle public funds.[35]

---

29 Nyika et al, "Covid-19 Pandemic: Questioning Conspiracy Theories", 3. Also see Michael MG. 2010. "Demystifying the Number of the Beast in the Book of Revelation: Examples of Ancient Cryptology and the Interpretation of the '666' Conundrum", *International Symposium on Technology and Society* 1:23-41.

30 Nyika et al, "Covid-19 Pandemic", 5.

31 Burnard M and Richards A. 2020. "Covid-19 and 5G: Biggest cover-up in history? True or False?", *INcontext International*, 21 May.

32 Burnard and Richards, "Covid-19 and 5G: Biggest cover-up in history? True or False?". See also Nyika et al, "Covid-19 Pandemic", 5.

33 Aladekomo A. 2021. "Covid-19, A New World Order, Vaccine Safety, Effectiveness and Our Human Rights", Social Science Research Network (SSRN), 27 March.

34 Kalu N, Oduadu-Erameh E and Thomas E. 2021. "Attacking Gates, Attacking Vaccines: How Conflict, Religion and Conspiracy Theories Drive Covid-19 Misinformation in Nigeria", *The Guardian*, 23 September. See also Donnelly E and Hassan I. 2021. "Nigeria's Political Leaders Need to Win Trust to Tackle COVID-19", *Chatham House*, 23 April. See also Archibong B and Annan F. 2021. "What do Pfizer's 1996 drug trials in Nigeria teach us about vaccine hesitancy?", *Africa in Focus* (blog), 3 December, Brookings Institution.

35 Olatunji OS, Ayandele O, Ashirudeen D and Olaniru OS. "'Infodemic' in a pandemic: Covid-19 conspiracy theories in an African country", *Social Health and Behaviour* 3(4):153.

In addition, Pfizer, one of the leading companies that manufactured the Covid-19 vaccine, had earlier undertaken a drug trial on Nigerian children in 1996 that left 11 children dead and dozen others disabled.[36] Although Pfizer paid compensation to the families, it was widely rumoured that it paid bribes to the authorities to avoid criminal charges.[37] The company, however, insisted that the cases were resolved by mutual agreement and that its conduct was proper at all times. Viewed from this perspective, it was therefore not surprising that many Nigerians bought the idea that a foreign billionaire and foreign drug companies were trying to harm the Nigerian population with the permission of their government.[38] In fact, the situation was so bad that *The Guardian* reported that were Bill Gates to have visited Nigeria at the time, he might have received a less than favourable welcome. Indeed, some Nigerian commentators described Gates as being in league with Satan himself.[39]

The belief that governmental authorities conspired with foreigners to use their citizens for some kind of biological experimentation was not limited to Nigeria. In fact, most members of the African society held this view at one time or the other during the pandemic,[40] so much so that John Magufuli, the president of Tanzania, remarked that he would not allow the citizens of his country to be used as guinea pigs.[41] Such remarks from a well-known and respected political figure accounted for vaccine hesitancy in these parts.

Radiation from 5G transmission

Research has shown that one common theory associated the pandemic with radiation from the 5G transmission.[42] According to Nyika and colleagues, this theory, claimed that radiation emitted by 5G transmitters caused the pandemic.[43] In Nigeria, some believed that radiation emitted by 5G transmitters caused the pandemic or that the pandemic was a hoax perpetrated by media and technology companies seeking

---

36 Wise J. 2001. "Pfizer accused of testing new drug without ethical approval", *British Medical Journal* 322(7280):194.

37 Stephens J. 2000. "Where Profits and Lives Hang in Balance", *Washington Post*, 17 December; "Pfizer: Nigeria drug trial victims get compensation", *BBC*, 11 August.

38 Lenzer J. 2006. "Secret report surfaces showing that Pfizer was at fault in Nigerian drug tests", *British Medical Journal* 332(7552):1233. Also see Kovac C. "Nigerians to sue US drug company over meningitis treatment", *British Medical Journal* 323(7313):592 and Archibong and Annan, "What do Pfizer's 1996 drug trials in Nigeria teach us about vaccine hesitancy?"

39 Kenechi S. 2020. "Chris Okotie says Bill Gates leading agenda to destabilise the world with Covid-19", *The Cable*, 13 July.

40 In South Africa, for instance, there was a protest at the University of the Witwatersrand in Johannesburg. The reason for the protest was that the protesters did not want Africans to be used as guinea pigs. See "'We are not Guinea Pigs' say South African Anti-Vaccine Protesters", *Reuters*, 1 July 2020.

41 "Coronavirus in Tanzania: The Country that's Rejecting the Vaccine", *BBC News*, 6 February 2021.

42 Nyika et al, "Covid-19 Pandemic", 4.

43 Nyika et al, "Covid-19 Pandemic", 4.

to install a new 5G network facility that would harm the world.[44] Pastor Chris Oyakhilome, a well-known Pentecostal pastor in Nigeria and the general overseer of the Believers Love World Ministries (also known as Christ Embassy), a Nigerian church with branches in South Africa, was among those who believed in this conspiracy theory. Oyakhilome's religious media empire enabled this charismatic figure to speak to global audiences.[45] He stated that the virus attack was a ploy by the technological giants to divert human attention to facilitate the setting up of their 5G infrastructure around the world.[46] The spread of this conspiracy theory that associated Covid-19 pandemic with the development and launching of 5G networks compelled the Office of Communication (OFCOM), the British broadcast regulator, to sanction and prevent Pastor Chris Oyakhilome's Love World Television from airing in the British air space in May 2020.[47] The belief in this conspiracy theory was widespread and some people took to social media to propagate it.[48] Interestingly, Pastor Chris Oyakhilome later abandoned this claim and stated that he was only opposed to the 5G initiative because of its perceived health risks and the silence of authorised regulators to address its advantages and disadvantages.[49]

Staged health crisis propagated by the media

Nyika and fellow researchers also revealed that another conspiracy theory that was widely circulated in Africa was the claim that the devastating effects of Covid-19 and the critical shortages of required equipment and infrastructure shown by the media were a stage-managed programme aimed at creating fear and chaos for sinister purposes.[50] According to social and legal psychologists Roland Imhoff and Pia Lamberty, it was unclear what these sinister purposes were, but some alluded to the ensuing fear being used to hurt national economies or pass unpopular or restrictive laws.[51] Inobemhe et al indicated that this was also the case in Nigeria.[52] The common believe in Nigeria was that the Covid-19 pandemic was exaggerated.

---

[44] Adekanye M. 2020. "Nigerians react to the claim that 5g network causes coronavirus", *The Guardian*, 4 April.

[45] Asamoah-Gyadu JK. 2021."Pentecostalism and Coronavirus: Reframing the Message of Health-and-Wealth in a Pandemic Era", *Spiritus* 6(1):162.

[46] Aworinde T. 2020. "5G controversy: Oyakhilome makes U-turn, cites health risks", *Punch*, 12 April.

[47] Okoye and Obulor, "Religious organizations and fight against the spread of Covid-19 in Nigeria", 68.

[48] Inobemhe K, Santas T and Udeh TS. 2022. "Influence of Social Media on the Fight against Covid-19 in Nigeria", *Journal of Media and Information Warfare* 15(2):9; Ovenseri-Ogbomo GO et al. 2020. "Factors associated with the myth about 5g network during Covid-19 pandemic in Sub-Saharan Africa", *Journal of Global Health Reports* 4:2.

[49] Aworinde, "5G controversy: Oyakhilome makes U-turn, cites health risks".

[50] Nyika et al, "Covid-19 Pandemic", 12.

[51] Imhoff and Lamberty, "A Bioweapon or a Hoax?", 1112.

[52] Inobemhe, Santas and Udeh, "Influence of Social Media on the Fight Against Covid-19 in Nigeria", 9.

The general perception of the pandemic by people who held this belief was that the virus was not a real threat. They played down on the danger of Covid-19, calling it no worse than a flu, and suspected others to purposefully claim otherwise for their own advantage.[53]

In Nigeria, many claimed that the figures of cases of infections and deaths given by the Nigeria Centre for Disease Control was exaggerated.[54] In southeastern Nigeria, the governor of Abia State claimed that the state had been promised by God that Covid-19 won't get to it. A month later, he tested positive with the disease and was admitted into an isolation centre.[55] Similarly, the Kogi State government claimed was free from Covid-19 and accused the Nigeria Centre of Diseases Control (NCDC) of cooking up figures about the pandemic in Kogi State. In Kano State, the government refuted allegations that the deaths recorded during the pandemic were Covid-19 related,[56] and Yobe State, in Northeast Nigeria, declared zero cases of Covid-19 admission and discharged all patients without negative test results.[57] The high level of denial by political leaders at the state level about the disease likely promoted the belief in conspiracy theories. One version claimed that what was declared to be a Covid-19 pandemic was part of global economic competition and and geopolitical wars between leading countries, such as China and the United States of America.[58] Another version of the claim was that the purpose of the purported stage-managed pandemic was to weaken the global economy in order to enable the powers that be to take over critical sectors of the global economies when share prices became extremely low.[59]

A disease for them, not us

In some African countries, including Nigeria, the coronavirus was proclaimed to be a disease that affects people in the temperate regions and not the tropics. Some even claimed that the virus could not survive the African heat.[60] These claims were widely held in the early days of the pandemic, when it was winter in Europe, but they lost some of its credibility when millions of deaths were reported in hot

---

53 Imhoff and Lamberty, "A Bioweapon or a Hoax?", 1112.
54 Olatunji et al. "Infodemic in a pandemic", 153.
55 Omilana T. 2020. "Abia Governor Okezie Ikpeazu Tests Positive for Covid-19", *The Guardian*, 8 June.
56 Abdullahi M. 2020. "Study says Kano deaths linked to Covid-19, experts worry over community transmission", *HumAngle*, 5 May.
57 Saharareporters. 2020. "Yobe Discharges all COVID-19 Patients, Declares Zero Case Admission", *Sahara Reporters*, 1 July 2020.
58 Bahi R. 2021. "The geopolitics of Covid-19: US-China rivalry and the imminent Kindleberger trap", *Review of Economics and Political Science* 6(1):76-94.
59 Imhoff and Lamberty, "Covid-19 related Conspiracy Theories", 1112.
60 Raistrick N. "Debunking Africa's Covid-19 Conspiracies", *IWPR- Institute for War and Peace Reporting*, 12 August.

countries, such as Brazil and India. Still, some people held on to this claim.[61] For a long time, the Tanzanian government insisted that the country was free from Covid-19.[62] Even when it became obvious that the pandemic was real in Tanzania, its minister for health, Dr Dorothy Gwajima, stated at a press briefing that citizens should improve personal hygiene and use herbal steam and other natural remedies, not because the virus was in Tanzania, but because it was ravaging neighbouring countries.[63]

Beliefs or claims about who was susceptible to Covid-19 infection came in several versions, based on various differentiating characteristics that included geographical location, socio-economic class, race, religious belief and others. Religious beliefs also caused some people to have a sense of protection against the Covid-19 infections.[64] Some religious leaders prophesied to their willing congregations that Covid-19 could not infect them since they are carrying corrosive anointing in addition to being covered by the special blood of Jesus.[65] Goodheart Val Aloysius of Father's House International Church in Calabar asked the government to assemble all the people who had tested positive for Covid-19 in an isolation centre so that he could heal them. To demonstrate his seriousness, he called on the government to hang him if he failed to heal them.[66] Socio-economic class was the basis for some theories, with poor people perceiving Covid-19 infection as a disease for the rich and vice versa.[67]

OTHER COVID-19 MISINFORMATION AND DISINFORMATION

Disinformation refers to the deliberate transmission of false or inaccurate information from person to person with the intent to deceive, while misinformation refers to false or inaccurate information or communication which may not have been passed with intent to cause deception. Conspiracy theories, on the other hand, are a particular kind of false information that attribute the root causes of events or trends to shadowy networks or cabals carrying out secret plots to control, undermine or exploit the public, governments or institutions.[68] In addition to conspiracy theories, there were other examples of misinformation and outright disinformation

---

61 Ibrahim I. 2021. "Debunking the Claim that Heat Kills Covid-19 in Nigeria", *African Resilience Network*, 5 August.
62 "Coronavirus in Tanzania".
63 "Coronavirus in Tanzania".
64 Okoye and Obulor, "Religious organizations and fight against the spread of Covid-19 in Nigeria", 67.
65 Okoye and Obulor, "Religious organizations and fight against the spread of Covid-19 in Nigeria", 67.
66 Nwaka JC. 2020. "Between religious freedom and the public good: Reactions to religious restrictions to prevent the spread of Covid-19 in Nigeria", *Kujenga Amani* (blog), Social Science Resarch Center, 20 May.
67 Nyika et al, "Covid-19 Pandemic: Questioning Conspiracy Theories", 14.
68 Wonodi C et al. 2022. "Conspiracy theories and misinformation about Covid-19 in Nigeria: Implications for vaccine demand generation communications", *Vaccine* 40(13):2115.

or propaganda about the Covid-19 pandemic, which influenced the response of Africans in general, and Nigerians in particular, to the pandemic and its subsequent vaccines. Some of the beliefs, claims and prophecies commonly held in some African societies are discussed below.

Traditional herbs or alternative traditional medicines to prevent or cure

In countries like Nigeria, Tanzania, Uganda and Madagascar, there were claims that some herbs or alternative medicines could prevent or cure Covid-19. These claims were not based on transparent and conclusive evidence apart from the word of those making the claims.[69] On 20 April 2020, the president of Madagascar claimed that the herbal tea produced from the artemisia plant, called Covid Organics, could cure Covid-19.[70] He even avowed in a press conference that tests had been carried out and two people were cured by the treatment.[71] Some countries even planned on importing it,[72] even though the remedy had yet to be tested by internationally accepted standards,[73] that is to say, in properly designed research and clinical trials in accordance with the standards set by national regulatory authorities, health ministries or international organisations, such as the African Union and the WHO.[74] Perhaps, one reason the Covid Organics was so popular was because it included a blend of artemisia,[75] a plant with proven efficacy against malaria, and some of those infected with the virus manifested symptoms similar to malaria, such as high fever.[76]

The use of hydroxychloroquine for treating Covid-19 patients before conclusive clinical trials had been completed was another example of a claim of a coronavirus cure. The drug generally used for treatment of malaria or autoimmune disease was promoted for the treatment of Covid-19 patients by some,[77] even though no conclusive evidence of their benefit had been demonstrated.[78] In fact, earlier studies

---

69 Wonodi, "Conspiracy theories and misinformation about Covid-19 in Nigeria", 2115.
70 "Coronavirus: what is Madagascar's 'herbal remedy' Covid-Organics?", *Al Jazeera*, 5 May; "Madagascar President Launches coronavirus remedy", *France24*, 21 April 2020.
71 Baker A. 2020. "'Could it Work as a cure? Maybe!' A Herbal Remedy for Coronavirus Is a Hit in Africa, But Experts Have Doubts", *Times*, 22 May 2020.
72 Tih F. 2020. "Madagascar Leader Urges Use of Supposed Covid-19 Cure", *Anadolu Agency*, 22 May.
73 Tih, "Madagascar Leader Urges Use of Supposed Covid-19 Cure".
74 Nyika et al, "Covid-19 Pandemic: Questioning Conspiracy Theories", 9.
75 Baker, "Could it Work as a cure? Maybe!".
76 Baker, "Could it Work as a cure? Maybe!".
77 Pastick KA et al. 2020. "Hydroxychloroquine or Chloroquine for Treatment of SARS-CoV-2 (Covid-19)", *Open Forum Infectious Diseases* 7(4):130.
78 Wright C, Ross C and Mc Goldric N. 2020. "Are Hydroxychloroquine and Chloroquine Effective in the Treatment of SARS-COV-2 (Covid-19)?", *Evidence-Based Dentistry* 21(2): 64-65.

had raised concerns about serious life-threatening adverse effects that could outweigh any potential therapeutic benefits the drugs might have.[79]

Beliefs in supernatural powers

Some claims were based on belief in the supernatural. For instance, adherents of African Traditional Religions in Nigeria, who believe in and worship gods and deities, claimed that the pandemic was caused by evil supernatural powers that could be conquered by benevolent supernatural powers. Their leaders claimed to have positive supernatural powers that could set people free from the clutches of the evil powers believed to be responsible for the pandemic.[80] Also, Elijah Ayodele, a pastor of a Pentecostal church in Nigeria, claimed he was in possession of holy water and oil that could cure the disease.[81] Others, adherents of the Christian faith, claimed that the pandemic occurred because the evil of the world had become too overwhelming and the only way to avert the disaster was for people to repent of their sins and turn to God. Claims that holy ashes could protect believers from the Covid-19 pandemic were spread by some religious leaders in Nigeria and Zimbabwe.[82] The tenacity of belief in the supernatural in some African societies was evident in the fact that the beliefs continued even after the religious leaders who claimed to have the supernatural power to cure Covid-19 died from it.[83]

Covid-19 prophecies

Several prophets spread various prophecies about the pandemic. Prophet Emmanuel Makandiwa, a pastor in a Pentecostal church in Harare, Zimbabwe, prophesied that the pandemic was going to be miraculously wiped away by rain on 27 March 2020.[84] In the same way, the late Prophet T.B. Joshua of the Synagogue of the Nations Ministry in Nigeria also predicted that Covid-19 would disappear after heavy rainfall on the same day.[85] There were also claims that the Covid-19 pandemic was

---

79 Luca S and Mihaescu T. 2013. "History of BCCG Vaccine", *Amaltea Medical, Editura Magister* 8(1):53-67.
80 Nyika et al, "Covid-19 Pandemic: Questioning Conspiracy Theories", 12.
81 Okoye and Obulor, "Religious organizations and fight against the spread of Covid-19 in Nigeria", 67.
82 See Lawal S. 2020. "What the Church in Africa is Doing to Combat the Coronavirus", *America Magazine*, 21 May; "Apostolic Sect Gives Church Members Ashes to Eat for Protection Against Covid-19", *New Zimbabwe*, 11 April 2020.
83 Petersen C. 2020. "Pastor Dies from Covid-19 Just Weeks after Holding a Packed Church Service", *News 24*, 14 April. See also Maqbool A. 2020. "Coronavirus: Pastor Who Decried 'Hysteria' Dies after Attending Mardi Gras", *BBC News*, 3 June; Boorstein M. 2020. "Covid-19 Has Killed Multiple Bishops and Pastors within the Church of God in Christ, the Nation's Largest Black Pentecostal Denomination", *Independent Tribune*, 22 April.
84 "Apostolic Sect Gives Church Members Ashes".
85 Okoye and Obulor, "Religious organizations and fight against the spread of Covid-19 in Nigeria", 67.

the disease that was referred to in a 2016 prophecy that a disease worse than HIV and cancer was going to come from underneath the ocean by a weed or a creature in the ocean or from eating seafood.[86] No time frame for the coming of the predicted deadly disease was given by the prophecy in 2016. Still, followers and believers in this prophecy claimed that it was the Covid-19 pandemic that was predicted.[87]

DEBUNKING CONSPIRACY THEORIES: RELIGION, MEDIA AND THE LAW

Role of religion

Although members of Pentecostal Christian churches played a part in the spread of some of the conspiracy theories above, they also had a significant role to play in debunking them. As noted by historian of religions Asbjørn Dyrendal and social psychologist Daniel Jolley, conspiracy theories are sometimes deeply rooted in religious and religion-like beliefs.[88] This is evident in some of the conspiracy theories discussed above. In most African societies, there is usually respect for and trust in the information presented by religious leaders. Most of the time, their words carry a lot of weight.[89] Most people who hold political conspiracy theories are likely to reject direct counterarguments from governments and other authorities because they are perceived to be part of the conspiracy.[90] Therefore, religious leaders can play a significant role in countering these theories by passing accurate information to audiences who hold them in high esteem.

This important role was evident in what played out in Tanzania in the early days of the pandemic. While the government was in denial of Covid-19 and gave the impression that it was a hoax, leaders of the Catholic Church warned the public of its existence and encouraged them to observe health measures to curb the spread of the virus.[91] The secretary of the Tanzania Episcopal Conference told BBC Swahili that the church had noticed a rise in funeral services in urban areas, which was indicative of the fact that something was definitely amiss.[92] As a result members of the church were encouraged to take public health instructions seriously in order to avoid the infection. Without doubt, this prompted positive action on the part of the congregation.

---

86 Chirisa S. 2020. "Prophet Makandiwa Coronavirus Prophecy which was made in 2016", *iHarare*, 21 May.

87 Munhende L. 2020. "Zimbabwe: Hands off My Coronavirus, Makandiwa Says to Fellow Prophets Fellow Prophets", *All Africa*, 22 April.

88 Dyrendal A and Jolley D. 2020. "Conspiracy Theories in the Classroom: Problems and Potential Solutions", *Religions MDPI* 11:494-501.

89 Ayandele O, Okafor CT and Oyedele O. 2021. "The role of Nigeria's faith-based organisations in tackling health crises like Covid-19", *Africa Portal*, 27 January.

90 Douglas KM. 2021. "Covid-19 Conspiracy Theories", *Group Processes & Intergroup Relations* 24(2):270-275.

91 "Coronavirus in Tanzania".

92 "Coronavirus in Tanzania".

Religious leaders also helped to debunk conspiracy theories in Nigeria. Nigeria is a multi-religious state with two predominant religions: Christianity and Islam.[93] Although there are other religious groups, such as the African traditional religions, Hinduism and atheists and other nonbelievers, they are in the minority, as the majority are either Christians or Muslims.[94] The dissemination of vaccines in places of worship helped a great deal in convincing anti-vaxxers of the importance of the vaccine in building herd immunity. This went a long way in countering the theory that the vaccine was a Mark of the Beast or a feature of the Antichrist. This accords with the results of a 2009 study, carried out by Matthew Nisbet, a professor of communications and public policy, which recommended the use of a "trusted messenger" to reduce the impact of conspiracy theories.[95] In other words, combatting conspiracy theories may have more success if the counterarguments come from trusted sources, such as valued in-group members, instead of out-group members who are typically associated with mistrust.[96]

Religion was also used to debunk conspiracy theories that decreased trust in science by showing that religion is not incompatible with established science. For example, the website of the Jehovah's Witnesses published religious materials and articles arguing that religion is compatible with science.[97] As a result, the over 230 000 members of the congregations of Jehovah's Witnesses across Nigeria were kept abreast of efforts to combat the pandemic, including the need to adhere to public health instructions. Jehovah's Witnesses do refuse blood transfusions and treatment made with blood products, but they were consistently or repeatedly informed that the vaccine did not contain blood or blood components in these updates.[98] The updates helped hesitant members of the group to reevaluate the benefits of vaccination and to counter theories that associated the vaccine with vampires and the drinking of blood. A recent article published in the website of Jehovah's Witnesses admonished readers to beware of misinformation, such as misleading news, false reports and conspiracy theories.[99] Since Jehovah's Witnesses are known for their door-to-door preaching in most parts of Africa, including Nigeria, the

---

93 "Religious Beliefs in Nigeria", World Atlas, 2019.

94 Onomrerhinor AF. 2019. "Addressing the Problem of Terrorism and Extremism in Nigeria: Secularism to the Rescue?", *African Journal on Terrorism* 8(1):122.

95 Nisbet MC. 2009. "Communicating Climate Change: Why Frames Matter for Public Engagement", *Environment* 51:12-23.

96 Douglas, "Covid-19 Conspiracy Theories", 272.

97 Examples of such articles include: "Reconciling Science and Religion", published in *Awake!* magazine, "Science Religion and the Search for Truth", published in *The Watchtower* in 1994, "Science-Mankind's Ongoing Search for Truth published in Awake of 1993, Evolution and Religion – The Debate Continues", published in *Awake!* in 1974. Online at: https://www.jw.org

98 See Jehovah's Witnesses. "JW Broadcasting Governing Body Updates 1-10". Online at: https://www.jw.org

99 Jehovah's Witness. 2022. "Protect Yourself from Misinformation". Online at: https://www.jw.org/en/library/series/more-topic/conspiracy-theories-misinformation/

fact that their preaching from house to house was stopped and only resumed in September 2022 served to inform the Nigerian society, including members of other religious groups, of the threat posed by the Covid-19 pandemic.

Just like the Jehovah's Witnesses group, the leaders of the Catholic Church, the Anglican Church (Church of Nigeria), the Redeemed Christian Church of God (RCCG), Dunamis International Gospel Centre (DIGC), the Living Faith Church Worldwide (Winners Chapel International), the Elevation Church of the Christian faith in Nigeria directly or indirectly helped to counter conspiracy theories. Specifically, they modified traditional rites and rituals associated with their style of worship in line with the lockdown guidelines. Some of the modifications included the suspension of services and masses, initiation of online worship channels and stations, splitting of congregation into smaller numbers, creation of home cells, provision of water and hand sanitisers at their places of worship, enforcement of mask wearing at worship centres and in public places, education of their congregants on how to stay safe during the period and other measures.[100] Most importantly, religious organisations supported government efforts towards preventing the spread of the virus by not only making financial and material donations, but also making their facilities available to the government for use as isolation and quarantine centres.[101] By preaching compliance with public health instructions and government regulations on the pandemic, they helped to counter the belief that the disease was a myth. Islamic religious leaders in Nigeria were also instrumental in countering Covid-19 conspiracy theories.

The president-general of the Nigerian Supreme Council for Islamic Affairs (NSCIA), Sultan of Sokoto Muhammad Sa'ad Abubakar, reminded the country's Muslim community that Prophet Muhammad himself had advocated for social distancing in times of disease. They temporarily suspended congregational prayers and Jumu'ah (Friday) prayers. Further, the Sultan stated that Muslims had a religious duty to prevent the spread of disease and admonished them to observe personal hygiene in order to contain its spread. Taking cognizance of the fact that festive periods often witness increased human movement, travels, congestion and contacts that created risk factors for escalating community transmission and spread of the virus, he directed all the imams and district heads in Sokoto State and the larger Muslim communities in the country to observe Eid prayers at the mosques in their towns and villages instead of at the customary Eid grounds. This measure, according to a press statement that was signed by the Chairman Advisory Committee on Religious Affairs, Sultanate Affairs, Sokoto, Professor Sambo Wali Junaidu, on behalf of the Sultan on Wednesday, 22 July 2020, was taken because of the outbreak of Covid-19 pandemic.[102]

---

100 Okoye and Obulor, "Religious organizations and fight against the spread of Covid-19 in Nigeria", 73.

101 Adebowale-Tambe N. 2020. "Covid-19: Catholic Church donates 425 health facilities as isolation centers – Official", *Premium Times*, 12 May.

102 Olisah C. 2020. Just in: Sultan of Sokoto declares July 31 as Eid-El-Kabir, no prayers at Eid grounds", *NairaMetrics*, 22 July; "Covid-19: Nigeria to get online lectures in Ramadan",

Role of the media

The media, that is, the various means of mass communication, such as radio, television, newspapers, magazines and the internet, played a very significant role in the fight against misinformation and conspiracy theories. At the height of the pandemic in Nigeria, both mainstream media and social media such as Facebook, Google, YouTube, Twitter and WhatsApp shouldered the heavy burden of ensuring that the public was informed about matters affecting people's health and lives.[103] Discharging this responsibility meant playing a leading role in debunking theories that were circulating both in the global community and in most African societies.

For instance, the Africa Resilience Network (ARN) brought together Kenyan and Nigerian journalists with African and international media trainers to combat Covid-19 misinformation and disinformation. The project was launched in February 2021 and focused on open-source intelligence and investigative journalism techniques to probe the sources of some of the most prevalent fake news stories.[104] It successfully challenged a considerable number of conspiracy theories, misinformation and disinformation.[105] This included the conspiracy theory that the Covid-19 vaccination programme was a plot involving Microsoft founder Bill Gates, the United Nations and Satan, which would end with the recipient "drinking blood consistently so that they become vampires for their sustenance."[106] In effect, that theory stated that Covid-19 vaccination turn people into vampires.[107]

The media reports of conversion of conspiracy theorists also played an important role in changing the narratives. For instance, reports in the media of the conversion of die-hard anti-vaxxer, such as Femi Fani-Kayode, a public figure with a strong media presence in Nigeria, was in itself a debunking of one of the Covid-19 vaccine conspiracies.[108] Before 30 March 2021, when he announced on Twitter that he had taken the Covid-19 vaccine, he was foremost among those who publicly opposed Covid-19 vaccination.[109] He described the vaccine as a ploy to create a new world order. He tagged vaccination an exercise that would result in the deaths of millions

---

  Andalu Agency, 21 April 2020; Adediran O. 2020. "Covid-19: Islamic leaders donate N2.5m to Ogun govt", *Blueprint Nigeria*, 9 April.
103 Nunziato DC. 2020. "Misinformation Mayhem: Social Media Platforms' Efforts to Combat Medical and Political Misinformation", *First Amendment Law Review* 19(1):32-98.
104 Raistrick, "Debunking Africa's Covid-19 Conspiracies".
105 Such as: Vaccines turn people into vampires; holy water prevents Covid-19; Covid-19 is the same as malaria fever; hydroxychloroquine and steam can cure Covid-19; the Covid-19 vaccines are being used to exterminate Africans: the coronavirus cannot survive the African heat, claims of home cures for Covid-19, raw onion and garlic cure Covid -19; and Covid-19 vaccine was created by Bill Gates to make Africans infertile or Covid-19 vaccine can cause infertility.
106 Raistrick, "Debunking Africa's Covid-19 Conspiracies".
107 Raistrick, "Debunking Africa's Covid-19 Conspiracies".
108 Raistrick, "Debunking Africa's Covid-19 Conspiracies".
109 Busari K. 2021. "Nigeria: Anti-vaccination Champion takes Jab", *Africa Resilience Network*, 11 August.

and dissuaded his followers from getting vaccinated by tweeting unconfirmed information and conspiracy theories about Covid-19.[110]

In addition to mainstream media, social media platforms, which played a significant part in spreading the Covid-19 conspiracy theories, were also instrumental in debunking them. Arguably the most important challenge for social media platforms at the height of the pandemic was responding to the rampant spread of medical misinformation. In contrast to their previous hands-off position, the major platforms rose to the challenge and took some decisive actions in response to misinformation about the coronavirus.

Role of law

African legal systems provided both a framework and tools with which a cross-section of actors, particularly governments, responded to the Covid-19 pandemic.[111] In South Africa, the emergency regulations protected persons living in urban poverty from eviction during the pandemic.[112] In Ghana, the Establishment of Emergency Communications System Instrument, 2020 (EI 63) was enacted to aid contact tracing in public health emergencies.[113] In Nigeria, President Muhammadu Buhari called upon his emergency powers under the Quarantine Act of 1926 to declare a state of emergency to address the pandemic. The Quarantine Act of 1926 gave the president sweeping powers towards preventing the introduction, spread and transmission of dangerous infectious diseases in Nigeria, as well as the power to make regulations for these purposes.[114]

Nigeria belongs to the category of nations with a constitutional framework for emergency powers. However, the Covid-19 pandemic did not meet the requirement for the declaration of a state of emergency under Section 305 of the Nigerian Constitution, hence the utilisation of the Quarantine Act, 1926, to declare a state of emergency and provide a basis for the president to issue the first set of regulations, the Covid-19 Regulations, 2020, which declared Covid-19 a "dangerous infectious disease" and made lockdown orders in the Lagos, Abuja and Ogun States.[115] Other relevant laws enacted to deal with the pandemic were the Nigeria Centre for Disease Control (NCDC) Act, which conferred information provision functions on

---

110 Busari, "Nigeria: Anti-vaccination Champion takes Jab".

111 Durojaye E, Lwabukuna O, Oette L and Williams-Elegbe S. 2021. "Introduction: Covid-19 and the Law in Africa", *Journal of African Law* 65(2):173-180.

112 Dube F and Du Plessis A. 2021. "Unlawful Occupiers, Eviction and the National State of Disaster: Considering South Africa's Emergency Legislation and Jurisprudence during Covid-19", *Journal of African Law* 65(2):333-346.

113 Gawu DA. 2021. "Covid-19 Contact Tracing and Privacy Rights in Ghana: A Critical Analysis of the Establishment of Emergency Communications System Instrument, 2020 (EI 63)", *Journal of African Law* 65(2):361-373.

114 Abdulrauf L. 2020. "Nigeria's Emergency (Legal) Response to Covid-19: A Worthy Sacrifice for Public Health?", *Verfassungsblog*, 18 May.

115 Abdulrauf, "Nigeria's Emergency (Legal) Response to Covid-19".

the Nigeria Centre for Disease Control (NCDC) and the public health emergency legislation.

These pieces of legislation did not specifically address the problem of misinformation and disinformation.[116] As a result, some questioned the role that the law should play in curbing misinformation and debunking conspiracy theories in Nigeria.[117] As already indicated, social media platforms played a large role in the spread of Covid-19 conspiracy theories and misinformation during the pandemic. Unfortunately, the bill to regulate social media presented before the pandemic was met with a lot of resistance because the public perception of the Nigerian society was that it focused largely on curtailing criticism of government. So, the public claimed that it was a threat to free speech.[118] In general, concerns around censorship and limitations on free speech become an issue when considering whether the law should intervene in limiting misinformation and spread of conspiracy theories. Perhaps this is why the ongoing legislative efforts on developing public health emergency legislation have not focused on misinformation or disinformation. However, the challenges that disinformation and conspiracy theories presents are such that efforts should focus on disseminating accurate and important information.[119]

The NCDC Act confers the role of communicating relevant public health information to the NCDC, thus it neither specified the role of the public nor addressed issues relating to misinformation. In this regard, the law needs to be revised so that it can adequately provide the right resources and incentives for spreading the right information. However, pursuant to the role assigned to it by the Act, the NCDC has played a significant role in countering misinformation and conspiracy theories by consistently disseminating timely and accurate information during the height of the pandemic. The law has a role to play in supporting the provision of the right information and the commendable efforts of the various social media platforms to counter misinformation, disinformation and conspiracy theories during the height of the pandemic, so that communication can be regulated without resulting in censorship.

Further recommendations

Debunking conspiracy theories is essential to curb misinformation and disinformation. To counter conspiracy theories and misinformation, one must explain why something is false and draw attention to the strategies used to deceive and providing facts, rather than simply labelling information false or misleading.[120] Social media companies tried to stop or limit the spread of misinformation, disinformation and

---

116 Onyemelukwe C. 2020. "Covid-19 Misinformation and the Law in Nigeria", *Bill of Health*, 20 August.
117 Onyemelukwe, "Covid-19 Misinformation and the Law in Nigeria".
118 Onyemelukwe, "Covid-19 Misinformation and the Law in Nigeria".
119 Onyemelukwe, "Covid-19 Misinformation and the Law in Nigeria".
120 Sherwin, "Anatomy of a Conspiracy Theory", 555.

conspiracy theories in Nigeria.[121] In general, the social media platforms undertook extensive measures to remove false or harmful information, such as posts that advocated drinking bleach to cure Covid-19, and they labelled and reduced the reach of posts that contained misinformation or conspiracy theories. The platforms' efforts thus far are commendable; however, they must act much more quickly to remove harmful false and misleading medical misinformation before it goes viral.[122]

In addition, social media platform should make deliberate efforts to counter conspiracies that are circulated on their platforms. For instance, videos that Covid-19 vaccine is associated with the Antichrist or that it contains implants that could make people magnetic or traceable were shared on Facebook. These videos accounted for vaccine hesitancy among the youth. Some Nigerian youths interviewed by *News Express* stated that these videos posted on Facebook led to their vaccine hesitancy.[123] Unfortunately, Facebook did not counter the information presented in the videos.[124] Some of those interviewed stated that they did not find videos on Facebook countering such content or tagging same as misinformation.[125] Therefore, social media platforms like Facebook needs to do more to counter or debunk conspiracy theories.

Commendably, though, the different approach taken by the social media platforms, such as labelling or deleting harming posts and establishing a coronavirus information centre (Facebook), deleting or suspending the account of users responsible for disinformation (Twitter) and adopting new misinformation policies that enabled service providers to delete posts containing disinformation and redirecting users to the official pages of the NCDC, showed that laws regulating communication can be made without censorship. Efforts should be made to balance the right to free speech with the necessity to curb misinformation, disinformation and conspiracy theories, especially during emergency or crisis, such as that presented by the Covid-19.[126] It is important to note that freedom should have limits, especially in a situation where freedom is likely becoming inimical to the growing society.

Given that internationally generated social media content are easily accessed by African audiences, including Nigerians, it is imperative that Nigeria adopt a strategy to counter such content. One way to achieve this is to adopt the redirect method that has proved successful in countering online-based or digital violent

---

121 Sherwin, "Anatomy of a Conspiracy Theory: Law", 578.
122 Nunziato, "Misinformation Mayhem", 37.
123 "Covid-19: How Facebook Contributes to Vaccine Hesitancy among Young Nigerians", *News Express*, 27 March 2022.
124 For reference to the video see "Covid-19: How Facebook Contributes to Vaccine Hesitancy Among Young Nigerians", *Daily Trust*, 27 March 2022.
125 "Covid-19: How Facebook Contributes to Vaccine Hesitancy among Young Nigerians".
126 Gambo S and Shem W. 2021. "Social media and the spread of Covid-19 conspiracy theories in Nigeria", *Journal of Ideas in Health* 4(3):432-437.

extremism.[127] The method should target audience members who actively look for Covid-19 conspiracy content and redirect them towards others disproving such content. To achieve this, the Nigerian government will have to partner with Google and other social media companies.

CONCLUSION

The Covid-19 pandemic presented unparalleled challenges to the world, including misinformation and disinformation. Conspiracy theories have serious consequences for how the public responds to Covid-19.[128] Conspiracy theories flourish in times of crisis, when people feel threatened, uncertain and insecure. The Covid-19 pandemic created the perfect circumstances for conspiracy theories, and research suggests that conspiracy theories have negative consequences for people's compliance with preventive behaviours.[129]

Most conspiracy theories stem from fear and existing tension between groups. In Nigeria, for example, the lack of trust between the ruling political elite and the public or masses helped to promote some conspiracy theories. As long as the pandemic continues, conspiracy theories and misinformation will continue to influence the level of adherence to public health instructions and Covid-19 guidelines, as well as decisions about whether to get vaccinated. This chapter has shown that countering misinformation and conspiracy theories requires that trusted and well-respected members of the African society provide accurate information that can help members including Nigerians to make informed choices about Covid-19 pandemic. It has highlighted the significant role of the media, religion and the law in debunking conspiracy theories and misinformation about the virus and its vaccine. It has also shown that religion and the media, in the context of the Covid-19 pandemic are a double-edged sword. They have contributed to the development and spread of conspiracy theories, and they have also played a significant role in debunking conspiracy theories and curbing the spread of misinformation.

The role of the media, both mainstream and social media platforms is commendable and should continue to be harnessed in the ongoing fight against the pandemic in order to ensure the survival of the African people. During times of crisis and instability, it can be difficult to know what information to trust. Given the anxiety and uncertainty that the pandemic occasioned, it was not surprising that the global community, including Africa, was caught in the web of unscientific theories of conspiracy and healing. The efforts of the governmental authorities and the media in ensuring that accurate information about the pandemic is made available should be applauded and regarded as a protection instead of censorship.

---

127 Amit S, Barua L and Al Kafy A. 2021. "Countering violent extremism using social media and preventing implementable strategies for Bangladesh", *Heliyon* 7:6.
128 Peitz, "Covid-19 Conspiracy Theories", 1.
129 Douglas, "Covid-19 Conspiracy Theories", 274.

The law played a significant role in supporting the provision of the right information. It is essential for the law to use culturally appropriate measures to encourage compliance. Progressive strategies, such as public education and risk communication, should be given a foundation in the law to support persistent communication of the current facts. In addition, deliberate spreading of false information should be sanctioned in order to punish the harm that misinformation and disinformation portends for all and to act as a deterrent to the spread of disinformation.

13 THE SOCIO-CULTURAL FOUNDATIONS OF THE WAABA PEOPLE'S RELUCTANCE TO VACCINATE AGAINST COVID-19 IN BENIN

Tchokomi Sabine Toungakouagou Sama[1]
N'koué Emmanuel Sambiéni[2]

INTRODUCTION

On 8 December 2019, the world discovered Covid-19, a new virus which originated from the Chinese city of Wuhan.[3] Subsequently, the World Health Organization (WHO) declared the existence of the virus in January 2020. The damage caused in Western countries was the subject of hyper-mediatisation by both traditional media and social networks.[4] Faced with the alarming Western social and health situation, African government authorities in general, and Benin in particular, put in place various barrier measures, including the closure of the land borders between Benin and the other countries of the sub-region in order to avoid any infiltration of the virus. Despite these precautions, Benin, a West African country, recorded its first case in March 2019 in Cotonou. From that moment, the virus, until then considered foreign and distant, became part of the daily life of Beninese people. Its detection created a wave of fear and involved a mobilisation of various actors, especially the government and health authorities of the country.

On 11 March 2020, in view of the damage caused by the virus, Covid-19 was classified as a pandemic by WHO. African countries, including Benin, were on general state of alert.[5] Various initiatives were taken at the national level to contain the spread of the virus. It was in this context that the first case of Covid-19 was

---

1 Tchokomi Sabine Toungakouagou Sama, Teacher-Researcher in Sociology-Anthropology, Faculty of Letters, Arts and Human Sciences, University of Parakou.
2 N'koué Emmanuel Sambiéni, Teacher-Researcher in Sociology-Anthropology, Faculty of Letters, Arts and Human Sciences, University of Parakou; Lecturer, CAMES Universities.
3 Borell J. 2020. "Covid-19: Le monde d'après est déjà là [Covid-19: The world after is already here]", *Institut Français des relations internationales/Politique étrangère* [French Institute of International Relations/Foreign Policy] 2:9-23; Al-Jayyousi GF et al. 2021. "Factors Influencing Public Attitudes towards Covid-19 Vaccination: A Scoping Review Informed by the Socio-Ecological Model", *Vaccines* 9:548.
4 Balard F and Corvol A. 2020 "Covid et personnes âgées: liaisons dangereuses [Covid and the elderly: dangerous liaisons]", *Gérontologie et Société* [Gerontology and Society] 42(162):9-16.
5 World Health Organization. 2020. "Listing of WHO's response to Covid-19", WHO, 29 June.

detected in the department of Atacora.⁶ At the sub-regional level, the management of Covid-19 by the Beninese authorities was considered a textbook case. Far from merely observing the measures applied in other African countries, Benin innovated by implementing a measure called the *"cordon sanitaire"*. This measure consisted in isolating potentially dangerous parts of the country from others. Covid-19 thus became a collectively shared evil, which implied the need to act together collectively.⁷ Beyond the ordinary measures and the establishment of the *cordon sanitaire*, a vaccination campaign was also introduced, as in European countries.⁸

The Waaba are a socio-cultural group from northern Benin made up of four tribes: the Waaba (Yimbopa), the Tangamba, the Daataba and the Naasiba. They are mainly from the department of Atacora, but have also settled in other regions of the country, such as Borgou, Collines and Zou, as well as outside Benin, such as the Saki regions of Nigeria, due to the rural exodus. The singular of Waaba is Waao, the spoken language is Waama. We write Waaba (plural) or Waao (singular) to designate the people and Waaba (plural) or Waao (singular) when it comes to the qualifying adjective. Attention is drawn to them here because of their resistance to vaccination against Covid-19. Faced with the reluctance of populations to be vaccinated, various strategies were tested, including awareness-raising through the media to convince communities at the national level. However, these initiatives were not successful in blunting the reluctance of the general population, including the Waaba of North Benin, to vaccinate against Covid-19.

From March 2021 forward, the fight against Covid-19 included a vaccination campaign in Benin. Despite communication and pressure actions, reluctance towards vaccination against Covid-19 has been notable within the Waao community. The research underlying this chapter aims to elucidate the socio-cultural foundations of this situation. The research is essentially qualitative, using interviews and questionnaires, and was carried out in 2022 in the towns of Natitingou and Toucountouna and in the villages of Yarikou and Pouya in the district of Kotopounga,⁹ with professionals and authorities of the health system, survivors of Covid-19 and other actors in their immediate social environment, including traditional healers, traditional religious leaders, other religious authorities and media representatives. The focus of the analysis was the socio-health context of the imposition of vaccination, beliefs about Covid-19, socio-cultural representations, the availability and

---

6   This department is located in the northwest of Benin. It is bounded to the north by Burkina-Faso and Alibori, to the west by Togo, to the east by Borgou and Alibori and to the south by Donga. The nine municipalities that it comprises are: Kérou, Kouandé, Péhunco, Natit.ingou, Toucountouna, Tanguiéta, Matéri, Cobly and Boukoumbé.

7   Rémon M. 2020."Covid-19, notre mal commun [Covid-19, our common evil]". CERAS/Revue Projet N° 375(2):1.

8   Le Bars S et al. 2021. "Covid-19: en Europe, la vaccination obligatoire s'impose comme l'ultime recours dans les pays qui résistent au vaccin [Covid-19: in Europe, mandatory vaccination is the last resort in countries that are resistant to the vaccine]", *Le Monde*, 8 December.

9   Kotopounga is a district of the commune of Natitingou.

accessibility of local recipes for prevention and treatment of the disease establish the level of adherence of affected communities to vaccination against Covid-19. This chapter, examining the vaccine resistance of the Waaba people, seeks to answer the following research question: What are the social and cultural foundations that justify the Waaba's reluctance to vaccinate against Covid-19? The hypothesis is that the local socio-health context and the socio-cultural representations of Covid-19 may explain the reluctance of the Waaba of North Benin in the face of vaccination against Covid-19.

UNDERSTANDING VACCINE HESITANCY AMONG THE WAABA

As noted above, the present research on the social and cultural foundations of Covid-19 vaccination hesitancy among the Waaba people of Benin is essentially qualitative in nature. Indeed, it focuses on personal representations of prevention and treatment practices, factors determining reluctance and adherence to Covid-19 vaccination recommendations, but it also employs statistical data relating to vaccination coverage rates. The research is based on empirical collection of data in the field, using interview scripts and an interview guide as working tools, as well as a literature review, which was ongoing throughout the process of conducting the research. The empirical data collection was carried out from December 2021 to February 2022.

The results of the study focus on the presentation of the national and local socio-health context, as seen through the traditional religious beliefs of the Waaba in the face of pandemics, the social representations of Covid-19 among the Waaba and the social and cultural factors behind vaccine hesitancy. These social and cultural factors are examined in connection with data on the national and local socio-health context of the unfolding of the vaccination campaign against Covid-19. The population surveyed was composed of professionals and authorities from the health system, survivors of Covid-19, traditional therapists and other actors in the immediate social environment. The theoretical approach used is the social constructionism of Berger and Luckman.[10] According to this sociological theory, social realities are artefacts constructed on the basis of the experience of social actors.[11]

The data for the present study was collected in Natitingou, Yarikou, Pouya and Toucountouna from fifty people, including twenty women. These sites were selected because they are characterised by a strong dominance of Waaba populations. The research was carried out in two communes of the department of Atacora, namely

---

10 Berger P and Luckman T. 1986. *La construction sociale de la réalité* [The social construction of reality]. Paris: Méridien Klienksiek.

11 The data has been manually stripped and the method of data processing and analysis is content analysis according to the method of Muchielli. See Muchielli A. 2013. *Dictionnaire des Méthodes qualitatives en sciences humaine et sociales* [Dictionary of Qualitative Methods in the Human and Social Sciences]. Third Edition. Paris: Armand Colin.

Toucountouna[12] and Natitingou.[13] Natitingou is the capital of the department of Atacora. Located in northern Benin, the communes of Natitingou and Toucountona are open to Burkina Faso and Togo by land borders. The main ethnic groups that inhabit them are the Waaba, the Bèètamaribè, the Nyendé, the Natemba and the Dendi, among others. Various religious practices are practised there, including Islam, Christianity and traditional religions. Similarly, these groups make use of various therapeutic remedies in case of disease, including self-medication, traditional therapy and modern health care. The population is predominantly young, a demographic that was seen as a barrier to the spread of Covid-19. The municipality of Natitingou has a health infrastructure, but it had no emergency management centre for Covid-19. The recourse infrastructures in this context were available in Parakou[14] in the department of Borgou.[15] It shares the latter with the commune of Toucoutouna, whose central district is 25 kilometres from Natitingou.

The implementation of the Covid vaccination campaign at the national level was characterised as a non-emergency situation. As of January 2022, there were 25 522 registered cases of Covid in Benin, with 24 823 cases presumed cured, 538 cases under treatment and 161 cases of death from Covid.[16] These data show that as of January 2022, two years after the outbreak of Covid-19 in Benin, the country had the capacity to successfully treat more than 97% of reported cases. Similarly, the death rate was very marginal (0.06%). All recorded cases have been cured, therefore, no cases of death have been recorded at the sites studied.

---

12 The commune of Toucountouna is located in the department of Atacora, twenty-five (25) kilometres from Natitingou. It has three districts namely Kouarfa, Tampègré and Toucountouna Centre. It is bordered to the north by the commune of Tanguiéta, to the south by that of Natitingou, to the east by the commune of Kouandé and to the west by the Atacora mountain. Commune of Toucountouna. 2015. *Communal Conservation Plan and Biodiversity of the Protected Areas System: Municipality of Toucountouna*, 63.

13 The municipality of Natitingou has nine districts namely Natitingou 1, Natitingou 2, Natitingou 3, Kotopounga, Pèporiyarikou, Perma, Kouandata, Kouaba and Tchoumi-Tchoumi. It is located in the northwest in the department of Atacora and is bordered to the north by Togo, to the south and east by the commune of Kouandé and to the west by the commune of Boukoumbé. INASAE. 2008. *Monograph of the municipality of Natitingou*, 131.

14 The city of Parakou is the capital of the department of Borgou, located in the North-East of Benin. It is a cosmopolitan city where several languages are spoken. It is located 435 km from Cotonou and is bounded to the north by the municipality of N'Dali, to the south, east and west by the municipality of Tchaourou. Ministry of State in Charge of Planning and Development (MPD). 2019. *Spatialisation of priority targets of the SDGs in Benin: Monograph of the communes of the departments of Borgou and Alibori. Summary note on the update of the diagnosis and the prioritisation of the targets of the communes*, 213.

15 The department of Borgou has seven municipalities, including Parakou, N'Dali, Bembèrèkè, Pèrèrè, Nikki, Kalalé and Sinendé. It borders Nigeria, the departments of Alibori, Atacora and Collines. The main languages spoken are Bariba, Dendi and Yoruba. MPD, *Spatialisation of priority targets of SDGs in Benin*.

16 Gouvernement de la République du Bénin. 2022. "Informations coronavirus (covid-19)". Online at: https://www.gouv.bj/coronavirus [Accessed January 2022].

Despite being faced with what seemed to be a non-emergency context at both national and local levels, a state of emergency was eventually declared and vaccination was made mandatory throughout the national territory. This imposition faced resistance from the populations. Beyond the general context presented above, various social factors have been mentioned in connection with vaccine resistance. In reality, death was experienced remotely via television and social networks, and there were not always actual cases in the immediate social environment of the those who were reluctant to be vaccinated. As one Catholic priest stated, "It is on TV that we see those sick with corona. We say we die from it, but no one in our environment has died."[17] There was also reported recovery from Covid-19 through the use of local medicinal plants. Presumptions from these reports, coupled with the lack of direct experience with Covid deaths, provided fertile ground for reluctance that was further induced by cultural factors. This situation was reflected in the present study recurrence of remarks relating to Covid deaths as mediatised and unlived. Covid-19, as an emergency, was simply not a part of people's perceived reality or lived experience.

CULTURAL DRIVERS OF COVID-19 VACCINE HESITANCY AMONG THE WAABA

The reluctance to vaccinate against Covid is rooted in the religious beliefs of the Waaba in the face of the disease and in the representations these communities had of the vaccine and Covid-19. These representations are multidimensional. After all, Africa has been, throughout its existence, a setting for the manifestation of epidemics. The latter profoundly mark the populations, because they result in deaths. However, in the popular mentality, certain forms of death are considered to be reaction of the deities against certain malicious behaviours of men. In Africa, especially Benin and particularly among the Waaba, epidemics are considered a form of manifestation of the discontent of the Supreme Being (Ouin-Ouro) against humans. This perception of epidemics is reflected in the response to Covid-19. Taking account of the socio-cultural representations, requires focused reflections on: (1) the belief or non-belief in the existence of Covid-19 by the survey participants, (2) the vocabulary associated with Covid-19, (3) the cultural referents surrounding vaccination among the Waaba and (4) the perception of the vaccine.

Existence of Covid-19

Reluctance to adopt a given practice may stem from a contradiction of perceptions between stakeholders. Regarding the existence of Covid-19, divergent positions are juxtaposed – that of the medical profession and survivors of Covid-19, on the one hand, and that of most Waaba, who lacked direct experience with the virus, on the other. Medical professionals and survivors understood Covid-19 through

---

17 Interview with D.C., a Catholic Waao priest, by TS Toungakouagou Sama, Natitingou, Benin, January 2022.

the registration of cases, mainly serious, which were treated in hospital, as well as through the interest shown by the authorities and media, especially television media, to disclose information about Covid-19. These groups believed in the existence of the disease. But for some of the communities studied, Covid-19 did not seem to exist. This position can be explained by the disproportionate involvement of the political and health authorities in the matter and the non-existence of Covid-19 cases and deaths in their families and immediate social environment.

Vocabulary of Covid

For those who were less sceptcal, in connection with the health and therapeutic referents of the Waaba, the coronavirus, even if it existed, was not perceived as a new disease. It was likened to a chronic malaria and therefore considered to be curable and not dangerous. As a result, the vocabulary developed around the disease, included referents such as malaria (*kpawago*) and colds (*mimbu*), which can be chronic (*kpèbu*) or benign (*minditafa*). In a nutshell, Covid-19, among the Waaba, seemed to be nothing but chronic malaria or a more benign infection, such as a cold with cough. In their experience, Covid had about the same symptoms as malaria, to which were added the symptoms of cough, cold and flu, leading to widespread fatigue. The name ultimately adopted was the same one used at the international level: coronavirus. However, several associated terms were in circulation in Waaba social environments, relating to the novelty of the disease (*bèètchatu*), its distant and white origin (*yiiboribèètu*), its symptoms and manifestations (*Korona* or *Korona bètu*) and its announced consequences (*tikpitibètu*).

Cultural referents for the vaccine

For critics of the vaccination campaign, the Covid-19 vaccine was not the solution to the situation they were experiencing. While vaccines are sometimes beneficial, the Covid vaccines were perceived as unprotective, possibly even dangerous and deadly. For those who were hestitant about the vaccine, the rush to develop the vaccines and noncompliance with lengthier periods normally required for validation of a vaccine made them sceptical about both the effectiveness and the safety of the vaccine. As one business executive in Yarikou stated: "I do not know why the government is forcing us to vaccinate. The research is not conclusive. Everywhere we say that it takes a certain amount of time and experimentation to know if the vaccine is good. All of this is not settled, but we are pressed."[18] This lack of confidence in the vaccine contrasted with their certainty about the availability and accessibility of traditional local care, based mainly on plants.

---

18 Interview with S.Y., a Waao executive, by TS Toungakouagou Sama, Yarikou, Benin, January 2022.

Availability of alternative treatments

Still another factor that was unfavourable to vaccination was the perceived existence and accessibility of alternative remedies for the prevention and treatment of Covid-19. As a housewife in Toucountouna stated, "Traditional healers offer plants and recipes that work. A traditional healer went on the radio to advertise a recipe that healed his family. The most effective remedy is hot water, plus ginger, plus aye, onion and sport. But many do not know it because everything must be done to eliminate by pigs. This is why infusion with neem is important."[19] Likewise, a Catholic priest stated,

> I take herbal teas to boost my immunity. The flu is related to the lungs, it is necessary to take ginger, aye and powder of the *cailcédrat*; I drink a lot of hot water and lemongrass. I personally believe I had Covid, but I treated myself with hot neem water that I inhaled using a loincloth for two days. Papa Valère gave me leaves that I boiled and drank.[20]

Among these were plants that were prepared and taken in the form of baths or drinks. Beverages came in various forms, namely hot, cold and alcoholic. The plants considered to be sufficient themselves against Covid were: *barikataka, baroma* (bush bean), *neem (Azadirachta indica)* leaves, artemisia and *pututunan* and *tokotu* (king of herbs). However, some were taken in combination with other plants, including mixtures such as: (1) *quinquelibat (combretum micanthum* plant), papaya leaves and *cailcedrat (Khaya senegalesis* tree); (2) lemon, *yayanon*, and papaya leaves; (3) ginger, garlic, and Guinea sorrel; (4) moringa, basil and garlic; and (5) lemon and moringa.

IMPACT ON VACCINATION ADHERENCE

This logic, forged by the context of the vaccination campaign and amidst the prevailing representations of Covid and the vaccine, explained the low adherence of the Waaba to vaccination against Covid-19. The national and local socio-health context of the implementation of the vaccination campaign, religious beliefs about pandemics, representations of Covid-19 and the vaccine, and the accessibility and availability of local herbal recipes for the prevention and treatment of Covid-19 had repercussions on the adherence of Waaba communities to Covid-19 vaccination campaigns.

As a result, particular strategies were developed by health authorities. These strategies included information sessions, awareness-raising and the establishment of mobile teams for targeted vaccination as a means of exerting pressure on civil servants and public and private vaccination service delivery. As a health care worker in Natitingou put it, "We are developing various strategies to convince people, including door-to-door work carried out by mobile teams. These teams

---

19 Interview with S.M., a housewife, by TS Toungakouagou Sama, Toucountouna, Benin, January 2022.

20 Interview Y.P., a Waao priest of the Catholic Church by TS Toungakouagou Sama, Pouya, Benin, January 2022.

are paid by the results and collectively. This is a means of ensuring that results are achieved. If there is a sloth in a team, the other members feel unsafe and motivate him to the task."[21]

For most respondents, these strategies were counterproductive. Only 20% of participants in the study report being vaccinated. These included users of public and private services, healthcare workers and people who had either been infected with Covid-19 or had exposure through their social environment. The reasons for their adherence to the vaccine were varied and included the need to protect themselves and others, their concern to access public services and their confidence in the government's initiatives. The other 80% of the study participants said they were not vaccinated. They gave as reasons the supposed dangerous nature of the vaccine, the perceived mildness of the disease that did not require the use of a vaccine, the comorbidity associated with susceptibility to Covid-19 and the unconvincing discourse of the country's public and health authorities. As one unvaccinated woman confided, "I didn't get vaccinated. It doesn't convince me. The vaccine requires at least five years to validate. Today, it's something in experimentation that they call vaccine. However, there are proven remedies. Pharmaceutical companies are encouraged."[22] Overall, the imposition of vaccination took place in an unfavourable social and cultural context.

A SOCIAL AND CULTURAL CONTEXT OF VACCINE HESITANCY

The imposition of the Covid-19 vaccination as a sustainable Covid-19 prevention strategy has faced a difficult social and cultural context. These include both the national and local regulatory context and cultural factors. In combination, these resulted in the low vaccination adherence among the Waaba.

National and local regulations

The Covid-19 vaccination campaign was implemented in a social context with multiple hesitancy factors. The social context was characterised by the non-emergency state of affairs in response to the disease, the real inexperience of death resulting from the virus and the exaggerated commitment of the country's health and political authorities to a non-emergency socio-health situation. Thus, the vaccination campaign was imposed in a national social context where the national health system had the capacity to successfully treat more than 97% of reported cases and where only 0.06% of people declared affected had died. It should be noted that Covid-19 was even less of a concern at these local sites than it was at the national one. According to official figures, very few cases were recorded, and all were cured.

---

21 Interview with a medical professional by TS Toungakouagou Sama, Natitingou, Benin, January 2022.
22 Interview with Y.R., a female, by TS Toungakouagou Sama, Natitingou, Benin, January 2022.

Added to this was the counter-campaign orchestrated by both traditional media and social networks and the capacities for prevention and cure of Covid-19 cases from local medicinal plants.

Several studies have focused on social factors underlying attitudes towards vaccination, but rarely in isolation from other demographic factors, despite the importance of the social environment.[23] Other social factors relate to the level of trust given to the authorities have also been cited, including the trust given to science and the health institutions, on the one hand, and conspiracy theories, on the other.[24] One of the few studies that addressed social factors in isolation, highlighted the role of family, friends, relatives, traditional media and social networks.[25] Although they concern the social aspects, these results of these studies do not focus on the same of analysis as the results of the present study. However, they agree on the role of traditional media and social networks. The particularity of the present study is that it highlights, beyond the social factors mentioned above, the real inexperience of the pandemic, the alternatives offered by traditional medicine and the capacity to manage cases recorded by the country's health and political authorities.

Cultural factors

Cultural factors, in particular, stand out as barriers to communities' full adherence to Covid-19 vaccination. These include religious beliefs about pandemics and therefore about Covid-19, sociocultural representations of Covid-19, the existence and accessibility of natural resources for prevention and treatment and perceptions of the vaccine. Regarding religious beliefs, the Waaba believe that in the face of any disease and therefore in the face of Covid-19, the Supreme Being (Ouin-Ouro), which promotes the advent of a pandemic, also makes available to particular social actors the means to overcome it through natural remedies such as plants. When it comes to representations of the pandemic, the Waaba and their caregivers had an identical view of the origin of Covid-19, but they had different perceptions about the dangerousness of the disease. While caregivers, particularly medical personnel, described it as dangerous and deadly, for the Waaba, the harm was benign and treatment was accessible. Among the Waaba, Covid-19 was considered to be no more severe than chronic malaria or more benign infectious disease, such as colds and coughs. An associated vocabulary developed to justify their perception of the

---

23 Al-Jayyousi et al, "Factors Influencing Public Attitudes towards Covid-19 Vaccination", 548.

24 See Schmelza K and Bowles S. 2021. "Overcoming Covid-19 vaccination resistance when alternative policies affect the dynamics of conformism, social norms, and crowding out", *PNAS* 118(25):e210491218; Okoro O et al. 2021. "Exploring the Scope and Dimensions of Vaccine Hesitancy and Resistance to Enhance COVID-19 Vaccination in Black Communities", *Journal of Racial and Ethnic Health Disparities* 9:2117-2130.

25 Al Shurman BA et al. 2021."What Demographic, Social, and Contextual Factors Influence the Intention to Use Covid-19 Vaccines: A Scoping Review", *International Journal of Environmental Research and Public Health* 18(17):9342.

disease. In the same vein, they considered the vaccine to be non-protective, but rather dangerous and deadly given the availability of local traditional care.

Some of these findings are consistent with previous studies that have addressed the cultural drivers of Covid-19. Thus, cultural factors are related to conflicting beliefs about Covid-19, and these deep beliefs function as systems of representations that impact attitudes on whether or not to adhere to vaccination.[26] It should be noted that the present research evokes, beyond these aspects, the dimensions related to the representation of the vaccine as dangerous and non-protective, the availability of local natural recipes involving a traditional therapeutic recourse and the perception of Covid-19 as a curable and controllable evil.

Low vaccination adherence of Waaba

The combined factors of the national and local socio-health context, the beliefs and cultural representations of the Waaba regarding the pandemic and the vaccine and the accessibility and use of natural resources have been obstacles to the adherence of vaccination by these communities. Previous work has focused on statistics on vaccination adherence and hesitancy, but in different contexts.[27] This work allowed countries to be classified into two categories regarding vaccination: highly reluctant and highly favourable. Analysis showed much lower levels of concern to be vaccinated among African countries and higher ones in Western countries,[28] with the rare exception of some countries, such as Australia, where the accession rate to the vaccine was 6%.[29] A study conducted in nineteen Western countries, found global vaccination rates generally varying between 63% and 93%,[30] while it is 89% in China and 55% in Russia.[31] In Senegal, the vaccination rate was 32.80%.[32] There were general trends towards low vaccination rates of African states and African-Americans in the United States.[33] This contrasts with high vaccination rates in Europe and Asia, which are explained by different socio-health contexts. On the one hand, the pandemic has imposed itself as a health, social and economic shock

---

26 Al-Jayyousi, "Factors Influencing Public Attitudes towards Covid-19 Vaccination", 548. See also Okoro et al, "Exploring the Scope and Dimensions of Vaccine Hesitancy and Resistance".

27 Ba MF et al. 2022. "Factors associated with Covid-19 vaccine hesitancy in Senegal: a mixed study", *Human Vaccines & Immunotherapeutics* 18(5):2060020.

28 Hyland P et al. 2021. "Resistance to Covid-19 vaccination has increased in Ireland and the United Kingdom during the pandemic", *Public Health* 195:54-56.

29 Edwards B, Biddle N, Gray M and Sollis K. 2021. "Covid-19 vaccine hesitancy and resistance: Correlates in a nationally representative longitudinal survey of the Australian population", PLoS ONE 16(3): e0248892.

30 Hyland et al. "Resistance to Covid-19 vaccination has increased in Ireland and the United Kingdom during the pandemic".

31 Alshurman et al, "What Demographic, Social, and Contextual Factors Influence the Intention to Use Covid-19 Vaccines".

32 Ba et al, "Factors associated with Covid-19 vaccine hesitancy in Senegal: a mixed study".

33 Okoro et al, "Exploring the Scope and Dimensions of Vaccine Hesitancy and Resistance.

and has profoundly changed the relationship between human beings and their relationship to death in many parts of the word, but, on the other hand, there are African communities where it has not spread.[34]

CONCLUSION

Covid-19 imposed itself on the world in different ways. The manifest evil of the pandemic had different impacts in different regions of the world. The health, social and economic shock has been intense in the West, but it was less so in Africa. In Benin, although official public health data showed that Covid-19 was under control, vaccination was imposed by the political and health authorities as the effective remedy for the spread of the disease. This imposition was perceived as an inappropriate and irrelevant recommendation in the face of a non-emergency situation, the availability and accessibility of local remedies and massive awareness against the vaccine through traditional media and social networks. It was therefore at the level of the public health context that the first obstacles to the achievement of vaccination results were encountered.

Social barriers encountered a favourable terrain in terms of cultural representations and practices. The combined effects of these social and cultural factors gave rise to a system of representations that resulted in vaccine hesitancy. Cultural factors translated into religious beliefs and representations about Covid-19 and the vaccine, the availability and accessibility of local natural remedies. Faced with this unfavourable system of socio-cultural representations, local authorities developed many strategies including information, awareness-raising and even pressure. However, these strategies were effective because, the vaccination remained low, including just 20% of the Waaba population.

---

[34] Borell, "Covid-19: Le monde d'après est déjà là".

IV. Sex, gender and vulnerability in the Covid-19 pandemic

14 TAMAR'S VOICE IN THE CONTEXT OF COVID-19: RE-READING 2 SAMUEL 13 FOR THE DIGNITY OF WOMEN'S SEXUALITY

Dorcas Chebet Juma[1]

INTRODUCTION

Application of Old Testament laws in matters sex and sexuality has been highly biased and gendered when it comes to women. By analogy, in Kenya, a patriarchal society, reported that cases of sexual and gender-based violence (SGBV) against women and girls escalated in 2020, after the government ordered a lockdown and restricted mobility by imposing a curfew to mitigate the spread of the virus that causes Covid-19. Just like in the case of Tamar in 2 Samuel 13, many women and girls found themselves confined in spaces that have constantly made them vulnerable to SGBV. Tabitha W. Kiriti-Nganga, a scholar of gender and economics, points out that "Kenya is a patriarchal society with widespread discrimination against women."[2] The vulnerability of women and girls to SGBV continues to be a barrier towards accessing justice and health services, putting the lives of many victims of SGBV at risk. According to legal scholar Christine Wanjiru Kung'u, marital rape is not a criminal offence in Kenya.[3] A report of human rights communications strategist Audrey Kawire Wabwire shows that during Covid-19 era, one hotline saw a 300% increase in reports of SGBV in 2020.[4] Yet not much was done by the Kenyan Government to address the issue. Many healthcare facilities in Kenya are not well equipped to handle cases of SGBV. With escalated cases of SGBV during Covid-19, the situation of healthcare facilities is not different from the way they were in 2015, when Adelaide Ndilu, a religious sister, broadcast producer and radio producer on church and justice issues, observed that some healthcare facilities lack basic awareness about patients' rights, and transparent and effective oversight mechanisms.[5]

---

1 Senior Lecturer, Department of Philosophy and Religious Studies, School of Humanities and Social Sciences, Pwani University, Kilifi, Kenya.
2 See Nganga KTW. 2008. "Institutions and Women's Empowerment in Kenya", in Roy CK, Clark C and Blomqvist HC (eds). *Institutions And Gender Empowerment in the Global Economy*. Singapore: World Scientific, 178.
3 See Kung'u CW. 2011. *Criminalization of Marital Rape in Kenya*. Toronto: University of Toronto.
4 See Wabwire AK. 2021. "Witness: Sexual Violence During Kenya's Covid-19 Lockdown", *Human Rights Watch*, 21 September.
5 See Ndilu A. 2015. "Kenyan laws still fail to protect women against violence", *Global Sisters Report* (blog), National Catholic Reporter, 7 January.

In Deuteronomy 25:11-12, we encounter a strongly gender-biased law against women. In a fight between two men, the wife of one of the men is warned against rescuing her husband from the grip of his opponent by reaching out and seizing the genitals of the opponent, or else her hand shall be cut off with no pity.[6] In this text, value, honour and dignity are placed on the sexuality of men. On the other hand, in Numbers 31:17-18, Moses instructs the soldiers to kill all women who have had a sexual encounter and to spare virgins for their sexual pleasure. Even today, Old Testament gender-biased laws continue to be used in patriarchal settings like Kenya to reinforce the oppression of and male dominance over women. Yet, it is in the context of power imbalance that SGBV thrives. Biblical scholars Frederick Mawusi Amevenku and Isaac Boaheng argue, that "if the Bible is thus interpreted to reinforce the African stereotype of women and the validation of patriarchy, then we have a huge problem on our hands."[7]

This chapter builds on the contribution of gender and religion scholar Charlene van der Walt, who enables readers to hear Tamar's voice through a contextual reading of the Old Testament to 2 Samuel 13:1-22.[8] According to Van der Walt, the voice of Tamar in 2 Samuel 13 is an embodiment of resilience and resistance for "many modern women who are the victims of rape or incest, yet whose experience has been denied or hidden."[9] Through the power of her voice, Tamar uses two strategies to try and protect her sexual dignity from being taken away. Firstly, Tamar pleads with Amnon not to disgrace her. In a resistant voice, we hear her scream: "No, my brother! Don't force me! Don't do this wicked thing!" Her resistant voice gives her the opportunity to try dialogue as a mode of calling the attention of Amnon to the dignity of her sexuality as a woman. She says: "What about me? Where could I get rid of my disgrace?" as seen in 2 Samuel 13:12-13. Yet Amon could not listen as seen in 2 Samuel 13:14. Secondly, Tamar negotiates with Amnon. Tamar brings the attention of Amnon to the dignity of his own sexuality as a man, a brother, and a child of royalty. Tamar uses a negotiating strategy to appeal to their blood relationship and the royal position of Amnon in King David's family. Theologian Gerald O. West argues that Tamar's direct speech to his brother is an embodiment of resilience and resistance in a context in which women are presented as though they are silent victims of SGBV.[10]

One therefore asks: why does Tamar use her blood relationship and the royal position of Amnon in King David's family to negotiate for the dignity of her sexuality?

---

6 Biblical citations in this chapter are to the New Revised Standard Version (NIV).

7 See Amevenku FM and Boaheng I. 2021. *Biblical Exegesis in African Context*. Wilmington, DE: Vernon Press, 108.

8 See Van der Walt C. 2012. "Hearing Tamar's Voice: Contextual Readings of 2 Samuel 13: 1-22", *Old Testament Essays* 25(1):182-206.

9 Van der Walt, "Hearing Tamar's Voice.

10 See West GO. 2020. "A Trans-Textual and Trans-Sectorial Gender-Economic Reading of the Rape of Tamar (2 Sam 13) and the Expropriation of Naboth's Land (1 Kgs 21)", in Choi JY and Rieger J (eds). *Faith, Class, and Labor: Intersectional Approaches in a Global Context*. Eugene, OR: Wipf and Stock Publishers, 118.

Amnon from the Hebrew word אַמְנוֹן (*amnon*) is literally translated as faithful.[11] Born circa 1000 BCE, Amnon was the oldest son of King David to his second wife, Ahinoam of Jezreel. Amnon was the apparent heir to the throne of Israel. Old Testament scholar Eugene H. Merrill has observed, that, "by virtue of this position, Amnon enjoyed immunity from prosecution and punishment."[12] By virtue of being David's daughter, Tamar was an insider in King David's family and the Israelite society. Arguably, she is fully aware of this information and therefore uses the politics of royal power to bargain for her sexual dignity.[13] Tamar reminds Amnon that there is nothing as disgraceful in Israel as going down in the records of Israel's history as one of the fools of Israel. And not just an ordinary fool. It is more serious if the fool is "foolish" on matters human sexuality, and even more so if he is from the royal family and a potential heir to the throne who does not even know that he has the power as an apparent heir to the throne to ask anything from the King and it will be given to him. In 2 Samuel 13:13 Tamar uses her wisdom to beg the "very fool" Amnon to speak to the king and ask her hand in marriage.

A foolish man in Israel is one who is harsh, hard-headed, cruel and stubborn and does not listen.[14] A foolish man in Israel is stiff-necked and evil in his doings. He disregards the law of God, especially on matters of sex.[15] He pays evil for good, does not walk in the ways of the Lord and he usually dies a sudden death.[16] Is this the kind of man to whom Tamar was bringing Amnon's attention? Though it is not immediately clear from the text, it is possible to see in the story that Tamar's voice stands strong in a context in which women and girls are seen as objects of sexual desire and passive recipients of SGBV.[17] The scene of the incident of Tamar's rape is set within the confinement of a house of royalty, where it is expected that Tamar, being Amnon's sister, is also a royal daughter. Thus, she deserves to be treated as a child of royalty, just like Amnon.[18] The setting of the house of royalty is supposed to provide legal protection to a daughter of royalty in accordance to the legal provisions of Deuteronomy 22:23-29. This particular law provides an interpretation

---

11 See Strong's Concordance, Hebrew Dictionary. "Amnon (or Aminon), a son of David. Hebrew: אַמְנוֹן, 'amnôn (H550)". Online at: https://www.quotescosmos.com/bible/bible-concordance/H550.html [Accessed 22 November 2022].

12 See Eugene MH. 2008. *Kingdom of Priests: A History of Old Testament Israel*. Ada, MI: Baker Academic, 278.

13 See Halbertal M and Holmes S. 2019. *The Beginning of Politics: Power in the Biblical Book of Samuel*. Princeton and Oxford: Princeton University Press, 27-35

14 See Barber CJ. 2003. *The Books of Samuel, Volume 2: The Sovereignty of God Illustrated in the Life of David*. Eugene, OR: Wipf and Stock Publishers, 207.

15 See Bible, Leviticus 18.

16 See Bible, 1 Samuel 25. See also Unknown. "Married to a Fool: Abigail and David, Part I", *Thinking Girl's Bible Study*, 3 July 2017. http://www.thinkinggirlsbiblestudy.com/2017/07/married-to-fool-abigail-and-david-part-1.html [Accessed 22 May 2020].

17 See a similar silenced voice in Bible, Judges, 19:25-29.

18 See Malliett LA. 2013. *Tamar's Closet: A Journey of Healing*. Bloomington, IN: WestBow Press, 93

that should grant justice to Tamar because she screamed. And yet, ironically, it is Tamar's rapist, Amnon, who enjoys immunity to the law of justice against rape. The royal house should enable justice to Tamar; yet it is the perpetrator who is protected and the voice of the victim silenced.

The household and family setting becomes the best setting for her to be sexually abused, denied justice and her voice silenced.[19] In the words of Amnon, "Get this woman out of my sight and bolt the door after her", as seen in 2 Samuel 13:17 and the narrator's words in 2 Samuel 13:17-20, it is possible to imagine the psychological trauma that Tamar went through. Just like Tamar, many victims of rape in Kenya suffer a double tragedy. The patriarchal structures prevent them from seeking justice, while at the same time some cannot access quality healthcare services. In fact, in some cases, the socio-economic status of some perpetrators grants them immunity against the legal laws that are supposed to protect women and girls from being raped. Additionally, the stigma associated with rape prevents many from seeking medical treatment; hence, some even die from injuries or sexually transmitted infections.[20]

Even so, the power of Tamar's voice against Amnon's action creates a conversational platform for steering conversations on sexual dignity and the need to sensitise women and girls to: (1) the fact that SGBV is a criminal offence that should not be spiritualised by praying the pain away; (2) the short-term and long-term social, physical and mental health implications that are attached to SGBV; (3) possible unusual behaviours that may lure unsuspecting women and girls in the family setting to SGBV; (4) the importance of sensitising family members on proper response mechanism on matters SGBV; and (5) the need to be watchful over the role of the "Jonadabs" of our contemporary Kenyan society who conspire to lure unsuspected victims to SGBV or aid SGBV through sex trafficking. Tamar's voice in the context of Covid-19 opens up opportunities for challenging religious settings and theological discourses to be sensitive to the legal and health implications of SGBV. In order to read and re-read 2 Samuel 13 as standing for the dignity of a woman's sexuality, it is first important to analyse Tamar's voice from the Kenyan context of Covid-19.

---

19 See Krafft EK, Giustina JAD and Krumholz ST. 2021. *Gender, Crime, and Justice: Learning Through Cases*. Lanham, MD: Rowman & Littlefield.

20 See Warenga N. 2021. "Access to Justice for Sexual Violence Against Women: A Socio-Legal Analysis of Case Reporting in Kenya", in Lubaale EC and Budoo-Scholtz A (eds). *Violence Against Women and Criminal Justice in Africa: Volume I: Legislation, Limitations and Culture*. Berlin, Germany: Springer Nature, 148-176; Gatuguta A et al. 2018. "Missed treatment opportunities and barriers to comprehensive treatment for sexual violence survivors in Kenya, a mixed study", *BMC Public Health* 18:769.

TAMAR'S VOICE IN 2 SAMUEL 13 FROM THE CONTEXT OF COVID-19

The story of Tamar in 2 Samuel 13 has been shared by many women and girls in Kenya during the context of Covid-19. Silenced voices, conspiracy among family members to conceal SGBV crimes and the difficulty in accessing healthcare services became the plight of many victims of SGBV. Available information shows that "the devastating SGBV impact of Covid-19 on women and girls is widely underreported."[21] Additionally, perpetrators of SGBV escape criminal justice through bail. Law enforcers are bribed to delay cases of SGBV. Thus, perpetrators are remanded beyond the mandatory period hence being enabled to apply for bail.[22] Some criminals take advantage of the bail to flee to neighbouring countries and escape the hand of justice. In some family settings, men conspire to commit SGBV and walk freely in the street without being charged. Kenyan lawyer, politician, and parliamentarian Millie Odhiambo notes, that "there is a general lack of information about sexual abuse, the likely predators, how to prevent abuse and lack of a solid legal and policy framework to eliminate abuse in Kenya."[23] The Kenya Covid-19 period witnessed increased cases of SGBV in which perpetrators were family members.[24] In some case, household duties have been used to lure victims into SGBV.[25] Kenya has a high HIV/AIDS prevalence in the general population yet, due to poverty, ignorance and powerlessness, rape victims may not escape HIV infection. Thus, SGBV is a justice issue and a terrible crime against women and girls, with potential lethal effects if the rapist is HIV positive.

In a patriarchal society like Kenya, men rely on their power of position and authority to commit sexual crimes against women.[26] The status of a man in the society or family can be a fertile ground for sexual violence to thrive. By analogy, in 2 Samuel 13, Amnon was told by Jonadab, his adviser and son of Shimeah, who was also a brother of King David, to ask Amnon's father King David to ask Tamar to prepare a meal for him as described in 2 Samuel 13:3-6. Having been brought up

---

21 See Bufacchi V and Byrne EC. 2022. "Covid-19 and Social Justice", in Schweiger G (ed). *The Global and Social Consequences of the Covid-19 Pandemic: An Ethical and Philosophical Reflection*. London, UK: Springer Nature, 146.

22 See Kabaseke C and Kitui B. 2021. "Access to Justice for Female Victims of Sexual Violence in Uganda", in Budoo-Scholtz A and Lubaale EC (eds). *Violence Against Women and Criminal Justice in Africa: Volume II: Sexual Violence and Vulnerability*. London: Springer Nature, 69.

23 See Odhiambo M. 2004. "Protecting Children's Rights in Kenya: Advancing the Case of a Sexual Offences Bill", in Kumari V and Brooks SL (eds). *Creative Child Advocacy: Global Perspectives*. New Delhi: SAGE, 141.

24 United Nations Children's Fund (UNICEF). 2020. "Violence against children and adolescents in the time of Covid-19", *UNICEF.org*, 31 August.

25 See McMillin DC. 2009. *Mediated Identities: Youth, Agency, & Globalization*. New York: Peter Lang, 159.

26 See Onyango JO. 2008. "The Masculine Discursive Construction of Rape in the Kenyan Press", in Uchendu E (ed). *Masculinities in Contemporary Africa*. Oxford OX: African Books Collective, 65.

in a patriarchal society, it seems that Jonadab knows that if Tamar was asked by her father to prepare food for his brother Amnon and she refused, the King would use his power as a father and head of the family to command Tamar to prepare a meal for her brother Amnon. In the Song of Songs 1:5-6, one hears a similar complaint against the use of anger and power by men to force a woman to work in the vineyards under hot sunshine. She was powerless and she worked in the vineyards and neglected her body to the extent that the daughters of Jerusalem looked down upon her. In the Song of Songs, we do not hear of any legal action against men who hurt women.[27] It is interesting to also see how the king aids in committing a crime yet "there are no laws" in Israel to also make the king answerable.[28] We thus see that in the Kenyan patriarchal setting, a daughter is not expected to say no to the instructions of a father. In the absence of a father, a brother can use the name and authority of a father to lure unsuspecting female sibling to SGBV. One can argue that SGBV usually arises from unequal power relationships.

In Kenya, perpetrators of SGBV can still walk freely within the family and also be set free on very affordable bonds. This has contributed to the continuing circle of perpetrators committing SGBV.[29] According to 2 Samuel 13:21, King David hears that Amnon has raped Tamar. He becomes furious, but he does not use his authority as the king to take any legal action against Amnon in accordance with Jewish law as provided for in Deuteronomy 22:22-23. In many Kenyan communities, perpetrators enjoy the protection of their fathers – a strong strand of patriarchy. Additionally, in many patriarchal settings like Kenya, sex is a taboo issue. In the Old Testament and in many African communities, it is shameful to speak about sex in both the public and the private spheres. Is this why Amnon suffers in silence with sexual feelings without sharing it in public? In 2 Sam 13:9, Amnon asks everybody to get out after Tamar has served him with food. This makes it possible for Amnon to sexually abuse Tamar without any witnesses. This way it will be Tamar's word against Amnon's. By analogy, many victims of SGBV never get justice on account of the lack of witnesses or concrete evidence. Even in cases that successfully get convictions, criminals sometimes find ways of appealing against the judgment on account of irrelevant, contradictory and inconsistent evidence and the categorisation of sexual abuse in relation to penetration of the penis through the virgin.[30] Some victims therefore choose to suffer in silence for fear of being victimised for falsely accusing perpetrators of SGBV. Thus, the silences voices on matters of sex become a fertile ground for SGBV.

---

27 See also Bible, Song of Songs, 5:7.
28 See the role of King David in the rape of Tamar in Yamada FM. 2008. *Configurations of Rape in the Hebrew Bible: A Literary Analysis of Three Rape Narratives.* New York: Peter Lang, 129.
29 See Onyango JO. "The Masculine Discursive Construction of Rape in the Kenyan Press", 65-68.
30 See, for example, the appeal of *Mohamud Omar Mohamed v Republic of Kenya*, "Criminal Appeal 2 of 2020", [2020] eKLR, that took place on 28 October 2020.

In Kenya, sexual violence within the context of the family setting is kept a secret, and victims remain desolate and depressed. In many African communities, protecting the family name against scorn is taken very seriously. Just like in the case of Jonadab, who aided Amnon to rape Tamar, brothers can conspire to lure unsuspecting victims into SGBV. On 18 November 2020, for example, Cheti Praxides, a newspaper reporter for *The Star*, documented the story of a nameless 14-year-old girl who was raped and impregnated by two brothers in Lamu at the coastal area of Kenya. The suspects were arrested, but they were unfortunately released on bond.[31] Incest is considered a sexual perversion, so much so that when sexual abuse happens, care is taken to make sure the matter stays within the family.[32] This makes it very difficult for victims of incest to seek professional help in case of serious health risks. The situation is even worse if the victim is infected with STIs or HIV. For fear of being profiled as a prostitute, many young girls do not seek medical help. This is because virginity is highly valued in Kenya, as in many African societies. Thus, any young girl who is diagnosed with a sexual infection is associated with sexual immorality. Unfortunately, sexual offenders, some of whom who are HIV positive, target virgin girls because of the belief that if they have sex with a virgin girl, they will be cured from HIV infection.[33] In such circumstances, it will be difficult for the girl to seek medical attention for fear of being victimised and or blamed.

In 2 Sam 13:20, Absalom confirms that Amnon has raped Tamar. Yet he asks her to be quiet and not to be bothered by the matter for now, because Amnon is Tamar's brother. The dominance of men's voices and the silenced voices of women in patriarchal settings cannot go unnoticed.[34] In 2 Samuel 13, the voices of men dominate throughout the narrative. This is typically the case in the Kenyan patriarchal settings, where even issues of reproductive health, are decided by men on behalf of women. In fact, in Kenya, men dominate the reproductive health facilities, making it very difficult for women to be helped by women professionals who may have a deeper understanding of sexual issues that have a direct impact on the health of fellow women. That is why SGBV occurs throughout the women's life cycle, from conception to old age, in different ways.

Even with prevalent cases of SGBV in Kenya during the Covid-19 lockdown, the Kenyan government did not do much to protect women and girls against SGBV during this crisis. On a daily basis, the government shared with the public measures put in place to minimise the spread of Covid-19. Key among the measures was the emphasis on curfew hours, the extension of lockdown days and the "stay-at-home"

---

31 See Praxides C, 2020. "Lamu girl gang raped by two brothers gives birth to twins", *The Star*, 18 November.

32 See Rugene N. 2022. "Incest: A tale of families' dark secrets behind closed doors", *The Standard*, 22 March.

33 See Mathai MA. 2006. *Sexual decision-making and AIDS in Africa: A look at the social vulnerability of women in Sub-Saharan Africa to HIV/AIDS: A Kenyan Example.* Kassel, Germany: Kassel University Press GmbH, 276.

34 See Silberschmidt M. 1999. *"Women Forget that Men are the Masters": Gender Antagonism and Socio-economic Change in Kisii District, Kenya.* Stockholm: Nordic Africa Institute.

measures. Unfortunately, even with the outcry of increased SGBV, there is no single script, written or oral, that stipulates measures put in place by the government to protect women and girls against SGBV. Available published reports indicate for example that the Kenyan government failed to provide timely access to quality health care for victims of SGBV, such as emergency sexual, reproductive and psycho-social care. In fact, some law enforcers also sexually abused women and girls.[35] In Kenya, many households are headed by women. Unfortunately, Covid-19 lockdown measures, made it difficult for some women to economically provide for their families; yet the Kenyan government failed to provide protection services and financial assistance to women who were bread winners to their families. The reports also observed that crimes were also not properly investigated or prosecuted.[36]

Notably, quarantine measures against Covid-19 have created stress and anxiety, causing some men to project their anger on women.[37] Many men have taken advantage of the generalised confinement period and courts not being in session to abuse women and girls. Many women and girls have had no choice but to stay confined in their homes with their abusers, fearing that they will be infected with coronavirus if they leave their home. Even if some women and girls have the option of leaving the house, survival is hard in the harsh economic times caused by Covid-19. In Kilifi, for example, a number of women are fishmongers, who depend on selling fish to survive. They sell the fish to Pwani University staff and students. When the university is not in session, they have no customers. Hence, the only choice is to stay at home and depend on the very perpetrators of SGBV. Notably, SGBV increases in times of crisis, such as natural disasters, wars and epidemics.[38] African traditional oral law demands total submission of women towards men. Through socialisation women believe that submission demands being silent on matters SGBV. Thus, if the father silences victims of SGBV to protect the name of the family, the mother will be afraid to seek legal justice in the name of submission to the father as the head of the family. The submission is further reinforced in Christian settings, with biblical laws requiring total submission of wives to husbands as unto the Lord, as shown in Ephesians 5:22-33.

PROBLEMATISING THE DIGNITY OF WOMEN'S SEXUALITY

In Deuteronomy 25:12, if a woman grabs the testicles of a man, with an intention of rescuing her husband, the hands of the wife rescuing her husband must be chopped off without pity. Yet, cases of SGBV are prevalent in the Old Testament. The dignity

---

35 See "Kenya police arrest prison warden over rape of patient in Covid-19 quarantine", Reuters, 17 July.
36 See Jerving S. 2021. "Report: Kenya failed to protect GBV survivors during pandemic", Devex, 21 September.
37 See Salari N et al. 2020. "Prevalence of stress, anxiety, depression among the general population during the Covid-19 pandemic: a systematic review and meta-analysis", Global Health 16:art 57.
38 See UNICEF. 2022. "Gender-based violence in emergencies", UNICEF.org, 31 January.

of women's sexuality is human dignity, hence the need to problematise the concept of the dignity of human sexuality. This way, it will be possible to present the dignity of women's sexuality as human dignity. Notably, the meaning of human dignity is heavily contested, contingent and fragile.[39] Even so, it is worth underscoring the fact that the sexuality of a woman is part of her totality as a human being that cannot be ignored or obscured. God caused Adam to fall into deep sleep so that God could take time to create a suitable companion for him, as in Genesis 2:21. That is why when Adam woke up from his deep sleep, he saw God's masterpiece of creation in the nakedness of a woman and exclaimed, "This is now bone of my bones and flesh of my flesh", as shown in Genesis 2:23. In fact, because Adam and Eve were from one flesh, they were naked yet, felt no shame, as in Genesis 2:25.

It is the negative attitude of some men towards the sexuality of women that continues to socialise women to be ashamed of their sexuality, thereby presenting women's sexuality as an overriding "problem", which defines their access to legal justice, health and spirituality. The women's sexuality continues to be a riddle that must be defined in order to fully comprehend its mystery. In the process of addressing the mystery of the sexuality of women, most story lines are so full of violence that they do not respond to the diversity of women's desires, health, sexuality, spirituality and experiences of sexual encounters.[40] In 2 Samuel 13, one encounters the worldview of men towards the sexuality of women. It is a world where the voices of women are suppressed, the power of men prevails to prevent the crime of SGBV and the prevailing worldview that relegates the voices of victims of SGBV to the periphery, condemning victims of SGBV to a life of solitude. At the centre of the story is the power of men over the sexuality of women and the craftiness of a man like Jonadab in the conspiracy to commit a sexual crime without being punished by the laws of the land.[41] Jonadab is described in 2 Samuel 13:3 as a son to Shimeah, David's brother. Jonadab is therefore a cousin to Amnon besides being referred to as his friend. Is there a family complicity and conspiracy in the rape of Tamar in relation to matters royal power?

Just like in Tamar's case, there were such similar cases in Kilifi during the Covid-19 period. Many women and girls were raped by very close relatives, and their voices silenced by very close family members to protect the family from shame. Many victims were prevented from seeking criminal justice. On the other hand, those who were prosecuted were granted bail and are interacting with members of the society freely, putting the lives of many victims of rape at risk.[42] Kenya being a patriarchal

---

39 See Cunningham S. 2016. "Reinforcing or Challenging Stigma? The Risks and Benefits of 'Dignity Talk' in Sex Work Discourse", *International Journal for the Semiotics of Law* 29(1):45-65.

40 See Jantz G. 2010. *Too Close to the Flame*. Brentwood, TN: Howard Books, 163.

41 See West, "A Trans-Textual and Trans-Sectorial Gender-Economic Reading of the Rape of Tamar", 113.

42 See Warega N. 2021. "Access to Justice for Sexual Violence Against Women: A Socio-Legal Analysis of Case Reporting in Kenya", in Lubaale EC and Budoo-Schultz A (eds). *Violence Against Women and Criminal Justice in Africa: Legislation, Limitations and Culture*, vol I. First Edition. London: Palgrave Macmillan, 148-176.

society, the mothers of female victims of rape are usually silenced and threatened. In fact, in African oral history traditions, sex is a taboo subject, and matters of sex cannot be verbalised in the private or public sphere. The sexuality of a woman in particular is treated mysteriously. This continues to make it difficult for victims of SGBV in Kenya to have a voice on matters of sex and to seek legal justice or healthcare services. In Tamar's story, her voice is silenced, yet we also don't hear the voice of the victim's mother. 2 Samuel 3:3 and 1 Chronicles 3:2 show that Tamar's mother, Maacah, was David's third wife, and daughter to King Talmai of Geshur. Thus, Tamar was also from a linage of royalty from her maternal family a matter that would have given Tamar's mother a voice on matters criminal justice for her daughter. Yet, the dominance of male voices remains a strong element of patriarchal power over women's sexuality in the story.[43] Tamar is raped and thrown out of the house with a bolted door behind her.[44] Has Tamar been banished and her fate doomed because she has lost the dignity of her sexuality through the loss of her virginity? In Kenya, the African traditional oral law provides that a daughter who loses her virginity is supposed to be banished since she has brought shame to her father and brothers.[45]

In many African communities too, the dignity of a woman's sexuality is directly linked to her virginity. It is interesting to note that the same men who insist upon marrying virgin girls are the same men who break the virginity of girls through rape. Arguably, problematising the dignity of women's sexuality means categorising the dignity of a woman's sexuality as human dignity. When it comes to matters of health, the sexuality of a woman plays a key role in the flourishing of life since; sexuality is part of the human person's totality. Safe sexual experiences are an integral part of the health of a woman. Kenyan society, just like many other patriarchal societies, should be sensitised on the importance of the legal aspects and health components of a woman's sexuality for the well-being of the whole society. Problematising women's sexuality means naming, exposing and criticising the negative world views that undignify women's sexuality. It means dignifying women's life and nurturing by creating conducive environments that allow for justice for victims of SGBV to flow like a river and for women's health and spirituality to flourish.[46] Kenyan women should also be sensitised on legal rights that pertains SGBV. It is difficult for an African woman to live a life of dignity if she is unwell mentally, physically and if she spiritually feels alienated from God. It is important to note, that in African Christian settings, the stigma that is associated with SGBV is linked to the legal and holiness code of the Bible. Thus, when a woman is raped, she

---

43 West, "A Trans-Textual and Trans-Sectorial Gender-Economic Reading of the Rape of Tamar", 113-115.

44 See Van der Walt. "Hearing Tamar's Voice".

45 The emphasis here is that most of the laws that are used to reinforce SGBV are not written down; yet through the social structures of the Kenyan patriarchal society, the laws continue to be orally passed on from one generation to the other

46 Nynäs P. 2016. *Religion, Gender and Sexuality in Everyday Life*. London and New York: Routledge.

will suffer physical injury, mental illness and spiritual alienation. Hence, without a holistic approach that paves the way for victims of SGBV to access justice, it will be difficult for victims of SGBV to feel reconciled to themselves, to society and to God.

LOVE, PASSION OR ENDOGAMY: A SEXUAL ANALYSIS OF 2 SAMUEL 13

A sexual analysis of the biblical text is one that creates a link between love, sex, passion, law and health from the context of power, explicit sexual expression and dialogue. It is the responsibility of every progressing country, including Kenya, to ensure that gender norms and unequal power relationships fuelling SGBV are criminalised. For any sustainable development goals to be realised, women's health should be prioritised from a legal and criminal point of view. The family institution is at the centre of life continuity in every society. Unfortunately, it is also the very place where the health of women continues to be fragile as a result of increased cases of SGBV that were witnessed during the measures taken to curb the spread of Covid-19 in Kenya. A sexual analysis, in dialogue with 2 Samuel 13, is a strong dialogical approach that can allow for the integration of spirituality, health and legal perspectives on SGBV in the Kenyan Covid-19 context. This way, care is taken also to bring charges of conspiracy to commit a crime to the Jonadabs.[47] As used in the context of this chapter, the Jonadabs are family members who make it possible for women and girls to be raped; yet these very enablers are never prosecuted. Some of them include relatives who ask victims not to seek criminal justice on matters of rape. This they do in order to protect the name of the family. In this way, it will be possible to read 2 Samuel 13 for the dignity of a woman's sexuality.[48] When one applies a sexual analysis to 2 Samuel 13, one gets the opportunity to ask: is it love, passion, or an endogamous event?[49] Endogamous is the practice of allowing marriage only within a specific tribe, caste, ethnic or religious group.[50] Thus, a sexual analysis of 2 Samuel 13 allows for one to question whether Amnon's feelings towards Tamar were flames of sexual obsession or true love as indicated in 2 Samuel 13:1.

In the Old Testament, women are in most cases portrayed as objects of sexual desire whose bodies are at the disposal of men. Thus, we see that in 2 Samuel 13, Tamar does not initiate sexual encounters the way a woman does in the Song of Songs 1:2. Even in a marriage, we are told that Adam knew his wife and she conceived and bore Cain as seen in Genesis 4:1. In Genesis 21:1-3, we are not told that Abraham

---

47 See West "A Trans-Textual and Trans-Sectorial Gender-Economic Reading of the Rape of Tamar", 113.

48 See Cook R and Cusack S. 2011. *Gender Stereotyping: Transnational Legal Perspectives.* Philadelphia: University of Pennsylvania Press.

49 The word "event" is used with caution as an alternative, for lack of a better word, to a relationship because what happens in 2 Samuel 13 is not a relationship but more of a staged episode.

50 See Rao CNS. 2012. *Sociology.* New Delhi: S. Chand Publishing.

had sex with his wife Sarah. We only hear that God visited Sarah and did unto Sarah according to what God had spoken, and Sarah conceived and bore Abraham a son in his old age. Thus, women's voices are constantly silenced on matters sex. Yet, it is in the contexts of silenced voices on matters of sex and the mysterious treatment of God's gift of human sexuality to humanity that SGBV thrives.[51] In the Song of Songs, one encounters the voice of a woman who unapologetically and explicitly initiates sexual encounters, presenting a romantic love that is stronger than death, as we see in Song 1:2-4 and 8:6. While love in the Song of Songs conquers death, sexual desire and the flames of passion, the narrative of 2 Samuel 13 leads to a desolate life for Tamar. It is from this perspective that one might argue that sex is a power issue that can give life or take away life.

In 2 Samuel 13, sex has the power to take away life, because the power for legal jurisdiction against SGBV as provided for in Deuteronomy 22:23-27 is in the hands of men. David H. Jensen, an Old Testament scholar, speaks of "how many men it takes to rape a woman and escape legal action."[52] The conspiracy of Jonadab and the passion of Amnon shutter Tamar's desire to enjoy a life of marriage.[53] In the Old Testament, an ideal marriage was usually an endogamous marriage to a cousin. The eldest daughter was often forbidden to marry outside the family.[54] Abraham married his half-sister as indicated in Genesis 20:12. In Genesis 24, when Isaac needed a wife, Abraham sent his servant back to his homeland to find a woman from his relatives. In Genesis 27, Rebekah convinced Isaac to send their son Jacob away to her family to find a wife. Thus, a sexual analysis of 2 Samuel 13 arguably shows a possibility of a proposed endogamous marriage from Tamar's direct speech to Amnon in 2 Samuel 13:13. In a sexual analysis of 2 Samuel 13, one sees a possible proposal of a love that can heal sexual desire through love that conquers death as in Song 8:6. From Tamar's direct speech to her brother, it is obvious that she loved him genuinely as a sister that she wanted to protect him from his foolishness that was eventually going to lead to his death as provided for in the Old Testament's legal code of Deuteronomy 22:23-27. The very opening words in 2 Samuel 13:1, "Some time passed", arguably prepare the readers to the politics of love, passion, sex and power.

In 2 Samuel 12:10, King David had just been warned that the sword will never depart from his house following his adultery with Bathsheba and his wholesome murder of eighteen men, including Bathsheba's husband Uriah. The question is: why should the rape of Tamar be staged in preparation for David to pay for his sins through the death of David's children, as seen in 2 Samuel 13:23-39 and 2 Samuel 18?

---

51 Clark A. 1987. *Women's Silence, Men's Violence: Sexual Assault in England, 1770-1845*. London: Pandora, 15.

52 Jensen DH. 2015. *1 & 2 Samuel: A Theological Commentary on the Bible*. Louisville, Kentucky: Presbyterian Publishing Corporation, 232.

53 deSilva DA. 2000. *Honor, Patronage, Kinship & Purity: Unlocking New Testament Culture*. Downers Grove, IL: InterVarsity Press, 176.

54 DeSilva, *Honor, Patronage, Kinship & Purity*, 176.

Tamar's voice has been celebrated by a number of feminist scholars as a resilient voice that can empower women not to take sexual violence lying down.[55] In the same spirit, Tamar's proposal is another strong conversational tool on matters about women's sexual health, passion, love and marriage. This is particularly important in patriarchal contexts such as Kenya where women have no voice when it comes to matters sex and sexuality. The guiding question is: can Tamar's voice and proposal be used in a Kenyan context as a life and safety negotiation tool in ways that can enable the lives of female victims of SGBV to flourish?

HUMAN DIGNITY AND THE DIGNITY OF WOMEN'S SEXUALITY

It is difficult to speak about the dignity of human sexuality and the dignity of women's sexuality without situating the two concepts within the context of the biblical concept of human dignity. The Bible does not directly speak about human dignity. However, in Genesis 1:27, God creates man and woman in God's image and likeness. This does not make it easy to define the term human dignity. German constitutional law, for example, has addressed the problem of whether to regard human dignity as a constitutional value or a constitutional right.[56] There is a premium placed on the monetary aspect of value as a principal standard for judgment. Viewing this German concept through a Kenyan hermeneutical lens uncovers the need to underscore human dignity beyond strictly monetary or economic value as a universal human right that transcends borders and contexts. Seen this way, it is possible to conceptualise the place of human dignity as a normative standard, principle and right in domestic and global healthcare decision-making especially when it comes to SGBV.[57] Human dignity is an inherently inalienable right. It is the unconditional right of a person to be valued and respected for their own sake regardless of gender, sex, race, status or circumstances. Thus, "human dignity is denied when any one is subjected to devalue based of their sexuality, exposed to SGBV, torture, degradation, discrimination or cruel punishment."[58] The dignity of a woman's sexuality is a positive aspect of the concept of human dignity.[59]

Human rights activist Lukman Harees argues that "human dignity is a notoriously slippery term with ambiguous interpretations and that if such a term must be used; it should be conveyed through stories."[60] However, even with the notoriousness of the term, a sexual approach to the concept of human dignity allows for one to see

---

55 Claassens JLM. 2016. *Claiming Her Dignity: Female Resistance in the Old Testament.* Collegeville, MN: Liturgical Press.

56 See Barak A. 2015. *Human Dignity.* Cambridge: Cambridge University Press, 235.

57 See a detailed discussion in Smith GP. 2018. *Dignity as a Human Right?* Washington, DC: Rowman & Littlefield.

58 See Valdés E. 2021. *Biolaw: Origins, Doctrine and Juridical Applications on the Biosciences.* London: Springer Nature, 68.

59 Based on Barak, *Human Dignity*, 235.

60 See Harees L. 2012. *The Mirage of Dignity on the Highways of Human "Progress": The Bystanders Perspective.* London: AuthorHouse, 93.

the dignity woman's sexuality in Genesis 1:27. This text provides that the dignity of all human beings originate from God. Every human being is linked to the other through the image of God an affirmation of our natural born right and our sacred right.[61] Implicit in this is the fact that human beings should treat each other with a sense of awe. Thus, women have the right to be valued, respected and treated with dignity. By virtue of this, the concept of human dignity should be integrated into issues of SGBV.

Firstly, a woman's sexuality is connected to human dignity because it is God's masterpiece of creation. In Genesis 2:23, Adam celebrates the uniqueness of Eve through the exclamation: "This is now bone of my bones and flesh of my flesh." The exclamation is done with a dignifying attitude, a language of reverence and endearment. Thus, a woman's sexuality should be conceptualised beyond the value attached to procreation, as is the case in the Israelite and in the Hebrew context and the Kenyan patriarchal contexts. The Kenyan Law of Succession (Amendment) Bill, 2019, which is the primal law on inheritance, puts the value of a woman's sexuality in procreation. The amendment of the law was skillfully done in a way that can allow men to enjoy sexual pleasure without taking responsibility for childcare support in case of pregnancy. Since former president Uhuru Muigai Kenyatta ascended the bill into law on 17 November 2021, the law has come under sharp criticism for fostering gender inequality, as has been observed by Kenyan lawyers on legal matters and ethical issues Jessica Oluoch and Gaudence Were.[62] In Genesis 1:27-28, the blessings accompanying procreation are only pronounced after God has created human beings in God's image and likeness. Thus, there is a strong theological statement in patriarchal contexts like Kenya that connects a woman's value, and therefore her dignity, to her sexuality in terms of procreation. On the same note, just like in the case of Tamar in 2 Samuel 13, women should not just be used and disposed of as though they are sexual objects.

Secondly, connecting human dignity to the dignity of a woman's sexuality creates a criterion for seeking justice for victims of SGBV. SGBV is a justice issue. Unfortunately, because Kenya is a highly religious nation, culture and religion combine to prevent victims of SGBV from seeking justice. Notably, preventing mitigating and responding to SGBV has moved to the top of the global agenda; yet SGBV remains one of the most pressing justice challenges in many nations.[63] Starting conversations on the dignity of women's sexuality from the context of human dignity opens up possibilities for urgency when it comes to the sensitisation programmes that target women and girls and their legal rights in matters of SGBV. To understand a woman's sexuality as human dignity opens up a liberating approach towards

---

61 Hopkins DN. 2017. *Black Theology-Essays on Global Perspectives*. Eugene, OR: Wipf and Stock Publishers, 99.

62 See Kenya Legal & Ethical Issues Network on HIV and AIDS (KELIN). 2021. "Inheritance Rights in Kenya: Law of Succession (Amendment) Bill 2019", *KELINKenya.org*, 19 November.

63 See Leach M (ed). 2015. *Gender Equality and Sustainable Development*. New York, NY: Routledge.

sacred texts that are used to demand total submission of women and girls towards men. It means giving women voice to speak out against SGBV and to seek justice for fellow female victims of SGBV.

Thirdly, underscoring a woman's sexuality as human dignity opens up sexual dignity talks that can allow all to see human sexuality as a gift from God. It provides dignified guidelines for introducing sex education and conversations about the dignity of human sexuality in schools that can help to prevent and mitigate SGBV in the society. SGBV is a life-altering experience for women in matters of health, sexuality and spirituality. The Nationwide Children's Hospital (NCH) Children and Families Project has pointed out that victims of SGBV need a safe space in which they can make sense of their experiences and gain supremacy over their life-altering traumatic experiences.[64] There is need for safe spaces that can be used to steer sexual dignity talks in a way that values the sexuality of both men and women. This can be achieved by deconstructing the negative worldview of women's sexuality and reconstructing a positive concept of women's sexuality in particular and human sexuality in general. Sexual dignity talk has the potential to create a foundation for legal and religious systems that responds to SGBV.

CONCLUSION

In 2 Samuel 13, one sees how patriarchy gives absolute power to men over women. That is why, even though the Old Testament in Deuteronomy 25:11-12 has legal provision that would have granted Tamar justice over Ammon, it is Amnon who enjoyed immunity. In the same way, we see that there were escalated cases of SGBV during Covid-19 in Kenya. The patriarchal nature of Kenyan society silences women on matters of sex because of the power of men over women and the negative worldview of men over the sexuality of women. SGBV transcends context, class, race, time, religion and culture. In Tamar's voice and through the context of Covid-19, one sees the importance for re-reading 2 Samuel 13 for the dignity of women's sexuality. The strategies that Tamar uses to protect her sexual dignity arguably present a woman's sexuality as theological phenomenon and an issue of justice, health and human dignity. Locating Tamar's voice within the context of Covid-19 and re-reading 2 Samuel 13 for the dignity of women's sexuality is to vindicate equality, and to express respect for the value of life itself. It is an opportunity to use an African women's approach and a sexual lens to interrogate gender bias in the application of the Old Testament laws on human sexuality.

---

64 Nationwide Children's Hospital (NCH), Children and Families Project. 2001. *Creating a Safe Place: Helping Children and Families Recover from Child Sexual Abuse.* London and New York: Jessica Kingsley Publishers, 59.

15 THE KENYAN COVID-19 PREVENTION PROTOCOLS: AN UNEXPECTED BOOST IN THE OBSERVANCE OF THE FEMALE HIJAB

Moza Ally Jadeed[1]

INTRODUCTION

When the outbreak of Covid-19 was announced in Kenya on 12 March 2020,[2] both the president and the National Emergency Response Committee on Coronavirus (NERCC) issued directives to curb the transmission of the virus and reduce its related fatalities.[3] The Cabinet Secretary for Health, who chairs the NERCC,[4] made a press release on 13 March 2020 and called for maintenance of social distance by one metre from persons who are coughing or sneezing.[5] Shortly thereafter, the president made a national address on 15 March 2020 and put in place further public health measures. These included: travel restrictions, quarantine, closure of schools and alteration of working schedules. Both public and private institutions were encouraged to allow their staff, except for staff in critical or essential services, to work from home and to avoid congregate meetings, such as social gatherings, congestion in public transport and crowding in shopping malls.[6]

All these measures were heightened or relaxed, depending on the prevalence rate of the disease in the country, via subsequent directives until 11 March 2022, when a majority of the measures were lifted up. The requirement to social distance, for example, increased to one and a half metres, regardless of whether the other person was coughing and sneezing or not.[7] It also became mandatory for every

---

1 Lecturer, Faculty of Law, University of Nairobi. The author thanks Badru Jaffar and Ali Dzimba for their insightful comments during the writing of this chapter. She dedicates this chapter to Dr Mwanakombo Mohammed Noordean who introduced the author to the conference. Until her demise, Dr Noordean was a Senior Lecturer of Swahili Studies at Moi University (Kenya). She brainstormed with the author on the possible contents of the chapter and reviewed the first draft of its abstract. Dr Noordean died in February 2022.
2 Kagwe M. 2020. "First Case of Coronavirus Disease Confirmed in Kenya", *Ministry of Health*, 13 March, 1.
3 NERCC is an ad-hoc multi-agency structure for coordinating, among other things, "Kenya's preparedness, prevention and response to the threat of the coronavirus disease". See National Emergency Response Committee on Coronavirus (Executive Order No 2 of 2020), para III. The president created NERCC on 28 February 2020.
4 See NERCC Executive Order No 2 of 2020, para V.
5 Kagwe, "Confirmed First Case", 2 n2.
6 See generally Kenyatta U. 2020."Address to the Nation on Covid-19, Commonly Known as Coronavirus, at Harambee House, Nairobi", 15 March.
7 Kenyatta U. 2020."Presidential Address on Enhanced Measures in Response to the Covid-19 Pandemic", 6 April, para 16.

person to wear a face mask in public.[8] A nationwide curfew also ran from 7:00 pm to 5:00 am to minimise the spread of the virus during nighttime social gatherings.[9] The curfew applied to every individual except personnel engaged in work designated "essential".[10] The government further locked out highly infected administrative counties from the rest of the country.[11] The Ministry of Health also developed guidelines to assist healthcare workers when managing a suspected or confirmed Covid-19 patient.[12] One of these guidelines included the usage of personal protective equipment (PPE), such as a medical mask and long-sleeved gown, to protect the healthcare personnel from contamination.[13]

The observance of these preventive measures was strict, and noncompliance attracted penal sanctions. In line with the social distancing measures, for instance, public transport commuting vehicles had to carry up to a maximum of 50% of their licensed capacity.[14] Contravening this directive constituted a criminal offence. And its penalty was a fine of Kenya shillings 20 000 (approximately 172 US dollars)[15] or a jail term of not more than six months.[16] This same punishment extended to users of both private and public transport systems who failed to don a face mask that covered the mouth and nose.[17] On the other hand, employers were mandated to release their non-essential staff from work by 4:00 pm to enable the latter to conform to the curfew rules.[18] Otherwise, the employers risked the cost of accommodating these employees should the latter fail to make it to their homes by 7:00 pm.[19] In fact, the police received strict instructions to implement the curfew.[20] Some people

---

8   Kenyatta, "Presidential Address on Enhanced Measures", paras 16 and 17.
9   See Public Order (State Curfew) Order, 2020 (Legal Notice 36/2020), para 3.
10 See Public Order (State Curfew) Order, 2020, para 5 and the schedule (i.e. addendum to the order).
11 Kenyatta, "Presidential Address on Enhanced Measures", para 30. The 2010 Constitution divided the country into 47 self-governing units called counties. See Constitution of Kenya, art 6(1).
12 See generally Ministry of Health and University of Nairobi. 2021."Interim Guidelines on Management of Covid-19 in Kenya: Covid-19, Infection Prevention and Control (IPC) and Case Management". Nairobi: Ministry of Health and the University of Nairobi.
13 MOH and U Nairobi, "Interim Guidelines on Management of Covid-19 in Kenya", 67.
14 See Rule 5(3) of The Public Health (Covid-19 Restriction of Movement of Persons and Related Measures) Rules, 2020 (Legal Notice 50/2020).
15 This is as per the exchange rated issued by the Central Bank of Kenya on 13 May 2022. See Central Bank of Kenya. 2022."Forex", 13 May. Online at: https://www.centralbank.go.ke/forex
16 See Public Health (Covid-19 Restriction of Movement of Persons and Related Measures) Rules, 2020 [hereinafter Restriction of Movement Rules], rule 11.
17 See Restriction of Movement Rules, rule 5(4).
18 See Public Order (State Curfew) Variation Order, 2020, para 2.
19 Kagwe M. 2020. "Press Release on the Update of Coronavirus in the Country and Response Measures as at 28 March 2020", *Ministry of Health*, 28 March.
20 Kagwe M, "Press Release on the Update of Coronavirus", 5.

suffered severe physical injuries or died in incidents of police brutality when they failed to be at home at 7:00 pm.[21]

Unexpectedly, however, the enforcement of some of these public health protocols benefitted Muslim women who observe fully or nearly all the Islamic rules on modesty. Measures such as outlawing handshakes, wearing a face mask, lockdown except to go out for essential services, social distancing in public spaces and the wearing of long-sleeved gowns by healthcare practitioners favoured these *hijabi* women. These containment rules aligned with five *hijab* rules.[22] And these rulings addressed: wearing a *niqab* (face veil),[23] a *jilbab* (an outer garment covering the head through the neck to the bosom or beyond) or *abaya*, (an outer garment covering the neck to the feet often worn with a separate head gear), staying at or working from home and keeping a distance from or shaking hands with unrelated males. Subsequently, there was a significant reduction of jeers, side-eyes and lack of appreciation of these women's expression of their Islamic faith in the country. Prior to the pandemic, *hijabi* women faced difficulties explaining to both Muslim and non-Muslim compatriots their choice to observe these forms of the *hijab*.

This chapter examines how the enforcement of these public health measures saved *hijabi* women from past psychological and physical injuries. It argues that the indifferent treatment suffered by these women before Covid-19 was discriminatory and that the limitations placed against the observance of the *hijab* served no objective purpose. Nor was the means to achieving that purpose proportionate. In essence, the chapter reveals that the response to the Covid-19 pandemic exposed the hypocrisy of both state and non-state actors towards the *hijab*. During the pandemic, it became normal to observe certain body coverings and societal behaviours akin to the *hijab* rulings.

Guided by the Muslim feminist method of a thematic reading of the Quran,[24] this chapter first traces the obligation to observe the *hijab*. The chapter conjoins this intratextual reading of the Quran with relevant pieces of Prophet Muhammad's *hadith* (sayings) to collate the *hijab* rules and to define a *hijabi* woman. The chapter also shares the popular conception of the *hijab* in Kenya. Working with an equivalent minority rights theory, that of critical race feminism,[25] the chapter then narrates the

---

21 "Nine Weeks of Bloodshed: How Brutal Policing of Kenya's Covid Curfew Left 15 Dead", *The Guardian*, 23 October 2020.

22 An Arabic word which means a veil, a drape or a screen. All the meanings of Arabic words in this chapter, unless contained in a quote, are derived from Baalbaki R. 1995. *Al-Mawrid: A Modern Arabic-English Dictionary*. Seventh Edition. Beirut: Dar El-Ilm Lilmalayin.

23 A discussion on the Islamic legal position of the face veil follows in the subsequent parts of the chapter.

24 Barlas A. 2002. *"Believing Women" in Islam: Unreading Patriarchal Interpretations of the Qur'an*. Austin: University of Texas Press, 15-19; Wadud A. 1999. *Qur'an and Woman: Rereading the Sacred Text from a Woman's Perspective*. Second Edition. New York: Oxford University Press, xii and 2.

25 See, for example, Wing AK and Smith MN. 2005."Critical Race Feminism Lifts the Veil? Muslim Women, France, and the Headscarf Ban", *University of California Davis Law*

different experiences of *hijabi* women before, during and after the Covid-19 containment measures. In particular, the chapter interrogates victims' stories and the author's observations in detailing these experiences. The chapter further embraces justice as plural and calls for the observance of both constitutional and legislative provisions which protect the *hijabi* women of unnecessary hindrances.

DEFINING A *HIJABI* WOMAN

This chapter construes a *hijabi* woman as any adolescent or older Muslim female who embraces all or nearly all the *hijab* rules. While the word *hijab* is understood conventionally to meaning a headscarf or a covering of a Muslim woman's head,[26] it is more than that. An intratextual reading of the Quran and a collation of the Prophetic sayings reveals that the requirement for *hijab* is for both sexes.[27] But as it relates to women, the stipulation entails covering the head, covering the bosom, wearing a loose-fitting outer garment, covering the face, lowering the gaze, concealing ornaments and decorations, except for what is apparently visible, along with keeping a distance from males within permissible degree of marriage,[28] avoiding shaking hands with such males, avoiding speaking with a melodious voice, refraining from wearing incense or perfume, refraining from striking one's feet when walking, walking on the roadside instead of the middle of the street, refraining from strutting before strange males and leaving one's house only to perform or seek an essential duty or need.[29]

Importantly, the observation of this array of rules happens when the Muslim woman is in public.[30] And the word "public" in Islam means in the presence of an *ajnabiyy* (a strange member of the opposite sex). Thus, a woman may still be deemed to be in public, even in the privacy of her house, if an unrelated male (or related but within permissible degree of affinity) is present. Otherwise, in the absence of any of these males, a Muslim woman's obligation to the *hijab* fades. She uncovers and conducts herself appropriately,[31] depending on the sex and her familial closeness with that other person(s) and the context within which they are interacting. But, even then,

---

Review 39:743-790; Crenshaw K. 1991. "Mapping the Margins: Intersectionality, Identity Politics, and Violence against Women of Color", *Stanford Law Review* 43(6):1241-1299.

26 Cohen-Almagor R. 2022. *The Republic, Secularism and Security: France versus the Burqa and the Niqab*. Cham: Springer, 8.

27 Barlas, *"Believing Women" in Islam*, 159. See also Quran 24:30 and 58. The first number in Quranic citations refers to a *surah* (Arabic word for a chapter of the Holy Quran), while the second relates to an *ayah* (plural *ayat*) which means a verse.

28 "Strangeness" means permissible degree of marriage. Once married, however, a husband and a wife move out of this category of distantness. Quran 24:31 outlines males within the private fold of women.

29 See generally Quran 24:31 and 33:59.

30 Cohen-Almagor, *The Republic, Secularism and Security*, 8.

31 Hafiz Ibn Kathir. 2003. *Tafsir Ibn Kathir (Abridged)*, vol VII. Second Edition. Riyadh: Darussalam Publishers, 70.

the Muslim woman remembers that she can only reveal her *awrah* (private parts) to her legitimate spouse.[32] This last rule can, however, be suspended in case of an exigency, such as medical attention.

Basically, all of the *hijab* rulings derive from the Quran and the *sunnah*,[33] which are the elemental sources of *sharia* (Islamic law).[34] The institution of *hijab* is to establish and preserve sexual purity in the society. This is achieved by arresting any possible triggers to sexual corruption and sexual immorality and by moulding a character of bashfulness for both sexes.[35] Quran 24:30, 31 and 58, and 33:59 highlight this message, as do the prophetic sayings on separating the males and females,[36] avoiding handshakes and women's refraining from wearing incense or perfume.[37]

Scholars, however, differ on the legal position of the *hijab* generally and each of its rulings. The pioneers of Muslim feminism,[38] for instance, dismiss the obligation of the *hijab*. They further opine that the ruling on covering the head is limited to seventh-century Muslims.[39] These scholars construe the word *khumuur*,[40] in Quran 24:31 to limit the reigning *hijab* ruling as covering of the bosom. While Sunni Muslims accept the *hijab* as obligatory, divergence exists among reputable contemporary orthodox scholars on the place of the face veil and gloves. Some find these two pieces of clothing obligatory.[41] Others, however, construe these items as highly recommended.[42] And both camps predicate their opinions on Quran 24:31 and relevant prophetic sayings.

Despite these varied theological and scholarly opinions, this chapter embraces the view that *hijab*, in itself, as a symbol of modesty, is an Islamic requirement. This

---

32 See Hadith 4017 in Abu Dawud SA. 2008. *English Translation of Sunan Abu Dawud*, vol IV. Khattab N (transl). Riyadh: Darussalam Publishers, 381-382.

33 The *sunnah* is made up of Prophet Muhammad's sayings, deeds, and his approval of the deeds of others.

34 Jadeed MA. 2020.*The Inheritance Rights of Muslim Women in Kenya: Reality or Rhetoric?* DPhil Thesis, University of Nairobi, 28. See also Quran 53:3-4, which expresses that the Prophet related "inspiration sent down to him".

35 Robert NB. 2005. *From My Sisters' Lips: A compelling celebration of womanhood – and a unique glimpse into the world of Islam*. London: Bantam Books, 185.

36 See Hadith 462 and 678 in Abu Dawud SA. 2008. *English Translation of Sunan Abu Dawud*, vol I. Qadhi Y (transl). Riyadh: Darussalam Publishers, 284 and 404.

37 Hadith 565 in Abu Dawud, *English Translation of Sunan Abu Dawud*, Qadhi (transl), I:349.

38 See, for example, Barlas, *"Believing Women" in Islam*; Mernissi F. 1992. *The Veil and the Male Elite: A Feminist Interpretation of Women's Rights in Islam*. Reprint Edition. Lakeland MJ (transl). New York: Basic Books.

39 See, for example, Mernissi, *The Veil and the Male Elite*, 85-101.

40 A derivative of the Arabic word *khimar*, which means a veil.

41 See, for example, Ibn Bazz AAA. 2016. *English Translation of Majmoo Al-Fatawa* [Collection of Legal Verdicts] *of Ibn Bazz*, vol I. Riyadh: Alifta, 205.

42 See, for example, Albani MND. 1974. *Hijab al-mar'ah al-Muslimah fi al-Kitab wa-al-Sunnah* [The Muslim Woman's *Hijab* from the Quran and Prophetic Tradition]. Beirut: al-Maktab al-Islami.

inference emanates from several Quranic verses, including the four mentioned above.[43] Quran 33:59, for instance, instructs the Prophet to tell his wives, daughters "and the believing women" to wear an outer garment whenever in public.[44] The precept identifies the reason for this garment as identifying these women as respectable. The phrase "and the believing women" lends itself to all ages.

This is so because the *asbab ul nuzuul* (the reasons for revelation) of Quran 33:59 persist today. While the letter of Quran 33:59 addressed the prevailing situation, when female slaves and non-Muslim women went out immodestly in seventh century Arabia, its spirit continues today. More than ever, it is important for Muslim women to cover their body and decorations to convey their modesty and keep off unsolicited male approaches.[45] Quran 33:39 is explicit that when Muslim women observe the *hijab*, they would be identified as respectful "and not molested".[46]

But while hiding that observing modesty is obligatory, the argument of the present study is that the body of *hijab* rulings has both *wajib* (obligatory) and *mustahab* (recommendable) acts. This deduction stems from the very language of the Quran and prophetic sayings.[47] With respect to the five *hijab* rules under discussion, the argument is that obligations include covering the head, wearing an outer garment that at least covers the bosom, keeping a distance from strange males and avoiding shaking hands with strange males. Meanwhile, covering the face and leaving one's home only to perform or seek an essential duty or service are highly recommended acts.[48] Moreover, the face veil only becomes obligatory when a woman accessorises her face through make-up or other decorations, such as false eyelashes.[49] This perspective fits well with Quran 24:31, which says of women that "they should not display their beauty and ornaments except what (must ordinarily) appear thereof", meaning what is apparent.[50]

As it differs among scholarly opinions, the construction of the *hijab* also differs among Kenyan Muslim women. But the common view is that the *hijab* relates to head coverings.[51] Thus many Kenyan Muslim women, both Sunni and Shia, cover

---

43 Other precepts on the *hijab* are Quran 33:32, 33 and 53.
44 Ali AY. 2001.*The Meaning of the Holy Qur'an*. Eleventh Edition. Beltsville, MD: Amana Publications, 1077.
45 Wing and Smith, "Critical Race Feminism Lifts the Veil?", 764.
46 Ali, *The Meaning of the Holy Qur'an*, 1077.
47 See Hadith 1825, 1833 and 1833 in Abu Dawud, *English Translation of Sunan Abu Dawud*, Khattab (transl), II:387-388, 391-392 and 422; and Hadith 641 in Abu Dawud, I:387.
48 See Quran 33:33. See also Hadith 565 in Abu Dawud, *English Translation of Sunan Abu Dawud*, I:349.
49 Abdul-Wahid AK. 2021."Al-Albānī on the Niqab of the Muslim Woman, Whether It is Wajib or Not, the Permissibility of Uncovering Her Face and Hands – and the Danger of Displaying Her Beautifications in Public", *Abu Khadeejah*, 7 April, 5.
50 Ibn Kathir, *Tafsir Ibn Kathir*, 68.
51 See, for example, Wangila MN. 2012. "Negotiating Agency and Human Rights in Islam: A Case of Muslim Women in Kenya", *Contemporary Islamic Studies*, 5; Abdi ZA. 2021. "Let Us

their heads, but these coverings range from covering the hair, to parts of the hair or the full head, including the ears. Women with strong religious background, through school or family, wear an outer garment too. And some of them add the face veil and gloves.[52] Muslim female students often observe the *hijab* through wearing a headscarf or a *jilbab* extending over the bosom or to the knees, with a pair of pants under their school skirts and dresses. Other Muslim women, however, do not find the *hijab* an obligation and do not cover their heads. They may wear tight-fitting clothes and other decorations in public.

KENYAN *HIJABI* WOMEN'S EXPERIENCES

Because of their different understandings of the *hijab*, Kenyan Muslim women have had a mixed experience with it. While some experiences have been positive, other experiences have been negative. This section of the chapter examines both the law and *hijabi* women's experiences before, during and after the Covid-19 pandemic, interrogating the prevailing law during each period to assess whether it is a driving force in these experiences.

Law in the pre-Covid-19 moment

While the law permitted Muslim women to observe the *hijab*, a number of them did not. From the time of colonialism until the advent of Covid-19 in March 2020, the law has favoured *hijabi* women. The law permitted women to observe any form of *hijab*. The Mohammedan Marriage and Divorce Registration Act (MMDRA),[53] for example, allowed *purdah-nisheen* women to send their agents to register their marriages or divorce on their behalf.[54] *Purdah-nisheen* women were adult females of Indian heritage, who secluded themselves in their homes and objected to attend public offices.[55] Women could also cover their heads and faces, as well as wear outer garments whenever they left their houses.[56]

The now repealed 1963 Independence Constitution of Kenya cemented the observation of the *hijab* rulings through the recognition of freedom of conscience. Both Section 22 of the original constitution and Section 78 of the later amended version guaranteed a *hijabi* woman the right to observe any form(s) of *hijab*. This freedom, however, was subject to the interests of public safety, defence, public health, public

---

Muslim Women Wear *Hijab* in Peace, We Are Not Complaining", *Nation*, 24 March.

52 Dluzewska A. 2007. "The Impact of Islamization on the Interaction between locals and tourists in Kenya". Warsaw: Muzeum Historii Polski, 148 and 149.
53 Mohammedan Marriage and Divorce Registration Act (MMDRA), ch 155 (repealed).
54 MMDRA, s 10 (repealed).
55 MMDRA, s 2 (repealed).
56 See Hirsch SF. 1998. *Pronouncing and Persevering: Gender and the Discourses of Disputing in an African Islamic Court*. Chicago: University of Chicago Press, 50.

morality, public order and the rights and freedoms of others.[57] But such exceptions only merited if they were "reasonably justifiable in a democratic society" and contained in legislation.[58]

When Kenya adopted the Constitution of Kenya, 2010, the rights of *hijabi* women were protected by Articles 32 and 27(4) and (5).[59] While Article 32 safeguards freedom of religion or belief (FoRB), Articles 27(4) and (5) proscribe discrimination on the basis of religion, belief and dress by both the state and individuals. Just like Section 78 of the repealed constitution, Article 32 permits a *hijabi* woman to observe any form(s) of *hijab*. But Article 32 of the 2010 Constitution is broader than Section 78 of the Independence Constitution because its proscription against forcing someone to act contrary to her religion is all encompassing.[60] It extends to innumerable situations and places. This includes compelling a *hijabi* to stop observing any of the *hijab* rules at any area, building or institution. Another important addition in Article 32 is the prohibition against denying someone employment, entry into an institution or the enjoyment of such other human rights and fundamental freedoms because of the expression of her faith.[61]

The limitations to enjoying FoRB under the Constitution of Kenya, 2010, are almost similar to those in the repealed law. But the present ones drop the grounds of public safety, defence, public health, public morality and public order. Again, for a limitation to succeed, it must meet three further concurrent conditions. First, the limiting legislation must contain a provision stating explicitly its "intention to limit that right" and "the nature and extent of the limitation".[62] Second, that provision must clarify and specify that FoRB is the subject of limitation. The provision must also be clear and specific about the "nature and extent of the limitation".[63] Finally, that limitation must not be so constricting that it renders the bearer as if she had no such right in the first place.[64]

The first dual preconditions to limiting FoRB in the present 2010 Constitution are similar to those in the repealed Independence Constitution. First, such limitation must be mandated by legislation.[65] Second, such limitation must be objective and merited in a country possessed of ideals such as human dignity, freedom and

---

57 Constitution of Kenya, 1963, s 22(5) (original independence constitution) and Constitution of Kenya, 2010, s 78(5).
58 Constitution of Kenya, 1963, s 22(5) and Constitution of Kenya, 2010, s 78(5).
59 The Constitution of Kenya, 2010, became operative on 27 August 2010.
60 Constitution of Kenya, 2010, s 78(3) and (4) cover oaths and religious instruction or observance in learning institutions only.
61 This provision was embodied in the freedom from discrimination clause in the repealed constitution.
62 Constitution of Kenya, 2010, art 24(2)(a).
63 Constitution of Kenya, 2010, art 24(2)(b).
64 Constitution of Kenya, 2010, art 24(2)(c).
65 *Seventh Day Adventist Churches (East Africa) Ltd v Minister for Education & 3 Ors* [2017] eKLR 15.

equality. This objectivity and merit, however, are discerned when all relevant factors are weighed. Examples of such cogent considerations are the relationship between the denial of the observance of *hijab* and its purpose – and whether there are other means of achieving this purpose without denying *hijabi* women the right to observe the *hijab* rules.

The Constitution of Kenya, 2010, also protects *hijabi* women under the nondiscrimination clause.[66] Under Article 27(4) and (5), the constitution outlaws both direct and indirect discrimination on the basis of religion, belief and dress by state and non-state actors respectively.[67] Direct discrimination is any different treatment, rule, law or policy which is predicated primarily – that is, intentionally – on any of these protected characteristics.[68] Indirect discrimination, on the other hand, occurs when an otherwise neutral treatment or policy nonetheless impacts *hijabi* women negatively because of any of these protected identities.[69] As is the case with FoRB, this protection from discrimination can also be limited. But its limitation must meet the rigours of the constitution. In addition to the Constitution of Kenya, 2010, several statutes further protect *hijabi* women. These include the National Gender and Equality Commission Act,[70] the Kenya National Human Rights Commission Act,[71] Kenya Medical Training College Act[72] and the Basic Education Act.[73]

The pre-Covid-19 hijabi experience

Notwithstanding these legal guarantees and the absence of any legislation limiting FoRB or freedom from discrimination, *hijabi* women suffered scorn and negative differentiation. Some tertiary institutions and employment facilities that have a uniform code restricted the *hijab* to a headscarf that covers the head, ears and neck only. Meanwhile, other establishments insisted on the removal of the face veil before entry as a security measure. The reluctance of some women to shake hands with strange male colleagues, acquaintances and relations evoked side-eyes, disbelief and taunts. The decision of other *hijabi* women to stay in or work from their homes

---

66 Cleveland SH. 2021. "Banning the Full-Face Veil: Freedom of Religion and Non-Discrimination in the Human Rights Committee and the European Court of Human Rights", *Harvard Human Rights Journal* 34:227-228 (discusses the interplay between FoRB and freedom from discrimination).

67 But characteristics such as culture, ethnicity and race can also work. See generally *Watkins-Singh, R (on the application of) v Aberdare Girls' High School & Anor* [2008] EWHC 1865.

68 See, generally, UN Human Rights Committee, "General Comment 28" in *Note by the Secretariat, Compilation of General Comments and General Recommendations Adopted by Human Treaty Bodies* (UN Doc HRI/GEN/1/Rev9 (Vol I), 2008) para 16.

69 See, generally, International Centre for the Legal Protection of Human Rights (Interights). 2011. *Non-Discrimination in International Law: A Handbook for Practitioners* 1. London: Interights, 8.

70 National Gender and Equality Commission Act (No 15 of 2011), s 8.

71 Kenya National Human Rights Commission Act (No 14 of 2011), s 8.

72 Kenya Medical Training College Act (Chapter 261), s 6.

73 Basic Education Act (No 14 of 2013), ss 4, 27(d), 39(c) and (h), 59(1) and (k).

caused them to be perceived as submissive and housebound in a pejorative sense.[74] In a similar way, the introduction of the female-only public transport vehicles was dismissed as divisive and economically unsound. This section details some of these *hijab* violations.

Education and employment hijab bans

One of the most conspicuous infractions against *hijab* observance was the refusal by the Kenya Medical Training College (KMTC) to allow its students in the Department of Nursing to wear a *jilbab*. Until August 2018, some Muslim female nursing students across all the KMTC campuses in the country wore a *jilbab* – sometimes extending down to the knees – on top of their uniform both in the lecture rooms and during hospital rotations.[75] The uniform is a blue dress which has the institutional badge affixed on or just below the position of the left breast. Beginning September 2018 and after the summer vacation, however, most of the KMTC campuses issued a directive which banned the *jilbab*.[76] Instead, the administration called on the Muslim female students to wear a headscarf, which only covered the head, ears and neck. According to the principals of the various campuses, this change emanated from a letter from the Deputy Director (Academics) of KMTC. The letter had forbidden the *jilbab* as part of the nursing students' uniform and insisted on the headscarf.

The letter gave four reasons for banning the *jilbab*. First, the *jilbab* concealed the institutional badge on the students' dress. Second, the length of the *jilbab* posed a health risk. It was probable that its flowing nature would allow it to touch a patient and carry micro-organisms when the nursing student is attending to other patients. Third, the length of the *jilbab* also made the wearer take longer time to manage a patient, because they would need to adjust it every time it drooped. Fourth, the *jilbab* covered some students' chins.[77] The institution wanted the entire face visible.

Thus, in keeping with the letter's requirements, the campuses' principals implemented the *jilbab* ban, albeit in different ways. While some ordered an immediate switch to the headscarf, some principals first discussed it with both male and female Muslim students and with the Muslim leadership, deciding to keep the ban when no consensus was reached. Others staggered the change, providing two weeks to reflect on it and then requiring a short *jilbab* up to the waist to acclimatise the students to the shorter headscarf. Yet still other principals complained of the length of the *jilbab*, but they did not outlaw it. The ban on the *jilbab* was implemented on innumerable KMTC campuses. Students who defied the ban were ejected from

---

74 Beydoun KA and Sediqe N. 2023. "Unveiling", *California Law Review* 111:29.

75 KMTC has 71 campuses. See https://kmtc.ac.ke/campus-list [Accessed 20 April 2022].

76 The author, alongside other Muslim lawyers, received complaints of *hijab* violations in KMTC campuses in 2019. She then collected information from *hijabi* students from Mwingi, Embu, Makueni, Siaya and Nairobi campuses.

77 Depending on how a *hijabi* covers, it is possible to cover the chin – even when the rest of the face remains uncovered.

classes, denied entry into hospitals to do rotations and faced disciplinary action. Many chose to wear the headscarf to avoid disruption of their studies.

Handshakes, transport, homework, face veils

Hijabi women also suffered sneers from distant males with whom they expressed reluctance to shake their hands, as well as from people who witnessed the refusal.[78] Those taking offence verbalised their displeasure or grudgingly remained mum. The misunderstanding arising from the refusal to shake hands with distant males has impacted some *hijabi* women's participation in public activities. A number of professional women would rather abdicate attending professional functions instead of appearing impolite or extreme for refusing to shake hands with male colleagues. When some Muslim private investors set up a fleet of women-only *matatus* for public transportation in the traditional Muslim port city of Mombasa in the 1990s, jeers also erupted.[79] Critics dismissed this arrangement as alienating. The initiative was faulted as reinforcing gender inequality and the belief that women are in need of protection from males. The resumption of similar taxis in Nairobi in 2019 was also discredited as unsustainable because of its high fares.[80] The decision by a majority of Muslim women to be stay-at-home mothers or to work from home received censure. Critics dismissed such women as '"lazy" or taking the "easy" option.[81] They also labelled them as subjugated and secluded. These labels exerted pressure on some Muslim women to value more their participation in the economy outside their homes. Such women would seek employment outside their homes, regardless of whether such pursuit was less cost-effective, was having a toll on their mental health or was preventing them from observing their *hijab*.[82] The face veil also received criticism by some people, who decried it as extremism.[83] Some regarded it as a conduit of terrorism and treated its wearers as a security threat

---

78 Devlin P. 2017. "Australian Universities Back Handshake Ban for Muslims", *Mail Online*, 22 February.

79 *Matatu* is the Swahili word for the 14-seater vans – the popular means of public transport then. The 2019 Census estimated the Muslim populace in Mombasa at 37.8%. See Kenya National Bureau of Statistics. 2019. *2019 Kenya Population and Housing Census Volume IV: Distribution of Population by Socio-Economic Characteristics*. Nairobi: KNBS, December, 422. But the identity of Mombasa remains predominantly Muslim because of its relatively high Muslim population compared to many parts of mainland Kenya since pre-colonial era. Cussac A. 2008. "Muslims and Politics in Kenya: The Issue of the Kadhis' Courts in the Constitution Review Process", *Journal of Muslim Minority Affairs* 28(2):292.

80 Chason R. 2021. "Kenyan Women Love the Idea of a 'Women-Only' Rideshare. They Hate that the Option Costs More", *Washington Post*, 12 September.

81 Khattab H. 2001. *The Muslim Woman's Handbook*. Second Revised Edition. London: Ta-Ha, 30.

82 Shepherd-Banigan M et al. 2016. "Workplace Stress and Working from Home Influence Depressive Symptoms Among Employed Women with Young Children", *International Journal of Behavioral Medicine* 23:103.

83 See Ali FA. 2018. "Understanding the Role of Gender Relations in Radicalising and Recruiting Young Muslim Women in Higher Learning Institutions in Kenya", *The African Review* 45:90.

if they did not reveal their faces fully.[84] Others found that the face veil obscured the identity and communication of the wearer.[85] Consequently, some *hijabi* women were denied entry into buildings until they revealed their faces or removed the veil completely. Their production of identity documents was rendered inadequate. Security personnel in a local university, for example, prevented *hijabi* women from entering the university premises until the students revealed their faces.

All these infractions were painful and caused the *hijabi* women, what Adrien Wing, a critical race feminist, terms as "spirit injuries", which are the "psychological, spiritual, and cultural effects of multiple types of assaults upon women".[86] As demonstrated in their experiences, some *hijabi* women underwent self-doubt, denial, helplessness and shame and they made self-destructive career decisions.

Law in the Covid-19 moment

The outbreak of the pandemic was in many ways beneficial for *hijabi* women. The enactment of public health measures facilitated the observance and wearing of the *hijab*. During the pandemic, both the constitutional and legislative provisions protecting the *hijab* remained operational. What changed was the introduction of fresh rules and policy directives to help manage the infection. Through the advice of the National Emergency Response Committee on Coronavirus (NERCC) and medical practitioners, both the president and the Cabinet Secretary for Health (CS Health) put in place a number of public health protocols. Most of these measures targeted everyone in the country. There were lockdowns, social distancing, bans on handshaking, and wearing of a face masks. Healthcare personnel had to wear long-sleeved gowns when attending to an infected or suspected Covid-19 patients under these public rules. Generally, the observance of all these measures was mandatory or highly recommended, and failure to adhere to them attracted penal sanctions.

Social distancing

The first measure in addressing the Covid-19 pandemic was social distancing. This began with advice to keep a distance of about one metre from persons who were coughing or sneezing. But when some infected cases were found to be asymptomatic, the CS Health directed people to keep a distance away from others who did not come from the same households as themselves.[87] The president enhanced this distance to one and a half metres in his later address. And it became the law to maintain social distance in all public spaces including in public transport, shopping

---

[84] Begum T. 2020. "How Making Face Masks Mandatory in England Makes Muslim Women Feel", *The Independent*, 28 June.

[85] Smith J. 2013. "Let's Face It – the Niqab is Ridiculous, and the Ideology behind It – Weird", *The Independent*, 21 September. See also Begum, "How Making Face Masks Mandatory in England Makes Muslim Women Feel".

[86] Wing and Smith, "Critical Race Feminism Lifts the Veil?", 779.

[87] Kagwe, "Press Release on the Update of Coronavirus 20 March 2020", 6.

malls, supermarkets, workplaces, schools and all learning institutions.[88] The Public Health (Covid-19 Restriction of Movement of Persons and Related Measures) Rules, 2020, required that public transport commuting vehicles had to carry up to a maximum of 50% of their licensed capacity.[89]

As part of the social distancing measures, the government encouraged both public and private institutions to alter their working schedules. Thus, all staff, except those offering essential services, were advised to work from home.[90] Employees who had underlying health conditions and those aged 58 years and above were mandated to work remotely from home. Both corporations and businesses were encouraged to introduce a 24-hour shift in place of the usual 8:00 am to 5:00 pm shifts to facilitate implementation of the social distancing rules, both at the offices and in the public transport system.[91] Where employees were operating from the office, they similarly had to keep a distance from each other.[92]

Contravening the social distancing rules amounted to a criminal offence, which was punishable under the Public Health Act. Such a contravention was construed as intent to spread the virus.[93] Thus, for instance, where *matatu* operators defied the rules, they suffered prosecution, suspension or revocation of their SACCO licences and bonding of their vehicles.[94] The penalty for failing to observe social distance in other public spaces was a fine of Kenya shillings 20 000 (approximately 172 USD)[95] or a jail term of not more than six months.[96] The social distancing directives also extended to some common social behaviour, such as shaking of hands. While no law prohibited handshaking when exchanging greetings, both the president and healthcare personnel discouraged the habit.[97] Instead there was a growing

---

[88] Kagwe, "Press Release on the Update of Coronavirus 20 March 2020", 4.
[89] See Public Health (Covid-19 Restriction of Movement of Persons and Related Measures) Rules, 2020 (Legal Notice 50/2020), rule 5(3)).
[90] Kenyatta, "Address to the Nation on Covid-19 15 March 2020".
[91] Kagwe, "Press Release on the Update of Coronavirus 20 March 2020", 6.
[92] Kagwe, "Press Release on the Update of Coronavirus 20 March 2020", 6.
[93] Kagwe M. 2020. "Update of Coronavirus in the Country and Response Measures as at 5 April 2020", NERCC, 5 April. 6.
[94] Kagwe, "Press Release on the Update of Coronavirus 20 March 2020". A SACCO is a member-driven Savings and Credit Cooperative Organisation. As part of regulating the public transport system, the National Transport and Safety Authority requires every *matatu* operating publicly to join a SACCO before it licenses it to operate.
[95] This is as per the exchange rated issued by the Central Bank of Kenya on 13 May 2022. See CBK, "Forex", 13 May.
[96] See Public Health (Covid-19 Restriction of Movement of Persons and Related Measures) Rules, 2020, rule 11.
[97] See Kenyatta U. 2020. "President Kenyatta Urges Kenyans to Observe Government Directives on Coronavirus", Office of the President of the Republic of Kenya, 7 April.

encouragement to use the fist-bumping, elbow-bumping or employing the *namaste* gesture (a non-contact Hindu greeting).[98]

Lockdown and curfew

The nationwide lockdown was another form of social distancing. About three days after the emergence of the disease in the country, the president ordered the closure of all learning institutions.[99] About three weeks later, the president directed the closure of four highly infected areas for 30 days. These were: Nairobi Metropolitan Area (82% infection) and Kilifi, Mombasa and Kwale Counties (combined 14% infection).[100] There was also restriction of movement in and out of these areas whether "by road, rail or air".[101] The movement of food supplies and other goods by any of these means, however, continued.

Earlier, on 27 March 2020, the Cabinet Secretary for Interior and Coordination of National Government (CS Interior) had declared a nationwide dusk-to-dawn curfew. Under the Public Order (State Curfew) Order, 2020, the CS Interior mandated everybody to be indoors between 7:00 pm and 5:00 am.[102] The initial curfew was to run for 30 days. But it was extended from time to time until 20 October 2021.[103] During this period, however, the timings of the curfew changed to between 10:00 pm and 4:00 am. At all times, nonetheless, the government encouraged people to stay at home.[104] The only workers who were exempted were those providing essential services, such as medical professionals and healthcare workers; national security, postal and courier services; and licensed banks, financial institutions and payment service providers.[105] The government ordered the police to enforce the curfew strictly.[106] Thus a person not in the essential category list could only be outdoors with the written permission of the police.[107]

Wearing face masks

The directive to wear a face mask in public spaces was one of the heightened measures to curb the spread of Covid-19. Initially, the CS Health had called for a good respiratory hygiene. Thus, when announcing the first case of the coronavirus

---

[98] See "Return of the Handshake as Covid Measures Put on the Back Burner", *Daily Nation*, 20 February.

[99] Kenyatta, "Address to the Nation on Covid-19 15 March 2020".

[100] Kenyatta, "Presidential Address on Enhanced Measures in Response to the Covid-19 Pandemic 6 April", para 27.

[101] "Presidential Address on Enhanced Measures in Response to the Covid-19 Pandemic 6 April", para 29.

[102] See Public Order (State Curfew) Order, 2020 (Legal Notice 36/2020), para 3.

[103] Kimuyu H. 2021."President Kenyatta Lifts Nationwide Curfew", *Daily Nation*, 20 October.

[104] Kagwe, "Press Release on the Update of Coronavirus 28 March 2020", 5.

[105] See schedule to The Public Order (State Curfew) Order, 2020.

[106] Kagwe, "Press Release on the Update of Coronavirus 28 March", 5.

[107] See Public Order (State Curfew) Order, 2020, para 4.

patient in the country, the CS Health asked all those found in Kenya to cover their mouths when coughing.[108] The CS Health also called on people to sneeze "with a handkerchief, tissue or into flexed elbow".[109] When the president announced enhanced public health measures three weeks later, he instructed everyone to wear a face mask "when outside the house".[110] The president indicated that he sourced this directive from medical professionals and experts.[111] The breach of any of these rules was an offence, and the penalty was similar to that of breach of social distance.

PPE for healthcare personnel

A medical face mask was a personal protective equipment (PPE) item that was essential for healthcare workers to prevent them from contracting Covid-19.[112] The rest of the PPE included eye-protection, gloves and a long-sleeved gown with a hood. Through guidelines on managing suspected or confirmed Covid-19 patients, the Ministry of Health mandated healthcare workers to use PPE.[113] Specific areas where the employment of the PPE was mandated were when performing aerosol-generating procedures, such as intubation and cardiopulmonary resuscitation, and when collecting specimen from the upper respiratory tract.[114] The government permitted the use of both disposable and reusable gowns.[115] One of the recommended reusable gowns was a long-sleeved water-resistant, plastic-like gown, which was knee-length – very much like the *jilbab*.[116]

The Covid hijabi experience

The public health measures were largely observed. Both individuals and companies, for example, maintained the social distancing rules. Thus supermarkets, banks, utility companies and public spaces marked the queuing spots leading to the cashiers at least one and a half metres apart. And these facilities reminded their

---

108 Kagwe, "First Case of Coronavirus Disease Confirmed in Kenya", 2.
109 Kagwe, "First Case of Coronavirus Disease Confirmed in Kenya", 2.
110 Kenyatta, "Presidential Address on Enhanced Measures", para 16. See also Public Health (Covid-19 Restriction of Movement of Persons and Related Measures) Rules, 2020, rule 6(1)(b).
111 Kenyatta, "Presidential Address on Enhanced Measures", para 17.
112 MOH/U Nairobi. 2021."Interim Guidelines on Management of Covid-19 in Kenya", 67.
113 MOH/U Nairobi. 2021."Interim Guidelines on Management of Covid-19 in Kenya", 26.
114 MOH/U Nairobi. 2021."Interim Guidelines on Management of Covid-19 in Kenya", 27 and 31.
115 MOH/U Nairobi. 2021."Interim Guidelines on Management of Covid-19 in Kenya", 51 and 61.
116 MOH/U Nairobi. 2021."Interim Guidelines on Management of Covid-19 in Kenya", 62 (with a photo showing the gown).

customers constantly to observe the demarcations. Many people also refrained from handshaking.[117]

Meanwhile, the police enforced the nationwide curfew strictly. They were so strict that they employed excessive force on persons found outside beyond the curfew hours. Thus, as of October 2020, at least 15 people had been killed and several others had been injured by the police.[118] On the first day of the curfew, Kenyans witnessed police beating men and women who were about to cross the Likoni channel to get to their homes.[119] Following local and global outcry over this incident, the CS Interior varied the curfew order and mandated all employers to release their non-essential workers by 4:00 pm.[120]

Law and the hijabi experience in the post-Covid-19 moment

When the country's infection rate remained below 5% for several months, the CS Health revised the public health protocols on 11 March 2022.[121] Incidentally the rules relating to wearing face masks and social distancing in public spaces were adjusted. And these adjustments impacted *hijabi* women, too. As was the case before the disease, the constitutional and legislative provisions protecting the *hijab* remained unchanged. The government did lift the obligation to wear masks in public spaces. Instead, the CS Health encouraged the use of the masks in indoor functions. All public transport services were allowed to resume to full capacity, provided that their passengers wore face masks. Kenyans interpreted the adjustments of the containment measures differently. They stopped wearing the face masks both indoors and outdoors. Only air transport maintained the mask. Other public transport systems and utility facilities no longer separated their clients. Gradually, the handshake resumed too.[122] And there is a growing unease for some *hijabi* women's refusal to shake hands with unrelated males.

DEMONSTRATING SIMILARITIES BETWEEN THE COVID-19 PROTOCOLS AND *HIJAB* RULINGS

Hijabi women's experiences before, during and after the pandemic reveal the hypocrisy of both state and non-state actors towards the *hijab*. In a bid to safeguard the right to health, the government and individuals permitted Muslim women to

---

117 Limboro CM. n.d. "Kenya's Response to Covid-19", Azim Preji University Practice Connect.
118 "Nine weeks of bloodshed".
119 Olingo A and Ahmed M. 2020."Dozens Injured as Police Brutality Marks Start of Curfew", *Daily Nation*, 30 March.
120 The Public Order (State Curfew) Variation Order, 2020 (Legal Notice 43/2020).
121 Kagwe M. 2022."Update on Covid-19 in the Country and Response Measures, as at 11 March 2022", NERCC, 11 March, 3.
122 "Return of the Handshake as Covid Measures Put on the Back Burner", *Daily Nation*, 20 February.

observe a myriad of measures alongside other Kenyans. Though these protocols mirrored some hitherto discredited *hijab* rulings, the Kenyan society was comfortable with the new arrangements.

The face mask, for example, covered the face. And while the authorities insisted the mask had to screen the nose and the mouth, it nonetheless covered the chin and parts of the cheeks. The physical effects of the mask were similar to those of the face veil.[123] As in the case of the face veil, the mask was questioned initially for obscuring the wearer's identity, facial expressions and ability to relate with others.[124] But unlike the negative reaction extended to the face veil, Kenyan society navigated these concerns and embraced the face mask. The face mask became a mandatory ticket for entering the public space. It was regarded as a safety measure, rather than a security scare. It became acceptable that the face mask was not necessarily a physical or psychological barrier to communication.[125]

The long-sleeved reusable gown in health facilities has proven to be an alternative means to eliminating the health scare supposedly caused by the *jilbab*, without denying the *hijabi* nursing students the right to observe their *hijab*. The Covid-19 pandemic revealed the importance of this outer covering for healthcare professionals. That lesson now provides an opportunity for institutions like KMTC to introduce an overcoat alongside a headscarf as part of the nursing students' uniform during hospital rotations. KMTC can also require the students to tuck in the headscarf in the overcoat. Meanwhile, KMTC should allow the *jilbab* in the lecture rooms. Failing to consider these proposals gives KMTC's outright *jilbab* ban the appearance of sheer discrimination.

The social distancing directives of lockdown and curfew further showed parity between non-essential workers and *hijabi* women who chose to be stay-at-home mothers or those working remotely from home. Both groups have been mandated by circumstances or the law to stay at home or to work from the house. While the government implored employers to allow their non-essential staff to work from home, these employees could still enter the public space to seek essential goods, such as food, and services, such as medical attention. These are the same opportunities available to *hijabi* stay-at-home mothers or those working from home, even for those with a greater need to engage in activities outside the home, such as visiting relatives, attending funerals, pursuing knowledge and meeting clients.

Meanwhile, the social distancing rule requiring public transport systems to carry up to 50% of their licensed capacity required spacing of the passengers. This decongestion augured well with the *hijab* rule of keeping a distance from males within permissible degree of marriage. And thus, as it did in shopping malls and banks, the rule guaranteed absence of unnecessary groping and inappropriate

---

123 Ong S. 2020."How Face Masks Affect Our Communication", *BBC*, 8 June.
124 Gori M. 2021. "Masking Emotions: Face Masks Impair How We Read Emotions", *Frontiers in Psychology*, 8.
125 Gori, "Masking Emotions: Face Masks Impair How We Read Emotions".

touching of females while receiving services. It was this very concern for the safety of female passengers that saw the introduction of women-only transport vehicles prior to the pandemic.

Finally, the social habit of handshaking when exchanging greetings was discouraged during the peak of the disease. As the president alluded, the absence of shaking hands did not mean loss of love or respect between the two people. As noted above, this reasoning was widely accepted. But *hijabi* women have argued similarly with regard to their hesitance to shake hands with unrelated males. It is not a show of disrespect, but rather an expression of higher ideals. And for *hijabi* women, it allows for conformity to their religious beliefs.

These similarities between the containment measures and the *hijab* rules demonstrate that it was unnecessary, and moreover illegal, to deny *hijabi* women the right to observe any form of their chosen *hijab* prior to the pandemic. The health exigencies during the pandemic made it possible for the rest of the citizenry to accommodate pieces of cloth, garments and social conduct hitherto described as antisocial. It gave *hijabi* women an unexpected boost and a welcome serenity in observing the tenets of their faith.

CONCLUSION

This chapter has demonstrated the similarities between some Covid-19 prevention protocols and five *hijab* rules. It has shown that the face mask can be likened to the face veil. The loose-fitting gown worn by healthcare professionals when attending to Covid-19 patients can be made an alternative to the outer garment long sought by the KMTC Nursing Department students during hospital rotations. The discouragement of shaking hands during greetings is no different from *hijabi* women's reluctance to shake hands with unrelated males. The social distancing in all public facilities, including transport, is not far removed from the interest in women-only vehicles that predated Covid. The curfews and orders to work or remain at home, except for those seeking or rendering essential services, mirrored the choices of some *hijabi* women to be stay-at-home mothers or to work from their houses.

This chapter has thus revealed that the pandemic presented a silver lining in the observance of the *hijab* in the country. Before the outbreak of Covid-19, *hijabi* women – whether students, professionals or ordinary women – faced difficulties in observing the five forms of *hijab*. Learning institutions, professional colleagues, utility companies and the general populace failed to accommodate some of the *hijabi* women's positions on their observance of the *hijab*. This failure pushed some of these women to make painful choices between their right to express their faith and to pursue such other rights such as education, freedom of movement and freedom of association. Yet the law, both legislative and constitutional, has upheld, since colonial days and up to the start of Covid-19, both freedom of religion and the freedom from discrimination on the basis of religion. And there has been no legislation limiting any of these freedoms to justify the exclusions suffered by the *hijabi* women.

This chapter has shown that the *hijabi* women insisted on the five forms of *hijab* because they deemed them to be religious edicts for every adolescent or older Muslim female. While divergence exists among theologians and academics over the obligation of the *hijab* and some of its forms, the *hijab* as a symbol of modesty remains a requirement for Muslim women. While many Kenyan Muslims limit their obligation to headgear, a sizeable number, especially those from strong religious backgrounds also wear an outer garment, either an *abaya* or *jilbab*. Some also add the face veil. In the end, both the Kenyan government's containment measures and Kenyan *hijabi* women's experiences offer good moments for reflection for the country as it emerges from the pandemic. The strict observance of the health protocols created platforms for these women to observe their *hijab* without censure or explaining their positions. Even after the pandemic waned in March 2022 and the government lifted most of the Covid-19 regulations, the face veil has remained acceptable. But the resumed grimaces against *hijabi* women's reluctance to shake hands with distant males and the continued disapproval of an outer garment for Nursing Department students at KMTC both in the classrooms and during hospital rotations suggest that the issues are not entirely resolved. These double standards in the face of the right to health and freedom of religion or belief defeat Kenya's constitutional conviction to uphold the Bill of Rights.

16 THE IMPACT OF THE COVID-19 LOCKDOWN ON THE INFORMAL ECONOMY IN ZIMBABWE: A LEGAL PERSPECTIVE

Lillian Mhuru[1]

INTRODUCTION

A World Health Organization (WHO) fact sheet in January 2020 designated the new Covid-19 coronavirus as a "public health emergency of universal concern".[2] As a measure to reduce the spread of the pandemic, WHO developed guidelines advising people to maintain social distance and practice sanitary precautions. African countries were not immune to the pandemic. In Zimbabwe, the first verified cases were reported in March 2020. Zimbabwe, like other countries, announced its first 21-day lockdown measures starting on 30 March 2020. Additional measures were promulgated and passed in the form of statutory instruments. Some of the extraordinary measures introduced to combat Covid-19 were considered drastic, as they infringed on basic human rights.[3] These include rights such as freedom of movement and assembly, restriction of which halted various business, religious and cultural activities. The lockdown regulations, however, were supposed to be proportionate and reasonable.[4] Measures that were put in place include but are not limited to: (1) the Civil Protection (Declaration of State of Disaster: Rural and Urban Areas of Zimbabwe) (Covid-19) Notice, 2020, which declared the Coronavirus an infectious disease and a state of disaster;[5] (2) the Public Health (Covid-19 Prevention, Containment and Treatment) Regulations, 2020, which declared the disease to be a formidable epidemic disease;[6] and (3) the (Covid-19 Prevention, Containment and Treatment) (National Lockdown) Order, 2020, declared a period of twenty-one days of lockdown, except for essential services and exempted cases.[7] Despite the measures taken to combat the spread of Covid-19 in the early days, the pandemic continued to spread across the globe, and that led to the extended lockdown and closure of national borders.

---

1 Zimbabwe Open University, Faculty of Law, Department of Public Law.
2 World Health Organization (WHO). 2020. "Covid-19 as a Public Health Emergency of International Concern (PHEIC) under the IHR", Fact Sheet 16A.
3 Mavhinga D. 2020. "Lockdown laws draconian, excessive", *The Independent*, 3 April.
4 Harris LB. 2020. "Jail Time for Breaking Covid-19 Regulations", *CITE News*/Center for Innovation and Technology Zimbabwe, 24 March.
5 Civil Protection (Declaration of State of Disaster: Rural and Urban Areas of Zimbabwe) (Covid-19) Notice, 2020 (Statutory Instrument 76 of 2020).
6 Public Health (Covid-19 Prevention, Containment and Treatment) Regulations, 2020, published as Statutory Instrument 77, 2020.
7 (Covid-19 Prevention, Containment and Treatment) (National Lockdown) Order, 2020, contained in Statutory Instrument 83 of 2020.

The WHO's Covid-19 prevention guidelines on hygienic sanitation and the stay-at-home orders that were issued by the state implied that everyone enjoys access to the requisites of socio-economic livelihood, such as adequate housing and access water and adequate food, yet millions of people in Africa live in absolute poverty, without access to the basic needs necessary to lead a dignified life. According to Lovemore Chikazhe and fellow researchers,[8] who are experts in the area of service marketing and strategic marketing in Zimbabwe, the pandemic pushed the plight of the jobless to extreme poverty and helplessness. With an unemployment rate of over 80%, many Zimbabweans who depended on informal business for survival found themselves in a futile and untenable situation. The pandemic caused unprecedented economic challenges in people's livelihoods for the economically vulnerable groups in Zimbabwe – especially on the informal sector. The International Labour Organization (ILO) estimated that relative poverty among informal workers increased by 56% in the first month of the crisis.[9]

Given the population's reliance on the unorganised and informal labour sector in Zimbabwe, it was expected that the pandemic and the subsequent ban on many unofficial activities during the state-imposed lockdown would cause a significant portion of the country's population to fall into utter poverty and increase their risk of contracting Covid-19. Zimbabwe most definitely did not escape the socioeconomic effects of national lockdowns, as sociologists Emmanuel Ndhlovu and Archiford Tembo have noted.[10] Further, research on the effects of the Covid-19 lockdown on the informal trading in Zimbabwe was warranted. The purpose of this chapter is to examine these effects, given the already precarious economic situation of the majority of the Zimbabwean population and the dependence of many in the nation to generate their livelihoods within the informal sector. To accomplish the goals of the present study, in-depth interviews with people running various informal businesses, particularly in the informal trade and informal transportation sectors, were conducted in Harare, using a qualitative design. Three overarching goals were intended to be attained by the question guidelines: (1) to determine the changes the lockdown brought about in the business of informal workers, (2) to examine how the lockdown affected the informal workers, and (3) to identify the survival techniques used during the lockdown. With the help of this design, the researchers were able to investigate and offer in-depth insights into how the Covid-19 lockdown affected the informal sector and how it made those who work in it more susceptible to poverty. The study's design also facilitated taking into account how people felt during the lockdown. The sixteen participants in the present study are members of the informal sector who were involved in informal cross-border trade and informal

---

8   Chikazhe L, Mashapure R, Chavhunduka D and Hamunakwadi P. 2021. "Socio-Economic Implications of Covid-19 Pandemic to Informal traders Entrepreneurs: A Case of the Informal Sector in Zimbabwe", *Business Management and Strategy* 12(1):1-5.
9   International Labour Organization (ILO). 2020. "COVID-19 crisis and the informal economy immediate responses and policy challenges", *ILO Brief*, May.
10 Ndhlovu E. and Tembo A. 2020. "Gendered socio-economic implications of the COVID-19 pandemic in rural Zimbabwe", *BizEcons Quarterly* 12:21-40.

transportation. Pseudonyms were used in the study to protect the confidentiality and anonymity of the respondents as well as to present the practical and ethical issues of the research.

THEORETICAL FRAMEWORK FOR STUDYING THE INFORMAL ECONOMY

The four main schools of thought regarding the nature and make-up of the informal economy are the dualist, structuralist, legalist and voluntarist theories, but the focus of this study is on the legalist theory.[11] The theory of legalism is thought to have originated from a Chinese philosophy whereby people are ruled by regulating the volatile and impulsive behaviour of individuals through strict and stringent laws.[12] This is mainly because it is assumed that humans naturally are attracted to doing wrongs over right as they are driven by impulses and selfish interests. Therefore, in respect of the informal economy, legal scholars contend that the self-employed operate formally and create their own informal extra-legal norms as a result of a hostile legal system.[13] People decide to work in the informal sector in order to escape the formal sector's burdensome rules and high taxes. One could argue that the country of Zimbabwe's sizeable informal sector developed in response to rules and regulations.

In an effort to stop the coronavirus from spreading, the Zimbabwean government introduced policies that indirectly promoted activities that raised the risk of people in this sector contracting the virus as they desperately tried to feed their families. The government also took advantage of the lockdown to enact policies aimed at eliminating the black markets, which led to the sudden and unannounced demolition of many informal trader stalls. According to researchers of the planning and management of human settlements,[14] Zimbabwe's decision-makers have long struggled with urban informality. Similarly, the government destroyed unauthorised urban settlements in 2005 as part of Operation Murambatsvina, as recently described by Abraham Matamanda and his research colleagues.[15] Concerns are usually raised about the way in which power can be abused to stifle unofficial activities in urban Zimbabwe by using this approach to dealing with the informal sector.

---

11 Chen MA. 2012. "The informal economy. Definitions, theories and policies", *Women in Informal Employment, Globalizing and Organizing*, Working Paper No. 1, August. Cambridge, MA: WIEGO.

12 Pines Y. 2018. "Legalism in Chinese Philosophy", *Stanford Encyclopedia of Philosophy*. Winter 2018 Edition. Zalta EN, (ed).

13 Pines, "Legalism in Chinese Philosophy".

14 Matamanda AR, Chirisa I, Dzvimbo MA and Chinozvina QL. 2019. "The political economy of Zimbabwean urban informality since 2000: A contemporary governance dilemma", *Development Southern Africa* 37(4):694-707.

15 Matamanda et al, "The political economy of Zimbabwean informality since 2000".

UNDERSTANDING THE INFORMAL ECONOMIC SECTOR IN ZIMBABWE

Zimbabwe has the largest informal sector in Africa, accounting for 60.6% of the country's GDP, and nothing indicates that this will be reversed within the next ten years or so.[16] With such a backdrop, the arrival of the Covid-19 pandemic wreaked havoc in other sectors of the informal economy in Zimbabwe. Two groups of informal workers represented by participants in the present study, who particularly suffered from the effects of the lockdown, were informal traders and informal transportation workers. The informal traders were mostly women, whereas the informal transportation workers were mostly male. The remainder of this chapter presents and compares the experiences of these two groups of informal sector workers.

Informal trade

The traders in the city of Harare who ran flea markets stopped doing cross-border business during the lockdown, as they were unable to get goods from abroad, and they did not start back up until the lockdown rules were relaxed in 2021. They claimed that city officials, working with the government, took advantage of the lockdown by using it as an excuse to destroy their market stalls while they were following the orders to stay at home. This confirms Prashanth Kulkarni's findings from 2021 that authorities in Zimbabwe's major cities destroyed thousands of vending stalls as part of a campaign to renovate and cleanup workplaces used by informal traders prior to the resumption of business after the lockdown.[17] However, from the time of their demolition in April 2020 until February 2021, these workplaces had not undergone renovations. This backs up the claim that Zimbabwean decision-makers find it difficult to deal with some aspects of urban informality.[18] But when the government relaxed its restrictions in February 2021 and the owners of the privately owned flea markets complied with its requirements, the traders who had stopped operating during the total lockdown started doing so again.

Informal transportation

Nyasha Chinyora and Tanaka Kusi, two of the eight respondents in the present study, worked in the sector of informal transportation as conductors on commuter omnibuses. Four were private car owners, and two were commuter omnibus drivers. Males made up every participant in this industry, which was based out of the Mbare Musika bus terminal. According to the respondents, informal transportation was prohibited during the lockdown in an effort to stop the spread of Covid-19. While the state-owned Zimbabwe United Passenger Company (ZUPCO)

---

16 Medina L and Schneider F. 2018. "Shadow Economies Around the World: What Did We Learn Over the Last 20 Years?", *International Monetary Fund Working Paper*, 24 January.

17 Kulkarni P. 2020. "Small vendors hard hit by government ordered demolitions in Zimbabwe", *Peoples Dispatch*, 29 April.

18 Matamanda AR. 2020. "Battling the informal settlement challenge through sustainable city framework: Experiences and lessons from Harare, Zimbabwe", *Development Southern Africa* 37(2):217-231.

and operators franchised by ZUPCO were allowed to operate after the lockdown was relaxed in September 2020, the informal transportation sector was prevented from resuming operations. According to legalist theory, it is precisely this kind of governmental regulation that leads to an increase in illegal undercover activities, as people whose undercover businesses were shut down looked for other undercover ways to survive. Unlicensed drivers were seen transporting people, bribing police officers at roadblocks to let them pass and thus exposing both themselves and their passengers to the virus because they were not abiding by Covid-19 regulations.

EXPERIENCES OF INFORMAL SECTOR WORKERS IN ZIMBABWE UNDER COVID-19

The lockdowns presented a great threat to the country's deepening socio-economic crisis, precisely because of this impact on Zimbabwean informal workers. The informal sector was found to be vulnerable due to the Covid-19 lockdowns.[19] When the lockdown was implemented, stalls of vendors were removed from the streets of Zimbabwe as one of the containment measures. As a result, key socioeconomic rights, such as the right to enough food and the right to work, as provided in the Constitution of Zimbabwe, 2013, were jeopardised.[20]

The announcement of the lockdown meant that vendors needed to stock up on food and other household necessities, but the majority could not afford to stay home from work even for a day in order to afford these necessities. Going to work or to the markets meant exposure to the virus as well as to police intervention; however, informal sector workers needed to feed their families on a daily basis. Therefore, the impact of the lockdown hit the informal traders the hardest, being the majority of players in the informal economy.

Zimbabwean sociologist, Perpetua Gumbo observes that around 80% of informal traders in Zimbabwe work in the informal sector through street vending, flea-market selling, cross-border trading, piece work at people's homes and working in small to medium firms.[21] Gumbo, therefore, claims that the shutdown resulted in a drop in people's livelihoods in a country that was already poor before the Covid-19 crisis, since the country was food-insecure, had a high unemployment rate and was experiencing economic disaster.

Informal trade

A single mother of four who is a cross-border trader and sells clothes at a market in Kambuzuma, Harare, was interviewed on 22 February 2022, and she indicated that

---

19 Zhanda K, Garutsa M, Dzvimbo MA and Mawonde A. 2022. "Informal traders in the informal sector amid Covid-19: implications for household peace and economic stability in urban Zimbabwe Informal traders in the informal sector amid Covid-19: implications for household peace and economic stability in urban Zimbabwe", *Cities & Health* 6(1):37-51.

20 Constitution of Zimbabwe, 2013, ss 77 and 64.

21 Gumbo O. 2020. "Covid-19 Lockdown Measures on Zimbabwean Populace", *Advances in Social Sciences Research Journal* 7(7):797-814.

she lost more than 95% of her income the moment the regulations were introduced by the government, as social distancing guidelines drastically reduced the number of people visiting the market. These circumstances led a number of people in Zimbabwe to violate the lockdown regulations. For instance, some vendors continued to open their businesses and some shoppers continued to visit the markets without the lawful permission from the law enforcement agents, and they were criminally prosecuted.

A forty-year-old woman with eight children, who lives in Kambuzuma, Harare, was also interviewed on 22 February 2022. She is the owner of a flea market which is not yet registered, and her source of income was drastically reduced due to the coronavirus pandemic. Her clothes were imported, mainly from South Africa, by road transport. With land border closures and restrictions on movement since March 2020, her business suffered a major setback, as she was not able to import her clothes from South Africa. Subsequently, the capital for the business was depleted through diversion to other immediate and household needs. Prior to the pandemic, the woman would earn on average two hundred to five hundred United States dollars per month as profit from sales. Since the lockdown measures were introduced in March 2020, her income dwindled to almost nothing. As a result, she was now struggling to make ends meet, as her only source of income and livelihood was disrupted by the Covid-19 pandemic. The most painful thing was that the woman received no assistance from the government, and maintained that the government should have helped them with financial assistance to sustain their families during the lockdown.

Nyasha Mukoweni, a forty-five-year-old woman with two children aged fifteen and thirteen, who resides in Rugare, Harare, was interviewed on 23 February 2022. She indicated to the researcher that as a cross-border trader who sources clothes and kitchenware items from neighbouring countries, such as Botswana, she encountered travelling challenges the moment the lockdown measures were introduced. Prior to the pandemic, she travelled three to four times per month to source goods for resale in Zimbabwe. Being a single mother, the coronavirus pandemic severely harmed her business and way of life, making it impossible for her to send her two kids to school. Despite the fact that schools have resumed operations, it is now difficult to meet basic needs for food and clothing. All her capital was utilised to stock up on food and other household essentials during the prolonged lockdown. Since then, the capital has been totally depleted. Nyasha tried to diversify her business by sourcing and trading goods locally, since she was unable to travel to any country to source goods for resale in Zimbabwe due to border closures and travel restrictions. This was unsuccessful because she was unable to sell her goods on the street because city council officials were constantly pursuing street vendors. She also didn't get any food or financial aid from the government or any other organisation to protect her from the pandemic's effects. An independent journalist, Tonderayi Mukeredzi, correctly questions how traders confined to their homes would be able to feed their families.[22]

---

22 Mukeredzi T. 2020. "'Dying of hunger: Zimbabwe street vendors hit by coronavirus clampdown", *Reuters*, 16 June.

Informal transportation

Participants in the informal transportation industry reported that the country's economic hardship had already made it difficult for them to support their families before the lockdown. Their economic situation deteriorated as a result of the lockdown, with little hope of improvement. One driver of a commuter omnibus in Harare on 27 February 2022 explained: "We found the announcement of the lockdown to be very unfair. Most of us were struggling to make ends meet. Since we haven't been in the wilderness since the lockdown started, there is no food in this economy if you don't hustle, making hunger a more lethal threat than the Covid-19 virus." The statement provides more proof that informal workers were having trouble following the Covid-19 containment procedures.

According to legalist theory, this statement implies that the government's decisions to contain the virus were harsh on the informal economy, to the point where it threatened their means of subsistence. For informal transport providers, for instance, operating was a life-or-death decision because remaining inside during the lockdown meant starving to death. Since the threat of hunger and starvation was just as real as the threat posed by the coronavirus itself, unofficial workers engaged in illegal activities to survive during the lockdown. According to the legalist theory, informal workers use illegal methods to survive rather than rebel against society.[23] In other words, acting outside of the law in Zimbabwe by the informal traders became the only option available because it was more beneficial for their survival to break the law, since the cost of following the lockdown regulations was greater than the benefits. According to economists Louise Fox and Landry Signé, the implementation of a lockdown presents a significant conundrum that forces a trade-off between the lives and livelihoods of informal economy workers, because 68% of informal sector workers in Africa resided in nations that had fully implemented full lockdowns as of April 2020.[24] Because of the disruption to their source of income, many workers in the informal economy were forced to choose between the risk of infection and starvation.[25]

An entire network, including the owners of the vehicles, the drivers, conductors, touts and mechanics, whose livelihoods depended on the informal transportation sector, was upended when commuter omnibuses were removed from the streets. Those who rely on the unofficial transportation network to get to work were also impacted by this situation. Molly Manyonganise describes how the pandemic affected people in Zimbabwe economically in a study she conducted.[26] Manyonganise claims that

---

23 Gano-An, "On becoming creative solopreneurs"; Matsongoni H and Mutambara E. 2018. "An assessment of informal SMEs' potential in an African economy: Theoretical and conceptual framework", *Public and Municipal Finance* 7(2):1-13.

24 Fox L and Signé L. 2020. "COVID-19 and the future of work in Africa: How to shore up incomes for informal sector workers", *Africa in Focus* (blog) Brookings Institution, 26 May.

25 Bonnet F, Vanek J and Chen MA. 2019. "*Women and Men in the Informal Economy: A Statistical Brief*". Manchester: WIEGO and ILO, January.

26 Manyonganise M. 2022. "When a Pandemic Wears the Face of a Woman: Intersections of Religion and Gender during the Covid-19 Pandemic in Zimbabwe", in Sibanda F,

because of the closure of the informal sector, the lockdown has led to the economic disempowerment of informal traders.[27] She continues by describing how Epworth residents were cited in the media as having walked with loads of vegetables to and from Mbare for resale because the human transporters were no longer in operation.[28] Buses were unable to provide an adequate or dependable service, despite the fact that the ban on commuter omnibuses was intended to restrict movement to and within urban centres. Once more, the government was to blame for the destruction of the informal sector without providing better living conditions for those who worked in it. As a result, those who were impacted were likely forced to find other (illegal) ways to survive in the informal sector. This supports legalist theory once more, which contends that increased participation in the informal economy is a result of government efforts to make it more challenging for businesses to operate there.

STRATEGIES FOR SURVIVAL USED DURING THE COVID-19 LOCKDOWN

According to the World Bank, legalists view the informal economy as "a rational response by micro entrepreneurs to over-regulation by government bureaucracies."[29] This was evident in Zimbabwe during the Covid-19 lockdown, where informal traders were violating the regulations for survival. This is supported by economic anthropologist Julia Elyachar, who contends that informal workers turn to illegal methods not to act against society or by choice, but to survive.[30] Further, she postulates that people base their decision on whether or not to enter the legal system and remain there based on a broad assessment of what it could cost to comply with legal requirements and what they could gain from doing so.

Informal traders

When their market stalls were destroyed, the informal traders who were vending at flea markets run by the city council said they had to continue doing business from their homes. According to the legalist theory, this demonstrates unequivocally that the Zimbabwean government encouraged the growth of the informal sector and illegal activities during the lockdown period, since they did not give the people whose sources of income they had destroyed any way to survive. Informal traders on social media promoted whatever inventory they had, and customers would visit their homes to buy products. They were unable to buy more stock for resale due

---

Muyambo and Chitando E (eds). *Religion and the Covid-19 Pandemic in Southern Africa*. London: Routledge.

27 Manyonganise, "'When a Pandemic Wears the Face of a Woman'", 236.
28 Manyonganise, "'When a Pandemic Wears the Face of a Woman'", 236.
29 World Bank and International Finance Corporation (IFC). 2009. *Doing Business 2010*. Washington, DC: World Bank/IFC/Palgrave MacMillan.
30 Elyachar J. 2003. "Mappings of Power: The State, NGOs, and International Organizations in the Informal Economy of Cairo", *Comparative Studies in Society and History* 45(3):517-605.

to their limited mobility, which also decreased their income. At privately run flea markets, the informal traders admitted that they had to borrow money to buy new stock. They used *malaicha* (Ndebele slang for the traditional way of sending goods over the border with bus and taxi drivers), who served as go-betweens between them and the police, helping them cross the border illegally by bribing officials. However, this tactic exposed them to the virus because no tests were done, and when they returned home, their families and clients were also at risk.

The most obvious problem is how corruption and, more specifically, bribes, have damaged the rule of law and good governance. The concept of authority is undermined when state employees are corrupt, and it becomes challenging for the state to continue playing a legitimate role in enforcing the law. Actors in the informal economy try to avoid the state or co-opt it through bribes and incentives, resulting in a relationship of "inevitable conflict" between the state and the informal economy. Thus, despite attempts by the government to restrict their business activities, informal cross-border traders were willing to do anything to survive. They would occasionally hire cross-border agents, paying them with money to purchase the goods they desired from neighbouring South Africa. While this activity was illegal, traders would not be able to report theft of this nature, so the main risk was that there was no assurance or guarantee that the agents would bring back the promised goods.

Although they had given their information to the government at the beginning of the lockdown for potential financial assistance, the cross-border traders claimed that they had not received any kind of assistance from the government. Further, the government promised a one-time cushioning allowance to vulnerable people, but more than four months into the lockdown only 208 000 of the 1 million households identified for assistance had received it. Therefore, no one who took part in the present study claimed to have gotten help from the government. Without any help and without any means of support, the informal workers are unable to escape the rising levels of poverty. Since the informal sector is what the majority of Zimbabweans rely on for survival, all of the participants agreed that the government of Zimbabwe should not have used the lockdown to destroy it. They also believed that the traders whose market stalls had been destroyed should have been given access to new working spaces as soon as the lockdown regulations were relaxed by the city officials.

Informal transportation

One private driver who lives in Rugare, Harare, narrated to the researcher that he sold his car and used the proceeds to get through the lockdown, while other drivers, who had no other sources of income, converted their cars into mobile stores, where they sold the scarce groceries that were available during the lockdown. Since this was illegal, he went on to say that they had to sneak into neighbourhoods where they had regular clients to sell their goods. Others, on the other hand, claimed that they were doing whatever was offered to them as long as it generated income. These responses, too, indicated the applicability of the legalist theory, providing convincing evidence that the government's attempt to suppress the use of illegal transportation led to the emergence of other illegal activities.

The government had urged private transportation providers to join the established transportation industry, but participants noted that not all private providers could comply, because their vehicles would then need to meet strict safety requirements. Additionally, they claimed that when working in the formal transportation industry, their profits were lower and they were unable to support their families financially, let alone pay for the upkeep of their fleets. They added that some commuter omnibus owners who had signed up for the official transportation franchise had already voiced their dissatisfaction with the government for not paying them on time and for paying them with money that had depreciated in value due to inflation. Many were discouraged from franchising their cars as a result. According to the legalist theory, microbusiness owners find it difficult to adhere to formal requirements because they are inefficient, expensive, and burdensome, and as a result they prefer to operate formally. While many people who work in the informal sector avoid these requirements, formal participants in the economy pay costs to maintain their status as such. Many of those surveyed believed that those who follow the law incur additional expenses, and this extra financial burden served as a strong incentive to reject or disobey laws that were thought to be inconvenient.

Participants claimed they had no other means of support and that the government had not offered them any assistance. They recommended that instead of outright banning this industry, the government create an effective system that can accommodate all nonconventional transportation providers. This recommendation, which again supports the legalist theory, indicates that the informal workers were unwilling to leave the informal sector, despite the government's continued efforts to make it challenging for them to do so by the stringent lockdown regulations.

It was clear that the formal transportation model was not the best option for private operators, who were required to provide their own vehicles, but are instead managed by the government under subpar circumstances that have a negative impact on their profitability. Any informal transport provider cannot reasonably expect monthly payments in local currency as the exchange rate in the country continues to decline. Furthermore, the government was already unable to pay the few individuals who had joined the formal sector, and the majority of them have since terminated their contracts with the government.

CONCLUSION

Informal workers and their families in Zimbabwe were severely vulnerable and unable to make a living as they had been able to do before during the Covid-19 lockdown, which resulted in some being charged with crimes and imprisoned as a result. Many people in the informal sector engaged in illegal activities during the lockdown in order to survive, which continued the dominance of the informal sector in Zimbabwe. Most of the individuals were detained and charged with crimes. The legalist theory contends that the expansion of the informal sector is the result of governmental regulations. The Covid-19 pandemic offers a chance for the government and local authorities to reevaluate their relationship with those employed in the informal sector, according to the study's findings. The socioeconomic crisis brought on by the lockdown has highlighted the crucial roles played by local governments and national governments in responding to emergencies in urban areas. Accordingly, the research findings are used to support the following recommendations, which must be implemented more thoroughly in Zimbabwe in order to reduce the negative effects of crises like the pandemic on the unorganised sector.

First of all, instead of attempting to completely eradicate the informal sector, the government of Zimbabwe should provide a workable policy framework that accommodates it and promotes economic activity by allowing it to operate under restraints during the Covid-19 pandemic. Decongesting markets or other locations where informal workers congregate and ensuring that they adhere to new health regulations can help achieve this. Since the informal sector is the largest source of employment for many people in an economy where formal employment has collapsed, the government should do more to foster its growth and development. The nation will benefit from this as it works to combat poverty and advance the Sustainable Development Goals (SDGs). Above all, the Zimbabwean government must work with local councils to persuade participants in the informal sector to register their businesses so they can receive aid from the government in the event of a similar national or international catastrophe because their operations will be seen as legal. The government can make this process easier by allowing the informal sector to register their businesses for free and by enacting a minimal tax rate that has little impact on their bottom lines.

A weak social contract between the state and those working in the informal sector in Zimbabwe has made them more vulnerable to the Covid-19 pandemic. The public services that matter to informal workers, like infrastructure in markets and safe water and sanitation systems, must be funded with the taxes that informal workers' pay. Doing so would help to contain the effects or spread of Covid-19. Numerous unregistered workers will be encouraged to do so by the increased accountability and transparency. Further, it is also recommended that the government should introduce economic support packages, including direct cash-transfers, expanded unemployment benefits and child benefits for vulnerable informal traders and their families. Direct cash-transfers, which would mean giving cash directly to informal traders who are poor or lack income, can be a lifeline for those struggling to afford day-to-day necessities during pandemics.

17 PUSHED TO THE MARGIN: THE RIGHTS OF WOMEN LIVING WITH HIV AND AIDS DURING LOCKDOWN IN ZIMBABWE

Priccilar Vengesai[1]

INTRODUCTION

Covid-19 has been a global challenge, with developing countries such as Zimbabwe being the most vulnerable. Zimbabwe recorded its first Covid-19 positive case on 20 March 2020, involving a male resident of the town of Victoria Falls who had a travel history to the United Kingdom and South Africa. The second Covid-19 case was recorded immediately afterwards. It involved a journalist who also had a history of travelling to several countries.[2] The World Health Organization (WHO) encouraged countries to adopt concerted measures to prevent and contain Covid-19.[3] As a result, Zimbabwe implemented measures, such as lockdowns, that were targeted at containing the virus's spread and its effects. The objective of this chapter is to discuss the manner in which the rights of women with HIV and AIDS were affected during lockdowns with a particular focus on Zimbabwe.

Statutory Instrument 83 of 2020 introduced the first lockdown in Zimbabwe.[4] In Section 2, the statute provided that: "'National lockdown' means the restrictions on the movement of persons and on intercity, terrestrial, airborne and cross-border traffic prescribed by this Order." This definition of lockdown emphasises the restriction on the movement of people. However, it should be noted that Zimbabwean lockdowns came in different levels, with level one being the most restricted one and level five the least restricted. The first lockdown in Zimbabwe was implemented on 30 March 2020, when the country had recorded only one death and nine confirmed cases.[5] The first lockdown was a level one lockdown. A second-level lockdown was then imposed on 14 April 2020, following the provisions of Section 4 of the Statutory Instrument 110 of 2020.[6] According to the Statutory Instrument,

---

1 Law Lecturer at Herbert Chitepo Law School, Great Zimbabwe University.
2 Chipenda C and Tom T. 2021. "Zimbabwe's Social Policy Response to Covid-19: Temporary Food Relief and Cash Transfers" (CRC 1342 Covid-19 Social Policy Response Series, 23). Bremen: Universität Bremen, SFB 1342 Globale Entwicklungsdynamiken von Sozialpolitik / CRC 1342 Global Dynamics of Social Policy.
3 Xiong J et al. 2020 Impact of Covid-19 pandemic on mental health in the general population: A systematic review", *Journal of Affective Disorders* 277:55-64.
4 Statutory Instrument 83 of 2020 [CAP. 15:17] Public Health (Covid-19 Prevention, Containment and Treatment) (National Lockdown) Order 2020.
5 Mavhunga C. 2020. "Zimbabwe Begins Lockdown to Fight COVID-19", *VOA*, 30 March.
6 Statutory Instrument 110 of 2020. [CAP. 15:17] Public Health (Covid-19 Prevention, Containment and Treatment) (National Lockdown) (Amendment) Order, 2020 (No. 8).

the level one lockdown of March 2020 meant that everyone would stay home and would only go outside for food and health reasons within their neighbourhood. This lockdown saw the erection of numerous checkpoints and roadblocks to regulate the flow of people. A curfew from 6:00 pm to 6:00 am was put in place. It is in the context of this first-level lockdown that women with HIV and AIDS faced surmounting challenges that violated various constitutionally enshrined human rights.

While everyone was vulnerable to Covid-19, people were far from equally affected by the pandemic responses. There were stark gendered disparities, and women with HIV and AIDS already among the most marginalised people in a patriarchal society, were hit the hardest in Zimbabwe. Stigmatisation, coupled with intersectional discrimination, has always been exerted towards women living with HIV and AIDS. Their challenges are a mirror to stark inequalities and injustices, which were intensified by Covid-19 responses.[7] As the Covid-19 pandemic exposed entrenched inequalities and gender power dynamics, women living with HIV and AIDS experienced the greatest health and human rights impacts.

With the above factors in mind, this chapter focuses on how women living with HIV and AIDS were affected by the curtailment of certain rights during lockdowns in Zimbabwe. These realities suggest recommendations that may be useful in future measures against emerging pandemics. This research used a qualitative mixed method of legal doctrinal approach. S.N. Jain, a legal researcher, defines doctrinal research as analysis of case law, arranging, ordering and systematising legal propositions and study of legal institutions through legal reasoning or rational deduction.[8] This approach helps one to understand the legal framework and judicial precedent relevant to the plight of women living with HIV and AIDS. According to Amrit Kharel, another legal researcher, availability of the reliable data is the biggest challenge in conducting legal doctrinal research.[9] To bridge this gap, semi-structured key interview questions were devised for five key non-governmental organisations dealing with women living with HIV and AIDS. This research also used a human rights-based approach. Human rights theory requires governments and authorities to focus in their programmes on the rights of those who are most marginalised, excluded or discriminated against in society, in order to ensure that they are not deprived of their rights.[10] The broad objective of the lockdown was to guarantee Zimbabweans the right to health by harnessing the spread of Covid-19. However, in the process, the government took away more rights from women living with HIV and AIDS than they gave them.

---

7   UN Committee on Economic, Social and Cultural Rights (CESCR), General Comment No. 14: The Right to the Highest Attainable Standard of Health (Art. 12 of the Covenant), 11 August 2000, E/C.12/2000/4.

8   Jain SN. 1972. "Legal research and methodology", *Journal of the Indian Law Institute* 14(4):487-500.

9   Kharel A. 2018. "Doctrinal Legal Research", *SSRN Electronic Journal* January:12.

10 United National Population Fund. n.d. "The Human Rights Based Approach", *UNFPA. org*. [Accessed on 31 March 2022].

RIGHTS CURTAILED DURING THE LOCKDOWNS

Right to health

The right to health care is enshrined in the Constitution of Zimbabwe.[11] Section 76(1) provides that "every person living with a chronic illness has the right to have access to basic health care for the illness". This section directs the state to accord the right to health to people with chronic diseases, such as women with HIV. Numerous international instruments to which Zimbabwe is a signatory recognise the right to health.[12] Equally binding on Zimbabwe are regional instruments that also recognise the right to health.[13] Under Section 46 of the Constitution, Zimbabwe is obliged to abide by these international and regional instruments, since this provision requires domestication of international instruments and treaties.[14] According to Admark Moyo, a human rights lawyer, this provision mandates the consideration of the norms and values of the international community, as given in international treaties and customary international law and general principles of international law.[15] Moyo further points out that Zimbabwe's obligation to observe and apply international and regional law is apparent by the virtue of it being a member state to international and regional human rights treaties.[16] On the basis of the established Zimbabwe's international obligations, the importance of the right to health as elaborated in General Comment 14 to the International Covenant on

---

11 Constitution of Zimbabwe Amendment (No. 20) Act 2013, s 76.

12 Universal Declaration of Human Rights, G.A. res. 217A (III), U.N. Doc A/810at 71 (1948), art 25. (Article 25 affirms that: "Everyone has the right to a standard of living adequate for the health of himself and of his family, including food, clothing, housing and medical care and necessary social services."); International Covenant on Economic, Social and Cultural Rights, GA Res. 2200A (XXI), 21 UN GAOR Supp (No 16 at 49, UN Doc A/6316 (1966), 993 UNTS 3, *entered into force* 3 Jan 1976, art 12.1. (Article 12 provides the most comprehensive article on the right to health in international human rights law. States parties must recognise "the right of everyone to the enjoyment of the highest attainable standard of physical and mental health", while Article 12.2 enumerates, by way of illustration, a number of "steps to be taken by the States parties ... to achieve the full realization of this right"). See also International Convention on the Elimination of All Forms of Racial Discrimination of 1965, 660 U.N.T.S. 195, *entered into force* Jan. 4, 1969, art 5 (e) (iv); Convention on the Elimination of All Forms of Discrimination against Women of 1979, G.A. res. 34/180, 34 U.N. GAOR Supp. (No. 46) at 193, U.N. Doc. A/34/46, *entered into force* Sept. 3, 1981, art 11.1 (f) and art 12, Convention on the Rights of the Child of 1989, G.A. res. 44/25, annex, 44 U.N. GAOR Supp. (No. 49) at 167, U.N. Doc. A/44/49 (1989), *entered into force* Sept. 2, 1990, art 24.

13 African [Banjul] Charter on Human and People's Rights adopted June 27, 1981, OAU Doc. CAB/LEG/67/3 rev. 5, 21 I.L.M. 58(1982), *entered into force* Oct 21, 1986, art 16.

14 Constitution of Zimbabwe, 2013, s 46(1)(c) provides that when interpreting this Chapter [The Bill of Rights], a court, tribunal, forum or body must take into account international law and all treaties and conventions to which Zimbabwe is a party.

15 Moyo K. 2019. "Socio-Economic Rights under the 2013 Zimbabwean Constitution", in Moyo A (ed). *Selected Aspects of the 2013 Zimbabwean Constitution and the Declaration of Rights*. Lund: Raoul Wallenberg Institute, 163-181.

16 Moyo "Socio-Economic Rights under the 2013 Zimbabwean Constitution", 168.

Economic, Social and Cultural Rights (ICESCR) becomes instructive.[17] This general comment, first and foremost, appreciates that "health is a fundamental human right indispensable for the exercise of other human rights and that every human being is entitled to the enjoyment of the highest attainable standard of health conducive to living a life with dignity".

In accordance with General Comment 14, the realisation of the right to health may be pursued through numerous, complementary approaches, such as the formulation of health policies, the implementation of health programmes developed by the World Health Organization (WHO) or the adoption of specific legal instruments. Zimbabwe has put in place legislation and policies for the realisation of the rights of people living with HIV.[18] These legal frameworks generally posit and accept the vulnerability of people living with HIV and appreciate the need for their protection. These legal frameworks signal an intent to protect both men and women living with HIV.

However, the right to health requires more than simply putting a legal framework in place. The provision and access to the treatment form part and parcel of the obligation of the state to provide the right to health.[19] In *Minister of Health v Treatment Action Campaign*,[20] a South African case which has a persuasive value in interpreting Zimbabwean law,[21] the court made it clear that the unavailability of nevirapine drug in hospitals was unreasonable, given that they had a policy in place. In this case, justifications for the failure to provide a comprehensive programme for the prevention of mother-to-child transmission were found by the court to be inadequate to meet the tenets of the state's obligation to provide for the

---

17 Convention on Economic Social Cultural Rights General Comment No. 14: The Right to the Highest Attainable Standard of Health (Art. 12) Adopted at the Twenty-second Session of the Committee on Economic, Social and Cultural Rights, on 11 August 2000 (Contained in Document E/C.12/2000/4).

18 Health Service Act Chapter 15:17 of 2018 s 37 gives guidelines regarding health services operations that include:
   (a) the types and availability of health services
   (b) the operating schedules and timetables of visits
   (c) procedures for access to the health services
   (d) other aspects of health services which may be of use to the public
   (e) procedures for laying complaints.
   This is of importance to people who have HIV as it helps to inform them about where they can get treatment. See also the National Aids Policy of 1999, which introduced the Aids levy was introduced by the government. Also, the Statutory Instrument 202 of 1998, which was enacted under the Zimbabwe Labour Relations Act, was regarded as a giant stride in protecting employees with HIV.

19 *Minister of Health v Treatment Action Campaign* 2002 (5) SA 721 para 17 (CC).

20 *Minister of Health v Treatment Action Campaign*, para 17.

21 Constitution of Zimbabwe, 2013, s 46(1)(e) permits the consideration of relevant foreign law when interpreting the Bill of Rights.

right to health.[22] This is buttressed by the General Comment 14 on Paragraph 12 of the ICESCR, echoing the need of accessibility to treatment and drugs as a crucial component of the right to health.[23] The general comment further states that accessibility must be nondiscriminatory, thus health facilities, goods and services must be accessible to all, especially the most vulnerable and marginalised sections of the population, such as ethnic minorities and indigenous populations, women, children, adolescents, older persons, persons with disabilities and persons living with HIV.[24]

While lockdown was a health measure implemented to prevent a health disaster by harnessing the spread of Covid-19, it also compromised the right to health of women living with HIV by limiting their access to healthcare facilities and anti-retroviral (ARV) medication. It is argued that the Zimbabwean government failed to ensure access to both medication and health facilities by women living with HIV during the lockdown. The results were a two-dimensional violation of the right to health.

Access to drugs

With respect to access to drugs, lockdowns brought about travelling restrictions across borders and between cities. For example, if A from Bindura decides to visit his uncle in Marondera and the lockdown goes into effect before he can return home, then he must stay there until the end of the lockdown. Travelling from one city to the other was only allowed where there was a letter from the police, which was not easily obtainable. Even though movement for medication purposes was allowed,[25] the effect of these difficulties and undue delays in obtaining police clearance letters was to render the authorisation unhelpful.

These travelling restrictions, as Nyashanu and fellow researchers have shown, led women to miss appointments because of the difficulty in travelling to health facilities to collect their supply of antiretroviral drugs (ARVs).[26] Women living with HIV in Harare had to negotiate with police officers so that they could be let into town to collect ARVs.[27] These women were not always successful in such negotiations, and some were turned back to their residential areas. Furthermore, upon the pronouncement of the lockdown, some people collected the ARVs for

---

22 Currie I and De Waal J. 2017. *The Bill of Rights Handbook*. Cape Town: Juta and Company (Pty) Ltd, 578.
23 CESCR, General Comment No. 14.
24 CESCR, General Comment No. 14.
25 See Public Health (Covid-19 Prevention, Containment and Treatment) (National Lockdown) (Amendment) Order, 2020 (No. 5) Section 4(1).
26 Nyashanu M, Chireshe R, Mushawa F and Ekpenyong MS. 2021 "Exploring the challenges of women taking antiretroviral treatment during the Covid-19 pandemic lockdown in Peri-urban Harare, Zimbabwe", *International Journal of Gynecology and Obstetrics* (154):222.
27 Nyashanu et al, "Exploring the challenges of women taking antiretroviral treatment".

3-6 months, and when others went to collect, the clinics had run short.[28] The police clearance letters also did not serve any legitimate governmental purpose in fighting the spread of Covid-19. The issuance of these letters at police stations was not pre-conditioned by any medical examination of the intended travellers, hence there was no guarantee that they would not spread the coronavirus to other areas. Such medical examinations are the sole domain of the country`s health profession and not the police.

The unavailability of public transport in remote areas also forced women to miss their treatment. A rapid HIV-specific assessment from Zimbabwe found that 19% of people living with HIV were unable to get antiretroviral therapy (ART) refills.[29] In an interview, Samuel, the Director of Tariro Youth Development Trust, whose organisation was serving young people living with HIV before and during the pandemic, noted that in Zaka District, Masvingo Province, some women living with HIV resorted to walking long distances to get their ARVs refilled.[30]

Access to healthcare facilities

Many women living with HIV have other comorbidities and require regular access to healthcare facilities for clinical treatments. They require constant viral load checks, routine tuberculosis (TB) checks and cervical and breast cancer screenings, as they are more susceptible to these cancers. Lack of access to health facilities due to travel restrictions accelerated the deterioration of their health conditions. Opportunistic Infection Centres were closed in many places and there were reduced clinic hours.[31] It was also reported that women living with HIV who had underlying cardiac or respiratory conditions and older women living with HIV may be at higher risk of acquiring the coronavirus and developing more serious symptoms.[32] These problems prevented women from accessing care for HIV-related conditions thus left them much prone to contracting coronavirus itself.

Right to water

Another right that was tempered with during lockdown is the right to water. According to General Comment 14 to the ICESCR, Paragraph 11, the right to health is an inclusive right, extending not only to timely and appropriate health care, but also to the underlying determinants of health, such as access to safe and

---

28 Nyashanu et al, "Exploring the challenges of women taking antiretroviral treatment".
29 Cairns G. 2020. "Disruption to HIV treatment in Africa during Covid-19 during Covid-19 pandemic could double HIV deaths, modelling studies warn", *Aidsmap.com*, 13 May.
30 Interview with Samuel, Director of Tariro Youth Development Trust, by P Vengesai. Zaka, Zimbabwe, 14 April 2022.
31 Universal Health Coverage (UHC) Partnership. 2021. "Zimbabwe: Data-driven decisions maintain availability and access to essential health services during the Covid-19 Response", *ExtranetWHOint*, 31 March.
32 UNICEF. n.d. "Technical Note on Covid-19 and Harmful Practices", UNICEF.org.

potable water.³³ While the committee on the ICESCR frames the right to water as right to health, this is not the case with Zimbabwe. The Zimbabwe Constitution, in Section 77(a), makes the right to water a stand-alone right. It unambiguously states that "every person has the right to safe, clean and portable water".

The importance of the right to water in the Zimbabwean context can be derived from its wording. The relevant section provides for the *right* to safe, clean and potable water, as opposed to the *right of access to* water in other constitutions.³⁴ Zimbabwe is therefore obligated to guarantee the right to water, and not merely the right of access. The right to access to water was explained by Gabru to mean that the state's obligation is to provide the means to ensure access to water.³⁵ It can be argued that this may not be the case where the state must guarantee right to water.

The court in *City of Harare v Mushoriwa* noted that Section 77 of the Zimbabwe Constitution is a fundamental human right, such that the state is enjoined to take reasonable legislative and other measures to achieve the progressive realisation of this right.³⁶ The brief facts of the case are that the City of Harare issued a water bill of $1700 to Mr Mushoriwa who disputed the bill on the basis that it was a bulk water bill and not for his premises, leading to the disconnection of the water. Mr Mushoriwa made a chamber application for the restoration of the water supply pending the resolution of the water bill dispute, which interim relief was granted by the court *a quo* on the basis that the disconnection of the water was in violation of the right to water.

In interpreting Section 77, the court stated that:³⁷

> Possible violation of its provisions is only implicated where the State or a local authority fails to provide any or adequate water supply to any given community or locality. It might also arise where, as appears to have been recently admitted by the appellant itself, having afforded an adequate water supply to most inhabitants, it is then discovered that such supply is in fact contaminated and therefore only potable at great risk.

It is argued that the government of Zimbabwe failed to provide adequate water during lockdowns. The Women's Coalition of Zimbabwe reported that women were "beaten and barred" by law enforcement agents from accessing water at communal boreholes. This was particularly reported in Masvingo in the Aphiri area.³⁸ There

---

33 CESCR, General Comment No. 14.
34 Constitution of the Republic of South Africa, 1996, s 27 (provide for the right to access to water, as opposed to the right to water as provided by the Constitution of Zimbabwe).
35 Gabru N. 2005. "Some comments on Water Rights in South Africa", *Potchfstroomse Elektroniese Regsblad/Potchefstroom Electronic Law Journal* 8:12-14.
36 *City of Harare v Mushoriwa* 2018 ZWSC 54 at 27.
37 *City of Harare v Mushoriwa.*
38 Parliament of the United Kingdom. 2020. "Womankind response to IDC inquiry on the impact of corona virus (Covid-19) on developing countries". Online at: https://committees.parliament.uk/writtenevidence/1931/pdf

were reports of men using violence and force against women queuing at water points in attempts to jump the queue.

Right to food

In the same section as the right to water, the Zimbabwean Constitution, in Section 77(b), provides for the right to sufficient food and mandates the state to take reasonable legislative and other measures, within the limits of the resources available to it, to achieve the progressive realisation of this right. The right to food has been described by Kirsteen Shields, a lawyer, as a right that is corporeal, intimate and essential to all of life.[39] The focus on assessing whether this right has been met must be on the adequacy of structures surrounding the production of and access to food as opposed to the metrics of physical access and consumption.[40] Since it is an internationally recognised right, the scope of the right to food can be found in international law.[41] An interpretation of the international right to food is given in General Comment 12 of the Committee on Economic, Social and Cultural Rights to the ICESCR.[42] It defines the right to food as: "the right of every man, woman and child alone and in community with others to have physical and economic access at all times to adequate food or means for its procurement in ways consistent with human dignity".[43]

The heart of the right to food is access to food that is adequate in terms of both quality and quantity.[44] The threefold obligation of government is to respect, protect and fulfil the right to food.[45] This threefold obligation is corroborated by Section 15 of the Zimbabwean Constitution, which requires the state to encourage people to

---

39 Shields K. 2017. "Methods of Monitoring the Right to Food", in Andreassen BA, Sano H-O, and McInerney-Lankford S (eds). *Research Methods in Human Rights: A Handbook*. Cheltenham: Edward Elgar Publishing, 333-353.

40 Shields, "Methods of Monitoring the Right to Food".

41 Universal Declaration of Human Rights, G.A. res. 217A(III), U.N. Doc A/810at 71 (1948), art 25(1). (Article 25(1) provides that: "Everyone has the right to a standard of living adequate for the health and wellbeing of himself and of his family, including food, clothing, housing and medical care and necessary social services, and the right to security in the event of unemployment, sickness, disability, widowhood, old age or other lack of livelihood in circumstances beyond his control."). See also International Covenant on Economic, Social and Cultural Rights, GA Res. 2200A (XXI), 21 UN GAOR Supp (No16) at 49, UN Doc A/6316 (1966), 993 UNTS 3, *entered into force* 3 Jan 1976, art 11(1). (Article 11(1) states that: "The States Parties to the present Covenant recognize the right of everyone to an adequate standard of living for himself and his family, including adequate food, clothing and housing. Moreover, article 11(2) recognizes the fundamental right of everyone to be free from hunger.").

42 Convention on Economic Social Cultural Rights, General Comment No. 12 (1999) (on the right to adequate food as set forth in Article 11 of the Covenant).

43 Convention on Economic Social Cultural Rights, General Comment No. 12.

44 Zimbabwe Human Rights NGO Forum. 2009. "Human Rights Bulletin No. 42: The right to food and Zimbabwe", *Reliefweb*.

45 HRForumZim, "Human Rights Bulletin No. 42: The right to food and Zimbabwe".

grow and store adequate food, secure the establishment of adequate food reserves and encourage and promote adequate and proper nutrition through mass education and other appropriate means. It is this threefold obligation which the Zimbabwean government failed to accord its citizens, and women living with HIV and AIDS suffered the most.

Covid-19 had drastic impact on food consumption and nutrition security as households lost income while food prices went up due to the inflationary shocks of the pandemic.[46] This scenario came in the midst of a situation where women with HIV and AIDS are economically disadvantaged more than men. Women living with HIV aged 25-34 years are 22% more likely than men to live in extreme poverty.[47] This economic inequality increased further during the Covid-19 pandemic and its aftermath.[48] The Zimbabwean economy, which is largely informal, could not sustain livelihoods of those who make a daily living off the streets. In a report, UNAIDS indicated a great concern for the worsening humanitarian situation in Zimbabwe, where people living with HIV are disproportionately affected by food insecurity and shortages of essential medicines.[49]

Right to privacy

A pertinent section of the right to privacy as provided for in the Zimbabwean Constitution is Section 57(e), which clearly forbids unwarranted intrusion into a person's health condition. The right to privacy is a civil and political right, and its wording in the Constitution is even clearer in its intention to protect the privacy of a person's health condition than it is in the international law.[50] General Comment No. 16 and Article 17 of the International Covenant on Civil and Political Rights (ICCPR) require member states to take effective measures to ensure that information concerning a person's private life does not reach the hands of persons who are not authorised by law to receive, process and use it, and is never used for purposes incompatible with the Covenant.[51]

---

46 Zimbabwe Peace Project. 2021. "The impact of COVID-19 on socio-economic rights in Zimbabwe", *Reliefweb*, 18 May.

47 McCarthy J. 2018. "Women Are More Likely Than Men to Live in Extreme Poverty: A Report", *Global Citizen*, 16 February.

48 Ferreira FHG. 2021. "Inequality in the Time of Covid-19", International Monetary Fund, Summer.

49 "People living with HIV face major challenges in Zimbabwe", UNAIDS, 8 March 2019.

50 UDHR, art 12 (Article 12 states: "No one shall be subjected to arbitrary interference with his privacy, family, home or correspondence, nor to attacks upon his honour and reputation. Everyone has the right to the protection of the law against such interference or attacks." See also International Covenant on Civil and Political Rights art 17 which states that "No one shall be subjected to arbitrary or unlawful interference with his privacy, family, home or correspondence, nor to unlawful attacks on his honour and reputation.").

51 UN Human Rights Committee (HRC). 1988. CCPR General Comment No. 16: on Article 17 (Right to Privacy), The Right to Respect of Privacy, Family, Home and Correspondence, and Protection of Honour and Reputation, 8 April.

In order to enforce travelling restrictions, Zimbabwean roadblocks, especially on roads entering the major cities, were manned by soldiers and police.[52] As people would try to make their way to health care centres, they would inevitably encounter these roadblocks. Confidentiality in this regard was breached in two ways. Women with HIV were asked to present medical cards to the police at the roadblocks to prove that they were HIV positive, hence their intention to visit health facilities, or they would be required to disclose their status in order to be issued travelling letters at the police station. The breach of confidentiality is confirmed by reports of public health researcher Mathew Nyashanu and colleagues that police would ask to see hospital cards from women living with HIV if they alleged that they were visiting a hospital for medical treatment.[53]

Freedom of religion

The Zimbabwe Constitution does not provide for a stand-alone right to religion. However, it is included in the guarantee of freedom of conscience in Section 60(1)(a), which provides: "Every person has the right to freedom of conscience, which includes freedom of thought, opinion, religion or belief. In the same fashion, this right is provided for in both the African Charter on Human and Peoples' Rights and the ICCPR.[54] General Comment 22 of the Committee on Civil and Political Rights interprets the right to freedom of thought, conscience and religion in a far-reaching and profound manner.[55] In its interpretation, the Committee emphasised that the right to religion encompasses personal conviction and the commitment to religion or belief, whether manifested individually or in community with others.[56] The same general comment further provides that the freedom to manifest religion or belief may be exercised "either individually or in community with others and in public or private." A South African case of *S v Lawrence*, which has a persuasive value to Zimbabwe, established the scope of the right to religion as: "The right to entertain such religious beliefs as a person chooses, the right to declare religious beliefs

---

52 Nyashanu et al. "Exploring the challenges of women taking antiretroviral treatment".

53 Nyashanu et al. "Exploring the challenges of women taking antiretroviral treatment".

54 See African (Banjul) Charter on Human and Peoples' Rights (Adopted 27 June 1981, OAU Doc. CAB/LEG/67/3 rev. 5, 21 I.L.M. 58 (1982), *entered into force* 21 October 1986, art 8 (providing for freedom of conscience); International Covenant on Civil and Political Rights, GA Res 2200 (XXI) of 16 Dec 1966, 21 UN GAOR Supp (NO 16) at 52, UN Doc A/6316, 999 UNTS 171 *entered into force* 23 Mar 1976, art 18:1 (provides that: "Everyone shall have the right to freedom of thought, conscience and religion. This right shall include freedom to have or to adopt a religion or belief of his choice, and freedom, either individually or in community with others and in public or private, to manifest his religion or belief in worship, observance, practice and teaching.").

55 UN Human Rights Committee (HRC), CCPR General Comment No. 22: Article 18 (Freedom of Thought, Conscience or Religion), 30 July 1993, CCPR/C/21/Rev.1/Add.4.

56 UN HRC, CPPR General Comment No. 22.

openly and without fear of hindrance or reprisal, and the right to manifest religious belief by worship and practice or by teaching and dissemination."[57]

The right to gather for religious purposes can also be found in the right to freedom of assembly and association.[58] In another South African case, *Minister of Home Affairs v Fourie and Another*, the role of religion was perceived to have the capacity to awaken concepts of self-worth and human dignity.[59] Section 58 of the Zimbabwe Constitution provides for the right to freedom of assembly and association, and if this right is read together with the right to religion, then the right to religion would guarantee a degree of autonomy for religious groups to run their affairs without interference.[60] This view was corroborated by legal scholar Pierre De Vos and colleagues, who highlighted that freedom of religion includes also the right to act in accordance with those beliefs and to organise one's life in a manner that demonstrate allegiance to one's beliefs.[61] Thus, where a certain religion believes in congregating and is banned from gathering, it means that their right has been violated.

During lockdown, women with HIV were deprived of this right, despite its benefits to their status and healing process. Research has shown that spirituality and religion play an important role in women living with HIV.[62] Churches in collaboration with community-based organisations (CBOs) have been known to hold special programmes at clinics and in the communities to encourage adherence to medication. Some CBOs also belong to churches. As well, spirituality has been defined by sociologist Magdalena Szaflarski to be the "internal, personal and emotional expression of the sacred and often assessed by spiritual wellbeing, peace/comfort derived from faith, and spiritual coping", while religion has been defined as "the formal, institutional and outward expression of the sacred, and has been measured by importance of religion, belief in God, religious attendance, and prayer and meditation".[63] Szaflarski appreciates the interrelatedness of religion and spirituality. The importance of spirituality and religion to women living with HIV is centred on the fact that they slow disease progression.[64]

According to theologian Francisco Dimitre Rodrigo Pereira Santos and fellow researchers, "the moment that a woman receives a positive diagnosis for HIV, she experiences fear, not only the fear of death as a result of the disease, but also fear of prejudice, fear of not receiving social support, and fear that other people might

---

[57] *S v Lawrence* 1997 (4) SA 1176 (CC) para 92.
[58] Currie and De Waal, *The Bill of Rights Handbook*. 317.
[59] *Minister of Home Affairs and Another v Fourie and Another* 2006 (3) BCLR 355 (CC) para 89.
[60] Currie and De Waal, *The Bill of Rights Handbook*, 317.
[61] De Vos P. and Freedman W. 2017. *South African Constitutional Law in Context*. Cape Town: Oxford University Press, 484.
[62] Szaflarski M. 2013. "Spirituality and Religion among HIV-Infected Individuals", *Current HIV/AIDS Reports*, 10:324-332.
[63] Szaflarski, "Spirituality and Religion among HIV-Infected Individuals".
[64] Szaflarski, "Spirituality and Religion among HIV-Infected Individuals".

know her condition. The patient then begins to re-evaluate her life and goals."[65] Santos and his research colleagues posit that religious groups and spirituality are among the means by which people living with HIV cope with the condition.[66] Many women living with HIV use spirituality as a fundamental resource for overcoming the stress and demands associated with disease.[67] In many cases, spirituality can enhance the lives of women living with HIV, as such women seek spirituality as a coping mechanism for their illness, entrusting to God all their chances for cure.[68] In this way, women can cope with the negative thoughts brought about by illness, as well as the stressful situations brought on by the disease, maintaining calmness even in the face of adversity.[69]

The lockdown brought a ban on religious gatherings to Zimbabwe. Religious leaders switched to online church services. Online conduct of business has been found to be exclusionary on its own due to lack of resources such as devices and data required for online engagement. Therefore, the banning of church gatherings impeded stress management of women living with HIV. These women were left in the confinement of their homes, where they were also susceptible to gender-based violence (GBV). Globally, women living with HIV experience higher rates of GBV than the general population.[70]

For women living with HIV, gender-based violence can hinder HIV prevention and access to services.[71] The fear of violence makes it difficult for women to decide whether and with whom they will have sex or to be able to negotiate safer sex. Violence and the potential for it, discourages many women living with HIV and AIDS from disclosing their HIV positive status to their partners, families and health providers, making it more difficult for women to stay on HIV treatment. Thus, the ban on religious gatherings exacerbated and increased other social problems especially GBV.

HOW WOMEN LIVING WITH HIV WERE AFFECTED BY THE CURTAILMENT OF THESE RIGHTS

Based on the interviews, challenges faced by women with HIV during lockdowns are several. According to one of the interviewees, Ottinah Matafi, a Community

---

65 Santos FDRP, Gurgel do Amaral LRO, Dos Santos MA, Ferreira AGN, Ferreira de Moura J and Brito LB. 2019. "Repercussions of Spirituality in the lives of women living with HIV", *Revista Cuidartre* 10(3):71.

66 Santos, "Repercussions of Spirituality in the lives of women living with HIV".

67 Szaflarski, "Spirituality and Religion among HIV-Infected Individuals".

68 Szaflarski, "Spirituality and Religion among HIV-Infected Individuals".

69 Ironson G, Kremer H and Lucette A 2016 "Relationship Between Spiritual Coping and Survival in Patients with HIV", *Journal of General Internal Medicine* 31(9):1068-1076.

70 Orza L et al. 2015. "Violence Enough already: Findings from a global participatory survey among women living with HIV", *Journal of the International AIDS Society* 18(5):20285.

71 "What is the link between HIV and gender-based violence?", *ReliefWeb*, 1 December 2014.

Adolescent Treatment Support mentor from Zimbabwe Young Positives (ZY+), young women living with HIV were forced to disclose their statuses.[72] The confidentiality of the women's HIV status was compromised when they had to show hospital cards to police officers to show that they were travelling to collect ART. Some of the women were denied access at roadblocks despite showing hospital cards. This was made worse by the fact that most of the police officers at roadblocks were from the same communities as the women. Most feared it would end up being a topic of gossip with their neighbours. According to an interview with Charmaine Matanda a monitoring and evaluation officer with ZY+, "Some of the women had to suffer accidental disclosure at home as families began to see that a family member was constantly taking medication as people had to spend more time together at home than before. These disclosures came with a lot of mental challenges which caused some to abandon their medication."[73]

People living with HIV must also constantly access medical facilities for other medical service, according to an interview with Fadzai Tawonangwere the advocacy and communications assistant for ZY+.[74] This include, viral load checks, cervical cancer screening and general medical check-up, so that practitioners may know if the women are experiencing challenges with their health. Some clinics had to be closed in Shamva District, as cited by Wellington Bakaimani, the Director for Simukaupenye Integrated Youth Academy, which is working with young women living with HIV, especially single mothers.[75] There arose gaps in medical treatment with more people skipping appointments, as some were locked down in other places far from their local clinics with their medical records elsewhere. This led to some women who had low viral loads ending up with high viral loads, as well as opportunistic infections and death for some.

This prompted most women to travel long distances to access their medication. They had to walk, because in their area was not served by the Zimbabwe United Passenger Company (ZUPCO), which was the transport service that had been exempted from Covid-19 restrictions. If they boarded unregistered taxis, at some point they would be ordered to disembark on the way. The women from the rural areas were hit doubly, as their local facilities were closed with no alternative transport. The transport challenges faced by urban women were generally among the few who used facilities outside of their local communities, as was noted by Yvonne Shumbanhete of Africa Asia Youth Foundation in an interview.[76]

---

72 Interview with Ottinah Matafi, a Community Adolescent Treatment Support mentor from Zimbabwe Young Positives (ZY+), by P Vengesai. Harare, Zimbabwe, 2 May 2022.
73 Interview with Charmaine Matanda, a monitoring and evaluation officer with ZY+, by P Vengesai, Harare, Zimbabwe, 2 May 2022.
74 Interview with Fadzai Tawonangwere, the advocacy and communications assistant for ZY+, by P Vengesai, Harare, Zimbabwe, 2 May 2022.
75 Interview with Wellington Bakaimani, the Director for Simukaupenye Integrated Youth Academy, by P Vengesai, Shamva, Zimbabwe 5 May 2022.
76 Interview with Yvonne Shumbanhete, the Director of Africa Asia Youth Foundation, by P Vengesai. Masvingo Zimbabwe, 20 April 2022.

Shumbanhete further noted that "these women resorted to defaulting because most of them opted for out of community facilities as they shun nursing staff who live within their communities for fear of being known".[77]

During the pandemic, they reduced the meals to one due to financial hardship. This resulted in malnutrition and mental health challenges. According to Shumbanhete, malnutrition and mental health challenges have a relationship with a high viral load.[78] The right to food was thus not respected during the pandemic, as even the safety nets offered by government could not last a family a fortnight. Shumbanhete further noted that women are already economically marginalised in many different ways and particularly noted that traditionally women cannot own the means of production like communal land. Many traditional leaders are sceptical to give land to women. Traditionally, the inheritance of deceased spouse's estate is handled by the family and husband's families disregard the widowed wives. Many women living with HIV are widows and single mothers. They are living in poverty. Before the pandemic, they were living on two meals a day. As Shumbanhete put it, "When we say meals, we are not talking about the substance, but just something to eat. It may be a whole carbohydrate meal only or something. During the pandemic, some barely had a single meal, though they still had to take their medication."[79] Tafadzwa Mupfumi, a programmes officer at the Africa Asia Youth Foundation, emphasised the exacerbation of economic hardships during lockdowns and linked it with gender-based violence.[80] Of this connection, Mupfumi said, "We saw more cases of gender-based violence during the pandemic, some of which culminated into domestic violence as the women turned to victimise children due to the GBV. One case in Chivhu was recorded where a woman murdered four of her children because of their father's infidelity."[81]

Due to the financial challenges posed by the Covid-19 pandemic, many households could not afford to pay for their water bills. Many households saw their safe, clean water being disconnected. Generally, the right to water has been questionable even in the pre-Covid-19 era, with taps only having water very early in the morning and going the rest of the day without. During the pandemic, most people faced water disconnections, such that they relied on boreholes which are far from where they were residing. Angeline, as a woman living with HIV, had this to say:

> My worst nightmare during the pandemic was a time I could not even pay for my rent. My landlord wanted at least money to settle the bills, which I didn't have at that time, and she insisted I leave if I could not raise the money. I had to move to another area where rentals are much cheaper but there is no water connection. People there rely on boreholes. There is no

---

77 Interview with Yvonne Shumbanhete.
78 Interview with Yvonne Shumbanhete.
79 Interview with Yvonne Shumbanhete.
80 Interview with Tafadzwa Mupfumi, a programmes officer at the Africa Asia Youth Foundation by P Vengesai. Masvingo, Zimbabwe, 20 April 2022.
81 Interview with Tafadzwa Mupfumi.

> electricity. They rely on gas, but I still couldn't afford it. So, I had to use fire, but I cannot really go out to look for firewood due to my health condition. I have a heavy chest, which is why I can't opt to use paraffin for cooking. It has been difficult to access water, but I have to go to fetch water several times, as I can only use a smaller container. I do not have anyone to help, so I have to do it myself.[82]

When asked to clarify on what a heavy chest would mean, Angeline indicated that it is a respiratory problem. The problem of water and other utilities was affecting everyone; however, women with HIV, because of their underlying conditions, were affected more than others.

The cessation of gatherings, including religious gatherings and all forms of clubs, affected many young women who relied on these to relieve their stress and get inspiration from others. Clinics relied more on giving lessons when people came to collect medication. In these lessons, they reminded everyone to adhere to medication and other ways of living positively. It is in these lessons that experts were called to teach on other ways to live positively. Church attendance also helps people to remain positive – and without it, many lost hope. Jacqueline, another woman living with HIV had this to say:

> Closing of churches during the pandemic was not for anyone's benefit. I love church, and I have always found solace in church since I found out I was HIV positive. The very week I discovered my status I went to a new church. I was looking for healing from HIV, but I found something better than a healing. It became family and it has helped me stay positive. Online services were not accessible to many, as it required data at a time when money was hard to come by. For most of us, online services were difficult to follow, though it became normal.[83]

Many of the women could relate to this reality. Non-organisations serving these women also experienced hurdles in delivering services to their beneficiaries. Total lockdown meant that they could not help women living with HIV directly, since there was no physical access to them. Some women living with HIV became reluctant to collect ARTs, leading to high viral loads and low CD4 count.[84] The organisations could neither provide counselling services, nor make follow ups with women who had been recently tested positive for HIV. They also could not conduct CD4 counts on women living with HIV.

---

82 Interview with Angeline (not her real name) by P Vengesai. Masvingo, Zimbabwe, 15 September 2022.

83 Interview with Jacqueline (not her real name) by P Vengesai. Masvingo, Zimbabwe, 15 September 2022.

84 A CD4 count tells you how many CD4 cells there are in a drop of blood. The more there are, the better. A healthy immune system normally has a CD4 count ranging from 500 to 1 600 cells per cubic millimetre of blood (cells/mm^3), according to *HIV.gov*. When a CD4 count is lower than 200 cells/mm^3, a person will receive a diagnosis of AIDS. AIDS is a separate condition that can develop in a person with HIV.

Most medical facilities working with people living with HIV rely greatly on volunteers from different organisations to complement their programmes' efforts. During the programmes is where much advocacy is done to encourage people to get tested and adhere to medication, as well as on ending stigmatisation and discrimination. In the absence of these organisations, facilities became overwhelmed with just a few people. According to Sam Mzenda of Tariro Youth Development Trust, it was very hard to keep working in the pandemic, thus he observed, "We had members who were working directly from the medical facilities. They had to struggle as the nurses there did not have enough PPE; hence, we could not even think of having it. There was general fear among the staff members, especially at a time when medical staff was hard hit and were dying from the pandemic. It was a difficult time. Organisations could not keep encouraging the staff to face the danger. It was a trying time."[85]

Above all, the findings from the interviews emphasised the way in which the rights of women living with HIV were violated. One dimension of the violation of the right to privacy arose from the home visits that the organisations initiated in trying to reach out to their patients. These visits had the effect of informing other family members about the client's HIV status. Also, when they sent personnel to an area for purposes of collection and treatment, the client's status was exposed to the person bringing the treatment. This then amounts to violation of medical confidentiality.

All the research participants agreed that society should have some understanding of the plight of those suffering from other chronic diseases and that people should not suffer any stigma or stigmatisation when they discloser their health status in a bid to look for health assistance. Women with HIV or AIDS are perceived by the society to have contracted it through promiscuity. For that reason, women with HIV and AIDS felt that they should not have disclose their status to police for the purpose of obtaining travelling letters. One woman living with HIV said, "Telling the police that I need a letter to visit clinic to collect my treatment was a major challenge, because my condition is different from blood pressure, sugar diabetes or any other disease which people consider to be of natural cause. If you tell people that you have HIV in my society, you will be considered to have contracted it through sexual promiscuity."[86] Mary T. Bassett, an American public health researcher who has administered HIV/AIDS programmes in Africa, buttresses this position in arguing that the emergence of AIDS pandemic in the early 1980s was gendered and those women who were positive were perceived to have contracted it through sex work. This kind of discrimination and stigmatisation persisted in the Covid-19 pandemic and led to women living with HIV to avoid seeking assistance, as that was only possible after disclosing the status. This fear of disclosure of health status resulted in women living with HIV suffering in the confinement of their houses.

---

85 Interview with Sam Mzenda of Tariro Youth Development Trust by P Vengesai. Zaka, Zimbabwe, 14 April 2022.
86 Interview with a woman with HIV by P Vengesai. Masvingo, Zimbabwe, 2 October 2022.

Globally, women carry the burden of domestic work at the rate of 2.5 times more than men.[87] Women generally have borne the brunt of house chores, coupled with the need to help their children with schoolwork, among other domestic tasks. Due to the increased care responsibilities during the Covid-19 pandemic, all women were hard hit. However, women with HIV, like other patients with chronic diseases, needed to work less and find some rest. Because of their fear of disclosing their condition to their family members so that they could be relieved of domestic duties to nurse their health conditions, they had to endure the burden of domestic work. Maria, a community care supporter and peer counsellor interviewed in Masvingo, had this to say, "Through my counselling sessions, I discovered that most of my HIV patients went through traumatisation and stress due to the burden of domestic work, as they did not disclose their status to family members in fear of stigmatisation."[88]

Maria indicated that, by the time that the Covid-19 restrictions were relaxed, most of their women patients had run out of treatment due to lack of accessibility. She indicated that most men would find their way to the centres to collect their medication, yet women found it very difficult to negotiate with police at the roadblocks. As Maria described it:

> In the second phase of the lockdown, when we had processed the paperwork to open the centre, most of our male patients would come to collect their medication, and when I asked them how they would have passed the roadblocks, they would say "I am a man I know how to find my way out." Yet it was very unfortunate most women could not visit us for their treatment and our efforts to visit their homes were hampered by their fear of stigmatisation and discrimination.[89]

These contentions were backed by another women living with HIV, who was asked if she managed to consistently take her medication during the Covid-19 lockdown. In her own words Maria in an interview said, "At some point I went for a week without medication, as there was nowhere to find the treatment in my suburb. I tried to go to town to get my medication and the police sent me back indicating that I did not have a letter to go to town."[90]

Some of the research participants indicated that they run out of medication during lockdown. Generally, most people living with HIV could not afford to buy medication in pharmacies, and the pharmacies generally do not stock ARVs, as they are free in public institutions because of health aid offered by international organisations, such as the Global Fund and PEPFAR. But even if the medication was available in pharmacies, it was difficult for them to buy over the counter with their cards, as any

---

87 UN Women/Women Count. 2021. Progress on the Sustainable Development Goals: The Gender Snapshot 2021. New York: UN Women/ UN Department of Economic and Social Affairs, 16.
88 Interview with Maria by P Vengesai. Masvingo, Zimbabwe, 2 October 2022.
89 Interview with Maria.
90 Interview with Maria.

other patient with a chronic disease would do, because they did not want the local pharmacists to know their conditions. The idea of having the ARV bottle thrown on the counter and having to pick it up and walk out was too farfetched. In clinics, people living with HIV have long battled the need to be assisted in rooms that are secluded, especially the back of the facilities where they are not seen by others. As Ivy in an interview said, "I waited for an opportunity to access the clinic so that I can get my medication instead of me going to the pharmacy and be known by the whole suburb that I am positive."[91] Agreeing with Ivy, Angeline said, "At the pharmacy you will see a board written 'we check BP and sugar', but they won't include HIV, because it is a sacred disease that one cannot disclose in our culture. Even bringing the medication from the local pharmacy with your card is not something I would do. Besides where would I find that kind of money to purchase the drug for about US$30.00."[92]

CONCLUSION

In light of the above, it is recommended that the Government of Zimbabwe should improve drug restocking at all health centres, allowing patients to access medication and needs locally. It is essential that ARV stocks and prevention supplies are prioritised. It is also important for the government to provide for training and deployment of larger numbers of village healthcare workers, peer counsellors and ART counsellors who bring all the HIV and opportunistic infections (OI) clinic services into the communities. Many women living with HIV and AIDS need constant counselling and frequent check-ups in order to prevent and overcome depression, stress, anxiety and psychosocial challenges. Portable water must also be made available to communities through the use of increased number of boreholes and mobile tanks. Municipalities must be assisted to increase their capacity in water provision to avoid cut offs and interruptions. Social assistance funding must also be increased and be extended to women living with HIV and AIDS. This will help them to secure food and be able to participate in church services that are done online for instance through WhatsApp and Facebook.

While it is accepted that Covid-19 epidemic affected everyone, vulnerable groups within communities, such as people with chronic diseases, were the most affected. People with chronic diseases need to have access to health care systems, sanitation and hygiene, safe water and a healthy food supply. As discussed above, during lockdown, access to such critical services was limited. Although both man and women with chronic diseases were affected due to lockdown, women living with HIV and AIDS suffered the brunt of the challenges. Public health researchers and clinician Mathew Nyashanu and his fellow researchers posit that HIV and AIDS still has the status of a global health challenge despite numerous efforts, at international,

---

91 Interview with Ivy (not real name) by P Vengesai. Masvingo, Zimbabwe, 2 October 2022.
92 Interview with Angeline.

regional and national levels, to contain it.[93] The gains realised from these efforts faced setbacks in the Covid-19 era. Women with HIV and AIDS suffered more because of the factors identified in this chapter.

---

[93] Nyashanu et al, "Exploring the challenges of women taking antiretroviral treatment".

18 THE EFFECTS OF THE COVID-19 PANDEMIC ON WOMEN IN THE UNITED CHURCH OF ZAMBIA

Upendo Mwakasenga[1]

INTRODUCTION

The first Covid-19 case in Zambia was reported on 18 March 2020 at Kenneth Kaunda International Airport in Lusaka.[2] These first infected Zambians were a couple who went to France for a two-week holiday with their two children.[3] Later on, cases were confirmed in Lusaka City and then eventually from all the ten Zambian provinces.[4] The United Church of Zambia (UVZ) is the largest Protestant church in Zambia. With a Presbyterian type of governance, the UCZ has three million members with 1 060 congregations, and it has grown from the time of the union to today. The UCZ is now found in all ten provinces of the country, and according to church annual reports 60% of its members are women. It has been observed that in the UCZ, women are the majority, but they are not involved in decision-making positions.[5]

The present study of the effects of Covid-19 on UCZ women was done at Calvary Congregation and St. Marks Congregation in Lusaka.[6] The study examined how Covid-19 laws and policies affected women in the UCZ. Women, who form the majority in the church, are often responsible for cleaning and offer hospitality to the members. Women are the ones who take care of the sick and manage activities related to funerals and weddings. These activities made women more vulnerable health-wise during the Covid-19 pandemic.

Covid-19 affected both male and female, and rich and the poor alike, in the country. Since a majority of UCZ members are women, they were more directly and

---

1 Reverend, United Church of Zambia; Master's Student in Systematic Theology, School of Religion, Philosophy and Classics, University of KwaZulu-Natal.
2 Kayula J. 2020. "Covid-19 and Labour Law: Zambia", *Italian Labour Law e-Journal* 13(1).
3 Simulundu E et al. 2021. "First Covid-19 Case in Zambia – Comparative Phylogenomic Analysis of SARS-CoV-2 detected in African Countries", *International Journal of Infectious Diseases* 102:455-459.
4 Sialubanje C et al. 2022. "Perspectives on Factors Influencing Transmission of Covid-19 in Zambia: A Qualitative Study of Health Workers and Community Members", *BMJ Open* 12:e05789.
5 Kabonde PM. 2014. *Ordination of Women: Partnership, Praxis and Experience of the United Church of Zambia*. PhD Thesis, University of KwaZulu-Natal, 5.
6 St. Marks and Calvary are congregations within the UCZ from which participants in this study were selected. The two congregations are located within Lusaka presbytery. St. Marks congregation is in a peri-urban area in Chisamba District, fifteen miles from Lusaka city, while Calvary congregation is in Lusaka District urban area.

immediately affected, but children other family members were not spared, with many eventually testing positive for Covid-19. While the majority who were infected recovered, others lost their lives. According to Bernadette Deka-Zulu, the executive director of the Policy Monitoring Research Centre (PMRC) in Lusaka, "the disease outbreak affected women and men differently and make existing inequalities for women and girls worse as the impact of Covid-19 has not been gender neutral".[7] This is because "women not only provide care formally as healthcare workers, but have observed most of the work of informal and unpaid care in the Covid-19 response at domestic and community level".[8]

Using a specifically feminist approach, the present study examines: (1) how Covid-19 laws and policies made by the government affected women in the Church, (2) how women in the Church responded to Covid-19 laws and policies made by the government, and (3) how the church responded to the government Covid-19 laws and policies made in helping the women socially, economically and spiritually. The intent of the study is that the government and the church may find ways and means of helping women to be self-reliant and self-sustaining during future pandemics.

ASSESSING THE EFFECTS OF COVID-19 ON UCZ WOMEN

Scholars in Zambia and other parts of Africa have written on Covid-19 and the particular challenges faced by women. Bernadette Deka-Zulu in her research has chronicled in her research how Zambian women in business were affected by the pandemic.[9] Mathew Nyashanu and fellow researchers examined the impact of the Covid-19 lockdown on Christian self-employed women, businesswomen, civil servants and housewives in the city of Ndola, looked at the gender inequalities which makes women more vulnerable during pandemics.[10] Nelly Mwale has studied the responses of Roman Catholic religious sisters to Covid-19 and how this was portrayed in Zambian media. Mwale argues that the role Roman Catholic sisters played in the pandemic reveals the active role women have played in combatting Covid-19 in the church.[11] Bridget Mukuka has written on violence against women and children in Zambia during the pandemic from a gendered perspective.[12] In addition, Ogechi Adeola has written on gender and sustainable

---

7   Deka-Zulu B. 2021. "Overview of the Challenges caused by Covid-19 on Women-Led Enterprises in Zambia". Lusaka: Policy, Marketing and Research Center (PMRC), 6.
8   Deka-Zulu, "Overview of the Challenges caused by Covid-19 on Women-Led Enterprises", 7.
9   Deka-Zulu, "Overview of the Challenges caused by Covid-19 on Women-Led Enterprises".
10 Nyashanu M, Ikhile D, Karonge T and Rumbidzai C. 2020. "The impact of Covid-19 lockdown in a developing country: narratives of self-employed women in Ndola, Zambia", *Health Care for Women International* 41(11-12):1370-1383.
11 Mwale N. 2022. "Representation of Roman Catholic religious sisters Response to Covid-19 in the Zambian Media", *HTS Theologiese Studies/Theological Studies* 78(2):1.
12 Mukuka BNM. 2021. "Covid-19 and Violence against Women and Children in Zambia. A Gendered Perspective", in Chammeh JK (ed). *Religion Gender and Wellbeing in Africa*. New York, London: Lexington Books, 49-59.

development and the political, social and economic effects of Covid-19 recovery in Africa.[13] Although this existing literature shows the economic, social and religious challenges of women during the Covid-19 pandemics, these scholars write from a gender perspective, but not from a feminist narrative perspective.

While scholars of other African churches have written on Covid-19 effects on women, there is no literature found on the effect of Covid-19 on women in the United Church of Zambia. Hence, there is a gap in the literature in terms of the experiences of women in the UCZ that this study fills, for Lilian Siwila, a scholar of theology and gender studies, has observed that "most churches in Africa are filled with women and children".[14] Siwila's statement is very true, especially in the UCZ, where majority are women. While Covid-19 certainly had effects on men in the church, women, constituting the majority of the church, were disproportionately affected. Thus, the objective of the present study is to investigate the effects of Covid-19 pandemic laws and policies made by the Zambian government on UCZ women. It has been observed that "religion and theology are part of the fabric of African life, and therefore a crucial part of understanding, responding to, confronting and overcoming Covid-19".[15] The study contributes to the already existing literature by adding UCZ women's voices. It is also a contribution to African feminist theological responses to the Covid-19 pandemic.

The present study used qualitative methodology in which twelve women from the UCZ were interviewed on the effects of Covid-19 in their lives. Using a feminist narrative theory, the study analysed the effects of laws and policies on women in the church. Primary data was obtained through one-to-one and group interviews by using open-ended questions, along with a questionnaire distributed to all participants, both observation and analysed through thematic analysis. These interviews were very important in order to hear women's narratives during the Covid-19 pandemic. Primary data from the interviews was then supported and corroborated by a range of secondary sources.

Of the original twelve women, nine from St. Marks and Calvary congregations participated in this research, as the other three withdrew due to other commitments. The interviews were done in two parts. Six women answered the questions as a group and three were given a questionnaire to answer individually and later submitted. The group discussion interview with six women from St. Marks Congregation women's group was done on Sunday, 27 March 2022. The women who took part in the group discussion at St. Marks were approached through the

---

13 Adeola O. 2021. "Introduction: Gendered Perspective on Covid-19 Recovery in Africa: Towards Sustainable Development", in Adeola O (ed). *Gendered Perspective on Covid-19 Recovery in Africa. Towards Sustainable Development*. Switzerland: Springer, 1-38

14 Siwila CL, Mukuka S and Mwale N. 2022. *Chikamoneka!: Gender and Empire in Religion and Public Life*. MalawiMzuni Press, 50.

15 Stiebert J. 2021. "Introduction", in Labeodan HA, Amenga-Etego R, Stiebert J and Aidoo M. (eds). *Covid-19: African Women and the Will to Survive*. Bible in African Studies 31. Bamberg: University of Bamberg Press, 11-13.

congregation secretary, who announced interviews and those who were interested were approached. Six women agreed to sit for the group interview on the agreed date. The study group thus consisted of six women who were members of the UCZ and were farmers and businesswomen between the ages of 30 and 60. The other three participants from Calvary Congregation were teachers and businesswomen between the ages of 45 and 55 years. These three were not interviewed in person, but were given a questionnaire, which they answered on their own time and submitted to the researcher on the agreed date between 26 and 30 March 2022. Since these three participants were working, it was difficult to meet them during the day. Hence, questionnaires were given to them to allow participants to answer at their own convient time.

It should be noted that confidentiality was observed in this research, in that the names of the participants are not attached to any information. We agreed that their names be withheld for privacy purposes, and this gave the participants confidence to open up and share the stories and challenges they experienced as a result of Covid-19 laws and polices imposed by the government during the lockdown. The data is limited in the sense that it comes solely from the two UCZ congregations indicated above. However, the study represents a lot of silent voices of women on effects of Covid-19 in the UCZ. As an insider and leader in the church, I was aware that participants might feel influenced to be part of the study because of my leadership role in the church; however, I informed the participants my role within the church should be set aside so that they might feel free to participate and share openly within the context of the study with my role being that of a participant-observer.

The feminist theory approach that was used in the study to elicit narratives from women experiences during the Covid-19 pandemic was grounded in the understanding that traditionally "knowledge, truth and reality has been constructed as if men's experiences were normative".[16] Feminist narrative theory helps to investigate how masculinities and femininities come to play through women experiences as mothers, wives and Christians. This research is located within the tradition of African feminist theology, which believes in listening to women's experiences in religious spaces and encourages them to narrate their own stories. For purposes of the present study, narratives are "the stretch of stories that are told orally, and are descriptive of personal experiences of individual sharing their stories or related oral texts".[17] Feminist narrative theory is important because "narratives of women during the pandemic are significant for constructing women as active players in the making of contemporary church history".[18] Though examining women telling their

---

16 Barbre JW and Personal Narratives Group (eds). 1989. *Interpreting Women's Lives: Feminist Theory and Personal Narratives*. Bloomington: Indiana University Press, 3.

17 Smith FC. 2014. *African American Female Narratives and Identity Development: A Case Study of Language, Literacy, and Identity Development in the Beauty Salon*. EdD Diss, University of Kentucky. See also Bal M. 2004. *Narrative Theory: Critical Concepts in Literary and Cultural Studies* vol 1. New York: Routledge, 1.

18 Mwale, "Representation of Roman Catholic religious sisters Response to Covid-19".

experiences, the present study examines the social significance of religious spaces in how women narrate the effects of Covid-19 and the role the church played in helping them during the pandemic.

LAWS AND POLICIES ON COVID-19

The Zambian government

It should be noted that the pandemic was global, and all countries had to take their own measures to prevent their citizens from the spread of this disease. It has also been observed that "several African nations have stood out for their highly organised and effective large-scale public campaign".[19] The Minister of Health, Dr Chitalu Chilufya, had a press briefing on Covid-19 prevention and control measures. In his statement, he announced the restrictions on all foreign travels and public mass gatherings.[20] In his statement, the minister also informed the media that the measures taken was in line with the Public Health Act, for as Kachikoti Banda and other public health officials and researchers have stated, "The Public Health Act Cap. 295 of the Laws of Zambia is a guiding law for public health matters in the country".[21] In addition, then-president of the Republic of Zambia, Edgar Lungu, in his 25 March 2020 address to the nation, made further pronouncements that were meant to cement the already existing measures.[22]

Through the Ministry of Health, the government of Zambia put some measures in place to preserve the lives of people in the country. These were known as the "five golden rules" to which every citizen was supposed to adhere or face punishment of the law. Then Minister of Health Dr Jonas Chanda highlighted the five golden rules' requirements of: (1) masking up consistently and correctly in public; (2) hand hygiene, including washing your hands with soap and water or using sanitised; (3) observing social or physical distancing; (4) avoiding crowded places whenever possible and staying home if without business to be about; and (5) in case of Covid-19 infection, seeking medical care early when symptoms develop.[23] According to Part III of the Act on notification of infectious diseases, the minister of health is mandated to "declare that any infectious disease other than those specified ... shall be notifiable

---

19 Stiebert, "Introduction", in *Covid-19: African Women and the Will to Survive*, 12.
20 Republic of Zambia. Ministry of Health. 2020. "Press Briefing on Covid-19 and Additional Preventative and Control Measures", 17 March.
21 Banda KW, Mwanza BG, Mwananumo EM and Banda IN. 2021. "Governance Mechanisms for Managing Municipal Solid Waste: A Review", Proceedings of the 11th Annual International Conference on Industrial Engineering and Operations Management Singapore, 7-11 March.
22 Kayula, "Covid-19 and Labour Law: Zambia".
23 Republic of Zambia. Parliament. 2021. "Ministerial Statement on the Status of Covid-19 Situation in the Country", 3 February.

diseases under this Act".²⁴ Although the Public Health Act passed in 1995, did not mention Covid-19, which was not yet on the horizon, the Ministry of Health provided two statutory instruments in 2020 to address the emergence of Covid, including SI 21 designating Covid-19 as a notifiable disease and SI 22 providing additional regulations to facilitate management and control of the pandemic.²⁵ The statutory instruments provided for the inspection, permitting or closer of public places to ensure that rules are followed.

The Ministry of National Guidance and Religious Affairs also released a letter to all religions in Zambia to guide religious leaders on the guidelines from the Ministry of Health and the five golden rules are repeated in the letter.²⁶ In the letter from Religious Affairs, all churches who used classrooms for worship were suspended. However, the churches in this study were not affected by this rule, because they had their own church building. Nevertheless, in the letter, children and elderly people above 70 years were not allowed to come to church. The suspension of children going to church prevented nursing mothers to attend church services while their husbands attended. The decision was to prevent children as well as mothers from being infected, but the husband going for gatherings and coming back home also put women and children at risk of being infected.

As Nelly Mwale has noted, "The prevention and control measures had implications on different spheres of life."²⁷ Although the above measures were put in place by the government, it was difficult to maintain social distance in public places, such as churches, public buses and markets. Therefore, guidelines from the Ministry of Health were reinforced by the police, who monitored the people, especially in public places. In some cases, police harassed people in the churches who were found not observing five golden rules, even if just a single one. This prompted then-president Lungu to issue a statement in which he "directed that agencies entrusted with enforcement of Covid-19 guidelines should refrain from abusing and harassing citizens found breaking the rules".²⁸ Luckily enough, the churches that participated in this study were not harassed by police.

---

24 Republic of Zambia. Ministry of Legal Affairs. "The Public Health Act. Chapter 295 of the Laws of Zambia".

25 Republic of Zambia. Ministry of Health. 2020. "Press Briefing on Covid-19 and Additional Preventative and Control Measures", 17 March. See also Republic of Zambia. 2020. "The Public Health (Infected Areas) (Coronavirus Disease 2019) Regulations, 2020", Statutory Instrument 22 of 2020, *Government Gazette*, 13 March.

26 Republic of Zambia. Ministry of National Guidance and Religious Affairs. 2020. "Letter to Churches on Covid-19, 2020", 22 September, 1-2.

27 Mwale, "Representation of Roman Catholic religious sisters Response to Covid-19 in the Zambian Media", 3.

28 "Police harassing faithful? (Pictures)", *The Zambian Sun*, 15 April 2022.

The United Church of Zambia

Because of the pandemic in the country, the United Church of Zambia issued a pastoral letter through its synod general secretary Rev Dr Mulambya Kabonde. The first pastoral letter was issued in March 2020, after the Ministry of Health restricted all public gatherings in the country including churches. The second pastoral letter was not so different from the first letter, despite the fact that President Lungu, on 24 April 2020, had announced the opening of the churches subject to observing the five golden rules. Nevertheless, the pastoral letter indicated that, worship services, group meetings, Holy Communion and other activities remained suspended.[29] The suspension of church gatherings came at a time when churches come together to celebrates Palm Sunday in the streets. This created tension between the government and the Christian community, as well as between church members and leaders. The members condemned the clergy for allowing the government restrictions on church worship. In 2020, a third pastoral letter allowed the opening of the UCZ churches in the country with strict measures.

However, in June 2021, the UCZ, through its newly elected General Secretary, Rev Chipasha Musaba, released a fourth pastoral letter, which allowed gatherings after each congregation obtained permission from government through Ministry of Health who inspected the building and declared it clean.[30] Surprisingly, after one year and some months, the church still did not allow children or the elderly to come to church. There was no Holy Communion, no funeral or wedding gatherings at home or church and weddings were restricted to family members. Since all church group gatherings were suspended, including catechumen class, there were no baptisms. What is notable about the above pastoral letters was that the two sacraments of the church, baptism and Holy Communion, were suspended in a way that shook and tested the faith of the church. These church restrictions were not welcomed by the members, who thought the church failed to stand its ground in support of the worship of God even in difficult times. Members also felt that leaders of the church failed to protect its faith and doctrines, leaving the people vulnerable to temptations. Bridget Mukuka observed that, "For many Church members, partaking holy communion brings them closer to God … . Hence, no one can be stopped from partaking holy communion unless there are serious offences that a person has committed."[31] Indeed, the government restrictions and church responses affected these long-standing church traditions. However, the church suspension of sacraments of Holy Communion and baptism protected church members and the clergy from the virus, as such church services are fully packed and observing social distance would have been difficult.

---

29 United Church of Zambia, Synod Headquarters Lusaka. 2020. "Second Pastoral letter on Covid-19", 25 April.
30 United Church of Zambia, Synod Headquarters Lusaka. 2021. "All One in Christ", Council for World Mission. Fourth pastoral letter on Covid-19, 17 June.
31 Mukuka, "Covid-19 and Violence against Women and Children in Zambia", 51.

The suspensions of other church activities were not easy to resolve through online means. Many people went through difficult times without the presence of the church encouragement. This was very difficult in the context of African religiosity. Pastor and theologian Chammah Kaunda observes, "spirituality in all its various manifestations and aspects of life, should not be regarded as separate from the totality of African human life."[32] This observation brings to light the spiritual effects that the government Covid-19 laws and policies touched by not allowing churches to gather. Kaunda suggests that since African spirituality include all aspects of life, then its hindrance results in moral decay in the community.

The laws and policies made not only affected the churches, but also other cultural practices of African and Zambian people. For example, Zambian women are sociable, and when someone has a funeral they will go and gather at the funeral house and spend nights there. But Covid-19 laws and policies restricted such gatherings, further isolating people who were mourning, especially if people heard that the deceased's death was due to Covid-19. Women were particularly affected by the lockdown, since they were more exposed, more than men, to diseases as frontline workers. The lockdown also created a great challenge economically in sub-Saharan Africa, with women being hit harder because of lower income and higher poverty rates.[33] Women were vulnerable to disease, because they are the ones who take care of the family. That is why the lockdown was such a big challenge to women in the church, community and health sectors. To take another example, it was observed that during the periods of the lockdown and other restrictions, the police and other security forces recorded large numbers of incidents of gender-based violence.[34] That could have been due to couples stuck together at home for long periods of time.

ZAMBIAN WOMEN'S EXPERIENCES DURING THE COVID-19 PANDEMIC

Laws and policies on Covid-19 by the Zambian government affected women socially, economically and spiritually. Participants in the present study acknowledged that in the beginning, there was a lot of resistance, because no Covid-19 cases were recorded in their families, community and churches. This made it difficult to convince people to follow the "five golden rules". Even so, the women made it clear that even though the laws and policies were very hard and harsh on them, they still appreciated how the government handled the pandemic and put in place to protect all.

---

32 Kaunda CJ. 2021. "Introduction: Encountering the 'Voice' of Well-being in African Contexts", in Kaunda CJ (ed). *Religion, Gender and Wellbeing in Africa*, 2.

33 Aoyagi C. 2021. "Effect of Covid-19 on Region and Gender Equality in Sub-Saharan Africa. Evidence from Nigeria and Ethiopia", Working Paper No. 2021/169 Washington, DC: International Monetary Fund.

34 Mukuka, "Covid-19 and Violence against Women and Children in Zambia", 51.

Social experiences

The Greek philosopher Aristotle observed, "Man is by nature a social animal."[35] The Covid-19 regulations issues by the government through the ministry of health made life difficult by preventing socialising with others. Participants in the present study indicated through the interviews that laws and policies put in place had good and bad sides. Both the group discussion and individual respondents indicated that, the laws and policies were good because the prevented the disease from spreading and they kept people in good health. Asked what was good about the government Covid-19 laws and policies, one woman said, "Without those restrictions by the government no one would be alive today. You know, us women, we like socialising with a lot of people through *ichilangamulilo*, *amatebeto*, kitchen parties, weddings and funerals. The government did well."[36] (*Ichilangamulilo* is food prepared by the bride's family to be given to the gloom showing them how the bride cooks, and *amatebeto* is food prepared by the in-laws to appreciate their son-in-law for how he has kept their daughter well.) Suspension of weddings and kitchen parties had an economic impact on couples who did not see the restrictions coming.

With regard to family care responsibilities, another woman maintained, "The restrictions brought the disease under control, and it encouraged people to have more sense of care and responsibility, especially women, because of their role of being frontline caregivers in their homes, churches, and the community. It improved the level of hygiene and behavioural change in our homes, church and community."[37] Raymond Hamoonga and fellow researchers have stated that "the success of Zambia's Covid-19 response is premised in communities adhering to good hygiene practice".[38] Participants in the group discussion indicated that men were better than women when it comes to following Covid-19 health guidelines. But in Zambia, women are usually the ones who take care of family members of all ages when they are sick, a task that fewer men can manage. Overall, women are more sociable than men in Zambian society, and that is why it was harder for them to keep the rules.

In the focus group discussion, it was discovered among some of the women that when their husbands tested positive with Covid-19, they were the ones at their husband's bedsides taking care of them throughout until they recovered. Unfortunately, when the women tested positive for Covid-19, their husbands followed the rules of social distance upon hearing it and prepared a room to keep their wives in isolation while they remained in the bedroom alone. It turned out that some men love their wives only when they are in good health, which meant that the laws and policies had a negative impact on marriages, as some members of couples felt neglected by their loved ones. The findings suggested that women risked their

---

35 Aristotle, *Politics*, 1253a.
36 Group Discussion. St. Marks Congregation Lusaka, Zambia, 27 March 2022.
37 Questionnaire from Calvary Congregation, Lusaka, Zambia, 26 March 2022.
38 Hamoonga R et al. 2020. "Hygiene Behaviour Change in Response to Covid-19 in Zambia: A cross-sectional survey", *Health Press Zambia Bulletin* 5(1):3.

lives just to show love by taking care of their sick family members, but they never received same care from men in return.

Economic experiences

The seventeenth-century English poet John Donne wrote, "No man is an island." There is a need for interconnectedness of all people to God and to each other. The economic effect that the pandemic brought affected not just individuals, but families, communities, nations and the entire globe. Many women and men lost their jobs because of the lockdown. Those who engaged in cross-border trade saw their business shut down, since borders were closed from March through October 2020. This led to high consumer prices, since goods from outside the country become scarce and the few who had them hiked the prices. These policies of the government were hindrances to women's work both in the private and public sector. In the focus group discussion, it was evident that women were financially affected during the Covid-19 pandemic period. Deka-Zulu states that, "when compared to men 49% women entrepreneurs reported temporary suspension of business activities due to Covid-19 against 35% men.[39]

During data collection, I discovered that one of the three participants who were teachers was teaching at a private school, while the other two were at the government school. Teachers at private school were affected differently economically from those in government schools. Teachers from private schools never received their salaries, because parents did not pay tuition fees, as pupils were not learning. It was through payment of tuition fees that private schools were able to pay their workers, while in government schools it was the responsibility of the government to pay teachers and not the school. The private school teacher was used to having her own money, but Covid-19 reduced her to a housewife and asking for money from her husband. This made women feel even worse. Some women stopped even giving Sunday offerings, group gathering offerings, tithes and to other programmes that needed monies to support the kingdom of God. Thus, the church was also affected economically.

The experiences of these women bring to light the challenges that they experienced in the private sector. The government did not consider how those in the private sector would survive. The interviews revealed that the women felt bad staying out of employment, but they were more free to ask for assistance from their husbands than men from their wives. The financial challenges of an individual member of the church also affected the offerings in the church negatively. Most of the women reported that they stopped attending women's fellowship, even after the lockdown was over. The financial capacity of the women's group was low as was that of the church.

During the Covid-19 lockdown, the government was forced to close all salons, barbershops, restaurants, bars, liquor stores casinos, kitchen parties, wedding

---

[39] Deka-Zulu B. 2021. "Overview of Challenges Caused by Covid-19 on Women-Led Enterprise in Zambia". Lusaka: Policy Monitoring and Research Centre.

ceremonies. Some women took advantages of the Covid-19 lockdown and started making face masks and selling them in bulk. The made not only masks, but also hand sanitisers, and they also sold lemons, ginger roots and other herbs believed to cure Covid-19. In fact, some women were never negatively affected by the lockdown of Covid-19, even when most of the business entities were closed, because they found other means of surviving. A few women reported that they made a lot of money; thus, it could be said that they were economically positively affected by the laws and policies made by the government of the Zambia during the pandemic. Covid-19 prompted the women to be resourceful and seek new avenues of income.

Spiritual experiences

The laws and policies put in place by the government and the church had both positive and negative impacts on the women who were the majority of the members of the church. The most important point that the participants pointed to was the decline in membership, since the few who came to church after lockdown still feared contracting the disease. Concerning the spiritual life of women, there was a decline in participation and membership, as activities planned for the year were disrupted. The participants observed that worshipping during Covid-19 lockdown made the situation worse for those who were not very active in the women's fellowship group. In addition, house prayers proved unfruitful to majority of the members, because the home environment was not conducive for prayers during the day.

When services were allowed to be done for the limited duration of an hour, some people still cited Covid-19 as an excuse for not attending. Many of the women who participated in the presented study said that they missed church and wondered why the church agreed to the government's the conditions. They continued to say that they were most upset about suspending Holy Communion, which brings the people closer to God. Church members were encouraged to continue to give offerings, when spiritually they were backsliders.

The clergy were asked a lot of questions as to why members had to give offerings despite not coming to church. However, the church did engage in helping the needy in the society, especially women, by giving them foodstuffs. Such activities encouraged members to give more. The work of the clergy and church leaders during and after lockdown was difficult in terms of convincing people to come back and worship God while observing social distance. A lot was done to convince people to start going to church, such as encouragement through WhatsApp groups, Facebook pages and phone calls from different church leaders to assure people that God's presence was with them despite of the pandemic. Other participants pointed out that Covid-19 helped them to learn on how to be strong, and how to stand on their own and trust God in every situation. It was a time that brought people closer to their families and helped them understand and know Jesus as their personal saviour.

When asked how vulnerable they were as women in the church, most of the women in the focus group discussion, said that, as women, they were responsible for cleaning the church. The Covid-19 pandemic required them to develop hygiene consciousness, but at the same time they were scared that they might contract the disease. Indeed, Covid-19 helped in improving cleanliness in the church, because the health inspectors inspected the churches to see if they were complying to health guidelines. Other participants noticed that the government law and policy were a bit loose, with health inspectors and police being strict with the churches, but leaving the markets, bars and public transport unchecked and as far as observing social distance.

ANALYSIS OF THE RESPONSE OF WOMEN AND CHURCHES

Using a feminist lens, the general view from the data collected was that the laws and policies taught women the value of cleanliness, innovation, physical, spiritual and self-reliance. These values clustered around several different themes.

Gender-based violence

Though the lockdown solved one problem of health in the form of the pandemic, it created a new one in the rise of gender-based violence. Chammah Kaunda and Benjamin Pokol, writing from a feminist perspective, observed that, "gendered inequalities and relations of dominion shapes African Cultural systems, makes women vulnerable to various forms of violence."[40] Covid-19 sent husbands, children and businesswomen home. Bridget Mukuka states that, "Staying indoors brought about many types of abuse against women and children".[41] The question Bridget Mukuka posed was: where was religion when women and children were abused? She forgot that churches were also closed and there was little or no communication with members and leaders. In some cases, this fostered good family fellowship, that had been lost due to parents and children being kept busy and apart. These families cemented their relationships, but in others the loss of jobs created frustration which led to gender-based violence.

The picture of a woman being treated at the University Teaching Hospital (UTH) in Lusaka Zambia was reported in the newspaper by journalist Mwaka Lengalenga on 21 December 2021. Lengalenga reported that the Young Women's Christian Association (YWCA) was one of the key actors in the fight against gender-based violence. However, due to the Covid-19 pandemic, the organisation recorded an increase in gender-based violence cases. Lengalenga further reported that the organisation received 587 clients in 2020 compared to 398 in 2019 and 431 in 2018.[42] Deka-Zulu has noted that GBV cases increased by 19.8% with 6 788 cases in 2019

---

[40] Kaunda C and Pokol B. 2019. "African Christianity, Myth of Creation, and Gender Justice: An African Feminist Re-Inculturation Perspective", *Journal of Feminist Studies in Religion* 35(1):6.

[41] Mukuka, "Covid-19 and Violence against Women and Children in Zambia", 53.

[42] Legalenga M. 2021 "Addressing Gender-Based Violence amid Coronavirus Pandemic", *Zambia Daily Mail Limited*.

and 7 640 in 2020 and that one contributing factor might be due to lockdown and frustrations that come with the loss of income, further acknowledging that "these measures had weakened women protection and increased women exposure to higher risk of gender-based violence."[43] These observations indicate that laws and policies during the pandemic can be correlated to an increase in gender-based violence. In this study, participants also acknowledged that men staying at home caused a lot of relationship misunderstanding among the couples. Some issues which caused misunderstanding were shortages of food supply for the family. In their research on women in Ndola, Mathew Nyashanu and research colleagues reported that participants in their study "had inadequate food supplies as a result of closing down their self-run of businesses" and "never received any help from the government".[44]

Women's use of African medicine

UCZ women expressed fear of dying from Covid-19. The fear went to such an extent that they did not want to go to the clinic for fear of catching Covid. Participants in the discussions conducted for the present study revealed that it was this fear that prompted them to seek solutions by going back to their roots and what their foremothers and forefathers had used to keep themselves healthy. Media reports suggest that there was an increase in the use of medicinal plants commonly used in African traditional medicine and that sellers in Lusaka were running out of stock.

Steaming inhalation therapy, known as *ukufutikila* in the Bemba language, was reported to be on the rise in Zambia in home-based care solutions as a prevention measure against Covid-19. The Minister of Health, then Mr Jonas Chanda, was reported having said that, "Local based traditional remedies were vital in managing less severe cases at home. Among the recommended preventative remedies are included hot steaming, vitamin C, ginger, garlic, honey and cinnamon concoctions."[45] Steaming inhalation, which was seen as old-fashioned by this generation, again became part of their lives, as women learnt how to use these techniques properly on their children. In his ministerial statement on the status of the Covid-19 situation in the country, Minister of Health Chanda said that for home-based care management of patients who were symptomatic, the advice was to use supplementation with vitamins, a balanced diet with additional fruits and vegetables, taking plenty of fluids to ensure that they were well hydrated at all times, engaging in light exercises and the steaming up commonly known as *ukufutikila*.

What was surprising was that, in the past and before Covid-19, women of faith were the ones who condemned African medicine as being evil. David Mutemwa states that "The limited access to the health care system, left many to resort to traditional

---

43 Deka-Zulu, "Overview of Challenges Caused by Covid-19 on Women-Led Enterprise in Zambia", 12.
44 Nyashanu, "The impact of Covid-19 lockdown in a developing country", 1374.
45 "Feature: Home-based care solutions for Covid-19 prevention in Zambia on the rise", *Xinhua* 20 January 2021.

remedies. Home-based care in Zambia includes the use of local based solutions such as steaming.[46] In the same way that the former president and Ministry of Health recommended the use of African traditional medicine, Mutemwa further clarifies the recommendation of steaming as involving "putting leaves of trees such as mangoes, guavas, and eucalyptus into boiling hot water from which the team raises".[47] In light of the resurgence of these African traditional healing methods would also recommend that the government promote African medicines be used even more to control diseases. However, there is need for the Ministry of Health to research the African medicines and therapies that enabled our mothers to live without clinics.

Church traditions tested

The suspension of Holy Communion, baptism, funeral services and group fellowship made people question the church for not defending what they believed during such hard times. The church seemed not to have a say with what the government had put in place. This made a lot of people question whether the church was really the mouthpiece of the vulnerable people in the society. The doctrines and traditions of the church were challenged by the Covid-19 pandemic. The measures the church had put in place were to protect members and church workers from being infected. The United Church of Zambia constitution, rules and regulations pertaining to the sacrament of Holy Communion state, "This sacrament has from the earliest days been recognised as the central act of worship of those who are fully committed to the services of Christ and are therefore termed 'Communicant Members'."[48] What the church considered to be the central part of worship, for which communicant members are suspended if they miss three consecutive months, was no longer being administered. The other implication of not partaking Holy Communion was that if such a person dies, they will not be accorded a Christian funeral service. For a UCZ member, a Christian funeral service is an important rite of passage for the deceased of which they were deprived during the Covid-19 pandemic.

Self-reliance and self-sustenance of the church and its members

Though the church had experienced financial problems, it still extended its helping hand to women and men who lost their jobs and businesses due to Covid-19. Early in the pandemic, personal protective equipment for healthcare workers were expensive and difficult to acquire. However, the church provided personal protective equipment

---

46 Mutemwa D et al. 2021. "The Role of Women, Philosophy of Life, Global Health, Traditional Medicine and Past Experiences in the Covid-19 Pandemic Response: Zambia Case Study", *Caritas e Veritas* 11:34-49.

47 Mutemwa et al. "The Role of Women, Philosophy of Life, Global Health, Traditional Medicine and Past Experiences", 45.

48 The United Church of Zambia, "Constitution Rules and Regulations. 2014". Article 5.2. On importance of Holy Communion, see also Mukuka, "Covid-19 and Violence against Women and Children in Zambia", 51.

for frontline workers in its church-owned hospitals. By doing so, they helped women who were nursing husbands, children or family members who were admitted to the hospital. Though such help rendered by the church to vulnerable families and church-owned hospitals seemed to be a drop in the ocean, the study suggests that there is a need for both the church and churchwomen to be self-reliant and self-sustaining in the context of financial crisis and pandemics.

Mathew Nyashanu and research colleagues have suggested that "there is need to make training available for self-employed women in entrepreneurship skills to ensure that they have skills to protect their business during pandemic times".[49] Women being empowered with skills to keep their businesses intact during a pandemic is only possible if they are trained to know how to turn bad situations into business opportunities. The government, together with religious institutions, can work together to find a lasting solution for pandemics. Some women who were tailors saw a business opportunity during Covid-19 by sawing face masks and selling them to the public.

Communication

The main lesson learnt from the Covid-19 pandemic by study participants was that phones become more important than ever before. People learnt how to use WhatsApp messages and video, send and receive money and they communicated to their friends and fellow church members. The church no longer relied on hard copy letters to communicate; instead, emails and WhatsApp were used to communicate with congregants. Felesia Malauzi and Kendra Albright have maintained that the ability of a society to develop "depends on the ability of individuals, including women to access information and knowledge".[50] Malauzi and Albright further observe that "information access is critical for women in many regions because they are key players in the development process."[51] However, Ngabo Nankonde and research colleagues have noted that "the ownership of mobile phones across genders revealed that there are relatively more 'male headed' households that own at least one working mobile phone than 'female headed' households".[52] The United Nations Secretary-General António Guterres has observed that "most of those who lack access to digital technology [are] women and girls in developing countries" and Hansen He, Huawei Zambia Director of Public Relations, has urged women in Zambia "not [to] be afraid to put themselves forward and prove that they can

---

49 Nyashanu M et al. 2020. "The impact of Covid-19 lockdown in a developing country", *Health Care for Women International* 41(11-12):1380.

50 Mulauzi F and Albright KS. 2009. "Information and Communication Technologies (ICTs) and Development information for Professional Women in Zambia", *International Journal of Technology Management* 45(1-2):177-195.

51 Mulauzi and Albright, "Information and Communication Technologies (ICTs) and Development information for Professional Women in Zambia".

52 Nankonde N, Banda B and Siluyele I. "Evaluating the Gender Gaps in Access & Usage of ICTs in Zambia". Lusaka: ZICTA/SPIDER, 16.

defy odds and break through that proverbial glass that espouses that ICT is a male field".[53] These data indicate that women have a long way to go to have the access to phones that men do.

The Covid-19 period prompted clergy and church leaders to make use of their phones to communicate with their members. The challenge was with women who lacked mobile phones, as indicated by Nankonde and fellow researchers. During the Covid-19 period, the clergy and church leaders used Zoom meetings to discuss affairs pertaining to the church and WhatsApp and Facebook to preach and communicate important information to church members. One member from the group discussion shared her experience of bad communication during lockdown. It was an instance in which she was sick and no member of the church visited her or called upon her to find out how she was coping, for fear of contracting the virus, even though she only had malaria. It made her feel bad – how Covid-19 disconnected the members and broke their fellowship and care for one another.

The pandemic did not just break communication among people in the church, but also in the wider society. Care was disrupted in cases of sickness, funerals and weddings. As a leader in the church, there was no other means to share the word of God without gathering. Hence, the church encouraged the church pastors to make use of social media to preach and restore hope in the lives of the people. Communication is very vital, as it unites the families and helps us to achieve our goals, but Covid brought the life of the church to a standstill.

CONCLUSION

The first objective of this study was to investigate how Covid-19 laws and policies made by the government affected women in the church. The results show that women during lockdown were affected both positively and negatively. The positive part was that the Covid-19 pandemic prompted women to be clean both at church and at home in a way that prevented them from being infected. In the church and at home, women played an important role in preventing the Covid-19 through practising good hygiene. The women had adequate time to spend with their spouses and children. In addition, house prayers encouraged fellowship in the family and built their faith in God.

However, as much as these laws and policies had positive effects, they also had negative effects on women and the family. It should be noted that the majority of the women who participated in the study were famers and businesswomen and a few were schoolteachers. When the lockdown was implemented, their business went down, resulting in a shortage of food supplies for their families. Some of the men in their families were also out of employment, and they stayed home with their wives all day. That resulted into increased gender-based violence among couples due to economic pressures. The effects were not just physical, but also spiritual.

---

53 Chiwila C. "Zambia: Not Leaving Women Behind in ICTS", *Times of Zambia*, 1 June 2021.

18. The effects of the Covid-19 pandemic on women in the United Church of Zambia

The second objective of the study was to assess how women in the church responded to Covid-19 laws and policies made by the government. The data collected revealed that it was difficult for women to keep the social distance rules the whole day, as they had many responsibilities at home. Women were vulnerable to Covid-19 at church, in the society and at home. This is because women are social beings who care for the family. When members of the family were sick, the women took care of them, but they were asked by their male partners to isolate when sick. The duty to care for the sick resulted in women returning to African traditional healing medicines and therapies, the preparation of which was mainly known by women in earlier eras. Women did everything possible to save lives. Though physical contact was discouraged, women used phones to communicate to their families and fellow church members.

The final objective was to analyse how the church responded to the government Covid-19 laws and policies and how these policies affected women socially, economically and spiritually. The church limits on time for worship affected women's group social activities. However, the church, through its social services, helped vulnerable by giving them food. In the hospitals run by the church, donations from members were made to health institutions to prevent the spread. Though the church did not give food to all, others were helped, and their faith was revived.

The study proved that Covid-19, as other pandemics, was gendered in a range of ways. Inasmuch as men were affected economically, socially and spiritually, women were more affected, as they had to look after the families and make sure that hygiene standards were followed both at church and at home. Women played and important role as home-based caregivers to symptomatic patients. But despite all the work they did and the pressure to look after the children at home, some women experienced gender-based violence. The violence was physical to some and mental to others, as they were not taken care of by their husbands when they were sick.

The UCZ women's stories indicate there is need for the church and the government to collaborate in any pandemic that may come and particularly to consider how women's experiences can be addresses. Trouble can result when the government closes churches, workplaces, markets and essentially the whole country, even in places where Covid-19 was not present. The government should make decisions according to the context of people living in the developing countries when it comes to lockdowns and medicines to be used. It is good that the use of herbal medicine was supported by the president and the Ministry of Health. The study shows that there was no change in women access to phones recorded. There is need comparative research on women access to phones before and during Covid-19. On the other hand, the lesson for the church is to learn to be self-reliant and self-sufficient and empower women in acquiring various skills and in accessing access to phones for business and spiritual purposes. Further comparison research on the effects of Covid-19 on men and women should also be done.

19 RELIGIOUS RESPONSES TO DOMESTIC VIOLENCE AND MENTAL HEALTH ISSUES DURING THE COVID-19 PANDEMIC

Opeyemi Oyewunmi Ekundayo[1]

INTRODUCTION

The World Health Organization (WHO) declared the novel coronavirus (SARS-CoV-2) or Covid-19, a global pandemic on 11 March 2020. The WHO thereafter began efforts to contain the disease through recommending preventive non-medical measures, such as frequent hand washing, wearing of personal protective equipment and physical and social distancing from others. In furtherance of the WHO's measures, different countries declared lockdown at different times.[2] The first case of Covid-19 in Nigeria was confirmed on 27 February 2020, after which several others were confirmed, and a lockdown was declared on 29 March 2020.[3] The lockdown kept family members together under the roof without the usual daily "escape" to social gatherings, schools and workplaces. On the home front, it led to excessive familiarity, frequent quarrels, and inadequate finances. Coupled with the physical and social distancing, the Covid-19 pandemic had significant implications on the mental health of people worldwide.[4]

Mental illnesses, like other medical problems, are based on a combination of physical, emotional and psychological factors. Women with mental health disorders are more likely to have experienced domestic abuse in the past, and domestic violence is seven times more likely for women with post-traumatic stress disorder (PTSD). Women who have schizophrenia, bipolar disorder, or obsessive-compulsive disorder (OCD) are also more likely to have witnessed at least a form of intimate partner violence.[5]

Domestic violence is a major public and social health issue all over the world. In their lifetimes, one in every three (30%) women in the world has been subjected to

---

1 Senior Lecturer, Department of Psychology, Faculty of Social Sciences, Obafemi Awolowo Univerity, Ile-Ife, Nigeria.
2 Xiaoni C, Pengxiang W and Zhun W. 2021. "Emergency use of Covid-19 vaccines recommended by the World Health Organization (WHO) as of June 2021", *Drug discoveries & therapeutics* 15(4):222-224.
3 Adegboye OA, Adekunle AI and Gayawan E. 2020. "Early transmission dynamics of novel coronavirus (Covid-19) in Nigeria", *International Journal of Environmental Research and Public Health* 17(9):3054.
4 Muktar S. 2020. "Mental health and emotional impact of Covid-19: Applying Health Belief Model for medical staff to general public of Pakistan", *Brain, Behavior, and Immunity* 87:28-29.
5 Dogar FA. 2021. "The impact of domestic violence on mental health", *OlaDoc.com*, 16 July.

physical, emotional and/or sexual assault by their intimate partner.[6] The Covid-19 pandemic lockdown is said to have exacerbated domestic violence all over the world because of the of lockdown orders that required victims to stay at home with their abusers,[7] reducing their chances of being able to escape a violent situation.[8] The lockdown altered the rhythms of everyday life for Nigerians who struggled with income deficits and the daily expenses of the family,[9] and it heightened social tensions leading to more aggression and violence.[10] Victims felt culturally compelled to remain silent,[11] and in a risky family environment that can lead to immediate and long-term adverse mental health effects.

Mental health issues are culturally stigmatised in Nigeria.[12] Thus, people are often forced to remain in silence until their situation gets worse. When domestic violence occurs, the perpetrator often uses religious justifications to justify their behaviour and attribute violence to their religion.[13] However, many of those who seek help seem to prefer help from religious communities, either because they are religious themselves or because they perceive health facilities to be inadequate and expensive. Some religious communities indirectly contribute to domestic violence by suggesting that a man is the family's leader and has the ability to reprimand rebellious family members, including his wife. Some religions believe that every

---

6   World Health Organization (WHO). 2013. "Global and Regional Estimates of Violence Against Women: Prevalence and Health Effects of Intimate Partner Violence and Non-partner Sexual Violence", *WHO.int*, 20 October.

7   UN Women. 2020. "Covid-19 and Ending Violence Against Women and Girls". New York: UN Women.

8   For global literature on the mental health effects of Covid-19 stay-at-home orders and the rise of domestic violence, see Hamadani JD et al. 2020. "Immediate impact of stay-at-home orders to control Covid-19 transmission on socioeconomic conditions, food insecurity, mental health, and intimate partner violence in Bangladeshi women and their families: an interrupted time series", *The Lancet Global Health* 8(11):e1380-e1389; Piquero AR et al. 2021. "Domestic violence during the Covid-19 pandemic: Evidence from a systematic review and meta-analysis", *Journal of Criminal Justice* 74:art 101806; Berniell I and Facchini G. 2021. "Covid-19 lockdown and domestic violence: Evidence from internet-search behavior in 11 countries", *European Economic Review*, 136:103775.

9   Onah NG. "Socio-cultural and religious impact of the Covid-19 pandemic in Nigeria", in Labeodan HA, Amenga-Etego R, Stiebert J and Aidoo MS (eds). *Covid-19: African Women and the Will to Survive*. University of Bamberg Press, 187-226.

10   See Nzeadibe A et al. 2022. "Nigeria's pandemic lockdown measures were hard on informal workers", *The Conversation*, 28 February; Fawole OI, Okedare OO and Reed E. 2021. "Home was not a safe haven: women's experiences of intimate partner violence during the Covid-19 lockdown in Nigeria", *BMC Women's Health* 21:art 32.

11   "Breaking the silence on domestic violence", *Vanguard*, 6 April 2017.

12   Armiya'u AY. 2015. "A review of stigma and mental illness in Nigeria", *Journal of Clinical case Reports* 5(1):1000488.

13   See Ngwoke PN. 2021. "Religious manipulation and domestic violence within Christian homes in Nigeria", *International Journal of Religion and Spirituality in Society* 11(1):121-136; Umar MA. 2012. "The perspective of Shari'ah on domestic violence", *Nnamdi Azikiwe University Journal of International Law and Jurisprudence* 3(2012):170-181.

member of the family deserves respect. Religion is, thus, perceived as both a cause and a cure for the mental health issues that can come from domestic violence.

It is argued by some authors that domestic violence is a theological and ecclesiastical issue, and that responses by religious organisations are necessary to lessen its high prevalence in Nigeria.[14] It is, therefore, imperative to investigate how various religious communities have responded to domestic violence in the face of the Covid-19 pandemic. What prevention and risk mitigation strategies do religious communities put in place as a response to domestic violence and tackle associated mental health issues during the Covid-19 pandemic? This is the key question of the present study, which contributes to the growing body of research on these issues by looking at the socio-ecological framework that the religious communities deploy to address reported incidents of mental health issue linked to domestic violence.[15]

FRAMING RELIGION, DOMESTIC VIOLENCE, MENTAL HEALTH AND COVID-19

The current study's data was acquired through narratives based on an average of one hour face-to-face, in-depth interviews conducted in English. Interviews were held at the offices of the participants and on the grounds of various religious institutions, as agreed. The interviews were conducted to learn about each participant's experience with domestic abuse and mental health issues as reported by their religious members. It was also to determine the forms of assistance that religious groups could provide to victims and abusers. To assure consistency and the study's reliability, the author conducted and audio-recorded all interviews, which were then transcribed for thematic analysis.[16]

Three religious leaders were included in this study, a Muslim imam, a Pentecostal pastor, and a chief priest from the Obatala traditional religion.[17] The rationale for recruiting participants from different religious groups was to represent the diversity of religious affiliation of southwestern Nigerians and the three major religions in Nigeria: Christianity, Islam and African traditional religion.[18] Participants were

---

14 Ogbuji HO. 2022. "Mitigating the prevalence of domestic violence in Nigeria: An Ecclesial and pastoral leadership response". Project Thesis, Boston University School of Theology.

15 For more information on the methodology of social-ecological frameworks, see Stokols D, Allen J and Bellingham RL. 1996. "The social ecology of health promotion: implications for research and practice", *American Journal of Health Promotion* 10(4):247-251; Tolley EE et al. 2016. *Qualitative methods in public health: a field guide for applied research*. Hoboken, NJ: John Wiley & Sons.

16 See Guest G, MacQueen K and Namey E. 2012. *Applied thematic analysis*. Los Angeles, CA: SAGE; Braun V and Clarke V. 2006. "Using thematic analysis in psychology", *Qualitative Research in Psychology* 3(2):77-101.

17 Obatala, according to the Yoruba mythology of deity, is the *orisha* of creation and healing. Obatala is the spirit of righteous kindness and justice – a peacemaker.

18 Ngbea GT and Achunike HC. 2014. "Religion: Past and present in Nigeria", *International Journal of Sciences: Basic and Applied Research* 17(2):156-174.

selected based on two primary factors: (1) preference for larger congregations and (2) the availability and willingness of the religious leader to grant interview. The imam was a 53-year-old man at the time of the interview and has been married for thirty-five years.[19] He is the circuit missionary of a Muslim sect and has been a religious leader for thirty-four years now. The pastor is a 62-year-old man, married for 32 years to his wife, who works in the same ministry with him.[20] The Obatala traditional priest is a 67-year-old man, married to several wives and a devoted worshipper of his deity.[21]

It would have been preferable if more religious leaders had been able to participate in the research and the perspectives of the victims could be considered in the study. Unfortunately, the participants were unwilling to share the contact information of the identified victims within their religious group, since it contradicted their principles and risked jeopardising the privacy of those victims of domestic violence and sufferer of mental illness. After concluding that their experiences were distinctive enough to justify further investigation, the three participants in this study volunteered to participate in the study. The goal of the study was made explicit to volunteers: it was to learn about the lives of victims of mental health issues as influenced by domestic violence during the Covid-19 pandemic.

RELIGIOUS RESPONSES TO DOMESTIC VIOLENCE

The study explored the relationship between domestic violence and mental health issues during the Covid-19 pandemic lockdown in religious settings from the perspective of diverse religious leaders and their organisations. The discussion below highlights the responses of selected religious leaders based on recurring themes, such as domestic violence from religious perspectives, types of mental health issues identified and kinds of religious care and social support provided.

Domestic violence as a religious problem

Domestic violence in this study refers to any type of abuse that occurs between spouses or partners, between parents and children or against older relatives. Participants in the study were asked to explain what their religion says about domestic violence and how their religion reacts to domestic violence. The participants affirmed that their religion preaches and advocates for peace, fairness and tolerance between a domestic couple and within the home.

---

19 Interview with a Muslim imam by OO Ekundayo, Ile-Ife, Nigeria, 7 April 2022. The imam was the most versed in Quranic understanding at the largest mosque visited in Ile-Ife, Nigeria as at the time of the interview.

20 Interview with a Pentecostal pastor by OO Ekundayo, Ile-Ife, Nigeria, 18 March 2022. The pastor was the most senior pastor of the largest and most populated church in Ile-Ife, Nigeria at the time of the interview.

21 Interview with an Obatala chief priest by OO Ekundayo, Ile-Ife, Nigeria, 30 March 2022. The chief priest was the traditional religion leader at the World Obatala Temple located in Ile-Ife, Nigeria.

The Muslim imam explained that Islam frowns at domestic violence and at violence in whatever form and encourages peaceful and happy homes. The Quran enjoins peace, equity and fairness. He emphasised the importance of peace, equity and fairness in families and within couples, as encouraged by the Quran. When each spouse or member of the family dutifully maintains their responsibilities in the home, as pointed out by the Quran, there can rarely be violence in the home. The imam further quoted from the Quran a passage which states that "among His wonders is that He created from you mates out of your own kind, so that you may incline toward them, and He engenders love and tenderness between you; in this, behold, there are messages indeed for people who think."[22] Muslim men are encouraged to assume complete responsibility for their wives, caring for them as much as possible. Wives are also admonished to sexually satisfy their husbands. If a husband or wife decides to defy the Quran's admonition by denying the other spouse the marital pleasure of sexuality, the partner is advised not to resort to violence.

The Pentecostal pastor similarly emphasised that domestic violence is against God's wish and that Christianity frowns at it. According to the scripture, humans are commanded, "Let everybody be slow to hear, slow to speak, slow to anger, for the anger of man does not propose the righteousness of God."[23] The pastor further reiterated that domestic violence comes with a lot of anger, and God is against it.

In the same view, the Obatala traditionalist maintained, "Our religion is a very peaceful religion. We don't condone violence in whatsoever form. We are peace lovers. A man and his wife cannot engage in any form of violence be it physical, sexual, or verbal because there are laid-down rules that guide relationships either with your spouse or your children. There are hierarchies and respect accorded to each person. Humans are treated with dignity and honour, even children because each person is an entity that MUST be respected."

Participants in the study attributed the importance of peace and tranquility in homes as attested to in all three religions. They rejected domestic violence, even in the tense times of the pandemic. They believed that religion should be the system that upholds society's morality and strong bonds, as well as teaching respect and defining the duties and responsibilities that people should have towards each other, essentially guiding how we behave in our homes, schools, communities, places of work and society at large.

Women as "weaker vessels"?

Domestic violence is a pattern in which one person attempts to dominate or control another. It is a pattern of abuse in which the perpetrator consistently seizes control of the victim. Domestic abuse manifests itself in a variety of ways. It is a fact that women and children are usually the victims of domestic violence. Although men

---

22 Quran, 20:21.
23 Bible, James 1:19-20.

also experience domestic violence, studies reveal that women and children are more likely to suffer physical or psychological harm from domestic abuse than men are. Could this be as a result of women and children being seen as weaker than men as implied in the biblical command: "You husbands likewise, live with your wives in an understanding way, as like a weaker vessel"?[24]

When asked why women are sometimes referred to as "weaker vessels", religious leaders express a number of different perspectives. The pastor said of the women as "weaker vessels" proposition, "Basically, I agree. I think I have a hundred per cent agreement … even according to the bible that women are weaker vessels and they should be treated with love. So, I agree that women are weaker vessels in marriage." The Obatala priest took a different view, saying, "Women are stronger than men … even the reign of women is stricter and better than that of men."

For his part, the imam stated that, as far as he is concerned, women are not weak. He elaborated, "You know they contribute their own quota to the society, so as far as I'm concerned, they are not weak in any form. They're stronger than men, because they take more responsibilities nowadays and absorb marital shocks. Women go through a lot of pain in childbirth, and some are even assaulted by their spouses, but they still come out stronger." Contrary to the pastor, who agreed strongly with the biblical notion of women as weaker vessels, the imam and the Obatala priest opined that women are most of the time stronger than men, because they are better leaders, emotionally stronger and absorb pressures associated with the responsibilities of life. Women are stronger than men, as against biblical claims. Nevertheless, they are weaker when it comes to dealing with their husbands or partners who threaten them and physically abuse them.

A victim of domestic violence, regardless of her religion, may suffer tremendously if no one helps her to come out of such a traumatic experience, especially during in the context of an event like the Covid-19 pandemic.[25] Unfortunately, most women continue to be the victims of domestic abuse and violence in Nigeria and around the world. Women often live under the rule of men and are treated as inferior and oppressed creatures in most parts of the world, including some religions.

Varieties of domestic violence

Religious leaders reported encountering varying types and degrees of domestic violence in their congregation, both before and during the Covid-19 pandemic. The different forms of domestic violence identified by the religious leaders among their congregation, particularly during the Covid-19 lockdown, was physical and sexual violence towards spouse.

---

24 Bible, 1 Peter 3:7
25 Linde A and González Laya A. 2020. "What the Covid-19 pandemic tells us about gender equality", *World Economic Forum*, 9 May.

Physical and emotional violence

Physical violence towards spouse involves punching, shoving, clutching, biting, pulling hair and similar actions. This sort of abuse also includes denying a partner medical care or pressuring them to use alcohol or drugs. According to the most recent, pre-Covid statistics of the Nigeria Demographic and Health Survey (NDHS), 14% of married women in Nigeria experienced physical violence over the course of a year in 2018.[26] But domestic violence, notably, also includes emotional violence. According to reports from the Nigerian national population commission, women are exposed to emotional IPV from their current partner or husband at a lifetime rate of 19%, physical IPV at a rate of 14%, and sexual IPV at a rate of 5%.[27] The use of words to undermine the self-confidence of the wife, husband, or other intimate partner victims is referred to as emotional abuse. Using coercion, deceit, stalking, name-calling, and other tactics on one's spouse occurs at a rate of between 31% to 61% of households in Nigeria.[28]

With regard to physical violence, the Pentecostal pastor interviewed for this study said, "We have seen cases of wives killing their husbands, we've seen cases of wives who have wounded their husbands. I think the most reported form of violence among my church members is from husbands to wives and you see wives report their husbands ... most times they raise their voices against their wives, even in public. That's a form of violence." This narrative from the pastor describes how both husbands and wives physically and verbally assault their spouses among his church members. The pastor reiterated that both women and men are victims of emotional violence, such as name-calling and humiliation. "The form of domestic violence that is often reported in our sect is verbal violence, and this goes both ways – the husband and wife verbally abusing each other."

Contrary to the pastor, the Obatala priest said that in his religion "there is no form of domestic violence, either between husbands and wives or from parents to their children." Among the Obatala worshippers, domestic abuse was rarely reported, since the group maintained a zero-tolerance policy against physical, verbal and sexual violence, says the Obatala priest. However, it could also be that the leader's strong position on the subject makes it difficult for members of this sect to disclose domestic violence, even when it occurs in their own homes. Members may also wish to avoid bringing up their wives or husbands for fear of setting a bad example in the congregation. In contrast to the extreme stance held by the Obatala priest, the pastor and the imam reported the existence of physical and emotional domestic violence

---

26 Nigerian Population Commission (NPC), Federal Republic of Nigeria and ICF International. 2019. *Nigeria Demographic and Health Survey 2018*. Abuja, Nigeria and Rockville, MD: NPC and ICF International.

27 National Population Commission (NPC), Federal Republic of Nigeria and ICF International. 2014. *Nigeria Demographic and Health Survey 2013: Final Report*. Abuja, Nigeria and Rockville, MD: NPC and ICF International.

28 Mapayi BM et al. 2013. "Impact of intimate partner violence on anxiety and depression amongst women in Ile-Ife, Nigeria", *Archives of Women's Mental Health* 16(1):11-18.

in their congregations. For them, when families or couples are cooped up in a house during a lockdown, there will undoubtedly be conflict, but misunderstandings and conflict should be resolved in love and peace.

Sexual violence

Sexual violence is any action that intimidates one's spouse into having unsafe sex or participating in sexual behaviour in which they do not want to or that otherwise utilises sex to control or degrade them. Forced intercourse, assaults, threats and other forms of sexual violence are all examples of sexual violence. According to the NDHS, a significant number of Nigerian women in the age bracket of 15 years to 49 years have been sexually abuse by an intimate partner.[29] Another study from Nigeria have shown the prevalence of intimate partner violence to range from 31 to 61% for psychological/emotional violence, 20 to 31% for sexual violence, and 7 to 31% for physical violence.[30] Based on the population of Nigeria, these statistics are high and scary.

The Pentecostal pastor claimed that sexual deprivation of a husband by his wife was a form of sexual violence towards the man. Hence, a sexually deprived man might want to claim his sexual right from his wife forcefully. According to the Muslim imam, the most reported forms of domestic violence in his congregations is sexual abuse by husbands to their wives. However, the Obatala priest claimed that sexual violence by husbands or wives had never been reported to him by anyone in his congregation. He feels it is because his congregation understands fully the sanctions meted out to anyone who goes against the doctrine of peace and "zero tolerance for violence". According to him, anyone who is violent, with bad temper, impatience and anger outburst will not enjoy the favour of Obatala.

RESPONSES TO DOMESTIC VIOLENCE DURING THE COVID-19 PANDEMIC

The two participants who had cases of domestic violence reported to them during the Covid-19 pandemic responded in diverse ways. For the Pentecostal pastor, the first step in case of life-threatening domestic violence situations was separation, with the survivor relocated to an apartment owned by the church until the perpetrator was properly rehabilitated. The Muslim imam and the Pentecostal pastor indicated that there was a system put in place in their congregations to handle domestic violence during the Covid-19 pandemic. These systems operated through committees consisting of legal personnel, security agencies, social welfare and spiritual heads. Both also indicated that the committee's members were duly respected by both genders. Both also referred the couple to counselling by committees involved with the welfare of congregation members with the involvement of legal and security

---

29 NPC and ICF International, *Nigeria Demographic and Health Survey 2018*.
30 Mapayi et al, "Impact of intimate partner violence on anxiety and depression".

personal. Various sorts of sanctions are also applied to the culprit within the Muslim community.

When the religious leaders were asked what their responses had been to domestic violence during the Covid-19 pandemic, the pastor said that in cases of life-threatening violence, they rescue the victim first and report the perpetrator to the appropriate law enforcement authorities. They provide support system for the victim through the welfare unit of the church or mosque. The pastor further explained that they have counsellors who can spiritually guide and counsel the spouse towards reconciliation. In a similar fashion, the imam said, "We actually investigate through the through the marital committees in conjunction with welfare officers. The only reaction is to use scriptures and prayers to settle the difference between the spouses." The imam continued, "If the husband beats the wife, the man is reprimanded for his actions by appearing before a committee that guides him to unlearn his actions and to relearn love and peace. Islam does not give permission to any man to beat any woman, Islam does not do that one."

Participants in the study were in agreement that violence, especially domestic violence, is not condoned by their religion in any way. The religious leaders asserted that domestic abuse is frowned upon throughout the three major religions and that perpetrators are punished and victims receive spiritual and physical rehabilitation when it occurs. When security and legal personnel are required, they are invited to participate to guide the religious body appropriately.

These religious leaders also reported that the most common types of mental health symptoms associated with domestic violence that were reported to them were sadness, outbursts of anger and physical violence towards children and social withdrawal during the Covid-19 pandemic. Most of the survivors of domestic violence in these religious groups reported symptoms of withdrawal from social interactions and social engagements. They also reported signs of depression, such as persistent sadness and social withdrawal. In light of this, the religious leaders posited that there is link between domestic violence and mental health outcomes based on the exposures they have had with of their members of their congregations who are victims or perpetrators of physical, sexual and emotional violence.

The pastor opined that the most common mental health symptoms that he noticed and identified among women who have been domestically violated or abused is withdrawal. "You see a lady who has been very vibrant in serving God and involved in the church's activities suddenly withdrawn. She rarely exchanges pleasantries after service. Most times they have been physically battered; they wear excess makeup and clothes to cover up", said the pastor. "During the pandemic lockdown, a lot of ladies withdrew into themselves and for those who didn't withdraw, they talked excessively". Pastors had to go out of their ways during the Covid-19 lockdown to encourage member to join virtual meetings and to look out for plausible signs of pain and withdraw from their members. Among the pastor's Pentecostal congregation, the most prevalent mental health symptoms documented among the women who have been abused or violated by their husbands include social withdrawal, social unreliability and mental instability. The imam also opined that domestic violence has caused havoc in his congregation, leaving the victims with physical injuries, with some becoming socially backwards and depressed as a result of being physically violated.

RELIGIOUS INTERVENTIONS FOR DOMESTIC VIOLENCE AND MENTAL HEALTH

The religious leaders who participated in the study described the different ways that they have worked in their congregation to care for survivors with mental health issues associated with domestic violence. Some of the prevention and mitigation measures that they highlighted included counselling, prayers, deliverance, medical care, financial care and support and collaboration with legal and security personnel in their town to protect the rights of survivors in their congregations.

Counselling sessions

Counseling is a well-established and viable style of therapy that is multifaceted and applies to a wide range of contexts and roles. During the therapy process, religion can aid in the facilitation of positive change. The three religious leaders emphasised the necessity of marital dispute counselling. The Pentecostal pastor opined that counselling is a means that has helped families in difficult times to adhere to the biblical admonition to live peaceably with all men. The pastor's counsellors were described as men and women of integrity who are knowledgeable in biblical doctrines and who have been happily married for decades.

According to the Muslim imam, counsellors have been readily available to counsel and help the distressed person who cries out for help. They engaged in counselling, prayers and activities for members during the Covid-19 pandemic. Victims of domestic violence are supported by the congregation, so that they may rehabilitated. There are two committees dedicated to family affairs within the congregation. The imam also described strategies put in place to curb the domestic violence menace, such as regular seminars to enlighten congregation members to enlighten them, including such as character seminars, marital seminars, orientation seminars and age-group seminars. "We teach men and women strategies to enjoy and cope in a relationship. We further encourage our women to join martial art to learn defence techniques against physical violence."

Based on the narratives of the imam and pastor, it is evident that there is a need for support groups to provide comfort, care and counselling to both the victim and the perpetrator until they are rehabilitated together and there is healing and restoration in the marriage. This process highlights the importance of organising seminars to educate and prepare youths towards building a happy and peaceful marriage. Both pre-marital counselling and marital or family counselling in times of distress helps build and restore peace in families.

Legal and security support

There is reportedly good collaboration between the selected religious communities and the legal and security agencies around them. The legal and security agencies have guided and advised religious leaders appropriately on the way out of dire situations prior to Covid-19 pandemic and they were also willing partners when crises erupted during the Covid-19 lockdown. According to the Muslim imam, there are legal teams in the congregation who are also overseeing the crisis that may likely arise in families. If the case is serious, such as husband beating or threatening the life of his wife, this can be reported to the legal authority. The legal agencies would then advise on the best way such situation can be handled. The Pentecostal pastor, in a similar view, said that "when it is a life-threatening situation, we report the perpetrator to the legal authority". In the case of the church, the legal team are not all members of the congregation but include respected members of the society who are police officers, civil defence and lawyers. These legal personals are most times employed or engaged as secular agents, who are working at either the state or federal level in Nigeria, but sometimes they are members of the congregation as the Muslim imam pointed out. The implication of engaging members who are legal or security agents as enforcers of law and order in these religious organisations is that there is likely to be smooth transition between the knowledge of the law of the land and the law of the religious organisation. The understanding of both laws – law of the state and religious law – can bring about a wholistic change.

Based on the imam's and the pastor's reports, it is critical to build a positive rapport and bilateral interaction between religious organisations and the town's security services because such services were specifically needed during the Covid-19 pandemic. The established relationship contributes to the development of law and order, as well as peace, in religious organisations, families, the home, and society as a whole.

Prayer and deliverance sessions

Prayer is a spiritual conversation with the highest divinity. Prayer and deliverance sessions are organised as part of the religious care against domestic violence and mental health issues resulting for violence within the family setting. Prayer and deliverance practices were common to all of the religious traditions and congregations consulted for this study.

The Muslim imam expressed his profound belief in the power of prayer for the couple whose marriage is affected by domestic violence such that their mental health is in jeopardy. The imam said, "Yes, we do have prayer sessions like *tahjud* (mid-night prayers) *solatul-duha* (prayer before sunrise) and so on for victims who have been abused domestically and are gradually displaying symptoms of mental illnesses." The imam further noted, "Usually members come together to organise prayers for distressed families in order to bring back together in peace. We harness all the resources to make sure that we retain that family in the congregation."

The imam pointed out that there are types of prayers offered at midnight and at sunrise to help restore peace and tranquility in distressed homes. In the same vein, the Pentecostal pastor said, "there are sessions of prayers and deliverance. Whatever the issue is, we pray because we are strong believers in the efficacy of prayer." The pastor and the imam both believed in the efficacy of prayers for the victims and the perpetrators of domestic violence. Particularly during the trials of the Covid-19 pandemic, they believed that such prayers would deliver the perpetrator from anger and rage and restore the victim to love and peace.

Medical care via religious organisation

Another collaboration that exists between the religious organisations and their communities is with health care personnel. The participants reported establishing rapport with medical personnel who are members of the organisation or who reside near them. The imam reported that doctors and other medical persons in his congregation attended to members who needed medical attention by doing the relevant medical examinations and assessments during the Covid-19 pandemic. Some of the medical personnel were trained in cases involving physical and sexual violence. Furthermore, as reported by the pastor, doctors and other medical professionals who have received training in handling cases of domestic violence provided care for members of his congregation who needed it. They also provided treatment in cases of sexually transmitted disease during the Covid-19 pandemic.

The Obatala priest also confirmed a strong collaboration between his religious organisation and local medical personnel. In his congregation, mentally disturbed members are sometimes treated with synthetic drugs, as prescribed by the invited medical doctors, along with local herbs. In this way, he claimed that mental health issues are treated wholistically – by prayers, administration of drugs, sacrifices, and by performance rituals peculiar to their religion.

The relationship between the religious and medical personnel makes healing and health effortless. Medical personnel who are members or reside around these religious organisations have been of tremendous assistance to members of who medical help. Some have personally visited victims of domestic violence in their homes to provide personalised care, such as treatment of physical injuries, monitoring of blood pressure and prescription of drugs, both before and during the Covid-19 lockdown.

Financial care and support

The three religious leaders in this study attested to giving financial aid to member of their congregation during the Covid-19 pandemic. More aid and necessary resources were given to families with particular hardship and distress during the lockdown. When asked what type of support the religious bodies gave to their members during the Covid-19 pandemic, the Muslim imam affirmed that the congregation was able to come together to donate financial resources and food items, which were then divided among those in need. The Obatala priest said members were taken care of during the Covid-19 pandemic and that members had access to the temple to seek any form of support, especially financial and food support. By his account, no one lacked, hence there was no aggression, anger or any form of mental breakdown among any community member.

The Pentecostal pastor also said that the congregation made sure that as many members as required financial and material help during the Covid-19 lockdown were given such assistance. Therefore no one had mental health issues as a result of domestic violence, which could come about through conflicts over lack of money or food items in the home. The pastor claimed that his church has an apartment where members who were in distress or homeless could be housed prior to Covid-19 and during the lockdown. Members who were separated from their spouses for some time due to domestic disputes were accommodated and fed until the process of reconciliation is concluded.

During the Covid-19 pandemic, the pastor's congregation appears to have received financial, monetary, feeding and lodging assistance, with special care and attention given to victims of domestic violence. The imam explained that during the Covid-19 pandemic, members of their congregation received assistance from contributions made by wealthy members of the congregation. The Obatala priest testified that during the Covid-19 pandemic, members were especially encouraged to live a communal life in which they shared resources. As a result, it was clear that the three religious groups offered a support structure for their members to live a stress-free life before and during the Covid-19 pandemic. Lack of resources – money, food, clothing and shelter – sometimes leads to frustration and aggression, as the Obatala priest noted.

UNDERSTANDING RELIGION, DOMESTIC VIOLENCE AND MENTAL HEALTH IN THE COVID-19 PANDEMIC IN NIGERIA

This study engaged religious leaders from different religious sects to report their members' experiences of domestic violence and mental illness during the Covid-19 pandemic in Nigeria. The results are particularly relevant for Nigeria, a multi-religious country where religion plays a crucial role in determining the fate of families and each family member in terms of social norms and morals. As a result, religious leaders are major stakeholders in the country's response to domestic abuse and related mental health symptoms. They are often the first point of contact for domestic violence survivors seeking help, healing and guidance during the pandemic. Considering the strictness of the Covid-19 pandemic lockdown measures, it was difficult for families and the religious sector to play these crucial roles. The prospect of poor mental health outcomes associated with domestic violence became menace in that context, but it was clear that religious leaders and their organisations had the capacity to play a major role in its eradication.

The study participants spoke of the views and perspectives on domestic violence from the three major religions in Nigeria – Islam, Christianity and African traditional religion. They referred to scriptures and teachings that emphasised peace in the home between spouses, parents and their children. No violence – physical, emotional or sexual – is encouraged by the three religions. The indigenous Obatala traditional religion particularly emphasised that each person is a spiritual being and must be respected as such; hence, battering of spouses and or children or wards is prohibited. All three major religions condemn domestic violence. When it occurs, offenders are reprimanded and victims receive both spiritual and physical rehabilitation and reconciliation where possible. This supports the view of other studies that when violence or divorce occurs, concerned couples should seek reconciliation.[31] Religious care has significant role in influencing domestic violence and mental health issues which result from it.

The present study suggests that domestic violence was rampant during lockdown, in line with existing studies.[32] Anxiety, depression and social withdrawal were the mental health issues caused by domestic violence, as reported by members of all three religions. Counselling sessions, prayer and deliverance, medical care, financial care, enlightenment and orientation programmes were some of the interventions the religious institutions deployed during the pandemic. The incorporation of religious care interventions within religious communities indicates that these communities had means to tackle the problem through measures that were helpful for victims and the perpetrators. These religiously based interventions had the same impact as other psychological and non-psychological treatments.[33] Forms of religious care and congregation-based support thus contributed to addressing domestic violence and mental illness during the pandemic and are worthy of further study.

It is important to note that, while religious care and support for victims of domestic violence and mental illness was a resource in the pandemic, it was not always without problems or as seamless as Nigerian religious leaders may have reported. In some cases, religious leaders tended to focus more on their congregants' visible and external representations of their well-being, most of which usually conformed to their religion's expected norms, especially during trying times like the Covid-19 pandemic. In that sense, religious leaders who insisted what there was no or little domestic violence in their communities may have reflected either a failure of religious leaders to pay closer attention to their members' actual mental health or attitudes that discouraged some victims from coming forward. Even, religious

---

31 Ademikuka SO. 2019. "Reading 1 Corinthians 7:10-11 in the context of intimate partner violence in Nigeria", *Verbum et Ecclesia* 40(1):art 1926.

32 Obeid S et al. 2020. "Factors associated with fear of intimacy among a representative sample of the Lebanese population: The role of depression, social phobia, self-esteem, intimate partner violence, attachment, and maladaptive schemas", *Perspectives in psychiatric care* 56(3):486-494; Mautong H et al. 2021. "Assessment of depression, anxiety and stress levels in the Ecuadorian general population during social isolation due to the Covid-19 outbreak: a cross-sectional study", *BMC psychiatry* 21(1):1-15.

33 Sorrentino AE. 2021. "Mental health care in the context of intimate partner violence: Survivor perspectives", *Psychological services* 18(4):512; Galovski TE. 2022. "Massed cognitive processing therapy for posttraumatic stress disorder in women survivors of intimate partner violence", *Psychological trauma: theory, research, practice, and policy* 14(5):769.

leaders who reported that domestic violence was rampant during the pandemic lockdown acknowledged that this also put additional strain on their procedures in place to address domestic violence, particularly because physically evacuating the victim was difficult in conditions of lockdown and social distancing. These factors also made it extremely difficult for the victims to request and accept assistance. Further, even though there were relations between religious organisations and local legal, security and medical personnel, there is need for improved coordination among key government agencies and religious institutions on how to respond to domestic abuse in order to reduce mental health issues during lockdowns or times of distress.

20 THE IMPACT OF COVID-19 ON INFERTILITY AND ASSISTED REPRODUCTIVE TECHNOLOGY IN NIGERIA: LEGAL CHALLENGES AND PROSPECTS

Zaynab Omotoyosi Shittu-Adenuga[1]

INTRODUCTION

Infertility impedes the realisation of essential human rights, especially by those who desire to become parents and build a family. All individuals have a right to the enjoyment of the highest form of physical and mental health. Infertility is a disease of the male or female reproductive system defined by the failure to achieve a pregnancy after twelve months or more of regular unprotected sexual intercourse.[2] Every person and couple has the right to decide the number, timing and spacing of their children. Both men and women can suffer from infertility, although women in Nigeria are perceived by the society to suffer more from infertility.[3]

Infertile couples typically face violence, divorce, social stigma, emotional stress, sadness, anxiety and low self-esteem. Infertility has a huge negative societal influence on their lives. Infertility affects millions of people who are of reproductive age, including 48 million couples and 186 million people who struggle with infertility worldwide,[4] and it can have a profound effect on their families and communities. Even though in vitro fertilisation (IVF) and other assisted reproductive technologies (ART) have been used to conceive more than five million children worldwide, they are still widely unavailable, difficult to access and prohibitively expensive in many parts of the world, particularly in low- and middle-income nations.[5]

During the final quarter of the twentieth century, assisted reproduction was first introduced into medical practice. Some religious groups, such as Roman Catholics, strongly opposed it, while others warmly embrace it. Although most Orthodox Jews reject third-party involvement, Judaism, Hinduism and Buddhism today permit assisted reproduction in almost all of its forms. On the other hand, Sunni Muslims, Anglicans Protestants and Coptic Christians tolerate assisted reproduction to the

---

1 LLB, BL, LLM, PhD (candidate) University of Ibadan; Barrister & Solicitor of the Supreme Court of Nigeria; Lecturer & Coordinator, Department of Private and Business Law, College of Law, Fountain University, Osogbo, Nigeria.
2 World Health Organization (WHO). 2018. *International Classification of Diseases*, 11th Revision (ICD-11). Geneva: WHO.
3 Zegers-Hochschild F, Dickens BM, Dughman-Manzur S. 2013. "Human Rights to In Vitro Fertilization", *International Journal of Gynecology & Obstetrics* 123(1):86-89.
4 Mascarenhas MN, Flaxman SR, Boerma T, et al. 2012. "National, Regional, And Global Trends In Infertility Prevalence Since 1990: A Systematic Analysis of 277 Health Surveys", *PLoS Med* 9(12):e1001356.
5 World Health Organization (WHO). 2020 "Infertility", *WHO.int*, 14 September.

extent that it does not involve gamete or embryo donation. Sunni Muslims accept all forms of assisted reproduction that do not require the involvement of a third party. This means that the egg and sperm must be from the intending couple themselves.[6]

This chapter seeks to examine assisted reproduction in Nigeria in the context of Covid-19. It examines the problem of infertility, its causes and effect and the operation of the assisted reproductive technologies during the pandemic and how the Nigerian government responded to problems accessing assisted reproduction. It reports the results of an online survey of Nigerians' experiences with assisted reproduction under Covid-19.

INFERTILITY: DEFINITION AND CAUSES

Infertility is a condition of the male or female reproductive system described as the inability to conceive after a period of twelve months or more of unprotected sexual activity.[7] Infertility can affect one or both partners. Sometimes, no cause can be found. The causes of male infertility may include: sexual problems with the delivery and quality of sperm due to premature ejaculation or genetic defects, such as cystic fibrosis; structural problems, such as a blockage in the testicle or damage or injury to the reproductive organs; or sperm quality problems from enlarged veins in the testes (*varicocele*) or other conditions. The production of sperm may also be impacted by excessive exposure to certain substances, such as pesticides, radiation and illegal narcotics.[8]

Female infertility may be caused by endometriosis,[9] ovarian problems,[10] cervical abnormalities[11] and fallopian tube damage or obstruction, frequently brought on by fallopian tube inflammation. Fallopian tube damage can also happen as a result of endometriosis, an infection that typically causes pelvic inflammatory disease.[12] Advancing maternal age is also one of the causes of infertility in women. The quality of the egg produced or the probability that an egg will be biologically normal declines as we age. Rarely is a woman fertile after the age of forty-five, especially if she wishes to use her own eggs rather than donor eggs.[13] Assisted reproductive technology (ART) has been defined as including all procedures or treatment strategies involving handling of human oocytes or sperm in vitro to establish clinical pregnancy by circumventing different pathological barriers in human

---

6   Sallam HN and Sallam NH. 2016. "Religious aspects of assisted reproduction", *Facts Views & Vision in Obgyn* 8(1):33-48.

7   WHO, *International Classification of Diseases*.

8   Mayo Clinic. 2022. "Infertility", *MayoClinic.org*.

9   This occurs when endometrial tissue grows outside of the uterus, may affect the function of the ovaries, uterus and fallopian tubes.

10 This affects the release of eggs from the ovaries.

11 This includes abnormalities with the cervix, polyps in the uterus or the shape of the uterus.

12 Mayo Clinic, "Infertility".

13 UCLA Health. 2022. "Infertility: Symptoms, Treatment, Diagnosis", *UCLAHealth.org*.

reproduction.[14] In vitro fertilisation, surrogacy, gamete donation, physiological intracytoplasmic sperm injection and intracytoplasmic sperm injection have evolved over time due to the development, commercialisation and global spread of assisted reproductive technologies, including cross-border reproductive care.[15] Due to changes in affordability, legislation, reimbursement and pregnancy and childbearing policies between countries, Europe is the largest market for assisted reproductive technologies.[16]

According to medical anthropologist Marcia C. Inhorn, lack of access to appropriate infertility therapy is the leading cause of untreated and intractable infertility in largely rural and low-resource settings in the developing world, and it was exacerbated by the recent Covid-19 outbreak.[17] Nigerian fertility expert Oladapo Ashiru has given his opinion on the reason for the increase in the cases of infertility among Nigerians.[18] Ashiru states that increased social interaction, unprotected intercourse and the resultant sexually transmitted diseases or infections (STDs or STIs) are some of the factors. Research has proven that STDs or STIs account for 70% to 80% of infertility in Africa. The most prevalent of these diseases is chlamydia, which is typically a hidden infection. Unfortunately, if it is not treated promptly, it can cause harm to the female fallopian tube and the male sperm tube. Gonorrhea is another infection that can result in irreversible tubal damage.[19] Reproductive problems can also be caused by a variety of other factors, including excessive consumption of sugar and fructose-containing foods like watermelon, apples and other sweet fruits as well as emissions from paint, diesel and aviation fuels, alcohol and cigarettes.[20]

With the rapid growth in Covid-19 transmission rates around the world, many governments implemented a lockdown approach, which had serious economic consequences. This lockdown process required individuals to remain indoors or at home. Many countries ordered the closure of educational institutions, religious institutions, clubs, restaurants, factories, salons and a variety of other establishments.[21] Only

---

14 Deep JP. 2014. "Assisted Reproductive Technology", *Journal of Chitwan Medical College* 4(7):1-10.

15 Palermo GD et al. 2012. "Development and Current Applications of Assisted Fertilization", *Fertility and Sterility* 97(2):248-259.

16 Ferraretti AP et al. 2008. "The European IVF Monitoring Consortium for the European Society of Human Reproduction and Embryology. Assisted Reproductive Technology in Europe; Results Generated from European Registers by ESHRE", *Human Reproduction* 27(9):2571-2584.

17 Inhorn MC. 2009. "Right to assisted reproductive technology: Overcoming infertility in Lowresource Countries", *International Journal of Gynecology and Obstetrics* 106:172-174.

18 Muanya C. 2020. "Infertility set to rise after Covid-19", *The Guardian*, 23 November.

19 Muanya, "Infertility set to rise after Covid-19".

20 Muanya, "Infertility set to rise after Covid-19".

21 Gopalan HS and Misra A. 2020. "Covid-19 Pandemic and Challenges for Socio-Economic Issues, Healthcare and National Health Programs in India", *Diabetes & Metabolic Syndrome* 14(5):757-759.

essential workers were exempted from being in public places if they followed the Covid-19 prevention guidelines. In a bid to flatten the curve and slow the spread of the disease, some governments extended the lockdown even farther.[22] The lockdown had both positive and negative consequences for individuals and the environment. The lockdown affected the mental well-being of people negatively in many respects, with many people experiencing anxiety, despair and abnormal sleep and eating patterns.[23] Stress itself has been found to decrease sexual behaviour and reproduction. However, during the lockdown, many couples were less weighed down by professional constraints and more likely to engage in sexual activity while confined at home.[24] Additional sexual activity among the homebound might be seen as a positive effect of the lockdown. However, increased sexual activity also meant increased experience of infertility when the sexual activity did not result in desired pregnancy.

THE IMPACT OF COVID-19 ON INFERTILITY AND ASSISTED REPRODUCTIVE TECHNOLOGY IN NIGERIA

In Nigeria today, virtually all forms of ART are available, namely: artificial insemination by husband (AIH), donor insemination (DI), in vitro fertilisation (IVF), intracytoplasmic sperm injection (ICSI), freezing and donating embryos, gamete intrafallopian transfer (GIFT), zygote intra fallopian transfer (ZIFT) and surrogate motherhood.[25] With respect to Covid-19, the Control of Infectious Disease Bill was introduced on 28 April 2020.[26] The Bill repealed the Quarantine Act.[27] It was enacted to make provisions relating to quarantine and make regulations for preventing the introduction into and spread in Nigeria of dangerous infectious diseases and other related matters. The bill is one of the measures put in place by the Federal Government to contain the spread of the pandemic within the nation's borders.[28]

During the Covid-19 pandemic, many fertility laboratories around the world developed plans for managing diseases and embryology cases,[29] including reducing

---

22 Kenyon C. 2020. "Flattening-the-curve associated with reduced Covid-19 case fatality rates: an ecological analysis of 65 countries", *The Journal of Infection* 81(1):e98-e99.

23 Dubey S et al. 2020. "Psychosocial Impact of Covid-19", *Diabetes & Metabolic Syndrome* 14(5):779-788.

24 Shilo G and Mor Z. 2020. "Covid-19 and the Changes in the Sexual Behavior of Men Who Have Sex with Men: Results of an Online Survey", *The Journal of Sexual Medicine* 17(10):1827-1834.

25 Giwa-Osagie OF, Nwokoro C and Ogunyemi D. 1985. "Donor insemination in Lagos", *Clinical Reproductive Fertility* 3:305-310.

26 Control of Infectious Diseases Bill, 2020.

27 Quarantine Act (CAP Q2 LFN 2004) Covid-19 Regulations, 2020.

28 Control of Infectious Diseases Bill (2020).

29 This is a branch of biology that studies the prenatal development of gametes (sex cells), fertilisation, and the development of embryos and fetuses.

labour needs, logistical arrangements and protective measures.[30] According to Abayomi Ajayi and fellow researchers,[31] economic conditions during the pandemic were the primary reason for limited access to in vitro fertilisation therapy, which was worsened by the Covid-19 pandemic. Pregnant women also encountered dangers and difficulties, including virus-induced pregnancy issues, vertical transmission to the fetus and the need to make the most of vital health care resources.[32] According to reports, the ability of coronavirus to persist in cryopreservation tanks poses a significant danger of gamete contamination, patient illness and embryo infection. Several pre-implantation genetic diagnoses were halted due to the Covid-19 pandemic.[33] During the pandemic, it was reported that that vertical transmission of Covid-19 from mother to the fetus during pregnancy was not recorded, but the possibility of transmission during delivery could not be ruled out.[34] Research revealed the possibility that the mother might develop different cardiopulmonary disorders alongside acid-base imbalance and postpartum hemorrhage.[35] It should be noted that the male reproductive organ has also been identified as a possible target for the novel coronavirus illness, as the coronavirus can infect the testis, producing orchitis,[36] inflammation, free radical production, oxidative stress, sperm failure, cytokine storm[37] and hormonal imbalance.[38]

The Covid-19 pandemic also had a devastating mental effect on patients, especially as some clinics or hospital facilities suspended reproductive treatment during this period. Government directives on Covid-19, such as social distancing, lockdown and travel restrictions, placed a huge burden on patients who wanted to seek physical medical attention for their reproductive issues. In a bid to communicate with patients during the Covid-19 pandemic, fertility clinics employed the use of

---

30 Choucair F, Younis N and Hourani A. 2020. "IVF Laboratory Covid-19 Pandemic Response Plan: A Roadmap", *Middle East Fertility Society Journal* 25:31.

31 Ajayi AB. 2020. "Influence of the awareness of Covid-19 pandemic on assisted reproductive technology clinic in Africa, South of the Sahara", *Obstetrics & Gynecology International Journal* 11(5):328–332.

32 Ory SJ et al. 2020. "The Global Impact Of Covid-19 On Infertility Services", *Global Reproductive Health* 5:43.

33 Ajayi et al, "Influence of the awareness of Covid-19 pandemic on assisted reproductive technology clinic".

34 Karimi-Zarchi M et al. 2020. "Vertical Transmission of Coronavirus Disease from Infected Pregnant Mothers to Neonates: A Review", *Fetal Pediatric Pathology* 39(3):246-250.

35 Karimi-Zarchi et al, "Vertical Transmission of Coronavirus Disease".

36 This is an inflammation of one or both testicles.

37 This is a physiological reaction in humans and other animals in which the innate immune system causes an uncontrolled and excessive release of pro-inflammatory signaling molecules called cytokines. Normally, cytokines are part of the body's immune response to infection, but their sudden release in large quantities can cause multisystem organ failure and death.

38 Younis JS, Abassi A and Skorecki K. 2020. "Is there an impact of the Covid-19 pandemic on male fertility? The ACE2 connection X", *American Journal of Physiology, Endocrinology and Metabolism* 318(6): E878-E880.

telemedicine. While some patients were relieved to have ample time to interact with their fertility experts, since majority were working from home, others were worried about being safe inside the fertility facility. People who were eager to continue their reproductive therapy flocked to the clinic, while those who were hesitant preferred to wait until the pandemic came to an end for fear of nosocomial infection.[39]

Furthermore, it was discovered that the global rate of conception decreased as a result of the extended lockdown of numerous healthcare facilities that provide high-complexity fertility procedures. According to reports, just 0.3% of babies are conceived each year using assisted reproductive technology; therefore, the number of infants projected to be conceived and eventually conceived during the Covid-19 pandemic was low.[40] Medical researchers David Swartz and Ashley Graham examined how Covid-19 infection affected maternal and reproductive health services. They discovered that in underdeveloped countries, shortages of medical supplies, ineffective service delivery and increased staff workload dramatically reduced the utilisation and quality of maternal and reproductive health care services.[41] In addition, human reproduction societies recommended that embryo transfers should be postponed, telecare use should be increased, and new treatment cycles should be stopped.[42] Evidence also suggested that the outbreak of Covid-19 may have increased the risk of infertility as a result of the stress of the lockdown process, postponement of treatment cycles, suspension of fertility treatments, scarcity and increase in the price of drugs during the pandemic.[43] Likewise, it was revealed that there was the possibility of Covid-19 vertical transfer from infected mother to fetus.[44]

ASSESSING THE EFFECTS OF COVID-19 ON INFERTILITY IN NIGERIA

The underlying study for this chapter was an online survey to examine the impact of Covid-19 on infertility and assisted reproductive technology in Nigeria. A total

---

39 Younis et al, "Is there an impact of the Covid-19 pandemic on male fertility?". Nosocomial infection is an infection you get while you are in the hospital for another reason. It is also called a hospital acquired infection.

40 Alviggi C et al. 2020. "Covid-19 And Assisted Reproductive Technology Services: Repercussions for Patients and Proposal for Individualized Clinical Management", *Reproductive Biology and Endocrinology* 18(1):45.

41 Swartz D and Graham A. 2020. "Potential Maternal and Infant Outcomes from Coronavirus – nCoV (SARS-CoV-2) Infecting Pregnant Women: Lessons from SARS, MERS, and Other Human Coronavirus Infections", *Viruses* 12(2):194.

42 Bateson DJ et al. 2020. "The Impact of Covid-19 on Contraception and Abortion Care Policy and Practice: Experiences from Selected Countries", *BMJ Sexual & Reproductive Health* 46(4):241-243.

43 Olaniyan OT et al. 2020. "Impact of Covid-19 on assisted reproductive technologies and its multifacet influence on global bioeconomy", *Journal of Reproductive Healthcare and Medicine* 2 (Suppl 1):92-104.

44 Olaniyan, "Impact of Covid-19 on assisted reproductive technologies".

of 60 individuals participated in the study, including 17 men (28.8%) and 42 women (71.2%), while one person did not identify with any gender. The participants were recruited via various social media platforms. The majority of the participants were in the age range of 25 years and above (96.6%), as against a smaller group (3.4%) who ranged in age from 18 to 25 years. Forty participants (67.8%) were married, while 19 participants (32.2%) were single.

The respondents were asked if they were trying to get pregnant, and while 76.3% answered no, 23.7% answered affirmatively. 27.1% of the respondents revealed that they had tried to seek medical attention for their condition. 1.7% of the respondent revealed that they have been medically proven to be infertile. When asked about the traditional or modern methods employed in getting pregnant, there were several findings: (1) 3.6% of the respondents claimed to have visited the hospital and conducted various test; (2) 3.6% of the respondents calculated their ovulation periods and avoided stress; (3) 3.6% of the respondents mentioned follicle tracking and ECG; (4) 3.6% of the respondents alleged to have resorted to local herbs; (5) 3.6% of the respondents claimed to submit to letrozole, varicoclectomy and the use of supplements; (6) 3.6% of the respondents reported using clomid and ovulation tracking, as directed by the physician; (7) 10.7% of the respondents are reported to have used modern techniques of getting pregnant; and (8) 3.6% of the respondents adopted both traditional and modern means.

The respondents were further quizzed on whether any of the traditional or modern methods worked. Unfortunately, only 15.2% of the respondents answered affirmatively and explained how it worked. Some of the responses were: (1) "After flushing my fallopian tube, I got pregnant the following month"; (2) "I got pregnant after the treatment"; and (3) "The treatment helped my hormones." The survey also revealed that 19% of the respondents did try to conceive during the Covid-19 lockdown and encountered challenges. Furthermore, 40.7% of the respondents admitted to having been fully vaccinated against Covid-19 and 24.2% of them believed that the Covid-19 vaccine may have aided their fertility journey positively. The study further revealed that all of the respondents attested to the fact that the Covid-19 vaccine did not disrupt their fertility journey.

When asked if the participants tried some of the techniques of assisted reproduction, such as surrogacy, in vitro fertilisation, artificial insemination and other methods during the Covid-19 lockdown, 16.7% stated that they tried artificial insemination. The survey revealed that 6.4% of the participants revealed that the Covid-19 outbreak had a negative psychological effect on them. In conclusion, 29.2% of the participants stated that they had unfettered and unrestricted access to medical care during the Covid-19 lockdown, while 70.8% claimed to have been denied access to medical care during this period.

It should perhaps be noted that overall, 60 participants participated in this study of the impact of Covid-19 on infertility and assisted reproductive technology in Nigeria. The low participation rate can be linked to the fact that issues of fertility and the use of assisted reproductive technology in Nigeria is still considered a sensitive topic, thus, women especially are shy to share their experience, which was perhaps the major limitation to this study. Overall, the study recorded a low success rate for participants who adopted any of the traditional or modern techniques of assisted reproduction. Furthermore, it was revealed that the Covid-19 vaccine did not disrupt individual's fertility plan or reproductive process. Unfortunately, a large percentage of the participants stated that they didn't have access to adequate medical care during the Covid-19 lockdown.

LEGAL CHALLENGES AND PROSPECTS AROUND INFERTILITY IN NIGERIA

In Nigeria, a couple's capacity to have children determines how successful their marriage will be. Thus, childless couples turn to assisted reproductive treatment facilities for assistance. Sadly, these ART practices are largely unregulated. The creation of the Association for Fertility and Reproductive Health (AFRH) has cushioned a little of the effect of the total absence of legislation in this aspect of the medical field by providing guidelines for ART practitioners.[45] AFRH is a non-profit organisation dedicated to improving and providing high-quality reproductive health education, with a focus on fertility services. The organisation aims to raise awareness of the importance of reproductive health among all people in Nigeria, Africa and the rest of the world. The Health Regulatory Agency in Lagos State is the only state agency to really enforce the AFRH's stated requirements; other states have yet to do so.[46] It is important for the Nigerian government to address ART in order to prevent unethical practices and abuse. ART centres need to be properly evaluated, and monitoring and quality assurance must be carried out regularly.

In sub-Saharan Africa, South Africa is the only country with a national law on assisted reproductive technology. In vitro fertilisation was initially used in sub-Saharan Africa by Nigeria in 1984, South Africa in 1986 and Ghana in 1995. Right now, there are more than seventy ART centres in Nigeria.[47] There exist well-trained ART specialists in Nigeria. Notwithstanding this, there have been complaints of fraud by the ART centres. Desperate couples have been taken advantage of because of their vulnerability.[48]

The National Health Act of 2014 is the main piece of legislation governing health care delivery in Nigeria. The requirements of the Act are supplemented by the Nigerian Code of Medical Ethics,[49] which focuses on ethical considerations in medical

---

45 See Association for Fertility and Reproductive Health. Online at: https://afrhnigeria.org
46 Ezeome IV, Akintola SO, Jegede AS and Ezeome ER. 2021. "Perception of Key Ethical Issues in Assisted Reproductive Technology (ART) by Providers and Clients in Nigeria", *International Journal of Women's Health* 13:1033-1052.
47 Bamgbopa KJ et al. 2018. "Public Perceptions On Ethics In The Practice Of Assisted Reproductive Technologies In Nigeria", *Global Reproductive Health* 3:e13.
48 Ezeome et al, "Perception of Key Ethical Issues in Assisted Reproductive Technology".
49 Dondorp W et al. 2013. "ESHRE Task Force on Ethics and Law 20: sex selection for non-medical reasons", *Human Reproduction* 28(6):1448-1454.

practice. Although they are limited, there are a few sections of both the Act and the Code that could have an effect on assisted reproductive technologies in Nigeria.[50] While other countries made advancements in the field of assisted reproduction during the outbreak of Covid-19 by putting in place adequate structures to address the challenges created by the pandemic, Nigeria is still struggling with the issue of codification, let alone putting in place a structure to address the reproductive health concerns of its citizens in a pandemic context.

Legal issues abound due to this lack of codification. One of it is on the issue of confidentiality, which creates problems for the child born through any of the assisted reproductive methods. Section 26(1) of the National Health Act protects a patient's confidentiality. It states: "All information concerning a user, including information relating to his or her health status, treatment or stay in a health establishment is confidential."[51] On the other hand, Regulation 44 of the Nigerian Code of Medical Ethics provides that the profession takes very seriously the ethic of professional secrecy, whereby any information about the patient that comes to the knowledge of the practitioner in the course of the patient-doctor relationship constitutes secret and privileged information, which must in no way be divulged by him to a third party, except with an informed consent of a patient given preferably in writing. However, the principles do not apply in circumstances where a discretionary breach of confidentiality is required to save the patient or the community.[52]

When the child reaches the age of majority, Section 24 of the National Health Act of 2014 and Regulation 44 of the Code of Medical Ethics will have the combined effect of keeping information regarding the request of a donor-conceived child private because the child is not regarded as a "user".[53] A user is defined as the person receiving treatment in a health establishment, and if the person receiving treatment is under the age of majority, "user" includes the person's parent or guardian or another person authorised by law to act on behalf of the parents, such as the person's spouse, grandparent, adult child, brother, sister or other family member. It is difficult to classify the donor-conceived child who has come of age as an adult child (conceived through traditional means) as stated under Regulation 44. This is not the case in other advanced jurisdictions, such as the United Kingdom. This may cause serious family problems for the donor-conceived child. The restriction on disclosure amounts to stigmatisation of the donor, the donee and the child. A child has the right to be aware of their birth parents. Such facts provide the child with an identity.[54]

---

[50] Ekechi-Agwu CA and Nwafor AO. 2020. "Regulating assisted reproductive technologies (ART) in Nigeria: lessons from Australia and the United Kingdom", *African Journal of Reproductive Health* 24(4):82.

[51] National Health Act of 2014, s 26(1).

[52] Ekechi-Agwu and Nwafor, "Regulating assisted reproductive technologies (ART) In Nigeria".

[53] National Health Act of 2014, s 24; Code of Medical Ethics, reg 44.

[54] Ekechi-Agwu and Nwafor, "Regulating Assisted Reproductive Technologies (ART) In Nigeria".

Further sections of the Health Act that touch on assisted reproductive issues can be found in Section 50, which states as follows:

(1) A person shall not:-
   (a) Manipulate any genetic material, including genetic material of human gametes, zygotes or embryos; or
   (b) Engage in any activity including nuclear transfer or embryo splitting for the purpose of the cloning of human being.
   (c) Import or export human zygotes or embryos.

(2) Any person who contravenes a provision of this section or who fails to comply therewith is guilty of an offence and is liable on conviction to imprisonment for a minimum of five years with no option of fine.

It is noteworthy that this section above prohibits reproductive and therapeutic cloning of humankind. This may be likened to the prohibition of creating a human embryo. The act is silent in situations where a human egg is fertilised by a human sperm outside of a woman's body with the goal of causing a woman to become pregnant. This is one of the negative consequences of the lack of codification of ART practices in Nigeria.

ART is very expensive in Nigeria, although the cost is still low compared to the Western world. In Nigeria, ART treatments are mostly carried out in privately owned hospitals, which buy modern equipment abroad at a seemingly high rate. Every nation in Europe offers some kind of cost health insurance coverage. The only countries having complete national health coverage are Denmark, France, Hungary, Russia, Slovenia and Spain, while Austria and Finland have two-thirds and forty per cent coverage, respectively. On the other side, health insurance coverage is based on the patient's unique characteristics. Despite strong government support in the majority of western European nations, all public and commercial Western health care systems have stringent eligibility standards that restrict patients' access.[55] In Nigeria, where people scarcely take out medical insurance policies and there is hardly any form of public subsidy, the financial burden is significantly greater.

Assisted reproductive technology is established in Africa, although a lot needs to be done, in terms of regulation, training of professionals, importation of modern equipment, medical insurance and adequate sensitisation of the public. Efforts must be directed at improving.[56] One of the challenges created by the lack of legislation is the problem of managing medical negligence and regularising the legal impact of intercontinental demand for ART services in Nigeria. Due to the cheaper cost of

---

55 Keane M, Long J, O'Nolan G and Farragher L. 2017. *Assisted Reproductive Technologies: International Approaches to Public Funding Mechanisms and Criteria. An Evidence Review.* Dublin: Health Research Board.

56 Dyer S et al. "African Network and Registry for Assisted Reproductive Technology. Assisted reproductive technology in Africa: a 5-year trend analysis from the African Network and Registry for ART", *Reproductive Biomedicine Online* 41(4):604-615.

ART in Nigeria, as a result of the Naira's value relative to other currencies, there appears to be an increase in the need for ART on the continent. There are no regulations governing the production of transatlantic ART services, as there are in most developed countries.[57]

Due to the lack of legislative backing, self-regulation in Nigeria is unlikely to succeed. According to a study in which clinic directors took part, the AFRH standards are insufficient. This is because AFRH has little influence in the other states of the nation outside of Lagos State. While it might be effective in Lagos, other states cannot use it. Because of Nigerians' ingenuity, unlicensed clinics can move to other regions of the nation and continue to wreak havoc. Instead of state-by-state regulation, there are reasons for a national law that will be binding on all practitioners.[58]

It is clear that the practice of assisted reproduction in Western countries has evolved to the point where an intending parent can simply go online and conduct the process of ART, as sperm and eggs selection from women can be done via delivery to the fertility clinic.[59] Globally, there has been considerable advancement in the development of ART. Despite this, the industry of assisted reproductive technologies is currently being threatened by the aftermath of the Covid-19 pandemic across many sectors, including pharmaceutical, medical, research, agricultural sector and others. In many jurisdictions, personal interaction was reduced to the barest minimum, as people were asked to stay home from work, school and public areas, and if there was any reason to be in a public space, then a well-fitting face mask was recommended.[60] Prospective parents who needed to travel could not travel as a result of flight restrictions or cancellation. Medicine companies producing reproductive health drugs closed their factories for economic reasons, while some countries suspended new treatment cycles.[61]

The American Society for Reproductive Medicine (ASRM) declared on 17 March 2020 that all cases of reproductive care must be stopped, unless they were extremely necessary.[62] Due to the limited evidence available at the time about Covid-19 and its effects on pregnancy, the European Society of Human Reproduction and Embryology (ESHRE) issued a warning on 19 March 2020 to infertile patients to use caution and advised against getting pregnant. Similar to this and on the same day, the Fertility Society of Australia (FSA) advised people to consult with their

---

57 Rozée-Gomez V and de la Rochebrochard E. 2013. "Cross-border reproductive care among French patients. experiences in Greece, Spain, and Belgium", *Human Reproduction* 28(11):3103-3110.
58 Ezeome et al. "Perception of Key Ethical Issues in Assisted Reproductive Technology".
59 Olaniyan et al, "Impact of Covid-19 on Assisted Reproductive Technologies".
60 Olaniyan et al, "Impact of Covid-19 on Assisted Reproductive Technologies".
61 Olaniyan et al, "Impact of Covid-19 on Assisted Reproductive Technologies".
62 American Society for Reproductive Medicine (ASRM). 2020. "Patient Management and Clinical Recommendations During the Coronavirus (Covid-19): Pandemic Update No. 11 – Covid-19 Vaccination", 16 December.

expert on the propriety of delaying treatment.[63] According to research, receiving the Covid-19 vaccine did not raise the risk of infertility, pregnancy loss, stillbirth or the need for treatment for congenital abnormalities.[64] However, many countries are still recovering from the economic impact of Covid-19. It is important to reiterate that while many jurisdictions were making important governmental policies to manage and evaluate reproductive techniques during the Covid-19 pandemic, Nigeria did not partake in such.

CONCLUSION

The process of assisted reproduction affords infertile couples the opportunity to bring forth a life. This process goes to the root of a family's existence, identity and happiness. In Africa, people's opinions about assisted reproduction are significantly influenced by their religious beliefs, and different religions have responded to assisted reproduction in different ways. The response ranges from partial approval to complete approval to complete rejection. Every Nigerian citizen has a right to life, and this right must be protected at all costs. The whole world witnessed the devastating impact of Covid-19 on all spheres of life, including the economic, social, political, public and private sectors, and even the research community. The Nigerian government needs to urgently begin the process of codifying the laws relating to the reproductive health of its citizens. This is indeed a wakeup call. It does not suffice to leave all matters pertaining to assisted reproduction in the hands of a professional body like the Association for Fertility and Reproductive Health (AFRH), especially during a pandemic. All existing challenges regarding assisted production are magnified and worsened by a pandemic.

The underlying study of this chapter revealed that the Covid-19 vaccine did not disrupt an individual's fertility plan or reproductive process, although a large percentage of the participants stated that they didn't have access to adequate medical care during the Covid-19 lockdown. The lack of access to medical care for women who were going through assisted reproduction during the Covid-19 pandemic is indeed worrisome. People were scared of contacting the disease; hence, they stayed at home, with some discussing treatment with their doctors online. Yet a challenge encountered in course of speaking with a physician was often the limitation of a poor mobile network. Above all, the Federal Government should set up a structure to provide support to infertility patients during a crisis or pandemic. Although the legislation brought about by the Control of Infectious Diseases Bill, 2020, was a much-needed improvement to Nigeria's public health laws, it is the task of government to see beyond the Covid-19 pandemic and to prepare in the event that we are faced with similar situation in the future.

---

63 Cutting E et al. 2021. "The Impact Of Covid-19 Mitigation Measures on Fertility Patients and Clinics Around the World", *Reproductive Biomedicine Online* 44(4):755-763.

64 ASRM, "Patient Management and Clinical Recommendations".

V. African churches and African traditional healing

21 AFRICAN CHRISTIANITY, HEALING AND COVID-19 IN ZIMBABWE: RE-THINKING THE EFFICACY OF AFRICAN TRADITIONAL MEDICINE

Molly Manyonganise[1]
Clemence Makamure[2]
Vengesai Chimininge[3]

INTRODUCTION

The discourse on healing in African Christianity in Zimbabwe has always been a complex one and has been made more complicated historically by the inclusion of African Traditional Medicine (ATM). Dominant narratives about ATM in Zimbabwe place it at the margins of formal health discourse. Scholars and health practitioners have been grappling with the challenge of integrating ATM within formal health care systems. Most African governments have been hesitant in bringing ATM into the formal health sector despite the enactment of various legislation. This could be a result of the historical Western and Christian constructions of ATM as primitive and evil.

In 2020, the advent of Covid-19 on the African continent in general and in Zimbabwe in particular challenged systems of primary health care and shook the very foundations of African Christianity when it comes to healing. The virus exposed both modern medicine and faith healing as ineffective, especially in Zimbabwe. This study investigates the resurgence, utilisation and efficacy of ATM during the Covid-19 era and the responses of African Christians in the Harare urban region to the popularisation of ATM in the same period. As Covid-19 landed on the continent, some people from the Western world who tend to have a negative perception on Africa expected the worst because of the dilapidated health delivery systems in most African countries, to the extent of predicting that once the pandemic reached its peak, dead bodies would litter the streets of African cities and towns. While the effects of the virus were felt in Africa, its effects were not to the expected magnitude, much to the bafflement of the rest of the world. Justin Maeda and John Nkengasong, an epidemiologist and a virologist, respectively, have observed how the Covid-19 pandemic puzzled many health experts, since Africa reported

---

[1] Molly Manyonganise is a senior lecturer at the Zimbabwe Open University, Faculty of Arts, Culture and Heritage Studies, Department of Religious Studies and Philosophy/ Research Associate, Department of Religion Studies, Faculty of Theology and Religion, University of Pretoria/Georg Forster Research Fellow, Alexander von Humboldt Foundation.

[2] Clemence Makamure is a senior lecturer at the Zimbabwe Open University, Faculty of Arts, Culture and Heritage Studies, Department of Religious Studies and Philosophy.

[3] Vengesai Chimininge is a senior lecturer at the Zimbabwe Open University, Faculty of Arts, Culture and Heritage Studies, Department of Religious Studies and Philosophy.

far fewer cases and deaths from Covid-19 than predicted.[4] Of all the reasons they proffered as having contributed to the low infection and death rates, however, they do not mention ATM.

The present study seeks to establish whether ATM was the "miracle" that enabled Africa to escape the brutality of the Covid-19 pandemic. It explores the possibility of integrating ATM in Zimbabwe's formal health discourse. The study represents a paradigm shift in how narratives of healing through the use of ATM in Africa have been presented by adopting a different perspective that offers insights into how the Covid-19 context has prompted African Christians in Zimbabwe to be accommodative and receptive of ATM. The study focuses on determining whether the popularisation of ATM during the Covid-19 era was a result of the view that Zimbabwean mega-prophets were grounded[5] and Western medicine floundering.[6] In this case, the study brings to light nuances of the Covid-19 context in Africa in general and in Zimbabwe in particular by asking three key questions as follows: (1) Was the popularisation of ATM, in fact, a result of the aforementioned view that Zimbabwean mega-prophets were grounded and Western medicine was floundering? (2) Did the very nature of Covid-19 fit the operational assumptions of ATM? (3) How have Christians in Zimbabwe responded to the popularisation of ATM due to Covid-19? The study approaches these questions at two levels: first, the resurgence of ATM after a century of demonisation by missionary Christianity, and second, the global marginalisation of Africa. It, therefore, becomes imperative for purposes of the study to determine the possible synergies between African Christianity, modern medicine and ATM as a response to Covid-19.

THEORETICAL FRAMEWORK

The study is in the field of African Christian Studies, focusing on the intersection of religion, healing, modern medicine and ATM through the utilisation of social scientific approaches. It seeks to move away from the use of narrow theological approaches when dealing with important subjects such as healing and ATM within African Christianity. The study is guided by phenomenological, sociological and grounded theology approaches.

With respect to the phenomenological approach, medical anthropologist Sjaak van der Geest has contended that for academic scholars to fully understand the attitudes of Africans towards ATM usage, proper field research needs to be carried out at the

---

4   Maeda JM and Nkengasong JN. 2021. "The Puzzle of the Covid-19 Pandemic in Africa", *Science* 371(6524):27-28.
5   Parsitau D. 2020. "Religion in the Age of Coronavirus", *The Elephant*, 6 April.
6   Dandara C, Dzobo K and Chirikure S. 2020. "Covid-19 Pandemic and Africa: From the Situation in Zimbabwe to a Case for Precision Herbal Medicine", *OMICS: A Journal of Integrative Biology* 24(0):1-4.

community level, so as to capture the views of the people.[7] The phenomenological approach is important for this study, as it allows for the capturing of the voices of African Christians in Zimbabwe, so that we understand their attitudes towards ATM and what informed those attitudes in both the pre-Covid-19 and Covid-19 context, as to whether attitudes were either changed or reinforced. The phenomenological approach nudges us to set aside our preconceived ideas on the phenomenon under investigation.

The study also adopts decolonial theory as part of its social scientific approach. Various scholars have made a clarion call for religion to critically engage with decoloniality.[8] Employing a decolonial theory to study religion is important for this study, because it enables us to analyse the persistent colonial influence of African Christianity's dealings with African traditions in the area of health, especially the attitudes towards the use of ATM in treating ailments. It helps the study to reconfigure the theological debates around African Christianity and ATM. This enables us to debunk the notion that ATM is a lesser alternative to Western medicine. Bringing a decolonial lens to the field of African Christianity, healing and ATM in the era of Covid-19, opens up crucial new sites of analysis and engagement as we take into consideration how Christianity enabled the perpetuation of the negative treatment of ATM in formal health discourses in Zimbabwe and how it can positively contribute to the study of decoloniality through alternative ways of theologising about ATM.

The grounded theology approach enables the embedding of the study in the experiences of the people. By doing this, the study augments already existing literature on African Traditional Religion (ATR) and health in Zimbabwe.[9] The study makes use of structured interviews to collect data and were analysed using content analysis.

---

[7] Van der Geest S. 1997. "Is there a role for traditional medicine in basic health services in Africa? A plea for a community perspective", *Tropical Medicine and International Health* 2(9):903-911.

[8] Fitzgerald G. 2020. "Introduction to Decoloniality and the Study of Religion", *Contending Modernities* (blog), Kroc Institute for International Peace Studies, University of Notre Dame; Ndlovu-Gatsheni SJ. 2018. "The Dynamics of Epistemological Decolonisation in the 21st Century: Towards Epistemic Freedom", *Strategic Review for Southern Africa* 40(1):16-45.

[9] Murray L and Chavunduka GL (eds). 1986. *The Professionalisation of African Medicine*. Manchester: Manchester University Press; Chavunduka GL. 1999. "Christianity, African Religion and African Medicine". Geneva: World Council of Churches; Shoko T. 2011. "Shona Traditional Religion and Medical Practices: Methodological Approaches to Religious Phenomena", *Africa Development* 36(2):277-292; Shoko T. 2018. "Traditional Herbal Medicine and Healing in Zimbabwe", *Journal of Traditional Medicine and Clinical Naturopathy* 7(1):254.

AFRICAN TRADITIONAL MEDICINE DURING THE COLONIAL ERA

In pre-colonial Africa, Africans in general and Zimbabweans in particular depended on ATM for healing. Sociologist Gordon Chavunduka explains how temporary illnesses could be dealt with using herbal treatment within the surroundings of the patient.[10] At times, the patient could administer the treatment with success. People would only get worried if the illness did not respond to the administered treatment. This called for consultation with renowned traditional healers within or without one's community. If the healer felt that the illness only required stronger medication, they would make this available to the patient. However, the Shona people had the belief that if an illness did not go away easily, there should be a cause. In their worldview, the cause can be located either with angered ancestral spirits or witchcraft. Hence, in consulting the traditional health practitioner, they did not only want the patient to get healed but to also get to the cause of the illness. Hence, the African traditional health practitioner played three roles at once; that is, as a diviner, herbalist and healer. It is, however, not the norm that every traditional health practitioner should possess the three skills. At times, some could possess just one or two of these skills.

One could become a health practitioner in different ways. As described by sociologist Michael Bourdillon, one could become a health practitioner through spirit possession.[11] Such a practitioner would be able to have dreams pertaining to some herbs and their exact location, as well as the disease they are able to treat. Usually, the spirit would be of someone who was a health practitioner during their lifetime. The other way that one could be a health practitioner was through training. A healer may have been a member of a family of healers; hence, knowledge was passed from one generation to the other. Bourdillon explains that a healer would be chosen by a senior relative who was also an established healer.[12] The child then would be taught about indigenous herbs from an early age until such a time that they could start to administer treatment even in the absence of the tutor. Eventually, they would become established as an experienced health practitioner who could build a clientele on the basis of their knowledge of a variety of herbs.

The onset of colonialism disrupted the African indigenous ways of disease prevention and cure. It is apparent that there has been conflict between Christianity and African Indigenous Religion(s) over the use of ATM in the formal and informal primary health care systems. Some early Christian missionaries sought to suppress the African traditional medical sector.[13] Cultural anthropologist Tony Cavender argues that during Zimbabwe's early colonial era, the Rhodesian government and

---

10 Chavunduka GL. 1986. "ZINATHA: The Organisation of Traditional Medicine in Zimbabwe", in Murray and Chavunduka (eds). *The Professionalisation of African Medicine*, 29-49.
11 Bourdillon MFC. 1989. "Medicines and Symbols", *Zambezia* XVI(i):29-65.
12 Bourdillon, "Medicines and Symbols".
13 Chavunduka, "Christianity, African Religion and African Medicine".

Christian missionaries devoted considerable effort to discrediting the traditional healer's role.[14] Sociologists Chavunduka and Bourdillon allude to the fact that colonial administrators and missionaries dismissed indigenous healing practices as superstition.[15] As a way of shutting out ATM and promoting Western medicine, missionaries in Zimbabwe established mission hospitals. Biblical scholar Helen C. John notes the close association between Christianity and mission hospitals.[16] She argues that missionary efforts were focused on eliminating the indigenous beliefs and practices of African Traditional Religion.[17] They confused Western cultures with biblical ways of life. Hence, they endeavoured to destroy indigenous beliefs and practices despite the absence of biblical texts condemning these cultural practices and beliefs. The missionaries' misunderstanding of witchcraft and witchcraft prevention led traditional healers, witches and sorcerers to be lumped together under the tag "witchcraft".[18] Resultantly, throughout Africa, traditional healers were perceived as agents of the devil. In Zimbabwe, to curtail the activities of the traditional health practitioners, legal instruments were put in place. In 1899, the Witchcraft Suppression Act[19] was enacted. It made it unlawful for anyone to practise as a "witchdoctor" or "witch-hunter".[20] Furthermore, the Medical Council of Rhodesia discouraged physicians from consulting and referring patients to a traditional health practitioner as a violation of ethics.[21] While acknowledging an abundance of literature on the impact of colonialism on Africa and African culture, Biblical scholar, Temba T. Rugwiji notes that very few scholars, or perhaps none, have succeeded in interrogating the Christian view of healing from a postcolonial perspective, with a particular focus on promoting African Traditional Medicine (ATM) in Zimbabwe.[22] Such an attitude has been persistent.

THE WORLD HEALTH ORGANIZATION AND AFRICAN TRADITIONAL MEDICINE

The World Health Organization (WHO) started to encourage the recognition of ATM during a time when most African countries were still under colonial rule. In its reference to traditional medicine, the WHO uses other terms, such as

---

14 Cavender T. 1988. "The Professionalisation of Traditional Medicine in Zimbabwe", *Human Organisation* 47(3):251-254.
15 Chavunduka, "ZINATHA"; Bourdillon, "Medicines and Symbols".
16 John HC. 2021. "Christianisation, The New Testament and Covid-19 in Owambo, Namibia", *Journal for the Study of the New Testament* 44(1):112-133.
17 John, "Christianisation, The New Testament and Covid-19", 114.
18 John, "Christianisation, The New Testament and Covid-19", 115.
19 Garbett, K. 1998. "Changing Perceptions of Shona Witch Beliefs and Practices", *The International Journal of Anthropology* 42(2):24-47.
20 Cavender, "The Professionalisation of Traditional Medicine in Zimbabwe", 251.
21 Cavender, "The Professionalisation of Traditional Medicine in Zimbabwe", 251.
22 Rugwiji T. 2019. "Faith-based Healing and African Traditional Medicine in Zimbabwe: A Post-Colonial Perspective", *Theologia Viatorum* 43(1):1-10.

nonconventional medicine or complementary medicine. It defines traditional medicine as the "sum total of the knowledge, skill and practices based on the theories, beliefs and experiences indigenous to different cultures, whether explicable or not, used in the maintenance of health as well as in the prevention, diagnosis, improvement or treatment of physical and mental illness."[23] In 1977, the Thirtieth World Health Assembly of the WHO adopted a resolution promoting the development, training and research into traditional health systems.[24] Such a declaration was significant in that it broadened the perception of health beyond doctors and hospitals to social determinants and social justice.[25] The Alma Ata Declaration noted the presence of traditional medical practitioners as well as birth attendants in most societies. It argued that with the "support of the formal health system, these indigenous practitioners can become important allies in organizing efforts to improve the health of the community".[26] Overall, the declaration was important in that it recognised the use of ATM in primary health care.[27] The following year, in 1978, the International Conference on Primary Health adopted the Alma Ata Declaration.

In 2001, the organisation declared 2001 to 2010 to be the Decade of African Medicine. It extended the declaration by another decade from 2011 to 2020. In 2008, the International Conference on Primary Health Care and Health Systems in Africa adopted the Ouagadougou Declaration, which was an affirmation of the Alma Ata Declaration of 1978. As the WHO Africa Directorate evaluated the progress made after the first decade of traditional medicine, it noted that by 2010, more than half of its 46 member states of the region had formulated national traditional medicine policies and regulatory frameworks to ensure the efficacy, safety and quality of traditional medicines and the regulation of the practice of traditional health practitioners. Some states established structures, programmes and efficacies in their ministries of health to institutionalise traditional medicine in health care systems. This was also the case with some institutions of higher learning, which introduced programmes on traditional medicine. For example, the Kwame Nkrumah University of Science and Technology in Ghana established a department of Herbal Medicine under the College of Health Sciences for the training of herbal medicine specialists and to provide continuing education for traditional health practitioners.

The WHO Traditional Medicine Strategy (2014-2023) set out to support member states in harnessing the potential contribution of traditional and complementary

---

23 World Health Organization (WHO). 2013. *World Health Organization Traditional Medicine Strategy (2014-2023)*. Geneva: WHO.

24 Le Roux-Kemp A. 2010. "A legal perspective on African traditional medicine in South Africa", *The Comparative and International Law Journal of Southern Africa* 43(3):273-291.

25 Rifkin SB. 2018. "Alma Ata after 40 years: Primary Health Care and Health for All- From Consensus to Complexity", *British Medical Journal Global Health* 2018:3:e001188.

26 World Health Organization and the United Nations Children's Fund. 1978. *Alma Ata Declaration: Primary Health Care*. Geneva: WHO/UNICEF.

27 Abrams AL et al. 2020. "Legislative landscape for traditional health practitioners in Southern Africa: A Scoping Review", *British Medical Journal Open* 10:e029958.

medicine to health care and in promoting the safe and effective use of traditional and complementary medicine through the regulation of products, practices and practitioners. Its objectives were to strengthen safety, quality and effectiveness through regulation and to promote universal health coverage by integrating traditional and complementary medicine services and self-health care into national health systems. The strategy, however, took note of the various challenges that states face, two of which are worthy of particular note. The first challenge is one of integration, especially the identification and evaluation of strategies and criteria for integrating traditional medicine into national and primary health care. The second challenge relates to the safety and quality, notably to the assessment of products and services, qualification of practitioners, methodology and criteria for evaluating efficacy.[28] As a result, the WHO called on states to craft policies around traditional medicine that speak to their own contexts. Zimbabwe's policies on ATM need to be understood in this framework.

AFRICAN TRADITIONAL MEDICINE IN INDEPENDENT ZIMBABWE: RE-STRUCTURING COLONIAL HEALTH DISCOURSES?

Zimbabwe got its independence on 18 April 1980. As the new government assumed power, a key focus was to dismantle the oppressive structures of colonial rule, including the health sector. Zimbabwe's independence saw the ushering in of a new vigorous thrust in health care based on the Primary Health Care (PHC) approach.[29] This approach emphasised the need for communities to consciously and actively participate in transforming their own health care systems. In analysing the PHC, public health specialists Alison Mhazo and Charles Maponga argue that the concept was steeped in the ideology of decolonisation, global solidarity and equity. As a result, in July 1980, the then Minister of Health, Herbert Ushewokunze, influenced the formation of the Zimbabwe National Traditional Healers Association (ZINATHA).[30] This act was seen as a positive step towards the integration of conventional medicine, though formal health practitioners viewed this as an unfortunate development. The aims of ZINATHA as listed by Cavender were: (1) to promote traditional medicine and practice, research into traditional medicine and methods of healing, including training in the art of herbal and spiritual healing; (2) to supervise the practice of traditional medicine and prevent abuse and quackery; and (3) to cooperate with the Ministry of Health and establish better working relations between traditional and conventional medical practitioners.[31]

---

28 World Health Organization (WHO). 2013. *World Health Organization Traditional Medicine Strategy (2014-2023)*. Geneva: WHO.

29 Saunders D. 1990. "Equity in Health: Zimbabwe Nine Years On", *Journal of Social Development in Africa* 5(1):5-22.

30 Mhazo AT and Maponga CC. 2022. "The political economy of health financing reforms in Zimbabwe: a scoping review", *International Journal of Equity Health* 21(1):42.

31 Cavender, "The Professionalisation of Traditional Medicine in Zimbabwe", 253.

In order to strengthen its resolve to recognise ATM, the government of Zimbabwe enacted the Traditional Medical Practitioners Council Act in 1981. The Act empowered the Minister of Health to constitute a twelve-member council. The council had to register and regulate all traditional medical practitioners. The council was expected: (1) to supervise and control the practice of traditional medical practitioners; (2) to promote the practice of traditional medical practitioners; and (3) to foster research into and to develop the knowledge of such practice.[32] In 1985, the government of Zimbabwe crafted a policy which it called the Zimbabwe Health for All Action Plan. It highlighted that the plan had been necessitated by the need to deal with colonial injustices in the health sector. The plan acknowledges that traditional health practitioners constitute a large corpus of people who are recognised, respected and trusted by the community in their activity. It also noted that the legal frameworks put in place in 1981 provided for the regulation, supervision, upgrading and investigation of traditional health practices through scientific ways. Epidemiologist Rene Loewenson notes that the exclusion of key groups inclusive of traditional health practitioners in the implementation of this plan led to its failure.[33] A situational analysis of the health sector carried out in the late 1990s resulted in the formulation of the National Health Strategy for Zimbabwe, 1997-2007.[34] However, none of the plans were implemented by the end of 2007. Another health policy strategy was crafted covering the period 2009 to 2015 focusing on universal health systems and the provision of quality health services to all Zimbabweans. The national health strategy covering the period 2016 to 2020 noted a significant negative influence of religious and other socio-cultural objectors on care seeking.[35] The strategic plan noted the continued use of traditional medicine within communities but acknowledged the challenges that remain in ensuring use of approved and registered medicines and promoting evidence-based practices. It recommended that research is required to ascertain the therapeutic value of traditional medicine. The objective of the strategy was to strengthen research frameworks for traditional medicine, as well as to conduct research on ATM in order to inform and promote evidence-based practices. However, despite all the promising legal frameworks and strategic plan, the implementation of policies on ATM have remained on paper.

Despite all of the above efforts, it is instructive to note that in contemporary Zimbabwe, African Christianity has by and large frowned upon ATM. Many African churches prohibit their members from using African herbs in curing health complications. Rugwiji notes that "African traditional herbs and the African way

---

32 Cavender, "The Professionalisation of Traditional Medicine in Zimbabwe", 253.
33 Lovenson R. 2000. "Public Participation in Health Systems in Zimbabwe", *IDS Bulletin* 31(1):14-20.
34 Nyazema NZ. 2010. "The Zimbabwe Crisis and the Provision of Social Services", *Journal of Developing Societies* 26(2):233-261.
35 Government of Zimbabwe, Ministry of Health and Child Care. 2015. *The National Strategy for Zimbabwe – Equity and Quality in Health: Leaving no one behind*. Harare: MOHCC.

of dealing with ailments are perceived as evil and satanic."[36] This has resulted in African Initiated Churches (AICs) and Pentecostal churches emphasising faith-healing and the performance of miracles, while Mainline churches favour Western medicine. Despite the emphasis on faith healing, these churches appear to be steeped in the African spiritual worldview where one is satisfied that they can get healed when they use certain tangible things. In this case, the use of healing water, stones, anointing oil, anointed cloths and other items is rampant in these churches. This shows that while they claim to have broken free from the past, the past still binds them. In order to accommodate African indigenous cultures, the Roman Catholic Church adopted inculturation as a practical approach. But in Protestant churches that continue to demonise indigenous ways of healing, members often sneak at night to either consult traditional health practitioners or to treat themselves using ATM.

Covid-19, however, has challenged and brought into question the claims of faith healing and miracles by some of the Christian formations. Damaris Parsitau, a scholar of religion focusing particularly on Pentecostal churches, postulates that Covid-19 has rendered the clergy in Africa incapable of healing the sick and praying away the coronavirus.[37] On the other hand, there has been a plethora of testimonies by people who claim to have used ATM in curing Covid-19.[38] In this study, we have called these "street narratives" on the effectiveness of ATM in curing Covid-19. Claims of ATM curing Covid-19 were challenged by the WHO when the government of Madagascar had advised that a particular herb in that country was capable of healing people infected with the virus. In that context, it is important to note that on the ground, Zimbabweans of all persuasions never completely abandoned their faith in ATM during the pandemic.

COVID-19 AND THE POPULARISATION OF ATM: A THEOLOGICAL DILEMMA FOR CHRISTIANITY?

Covid-19 was first discovered in China's Wuhan Province in December 2019, and it spread to the rest of the world in 2020. Various scholars have dealt with the historical background of the pandemic, which warrants no repeating in this study.[39] At the onset of the virus globally, most African nations were mere onlookers, as the

---

36 Rugwiji T. 2008. *Reading the Exodus Tradition from a Zimbabwean Perspective*. Master of Arts Diss, University of South Africa, Pretoria.
37 Parsitau, "Religion in the Age of Coronavirus".
38 They only remain narratives because they have not been proven scientifically.
39 Chigevenga R. 2020. "Commentary on Covid-19 in Zimbabwe", *Psychological Trauma: Theory, Research Practice and Policy* 12(5):S62-S64; Murphy MPA. 2020. "Covid-19 and emergency eLearning Consequences of the Securitisation of Higher education for post-pandemic pedagogy", *Contemporary Security Policy* 41(3):492-505; Rashid S and Yadar SS. 2020. "Impact of Covid-19 Pandemic on Higher Education and Research", *Indian Journal of Human Development*, 1-4; Sibanda F, Muyambo T and Chitando E (eds). 2022. *Religion and the Covid-19 Pandemic in Southern Africa*. London: Routledge.

pandemic was being reported in other continents. This prompted the peddling of conspiracy theories on why the virus would not affect black Africans. One of the theories pointed to African climate and black skin as offering resistance to the virus. It was argued that Africa's hot climate and the melanin that black Africans possess were enemies of the virus. Some Zimbabwean politicians, on the other hand, created their own narrative, in which they used propaganda to locate the origin of the virus in religious terms. Such narratives meant that Zimbabweans developed a false sense of security and did not invest in coming up with effective ways of responding to the virus in the event that it landed on their soil. Hence, when the first case of the virus was first reported in mid-March 2020, they were caught off guard. The first fatality was recorded on 24 March 2020. The government declared a lockdown starting 30 March 2020. Reports from media houses about the first fatality pointed to neglect of the patient by ill-equipped health personnel at Wilkins Hospital in Harare. The reality of the seriousness of the pandemic dawned on most Zimbabweans. Fear and uncertainty gripped the nation. Amidst the fear and uncertainty, people turned to local remedies to safeguard themselves from infection. The use of herbs and other forms of ATM shaped and continues to shape Zimbabweans' response to the virus.

As the pandemic ravaged through the country, different perceptions were expressed concerning the way Christians were navigating the effects of the pandemic. When it was reported that Madagascar had found a remedy for Covid-19 from one of its herbs, Zimbabweans, including Christians, quickly resorted to their own herbs for both prevention and healing. This study is aware that when talking of Christianity in Zimbabwe, we are making reference to a heterogeneous group in Zimbabwe; hence, we can talk of Christianities.

In order to understand how Christians in Zimbabwe responded to Covid-19, we sought responses from six families in Harare who belong to different Christian backgrounds: Roman Catholicism, Protestantism (United Methodist Church), Pentecostalism (Apostolic Faith Mission and the United Family International Church), new religious movements (Jehovah's Witness), as well as African Independent Churches (Johanne Marange). For purposes of anonymity, these families are given alpha-numerical codes A1 to F1. In cases where different members of a family responded, they carry the same alpha code but a different numerical one. The authors of this chapter carried the interviews simultaneously with each author interviewing two families. The interview questions sought to establish the following: (1) their general reaction as well as that of their communities when they found out that the coronavirus was now in Zimbabwe; (2) whether they adopted the use of traditional medicine and, if so, whether their churches condone such practices; (3) whether they utilised ATM openly with the knowledge of church leaders and fellow church members; (4) whether ATM was useful against the virus; (5) the type of ATM used and what it was used for; (6) whether they think Christianity should change its stance towards ATM; and, finally, (7) if Covid-19 had plunged Christianity into a dilemma concerning ATM.

Fears of death and dying alone

The research participants were unanimous in highlighting the fear that gripped them, as well as the members of their communities, when it was announced that the coronavirus was present in Zimbabwe. The drastic measures taken by the government of Zimbabwe to lockdown the country made them feel as if they were looking death in the eyes. Interviewee A1 indicated that she panicked, saw doom and gloom. She was sceptcal about the country's ability to pull out of the Covid-19 period with many citizens alive. In reference to the response of other members of her community, she said that many were doubtful. They believed that the virus would affect those who flew or travelled a lot. She was concerned about the critical situation they were in particularly in relation to the health care system in shambles.

On the issue of fear, Interviewee B1 said, "I was grappled with fear and anxiety; l didn't know whether l was also going to survive having watched how people were dying in China. It was a scary moment."[40] She also noted, "The community was very fearful of the pandemic. The introduction of the restrictions by the government made it worse; people were not allowed to visit each other, going to work and attend funerals of their close ones. It was a difficult time and it brought so much confusion amongst the community members, and everyone thought they were going to die of the pandemic."[41]

In concurrence, Interviewee C1 said, "When I first heard that Covid-19 was now in Zimbabwe, I was frightened. Considering our dilapidated health system, I wondered how we would survive this pandemic as a nation. As an individual or at family level, I wondered how my family would cope with the pandemic in the event we got infected factoring in our meagre financial resources. We were not going to be able to fund any medication or hospitalisation. It was like we had been put under a death trap."[42] Interviewee C1 said his community was equally fearful as they navigated the seemingly hapless situation. For him, the lockdowns exacerbated the fear as people felt like they were being sentenced to death, but it was death they were going to experience alone, as visits from loved ones were prohibited. The same sentiments were echoed by Interviewee D1, who said she quickly tried to find out how best to protect her family members from infection, while her community, though fearful, adhered to the government-pronounced Covid-19 protocols.[43]

The above responses are informative in that they reveal the fact that, inasmuch as the virus induced so much fear in people, for most Zimbabweans it was a double tragedy, because the formal health care system is decrepit. In case of infection, they were convinced that going to the government hospitals was not an option, as they were ill-equipped to handle coronavirus cases. Seeking treatment in the hospitals was like sentencing oneself to death.

---

40 Interviewee B1, interviewed by V Chimininge, Harare, Zimbabwe, 2 April 2022.
41 Interviewee B1, 2 April 2022.
42 Interviewee C1, interviewed by M Manyonganise, Harare, Zimbabwe, 3 April 2022.
43 Interviewee D1, interviewed by M Manyonganise, Harare, Zimbabwe, 4 April 2022.

Resort to alternative and traditional medicine

In such situations, people look for alternative ways to survive. In the case of research participants in this study, their families turned to ATM. Interviewee C1 indicated that he and his family used traditional herbs for prevention. They boiled *zumbani* (*Lippia javanica*) leaves and drank the water after draining. They also made concoctions that they put under their pillows when sleeping. They would also inhale the steam of some of the concoctions. He further indicated that they did steam inhalation (*kunatira*), a treatment where one covers themselves with a sheet or blanket while inhaling the steam.[44] Interviewee A2 said she also gargled warm water with salt to clear her throat and chest. He said *zumbani* was for boosting the immune system while steaming was intended to kill the virus, since the virus was said to be unable to withstand high temperatures.[45]

The use of *zumbani* appears to have been very common with interviewees. It was mentioned by all participants, though the way it was used may have differed. Interviewee B1 did not indicate how she used the herb, while Interviewee A1 indicated that she used *zumbani* mainly for steaming and drinking.[46] She noted that steaming techniques employed during Covid-19 differed. In her own home, they steamed with boiling water usually with eucalyptus oil or placing a piping red hot rock in water. Apart from this, she also indicated that her family also used concoctions of ginger, guava, eucalyptus leaves and lemon. Bicarbonate of soda in warm water was also used in order to make the system alkaline. Interviewee D1 said she used ATM for both prevention and cure.[47] For Interviewee E1, his family made it mandatory that *zumbani* with lemon was the new tea in the home.[48]

Trying to ascertain the efficacy of the ATM used by research participants in curing coronavirus was very problematic. Though some of them got flu, which for some was very severe, they were not tested for Covid-19. Only A2 and A3 were confirmed to have been infected with the virus.[49] The reason for not getting tested was mainly fear of being confirmed positive. For study participants, not knowing was much better, because psychologically they remained stable. From their analysis, some people died because they panicked after knowing that they had contracted the virus.

---

44 Interviewee C1, interviewed by M Manyonganise; Harare, Zimbabwe, 3 April 2022.
45 Interviewee A2; Interviewee A1, interviewed by V Chimininge; Harare, Zimbabwe, 3 April 2022.
46 Interviewee B1, 2 April 2022; Interviewee A1, interviewed by V Chimininge, Harare, Zimbabwe, 1 April 2022.
47 Interviewee D1, interviewed by M Manyonganise, Harare, Zimbabwe, 4 April 2022.
48 Interviewee E1, interviewed by C Makamure, Harare, Zimbabwe, 4 April 2022.
49 Interviewee A2, 1 April 2022; Interviewee A3, interviewed by V Chimininge, Harare, Zimbabwe, 1 April 2022.

Uncertainty of effect

Thus, some participants in the study were convinced that they had been infected, even though they were not tested, and they used ATM, at times together with conventional medicine, until they got healed. In such cases, they are not sure whether what got them healed was ATM or conventional medicine. Interviewee A1 only thinks that it worked, because none of her family members died of Covid-19. However, she is quick to highlight that they used a mixture of traditional and modern medicine. Hence, she is not sure of what really worked. When A2 and A3 got infected with the virus, they used both types of medicines. A1 pointed out the difference in severity of the virus was seen in that A3 who had been vaccinated had mild symptoms, while A2 who had refused the vaccine nearly died, and he rushed for it as soon as it was possible for him to get the vaccine. A2 is equally confused as to what really worked for him, while A3 believes that the vaccine made the difference.

Interviewee C1 said he could not vouch for the effectiveness of ATM against the virus. In this regard, he said, "On their effectiveness, I would not know for real because there were other methods of prevention that we were using such as isolation and maintaining social distancing and also other hygienic methods such as washing of hands with soap and sanitisers. Again, no one in my family was clinically diagnosed as having been infected with the virus, so it's difficult to tell the effectiveness of ATM at a personal level."[50] The same was echoed by Interviewee F1 who noted that she used both traditional and modern medicine.[51] Her own sister and her husband were infected with the virus. The sister is said to have used traditional medicine, and she was healed. However, the husband actually got worse, to the extent that when they finally took him to a private doctor, he was given seven injections all at once. She confirms that had they not taken him to the doctor and continued giving him ATM, he could have died.

Interviewees B1 and D1 are the only ones who are sure that ATM worked for them. Interviewee B1 said her whole household got sick with a heavy flu when the first wave of Covid-19 was at its peak. They were afraid of getting tested, because then the government was taking positive patients to Parirenyatwa Hospital in Harare where they were isolated in an area code-named "Red Zone". They had heard that very few people were coming out of that zone alive. The naming of that area alone was scary. It killed all the hope to live again. Hence, they resorted to ATM, and they were all healed from the flu. Interviewee D1 said, "ATM was useful. Personally, when I had a terrible flu which I suspect was Covid-19, though not tested, I used traditional medicines such as lemon, guava, *zumbani* and eucalyptus leaves for steaming and drinking. It really worked, together with honey and lemon juice."[52]

---

50 Interviewee C1, interviewed by M Manyonganise, Harare, Zimbabwe, 3 April 2022.
51 Interviewee F1, interviewed by C Makamure, Harare, Zimbabwe, 4 April 2022.
52 Interviewee D1, interviewed by M Manyonganise, Harare, Zimbabwe, 4 April 2022.

Church approval or disapproval

The crux of the matter centred on whether the participants' churches approve of them using ATM. All the participants except B1 said that their churches neither condone nor speak openly about ATM. B1 is a member of the Roman Catholic Church. She said her church do,es not see anything wrong with one using ATM; hence, she, together with fellow members used the traditional medicine openly.[53] Interviewee A1 indicated that while her Jehovah's Witness church is not against the use of traditional remedies, it discourages members from consulting indigenous health practitioners. She said her church allows the use of traditional medicine minus what she called "the spiritualistic position of traditional healing".

Interviewee C1 and D1 (Pentecostals) and E1 (Johanne Marange Apostolic Church) indicated that their churches emphasise faith healing. However, their families, as well as other members in their churches, also resorted to ATM from the beginning of Covid-19 until today. C1, a Pentecostal Christian in the UFIC, said the use of traditional medicine was never mentioned in his church, because when one is sick, they are always told to depend on prayer. This was supported by D1, who said her Apostolic Faith Mission in Zimbabwe (AFMZ) is silent on the use of traditional medicine. She indicated, however, that the original doctrine of her church forbade people from seeking medical attention in hospitals, directing them instead to have faith in prayer. It would then follow that the use of traditional medicine by members of their churches is not a subject for discussion.

Hence, C1, D1 and E1's use of traditional medicine during Covid-19 was a decision taken outside of official church doctrine. It is indicative of the fact that when faced with situations that are threatening to their lives, individuals will choose any path that (they think) will lead to their survival. The lockdown also enabled the free use of ATM without fear of being seen by church leaders. C1 joked that "who knows, maybe they were also using the same home remedies."[54] All participants indicated that they got the herbs either in the bushes, in supermarkets as well as from friends and family. When the country partially opened, they could buy these herbs from fellow employees at work as well as from those selling them along the streets. Hence, none of them consulted traditional or indigenous health practitioners, who appeared to be anathema to most of them.

All participants were of the view that the popularisation of ATM by church members across the denominational divide calls for the church in its generic sense to break the silence on ATM. Interviewee C1 gave two reasons for his views. First, he argued that the church needs to start conversations around ATM in order to assist members in distinguishing it "from those other traditional/spiritual healings associated with witches and wizards."[55] This was supported by Interviewee A1 who said the church

---

53 Interviewee B1, interviewed by V Chimininge, Harare, Zimbabwe, 2 April 2022.
54 Interviewee C1, interviewed by M Manyonganise, Harare, Zimbabwe, 4 April 2022.
55 Interviewee C1, interviewed by M Manyonganise, Harare, Zimbabwe, 3 April 2022.

should encourage the use of ATM without the traditional healers. For C1, traditional medicine on its own, in its purity, is just like any modern medicine.

The second reason was that many Christians died, as they could not accept the use of the medicinal remedies that are indigenous. He said this was due to many Christians listening to the voices of their pastors more than to the voice of reason or experts in the field of health. He further explained, "Generally the church has been silent concerning the use of traditional medicine for healing purposes. Whilst God can still heal through the laying on of hands, the silence of the church on the use of medicine in general seems to suggest that if one is to prove that he is healed of God, it only has to be by the laying on of hands. I believe God works in various ways and that he gives people different gifts – some in the use of traditional medicine and others in using effective modern medicines."[56]

In supporting the fact that the church should start talking about ATM, D1 argued that Covid-19 was an eye-opener concerning ATM. For her, traditional medicine "proved" to be very useful in the prevention and cure of Covid-19. For E1, the conversations on ATM in the church are crucial, because though AICs publicly denounce traditional medicine, many of them are using it clandestinely.[57] Hence, either way, some African Indigenous Church members are using ATM for Covid-19 treatment. B1 said the church needs to actually encourage its members to take traditional medicine, because, for her, it is the same as modern medicine with the difference only noticeable in the packaging. She further argued that all medicines, traditional or modern, are created by God; hence, people should use them freely. For F1, teachings on ATM are needed urgently in the church so that lives can be saved in the Covid-19 era rather than being lost unnecessarily. She cited Ezekiel 47:12, which states that the leaves of trees shall be for medicine.[58]

The data presented and interpreted above bring out key issues pertaining to the relationship between Christianity and ATM. One of the key issues is the continued demonisation and stigmatisation of both ATM and Christians who dare to use traditional medicine either for healing or prevention of disease. The other is the fact that churches that encouraged their members to depend on prayer alone for healing illnesses failed to prove that faith alone was what is needed to be healed. In other words, Covid-19 challenged narratives of faith healing. This was even made worse when some church leaders succumbed to the virus. Systematic theologian Robert Matikiti challenged the church in Zimbabwe to prayerfully and consistently interpret the Christian message in new situations.[59] For him, "brushing aside ... traditional medicines is a form of ahistoricism".[60] Gordon Chavunduka argues that when Africans are faced with threatening disease, though they are Christians, they

---

56 Interviewee C1, interviewed by M Manyonganise, Harare, Zimbabwe, 3 April 2022.
57 Interviewee E1, Interviewed by C Makamure, Harare, Zimbabwe, 4 April 2022.
58 Interviewee F1, Interviewed by C Makamure, Harare, Zimbabwe, 4 April 2022.
59 Matikiti R. 2021. "Confessing Jesus Christ in Cultural Context: The One-sided Politics of Covid-19 Vaccination in Zimbabwe", *History Research* 9(2):127-135.
60 Matikiti, "Confessing Jesus Christ in Cultural Context", 127.

revert back to their traditional medicines for cure and prevention.[61] For Matikiti, the continued utilisation of traditional medicines by Christians in Zimbabwe shows that their religion and culture make meaningful connections with their past that shape their identity in the present.[62]

The data also show the confusion that arises when one is talking about traditional medicine. People confuse traditional medicine with traditional health practitioners. However, as indicated before, none of the participants consulted a traditional health practitioner, even though they all utilised traditional herbs. In the age of technology, information about effective herbal medicine became viral on social media platforms. As indicated by both A1 and C1, Matikiti reinforces the fact that during Covid-19, Christians sought herbs and not divination.[63]

Research participants also raised the issue of the church at a crossroads. It appears from the responses that there is a lack of a clear theology of healing in the church, in the sense of a theology that is devoid of colonial influences and is able to accommodate indigenous healing systems in Zimbabwe. Matikiti argues that the "experiences of the pandemic highlight the theological deficiency of the church in Zimbabwe".[64] The church has failed to free itself from the clutches of colonial narratives that presented ATM as not only primitive, but demonic and a product of the devil. It becomes significant for the church in Zimbabwe to embark on a decolonial journey so that it is appreciative of some of the African cultural practices in the field of health. The lack of a solid legal framework from government is also instructive. When crafting the Zimbabwe National Health Strategy (2009-2013), the then Ministry of Health and Child Welfare noted that inroads on ATM had been made in other African countries, with certain governments having integrated traditional medicine into the public health system at various levels and with traditional medicine receiving official attention and funding with clear legislative and operational frameworks that ensure that the medicine is accessible and available to those who need the service.[65] The ministry, however, acknowledged that in Zimbabwe, the laboratory studies and clinical evaluations were being done at individual levels and were largely uncoordinated, thereby lacking any national agenda.

This leads to a number of challenges, one of which is the limited recognition of the role of traditional medicine as an important part of Primary Health Care (PHC). On 6 April 2020, the government of Zimbabwe announced that it had authorised certain traditional health practitioners to treat Covid-19. However, it was difficult to get a policy framework to support that announcement. Hence, reactions from conventional medical experts were mixed, resulting in conflicting messaging. This leaves other key stakeholders, like the church, in a dilemma of how to proceed. The announcement made by the now Ministry of Health and Child Care (MOHCC) that

---

61 Chavunduka, "ZINATHA".
62 Matikiti, "Confessing Jesus Christ in Cultural Context", 129.
63 Matikiti, "Confessing Jesus Christ in Cultural Context", 133.
64 Matikiti, "Confessing Jesus Christ in Cultural Context", 133.
65 Ministry of Health and Child Care, *National Strategy for Zimbabwe*.

some of the herbs were now being scientifically tested to determine efficacy were encouraging, despite the Medical Research Council moaning about inadequate funding for the process. However, for the church to respond to the existential challenges of members, it needs to rethink its silence over the use of ATM and come up with theologies of healing that respond to the contextual questions around Christianity, modern medicine as well as ATM. It would not help the church, even in a post-Covid-19 era, to continue hiding its head in the sand pretending that its members are shunning ATM, while their cupboards are overflowing with the same, albeit without declaring its usage openly. The government needs to assist in this matter by not only crafting legal frameworks that end up on shelves without meaningful implementation guidelines, but also taking seriously the issue of integrating ATM in formal health systems. Following in the footsteps of other institutions of higher learning, the mainstreaming of courses and programmes on ATM in relevant faculties would be a welcome development which would also assist in the preservation of critical indigenous knowledge systems.

CONCLUSION

This chapter's point of departure was to interrogate the contested position of ATM in Christianity and in formal health discourses in Zimbabwe. Using a decolonial lens, assisted by both phenomenology and grounded theological approaches, the study situated the marginalisation of ATM within the missionary as well as the colonial enterprise. It established that the colonial legislative frameworks on health were meant to shut out not only the traditional health practitioners, who were misnamed as "witch doctors", but also whole African indigenous epistemologies on healing. Missionaries, on the other hand, were shown to have felt that they were competing for converts with traditional health practitioners; hence, they demonised their practices as well as the general use of traditional medicine.

However, the continued use of traditional medicine not only in Africa, but also in other contexts, influenced policy shifts in organisations such as the WHO. The present study discussed the Alma Ata Declaration, which embraced traditional medicine as crucial for PHC. The study also traced the historical development of these attitudes, as well as the many declarations and policy frameworks that followed. It is, however, disheartening to note that despite much paperwork having been done, there is little to show for it within the Zimbabwean context. Covid-19 happened in such a context.

In spite of all this, the study participants were shown to prove what other scholars in other fields have already noted, that is, Africans have never abandoned ATM. This being the case, we can conclude that Covid-19 resuscitated the interest in ATM of a large number of Christians in Zimbabwe, including those who belong to churches that emphasise faith healing. Sentiments from participants point to the need for clear healing theologies within Christianity in Zimbabwe, namely, theologies that touch on the use of ATM. The pandemic was shown to have challenged the overdependence on both modern medicine and faith healing. Instead of buying ATM from unauthorised street sellers, is it not better to formalise ATM so that it can be purchased from authorised sources? While this study relied on a small sample of six families in Harare, further research may be required to cover other provinces as well. As health researcher Vibhu Paudyal puts it, "gathering ... perspectives and experiences on [African] traditional medicine is imperative in informing future practices, as well as policy direction."[66]

---

[66] Paudyal V. 2022. "Complementary and alternative medicines use in Covid-19: A global perspective on practice, policy and research", *Research in Social and Administrative Pharmacy* 18:2524-2528.

22 THE SYNCRETISM HEALING ATONEMENT MOTIF AND AFRICAN TRADITIONAL HEALING IN AFRICAN INDEPENDENT CHURCHES IN BOTSWANA: A RESPONSE TO COVID-19

Kenosi Molato[1]

INTRODUCTION

The coronavirus has recently ravaged the world in which we live, thereby taking the lives of our beloved friends and relatives. It was first considered as flu of no significance in the corner of the world located around Wuhan, China. In its inception, many thought it would not reach other parts of the world, let alone reach Africa, much less Botswana. Many argued that due to the heat in Africa, especially in Botswana and its Kgalagadi Desert, the coronavirus would not survive light and heat of the day. Some even argued that the black skin of Africans possessed the power to resist the coronavirus.[2] Indeed, the delayed arrival of corona in Botswana enabled the government to prepare and to put in place the procedures that would reduce its impact.

A World Health Organization (WHO) report stated that the organisation would work with the government of Botswana to make sure that the public health protocols were observed in the country for the safety of the citizens of Botswana.[3] This included developing a comprehensive multi-sectoral response plan and active engagement with other sectors and communities. However, these measures did not prevent the coronavirus from spreading into the country, and on 30 March 2020 the first case of coronavirus was reported in Botswana. By 22 April 2020, the government of Botswana declared a lockdown across the whole country for 28 days in order to stop the spread. However, as of 8 August 2022, there had been 325 684 confirmed cases of Covid-19 with 2 778 deaths recorded.[4] Furthermore, the speed by which the coronavirus reached other corners of the world was so remarkable that there is no place in the world today that has not been affected by the coronavirus.

---

1 Researcher, Botswana Circle, Gaborone, Botswana.
2 Vaughn L, Kiconco A, Quartey N, Smith CS and Ziz IS. 2021. "'Colonial Virus'? COVID-19, Black Immunity Myth and Africa", *Discover Society*, 1 February.
3 Siamisang K. 2021. "University of Botswana Public Health Medicine Unit contributes to the national COVID-19 response", *Pan African Medical Journal* 39:82.
4 "Covid-19 Tracker Botswana", Reuters, 15 July 2022 (last update). https://www.reuters.com/graphics/world-coronavirus-tracker-and-maps/countries-and-territories/botswana/ [Accessed 28 September 2022].

The pandemic produced claims by some in Botswana, and Africa more broadly, that they had means to heal people from corona.[5] African Independent Churches (AICs) are one of the major religious groups that has been on the forefront of claiming to heal Covid-19 in Botswana.[6] This chapter examines the Botswana AICs' claims of being able to heal people from the coronavirus through what I call the "syncretism healing atonement motif".[7] The chapter, first, sets forth the history of AICs in Botswana, noting particularly their service to Botswana in time of other pandemics, such as AIDS. Second, the chapter analyses the syncretism healing atonement motif in the AICs, pointing out the reason why this method persists in these churches. Third, it describes the impact of Covid-19 on the churches in Botswana, highlighting the strategies that they used to reduce the impact of coronavirus in their communities. Fourth, the chapter presents the methodology and the research design of its underlying study to capture the responses of the AICs church in their response to coronavirus, followed by discussion of the findings from the study and conclusions drawn from the analysis.

HISTORY OF AFRICAN INDEPENDENT CHURCHES IN BOTSWANA

Missionaries arrived in African countries in the last quarter of the eighteenth century, and they planted churches in different places, including among the Setswana-speaking communities.[8] Each denomination that participated in the missionary movement came to be associated with a particular ethnic group or groups in Botswana. This is demonstrated by the fact that each ethnic group had a direct link with the sending denomination through a missionary who was working among them. These ethnic groups benefitted from gaining resources for building school and hospitals through these missionary links. Historian Thomas Tlou notes that missionaries acted as advisors to the ethnic group chiefs, and they also brought educational systems, which the ethnic groups in Botswana perceived as important in allowing to engage with traders.[9]

While the missionary movement brought some positive and important changes in Botswana, there were conflicts with the indigenous people over Setswana practices condemned by the missionaries as pagan or satanic. This approach was not received well by the indigenous people.[10] Some indigenous Christians felt that the missio-

---

5 Baker A. 2020. "'Could It Work as a Cure? Maybe'. A Herbal Remedy for Coronavirus Is a Hit in Africa, But Experts Have Their Doubts", *Time*, 22 May.
6 Ekonde K. 2020. "The Challenge with African Countries Promoting traditional cures for Covid-19 without Research", *Quartz Africa*, 6 May.
7 This chapter uses the word "motif" of healing to mean a theory of healing in the AICs.
8 Ramsay J, Morton B and Mgadla T. 1996. *Building a Nation: A History of Botswana from 1800 to 1910*. Gaborone: Longman Botswana, 180.
9 Tlou T. 1973. "The Batawana of Northwestern Botswana and Christian Missionaries: 1877-1907", *Transafrican Journal of History* 3(2):112-128.
10 Amanze J. 2022. *African Christianity in Botswana: The Case of African Independent Churches*. Gweru: Mambo Press, 62.

nary churches did not fit with their African worldview. Among other things, the clash meant that African traditional medicine was prohibited by missionaries. The missionary movements emphasised that their Western healing methods comported with the gospel, while they perceived African traditional healing as pagan.[11] In this way, African traditional healing was pushed into the periphery, and out of traditional communities. Furthermore, certain concepts that are associated with the healing, such as prophecy, were also eradicated from church meetings. This move by the white missionaries entailed that the culture of the missionaries was perceived as superior to African culture and that African healing methods were perceived as unequal to those of the white missionaries.[12] This degradation of the African cultures and relegation of African to a position lesser than that of white missionaries left Africans with no option but to initiate and institute their own form of Christianity in ways that suited their culture. These African-initiated forms of Christianity took many forms, such as the mixture of Catholicism with the African culture in the Congo region and mixture of Protestant theology with African culture in others.[13]

These African Christianities believe in atonement-healing theology, which refers to the view that the efficacy of the death of Christ brings healing in the community. According to the theologian Bruce Reichenbach, this view perceives Jesus as a physician.[14] Therefore, Christ took on the task of bringing healing to the community that was facing pandemics.[15] In this view, Christ is still physician today and is concerned in bringing healing to the communities that are facing different maladies. As compared to missionary theology, which held to the view that the miraculous works of healing have ceased, the AICs hold to the view that Christ still heals today.[16] The AICs go further in emulating Christ in healing ministry, in the sense that Christ used mud to heal a blind man in John 9:1-7. Therefore Christ was syncretistic in his healing service in that he mixed his faith with traditional medicine. The syncretism healing atonement motif is the mixing of traditional medicine and Christian faith.[17]

---

[11] Kealotswe O. 1993. *Doctrine and Rituals in the African Independent Churches: A Study in Beliefs, Rituals and Practices in the Head Mountain of God Apostolic Church in Zion*. PhD Thesis, University of Edinburgh, 30.

[12] Thomas LE. 1997. "South African Independent Churches, Syncretism, and Black Theology", *Journal of Religious Thought* 53/54(2/1):39.

[13] Amanze, *African Christianity in Botswana*, 62.

[14] Beichenbach B. 2006. "Healing View", in Beilby J and Eddy P (eds). *The Nature of Atonement*. Illinois: IVP Academic, 118.

[15] Beichenbach, "Healing View", 118.

[16] Molato K. 2017. *Comparative Study of Prophecy between African Independent Churches and African Pentecostal churches: A Case Study of Botswana Healing Church and Maun Assemblies of God*. Master's Thesis, University of Botswana, 39.

[17] Ndhlovu J. 2020. *The Attitude of Evangelical churches towards Syncretism in Tshwane Townships"*. Unpublished PhD Diss, University of the Free State, 15.

The formation of the AICs was centred on the centrality of African culture in the practice of Christianity, while the missionary churches were European focused in their practices. Theologian Kofi Appiah-Kubi writes, "In contrast to a cold, frigid, professionally aired Christianity that is mainly interested in form, these churches are free, emotional, and to some extent fanatical in their Christian worship. Several of these churches are charismatic, lay, egalitarian, and are voluntaristic in contrast to the established, professional, hierarchical, prescribed religion of the missionary churches."[18] Church Historian Bengt Sundkler, who has done extensive research on the AICs in Southern Africa, argues that the AICs were a bridge between Christianity and paganism. Furthermore, Sundkler points out that the AICs are the "rebirth and revitalization of African culture in the guise of Christianity."[19] In his critique of the AICs, Sundkler argues that, in the AICs, the ancestral spirit has replaced the Holy Spirit in such a way that the role of a prophet in the AICs is that of a traditional healer. As such, the healing methods which are used by the AICs should be eradicated and never be used in the African communities. Missiologist Marthinus Daneel, however, takes a more gracious view than Sundkler. Instead of viewing the AICs as going back to African traditional belief, Daneel describes them as instance of biblical doctrine being transformed into the culture of the people.[20] When the biblical concept takes on the culture of the people, it creates a new sense of belief and a meaning, which is only relevant and understood by the practitioners. To an outsider, this might seem like a departure from the Christian faith, but to the practitioner, it is what Christianity is supposed to be in that context. The practices that the AICs espoused led the earlier missionary movement to perceive them as non-Christian and also to view them as the enemy of their flock, because they claimed that their practices might lead the flock astray.[21] Daneel argues that the acceptance of polygamy by the AICs made the missionary churches to believe that they were not Christian and that they were pulling people back into paganism of African practices.[22] This entail that the AICs beliefs and its practices, especially the aspect of healing, should not be accepted neither be used because it resembles some form of paganism practices.

In the AICs in Botswana, and in Africa more broadly, the paramount distinguishing mark is that they take African culture seriously.[23] Religion scholar James Amanze notes that the AICs in Botswana preserved Setswana culture and spirituality, which

---

18 Kofi AK. 1979. "Indigenous Christian Churches: Signs of Authenticity", in Appiah-Kubi and Torres S (eds). *African Theology En Route*. Maryknoll, NY: Orbis Books, 118.
19 Kealotswe ON. 2014. "Acceptance and Rejection: The Traditional Healer Prophet and His Integration of his healing methods", *Boleswa Journal of Theology and Religion* 1(1):109.
20 Daneel L. 1971. *The Background and the Rise of Southern Shona Independent Churches*. The Hague: Mouton & Co.
21 Nkomazana F. "The Botswana Religious Landscape", in Togarasei L, Mmolai SK and Nkomazana F (eds). *The Faith Sector and HIV/AIDS in Botswana: Responses and Challenges*. Cambridge: Cambridge Scholars Publishing, 13.
22 Daneel, *The Background and the Rise of Southern Shona Independent Churches*, 455.
23 Amanze, *African Christianity in Botswana*, 62.

the missionaries had condemned.[24] In the AICs, these key issues of African culture resurface in the practice of Christianity, and the Western culture that was paramount in the missionary churches was eradicated in these new churches. As well, the biblical doctrines come to be draped in the African cloth, such that they resemble the African way of life. This method of contextualisation is called "adaptation transformation theory". Through it a biblical doctrine become enmeshed in the cultural sitting to such an extent that that it totally resembles the culture of the people.[25] In this way, the AICs churches identified with the people on the ground. This is what South African theologian Helen Hlongwane calls "grass-roots theology".[26] The desire to reach the people with their theology and to incorporate African culture in their theological practice facilitated the growth of AICs in Botswana.

Writing in 1999, Amanze stated that AICs were the majority of the churches in the country.[27] Botswana theologian Fidelis Nkomazana, referencing a study done by the cultural globalisation scholar Wim van Binsbergen, has estimated that two out of three adults in Botswana are members of AICs.[28] One of the major theological concepts that arises from the AICs is the concept of healing, particularly the idea that God still heals today. This concept sets the AICs apart from the missionary churches that rely on the Western form of healing. In their inception, the AICs were built upon the prophets (*baporofiti*), who included both men and women. These AIC prophets, who were mostly founders of the AICs churches themselves, were spears that pierced the activities of the kingdom of darkness and established the kingdom of God in their society. As such, the concept of healing in the AICs established the point that God is active in the church and that he cares about his people. By definition, the prophets in the AICs are people who are endowed with the supernatural power to heal every sickness and also with the ability to diagnose sickness and the cause thereof.

In the present study, which I conducted in a Botswana healing church in 2017, these prophets were the shepherds of the congregation functioning under the bishops of the church, but they were also servants of the community in the sense that they diagnosed and healed people from the community who were seeking some assistance.[29] Zimbabwean biblical scholar Lovemore Togarasei and Botswana theologian Obed Kealotswe note that the AICs healers heal varieties of sickness, such as headache, diarrhoea and many other diseases that cannot be cured by Western medicine.[30] Furthermore, the AICs prophets not only cure diseases, but can also

---

24 Amenze, *African Christianity in Botswana*, 62.
25 Molato, *Comparative Study of Prophecy between African Independent Churches and African Pentecostal churches*, 92.
26 Hlogwane W. 1972. *Pentecostalism*. London: SCM.
27 Amanze, *African Christianity in Botswana*, 89.
28 Nkomazana, "The Botswana Religious Landscape", 12.
29 Molato, *Comparative Study of Prophecy between African Independent Churches and African Pentecostal churches*.
30 Togarasei L, Mmolai S and Kealotswe ON. 2016. "'Quinine', 'Ditaola' and the 'Bible': Investigating Batswana Health Seeking Practices", *Journal for the Study of Religion* 29(1):95-117.

determine the root or the cause of diseases. This corresponds with the African Setswana worldview, which assumes that nothing just happens – it has one way or the other to be caused by witchcraft. In this way, the AICs prophets acts as both traditional healers and pastors in the local church. In fact, during the HIV and AIDS pandemics, the AICs were in the forefront of trying to address the situation in Botswana. In this way, the modern form of healing was not only the means by which AIDS pandemic was addressed and healed. Thus, religion scholar Musa Dube notes that the HIV and AIDS pandemic called for the multiplicity of approaches in order to educate and heal the Botswana communities of this pandemic.[31]

SYNCRETISM AS A HEALING METHOD IN THE AICs

Syncretism is synthesis of cultural concepts with religious concepts in such a way that the religious concept is submerged into the cultural space, thereby losing its original religious form. Religious scholar Mark Mullis notes that syncretism is usually understood as a combination of elements from two or more religious traditions, ideologies or value systems.[32] In the social sciences, this is a neutral and objective term that is used to describe the mixing of religions as a result of cultural contact. In theology and missiological circles, however, it is generally used as a pejorative term to designate movements that are regarded as heretical or sub-Christian.[33] The legitimate cultural reshaping of Christianity is referred to as the "enculturation" or "contextualisation" of the gospel, though most social scientists would also include these cultural adaptations as examples of syncretism.[34] The term "syncretism", Mark Mullis asserts, is often viewed as a pejorative and derogative term used to demonise the practice of those who correlate cultural concepts with biblical concepts.[35] Mainline churches and missionary churches use this term to assert that the AICs should not be viewed as Christian churches and are to be viewed instead as heretical.

The question, however, is whether the term can be used in a positive manner in relation to the church for the purposes of the scientific study of religion. For it is only those who perceive themselves as superior in their way of doing theology who refer to those upon whom they look down upon as syncretists. It would seem that there can be a legitimate use of the term, in a scientific sense, to argue that any theological practice is shaped by the context in which it is presented.[36] As such,

---

31 Dube WM. 2019. "Remembering the Teacherly Moments of HIV and AIDS Texts", *International Bulletin of Mission Research* 43(4):320-333.

32 Mullis MR. 2001. "Syncretic movement", in Sunquest SW (ed). *Dictionary of Asian Christianity of Theology*. Grand Rapids, MI: William B Eerdmans, 809.

33 Ndhlovu, "The Attitude of Evangelical churches towards Syncretism in Tshwane Townships", 15.

34 Mullis, "Syncretic movement", 809.

35 Mullis, "Syncretic movement", 809.

36 Johnson PC. 2002. "Migrating bodies, Circulating Signs: Brazilian Candomblé: The Garifuna of the Caribbean and the Category of Indigenous Religion", *History of Religions* 41(4):302.

every practice on the ground is syncretistic in nature. It is in the positive sense that I analyse syncretism in relation to healing methods in the AICs in Botswana in this chapter.

Writing of the context of AICs in South Africa, theologian Linda Thomas has studied the St. John's Apostolic Faith Mission Church and the way that it uses syncretism in church practices.[37] Thomas notes that at the centre of the church is her ability to heal, and these healing practices are centred on the prophetic ministry. As such, the prophetic ministry encapsulates the traditional concept of divining and the biblical concept of prophecy. This concept is similar to one that I observed during my research in Botswana at the village called Maun in an AIC church called the Botswana Healing Church.[38] The prophetic ministry of this church is tied to the healing in the sense that, before the healing is practised, the prophet or diviner must diagnose the root cause of the disease. This is based on the cosmological worldview, which perceives that disease does not occur without cause in the spiritual realm. The question of why sickness and death has occurred calls upon the role of the diviner in African traditional religions, while the prophet fills this role in the AICs. In this sense, through the means of prophecy the prophet identifies the wrong doers of certain occurrence of evil deeds among the congregants.[39]

Relatedly, Botswana theologian Obed Kealotswe has studied the life of Doctor Ookeditse Batisani of Jerusalema Bethsaida Church. According to Kealotswe's research findings, Doctor Batisani is a traditional healer, who also functions as a prophet in his local church. In his role as a traditional healer, Doctor Batisani uses sticks to communicate with the ancestors in order that the ancestors may give him permission to heal those who seek help. If a patient is a witch, the ancestors will reveal to him that he should not touch the patient. As a traditional healer, Doctor Batisani uses *diwacho* (placebos), which are made out of seawater, and he also makes *diwacho* with a mixture of traditional herbs.[40] In this scenario, Doctor Batisani acts solely as a traditional healer, which entails that he consults the ancestors to guide him in his profession. In this form of healing practice, Doctor Batasani gives his patient from the church *diwacho* of seawater. In this sense, the *diwacho* of the seawater is not perceived as a healing element, but it is used to induce faith of the believers. Therefore, these elements become a form of contact in order to connect with healing forces that cannot be seen with the naked eyes. Kealotswe notes that most of the AICs in Botswana do not agree with the assertion that they mix prayer and traditional healing practices. Instead they revert to the idea that prayer is the

---

[37] Thomas, "South African Independent Churches, Syncretism, and Black Theology", 40-41.
[38] Molato, *Comparative Study of Prophecy between African Independent Churches and African Pentecostal churches*.
[39] Sundkler M. 1961. *Bantu Prophets In South Africa*. London: Oxford University Press.
[40] *Diwacho* is a plural noun for *Siwacho*. The mixtures which are used to make *diwacho* differ from one group to another.

most fundamental element of their healing services, and elements such as traditional herbs are used as a point of contact.[41]

THE IMPACT OF COVID-19 ON CHURCHES IN BOTSWANA

Covid-19 has caused stress in the society, because many people lost jobs due to the lockdown, and many people were affected by the threat of death to themselves and to their families and communities.[42] The financial constraints were also a key reasons why the anxiety among the Batswana increased during Covid-19, especially during the lockdown.[43] Many churches rely on the generosity of their members, and when the members have no form of income, the effectiveness of the church is limited.[44] Some Batswana called on Facebook for men of God, the pastors, to come forth to pray in order to stop the spread of coronavirus In Botswana, as in other countries, there were many hypotheses raised against coronavirus. Some argued that argued that it was the work of the devil and called for men of God stand against it. The argument that many Christians raised about corona being the work of the devil had much to do with the inability of the church to function.[45] Some of the pastors argued that since some of their public service were allowed to function and were deemed to be essential services, they should be given a permit that allowed them to attend their many congregation members who were suffering.[46] In the face of hindrances to their being allowed to do this, many pastors and church members argued that the government did not take the churches seriously.[47]

Some of the church leaders in Botswana advised their church members against the corona vaccine, arguing that it was an omen from the devil and that Western nations wanted to reduce the African populations. Rev Tsuaneng of the secretary of Botswana Council of Churches was quoted in *Botswana Gazette* issuing the following warning to pastors: "We are aware that there are those who peddle untruthful statements about the vaccine and it is quite unfortunate to be having such people within our community, I do not know of any sensible government across the world that can

---

41 Kealotswe, "Acceptance and Rejection", 114.
42 Stone LS, Stone MT, Mogomotsi PK and Mogomotsi MJ. 2021. "The Impacts of Covid-19 On Nature- Based Tourism in Botswana: Implications for community development", *Tourism Review International* 25:265.
43 Stone et al, "The Impact of Covid-19 on Nature-based Tourism", 265.
44 Amanze J and Madigele T. 2021. "Churches and Covid-19 in Botswana", in Sibanda S, Muyambo T and Chitando E. *Religion and the COVID Pandemic in Southern Africa*. London: Routledge, 7.
45 Sibanda F, Muyambo T and Chitando E. 2022. "Religion and Public Health in the Shadow of Covid-19 Pandemic in Southern Africa", in Sibanda et al (eds). Religion and Covid-19 Pandemic in Southern Africa. New York: Routledge, 6.
46 Mothobi T. 2020. Presidential (COVID-19) Task Force. *Botswana Bulletin*, Issue 93, 10 August.
47 Mpuang L. 2020. "The Church Clashes with Gov't over Covid-19 Relief Fund", *Botswana Gazette*, 23 April.

procure with people's money something that is intended to eliminate the whole nation."[48] This kind of behaviour reveals some of the concern from the public about the government procedures to reduce the impact of the corona in the country. The other concern that churches had, was in relation to the opening of churches after the lockdown. Attendance of church members was limited to fifty people per service and two services per week in Botswana.[49] Most of the churches pointed out that students were allowed to go back to school and workers have been allowed to go back to work. Their question was why the church was not being allowed to have their church members at full capacity at a time when they needed spiritual guidance and spiritual leadership. The attendance limits raised some concerns from church members, who complained that the church was being marginalised and being looked down by the government, which did not understand the role of the church in the community.[50]

In a study of church organisations in Botswana, included the Evangelical Fellowship of Botswana (EFB), the Botswana Council of Churches (BCC) and the Organization of African Instituted Churches (OAIC), theologians James Amanze and Tshenolo Madigele noted the impact that coronavirus had among the churches.[51] They noted that the churches experienced financial crises in this period. As such, some of the churches that were renting buildings closed because they did not have the finances to sustain themselves. Moreover, some of the church members experienced depression and stress because their loved ones were dying from coronavirus. The ministers of churches were confined to their houses and could not assist in the way they were used to. The *Botswana Gazette* writer Letlhogile Mpuang captured this point in observing, "The Church relies on offerings and tithes, and since there are no church services, things are now very difficult. Pastors' welfare has significantly changed as a result of the outbreak of the pandemic and also since the extreme social distancing protocols were put into effect."[52]

In their study, Amanze and Tshenolo observed that the churches in Botswana implemented strategies in order to take care of their members. Some of the strategies included forming WhatsApp groups to which sermons were uploaded so that each and every member had access to the word of God. Those living with their families were encouraged to pray and read the Bible as a family. This strategy played a big role in uniting the families, since they could now pray as a family and seek a ways assist one another in dealing with the stress of losing their loved ones to coronavirus.

---

[48] Molelo L. 2021. "Botswana Council of Churches Caution Delinquent Church Leaders Against Covid-19 Vaccine Falsehoods", *Botswana Gazette*, 11 March.
[49] Chikwanah E. 2020. "African church begin to reopen", *UM News*, 9 June.
[50] Amanze and Madigele, "Churches and Covid-19 in Botswana".
[51] Amanze and Madigele, "Churches and Covid-19 in Botswana".
[52] Mpuang, "The Church Clashes with Gov't over Covid-19 Relief Fund".

AFRICAN INDEPENDENT CHURCHES IN BOTSWANA AND THE RESPONSE TO COVID-19

For the present study, a qualitative method was used to undertake the measure of AICs response to Covid-19 in Botswana. As such, six churches were chosen from the different areas of Botswana in order to undertake this study. To capture the responses of the participants, the study used a phenomenological design with both in-person interviews and telephone calls. Phenomenological design is a method that is used in qualitative research, especially in the social sciences and health sciences. According to British researcher Stan Lester, phenomenological research is used "to illuminate the specific, to identify phenomena through how they are perceived by the actors in a situation".[53]

For the present study, the following questions were included in the interviews: (1) How did your church respond to COVID-19? (2) What were the healing method used to heal and help those affected by corona? (3) Are your methods reliable in comparison to Western methods of healing corona? The questionnaire was sent to six AICs in different parts of the country. The participants were required to provide the answers to the questions within a space of a month and half. This allowed them to think through the questions carefully and to process their answer to their own satisfaction. Researchers Mira Crouch and Heather McKenzie have noted that interview questions must guide research and provide valid information that will ultimately enhance the research project.[54] With this in mind, the data collected from the participants was thematised according to the literature review and the interview questions.

FINDINGS REGARDING AFRICAN INDEPENDENT CHURCHES' RESPONSE TO COVID-19 IN BOTSWANA

As the Covid-19 took hold in Botswana, the coronavirus was associated with flu by many AIC members. They argued that the symptoms of flu and Covid-19 were the same and that the effects are the same. The symptoms, such as headaches, sneezing and dizziness, were associated with the novel coronavirus, but they had been seen before in the person suffering with flu. Insofar as they argued that Covid-19 was like flu, they also argued that they already had remedies for coronavirus. The remedies they had used for years in dealing with the flu were same remedies that they could reduce the impact and the effect of coronavirus among their church members. This approach by the AICs practitioners prompted them to overlook Western healing methods, such as vaccination, for they argued that they had been dealing with these issues before the hype which is associated with the coronavirus. Some voices from the AICs argued that they could heal corona in the same way that they did the flu, even though the effects of the coronavirus were more devastating. This approach had a negative effect in neglecting the scientific investigations; however, it also

---

[53] Lester S. 1999. "An introduction to phenomenological research", *ResearchGate*, January.

[54] Crouch M and McKenzie H. 2006. "The logic of small samples in interview-based qualitative research", *Social Science Information* 45(4):485.

has some positive effects in reducing fears that engulfed the population.[55] Healing practitioners in the AICs used this psychological approach in dealing with those affected by corona to reassure them and reduce anxiety levels. The question was whether this approach could be replicated broadly to reduce both collective and individual anxieties.

Water

The main healing remedy that the AICs in Botswana use is water. Water is most often perceived as a link or a point of contact that induces faith and releases healing from God. The common use of water in the AICs involves sprinkling and also steaming, the latter process known as *go aramela*.[56] One of the study participants argued that they had been using *go aramela* steaming method for a long time, and now the scientific method of healing was attempting to hijack the traditional method, even though the latter was gaining new popularity during the time of Covid-19. Since one of the symptoms of coronavirus is fever and steaming has been used to cure fever, it was easy for the AICs' healers to recommend steaming as a cure for coronavirus.[57] Steaming came to be perceived as important in preventing coronavirus by opening up the nasal passages and thereby easing a stuffy nose; however, experts are divided with regard to its effectiveness.[58]

The AICs' recommendation of steaming is grounded in a theology of water that is common in African traditional religions.[59] In this way, the theology of water as a healing remedy is rooted in the African culture.[60] In the North-West District of Botswana, when the water flows from the river, people use it to clean themselves from things like bad luck and also to bring themselves fortune. Culturally, it is perceived as possessing powers that can heal even severe sicknesses. In some instances, some AIC healers prefer to use seawater.[61] This use of water is considered to be more powerful than the anointing oil that is usually used in the Pentecostal-charismatic churches.[62] In this way, the AICs drew on a theology and cosmology of water as a healing motif in the coronavirus pandemic.

---

55 World Health Organization (WHO). "Doing What Matters in Times of Stress: An Illustrated Guide", *WHO.int*, 29 April 2020.
56 Carrasco LN, Zulu M and Bukasa KP. "Steaming in the fringes; healing rituals in Johannesburg", *International Journal of Complementary & Alternative Medicine* 12(2):59.
57 Orisakwe OE, Orish CN and Owanaforo EO. 2020 "Coronavirus disease (Covid-19) and Africa: Acclaimed home remedies", *Scientific African* November:1-5.
58 Zeeman K. 2021. "Does steaming really help fight Covid-19?", *Sunday Times*, 9 July.
59 Kealotswe, "Acceptance and Rejection", 114.
60 Hagan G. 2020. "Water and Spirituality in some African Cultures and Traditions", Vatican Commission on Covid-19, 1. Online at: https://www.humandevelopment.va/content/dam/sviluppoumano/water-resources/33.pdf [Accessed 16 December 2022].
61 Kealotswe, "Acceptance and Rejection", 114.
62 Molato K and Dube M. 2021. "The Christic Okavango Delta of Botswana", in Chirongoma S and Kiilu W (eds). *Mother Earth, Mother Africa and World Religions and Environmental Imaginations*. Third Edition. Stellenbosch: African Sun Media, 46.

Plants

One of the plants that the participants note that it is helpful in reducing the effects of corona in the body is called *legala la Badimo*, literally translated as "coal of the ancestors". They note that this plant is mostly found in the mountainous and top of the hills. It is believed that this plant encapsulates smoke that has a touch of the ancestors, which no flu can withstand. According to the participants, the plant has been used from the time immemorial to deal with flu, and it has been found that it can also heal corona. The healing remedy from this plant is contained in its smoke. The sick person must inhale the smoke and allow the smoke to reach their lungs. The smoke reaches to the inner being of the person, including the lungs, which the AIC practitioners believe are hugely affected by coronavirus. These practitioners state that if the pain does not dissipate, they add additional plants known as *legala la Tshwane*, which is literally translated to "baboon coal".

The second plant that these practitioners think is helpful is a root of a tree called blackthorn (*Acacia mellifera*). The healing practitioners explain that when blackthorn is applied to chest, it relieves the pain from affecting someone who is sick. Scientifically, blackthorn is used to "treat colds, breathing conditions, cough, fluid retention, general exhaustion, upset stomach, kidney and bladder problems, and constipation; and to treat and prevent stomach spasms."[63] When I mentioned this to one of the participants, he noted that the problem with the scientific healing methods is that they always steal indigenous ideas and then present the effects without reference to their roots in the indigenous practices. AIC participants note that what makes the blackthorn roots effective, as compared to Western medicine, is that it is used and applied to a sick person mostly in the healing clinics. It is believed that the presence of God is significantly present in the healing clinics. One of the AIC members postulated that she might be sick when she is at home, but when she reaches the healing clinic, the sickness often disappears.

Syncretism

The question that is paramount to this study in linking the indigenous or the syncretic method of healing with the modern medicine is whether the remedies mentioned above can be replicated and confirmed in a scientific laboratory. This is crucial in trying to establish a link between the faith-healing method and the scientific method of healing. Undergirding this is the question of borrowing some healing remedies from the scientific healing motif and the syncretism healing atonement motif, which is the mixing Christianity and traditional African healing concepts. To be sure, there has been demonisation of the indigenous healing motif by many scientific healing practices.

Research carried out by Tongarasei and Kealotswe has noted that though the scientific method of healing is perceived as taking precedence over the faith-healing methods and indigenous healing method not only in theory, but also in practice,

---

63 "Blackthorn", Supplemented.co.uk, 2 October 2020.

the syncretic method of healing by the AICs healing practitioners is preferred by the people.[64] But even though the traditional methods described above are useful in dealing with coronavirus, study participants noted that they cannot heal or approach a person who is sick without God's guidance. Above all, they argue that it is God who guides on what to do when the person is sick, especially with relation coronavirus. So, whether the method is traditional or scientific, all healing ultimately comes from God in their view. Thus, there is an irreducible religious and spiritual element to healing.

CONCLUSION

The syncretic method, which is the mixing of Christian faith with the traditional means of healing, remained one of the leading methods of healing coronavirus in Botswana, even though the government ultimately required every citizen in the country to be vaccinated. The government of Botswana prohibited people to travel, especially those who were leaving the country, if they were not vaccinated. In places such as government offices, there was an obligation by the government to make sure that all their workers were vaccinated. However, the traditional means of healing practised in the African Independent Churches still remained the most relied upon means of healing in the country. Would AIC healing practitioners have used Western forms of healing coronavirus without the intervention of the government and to what extent would Batswana have used vaccination without the intervention of the government remain interesting questions for further research.

The objective of this study was to find out how the AICs in Botswana responded to the coronavirus using syncretic methods of healing. This chapter started by presenting the impact of the coronavirus in Botswana, focusing on the churches. Churches in Botswana, including the AICs, were affected in a tremendous way, which led to the closing of the churches in Botswana. The role of the church, especially the pastors' ability to attend to church members who were affected by coronavirus, was seriously constrained and the pastors were not allowed to attend their members. This was very different from history of AICs in Botswana and their previous responses to plagues and pandemics.

Though the syncretic healing method had long been described in derogatory terms by those who thought that their theological or scientific motif of healing were superior, positive use was made of syncretic methods by AICs in order to reduce the impact of coronavirus among their members. AICs in Botswana treated coronavirus as nothing more than a flu, which turned out to be an approach that actually had a positive impact upon those affected by coronavirus by reducing depression and anxiety levels through analogy to epidemics with which they had successfully dealt in the past. The AICs used traditional medicine methods, such as *go aremela*, *legala la Badimo* and *legala la Tshwane* that had been used to heal flu in a robust example of the syncretism healing atonement motif.

---

64 Togarasei et al, "'Quinine', 'Ditaola' and the 'Bible'".

23 HEALING AND DELIVERANCE IN THE CONTEXT OF THE COVID-19 PANDEMIC IN NOMIYA CHURCH, EASTLEIGH, KENYA

Fancy Cheronoh[1]
Telesia Kathini Musili[2]

INTRODUCTION

Pandemics are generally alarming and scary due to lack of adequate knowledge of their cause and treatment. Though there have been other pandemics in human history, such as influenza, swine flu and others, the Covid-19 pandemic shocked the whole world, including global economies, due to the contagious nature of its spread and the lack of knowledge of how the transmission would unfold, let alone the fatality rate envisaged. Kenya confirmed her first case on 12 March 2020.[3] Containment recommendations, such as wearing of masks, social distancing and closure of schools and churches, were issued by governments in collaboration with World Health Organization (WHO). In Kenya, physical worship was banned, and Kenyans were encouraged to observe social distancing. Some counties, such as Nairobi, were placed under lockdown and curfew was imposed in the country.

Myths and misconceptions about the virus were fronted from different circles. In Africa, particularly, due to low fatality rates reported in comparison to the Western world, myths were propagated regarding Africa's alleged resistance to coronavirus. Although there were fewer cases of Covid-19 related deaths reported in Africa in comparison to other parts of the world,[4] there is no scientific proof to support such myths. Unfortunately, some government leaders propagated these myths through their utterances and reactions towards measures issued by WHO to contain the spread of the virus. A leader of one Eastern Africa nation, for instance, reportedly championed the use of steam therapy as a form of treatment for Covid-19. Another was recorded declaring his nation corona-free due to the prayers made by the citizens.[5] Madagascar is perhaps the most notable nation in Africa for coming up with the Covid Organics (CVO) from the artemisia plant, which the country

---

1   Lecturer, Department of Philosophy and Religious Studies, University of Nairobi, Kenya.
2   Lecturer, Department of Philosophy and Religious Studies, University of Nairobi, Kenya.
3   World Health Organization (WHO), Regional Office for Africa. 2021. "Media Briefings on Covid-19", WHO. Online at: https://www.health.go.ke/wp-content/uploads/2020/03/Statement-on-Confirmed-Covid-19-Case-13-March-2020-final-1.pdf
4   https://www.science.org/content/article/pandemic-appears-have-spared-africa-so-far-scientists-are-struggling-explain-why
5   "Coronavirus: John Magufuli declares Tanzania free of Covid-19", *BBC*, 8 June 2020.

promoted as a remedy to Covid-19.[6] Some people believed these myths to be true, hence their rejection of the Covid-19 vaccination.

Health and well-being are part of our daily concerns. Governments have invested in the health sector, financially and legislatively, at the individual, regional and national levels. The right to health, first articulated internationally in the 1946 Constitution of the World Health Organization, remains one of the fundamental human rights in most nations.[7] The preamble of the WHO constitution further states that "the enjoyment of the highest attainable standard of health is one of the fundamental rights of every human being without distinction of race, religion, political belief, economic or social condition."[8] The 1948 Universal Declaration of Human Rights mentions health as part of the right to an adequate standard of living.[9] According to the Office of the United Nations High Commissioner for Human Rights (OHCHR) and the WHO "the right to health is relevant to all States: every State has ratified at least one international human rights treaty recognizing the right to health".[10] Furthermore, "states have committed themselves to protecting this right through international declarations, domestic legislation and policies, and at international conferences."[11] In Kenya, for example, the Kenya Health Act 2017 states in Section 5(1) that "every person has the right to the highest attainable standard of health which shall include progressive access for provision of promotive, preventive, curative, palliative and rehabilitative services."[12] In pursuance of this right, the government of Kenya, in collaboration with the WHO, introduced a universal health coverage programme. Its implementation has led to increased access to health services with an addition of more than 200 community health units, 7 700 community health volunteers and over 700 healthcare workers recruited.[13] The ongoing reforms in the National Hospital Insurance Fund (NHIF), the mandatory universal health coverage scheme and the provision of health coverage for low-income households, among other health reforms, require support from different sectors of the society, including religious institutions.

Health remains an integral focus of faith in all religions of the world. Religion has influenced health practices in societies throughout human history to a great extent. Adam Chepkwony, a professor of comparative religion and an ardent propagator of African indigenous religion, notes in this regard that, "the redemptive messages

---

6   "Coronavirus: John Magufuli declares Tanzania free of Covid-19".
7   Office of the United Nations High Commissioner for Human Rights (OHCHR). 2008. "The Right to Health", OHCHR/WHO Factsheet No. 31. Geneva: OHCHR.
8   OHCHR, "The Right to Health".
9   Universal Declaration of Human Rights, G.A. res. 217A (III), U.N. Doc A/810 at 71 (1948), art 25.
10 UDHR, art 25.
11 UDHR, art 25.
12 Health Act, 2017, 5(1).
13 World Health Organization (WHO). 2020. "Keeping to the Universal Health Coverage Path in Kenya", WHO.int, 11 December.

taught by all religions are expressed in terms of deliverance from a state of bad health to acceptable and full health as expected and intended by the creator."[14] Health and healing remain an important part of African spirituality, despite the introduction of other religions, such as Christianity, that sought to civilise Africans and to discourage beliefs and practices associated with traditional healing that were considered to be superstitious, barbaric and unscientific. The unique and strong affinity of African spirituality and holistic well-being caused many Africans to experience in the newly found Christian faith an emptiness of healing that they considered inadequate. This is because Christian faith introduced Western medicine and constructed hospitals to heal the sick using modern scientific methods of healing, disregarding African indigenous medicine. Consequently, "Africans who belonged to mission churches left and formed independent churches outside mission control to enable them infuse elements of African spirituality in their faith."[15]

One such church is Nomiya Church, the first African Independent Church {AIC} in Kenya. As African religion scholar Ezra Chitando rightly notes about AICs, these churches have achieved remarkable success in holistic health and healing through their religious teachings and rituals. They have adopted African interpretations of disease and use African approach to healing, thus providing an alternative therapeutic system of holistic healing.[16] Many have adopted the African cosmotheandric view of life propagated by African scholars, such as Chioma Ohajunwa.[17] The three-dimensional relational approach to life includes human beings, nature and spiritual beings. Well-being is understood holistically as encompassing multiple aspects of life, including individuals, family, kinship, community, ancestors, the physical world and future generations. A disturbance of the relationship among any of the above entities, such as through pandemics, affects the living, non-living and spiritual beings. Holistic healing in such contexts becomes paramount. This African indigenous approach to well-being and existence is used in this chapter to show how the Covid-19 pandemic, which disrupted life in its entirety, called for holistic healing. Furthermore, AICs such as Nomiya Church use African indigenous conceptions, experiences and practices of well-being which are cosmotheandric in nature. This chapter thus examines how holistic healing and deliverance was facilitated by Nomiya Church during the Covid-19 pandemic period, particularly when the government of Kenya banned physical worship and issued measures requiring social distancing and lockdown.

---

14 Chepkwony AK. 2019. "An Understanding of Healing in African Christianity: The Interface between Religion & Science", *East African Journal of Arts and Social Sciences*, 4(1):22.

15 Chepkwony, "An Understanding of Healing in African Christianity", 23.

16 Cox LT and ter Haar G (eds). 2003. *Uniquely African? African Christian Identity from Cultural and Historical Perspectives.* Asmara: African World Press, Inc.

17 Ohajunwa C. 2019. "Indigenous spirituality within formal health care practice", in Mji G (ed). *The walk without limbs: Searching for indigenous health knowledge in a rural context in South Africa.* Cape Town: AOSIS.

HEALTH AND HEALING IN AFRICAN INDEPENDENT CHURCHES

Health and well-being remain at the core of African being and existence. Rituals and ceremonies surrounding the rites of passage generally depict the central place of human life and well-being among Africans. Health and well-being among Africans concerns not only the living, but also extends to the unborn and the living dead. Africans thus feel at peace when their relationship with God, spirits, fellow human beings and the living and non-living things is good.[18] A broken relationship between these beings causes disaster, which affects not only the individual, but also the rest of the family, clan, community and even the nation at large. Sickness, illness and even pandemics may befall the living as a result of broken relationship with the spiritual beings.[19] It is from this strong belief that some Africans interpreted Covid-19 as a curse from God due to some evil committed by the living. Consequently, as Nahashon Ndung'u, a scholar of African Independent Churches, notes, there is a need for a remedy to bring back the wholeness of life to the people. Such a solution would be acquired through rituals that might include offering of animal sacrifices to seek absolution from the spiritual beings. This process of restoring the right relationship with the spiritual realm can be seen as a healing process.[20] In one county in Kenya, for instance, the Kipsigis elders, conducted a ritual by the river to cast out the spell of coronavirus in the country. They offered a ram, which was slaughtered and its blood poured into a river. The belief is that as the water flows, washing away the blood, so shall coronavirus be directed away.[21] Some AICs have adopted this form of healing, which at times is performed through exorcism.

Healing, understood in its wider sense as the restoration of the wholeness of life – social, personal, cosmic and communal – is thus not new to Africans. Africans have practiced health and healing in unique ways long before the introduction of Christianity, Western medicine and education. The uniqueness is founded in the African cosmotheandric perception of life which includes the spiritual realm, human beings and the environment – a mix of living and non-living things.[22] It is for this reason that Edwina Ward, a pastoral theologian, concluded from a comparative study of African and Western understandings of health and healing that "in the case of illness it is (not really much the individual who needs healing but) mainly the

---

18 Mbiti JS. 1969. *African Religions and Philosophy*. Nairobi: Heinemann, 2.
19 Mbiti, *African Religions and Philosophy*, 2.
20 Ndung'u NW. 2009. "Persistence of Features of Traditional Healing in the Churches in Africa: The Case of the Akurinu Churches in Kenya", *Thought and Practice: A Journal of the Philosophical Association of Kenya (PAK)* 1(2):87.
21 Kilonzo SM and Omwalo BO. 2021. "The Politics of Pulpit Religiosity in the Era of Covid-19 in Kenya", *Frontiers in Communication* 6: art 616288.
22 Panikkar R. 2006. *The Cosmotheandric Experience. Emerging Religious Consciousness*. Beijing: Beijing Religious Cultural Publishing House.

broken relationships."[23] Every African community therefore has ways of dealing with life-threatening forces, such as diseases, floods, droughts, barrenness, curses and witchcraft, among others. These forces are believed to be caused by evil spirits and human agents through witchcraft and magic.[24] According to prolific African theologians Laurenti Magesa[25] and John Mbiti,[26] anti-life forces can be seen as part of religious experiences. Consequently, they require religious approaches to be dealt with properly. As a renowned professor of religion with keen interest in AICs, Gerhardus Oosthuizen notes that, for diseases that are not peculiar to African cosmology, a combination of Christian and traditional methods might be used.[27] Rinaldo Rozani, a Roman Catholic priest and pastoral theologian, supports holistic approach to health and healing by asserting that "the combination of both scientific skills as well as resources from a spiritual view seems to be the last approach, as it deals with the whole person."[28]

The scientific approach to the Covid-19 pandemic no doubt required religious support, as it shook different pillars of the society. In African traditional societies, this approach would include the services of medicine people, who offer not only physical but also psychological healing. Psychological healing, in John Mbiti's view, is the equivalent of spiritual healing in the contemporary society.[29] The Covid-19 pandemic caused fear, anxiety, tension, confusion and stigmatisation, all of which affected people psychologically. Churches, including AICs, provided necessary support through prayers, counselling, home visits and material support, among other forms, to support holistic healing, despite the Covid-19 protocols of social distancing and bans on physical worship. In this chapter therefore, the term healing is used in a holistic sense to imply "putting in order those systems, structures and feelings which have been disrupted causing imbalances and suffering in the life of individuals and society at large."[30] Deliverance also implies and may entail exorcism of evil spirits believed to be involved in the Covid-19 crisis. Covid-19 measures on social distancing, lockdown and ban on physical worship disrupted holistic well-being, as human beings were alienated from one another. The physical, psychological, emotional and spiritual well-being was interfered with, prompting holistic approaches from churches as further discussed below.

---

23 Ward E. 2002. "Similarities and Differences in Cross-Cultural Pastoral Supervision", *Journal of Theology for South Africa* July:51-64.

24 Ndung'u, "Persistence of Features of Traditional Healing in the Churches in Africa".

25 Magesa L. 1997. *African Religion: The Moral Traditions of Abundant Life*. MaryKnoll, NY: Orbis Books, 159.

26 Mbiti, *African Religions and Philosophy*, 169.

27 Oosthuizen GC. 1992. *The Healer-Prophet in Afro-Christian Churches*. Leiden: EJ Brill, 86.

28 Ronzani R. 2007. *Christian Healing: The anointing of the Sick*. Nairobi: Paulines Publications, 18.

29 Mbiti, *African Religions and Philosophy*, 169.

30 Ndung'u, "Persistence of Features of Traditional Healing in the Churches in Africa", 89.

THE IMPACT OF SOCIAL DISTANCING AND THE BANNING OF PHYSICAL WORSHIP ON THE COMMUNAL OPERATIONS OF NOMIYA CHURCH, EASTLEIGH

Before delving into adaptive methods and mechanisms adopted by Nomiya Church towards the ends of holistic healing and deliverance during the pandemic period, it is imperative to consider the impact of the government measures of social distancing and the ban on physical church worship on the communal operations of the church. Social distancing, understood among Nomiya Church's members to imply physical distancing, affected the operations of the church, since it is highly communal in nature. Church fellowship in Nomiya is generally face-to-face human fellowship and interaction of people in a physical space. A typical worship gathering at Nomiya is where believers come to church, sit together and interact at a human level. Sharing personal experiences in the form of testimonies of what God has done or the tough experiences that one is undergoing is part of the church service. Believers share these experiences before the sermon is preached, so that in case one wants encouragement or prayers, the pastor can attend to it accordingly. Due to social distancing and the ban on physical worship, believers were prevented from sharing these experiences and feeling part of the community of believers. Though they could post prayer requests through the Facebook platform that the church adopted, they could not express themselves as fully as they would in a physical worship service.

In addition, Nomiya observes two important liturgical rites, male circumcision and infant baptism, which are celebrated communally. These rites are highly symbolic and provide a strong sense of identity to Nomiya members, distinguishing them from other African Independent Churches. Male infant circumcision at eight days, for instance, is the pride of every male adherent.[31] The rite involves different groups in the church, who are assigned specific roles during the celebration. The climax of the ceremony is *yepo*, a welcome and readmission service of the mother after childbirth, which is conducted in the church led by the *Simeon-Ka-Lawi*, the name given to the priest who takes the role of Simeon when he received baby Jesus and his parents during the purification and dedication ceremony in the gospel of Luke 2.[32] Social distancing and the ban on physical worship deterred believers from celebrating these liturgical rites, which had to be postponed or at times celebrated by the families with only a few church leaders in attendance.

The ban on physical worship further affected the church's financial position. Collection of offerings, tithes and funds to support the bereaved families is an important part of Nomiya's worship service. The church's treasurer, assisted by a member from the congregation, collects money from every member of the church, calling out names and the amount given by each member. A record is kept for the tithes and

---

31 Sudhe SO. 2018. *The Socio-Cultural and Theological Context of The Double Rite of Passage in Nomiya Church in Rarieda Sub-County, Siaya County*. Unpublished PhD Thesis, Maseno University, 115.

32 Sudhe, *The Socio-Cultural and Theological Context of The Double Rite of Passage"*, 115.

offerings for the purposes of transparency, accountability and tracking a believer's commitment. A special giving towards the bishop and the church's pastor is done on a Sunday set aside by the church. It is a special moment for the believers to receive blessings from church leaders through giving, both in cash and in kind. Believers feel that for them to get blessings from the church leaders, the gift should be hand-delivered to the church leader in the church. Giving through digital platforms, such as Mpesa, is thus perceived as a formality rather than a blessing. Some members thus slackened in their online giving, which affected the general operations of the church.

Visiting each other at homes during happy and sad moments is central to Nomiya's community. Believers visit each other when sick, bereaved or when celebrating graduations of their children. What defines love to them is how they treat each other, not only in church, but also in their homes. As an example, on one occasion, a member stood up during a church service and expressed dissatisfaction with church members who had not attended her daughter's graduation party at her home. This was long after the government had lifted the ban on physical gathering, and she had expected that most members would attend. During the lockdown and due to social distancing, believers could not visit each other to console one another or celebrate together. Only a few church leaders, most often the bishop, could visit the bereaved members.

Furthermore, believers in Nomiya accompany the bereaved families throughout the mourning period. They not only visit them in their homes, but also accompany them in burying the dead. They organise a common means of transport to accompany the funeral cortege from Nairobi to upcountry in western parts of Kenya. Covid-19 protocols that limited the number of people attending burials and the time limit within which a dead body was to be interred, denied Nomiya's believers opportunities to express love for one another during such sorrowful moments. One member who had lost a loved one during the Covid-19 period felt left out when his church members could not accompany him to bury his son. Though they took photographs and shared them with the church members through WhatsApp, but the absence of their physical presence meant a lot to him.

HEALING AND DELIVERANCE IN NOMIYA CHURCH IN THE CONTEXT OF THE COVID-19 PANDEMIC

As indicated earlier, Nomiya Church is the first African Independent Church in Kenya. The church is widely spread among the Dholuo-speaking people in Kenya. Nomiya Church, Eastleigh, is the headquarters of Nairobi diocese, which has four parishes and eight churches. Like other churches, Nomiya was greatly affected by the Covid-19 pandemic. The church, which is characterised by a convivial nature of worship with rigorous Luo dancing and clapping of hands, was forced to close her doors when physical church worship was banned in Kenya. The Covid-19 pandemic and subsequent containment measures, such as social distancing and the ban on physical worship, generally affected the communal operations of the church. Consequently, many churches, including Nomiya, had to adopt adaptive mechanisms to facilitate holistic healing among their members. The church had to move worship services to online spaces in order to address the needs of their members. In addition, they had to offer holistic support to their members, who were not only spiritually affected, but also socially, emotionally and physically deprived by the pandemic.

Prayers

Prayers receive a lot of attention in times of crises such as war, diseases, casualties, natural calamities and pandemics. The Covid-19 pandemic was no exception, especially given its contagious nature and spread. Prayers were offered in different parts of the world by the faithful, who sought divine intervention to a disease that shuddered the world. The president of Kenya declared 21 March 2020 a National Prayer Day, and he hosted religious leaders from different denominations led by Interreligious Council of Kenya (IRCK) at State House, Nairobi, for interfaith intercessory prayers dubbed "prayers of forgiveness". The prayers sought God's intervention to spare the nation from doom if the people turned away from their evil ways.[33] The president further called for a national holiday, dubbed Huduma (selfless service) Day, on 10 October 2020 and declared a weekend of prayer, with interfaith prayers held at State House, Nairobi. These two examples point to the significance of prayers during times of crisis. It further indicates the healing role of prayers, which is not necessarily physical, but importantly emotional, psychological and metaphysical.

Through prayers and messages of hope given by religious leaders through different forms of media, Kenyans felt encouraged to brace themselves through the pandemic, despite the challenges they had to endure. In these prayers, messages such as "Do not be anxious about anything, but in prayer and supplication, make your requests known to God and the peace of God, which transcends all understanding, will guard your hearts and your minds in Christ Jesus (Phil. 4:6-7)"[34] were repeatedly chanted. The Secretary General of Hindu Council of Kenya (HCK) encouraged Kenyans to be calm and to remain hopeful during the pandemic period using the following words from Hindu scriptures: "He takes care of all that breathes and all that does not breathe. He has got all this conquering power. He is the one and one alone and the only one. All these luminous forces of nature become one in him."[35]

Nomiya Church leaders prayed for their members and the nation at large in church and at home. They met in the church on Sunday morning to offer prayers before and after the service, which was streamed live through Facebook. In addition, the bishop visited members in their homes, especially the bereaved and the sick.

---

33 State House, Kenya. 2020. "The National Day of Prayer Service", *Facebook*, 21 March.
34 Inter-religious Council of Kenya. 2020. "Be Anxious of Nothing", African Council of Religious Leaders/Religions for Peace, May.
35 "Program for National Day at State House", *The Citizen*, 21 March 2020.

Social distancing and the imposed curfew limited such visits, which offered crucial emotional support. During these prayers, clergy and church members quoted passages from scripture, such as "You are the temple of the living God. Not the temple of weakness, decrepitude, sickness, dullness and distress, but the temple of strength, health and beauty",[36] by which they offered spiritual healing to those who were affected by the pandemic. These prayers were a source of hope and comfort to the sick in body and at heart.

Scholarly views from different fields, including sociology and psychology, indicate the importance of prayers in health and healing. Christian Science adherent Peter Ross notes that "we speak of man as both mind and body, mind being the upper, the more ethereal layer, and body the lower or grosser. But they are both mental, both parts of the same mentality."[37] Consequently, "since the body is mental and disease is mental, all types of disease respond to metaphysical or spiritual treatment."[38] In his view, spiritual healing addresses physical and mental distress. Spiritual healing, practiced in Nomiya Church through prayers aimed at exorcising the evil spirits, was necessary with Covid-19 pandemic, since people sometimes needed spiritual and mental deliverance from the myths, misconceptions and fears about the coronavirus. Some people were psychologically and mentally sick due to isolation, quarantine and lockdowns, which did not allow family members to interact with their loved ones. Furthermore, bereavement was made a family affair with the dead being hurriedly buried in the presence of a few family members. In fact, at the onset of the pandemic, those who died from Covid-19 pandemic were hurriedly buried even at night without any of the family members allowed to attend. Prayers offered during and after such sorrowful moments soothed the crying soul, thus facilitating holistic healing of the body, soul and mind. As Ross further notes, prayers offer metaphysical treatment to a sick body. Prayers permeated with sympathy, comfort, tenderness, compassion and cheer and soothe the soul and the body.[39] Nomiya Church transcended Ross's views of spiritual healing by addressing the holistic aspects of human beings by including physical, social and emotional healing.

Exorcism

Beliefs about evil spirits and demons and the practice of exorcism remain part and parcel of most AICs. These churches draw significantly from African spirituality and African experiences. According to African religion scholars, Hennie Pretorius and Lazio Jafta, exorcism is one of the main characteristics of many AICs, where

---

36 Interview with Nomiya adherent by F Cheronoh and T Musili in Eastleigh Parish, Nairobi Kenya, on 5 December 2021.
37 Ross PV. 1946. *Leaves of Healing: Method of Metaphysical Treatment*. New York: Hobson Book Press.
38 Ross, *Leaves of Healing*, 132.
39 Ross, *Leaves of Healing*, 133.

religious leaders cast out devils through examples drawn from biblical sources such as Matthew 10:1-8.[40]

The practice of healing through exorcism in most AICs has, however, taken different forms over time. Exorcism or deliverance from evil powers of the world in the Nomiya Church derives its impetus from deliverance practices in the Bible, which have greatly influenced their healing practices. An example commonly used at Nomiya and also used by preachers in other churches is the story of Simon's mother-in-law recorded in Luke 4:38-39. Drawing from different biblical versions, the following words, interpreted from the passage, would be heard in exorcism prayers: "As soon as the spirit behind the fever heard, understood and obeyed, the fever left her and she was healed." Church leaders commanded the evil spirit behind Covid-19 declaring God to be great, greater than any power in this world, through invocations such as *Nyasaye Duong', Duong' ni Duong'* (God is Great, His greatness is great).[41]

Exorcism, which takes the form of prayer in the contemporary Nomiya Church was offered through chanting of words meant to chase away the evil spirit. This is based on the belief that the real forces behind the world of physical matter are spiritual and that the real cause of sickness is neither mental nor physical, but rather spiritual. A spiritual approach is thus required in order to cast away the evil forces, hence exorcism. The use of anointing oil, holy water and handkerchiefs, among other symbolic materials, was not part of exorcism or healing procedures in Nomiya as was witnessed in other churches during the pandemic period. Prayers invoking God's name and his greatness to cancel the powers of coronavirus were offered by church leaders without much dramatisation. Church members would follow the prayers online through Facebook Live. The believers would at times meet in their homes and conduct prayers, even though government measures limited such physical gatherings.

Material support

The emergence of the Covid-19 pandemic brought dire social, economic, physical and mental issues. Many world economies faced a slowdown in their economic activities, at individual, organisational and national levels. Poverty levels increased, especially in developing countries. This can be attributed to the Covid-19 containment measures of lockdown, social-distancing and quarantine, which rendered many people jobless. A survey by Twaweza, a Kenyan nongovernmental organisation, in March 2021, showed that 60% of Kenyan families could no longer afford three meals per day.[42] During the first four months of the Covid-19 pandemic,

---

40 Pretorius H and Jafta LA. 1997. "Branch Springs Out: African Initiated Churches", in Elphick R and Davenport R (eds). *Christianity in South Africa: A Political, Social & Cultural History*. Cape Town: David Philip, 211-226.

41 Sudhe, *The Socio-Cultural and Theological Context of The Double Rite of Passage*.

42 Mulinya B. 2021. "Covid Plunging Many Kenyans Deeper into Poverty", *VOA News*, 7 March.

more than 1.7 million Kenyans experienced job losses.[43] Unemployment rates nearly doubled with the reduced job opportunities. The working hours and earnings of wage workers were cut, impacting families heavily. Most families that relied solely on the income of their small businesses experienced significantly reduced revenue, while others closed their businesses due to lockdown restrictions and hard economic times. Food security became a major concern for many families. Some families could not afford food, while others could only afford one or two meals per day. According to Twaweza, more Kenyans were worried about where their next meal would come from than their health care in the last six months of 2020.[44]

Families were also broken with increased cases of gender-based violence (GBV). A survey by Liverpool Voluntary Counselling and Testing (LVCT) Health, a Kenyan nongovernmental organisation, indicated that in one and half months following the Covid-19 lockdown in Kenya, a total of 793 adolescent and young women presenting to their clinics reported experiencing violence, a stark increase from pre-Covid times.[45] Physical violence increased from 33% to 43%, while sexual violence doubled from 2.5% to 5%. According to a report by the UN Country Team in Kenya, calls to GBV hotlines increased by 775% in March and April 2020.[46] This meant that an additional 3 650 cases of GBV were reported between March and the end of July.[47] Consequently, some families separated, while others divorced, challenging the core mandate of parenthood where both the mother and the father are expected to complement one another in parental responsibilities.

As a result, churches had to provide material support to those among their members who were greatly affected by the pandemic. At Nomiya, church leaders mobilised funds and basic commodities, especially foodstuffs, from their members who were able to contribute. It is worth noting here that a majority of Nomiya members in Nairobi County reside in informal settlements characterised by poor standards of living and high poverty levels, as affirmed by UN Habitat, which reported that "an estimated 60-70 per cent of Nairobi's more than 4 million residents reside in urban informal settlements".[48] Church members donated foodstuffs such as cooking flour, cooking oil, milk, baking flour and even maize. Some contributed cash, which was collected through the church's WhatsApp group.[49] Food items would be assembled

---

43 Mulinya, "Covid Plunging Many Kenyans Deeper into Poverty".
44 Mulinya, "Covid Plunging Many Kenyans Deeper into Poverty".
45 Ngunjiri A et al. 2020. "Covid-19 GBV Brief: Violence Against Women and Girls Amidst Covid-19 Pandemic – LVCT Health Experience". Nairobi: LVCT Health.
46 UN Office for the Coordination of Humanitarian Affairs (OCHA). 2020. "Emergency Appeal, Kenya, April-September 2020", *Reliefweb*, 9 April.
47 UN Office for the Coordination of Humanitarian Affairs (OCHA) 2020. "Kenya Situation Report – September 2020".
48 UN-Habitat. 2019. "Kenya Habitat Country Programme Document (2018-2021)". Nairobi: UN-Habitat.
49 Musili TK and Cheronoh F. 2022. "The African value of communality in virtual space amidst Covid-19: The case of WhatsApp welfare communities in Nomiya Church, Eastleigh", Chapter 24 in this volume.

in a central place in the church, where church leaders with the help of some church members would sort them out while noting the quantities. They would then list members whom they knew or had been reported by other church members as being vulnerable. Food items would then be packed in small bags and distributed to each household, depending on what had been collected. Some families would be given small sums of cash to purchase other basic commodities like soap or drinking water when finances allowed. The church did this solely from the contributions of their members and from the church account without the help of any other institution. In so doing, Nomiya provided physical, social and psychological healing to their members. In addition, it brought together the community of believers, including families who had separated or were living together unhappily. Holistic healing, of not just the physical hunger, but also social and communal bonds that had been broken by Covid, was provided by the church in this way.

The church thus fulfilled the greatest commandment, as instructed by Jesus in the Bible: Love one another. Love, they said, is best felt and seen when one is in need. The example of Jesus feeding the five thousand people with five loaves of bread and two fish (Matthew 14:13-21) was cited as a charitable work worth emulating, especially during times of crises, such as the Covid-19 pandemic. The church's theology on feeding her people was drawn from inspirational passages in the Old Testament imploring Israelites to consider the needs of others. For example, Isaiah 58:10 says: "If you give some of your own food to [feed] those who are hungry and to satisfy [the needs of] those who are humble, then your light will rise in the dark, and your darkness will become as bright as the noonday Sun." Likewise, Isaiah 58:7 says: "Share your food with the hungry, and give shelter to the homeless. Give clothes to those who need them, and do not hide from relatives who need your help."

Online communities

The Covid-19 pandemic has proven to be a catalyst for the growing importance of online communities globally. People have embraced online communities due to the desire for a strong sense of belonging. Though people were distanced socially and isolated from one another by the Covid-19 pandemic, online space gave them an opportunity to interact virtually. People connected and continue to do so in new and interesting ways which have hitherto appeared strange to many. Apps and online communities sprang up in the wake of the Covid-19 pandemic as if from nowhere, offering vital services to those who needed them. Meeting apps, such as Zoom and Google Meet, along with complex scientific research apps for collecting data on the spread of the virus, emerged. Zoom, for instance, was relatively unknown among many Kenyans, particularly those who were working outside corporate circles, before the Covid-19 crisis. Today however, church meetings, fundraising, tea parties and international meetings are held using the Zoom app. Apps aimed at encouraging communal ways of living are being introduced. For example, according to the founder of the community media platform Disciple, Benjamin Vaughan, the

National Health Service (NHS) in the U.K. has been promoting new app-based communities designed to give support to struggling parents and teenagers and to connect people with similar health conditions.[50] Though these have not been fully actualised and utilised in Kenya, they are important avenues for social support.

Within Nomiya Church, online communities were formed through WhatsApp and Facebook. The different groups in the church, similar to small Christian communities, held their meetings online with different groups, forming their own WhatsApp group to discuss church matters at group level. A general WhatsApp group for all the members of the Eastleigh church existed through which information concerning church progress, plans and vital Covid-19 information were shared. A Facebook page for the entire parish and a separate one for Nomiya youth within the parish also existed. Church leaders used these platforms to encourage their members, sharing prayers and inspirational messages drawn from the Bible and theological writings. They also encouraged their members to oblige to government Covid-19 protocols urging them to be safe. Church members would also encourage one another by sharing prayers and Bible inspirations among themselves through SMS or WhatsApp. Thus, they connected virtually and practised their spirituality online.

Online communities through WhatsApp groups would also be used to mobilise funds towards supporting bereaved members of the church. If a member lost a loved one, they would communicate this to the pastor, who would then form an online community together with other church leaders in order to communicate the news to the other church members. The church's treasurer would then receive the online contributions, updating every contribution in the WhatsApp group for purposes of transparency. Funeral arrangements would be made through these platforms, and a few church leaders would visit the bereaved families. Since death is inevitable, as noted by one of the members, most of the adherents participated actively in financially and emotionally supporting one another. As a result, online communities became an extension of physical communities, although without replacing, them as rightly noted by digital religion scholar Heidi Campbell in her analysis of religion online and offline.[51] Furthermore, as Benjamin Vaughan asserts, human beings generally are social and have a deep sense of belonging to a community. They thus want to help others and be pro-social at all times.[52]

Church members further supported church activities through online communities. Though tithes and offerings were given at individual level, church contributions, such as the annual contribution per parish, were done at group levels. Group leaders would mobilise their members through their WhatsApp groups to give their contributions, which would then be channeled to the church's treasurer on a given dateline. Church leaders however, noted that such financial support towards the church's activities decreased online in comparison to physical contributions,

---

50 Vaughan B. 2020. "How Online Communities Are Saving the World", *Forbes*, 13 May.
51 Campbell H. 2012. "Understanding the relationship between religion online and offline in a networked society", *Journal of the American Academy of Religion* 80(1):64-93.
52 Vaughan, "How Online Communities Are Saving the World".

where members would feel embarrassed if they remain seated while the rest were giving their support. In addition, economic crises and reduced income caused by the pandemic stretched the financial capacity of most households. Interestingly, these online communities remained active even after the government eased Covid-19 measures to allow full capacity in churches. Most of the members noted that there are times when one needs urgent help that cannot necessarily wait until members congregate together physically on a Sunday. Urgent cases, such as those involving a death, would thus be handled virtually and even physically. In this way, members feel being part of the community and are closely bound together by codes of alternative kinship.

There was also a general increase in ownership of smartphones and tablets and increased internet connectivity among Kenyans during the Covid period. In January 2020, it was estimated that there were 22.86 million internet users in Kenya, representing a 16% increase between 2019 and 2020, and a penetration of 43%. In addition, there were approximately 8.80 million social media users in January 2020, with an increase of 13% between April 2019 and January 2020. Around the same time, there were 52.06 million mobile connections in January 2020.[53] Although such statistics serve as an indication of exponential growth in Kenya's technology, not every Kenyan owns a smartphone. Some Nomiya Church members could not, therefore, utilise these online communities. Some members did not have smartphones that could support these apps. Consequently, these members would rely on their brethren from the church to pass vital information to them relating to church matters. Some felt left out due to mobile inaccessibility, which affected their relationships and interactions with other church members. Challenges of internet connectivity and lack of enough data bundles was a further hindrance to maximum utilisation of the online communities, especially in the informal urban areas that Nomiya Church dominates.

CONCLUSION

This chapter has examined healing and deliverance in Nomiya Church, Eastleigh, in the context of Covid-19 pandemic. The church's communal operations were adversely affected by the government's containment measures, such as social distancing and ban on physical worship. Consequently, the church adopted adaptive mechanisms, such as forming online communities, in order to address the needs of her members. Holistic approach to health and healing drawn from African spirituality and experience was adopted by Nomiya Church, Eastleigh. The psychological, emotional and spiritual needs of the adherents were addressed through prayers that were conducted to deliver people from anxiety, depression and distress caused by the pandemic. Material support was offered by the church to address arising physical and social needs, thus restoring the wholeness of life to her members. An African cosmotheandric view of life and well-being was affirmed

---

53   Kemp S. 202. "Digital 2020 Kenya", *DataReportal*, 18 February.

by Nomiya Church's adaptive mechanisms adopted to facilitate holistic healing of their adherents. The church embraced technology and formed online communities through which they shared vital information about Covid-19 and also provided emotional and financial support to their members. This affirms the assumption of the African religion scholar Lovemore Togarasei that "the histories, geographical spaces and traditions of most AICs have been permeated to a great extent by the Internet, WhatsApp, YouTube, Mobile Telephony, Mobile Money Transfers, and the like to transform the ways in which they access the gospel and interrelate".[54] African Independent Churches, such as Nomiya Church, Eastleigh, made use of these new digital spaces to meet the needs of their members towards healing and deliverance from the pandemic.

---

[54] Togarasei L. 2012. "Mediating the Gospel: Pentecostal Christianity and Media Technology in Botswana and Zimbabwe", *Journal of Contemporary Religion* 27(2):257-274.

24 THE AFRICAN VALUE OF COMMUNALITY IN VIRTUAL SPACE AMIDST COVID-19: THE CASE OF WHATSAPP WELFARE COMMUNITIES IN NOMIYA CHURCH, EASTLEIGH

Telesia Kathini Musili[1]
Fancy Cheronoh[2]

INTRODUCTION

The Covid-19 virus crept quickly into Kenya, causing sudden and numerous deaths. Armed with little information on how to inter the bodies of Covid victims, the Ministry of Health issued a directive that "the body must be buried as soon as possible under the supervision of the [healthcare personnel] (HCP), the local health care committee leader and religious leader".[3] Accordingly, the Ministry of Health sought "to provide general guidance and support in management (handling) of the dead in their response to increased deaths associated with the pandemic", particularly with regard to the disinfection of the surfaces and disposal of the bodies and tissues. Thus, the Ministry's guidelines were "developed to ensure the protection, dignity and respect for the deceased individuals and their next of kin".[4] Adherence to the directive was followed, with close family members buried hurriedly and without the customary rituals. However, most indigenous societies in Kenya have elaborate mourning rituals that accompany the departed to the ancestral world.[5] As such, hurried burials contravened African indigenous traditions intended to usher our loved ones to ancestorship.

Bereavement from death causes distress to families and friends. Burial rituals, both traditional and religious, accompany the bereaved families in releasing their loved one and also assist the healing process. As a result of the absence of these rituals, mandated by Covid-19 directives that banned social gatherings and normal burial ceremonies, grieving families were left psychologically traumatised by the hurried burials. Further, physical distancing deterred families from visiting their loved ones who were admitted to hospitals due to Covid-19. Quarantines and isolation centres

---

1 Lecturer, Department of Philosophy and Religious Studies, University of Nairobi.
2 Lecturer, Department of Philosophy and Religious Studies, University of Nairobi.
3 Ministry of Health (MOH) Kenya. 2020. "Interim guidelines on handling of human remains infected with Covid-19 in Kenya". Nairobi: MOH. 2 April, 11.
4 MOH, "Interim guidelines on handling of human remains", 9.
5 See Mbiti JS. 1996. *Introduction to African Religion*. Nairobi/Kampala: East African Educational Publishers; Mugambi J. 1989. "African Heritage: Change and Continuity", in Ojwang JB and Mugambi JNK (eds). 1989. *The S.M. Otieno Case: Death and Burial in Modern Kenya*. Nairobi: Nairobi University Press, 166-179; Mwiti P. 1999. *Understanding Grief as a Process: An Innovative Journey towards Growth and Reconciliation*. Nairobi: Uzima Publishers.

destabilised people's mental stability.[6] The mental health threat and ongoing psychological trauma posed by Covid-19 were unrelenting. This being the case, families and individuals continued to grapple with untold grief for their loved ones who departed during the unfortunate period of hurried burials.

Since adversity is the mother of invention, people came up with ways of navigating this saddening situation. The practice of social distancing forced many people stay at home, indoors and away from their coworkers and relations, a situation that caused disruption and harmony in communal life. The communal component deeply that engrained in African people's ethics would have rendered life almost dysfunctional were it not for virtual communities that were facilitated by a growth in internet technology. Sociologist Manuel Castells defines a virtual community as a "self-defined electronic network of interactive communication organised around a shared interest or purpose".[7] During the pandemic, people took their sociability to the internet, where networking continued remotely. Most families used virtual communities, such as Facebook groups, Zoom meetings, WhatsApp and others, as channels of communication. It is against this backdrop that this chapter examines how the value of communality was appropriated virtually and the effects of these virtual communities in cushioning people's health, well-being and resilience.

This study underlying this chapter employed hybrid ethnographic methods that included participant observation, interviews and virtual ethnography in Nomiya Church, Eastleigh, an African Independent Church in Kenya. The data is a result of a wider research project funded by Nagel Institute, Calvin University, USA, on engaging African realities. The wider project employed a comparative research design, focusing on the African value of communality and religious experiences in the virtual space during the Covid-19 pandemic among churches. Nomiya Church, Eastleigh, the first African indigenous church in Kenya, was selected purposively, since it adopted virtual modes of reaching it members during the Covid-19 pandemic.

Nomiya Church was started by Johana Owalo in 1912. From the Kenya National Archives, a letter from the District Commissioner's Office in Central Kavirondo, Kisumu, dated 9 August 1938, records that the religion was "started by one Johana Owala in 1918", and it was originally called the Nomiya Luo Mission. Johana Owala was a trained teacher, who is said to have incidentally taught Jomo Kenyatta, the first president of Kenya, at the Church Missionary Society (CMS) School in Nairobi. The main tenets of the cult the letter proceeds were: (1) belief in one God (the divinity of Christ is not accepted), (2) total immersion in baptism, (3) male circumcision 8 days after birth, (4) plurality of wives up to four and (5) a claim to preach obedience to

---

6   Hossain MM, Sultana A and Purohit N. 2020. "Mental health outcomes of quarantine and isolation for infection prevention: a systematic umbrella review of the global evidence", *Epidemiology and Health* 42:e2020038.

7   Castells M. 2000. *The information age: Economy, society and culture – the rise of the network society* vol I. Oxford: Blackwell, 386.

the government.⁸ The church is dominated by Luo ethnic group and is also the first independent church in Kenya to engage in secular education purely for her Nomiya members amidst challenges from the colonialists who wanted every child taught Christianity.⁹ The church can be classified as an Ethiopic or nationalistic movement, as it is both a breakaway group from missionary-led churches, such as the Roman Catholic Church and the Anglican Church of Kenya, and also a protest group against missionary paternalism and colonial oppressive structures.¹⁰ The majority of the church's adherents come from the western parts of Kenya, such as Nyanza, and they use their local dialect Dholuo, in their church services.¹¹ This explains why church services are conducted in Dholuo even in urban settings such as in Eastleigh, Nairobi. The church's worship is convivial in nature, with dancing, clapping of hands and drum beating. The movement is highly communal, celebrating life together through religious rituals, such as infant baptism, male circumcision and purification.

Since Nomiya Church is a traditional and patriarchal church, a research assistant was recruited to penetrate these distinct hurdles evident in Nomiya Church for the present study. The research assistant had to be male, an ordained minister and someone who speaks Dholuo. In Nomiya Church, women do not take pastoral leadership positions. The seriousness of the stance is depicted in the fact that no women can sit at the altar, but only in the pews. The research assistant and facilitated translations during interviews, though most leaders still opted to speak in Swahili or English.

At Nomiya Church, Eastleigh, oneness and togetherness resulted in solidarity, which gave rise to resilience in dealing with heartbreaking and emotionally draining events, such as hurried burials witnessed during the early days of Covid-19. The chapter is divided into three sections. The first section delves into the African value of communality as a moral tradition that expresses compassion, reciprocity, dignity, harmony and humanity in the interests of building and maintaining a community with justice and mutual caring.¹² The cases in point revolve around hurried burials

---

8   Letter of the District Commissioner, South Kavirondo, Kisii on African Religions, Nomiya Luo Mission, 19 August 1938. Kenya National Archives, Ref. ADM. 15/17 of 5/8/38.

9   Ndeda MAJ. 2005. "The Nomiya Luo Church: A gender analysis of the dynamics of an African Independent Church among the Luo of Siaya", *Gender, Literature and Religion in Africa*, CODESSRIA Gender Series 4, Dakar, Senegal: Council for the Development of Social Science Research in Africa (CODESSRIA).

10 Sudhe SO, Gumo S and Iteyo C. 2015. "The Socio-Cultural and Historical Basis for the Double Rite of Passage in the Nomiya Church in Kenya", *Sociology and Anthropology* 3(9):464-485.

11 For more information on Nomiya Church see Ndeda MAJ. 2011. *The Nomiya Luo Church: A gender analysis of the dynamics of an African Independent Church in Kenya*. Riga: VDM Verlag Dr Müller; Ndeda MAJ. 2003. "Nomiya Luo Church: A Gender Analysis of the Dynamics of an African Independent Churh in Siaya District, Kenya, c. 1907 to 1963", *Missionalia* 31(2):239-277; Opwapo M. 1981. *Nomiya Luo Church: The dynamics of an African Independent Church among the Luo of Siaya District*. Unpublished Doctoral Thesis, University of Nairobi.

12 See conceptualisation of *Ubuntu* by Nussbaum B. 2003. "African Culture and Ubuntu: Reflections of a South African in America", *World Business Academy* 17(1):2.

and the disruption they had on the value of communality as a result of Covid-19. The second section highlights the WhatsApp platform as a medium where virtual communities appropriated the value of communality after Covid-19 disruptions that destabilised peoples' mental well-being. The third section offers a descriptive analysis of these phenomena on the basis of qualitative data from adherents of the Nomiya Church, Eastleigh, and how they employed WhatsApp welfare groups as avenues of solace and accompanying platforms in upholding the value of communality.

AFRICAN VALUE OF COMMUNALITY AND VIRTUAL COMMUNITIES

Communality as an African worldview denotes the ability to hold relations, shared worldviews, consciousness, expected and acceptable behavioural patterns and socio-political and socio-economic norms to extend to all levels of societal complexity. African philosophers have debated the African's identity of communitarianism, with each taking diverging arguments though agreeing on the sociality that defines African people.[13] Kwasi Wiredu and Kwame Gyekye agree that communality cannot be equated to socialism or collectivism, as we may be lured to think, but that communality in its essence is the intrinsic value, the model personality that defines the undying desire to be one's keeper. It alludes to a warm concern for the well-being of the other.

The African communal ethic embraces the values of oneness, solidarity and well-being. Indigenous Africans express communal feelings, worldviews and moral and cultural values based on closed-knit relationship among their kith and kin within a socio-cultural setting. As an all-encompassing worldview, African communality is convoked in situations and contexts that call for concerted efforts, both good and evil. Philosopher Polycarp Ikuenobe asserts that, "a plausible African communal conception of moral dignity, which is founded on a moral conception of personhood and community, involves a combination of capacity and agency that is conceptually tied to communal responsibility and respect for self and others."[14] To assert this is to argue that human capacities and capabilities are morally good insofar as they are used to promote the moral good of communal well-being on which every individual's well-being or dignity depends.[15] Anything that distorts the balance and congruence in life's realities, such as the Covid-19 pandemic is considered disruptive, hence in need of concerted efforts to ward it off.

---

13 See Wiredu K and Gyekye K. 1992. *Person and community: Ghanaian philosophical studies* vol I. Washington, DC: Council for Research on Values and Philosophy (CRVP); Dismas Masolo DM. 2019. *African philosophy in search of identity*. Edinburgh: Edinburgh University Press.

14 Ikuenobe PA. 2016. "The Communal Basis for Moral Dignity: An African Perspective", *Philosophical Papers* 45(3):438.

15 Polycarp, "The Communal Basis for Moral Dignity", 439.

As Covid-19 ravaged communities, affecting the economic, political, and social well-being of many people, high mortalities and fatalities were witnessed in Nairobi County. Nairobi, the capital city of Kenya, was the most affected by the coronavirus (Covid-19) pandemic. Kenya registered 340 690 cumulative cases, with Nairobi County leading the other counties at 141 556 (41.5%). The total number of cumulative deaths reported since the beginning of the outbreak is 5 680 and Nairobi County recorded a high of 1 558 (27.2%).[16] Hurried and indecent burials devoid of the usual lengthy mourning periods and rituals became a painful new normal, as bodies were transported from the city to the village for hurried burials. Covid-19 infections surged, causing quarantines, isolations and hospital admissions that not only disrupted the oneness of the community, but also negatively impacted its economic, social and mental well-being. Hospital admissions drained families of their savings, leaving them financially unstable and unable to continue with their normal lives, since Covid-19 prevention protocols, such as handwashing with running water and soap and wearing masks, required money to sustain. Huge hospital bills and bereavements under restrictive conditions challenged the normalised communal manner of solidarity. Social stigma rose, as families whose members were known to have died of Covid-19 were segregated from society for several days. Covid-19 mitigation measures, such as quarantine, isolation, curfews, lockdowns and travel restrictions, resulted in the loss of income, disruptions to daily routines and social isolation, laying the ground for negative mental health outcomes among the populace.[17] Depression and suicide cases spiked mostly among caregivers and those affected as they tried to come to terms with the loss of their patients, parents, spouses, children, friends and co-workers.[18] In all manner of senses, communality and sociality were deeply challenged in the face of a foreign virus.

Hurried burials aggravated the situation. Most bodies were buried at night, wrapped in protective gear and not placed in caskets, as is the norm. In most cases, few or no members of the family were allowed at the burial site, especially at the onset of the pandemic. Only healthcare workers handled the body, which was said to be undignified, as no family members were allowed to dress and view the body as is the norm. In most cultures, when a loved one dies, people seek to grieve and to look for comfort and closure. Burial rituals are believed to offer all this, as they connect the living with the ancestral world – thus, they ought to be conducted respectfully.[19]

---

16 For comprehensive statistics on Covid-19 in Kenya, see Ministry of Health, Kenya. 2022. "Covid-19 Outbreak in Kenya: Daily Situation Report" [Accessed 13 November 2022].

17 Jaguga F and Kwobah E. 2020. "Mental health response to the Covid-19 pandemic in Kenya: a review", *International journal of mental health systems* 14(1):1-6.

18 For an elaborate study on mental health challenges in Kenya during Covid-19 see Angwenyi V et al. 2021. "Mental health during Covid-19 pandemic among caregivers of young children in Kenya's urban informal settlements. A cross-sectional telephone survey", *International journal of environmental research and public health* 18(19):10092.

19 See Mbiti JS. 1990. *African religions and philosophies*. Oxford: Portsmouth N.H. Heinemann Educational Publishers. See also Shino W. 1997. "Death and rituals among the Luo in South Nyanza", *African Study Monographs* 18(3/4):213-228, on spiritual connectedness between the living and the dead and the cycle of life from an African perspective.

But given the Covid-19's disruptive component, some members buried their loved ones "virtually" through Facebook, YouTube and Zoom livestreams. Even though these platforms were an option for purposes of closure and respecting the ancestral spirit world, internet data challenges loomed, leaving a majority of the relatives without the experience of accompanying their loved ones to the very end of their earth's journey. Indecent burials were also blamed on meagre resources, as many people had lost their jobs and others working from home with little or nothing to share. Nevertheless, the virtual platforms offered a ray of solace to grieving families, as virtual communities were formed to facilitate variant social events.

The name "virtual community" was coined by Howard Rheingold, a writer and a teacher who was fascinated by the internet, as the modern communication media that influenced the cultural, social and political milieu. In one of his seminal works, *The Virtual Community: Homesteading on the Electronic Frontier*, Rheingold defines virtual communities as "social aggregations that emerge from the [Internet] when enough people carry on those public discussions long enough, with sufficient human feeling, to form webs of personal relationships in cyberspace".[20] For Rheingold, the internet brought people together around shared values and interests that would later form lived experiences. Later sociologists, such as Manuel Castells and online religions renowned scholar Heidi Campbell,[21] agreed with Rheingold on the nature of the personalised human relationships in a digital common space where experiences are borne online.

The shared values and interests that draw people online are not a result of the internet but are a result of lived experiences that shape human values. Indeed, sociologists Barry Wellman and Milena Gulia point out that those virtual communities are not opposed to physical communities, they are just operating in a particular space with differing dynamics, though still keeping the component of sociability.[22] They further argue that virtual communities strengthen the "privatisation of sociability",[23] that is, the building of social networks around the individual both physically and online as guided by one's interests, values and experiences. The African value of communality as a shared value, in this case, becomes a motivating factor to want to connect to a virtual community after Covid-19 disruptions. As people navigated the loneliness and distress, their lone experiences got a platform where they could be shared and be bravely borne.

---

20 Rheingold H. 1993. *The Virtual Community: Homesteading on the Electronic Frontier*. Reading, MA: Addison-Wesley Publishing Company, 5.

21 Campbell H. 2010. *When religion meets new media*. London: Routledge; Castells, *The information age*, 404.

22 Wellman B and Gulia M. 1999. "Virtual Communities as Communities: Net Surfers Don't Ride Alone", in Smith MA and Kollock P (eds). *Communities in Cyberspace*. London: Routledge, 167-194.

23 Wellman and Gulia, "Virtual Communities as Communities", 176.

RELATIONAL THEORY AND AFRICAN SOLIDARITY

The humans desire to connect virtually resonates with the African ethic of Thaddeus Metz.[24] Metz, a philosopher and Africanist theorist, upholds a communal framework that infers identity to be a shared component in life where the quality of life for all members is paramount. Metz further argues that care for each other's well-being amounts to the value of solidarity, which is crucial not only in life's sustenance but also in its flourishing. This solidarity he argues involves "promoting others' well-being, being sympathetic, acting for the common good and showing concern for others",[25] as well as participating in their grief and joy.

In one of his latest publications, titled *A Relational Theory of Mental Illness: Lacking Identity and Solidarity*, Metz theorises mental illness from a relational perspective of psychological disorders. He argues that "the more one is mentally ill, the more one is psychologically unable to identify with others and exhibit solidarity with them".[26] This chapter employs Metz's line of thought that values of communality and solidarity, both from a subjective perspective and a towards the communal dimension, are crucial for mental well-being. Metz draws on the values of harmony, communality and cohesion as foundational for a good life. Even though Metz disassociates himself from the African conception of life and extending to the ancestral worlds in his moral considerations, a true African can never talk of peace and harmony without mentioning forefathers. Metz might have been influenced by his cross-cultural thinking in ways that fail to capture interrelational components of moral actions both among the living and the living-dead. Metz opts to concentrate on the value systems based on harmony. The communality, solidarity and harmony that shape our being is a product of their living. It is a heritage that we continue to shape in the spirit and ethic of *Ubuntu*.[27]

A renowned archbishop and former chair of South Africa's Truth and Reconciliation Commission, Desmond Tutu, grounding the ethic of *Ubuntu* among indigenous Africans, maintained, "We say, 'a person is a person through other people'."[28] It is not 'I think therefore I am'. It says rather: 'I am human because I belong'. I participate, I share … Harmony, friendliness, and community are great goods. Social harmony is for us the *summum bonum* – the greatest good."[29] A community for indigenous Africans includes our ancestors through naming. The living connect directly to the ancestors – the "living dead" believed to be kept alive through their loved ones

---

24 Metz T. 2021. "A Relational Theory of Mental Illness: Lacking Identity and Solidarity", *Synthesis Philosophica* 71(1):65-81.

25 Metz T. 2013. "The Western Ethic of Care or an Afro-communitarian Ethic", *Journal of Global Ethics* 9(1):81.

26 Metz, "A Relational Theory of Mental Illness", 66.

27 Manda DL. 2007. *The importance of the African ethics of ubuntu and traditional African healing systems for Black South African women's health in the context of HIV and AIDS*. Doctoral Thesis, University of KwaZulu-Natal, South Africa.

28 Tutu D. 1999. *No future without forgiveness.* New York: Random House, 35.

29 Tutu, *No future without forgiveness*, 35.

memory and in rituals – through the names they carry, which are also said to depict their behavioural traits. Thus, contrary to Metz's claims that moral actions are only able to be executed by the living, the values of harmony, solidarity and communality are believed to cut across both worlds: the living and the living dead.[30]

Metz's relational theory is relevant to the inquiry of this chapter, since mental stress is a natural result of grief of losing a loved one, made worse by indecent send-offs of ancestors that cause psychological disturbance to the living. As Metz alludes, "many mental illnesses cannot be fully understood without referencing such a failure" of identifying with others and exhibiting solidarity with them.[31] To exercise harmony and communality is therefore a step towards healing, as Metz illuminates in observing,

> Exhibiting solidarity with another (or acting for others' good, etc.) is similarly construed as the combination of exhibiting certain psychological attitudes and engaging in helpful behaviour. These specifications of what it is to commune or harmonise with others can ground a fairly rich, attractive, and useable African conception of the good life. Bringing things together, here are some concrete and revealing interpretations of "a person is a person through other persons": one should become a real person, which is a matter of identifying with others and exhibiting solidarity with them; or an agent ought to live a genuinely human way of life (exhibit *ubuntu*), which she can do if and only if she [he] honours relationships of sharing a way of life with others and caring for their quality of life.[32]

It therefore follows that if one is unable to self-identify with self and others and exhibit solidarity towards them, because of Covid-19 prevention protocols of quarantine, isolation and social and physical distancing, then a person, as Metz might note, "is not as much of a person as he could and should be".[33] This condition results in a mental health situation that calls for psychosocial accompaniment using all means available.[34]

Figure 24.1 below is a schematic diagram that Metz utilises to advance his notions of communalism, with an assertion that "all agents must treat others as having dignity

---

30   For more criticisms on the biased relational theorisation advanced by Metz, see Molefe M. 2017. "Relational ethics and partiality: A critique of Thaddeus Metz's 'Towards an African moral theory'", *Theoria* 64(152):53-76.
31   Metz, "A Relational Theory of Mental Illness", 66.
32   Metz, "A Relational Theory of Mental Illness", 73-74.
33   Metz, "A Relational Theory of Mental Illness", 74.
34   For insights on accompaniment of Covid-19 affected and infected persons, see Musili TK and Cheronoh F. 2021. "Ethical considerations for Community Based Psychosocial Accompaniment: Towards a Strengthened Mental Health Response Amidst Covid-19 Pandemic", *East African Journal of Arts and Social Sciences* 4(1):1-10; Musili T and Chamwama E. 2021. "Theology and ethics of pastoral accompaniment for patients with Covid-19 in the context of physical distancing", in Kaunda CJ, Longkumer A, Ross KR and Mombo E (eds). *Christianity and Covid-19: Pathways for Faith*. London: Routledge, 163-176.

in virtue of their capacity to enter in a communal life".[35] It is paramount that the value of communality incorporates identity and solidarity.

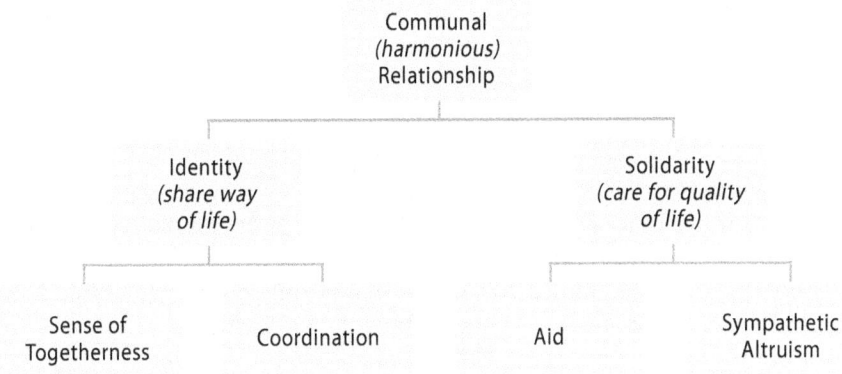

Figure 24.1: Schematic representation of communion (after Metz, 2017)[36]

WHATSAPP MESSENGER AND THE AFRICAN VALUE OF COMMUNALITY

WhatsApp is an American freeware, cross-platform centralised chat and instant messaging and voice-over service owned by Meta Platforms. It allows users to send text messages and voice messages, make voice and video calls, and share images, documents, user locations and other content using smart mobile phones. Given the versatility of this mode of communication, WhatsApp Messenger has become the most popular messenger application on the African continent. Kenya, for instance, is said to have the highest smartphone usage in Africa, estimated to encompass 74% of the entire population.[37] Kenyans are reported to spend close to three to four hours a day on social media, with the most used platforms identified as WhatsApp (74%), Facebook (70%), and Twitter (50%), based on users' own claimed activity.[38]

During the Covid-19 pandemic season, the platform was awash with useful information on mitigating the rapid spread of the coronavirus, such as washing hands with water and soap, but along with misinformation that caused panic among the populace. Nevertheless, it is a platform that was utilised well in the dire Covid-19 times in a range of ways, from tracking Covid-19 patients to receiving the ministry of health messages on good hygiene and inoculation tests. Given its promptness in communication, WhatsApp has an intergenerational following, including both the young and the old.

---

35 Metz T. 2017. "Replacing Development: An Afro-Communal Approach to Global Justice", *Philosophical Papers* 46(1):118.
36 Metz, "Replacing Development", 118.
37 Namunwa K. 2019. "Kenya leads Africa in Smartphone usage", *Business Today*, 19 March.
38 "Opinion. 2021. Social Media Platforms, Influencers and Internet Technology; Will Largely Influence the 2022 General Election Outcome", *Shahidi News*, 19 October.

The WhatsApp platform can send messages to one person or groups. WhatsApp groups form a virtual community of persons, family, friends, employees and all sorts of people sharing the same points of view. Social events are also organised and planned using WhatsApp platforms. A "virtual community" following the definition of sociologist Manuel Castells, occurs where a self-defined electronic network of interactive communication is organised around a shared interest or purpose, and this fits perfectly with the role that the WhatsApp platform plays for these communities. During Covid-19, communities assembled in WhatsApp groups to plan for pre-weddings, weddings and burials, as well as to cushion the strain on families in paying hospital bills prompted by the pandemic. It is against this backdrop that we examine how the WhatsApp platform advanced the value of communality virtually and its subsequent manifestations in cushioning people's health, well-being, and resilience for adherents of Eastleigh Nomiya Church, Nairobi County.

WHATSAPP VIRTUAL BEREAVEMENT COMMUNITIES AT EASTLEIGH NOMIYA CHURCH

The present study examines how the value of communality was appropriated virtually and its subsequent manifestations in cushioning people's health, well-being, and resilience among the Eastleigh Nomiya Church adherents. The church has an approximate population of 144 adult adherents and 56 children. Of 144 adult adherents, about 42% are men, while women are the majority at 58%. Notably, the majority of men had smartphones compared to women. Men dominate the leadership of the church, which is a key reason why Eastleigh Nomiya Church had a continuous presence in the virtual space. Livestreaming of services through Facebook was evidenced on the Eastleigh Nomiya Church Facebook page.[39] It was reported that, even though a Facebook page existed prior to Covid-19, a WhatsApp group for the entire church was created at the onset of the pandemic for communication purposes. After physical church attendance was prohibited, the WhatsApp platform became an efficient channel for the church leadership to reach out to the adherents. Communication and updates on one another's well-being and challenges were posted to the group. The bishop opined that communicating to church members about when to collect foodstuff, bereavement cases, sickness and Covid-19 infections were made easier among the adherents by the WhatsApp platform.

The Luo community exhibits elaborate funeral rituals.[40] They perform a series of rituals and many feasts for the dead because of their strong fear and respect for the dead, and these rituals were disrupted by Covid-19 pandemic protection protocols.

---

39 See Eastleigh Nomiya Church, *Facebook* [Accessed 28 November 2022].
40 See Otieno O, Ayako R, and Kandago D. 2021. "Luo rituals pertaining to ancestral spirits' veneration and their implication on christian worship – a study in the seventh-day Adventist church, Kenya lake conference", *Journal of Philosophy, Culture and Religion* 4(1): 28-42; Shino W. 1997. "Death and rituals among the Luo in South Nyanza", *African Study Monographs* 18:213-228.

The Kenyan government, through the Ministry of Health (MOH) press release of 6 March 2020,[41] banned with immediate effect all meetings, conferences and events where more than fifteen people would be gathering. Further, the Kenyan government issued a directive that interment must be conducted within 72 hours,[42] which worsened the financial burden to grieving families, who were no longer able to reach out to friends for support owing to time constraints and the ban on social gatherings. One Eastleigh Nomiya Church member opined, "We could not attend the burials of our loved ones, but a WhatsApp group was formed, where we contributed and sent to our brothers just to soothe them. You know the hospital people just came and buried him immediately."[43]

WhatsApp welfare communities emerged to cushion people not only financially, but also emotionally. Asked how the platform was of importance to them during mourning period, one respondent opened his phone and shared with researchers condoling messages that the other members of the church and from the wider community had shared in the WhatsApp group. The experience concurs with the observations of Johannes Cronje and Izak van Zyl, information and communication technologists, that "WhatsApp groups are considered useful for creating and supporting virtual communities".[44] Even though the virtual community on WhatsApp was not the same as in-person mourning rituals, the members asserted that it was a source of relief during the pandemic. Mobile money was another virtual venture that supported families during the pandemic, attesting to the value of communality that existed beyond the physical. Unlike previously, when mobile money platforms were largely used for person-to-person cash transfers, they were increasingly being used to support the welfare of family members within the church. The bishop explained, "Most of our members lost their jobs when this pandemic came in. They have wives and children to feed. We, as the church leadership, created a WhatsApp group and asked members to send money to the treasurer. We then used this money to buy food for our people. They would come one by one and collect from the church."[45] Thus, the use of social media enhanced giving of finances and other material things in different congregations a fact that fosters maturity of believers and enhanced spirituality.[46] Eastleigh Nomiya Church is a giving church. Church members give money towards various social events ranging from burials, hospital bills, graduations and family welfare upkeep. This is done together with a thanksgiving offering, development fund and tithes. WhatsApp and mobile money applications have been lauded for "contributing to the empowerment of women

---

41 Ministry of Health, Kenya. 2020. "Update on Covid-19 as at 6 March". Nairobi: MOH.
42 See MOH, Interim guidelines on handling of human remains".
43 Interview with Kayole pastor by T Musili, Nairobi, Kenya, October 2021.
44 Cronje J and Van Zyl I. 2022. "WhatsApp as a tool for Building a Learning Community", *Electronic Journal of e-Learning* 20(3):296.
45 Interview with Bishop of Eastleigh Parish by T Musili, Nairobi, Kenya, November 2021.
46 Kamau P, Kama J, Mwaura N and Njau M. 2019. "Effect of Utilisation of WhatsApp Social Media Platform on Spiritual Growth of Church Members a Case of New Life Church Kenya", *International Journal of Research and Innovation in Social Science* 3(5):347-351.

by enabling their freedoms to participate in developmental activities".[47] Eastleigh Nomiya Church leveraged these platforms during the pandemic. On one Sunday, for instance, it was observed that they had seven giving sessions. Every member was recorded in a book, for what was said to be accountability purposes. Once a contributor gave a certain amount, the person in charge of collection and writing would shout the name of the contributor and the amount. Other members opted to contribute through the WhatsApp group, for fear of shaming when the name and amount were mentioned.

The sharing and willingness to give however little money they had to these many social events was, however, a way of identifying with the grieving and showing solidarity with them. One woman observed, "Even if you have Kshs 200, give Kshs 50, 50 to each, at least you have your name in the book or in the WhatsApp group. It is a sign you are together and you belong to the church."[48] As Thaddeus Metz has observed, identity and solidarity are key factors that necessitate the well-being of persons. It is thus evident that new electronic media does not depart from or disrupt traditional cultures, but rather absorbs and appropriates them. The virtual communities formed as a result of grief, for instance, are not just for Eastleigh Nomiya Church adherents, but also draw membership from other institutions, as per the web of relationships that the affected belong to. Robert Putnam, an American political scientist, and educator refers to this web of relationships as "social capital", denoting the element of communities that forms affective bonds among people.[49] These relationships come in handy in times of need, since they can generate broader identities and reciprocity.

WhatsApp communities have become a norm not only in the Eastleigh Nomiya Church, but also in most societies in Kenya and across the globe. They are centred on shared norms, values and interests of all kinds. Eastleigh Nomiya Church leadership reported forming a lifelong WhatsApp welfare group for all church members for purposes of communication and eventualities. Since Covid-19 is easing up at the time of this writing, the groups are realised partially in the digital common space, but they also supported physically through the church welfare book, forming hybrid-facilitated welfare. The Eastleigh Nomiya Church WhatsApp groups are a testament to the vision of Howard Rheingold, in his pioneering book on virtual communities, because they exemplify the birth of a new form of community, bringing people together online around shared values and interests was necessitated by the pandemic.[50]

---

47 For more on WhatsApp as an empowering tool, see Abubakar NH and Dasuki SI. 2018. "Empowerment in their hands: use of WhatsApp by women in Nigeria", *Gender, Technology and Development* 22(2):164-183.

48 Interview with woman church member by T Musili, Nairobi, Kenya, November 2021.

49 Putnam P. 2000. *Bowling Alone: The Collapse and Revival of American Community*. New York: Simon and Schuster, 24.

50 Rheingold, *The Virtual Community*.

A virtual community, in line with Rheingold's vision, is generally understood as a self-defined electronic network of interactive communication organised around a shared interest or purpose, although sometimes communication becomes the goal in itself. Probed on how they maintained harmony with the ancestral world, given the elaborate nature of mourning among the Luo, the bishop, who always attended the burials on behalf of the entire parish responded, "Our God is one, he is understanding, our parents, brothers and sisters who have gone ahead of us are friendly and sympathise with us going through Covid-19. They understand. It is not our fault, they see we are doing our best."[51] The bishop's sentiments testify to the unity between the living dead and the living even in a technological age. As ancestors live among us, they were privy to the challenges the pandemic posed, thus confirming Barry Wellman and Milena Gulia's point that virtual communities are never opposed to physical communities, but rather should be understood as different forms of community with dynamic and distinct rules that interact with other forms of community. It thus follows that the living dead have a certain form of community, which is not detached from both the physical and virtual communities that serve their interests for the sake of identity and harmony.

So, in the end, one wonders whether virtual communities are real physical communities. Though they may not meet the physicality that they mimic, they are not unreal in terms of communality and solidarity, which are the driving human concerns in times of adversity. They do not exist in isolation from other forms of sociability, such as encounters, exchanges and interactions that ground opinions, attitudes and values. As communication is crucial in sociability, there is minimal or no separation at all between physical reality and the symbolic representation of the living dead and living communities. The Nomiya Church bishop alluded to this oneness as the ancestral community that is always living in our midst, understanding every real happening in society. Manuel Castells was therefore correct with his assertion that "there is no separation between 'reality' and symbolic representation. In all societies, humankind has existed in and acted through a symbolic environment".[52] Sheldon Richmond, a philosopher and information technology systems analyst, further confirms that virtual space "is a system in which reality itself (that is, people's materials/symbolic existence) is entirely captured, fully immersed in virtual settings in the world of make-believe, in which appearances are not just on the screen through which experience is communicated, but they become the experience".[53]

All realities are thus communicated through symbols. One church elder whose son had passed on explained, "We sent them (referring to church members) photos of his face, casket, and the grave. They have accepted that he died. They could see him lay peacefully, he never disturbed us." As if to say that even the ancestors

---

51 Interview with Bishop Eastleigh Parish by T Musili, Nairobi, Kenya, November 2021.
52 Castells, *The information age*, 403.
53 Richmond S. 2020. *A way through the global techno-scientific culture*. Cambridge: Cambridge Scholars Publishing, 34.

accepted him, "the laying peacefully and not disturbing them" is a testament that even though the rituals were not performed as expected, the virtually mediated assistance was enough. Thus, the reality of spiritual community online and its situated theologising was necessitated by the WhatsApp platform.[54] This is to say that in human life, in interactive communication, regardless of the medium, all the symbols convey meaning and an experience. In a sense, all reality can be and was virtually perceived. The WhatsApp platform had thus become the foundation for appropriating identity and solidarity in moments of adversity and beyond. It can be through words and *emojis* that express compassion, reciprocity, harmony and communality, values that are crucial for mutual caring both to the living and the living dead.

CONCLUSION

This chapter examined how the value of communality was appropriated virtually and its subsequent manifestations in cushioning people's health, well-being and resilience. Relational theory grounded the importance of identity and solidarity within African ethics, which extends beyond physicality to the virtual space. From the qualitative data, the WhatsApp platform was utilised to continue the African value of communality during the pandemic. Virtual communities, appropriated through social media, were powerful tools in combatting painful experiences and mental health challenges prompted by the Covid-19 pandemic. WhatsApp communities continued to service as platforms for communication and welfare spaces forming a formidable social capital for the community even as the pandemic was subsiding. The value of communality, as grounded in African ethics, survived Covid-19 and continues to blend well with technological innovations beyond this life. Its appropriation in social media platforms is a testament that communitarianism, as drawn from the African philosophy of *Ubuntu*, lives on, even under legal regulations and disruptive pandemics in a technological space as a healing tool for psychological pain and grief.

---

54 See Silverkors D. 2020. "Four Lessons I've Learned So Far in the Wake of the Pandemic", in Campbell HA (ed). *The distanced church: Reflections on doing church online*. College Station, TX: Digital Religion Publications/Texas A & M University. Online at https://jliflc.com/wp-content/uploads/2020/06/Distanced-Church-PDF-landscape-FINAL-version.pdf [Accessed 28 November 20220.

25 Digital ethnography and networked theology: new forms of religious experience in Covid-19 at CITAM Ngong, Kenya

Loreen Maseno[1]

INTRODUCTION

Coronavirus affected several sectors in Kenya in major ways. One sector that was especially affected was churches and other places of worship, as a result of social distancing and total lockdowns. The advent and subsequent growth of the internet, prompted computer-mediated communication in all spheres of human life, including religion. The period of the coronavirus forced people to embrace extenssive digitalisation. Religious rituals and behaviours were transferred and practised online. The pandemic and creation of virtual spaces became a challenge as a result of the foreclosure of social gathering areas, especially churches.[2] There were changes in the worship experience, interactions and other church rituals, such as tithing and offertory. Invention and extensive use of virtual spaces led most of the congregants of CITAM (Christ is the Answer Ministries) Ngong Church in Kajiado, Kenya not to visit churches and places of worship, but instead to follow proceedings through the mass media and social media services.

This chapter considers the new forms of religious experiences resulting from the Covid-19 pandemic and its impact in Kenya. It explores in subsequent sections the pandemic and its impact on Kenya's religious landscape. It introduces us to CITAM Ngong Church, which is one among many CITAM churches in Kenya that are commonly located within urban settings, such as Nairobi, and also in some smaller towns, such as Ngong. CITAM also has branches in Romania, East Timor and the United States. The chapter further considers the practice of digital ethnography in CITAM Ngong. The focus is on the practice of digital ethnography by concentrating on human experiences of what congregants felt and how congregants experienced the virtual practices and things.

COVID-19 IN KENYA

The Ministry of Health (MOH) Kenya first confirmed a Covid-19 case in Nairobi on 12 March 2020. The Kenyan government traced all the contacts of the patient since the individual's arrival in Kenya from the United States. Kenyans were reminded that most people who become infected may experience only mild illness and recover

---

1 Research Fellow, Faculty of Theology, University of Pretoria and Senior Lecturer, Maseno University.
2 Campbell HA. 2012. *Digital Religion: Understanding Religious Practice in New Media Worlds*. London: Taylor & Francis Group.

easily, but that the disease could be more severe in others, especially the elderly and persons with other chronic illnesses. The Republic of Kenya Ministry of Health, in a 13 February 2020 press release updating the coronavirus situation, insisted that people were to avoid close contact with people suffering from acute respiratory infections. In addition, anyone showing symptoms of respiratory illness, such as fever, coughing, difficulty in breathing and sneezing was to report to nearest health facility for assessment.[3]

Over the years, religious activities and gatherings across the country were the norm and taken for granted. However, with the sudden closure of places of worship in Kenya, there was profound impact on the across the country.[4] For example, the Ministry of Health ordered the closure of churches in a locality in Kisii County in southwestern Kenya following an upsurge in Covid-19 cases among church members and the surrounding community. In a letter addressed to church leaders, the local public health officer said that all places of worship would remain closed for a period of fourteen days beginning 11 June 2021.[5] Even after the government relaxed the rule on the right to attend church and allowed 100 people to gather, there was more confusion: "Who do you admit and who do you leave out? And just how many services can you hold on a Sunday?"[6]

Covid-19 in Kenya had an impact on the religious experiences of many. It is noted that in times of uncertainty and change, phenomena of prophecy, eschatology and miracles tend to be emphasised, since there are often few options for the majority who crave for consolation, empathy and motivation.[7] During this time, some Christians sought after prophecies about the pandemic, its longevity, end times, survival options and the like. Many people in Kenya, including Christians, lost their livelihoods, loved ones and access to health care and education. They also experienced gender inequality, social injustice and accelerated burdens of unpaid care work. In order to cope with these multi-faceted effects, many sought information about the disease, counselling services for anxiety and generalised fears. They also went after opportunities to connect and engage with family and friends through available technology.

---

[3] Republic of Kenya. Ministry of Health. 2020. "Update on Coronavirus Disease-19 (Covid-19), as at 13th February 2020".

[4] Maseno L. 2021. "Eschatological Prophecies before and during Covid-19: Female Pentecostal-Charismatic Preachers Self-Legitimation through Prophecy in Kenya", *Pharos Journal of Theology* 102(2):1-12.

[5] "MOH Orders Closure of Churches as Covid-19 Spike", *Kenya News Agency*, 11 June 2021.

[6] Kahura D. 2020. "Covid-19: The Great Disruptor of the Church in Kenya", *The Elephant*, 20 August.

[7] Maseno, "Eschatological Prophecies before and during Covid-19".

CITAM NGONG CHURCH

CITAM, or Christ Is the Answer Ministries, has its roots in Pentecostal Assemblies of Canada (PAOC), a result of revival witnessed in Canada during the early 1900s, which spread to Kenya as the Pentecostal Assemblies of God (PAG) in 1918. It is recorded that the first missionaries of PAOC in Kenya were the Reverend Otto Keller and his wife. Nyang'ori mission, based in Nyang'ori area of Vihiga County, served as its headquarters. CITAM churches are located within urban settings of Nairobi, Mombasa, Kisumu, Eldoret, Kakamega, Meru, Nyeri, Kisii, Naivasha, Thika and Nakuru. Others are located in in smaller towns that include Kiserian, Kikuyu and Ngong. It also has branches in Romania, East Timor and the USA where pastors were sent to plant churches.

CITAM Ngong was started in July 2003 within the precincts of the town on Ngong. The church started with a tent as its house of meeting and with Reverend Stephen Mutua as the first senior pastor. Mutua was succeeded by Reverend Jesse Mwai, before Reverend Edward Ngaira took over.[8] The church would later move from the tent to a sanctuary, which was completed in 2017. This transition from tent to sanctuary was termed as "Moving the Ark" and was popularly promoted by Bishop Dr David Oginde. CITAM Ngong is also referred to as God's habitation and the church conducts two Sunday services. The senior pastor at the time of this research was Reverend Josphat Shichende. The first service, which starts at 7:00 am, covers prayer and intercession. The youth service, New Believers class, doctrinal and Sunday school classes start at 8:30 am. The second segment of services begins at 11:00 am, and the main family, teen and Sunday Services are run simultaneously at this time. CITAM Ngong youth ministry targets the youth and young adults and takes care of their spiritual needs through Sunday church services. At CITAM Ngong, youth also have programmes for students who have just sat for their class eight and form four national examinations, as well as for university students and others. Mission and Outreach includes programmes of evangelism, local and international mission, drama, music and dance.

CITAM Ngong was the church selected for research sampling in the study on digital ethnography that is the basis for this chapter. CITAM Ngong was selected for its very close connection to the head and first church branch at CITAM Valley Road, whose virtual footprint is one of the greatest across the Pentecostal churches in Kenya. CITAM Ngong was also selected because it embraced a virtual presence even before the Covid pandemic. It is in an area slightly out of Nairobi and has a consistent membership of persons who reside in the locality. Access and formal permission to carry out research in this congregation was granted by the Deputy Bishop of CITAM.

---

[8] The CITAM Church leadership is rotated after three to five years. The pastors are moved across the CITAM branches and others are sent to start a Church plant, thus the frequent changes of leaders. Each pastor when hired is supposed to agree to be deployed across the CITAM assemblies at any time.

DIGITAL ETHNOGRAPHY METHODOLOGY

Digital ethnography in this chapter is both a methodology and a practice. As a methodology, it covers how to do ethnography in any environment in which digital media is unfolding. As a practice, elements of what differences the digital makes to the practices of communities come better into focus. As new media unfolds, it offers new ways of engaging with research environments, causing actual practices by the communities and researchers to also shift.

Digital ethnography, as outlined by Sarah Pink and others, is that approach to doing ethnography that considers how we live and research in a digital, material and sensory environment.[9] Clearly, the contemporary world and environment we live in is not static. Digital ethnography is a methodological import for how to do ethnography, even as the digital unfolds as part of the world that we co-inhabit with the people who participate in our research.[10] It involves doing research with, through and in an environment partially constituted by digital media. Pink adds that through digital ethnography, researchers ask "how digital environments, methods and methodologies are redefining ethnographic practice".[11] Digital ethnography also "takes the novel step of acknowledging the role of digital ethnography in challenging the concepts that have traditionally defined the units of analysis that ethnography has been used to study."[12] The intersection of the offline-online social world is an important dimension in unearthing the relationship between religious practice in a virtual space and religious change in terms of experiences.

Towards this endeavour, digital ethnography was used to collect rich data from CITAM Ngong Church. Primary data for this study involved obtaining data with, through and in an environment partially constituted by digital media. I carried out interviews and participant observation, which enabled me to determine whether the findings were substantiated. I chose interviews, direct observation and participant observation as the empirical methods to enable me gather what is commonly referred to as "thick description".[13] Thick description is detailed and informative and is acquired through sufficient probing.[14] In the context of interviews, questions were posed which were open-ended, and which avoided the eliciting of "yes" or "no" answers.

The objectives of the study were to examine the modes of operation and postures in relation to religious experiences in the virtual space in CITAM Ngong and to reflect on the adoption of virtual space and its effects on the religious experiences of congregants of CITAM Ngong. I sought to find out from the respondents how digital

---

9   Pink S et al. 2016. *Digital ethnography: principles and practice*. London: Sage, 20.
10 See Underberg NM and Zorn E. 2013. *Digital ethnography: Anthropology, narrative and new media*. Austin: University of Texas Press, 3.
11 Pink et al, *Digital ethnography*, 20.
12 Pink et al, *Digital ethnography*, 20-21.
13 Geertz C. 1993. *The Interpretation of Cultures: Selected Essays*. London: Fontana, 6.
14 Geertz, *The Interpretation of Cultures: Selected Essays*, 6.

environments impacted their services and worship experiences. I also sought to know how they felt in this new virtual space as congregants and their experiences of virtual practices and things. Although CITAM has a presence in different cities and towns, a choice was made to situate the study at CITAM Ngong, located in a smaller town, to facilitation the gathering data. This CITAM Ngong space was one where the present researcher had taken time to build a good rapport, close engagement and involvement within this religious milieu, in order to enhance the research.

Participant observation was a method to gather in-depth data for this study at CITAM Ngong. Participant observation is a scientific method that when combined with other methodologies enables the researcher to obtain systematic facts or data.[15] It is a method of verifying data acquired through other methods, such as interviews.[16] Through participant observation, I was enabled as a researcher to pick up not only verbal information, but also nonverbal cues, thus enriching data. CITAM Ngong is a 5 000-seat capacity church, and my presence in the distant balcony as an observer did not appear to influence the running of the services nor the behaviour of the persons present. I had been granted access by both the deputy bishop of CITAM and the senior pastor of CITAM Ngong, to carry out research of which the leadership was well aware. Through participant observation, I entered and experienced the world of the participants in their services. This was not just an experiential process, but also involved the recording of field notes throughout the process, which was important for the sake of the analysis of the collected data.

The Covid-19 pandemic in Kenya had different phases, such as the complete closure and partial shutdown of churches, as well as face-to-face services carried out under strict guidelines. This study was carried out from July 2021 onward when in-person services at CITAM Ngong were being conducted and in-person research was possible. Even as in-person services started picking up again, there was streaming of services and programmes, such as prayer, counselling, training and others, that continued to be carried out online. Data from participants observation and interviews enriched the digital ethnography.

Primary data from interviews for this study was obtained from a sample size of twelve youth, three church leaders and fourteen adult members. Purposive sampling was used to obtain the three church leaders, who included the senior pastor, the youth leader and the information technology (IT) officer in charge at the church. The youth pastor was allowed to invite the youth for the interviews, while the fourteen church members were selected from one of the *safari* (small groups) of the church. The research was consistent with the observations of feminist ethnographer Ruth Behar that in carrying out ethnography, there must be a real desire to engage

---

15 Kothari CR. 2004. *Research Methodology: Methods and Techniques*. New Delhi: New Age International Publishers, 9.

16 Kothari, *Research Methodology: Methods and Techniques*, 4.

with real people in real and usually forgotten places.[17] At the same time and at a fundamental level, embodied communities must be researched in their particular contexts. Data was collected for the study over a series of visits to CITAM Ngong over a period of six months. It was clear that the digital community was unfolding in a space which involved some view of the transcendent. Through this digital community at CITAM Ngong, it was possible to reflect upon immanent processes of cultural place-making, the negotiation of social identities and the formation of boundaries.

In doing research through and in an environment partially constituted by digital media, it was possible to unpack the practice of specific narratives regarding divine action, transcendent presence and supernatural reality in the immanent world. The presence of digital media in shaping the techniques and processes through which we carry out and practise ethnography itself became a focus of study and reflection, leading to various understandings of how the digital, methodological and practical dimensions of ethnographic research were increasingly intertwined. The study required mapping the technologies CITAM Ngong Church used to reach its congregants, along with assessment of how these have changed or been enhanced in the recent times due to Covid-19. Participant observation and conversation with the IT officer identified which Information Communication Technologies (ICT) were preferred at CITAM Ngong, as well as their limits. Respondents to the study also identified the expressions of spirituality produced through these technologies.

Using ethnography provided the opportunity to be directly involved with CITAM Ngong congregants to see how they understand, accounted for, took action and managed their day-to-day situation. When contact with a given community or group and concern for day-to-day events and direct or indirect participation in local activities is pursued, the name given to this research is fieldwork, which is also described "doing ethnography".[18] Ethnography is as a means of data collection in which the researcher is immersed in a social setting for an extended period of time in order to observe and listen with a view of gaining an appreciation of individual's perspectives and interpretations.[19]

A special feature of ethnographic approaches, namely directly observing situations through which congregants move, contributes significantly to understanding these congregations. Ethnographic method allows the gathering of rich collections of different kinds of information among different congregants, including the elders known as "golden-agers", adult women and men as well as youth to provide background information on the people and the locality in which the Church was situated. This background information permitted description aspects of the congregants' social milieu using a holistic gaze. This would not have been achieved if the

---

17 Behar B and Gordon DA (eds). 1985. *Women Writing Culture*. Berkeley: University of California Press, 10.
18 Agar MH. 1980. *The Professional Stranger: An Informal Introduction to Ethnography*. New York: Academic Press, 2.
19 Bryman A. 2004. *Social Research Methods*. Second Edition. London: Oxford Press, 267.

study had solely involved questions within the strict confines of oral interviews. Participant observation was crucial. Collecting these kinds of information from digital ethnography, supplemented with literature on ethnography, digital religion, Covid-19, gender and gender systems, intersectionality and networked theology was a stepping stone to the possibility of finding patterns and frames that could help describe new forms of religious experiences, rituals and solidarity during the Covid-19 pandemic and the practice of digital ethnography.

DIGITAL ETHNOGRAPHY AND NETWORKED THEOLOGY AT CITAM NGONG

Networked theology

According to media study scholar Heidi Campbell and theologian Stephen Garner, as digital media continues to find its way into church practice, we are increasingly faced with the challenge of how to evaluate and theologically reflect on these changes. Further, the new media technologies are situated in a unique cultural context, the networked society. It is from this networked society that a networked theology emerges as a framework for understanding the intersection between new media and theology.[20] According to Campbell and Garner, networked theology describes theologising about the digital, technological and network society in which many people live. It captures the way people of faith consume and are affected by digital media.[21] It is defined as, that which highlights and analyses how religion is practised both online and offline in an information-based society. It explores issues and trends that influence Christian beliefs and practices in a world wrapped in new media. Campbell and Garner argue that serious theological discourse is important to fully understand how new media shapes everyday lives.[22]

Networked theology provides a glimpse into the relationship between religion and the internet, with a focus on how religious communities have responded to and used the internet. Through studying networked theology, scholars are able to investigate the impact that online religious communities have on perceptions, church involvement, identity, authority and community. Network theology builds bridges between theology and media studies to create a vibrant interdisciplinary conversation which touches on rituals, community and identity in a globalised world.[23] In the context of the present study, examining of practices of digital ethnography allowed for concentration on human experiences of what people felt about their religious experiences and solidarity at CITAM Ngong during the Covid-19 pandemic.

---

20 Campbell H and Garner S. 2016. *Networked Theology: Negotiating faith in digital culture*. Ada, MI: Baker Academic Press, 2-3.
21 Campbell and Garner, *Networked Theology*, 2-3.
22 Campbell and Garner, *Networked Theology*, 15.
23 Campbell and Garner, *Networked Theology*, 15.

Congregant experiences

By some respondents' descriptions, the experience of the shift to digital forms of community and solidarity was fine. Others described the feeling as good in light of the digital community's expanse and reach and for the convenience that it afforded members during the closure of churches. Many felt that the virtual services expanded outreach to those members who could not make it to the sanctuary physically or who worked on Sundays. In addition, they could invite their friends and family from around the country and oversees to join in the services. To these respondents, the shift was a blessing and a convenience. In the framework of Campbell and Garner, these experiences are illustrative of the conditions of a networked society, in which digital technologies and their supporting culture are characterised and enabled by constant contact.[24] Accordingly, the instantaneous nature of digital communication allows easy transcendence of time-space boundaries and connection anytime and anywhere, with the possibility of plugging into several church services on any given day.

Other respondents experienced feelings of inclusivity in the digital services, such that those who did not have the possibility of coming in person could be part of the church without borders. This inclusivity was accorded to both members and non-members who may have felt odd attending a physical service. Some men who wear hairstyles such as braids, plaited hair, relaxed hair and uncommon haircuts that were different from the social norm reported feeling shunned or under a gaze when they walk into a sanctuary. The virtual church left all people feeling comfortable regardless of their habits, dress code and hairstyles. Mothers were comfortable breastfeeding and minding their children in the comfort of their homes. Thus, digital services facilitated this inclusivity.

Others felt a reluctance to attend the virtual services, since some were unable to concentrate on the services owing to a myriad of disruptions. For these respondents, being in the home came with a number of distractions. They would start the virtual service with others, but their attention wanes at the tail end of the service or they were tempted to walk to the kitchen to take a snack while the service was ongoing. The respondents added that they normally would not get distracted at a church service if they attended physically. For these virtual congregants, the home generated distractions to the detriment of their concentration. It is clear that the shift to a virtual space generated new experiences among different congregants. While others welcomed these churches, the practice of digital ethnography at CITAM Ngong brought to light variations in experience.

These findings from CITAM Ngong congregants' experiences were an indication of different people's religious experiences in an environment partially constituted by digital media. In this research, the practice of digital ethnography highlighted how the internet, social media, digital worlds, platforms, devices and content more broadly were experienced and engaged in ways that generate new experiential

---

24 Campbell and Garner, *Networked Theology*, 54.

configurations.²⁵ The congregants who embraced the internet and social media during the Covid-19 lockdown used specific narratives regarding divine action, transcendent presence and supernatural reality in the virtual world. Some congregants resisted or were uncomfortable to be involved in any religious environment partially constituted by digital media. Others became distracted in ways that made it clear that navigating both the embodied, sensory or affective realms of experience and the virtual church service was a challenge. Since these online services were accessed at home, it is important to reflect on the normally unspoken aspects and experiences of media in the home – what is referred to as "media presence".²⁶

According to ethnographers Sarah Pink and Jennie Morgan, in each home, there is a level of routine and sensory experiences from games or music played and programmes or movies watched and other activities.²⁷ For congregants at home and in a bid to help those distracted, it is important to inquire further, so as to begin to understand, and to some extent share, some of these routine and sensory experiences. This can help to consider media in the home environment beyond what conventional studies might uncover in relation to media as communication and content. When researchers focus on the experiential rather than material, they discover that what matters is the use of media to create sensory and affective environments not necessarily directly related to the particulars of the content or the technology itself.²⁸

When a virtual service is therefore streamed into the scene which already is laden with additional loud sensory and affective media environments, then there are bound to be unplanned distractions. For these congregants, such a mixture did have an effect on the flow of the service and served as a distraction to them. Congregants who were reluctant to attend virtual services, must also be understood from the perspective of the psyche and the spirit, where venues for normative religious encounters, such as the church building as a meeting place, are emphasised as a matter of theology. Such is the interdisciplinary conversation and dialogue that bridges theology and media studies. Can a virtual service replace what is normative for these congregants who prefer church buildings as the right and proper settings for worship?

These varied responses from congregants on where to partake a church service is a theological discourse worth examination and touches upon the perceptions relating to authority and community in religious circles. For many Christians, church has a meaning over and beyond an ordinary building and it must be designed in a certain way with respect to the pulpit, the altar, the position of the minister or priest and other factors. The plan of church-building is made so as to demarcate space and invite the divine. Traditionally, it was stated in both Pentecostal and

---

25 Pink et al, *Digital ethnography*, 59.
26 Pink S and Morgan J. 2013. "Short-term ethnography: Intense routes to knowing", *Symbolic Interaction* 36(3):351-361.
27 Pink and Morgan. "Short-term ethnography".
28 Pink et al, *Digital ethnography*, 59.

missionary-founded churches of Kenya in the early nineteenth century,[29] that people go to the "house of the Lord" and that the house of the Lord is distinct from one's own house. The sanctuary or the house of the Lord, is well laid out with sections distinctly set out for specific persons. The clergy sit at the front, while the laity sit facing the clergy. Emblems are shared from the front, and many rituals officiated in such spaces. Therefore, holding Sunday services and taking Eucharist and doing other Christian rituals in one's house, traditionally, has not been the norm in CITAM Ngong. This meant there was need for a mental and paradigm shift for these congregants to get into the flow of networked theology, especially under the Covid-19 pandemic. These feelings and persuasions are rather personal in nature and may not be generalised from one person to another.

Experience of the virtual practices and things

During the coronavirus pandemic period, CITAM Ngong congregants embraced the use of social media and online media worship. Findings showed that during the Covid-19 lockdown, CITAM Ngong church members, especially the youth and young adults between 18 years and 35 years old, became more conversant with the use of Facebook, WhatsApp, Twitter, Instagram and YouTube. These platforms existed and were functional before the pandemic, but they had not gained currency as the official broadcast channels for Sunday services to a large extent, since it had never been envisaged that a time will come when church attendance was banned. Many church meetings were done over Zoom. The preferred social media used among the CITAM Ngong youth, however, was Instagram. In fact, using other social media apart from Instagram hindered outreach among the youth.[30] Qualitative dimensions of youth values and behaviour affected how youth made choices and how they engaged with apps like Instagram and interfaces and devices in the context of the realities of everyday life.[31] Digital media and religious content were embedded in but also shaped everyday routines and habits of the CITAM youth, as well as their feelings, expectations and experiences of time and speed.

Youth indicated that they had to have the necessary gadgets to connect with their counterparts and plug into the sessions or announcements. It was clear that their engagement on various platforms, especially Instagram, required their ability to learn how to sign in and use them and that this required them to have the necessary WiFi to connect. Participant observation showed that most of the youth had

---

29 The mainstream churches are those founded by missionaries and include churches, such as the Roman Catholic, Methodist, Presbyterian, Seventh Day Adventist, Anglican, Quaker, Salvation Army, and Eastern Orthodox churches. Towards the independence movement, these missionary churches were seen as deeply integrated into a racialist society and thinking. See Maseno L. 2015. "Christianity in East Africa", in Bongmba E (ed). *The Routledge Companion to Christianity in Africa*. New York, Routledge, 112-119.

30 See, for example, Baym N. 2010. *Personal Connections in the Digital Age*. Cambridge: Polity, 10-24.

31 See also Campbell HA and Golan O. 2011. "Creating digital enclaves: Negotiation of the internet among bounded religious communities", *Media, Culture & Society* 33(5):709-724.

Android phones, which could capture and share images. Youth taught themselves how to use the technology and shared lessons on how to connect virtually. They even shared with each other how to use least amounts of money for connectivity when on the move. These lessons and actions among the youth were eye-openers to the researcher and the other youth.

The physical youth meetings at CITAM Ngong before Covid-19 included the Crossroad sessions, which comprised college and university students. This category of youth met every Sunday at 2:00 pm. The youth had a youth service from 11:30 am to 1:00 pm. Often, the university and college youth decide on a specific topic for focus or selected a book to study. Findings from the church leader in charge of youth indicated that most youth like what is trending, so they prefer to use the Instagram app more. They also continue to use WhatsApp and Facebook. The youth have continued to connect virtually for leadership meetings, announcements to the group and devotional messaging, even with Covid on the wane.

It was noted that young people easily get distracted by what is going on, for instance, using Facebook to listen to sermons and services. A respondent was quick to point out that, while on the Facebook live service, when messages come into their inbox, the youth end up getting distracted. One youth said that "the virtual church led to distractions, especially when we use our phones to watch sermons, and members instead get tempted to watch other kinds of stuff rather than the sermon".[32] In the event a gadget had several windows open, it was tempting to view the flashy adverts that popped up. Indeed, there were many in the wider digital audience, and through use of various media found that their attention and concentration could be hampered and limited. Another youth indicated that "virtual church has brought a new way of how the church can be administered and revealed or brought out the weaknesses or strengths in the church which were hidden before."[33] By this, the youth was pointing to how those churches, which did not have a clear service structure, well prepared sermons and music would be exposed when they streamed their content. At the same time, churches with good content and order would end up getting more views from people across the world.

At CITAM Ngong, relationships groups were formed in, through and with digital media and technology and the different forms of co-presence which are central to relationships. Co-presence involves the different ways of being together with others. The intersection of the offline-online social world can be understood through co-presence that allows persons to engage at a distance, for example, to play online games. These relationships create intimacy through particular communication technologies, and the fact that people are playing across physical distances is what makes online games so entertaining. Similarly, at CITAM Ngong, the particular ways in which co-presence become meaningful were shaped by different cultural contexts and norms around the ways in which intimacy is expressed. One congregant said

---

32 Interview with study participant by L Maseno. Ngong, Kenya, 8 November 2021.
33 Interview with study participant by L Maseno. Ngong, Kenya, 8 November 2021.

that "virtual services limited one-on-one experiences of fellowship".[34] Another noted that "the virtual space does not have the human touch as it feels distant".[35] Still another noted that with the advent of Covid-19, social life and relationships among congregants had been greatly affected. Particularly the loss of loved ones during Covid-19 put a strain on relationships in many ways. Friends who might have wanted to be close to the bereaved family or even the sick during this time were hindered. Many people could not condole with their friends due to the restrictions that were imposed at the time. Life includes walking with people during the tough patches, but under the circumstances of Covid, many were constrained to do so.

CONCLUSION

The Covid-19 realities in Kenya had an impact on religious experiences, beginning with lockdowns and the shutting of face-to-face church services. However, the innovation and creativity of the digital arena was quickly embraced by CITAM Ngong. Digital ethnography at CITAM Ngong invited reflection upon the experiences of the digital world in new ways. These included their experiences of what congregants felt and how congregants experienced the virtual practices and things. They experienced inclusivity and feelings from the engagement with the virtual demonstrated a somewhat new experiential configuration for them. Congregants were enabled to adapt although there were some challenges for others touching upon the perceptions relating to authority in religious circles. The experiences of the virtual practices brought about new ways in which digital media and religious content were embedded to the congregants. At the same time digital media with religious material shaped some everyday routines and habits, expectations and experiences of time and speed. Many acquired the necessary gadgets to connect with their counterparts and plug into the sessions.

The congregants at CITAM Ngong during Covid-19 period saw their services interface with the virtual. Findings showed that congregants not only consumed but were affected by digital media in their practice of religion. They were able to share new experiences from their online and offline engagements of religious purposes. Their reflections comprised networked theologies on authority, scope, jurisdiction and space. These dimensions appeared to be minimised in those environments where encounters with digital media was limited. However, findings from CITAM Ngong indicate some overflow between content from online and offline engagements.

These findings show what the congregants felt and how they responded to their experience of the shift to virtual practices and the ramifications of this for "doing Church". They present the implications of the digital world and ethnography for understanding the contemporary virtual contexts in which CITAM Ngong finds itself. They demonstrate the multiple ways in which religious content over digital space – as both a material culture and a set of media practices – is overlaid and

---

34 Interview with study participant by L Maseno. Ngong, Kenya, 7 December 2021.
35 Interview with study participant by L Maseno. Ngong, Kenya, 8 November 2021.

entwined in specific narratives regarding divine action and transcendent presence in the immanent world. They also shed light on the considered behind the church's adoption of the virtual space during the coronavirus pandemic and the impact on the religious experiences. It is clear that through the digital world, they experienced easy transcendence of time-space boundaries and were enabled to connect anytime and anywhere, and the possibility of plugging into several church services on any given day. Therefore, we note the amplification of transcendent presence and intimacies in the space.

VI. Theologies, spaces and solidarity in Covid-19

26 "BEHOLD, THE END OF ALL THINGS IS NEAR": AFRICAN THEOLOGIES AND BELIEFS ABOUT SIN AND DEATH IN THE TIME OF COVID-19

Milda Alberto Bernardo Come[1]
Marlino Eugénio Mubai[2]

INTRODUCTION

Since colonial times, Mozambique has experienced social distress that makes it fertile ground for religion. Moreover, its strategic location in the western Indian Ocean region and southern Africa, exposes Mozambique to various religious influences, from Islam to Hinduism to Christianity. In addition to these religions, a significant portion of the population adheres to syncretism of indigenous religious beliefs, characterised by a combination of traditional African practices and aspects of Christianity or Islam.[3] News outlets report the existence of more than a thousand registered religious denominations and a similar number of the unregistered.[4] This means that the government may not have the exact number of churches operating countrywide.[5] This religious landscape is in line with what Congolese Catholic Bishop Tharcisse Tshibangu Tshishiku has observed, namely that Africans are deeply religious. Thus, religion is not just a set of beliefs, but a way of life and the basis of culture, identity and moral values.[6] It is an essential part of the tradition that helps to promote social stability.[7] Considering that Mozambican society is embedded in such a cultural and religious context, this chapter sets its relevance

---

1 MA Candidate, Eduardo Mondlane University; Social activist for education and justice.
2 Assistant Professor, African History, Faculty of Arts and Social Science, Eduardo Mondlane University.
3 United States Department of State. 2019. International Religious Freedom Report, Mozambique.
4 Da Silva R. 2019. "As igrejas viraram negócio em Moçambique? [Have churches become a business in Mozambique?]", *Deutsche Welle*, 20 July.
5 Projections from the 2017 population census provided by the Instituto Nacional de Estatísticas, (INE), indicate that 26.2% of citizens were Roman Catholic, 18.3% Muslim (mostly concentrated in the northern part of the country), 15.1% Zionist Christian, 14.7% Evangelical/Pentecostal, 1.6% Anglican and 4.7% Jews, Hindus and Baha'is. The remaining 13.4% of the population did not list a religious affiliation.
6 Tshibangu TT, Ajayi JFA and Sanneh L. 1993."Religion and Social Evolution", in Mazrui AA (ed). *General History of Africa*, vol VIII, 501.
7 Alfredsson U and Linha C. 2000. *Onde Deus Vive: introdução a um estudo das igrejas independentes em Maputo, Moçambique* [Where God Lives: Introduction to a Study of Independent Churches in Maputo, Mozambique]. Maputo: Instituto Nacional de Desenvolvimento da Educação, 9.

in the literature by analysing the extent to which the Covid-19 pandemic and its effects changed the way that Mozambican people experience their faith.

Mozambique reported its first case of Covid-19 infection on 22 March 2020. Following that report, the government of Mozambique put in place several measures to stop the spread of the virus, including strict lockdown regulations. One of the preventive security measures adopted was the closure of social events, worshipping and religious ceremonies to minimise the transmission of the virus to the community. This decision affected people's spirituality and relationship with God in many ways. In fact, it brought to light questions about the theologies of sin and death.

This analysis focuses the discussion on Catholic, Pentecostal and Islamic denominations. One of the biggest differences between Catholicism and Protestantism is the concept of sufficiency and authority of Scripture. Pentecostal churches, many of which subscribe to the "prosperity gospel", claim to use the Bible to speak to real life situations by emphasising a theology of health and wealth. The Pentecostal churches believe that living in sin and non-fulfilment of tithing obligations favour evil to thrive.[8] Pentecostal churches are a string of the independent churches, which have experienced a dramatic proliferation over the last decade, mostly characterised by combining local religious knowledge with Pentecostal beliefs to mainly promote healing and financial stability. A common aspect among these churches is that they all have the Bible as their central scripture, they keep Sunday as the Day of the Lord and therefore perform crowded ceremonies on this day. Meanwhile, in the Catholic faith, the Bible, along with the traditions of the Roman Catholic Church, such as prayers to the saints and veneration of Mary are considered possible ways of communicating with God.[9] Islam has the Quran as fundamental source of scripture, uses a calendar of its own and performs prayers in a very particular way, with women separated from men and very rigorous prayer schedules.

The Covid-19 pandemic challenged these frameworks of religious practice, and all religious denominations were forced to change their routines and alter the way that sermons and services were performed, including using online platforms to broadcast messages or for worship, since people were encouraged to pray at home, as public gatherings either banned or restricted. These diverse strategies were observed in Mozambican churches as they struggled to cope with the adversities caused by the pandemic. Overall, in the religious response to Covid-19 in Mozambique, some denominations raised awareness about the severity of the disease and complied with government guidelines to keep their members from being infected, while others were sceptical about the seriousness of the problem, leading to disobedience in following safety regulations. Considering this background, this chapter analyses the response of churches to the regulation of religious activities due to Covid-19.

---

[8] Asamoah-Gyadu, J. 2021. "Pentecostalism and Coronavirus. Reframing the message of health and wealth in a pandemic era", *Spiritus* 6(1):160.

[9] Reesink ML. 2005. "Para uma antropologia do milagre: Nossa Senhora, seus devotos e o regime do milagre [Towards an anthropology of the miracle: Our Lady, her devotees and the miracle regime]", *Caderno CRH* 18(44):18527.

It looks particularly at measures taken to maintain the faith of church members amidst social distancing. It also looks at the impact of Covid-19 on scriptural teachings, with emphasis on concepts of healing and beliefs about sin and death.

THE MISSIONARY ENTERPRISE IN MOZAMBIQUE

Faith and beliefs were imbricated into the African social fabric long before European presence. Africans have a record of relying on faith and beliefs to deal with physical and social ills. Traditional rulers were endowed with sacred powers, including rainmaking and protection against evil forces. In sum, African societies had ritual experts who mediated between the visible and invisible worlds.[10] Thus, it was not surprising that Africans appropriated Christianity by incorporating elements of African traditional religions, such as spiritual possession and healing.[11] This shows that before European arrival, Africa experienced a vivid and functional religious foundation, which guided people's lives. This status quo was disturbed by the missionary actions, which downplayed African traditions. As is recorded in some missionary writings, African culture and social customs were depicted as the dark side of Africa by connecting them with the devil,[12] and thus indicating a clear disrespect and lack of understanding of African cultures. Following European conquest, Mozambique was colonised by Portugal, a country with a deep Christian tradition and belief in monotheism. Additionally, other independent churches, such as the Protestant, Pentecostal, and African Initiated Churches, were oriented towards healing – and practices of speaking in tongues, purification rites and taboos emerged.[13] The colonial government saw these churches as competitors to its Catholic missionaries, who were focused on converting Africans to Catholicism through a process of rejection of African religions. Moreover, religious proselytism was undertaken by Muslims and by Protestant churches, all of which endeavoured to evangelise Mozambique.[14] One thing to be noticed here is that regardless of the theological background these denominations brought, they overlapped local traditions and customs that existed a long time before the European expansion.

Many people were obliged to follow Christianity and other religions during the colonial period in Mozambique. Immediately after independence, religious organisations suffered interference from the newly installed Marxist-Leninist regime. Only after the Constitutions of 1990 and 2004 did religious organisations gain freedom to operate in the country. The easing of religious control created enabling conditions for

---

10   Ellis S and ter Haar G. 1998. "Religion and politics in Sub-saharan Africa", *The Journal of Modern African Studies* 36(2):187.

11   Ellis and ter Haar. 1998. "Religion and politics in Sub-saharan Africa", 199.

12   Ellis and ter Haar. 1998. "Religion and politics in Sub-saharan Africa", 197.

13   Alfredsson U and Linha C. 1990. "Where God lives. An introduction to a study of the independent churches in Maputo", *SEC Research Reports*, No. 20, April. Uppsala: SEC/ILU Uppsala University, 7.

14   Serapiao LB. 1993. "Mozambique Liberation Front in Mozambique (FRELIMO) and Religion in Mozambique, 1962-1988", *Istituto Italiano per l'Africa e l'Orient*, 48(1):112.

churches to thrive; thus, African Independent Churches and Protestants expanded countrywide. However, the 2004 Constitution made it clear that in the case of declaration of state of war, siege or emergency, the government could interfere in ways that religions should behave.[15] As is discussed below, when the pandemic hit Mozambique, the government interfered in religious freedoms, imposing many restrictions aiming to reduce interpersonal contact and curb Coronavirus infections.

SECURITY MEASURES IN MOZAMBIQUE DURING THE PANDEMIC

Following the diagnosis of the first Covid-19 case, the government of Mozambique declared a state of emergency on 30 March 2020. Thereafter, the president addressed the nation monthly to update the people on regulations concerning Covid-19 mitigation. After the expiration of the time stipulated by law to declare the state of emergency, the government declared a state of public calamity. The change from the state of emergency to state of public calamity meant a shift from partial commitment to a much more substantial one, because of the seriousness of the crisis and its direct effects on citizens. However, both policies focused on imposing strict social distancing measures. Table 26.1 provides a short chronology of main presidential decrees to curb the spread of Covid-19 in Mozambique.

Table 26.1: Main presidential decrees to curb the spread of Covid-19

DECREE NO.	CONTENT	IMPACT ON RELIGIOUS ACTIVITIES
11/2020 of 30 March	The President declares a State of Emergency due to public calamity in all territory.	Interdicts public events, including religious cults; imposes lockdown for preventive measures.
12/2020 of 2 April	Approves the administrative enforcement measures for the prevention and containment of the spread of the Covid-19 pandemic to be in force during the State of Emergency.	Suspends religious celebrations in all places of worship.
12/2020 of 29 April	Extends the State of Emergency, for reasons of public calamity, for another 30 days.	Suspends religious celebrations in all places of worship.
14/2020 of 28 May	Extends the State of Emergency, for reasons of public calamity, for another 30 days.	Suspends religious celebrations in all places of worship.
21/2020 of 26 June	Extends, for the third time, the State of Emergency.	Limits religious services.
51/2020 of 1 July	Extends the State of Emergency.	Suspends religious celebrations in all places of worship.

---

15 US State Department, IRF Mozambique 2019.

Decree no.	Content	Impact on religious activities
23/2020 of 5 August	Declares the State of Emergency due to public calamity in national territory.	Limits religious services.
79/2020 of 4 September	Declares the Situation of Public Calamity and activates the Red Alert.	Limits the number of participants in religious celebrations to 50% of the place of gathering as long as it does not exceed 150 people.
Resolution 73/2020 of 29 October	Approves the Communication from the President of the Republic to the Assembly of the Republic about the Terms of the State of Emergency.	The National Parliament states that the duration of the State of Emergency respected Article 292 of the Constitution.
102/2020 of 23 November	Establishes measures to contain the spread of the Covid-19 pandemic, while the Public Calamity Situation is in force.	Limits religious gatherings in places of worship to 50% of the maximum capacity as long as it does not exceed 150 people. It recommends the dissemination of Covid-19 prevention messages in church services.
110/2020 of 18 December	Establishes measures to contain the spread of the Covid-19 pandemic, while the Public Calamity Situation is in force and revokes 102/2020 of 23 November.	Limits gatherings for church services to 50% of the maximum capacity of the hall and imposes 2 metres social distancing.
1/2021 of 13 January	Reviews the measures to contain the spread of the Covid-19 pandemic, while the Public Calamity Situation lasts, and repeals 110/2020 of 18 December.	Limits gatherings for church services to 50% of the maximum capacity of the hall and imposes 2 metres social distancing.
2/2021 of 4 February	Reviews the measures to contain the spread of the Covid-19 pandemic, while the Public Calamity Situation lasts, and repeals 1/2021 of 13 January.	Closes places of worship in national territory for 30 days.
7/2021 of 5 March	Reviews the measures to contain the spread of the Covid-19 pandemic, while the Public Calamity Situation approved by 2/2021 of 4 February lasts.	Closes places of worship in national territory for 30 days.
17/2021 of 6 April	Reviews the measures to contain the spread of the Covid-19 pandemic, while the Public Calamity Situation approved by 7/2021 of 5 March lasts.	Closes places of worship in national territory for 21 days.

Decree no.	Content	Impact on religious activities
24/2021 of 26 April	Reviews the measures to contain the spread of the Covid-19 pandemic, while the Public Calamity Situation approved by 17/2021 of 6 April lasts.	
30/2021 of 26 May	Reviews the measures to contain the spread of the Covid-19 pandemic, while the Public Calamity Situation approved by 24/2021 of 26 April lasts.	The number of participants must not exceed 40% of the maximum capacity of each place and a maximum of 75 people in closed spaces and 150 people in open spaces.
42/2021 of 24 June	Reviews the measures to contain the spread of the Covid-19 pandemic, while the Public Calamity Situation approved by 30/2021 of 26 May lasts.	The number of participants must not exceed 40% of the maximum capacity of each place and a maximum of 40 people in closed places and 80 people in open places.
50/2021 of 16 July	Reviews the measures to contain the spread of the Covid-19 pandemic, while the Public Calamity Situation lasts and repeals 42/2021 of 24 June.	Closes places of worship in national territory for 30 days.
56/2021 of 13 August	Reviews the measures to contain the spread of the Covid-19 pandemic, while the Public Calamity Situation approved by 50/2021 of 16 July lasts.	Places of worship, conferences and religious celebrations are closed for 30 days throughout the national territory.
76/2021 of 24 September	Reviews the measures to contain the spread of the Covid-19 pandemic, while the Public Calamity Situation approved by 62/2021 of 27 August lasts.	Authorises the opening of places of worship nationwide for not more than 50 and 100 people in closed and open spaces respectively, not exceeding 30% of its capacity.
86/2021 of 25 October	It reviews the measures to contain the spread of the Covid-19 pandemic, while the Public Calamity Situation approved by 76/2021 of 24 September lasts.	Authorises the opening of places of worship nationwide for not more than 100 and 250 people in closed and open spaces respectively, not exceeding 50% of its capacity.
94/2021 of 20 December	Reviews the measures for the propagation of Covid-19 Pandemic, while the situation of public calamity approved by Decree no.86/2021 of 25 October prevails.	Authorises the opening of places of worship nationwide for not more than 100 and 250 people in closed and open spaces respectively, not exceeding 50% of its capacity.

Decree no.	Content	Impact on religious activities
2/2022 of 19 January	It reviews the measures to contain the spread of the Covid-19 pandemic, while the Public Calamity Situation approved by 94/2021 of 20 December lasts.	Authorises the opening of places of worship nationwide for not more than 100 and 250 people in closed and open spaces respectively, not exceeding 50% of its capacity.
4/2022 of 18 February	It reviews the measures to contain the spread of the Covid-19 pandemic, while the Public Calamity Situation approved by 2/2022 of 19 January lasts.	Authorises the opening of places of worship nationwide for not more than 500 and 1 000 people in closed and open spaces respectively, not exceeding 50% of its capacity.

This compilation of relevant legislation on the impact of Covid-19 on religious activities shows that in a period of two years, the government issued laws that closed the access to church facilities for ten months and imposed restrictions to the number of people that could assemble for fourteen months.

THE COVID-19 OUTBREAK AND INTERPRETATIONS ABOUT ITS ORIGINS

The Covid-19 infections and deaths shook the world terribly and suddenly, and they conditioned people's lives and livelihoods in different ways. The pandemic affected church organisations in respect of the way they explained the origins of the virus to their brethren. As the infectious circle expanded, churches and their clergy endeavoured to provide responses to people's questions and fears about the disease. Fundamentally, preachers and church members shared a belief that the pandemic was God's punishment, a result of the misuse of natural resources and an indication of the end of times.[16] A similar approach is taken by Maria Frahm-Art, a scholar of Pentecostal-charismatic Christianity, who points out that people's disobedience results in something going wrong in their lives, in this case, the pandemic.[17] Stephen Lubari, an historian of missions, goes further, stating that Christians compared imposed restrictions amidst pandemic to the end of the world and were reminded of the time of Noah when the flood occurred and the time of Jesus's temptations.[18] Moreover, Thembelani Jentile, a theologian, suggests that the pandemic molded people back to what they were supposed to be or to what they should have been.[19] These authors converge in seeing the pandemic as a propitious moment for people to come close to God and enhance their spirituality.

---

16 Lubari SE. 2020. "Covid-19 stories and experiences from South Sudan and Uganda", *Transformation: An International Journal of Holistic Mission Studies* (Special Issue: Mission During the Covid-19 pandemic) 37(4):319.

17 Frahm-Art M. 2021. "The practice of confessions and absolution as an agent of change in a prophetic Pentecostal church during Covid-19", *HTS Teologiese/Theological studies* 77(3):5.

18 Lubari, "Covid-19 stories and experiences", 321.

19 Jentile T. "*ICawa ivaliwe*: The church during the pandemic", *Pharos Journal of Theology* 101:6.

It is worth mentioning that until the beginning of March 2020, churches regulated their own activities, and the authorities did not interfere in this process at all. Even with the news about the propagation of the virus from China to the rest of the world, for some Mozambicans, these were just rumours and an invention of the modern world. When the first case was detected in Mozambique, churches registered divided opinions on how to administer preaching and how to act during this period. Nevertheless, there is a strong correlation among them regarding coronavirus connection to evil and actual sinful society.

Below are some examples of prayers to eradicate the Covid-19 pandemic:

> We, men here on earth, must confess that we are indeed sinners. We depart from your commandments to serve Satan and the sins he teaches. And so, sin took over the world. That is why we are suffering from so many evils of body and soul. As the shadow does not come out of the sun, neither do these evils come out of You: these are the consequences of your sins of the sin of the World increasingly distant from You, our CREATOR AND LEGISLATOR. Help us to repent of our sins, so that we can be forgiven in the Soul and healed in the body. We always want to follow Your Laws to improve the world. Afflicted, we ask for mercy. Drive away this coronavirus epidemic and all spiritual epidemics. They are what make us run away from You and hate each other. Mercy, our GREAT GOD. Amen.[20]

> We pray that restrictions will be lifted, so that the mass evangelism we planned for November together with the Malawian Fellowship of Youth can go ahead.[21]

> In Luke 10-19, Jesus said, behold, I give you power to tread on serpents and scorpions and every force of evil. At this moment we are going to pray so that all the demons and diseases behind the Covid-19 are paralysed, neutralised and all people infected by the virus are cured in the name of Jesus. I fight all demons behind coronavirus right now and paralyze them in the name of Jesus. Release humanity in the name of Jesus.[22]

> Lord Jesus, father of heaven, we have just ended this time that you have given us to interact with your people. Thank you so much for this privilege of being here in this place and we ask that lord Jesus at this moment extend your mighty hand on all those who are currently suffering from infirmities. Particularly in Mozambique, we hear that there are ten people sick with this epidemic of coronavirus, but I declare in the name of Jesus that the hand of God reaches upon these people and they are discharged to return to the family. I cry out for fire to break this curse in the name of Jesus and

---

20 Nossa Senhora de Fatima Cathedral. n.d. "Prayer to drive away coronavirus". Retrieved from the church 13 February 2022.

21 Zambezi Mission, York Baptist Church. 2021. "In Prayer", May-July, 3. Online at: https://zambesimission.org/wp-content/uploads/In-Prayer-May-July-2021-Print-Friendly.pdf

22 Igreja Ministerial Nações para Cristo. 2020. " Onório Cutane: Oração e Jejum contra Covid-19 por Moçambique e pelas Nações do Mundo [Prayer and Fasting against Covid-19 for Mozambique and the Nations of the World]", *Facebook*, 26 March.

once again my beloved brethren believe only in Jesus, give your testimony so that the name of Jesus may be glorified.[23]

My God will answer all things, we must stand firm for what is to come. Let us trust God completely. This is not the time to play in sin. It is the moment to walk in holiness so that our lives may be spared in the name of Jesus.[24]

Allah sends the storm to make us humble. The pandemic descends when sins are practised. The pandemic is a punishment that Allah sends to his people. Allah, push away this difficult situation that we are living, Allah helps us. Let's teach our children, our wives, brothers to do Istiftah (praise Allah) at least 500 times a day so that Allah has mercy on us and changes our situation, opens the madrassa and our masjids (mosques). We ask Allah that this pandemic will end in every corner of the world.[25]

These prayers were collected from websites from different churches and mosques in various provinces of Mozambique. They demonstrate how churches and mosques consistently explained issues provoked by the pandemic as a payback for people's sins. Furthermore, in what appears to be blaming of evil and demons, religious organisations also provided specific instructions to believers on how to halt the spread of the virus, which will be analysed below.

LOCKDOWNS AND SPIRITUALITY IN MOZAMBIQUE'S CHURCHES

Church leaders and members interpreted Covid-19 outbreak in varied ways. The main response was to point to sin, negligence and behaviour that was not approved in Christianity or other religions as being the roots of the problem. An analysis of the way the pandemic affected people's spirituality must be done, since for certain periods religious believers in Mozambique did not have access to physical worship places. This had effects not just on religion and religious organisations, but on spirituality more broadly.

It is important to this discussion to acknowledge the conceptual differences between religiosity and spirituality as a way of displaying the nuances that were verified during this period. Although sometimes difficult to distinguish, it can be said that the main difference between religiosity and spirituality has to do with the way faith is lived. According to American physician and medical professor Dale Matthews and fellow researchers, religiosity is "the involvement in, or endorsement of, practices, prayers, beliefs, attitudes, or sentiments that are associated with an

---

[23] A hora dos Pastores|Em directo|Ministerio Divina Esperança [The Hour of the Shepherds|Live|Ministerio Divina Esperança], *Ebenezer TV*, 8 April 2020.

[24] Igreja Ministerio de Deus com a Humanidade. 2020. *Facebook*, 23 March.

[25] Sheik Takdir Abdula. 2020. "Palestra sobre a Pandemia [Lecture on the Pandemic]", *Facebook*, 21 March.

organised community of faith".[26] Meanwhile, "spirituality seeks to facilitate communication between the transcendent and the believer" and "empowers individual introspection and provides hope".[27] Although religion and spirituality seem to function separately, there is an intrinsic relation between the two. For instance, a physical place of worship does not define people's spiritually; however, the whole environment can contribute to a deeper and intimate interaction with one's deity.

Mozambique has registered a rise in the number of religious organisations in recent years. One of the things that makes them popular is the "gospel of prosperity". One can hold the impression that people are always open to embrace a new religion when it promises to relieve social problems such as illnesses, spiritual problems and financial constraints. According to African religion and theology scholar Andreas Heuser, the feeling of financial unfulfilment and economic ambition can precipitate the search for solutions in churches of prosperity.[28] In 2011, a Protestant church and one the principal precursors of the prosperity gospel, the Igreja Universal do Reino de Deus (IURD) (Universal Church of the Kingdom of God), promoted an event called Dia da Decisão (Decision Day), a day that would grant a new life to whoever attended the event. On this day, people were invited to participate in the worship service irrespective of their religion, because that day would supposedly give a fresh start and resolve many problems. Reports show that there was an unprecedent peak in the number of attendants, which revealed how eager people were to resolve the problems they face in their daily lives.[29]

As the Covid-19 infections leaped ahead worldwide, nations did not stop in the search for a cure. Some believed in a scientific solution, and others saw salvation through repentance. Many people were affected by the pandemic, and in this context feelings of depression and desolation were recurrent. The updates on the number of deaths in Mozambique were provided daily, and many people saw the deaths of their relatives, friends and colleagues. In addition, companies shut down, leaving many families without sources of survival. While some lost their jobs, others were forced to work from home and also faced the closure of their churches, which could have been their haven, where they prayed for relief, understanding and comfort.[30] The reasons why people looked to prayer and why the search for

---

26 Matthews DA et al. 1998. "Religious commitment and health status: a review of research and implications for family practice", *Archives of Family Medicine* 7(2):118-124.

27 Da Silva J and Da Silva L. 2014. "Relação entre religião, espiritualidade e sentido da vida [Relationship between religion, spirituality and meaning of life]", *Revista da Associação brasileira de logoterapia e análise existencial* [Journal of the Brazilian Association of Logotherapy and Existential Analysis] 3(2):208.

28 Heuser A. 2016. "Charting African Prosperity Gospel Economies", *HTS Teologiese Studies/Theological Studies* 72(4):8.

29 "Dia da Decisão promovido pela igreja universal reúne cerca de 500 mil fiéis em Moçambique [Decision Day promoted by the Universal Church brings together around 500,000 faithful in Mozambique]", *GospelPrime.com*, 28 September 2011.

30 Bentzen JS. 2021. "In crisis we pray: Religiosity and the Covid-19 pandemic", *Journal of Economic Behavior and Organization* 192:542.

prayer increased amidst Covid-19 pandemic may be because praying provided a certain way of consolation for those who were troubled.

Timothée Bationo, a priest and missionary, asserts that people who go through traumatic experiences find in sacramental homilies insights on how to cope with them.[31] There is no direct relation between religion and spirituality as demonstrated before; however, it appears that people's spiritual life is stronger when attending church. As researcher Realito Adamugy Momade has demonstrated, the levels of spirituality decreased due to suspension of religious activities and ineffectiveness of activities done outside the churches.[32] Activities such as prayers at home, home worship and individual evangelism were not effective because people lacked expertise to perform accordingly.[33] These arguments make sense in the case of many Mozambican churches, which are organised in a hierarchal structure that is applied even in religious ceremonies. Before Covid began, prayers were performed by a consecrated person, but when everyone was confined home, people were challenged to become their own evangelisers and assume the role of spiritual leaders. Therefore, restrictions imposed on churches to hinder the propagation of the virus "were seen as an attack on the freedom to religion".[34] In Mozambique, the state of calamity extended for almost two years, depriving people of communal worshipping and reducing their spirituality.

It is important to emphasise that not everyone felt spiritually unfavoured by the pandemic repercussions. Some claim to have become sufficiently independent to continue worshipping by themselves. As one of our survey respondents maintained, "No, I always read on my own. I never allow them to do the interpretation for me, unless it is content that God is not revealing to me. As far as I know, leaders of my church maintained their scriptural organisation, because Scriptures cannot be adapted to any situation."[35] As it has been highlighted by religion and economics scholar Jeanet Bentzen, people tend to use their religion more intensively when coming across adversities.[36] Additionally, searches for prayer texts, which rose dramatically during the pandemic proved to be connected to spirituality and to a much lesser extent related to religious worship.[37] According to Jerry Pillay, a South African theologian, "Covid-19 has shown that faith survives without pastors, priests

---

31 Bationo T. 2004. "Preaching as a prophetic symbolic action. A case study of Luke 4, 14-22. In view of healing of the Sena People of Mozambique". Thesis for Ecclesiastic Baccalaureate in Theology, Tangaza College: The Catholic University of Eastern Africa, 35.

32 Momade RAU. 2021. "The impacts of Covid-19 on the Spiritual Life of Believers: case of Assembly of God Evangelical Church, Mozambique Island, 2020", *Academia Letters*, art 3329, August, 5.

33 Momade RAU. 2021. "The impacts of Covid-19 on the Spiritual Life of Believers", 7.

34 Jentile, "*ICawa ivaliwe:* The church during the pandemic", 2.

35 Online survey responses to religious adaptation during the Covid-19 pandemic, February-April 2022.

36 Bentzen JS. 2019. "Acts of God? Religiosity and Natural Disasters Across Subnational World", *The Economic Journal* 129(622):30.

37 Bentzen, "In crisis we pray", 544.

and bishops and that closure of churches reinforced the idea of 'priest' in each home."[38] As an illustration of this, one of the respondents to our survey reported that the pandemic was "serving to make some believers realise that it is not the beautiful church, spoken language or other aspects that guarantee faith."[39] Even though religious people somehow found a space apart from their churches to build or enrich their relation of intimacy with their God, this banalisation of worship places seems rather exaggerated, because group gatherings play an important role in making people firm in their beliefs through interaction with other followers. So, it would be reasonable to consider worship places an asset or tool to improve or maintain believers' commitment.

Churches implemented innovative methods to adapt to lockdown conditions and make believers self-reliant in matters of spirituality. For instance, some churches introduced the practice of introspection, which consisted of people reflecting upon their sins, then confessing to be absolved and forgiven by God.[40] Besides being exhorted to recognise their sins, people were alerted to avoid dual allegiance – the practice of mixing biblical principles with traditional rituals – because church leaders knew how people were desperate for immediate solutions. Since African traditions were never completely erased, this could be a propitious moment for a faith shift, and the pastors did not want to lose church members to private practice of traditional rituals at home.

Pillay, who is also a Reformed Church pastor and church leader, asserts that the Covid-19 experience drew people into a more appropriate understanding of Christian mission with the focus being not on the church but on the reign of God.[41] Up to a point, one can consider that the pandemic forced people to debunk or deconstruct their own faith and to build meaningful connection with their deities. However, in the view of church pastors, it was important to acknowledge that churches had an essential role, and they also paved the way of transformation during this period. This is also where interest in beliefs about sin and death revived, as church leaders and believers read and interpreted the scriptures to address the situation under Covid.

MOST-READ SCRIPTURES AND INTERPRETATIONS DURING THE PANDEMIC

Mozambique is a multicultural country in which religious denominations have been on the rise. Although they do not share the same principles, almost all follow

---

38 Pillay J. 2020. "Covid-19 shows the need to make church more flexible", *Transformation: An International Journal of Holistic Mission Studies* 37(4):272.

39 Online survey responses.

40 Frahm-Arp M. 2021. The practice of confession and absolution as an agent of change in a prophetic Pentecostal church during Covid-19", *HTS Teologiese Studies/Theological Studies* 77(3):art 6560, 2.

41 Pillay, "Covid-19 shows the need to make church more flexible", 279.

directives from a particular scriptural source, which might be the Bible, the Quran or another sacred instrument. In the context of the pandemic, Christians and Muslims, in particular, used a wide range of scriptures to instigate reflection, repentance and change of behaviour. These messages were transmitted via online sermons, phone calls and emails, since face-to-face interactions were suspended. According to Pillay, lockdown forced churches to close, and in the endeavour to keep contact with the faithful, they had to resort to creative ways of fulfilling their mission.[42] For instance, some religious denominations managed to create online services through Zoom meetings, virtual sermons and other events, in order to take the church to the people.[43]

In the time of Covid-19, churches followed two approaches, which can be regarded as anti- and pro-prevention. As reported by Jeff Levin, an epidemiologist, some religious organisations disseminated scripturally based messages contending that the virus was Satan's plan to eliminate Christians, and they dissuaded people from following public health recommendations and other crucial measures aimed at protecting people.[44] In this case, some churches remained open and performed services regardless of the dangerousness and disobedience to the government's rules. There were reports of imprisonment of church leaders in Manica Province, in central Mozambique, allegedly for assembling hundreds of people for prayers in violation of the presidential decree of the state of emergency.[45] This revealed certain scepticism towards Covid-19 restrictions, as these church leaders decided to keep performing service despite official prohibition. Other church leaders used their preaching and other means to influence believers' opinions to understand the importance of obeying the rules.[46] As one respondent to our survey noted, "Some religious denominations used scriptures to justify the emergence of Covid-19 and to encourage vaccination."[47] This was also in line with Article 16 of the Decree 102/2020 from the government, which suggested the use of worship place for dissemination of security measures.[48]

Theologians and faith leaders believe that scriptures will never be outdated; thus, one can find in them responses to actual problems that occur today. This would not be different with the pandemic. In theologian Edwin Odulio's assessment, the scriptures' stories are aimed at calling people back to Jesus Christ, advise repentance

---

42 Pillay, "Covid-19 shows the need to make church more flexible", 267.

43 Behera MN. 2020. "Mission during the Covid-19 pandemic", *Transformation: An International Journal of Holistic Mission Studies* 37(4):318.

44 Levin J. 2020. "The Faith Community and the SARS-CoV-2 Outbreak: Part of the problem or part of the solution?", *Journal of Religion and Health* 59:2218.

45 Jequete B. 2020. "Covid-19: Líderes religiosos detidos em Manica por cultos ilegais [Covid-19: Religious detained in Manica for illegal cults]", *Deutsche Welle*, 22 April.

46 Williams J et al. 2021. "Prioritizing health: churches to the Covid-19 pandemic", *Journal of Prevention & Intervention in the Community* 28 June, 5.

47 Online survey responses.

48 Boletim da República, Conselho de Ministros. Decreto no 102/2020 de 23 de Novembro, I Série, Número 224, art 16.

and inspire faith in the gospel.[49] Health and disease are seen and experienced in a religious perspective in Africa. In this context, people tormented with despair and fear resorted to all available means to cope with the pandemic. Researcher Jeanet Bentzen reports a massive rise of Google searches for prayers in the midst of the Covid-19 pandemic.[50] It was not clear who searched for prayers, whether it was churches' leaders or members, but it is reasonable to say that people sought and perhaps found relief in scriptures.

The messages spotlighted in the scriptures by religious denominations emphasised sin, repentance, hope, faith and healing. One of our survey respondents stated, "Scriptures were suited to the reality, thus there was emphasis on scriptures that teach about the need of repentance."[51] For example, the Catholic Church, besides advising on the need for compliance for security measures, highlighted sermons that included scriptures inspired by St. Paul's experience with the gospel, whereby he was convert from a persecutor of men to a hunter for souls.[52] Moreover, inspired by 1 John 4:8-16, Pope Francis preached on the necessity of leading people back to God based on a deeper relationship with Him.[53] This was a global directive shared from the Vatican that was also implemented locally. Catholic priest Henriques Bascones stated that in difficult times there are sacrifices that must be made for the common good. According to him, prevention was the fortune of all people, so everyone should follow the recommendations.[54]

Muslim religious leaders interpreted the outbreak in two different ways. One side, considered conservative, debated whether the pandemic was "divine punishment against nonbelievers", while the other side collaborated with authorities in providing practical advice on how to avoid contracting the virus.[55] In Mozambique, the Islamic Council disseminated messages of hope and solidarity to the worshippers through campaigns that also aimed to inform people about prevention methods.[56] This action was based on the *hadith*, "Make use of medical treatment, for Allah did not make a disease without indicating a remedy for it, with the exception of one

---

49 Odulio EB. 2020. "Developments and challenges in the use and interpretation of Scriptures in the study and teaching of Christian moral life", *MST Review* 22(1):28.
50 Bentzen, "In crisis we pray", 559.
51 Online survey responses.
52 Tavares PD. 2021. "Cartas Paulinas: Um exemplo de ação evangelizadora, em tempos de pandemia? [Pauline Letters: An example of evangelising action in times of pandemic]". Online at: https://repositorio.uninter.com/handle/1/704
53 Cezar Costa P. 2020. "Pandemia e Pós-pandemia: Dez pontos para reflexão" [Pandemic and Post-pandemic: Ten points for reflection], *Vatican News*, 8 May.
54 Bascones H. 2020. "Igreja Catolica-Paroquia da Polana", *Facebook* [Accessed 1 April 2022].
55 Hanna A. 2020. "What Islamists are Doing and Saying on Covid-19 Crisis", Wilson Center, 14 May.
56 "Visão Mundial e Conselho Islâmico juntos na luta contra a Covid-19 [World Vision and Islamic Council together in the fight against Covid-19]", *Jornal Noticias*, 12 June 2020.

disease: old age."[57] Muslim leaders strongly believed that the pandemic was God's punishment for people's sins. The message spread among Muslims on YouTube or Facebook was that the solution was obeying Allah's orders.[58]

Another clear usage of scriptures can be found in one of Pentecostal church Prophet Onório Cutane's sermons amidst the pandemic in which he exhorted believers to not be afraid, because fear could be worse than the virus itself. Beyond encouraging people to follow the instructions from the government he tells people to trust in God as the solution. Overall, Cutane's sermons rely on two principal scriptures. The first was Philemon 4:6 "Don't worry about anything! Present your concerns to God through prayer, supplication, and thanksgiving in all circumstances."[59] The prophet used this scripture to encourage worshippers to not give up praying and continue believing, so that that God does not abandon them.

The second was 2 Chronicles 7:13-14: "If I close the heavens, and there is no rain; or if the plague is ordered to consume the land; or if I send pestilence among my people; And if my people, which are called by my name, shall humble themselves, and pray, and seek my face, and turn from their wicked ways, then will I hear from heaven, and will forgive their sin, and will heal their land."[60] This scripture amplified the interpretation of the disease. The pestilence and plague mentioned above are depicted as evil diseases that can be sent to devastate humanity because of its sins and impurity. Prophet Onório compares the pestilence with the virus that killed thousands of people in short time. According to Prophet Onório, the plague was sent not to make people despair, but to trigger the faith inside them and inspire true Christianity.

Undoubtedly, the use of scriptures was accentuated during this period. Church leaders relied on a wide range of scriptures to trigger feelings of repentance and deliver sin. There were also abundant approaches about hope and healing, which would become a reality if people returned to their roots. Since not every church had the opportunity to conduct services in this period, due to the financial cost of creating and maintaining a virtual church, it can be said that this also defined how these churches interpreted the scriptures, sometimes to allay not only the peoples' fears, but the churches own concerns for institutional survival. As one survey respondence put it, "The message remained the same, the appeal for true belief, surrender to Jesus, end of times, hope. It was possible to notice some differences, especially in the type of message preached, the concern of some churches, the fear of failure of others, and the deviation of the focus."[61]

---

57 Soares P. 2020. "O islam, as pandemias, os conselhos do profeta e a medicina dos imames [Islam, pandemics, the prophet's advice and the medicine of the Imams]", *Carta Capital*, 21 April.
58 Yussuf Y. 2021. "Conselhos do Islam Compilacoes [Advice from Islam Compilations]", *YouTube*, 24 February.
59 Bible. Philippians 4.
60 Bible. 2 Chronicles 7:12-15.
61 Online survey responses.

SURVEYING SCRIPTURAL MESSAGING IN THE PANDEMIC

To gain further understanding of how churches adapted and interpreted scriptures, we conducted an online survey to capture the religious experience of people during Covid-19 pandemic. Web surveys have the advantage of collecting large amounts of data efficiently and economically within relatively short time.[62] Moreover, people feel free to respond online because they do not have the pressure of having someone in front questioning them, thus it can be convenient for some.[63] We used the electronic survey to respond to the complexity of the issue within the context of social distancing and limited resources to conduct face-to-face interviews. The survey was conducted online and targeted all eleven provinces of Mozambique. It used closed questions and open-ended options to capture any information that might have been left out. The survey covered 156 respondents, varying in age from 20 to above 50 years old. Among the respondents, 52.6% were female, 44.2% male and 3.2% did not reveal their gender. In terms of level of education, 66.6% of respondents had a bachelor's degree, 18.6% had completed secondary education, while 13.5% had a master's degree. The survey participants were asked eleven key questions about their viewpoints regarding articulation of the message of God and most-read scriptures during the pandemic.

The findings of the present study suggest that most religious denominations customised their ceremonies and sermons to respond to the new reality the pandemic brought, so this chapter has focused on this significant matter. When asked whether they noticed any changes in the interpretation of the holy scriptures in the period of Covid-19, at least 57.6% (90 out of 156) respondents denoted changes in the way the scriptures were broadcast and interpreted during the pandemic. On the other hand, 42.3% (66 out of 156) indicated the maintenance of normal preaching instruments.

Overall, respondents indicated that sermons revolved around messages and scriptures about sin, repentance and faith in times of turmoil, healing and salvation. Study respondents, reported that pandemic sermons: (1) justified the emergence of the virus as a result of humans' sinful nature and also emphasised the importance of forgiveness, (2) that exhorted repentance for sins committed and the need for a fortified faith in God and (3) promised healing through faith and salvation for those who follow God's teachings. Asked for examples of the most-read scriptural passages at church or in public events, respondents provided examples of scriptures they heard or read in compliance with church instructions or which they found through individual searches. According to these worshippers, these messages bred determination, hope and encouragement to cope. As one congregant put it, "Yes, more messages of encouragement were preached so that the sheep do not get lost and do not lose their faith in Christ Jesus."[64]

---

62 Lefever S, Dal M and Matthíasdóttir A. 2007. "Online data collection in academic research: advantages limitations", *British Journal of Education Technology* 38(4):575.

63 Evans JR and Mathur A. 2005. "The value of online surveys", *Internet Research* 15(2):198.

64 Online survey responses.

The results show that religious organisations and believers reacted to Covid-19 in various ways, but they did not lose their faith. In fact, it appears that Covid-19 brought people much closer to their religiosity and spirituality. These findings are in line with studies conducted in other African countries, which emphasised that Covid-19 has increased the spirituality of believers in their engagement and encounter with God for divine intervention, healing, protection, and provision.[65] In Mozambique, as in other Africans nations, responses to Covid-19 included: (1) calls for prayer, deliverance healing; (2) preaching gospels of faith and hope, (3) demystification and democratisation of the Holy Communion and (4) the challenges of loyal membership that came with the shift to virtual congregations.[66] Despite Mozambique's limited internet coverage, this study complements findings about the swiftness of Christians' responses using social media and digital networks.[67]

CONCLUSION

The purpose of this study was to access the experiences of religious leaders and religious laypeople concerning the Covid-19 pandemic that hit Mozambique from March 2020 onward, imposing severe restrictions on worship services. The results reveal that the closing of religious ceremonies affected the organisation of many religious denominations, forcing the innovation and significant changes in scriptures hermeneutics and performance of religious sermons. When the Mozambican government decreed the closure of worship places, the only way of coping was turning to virtual settings or shutting down for the period that the Covid-prevention rules prevailed. In fact, some religious congregations were forced to close for financial reasons or even for unpreparedness to deal with the situation because the pandemic challenged all religious institutions to be flexible and uncovered gaps in their structure. However, a substantial number of churches approached the "new normal" differently, and the use of scripture was a key part of it. As one congregant described the use of scripture messages, "They are used in a way that is appropriate to the moment. Through them, events were explained, and those who were afraid to lose their loved ones were comforted. In short, the scriptures have been perfected to meet current needs – the new normal."[68]

The Covid-19 context led to the adoption of innovative ways of broadcasting holy scriptures. At some point, religious leaders also began to interpret the scriptures

---

[65] Plüss JD. 2020. "Covid-19, the church, and the challenge to ecumenism", *Transformation* 37(4); Asamoah-Gyadu JK. 2021. "Pentecostalism and Coronavirus. Reframing the message of Health-and-wealth in a pandemic era", *Spiritus* 6(1); White P. 2022. "Pentecostal spirituality in the context of faith and hope (prosperity preaching): African Pentecostal response to the Covid-19 pandemic", *Dialog* 61(2):148-155; Djube PA and Burge RP. 2020. "The prosperity gospel of coronavirus response", *Politics & Religion*, 16 April.

[66] White, "Pentecostal spirituality in the context of faith and hope", 149.

[67] Pluss, "Covid-19, the church, and the challenge to ecumenism", 294.

[68] Online survey responses.

in a way that aligned with the pandemic phenomenon. For example, respondents indicated the intensification of messages of hope, repentance, self-reflexivity and end of times in church preaching, especially when infections reached alarming rates in the country. It is worth noting that Christian and Muslim congregations took different approaches in relation to liturgical practices. For instance, respondents indicated that some leaders challenged state lockdown regulations by encouraging their members to gather in groups for prayers. But, overall, the pandemic period showed that when the government and religious organisations come together, they effectively address unpredicted challenges.

What is unique about the study presented here of the theologies and beliefs about sin and death in the time of Covid-19 is its contextualisation in the historical development of religious institutions in Mozambique, a country that is relatively overlooked in African religious studies due to language barriers for most English and French speakers. The results are also interesting because, being a product of online survey, they captured the perceptions of educated people, a segment of the Mozambique population that is often portrayed as less prone to religiosity. The fact that most of the participants in the only survey revealed deep religiosity and spirituality shows that religion continues to play a major role for both spiritual and material well-being of many Mozambican people.

27 TOWARDS HEALING OUR BROKEN FOOD SYSTEM: A SOCIAL AND THEOLOGICAL RESPONSE TO FOOD INSECURITY IN SOUTH AFRICA

Linda Naicker[1]

> [T]he coronavirus has made the mighty kneel and brought the world to a halt like nothing else could. Our minds are still racing back and forth, longing for a return to "normality", trying to stitch our future to our past and refusing to acknowledge the rupture. But the rupture exists. And in the midst of this terrible despair, it offers us a chance to rethink the doomsday machine we have built for ourselves. Nothing could be worse than a return to normality. Historically, pandemics have forced humans to break with the past and imagine their world anew. This one is no different. It is a portal, a gateway between one world and the next. We can choose to walk through it, dragging the carcasses of our prejudice and hatred, our avarice, our data banks and dead ideas, our dead rivers and smoky skies behind us. Or we can walk through lightly, with little luggage, ready to imagine another world. And ready to fight for it.[2] – Arundhati Roy

INTRODUCTION

In this chapter, I address the structural and systemic nature of poverty in South Africa as it intersects with food insecurity and diet-related health disparities that disproportionately affect South Africa's poor. I concur with Roy,[3] who articulates how the pandemic has presented us with a unique portal, an opportunity anew to address our broken systems and structures and work collectively towards a better world. I argue that the pandemic heightened awareness of structural and systemic drivers of food insecurity and created opportunity for us to rebuild systems in a manner that foregrounds justice and equality for all. I further argue that given that the food security, health and well-being of all people in South Africa is enshrined in the Constitution of the Republic of South Africa, 1996, it is the prerogative of government to work closely with all stakeholders – including civil society, both the public and private sectors, nongovernmental organisations (NGOs) and faith-based organisations (FBOs) as well as other communities – to *re-envision* a more healthy and inclusive society, where poverty is holistically addressed and measured to eradicate food insecurity and food-related health disparities are decisively challenged and confronted. Moreover, from the perspective of the Christian faith, I maintain that in addressing food insecurity in South Africa, the Church needs to see itself as part of a larger whole and not operate in a silo with regard to food

---

1 Researcher, Institute for Theology and Religion, University of South Africa.
2 Roy A. 2020. "The Pandemic is a Portal", *Financial Times*, 9 April.
3 Arundhati Roy is a political analyst and human rights activist of Indian descent who challenges political and unjust power inherent in societies.

security. The Church must therefore work collectively with all stakeholders in order to envision theological innovations that cogently addresses the problem of food insecurity and related issues as a mandate of Christianity.

GOVERNMENT DEPARTMENTS AND THEIR REACTION TO THE CONSTITUTION

Section 27 of the Constitution of the Republic of South Africa, 1996, stipulates that the state, within the context of available resources, should take legislative measures to achieve proper health care services, inclusive of reproductive health care, food and water security and reasonable social security for all citizens.[4] Section 28(1) stipulates that every child has the right to basic nutrition, shelter, health care and social services, to protect them from malnutrition, neglect, abuse or degradation.[5] At the dawn of South African democracy in 1994, the need for drastic action to achieve food security for all South Africans was outlined in the Reconstruction and Development Programme.[6]

As constitutional mandate, the democratically elected government focused strongly on the food security of the nation. A national Integrated Food Security Strategy (IFSS) was adopted in 2002 in order to integrate the various existing food security programmes. The main aim of this policy was to achieve widespread access to enough nutritious food by all South Africans to meet daily dietary requirements and maintain health and well-being of all citizens.[7] The expected outcomes of this policy were that there would be greater participation and ownership of productive assets by those who were food insecure. There would be increased productivity and competitiveness in farming operations and initiatives that are owned and managed by or on behalf of food insecure people. A high level of nutrition and food safety would be attained thereby mitigating food insecurity. Better prevention and mitigation of food emergencies would be attained. There would be greater, more accurate and reliable tools of analysis, dissemination of information and communication on the status and conditions of food insecure people and the way in which improvements impact their status and lead to interventions. There would be a greater level of communication, collaboration and participation from all sectors of society in improving food insecurity interventions. The IFSS would stimulate greater governmental accountability and improve integration and coordination between government and the private sector as well as financial and administrative management.[8] The South African Department of Agriculture was appointed to

---

4   Constitution of the Republic of South Africa, 1996, s 27.
5   Constitution of the Republic of South Africa, 1996, s 28(1).
6   African National Congress (ANC). 1994. "A Basic Guide to the Reconstruction and Development Programme". Johannesburg: ANC.
7   South Africa. National Department of Agriculture (NDA). 2002. "Integrated Food Security Strategy". Pretoria: NDA.
8   Hendriks S. 2013. "Food Security in South Africa: Status Quo and Policy Imperatives", *Agrekon* 52(2):1-8.

oversee the IFSS, with a cluster of other social departments playing a supportive role. However, it has been argued that a serious disjuncture exists between institutional response mechanisms to food insecurity, as the IFSS is awkwardly positioned under the leadership of the South African Department of Agriculture, contributing to ineffective delivery.[9] Significantly, there has been no discussion on the complexities of food insecurity on an urban scale.[10] Furthermore, even though the IFSS proclaimed placing emphasis on both household and national food insecurity, it was critiqued for a lack of action.[11]

Housed within the South African Department of Health, the Integrated Nutrition Programme focuses on household food security, nutritional treatment and counselling that is disease specific, monitoring and promotion of growth, education advocacy, as well as the promotion of nutrition, breastfeeding protection and support, malnutrition control, food service management and nutritional interventions for HIV, AIDS and tuberculosis. However, this programme is deemed largely unsuccessful and has been critiqued for failing to engage the larger food system environment in South Africa.[12]

The National School Nutrition Programme housed in the South African Department of Basic Education is aimed at alleviating short-term hunger and enhancing learning capacity of school pupils through school feedings, nutritional education and the promotion of food gardens in schools. In 2012, the Department of Basic Education reported that the programme fed over eight million learners throughout all nine South African provinces. However, the programme is marred by issues of procurement.[13]

The National Policy on Food and Nutrition Security was instituted with the intention of working towards a Food and Nutrition Security Act for South Africa, and it aimed to provide a broad framework towards the fulfilment of the constitutional mandates of food security. While the focus is food security at national and household levels, there is no mention of urban food security within the policy. Despite multiple research initiatives indicating the dire sate of urban food security and the drastic increase in urban populations, the policy continues to identify rural food insecurity as the main problem.[14]

---

9 Drimie S and Ruysenaar S. 2010. "The Integrated Food Security Strategy of South Africa: An Institutional analysis", *Agrekon* 49(3):316-337.

10 Battersby J, Haysom G, Marshak M, Kroll F and Tawodzera G. 2017. "A Study on Current and Future Realities for Urban Food Security in South Africa", *South African Cities Network*. Braamfontein: SACities, 54.

11 Battersby et al, "A Study on Current and Future Realities for Urban Food Security", 55.

12 Battersby et al, "A Study on Current and Future Realities for Urban Food Security", 55.

13 Battersby et al, "A Study on Current and Future Realities for Urban Food Security", 55.

14 South Africa. Department of Agriculture, Forestry and Fisheries. 2014. "The national policy on food and nutrition security for the Republic of South Africa", *Government Gazette* No. 37915, 22 August.

The National Development Plan of 2012 is an overarching plan aimed at eradicating poverty and reducing unemployment and disparity by 2030 in South Africa by developing an inclusive economic policy, increasing state and societal capacity, endorsing strong leadership and engaging in partnerships with societal stakeholders. Connecting food security to wider food systems, the plan seeks to expand the concept of food security to include nutritional security. The plan also seeks to increase the production of fruit and vegetables and to work towards equalising power and ownership imbalances in the food sector. In sum, the National Nutritional Plan aims to offer a holistic approach to the nation's food security.[15]

In order to address the constitutional mandate of the Republic of South Africa to achieve food security and food health for all, several more strategies were adopted. These include the Zero Hunger Strategy, which was adopted in 2009. The Medium-Term Strategic Framework 2009-2014 sought to address priority areas for the implementation of a set of strategic objectives designed to realise food security for all. Research indicates that these and numerous other strategies and policies related to South Africa's food security cover the support for land reform, provision of social grants[16], boosting crop production, health and nutrition education.[17]

Notwithstanding all these governmental and constitutional interventions, numerous studies indicate that a large number of people, both rural and urban, living in South Africa are unable to access sufficient, nutritious food to meet daily dietary requirements and live healthy, productive lives.[18] Globalisation, international trade regimes, climate change and the poor storage and distribution of food coupled with an increasing population, poor coordination of interventions and food price volatility has led to a large percentage of the population having inadequate access to nutritional food on a sustained basis.[19]

---

15 Battersby et al, "A Study on Current and Future Realities for Urban Food Security in South Africa", 56.

16 The South African government pays a social grant to qualifying South African citizens on a monthly basis. The amount varies based on the type of grant such as old age grant, foster care, disability grant and child support. South Africans who earn minimum wage often do not qualify to obtain the grant and those without valid identification documents, foreigners and undocumented migrants do not qualify. See Western Cape Government. 2020. "Applying for a social welfare grant", 9 April.

17 Makwela M. 2019. "Why SA's food security policies have not lived up to their promises"' Cape Town and Pretoria: DSI/NRF Centre of Excellence in Food Security, 14 March.

18 Naicker L. 2021. *Food, Sex and Text: Exploring Survival Sex in the Context of Foods Insecurity through Communal Readings of the Book of Ruth*. PhD Diss, University of the Western Cape; Abrahams M and Smith J. 2016. PACSA Food Price Barometer; Pietermaritzburg: Pietermaritzburg Agency for Community Social Action; Crush J and Caesar M. 2014. "City without choice: Urban food insecurity in Msunduzi, South Africa", *Urban Forum* 25:165-175.

19 SA DAFF. "The national policy on food and nutrition security for the Republic of South Africa".

THE STRUCTURAL AND SYSTEMIC NATURE OF FOOD INSECURITY IN SOUTH AFRICA

Towards the end of the nineteenth century, both white settlers and black farmers responded to the growing demand for food in the country, particularly from new settlements and mining towns. By 1860, 80% of the almost half a million hectares of white-owned land were farmed by black tenants. White farmers began to complain that labour shortage and competition from black tenants hampered their progress and success. Resultantly, the Native Land Act of 1913 was instituted creating reserves for black people and prohibiting the sale of supposed *white land* to blacks. This served to meet the demands of white farmers for more land to farm and create a black labour force for the white agricultural and mining industries. In effect, this act eliminated all competition from black farmers in the agricultural industry. Under apartheid, national food security was equated with large scale commercial farming, which was dominated by white South Africans, who were given resources in order to develop and flourish.[20] Resultantly, black South Africans, to a large extent, became landless, impoverished and food insecure.

At the dawn of democracy in 1994, the Reconstruction and Development Programme (RDP) identified food security as a basic human right and food insecurity as a legacy of apartheid's socio-economic and political policies. At this point, it was largely understood that agriculture played a significant and historic role in the nation's food security. However, household food security in South Africa was, and still is, largely dependent on household income.[21] The IFSS, which was developed in order "to attain universal physical, social and economic access to sufficient, safe and nutritious food by all South Africans at all times to meet their dietary and food preferences for an active and healthy life", focused on availability of food, not access to food. This focus continues to inform policy and food security initiatives in South Africa. Yet, South Africa has adequate availability of food. The problem lies in access. Moreover, over 60% of South Africa is urbanised and urbanisation is growing rapidly. Gareth Haysom, an urban studies researcher, maintains that governmental interventions and policies do not reflect the rapid urbanisation of South Africa and continue to a large extent, to work from the perspective of rural development and agriculture.[22] Jane Battersby, an urban geographer, opines that, "despite the constitutional right to food for all and the specific right to basic nutrition for all children, we have shockingly high levels of long-term food insecurity

---

20 Hendriks S. 2013. "Food Security in South Africa: Status Quo and Policy Imperatives", *Agrekon* 52(2):1.

21 Shisanya S and Hendriks S. 2011. "The contribution of community gardens to food security in the Maphepetheni uplands", *Development Southern Africa*. 28(4):509-526.

22 Haysom G. 2017. "Climate change, food and the city: Agency and urban scale food system networks", in Thomas-Hope E (ed). *Climate Change and Food Security: Africa and the Caribbean*. London: Routledge, 145-155.

and devastatingly high levels of child stunting. A country like South Africa should not have more than a quarter of children under the age of five stunted."[23]

A myriad of intersecting factors determines the systemic nature of South Africa's food insecurity. In a cash-based society such as South Africa, income reliability is a key determinate of food security because people rely on markets to obtain food.[24] Yet rampant unemployment and enduring structural inequalities hamper the growth, development and food security of millions of South Africans. Urban infrastructure in under-resourced communities is limited or non-existent. A large percentage of urban dwellers live in informal settlements with limited or no access to basic services – such as sanitation, drainage, water supply and electricity, and, most importantly, land – that would enable them to live in a humane way and grow their own food. These inequitable social structures and arrangements put excessive strain on households, impinging on their health and well-being. In addition, rising inflation further hampers livelihoods.[25] Over 1.7 million households across the country experience hunger,[26] and food insecurity was declared a national crisis by the South African National Health and Nutrition Examination Survey in its 2013 publication. In urban South Africa, 28% of households are at risk of hunger and 26% of households are already experiencing hunger. Statistics in rural South Africa indicate that 32% of households are at risk of hunger and 36% of households are already experiencing hunger. In essence, roughly 50% of the South African population are food insecure or at risk of food insecurity, with urban household food insecurity growing at a rapid rate.[27] Battersby argues that within a rights-based framework, government has a responsibility towards its citizenry to defend, protect and realise the people's right to food through policies and programmes. However, government has failed to fully grasp its own role and has therefore failed to protect the right to food in South Africa.[28]

Women are most vulnerable to food insecurity, and pregnant women in particular face greater challenges in accessing adequate food to meet their nutritional needs and the nutritional needs of their unborn babies. Resultantly, there is a link between food insecurity and poor pregnancy outcomes, with numerous low-birthweight babies and occurrences of gestational diabetes and pregnancy-related complications. Children in food insecure households suffer poor health and increased probability

---

23 Battersby J. 2021. "Food Insecurity is not a COVID Related Shock but a Chronic, Systemic Problem in South Africa", *The Daily Maverick*, 15 October.

24 Warshawsky D. 2011. "Urban Food Insecurity and the Advent of Food Banking in Southern Africa: Urban Food Security Series", *AFSUN* 9:10.

25 Crush J and Franye B. 2010. "The Invisible Crisis: Urban Food Insecurity in Southern Africa", *African Food Security Urban Network* 1:6-47.

26 Statistics South Africa. 2019. "Towards Measuring the Extent of Food Security in South Africa: An Examination of Hunger and Food Inadequacy". Pretoria: Stats SA, 18.

27 Maluleke T et al. 2013. "South African National Health and Nutrition Examination Survey (SANHANES-1)". Cape Town: HSRC Press, 145; Kings S. 2018. "Food Insecurity Rising in Africa", *Mail & Guardian*, 21 September.

28 Battersby, "Food Insecurity is not a COVID Related Shock".

of hospitalisation. Children from these household types also suffer increased developmental delays, chronic hunger and chronic medical conditions, such as asthma, heart conditions, kidney disease and allergies. In addition, maternal health problems, such as postpartum depression, as well as psychosocial risk factors related to stressful life events, including intimate partner violence and other forms of abuse and trauma are associated with food insecurity.[29] In this context, on 23 March 2020, when the Covid-19 pandemic emerged worldwide, a state of national disaster was declared in South Africa, and the nation went into total lockdown on 26 March 2020. The Covid-19 pandemic brought into sharp focus a different long-term pandemic in South Africa – that of food insecurity promulgated through structural and systemic inequalities.

THE COVID-19 PANDEMIC: A KAIROS MOMENT IN TIME

The Covid-19 pandemic drew sharper attention to the dire state of food insecurity in South Africa. However, even before the coronavirus pandemic, as mentioned earlier, about half of the nation's population were already food insecure and unable to access a healthy diet as a result of chronic structural and systemic problems.[30] There has never been a more decisive time since the dawn of democracy to take seriously how the historic legacy of structural and systemic inequalities in South Africa continues to perpetuate food insecurity, malnutrition and ill-health. The coronavirus has brought to light the significant disparities in the areas of health and food security. Undoubtedly, the people who suffer the effects of food insecurity the most are those who were *previously* disadvantaged in South Africa.[31] Impoverished communities in the country remain largely black. The pandemic cast a spotlight on the spatial, health and food security inequalities of the nation. The burden of nutrition related disease, poor health care and chronic hunger continues to disproportionately affect poor, black communities.

During the lockdown phase of the pandemic, all activities, both economic and social, came to a halt. For the nation's poor, those who receive only a small social grant, low-income households and the unemployed, the situation became untenable. Where people were previously able to move around freely and forage for food, at the very least, under lockdown, they became prisoners to hunger in their own homes. Disconcerting images of winding queues stretching for kilometres, where people waited all day for food parcels, flooded social media and news outlets. The number of people who needed food assistance was staggering and an indication of the dire state of food insecurity in South Africa. In 2021, protest actions erupted

---

29 Ellis E. 2022. "Food Justice: The Shame of the Nation", *The Daily Maverick*, 29 March.
30 Battersby, "Food Insecurity is not a COVID Related Shock", 15.
31 I place the word "previously" in italics to indicate the untruthfulness of the term because a large percentage of those who were disadvantaged under apartheid is still disadvantaged in the present democratic dispensation.

across the country, as the poor demonstrated their frustration at their "long walk"[32] of never attaining food security and the economic freedom they expected to enjoy post-apartheid. The pandemic brought into strident focus the proportion of people vulnerable to hunger, poverty and lack of the goods necessary for survival. Journalist Tasmin Oxford has asserted:

> What makes this crisis worse is that South Africa has food. It has the food that could potentially transform lives, and yet it throws away 10 million tonnes of food a year – fruit and vegetables, grains, meat, roots and tubers. According to the Council for Scientific and Industrial Research the cost of this food loss is approximately 2% of the country's gross domestic product. In 2013, R71.4 billion was lost to inedible food waste … Far more needs to be done. Creating access to nutritious food will have a huge influence on this country's people, economy and future.[33]

Battersby asserts that the government lacks political will to decisively address the food and nutrition security of South Africa. Furthermore, it lacks understanding of how ordinary citizens access food. This, asserts Battersby, "was clear during Covid when one of the first responses of the state was to shut down informal food vendors, as well as the ongoing battle to get school feeding restarted. This is not a problem without history."[34] The pandemic made clear that there has never been a more pressing and opportune moment in time, a *kairos*[35] moment in South Africa's democracy, to institute progressive, sustainable and far-reaching changes to its social, economic and political policies in order to improve the health and food security of people in the country.

In 1985, at the height of apartheid oppression, inspired by the Aristotelian concept of *kairos*, a group of mainly black South African theologians, clergy and laypeople based predominantly in the South African township of Soweto, released a theological response to the injustices of apartheid known as the Kairos Document. The Kairos Document is a Christian, biblical and theological comment on the political crisis in South Africa under apartheid. It is a reflection on the political injustice, death and destruction meted out to black people in South Africa and a critique of the theological models particular Church denominations in South Africa used to promulgate apartheid and, in some instances, to attempt to resolve the country's

---

32 I use the term "long walk" as a reference to an autobiography credited to Nelson Mandela, freedom fighter and first democratically elected South African president. The work profiles the life and times of Nelson Mandela and his struggle for freedoms for all who live in South Africa from all forms of oppression. See Mandela N. 1994. *Long Walk to Freedom*. Boston: Little Brown.

33 Oxford T. 2018. "The Complex Insecurity of Hunger in South Africa", *Mail & Guardian*, 26 October.

34 Battersby, "Food Insecurity is not a COVID Related Shock".

35 "Kairos" is an ancient Greek term used to denote the proper or optimal moment in time to take action as opposed to "chronos" which refers to chronological time. See Valentine M. 2020. "Chronos vs Kairos: Understanding how the Ancient Greeks viewed time will make your life richer", *The Whippet*, 9 March.

problems. Creators of the document developed an alternative biblical and theological model in order to participate in the dismantling of apartheid.[36] In this chapter, I argue that, likewise, an alternative biblical and theological model must be developed through engaging conversations, strategies and interventions with a myriad of stakeholders in order to address the food insecurity crisis of the nation. From an ecclesial and theological perspective, there must be a concerted effort to engage public life and numerous relevant disciplines of knowledge that take the structural and systemic dimensions that contribute to food insecurity in South Africa seriously.

CREATING CONVERSATIONS, STRATEGIES AND INTERVENTIONS

According to Jane Battersby, two very important aspects are crucial if the nation's food security is to be realised. Firstly, collaborative action is key. Secondly, there is a need for concerted effort at addressing systemic drivers of food insecurity rather than addressing food security at sectoral levels.[37] Oxfam notes that in order to address the problem of food insecurity and its related health and livelihoods conditions, a national food act should be developed. The act should make provision for the eradication of hunger and food insecurity with "greater legal force than existing piecemeal policies to incentivise better coordination and implementation".[38] For such an act to be meaningful and fruitful, it must include all sectors of South African society, including communities suffering hunger, big business, both formal and informal sectors of the economy, institutions, NGOs, FBOs, and cultural and religious sectors of society. Such an act must include mechanisms that hold accountable the government and all stakeholders, including local and municipal governmental divisions. Within the act, provision must be made for the development and monitoring of a fair, accountable and sustainable food industry. Provision must also be made for a clearer understanding and evaluation of the food security needs in the country. Importantly, provision must be made for better coordination between local, municipal and national government, working in tandem with civil society and other stakeholders. Such an intervention measure will take seriously the structural and systemic nature of food insecurity and address price-fixing, cartels, food deserts[39] and food waste management, resulting in improvement in all levels of coordination and policy implementation. In this way,

---

36 The Kairos Theologians. 1985. "The Kairos Document: Challenge to the Church: A Theological Comment on the Political Crisis in South Africa", Kerkgrief.

37 Battersby, "Food Insecurity is not a COVID Related Shock".

38 Tsegay YT and Rusare M. 2014. "Hidden Hunger in South Africa". Nairobi: Oxfam International, 34-35.

39 The term "food desert" is increasingly used by academics and other stakeholders in the field of urban food security worldwide to describe areas where people cannot access affordable, nutritious food. While definitions of food deserts appear are varied and there appears to be no definitional consensus, food deserts have been defined as "poor urban areas", where residents cannot buy affordable, healthy food. Food deserts are, therefore, "areas of relative exclusion where people experience physical and economic barriers to accessing healthy food". See Cummins S and Macintyre S. 2002. "Food Deserts: Evidence and Assumption in Health Policy Making", *British Medical Journal* 325:436-438.

all stakeholders can work collaboratively in order to formulate a just and equitable food system in South Africa.[40]

I concur with Oxfam that collective action is necessary to repair the nation's broken food system. Battersby notes that the seeds for a better response to food insecurity in South Africa exist. At the beginning of the Covid crisis, Battersby observes, civil society organisations demonstrated how the shock of food insecurity should be addressed and plotted pathways towards a better food future for the country. Innovative and committed food activists began working together, engaging in discussions and establishing new and transformative action plans. In addition, activists have held government to account for its failure to effectively address the food insecurity crisis of the country and they have sought to work with government in order to address this crisis. It is clear that a more inclusive framework is necessary in order to alleviate food insecurity.[41] A comprehensive multi-tiered and transversal approach must be undertaken that takes into account and closely involves those on the margins of society, who experience food insecurity daily. In addition, all societal stakeholders must hold government to account and demand far greater action in the fight to eradicate food insecurity.

Liberation theologian Albert Nolan points out that in South Africa, the struggle itself produced hope through the successful dismantling of apartheid, the negotiated settlement and relatively peaceful transition into democracy, as well as the new Constitution and charismatic leadership of Nelson Mandela. However, laments Nolan, these hopes have been gradually eroded and the general mood in the country can be described as disillusionment and despair.[42] For Nolan, problems such as systemic food insecurity and other socio-economic disparities experienced in post-apartheid South Africa nullify true democracy. Nolan's insights raise important questions regarding the causes of food insecurity in South Africa. What can be done to address the historic structural and systemic drivers of food insecurity biblically and theologically? How can the overwhelmingly high unemployment rate and crushing poverty that perpetuates food insecurity be addressed biblically and theologically? How can theological engagement that demonstrates a *kairos* awareness contribute to the eradication of food insecurity? Focusing on theological responses to food insecurity, the next section expounds on how Christianity can and must be an active participant in addressing the food security crisis in South Africa.

THE CHRISTIAN MANDATE TO PARTICIPATE IN THE FOOD SECURITY OF THE NATION

To be socially and theologically relevant, Christian engagement with food insecurity and poverty must embody a kairos awareness that is contextually based, critical and

---

40 Tsegay and Rusare, "Hidden Hunger in South Africa", 34-35.
41 Battersby, "Food Insecurity is not a COVID Related Shock", 15.
42 Albert N. 2010. *Hope in an Age of Despair*. New York: Orbis Books.

socially relevant.[43] The Kairos Document explicitly states that prophetic theology commensurate with the contextual realities of struggle takes into consideration the lived realities of local communities and responds theologically, in a socially engaged manner.[44] From the perspective of Christianity, the Church and theological engagement must participate in measures and interventions that effectively address the broken food system of the country and the broken lives of the poor and the hungry. Theologian George Byarugaba contends that:

> The obligation of ensuring that each person is food secure calls on the state, communities and their leaders ... Religious communities in particular must remember that genuine religion is liberating, transforming and empowering to individuals and communities in order to realise God-given dignity. Both religious and civil society must work together to create conducive ethical environment in which every citizen subscribes to the principle that food is a basic human right – as it is stated in the South African Constitution and the Bill of Rights ... Because God is the God of life, and the guarantor of the fundamental rights of the poor, to believe in God is to believe in the life of all, especially the poor. Belief in God is incompatible with the death of hungry people. Where life is oppressed, God is oppressed.[45]

Charitable giving has for centuries been the hallmark of Christianity. Churches and Christian organisations have throughout the ages offered food aid to individuals, congregations, communities and countries in need. While such initiatives are needed and important in a country such as South Africa, where there is a necessity to address the immediate need of hunger, such actions must accompany a far greater social justice response. Liberation and contextual theologies have for decades paved the way towards an understanding that the Christian message of justice, hope and providence must be embodied within a socio-economic paradigm that calls for and works collectively towards radical social change.[46]

In order to achieve this, a Food Justice Theology from the South African perspective must be developed. The key aim of a South African Food Justice Theology must be the creation of a more sustainable and just food system. Such a theology must take into account how racialised societal arrangements intersects with capitalism to perpetuate food insecurity and other forms of injustice and inequality. A Food Justice Theology unique to the South African context will require the exploration, examination and investigation of how access to and ownership of land in South

---

43 Le Bruyns C. 2015. "The rebirth of Kairos Theology and its implications for Public Theology and Citizenship in South Africa", *Missionalia* 43(1):131.

44 West G. 2021. "Contextual Bible Study and/or as Interpretive Resilience", in Chitando E, Mombo E and Gunda MR (eds). *That All May Live! Essays in Honour of Nyambura J. Njoroge* Bamberg: University of Bamberg Press, 143-159; Haysom, "Climate change, food and the city".

45 Byarugaba G. 2017. "The influence of food symbolism on food insecurity in South Africa: how relevant is the Eucharistic celebration?", *Scriptura* 116 (1):1-19.

46 Astley J. 2000. *Ordinary theology: looking, listening and learning in theology*, Aldershot: Ashgate. See also Guterrez G. 1973. *Theology of Liberation*, New York: Orbis Books.

Africa is a key driver of food insecurity. The ways in which land in South Africa is racialised, resulting in race and class disparity that directly affects the food security of the economically oppressed must be addressed.[47] A South African Food Justice Theology must ask critical questions regarding the food consumptions patterns based on race and class and why healthy food is inaccessible to some and easily accessible to others. Moreover, the ideological construction of a racialised working class, rampant unemployment and below minimum wage earnings must be interrogated and confronted. A South African Food Justice Theology must address and seek to dismantle racism through sustainable food systems and theologically address how a sustainable food security system can be achieved. Race and class privilege in terms of food consumption and food movements must be analysed against the backdrop of prioritising access to fresh, healthy, culturally appropriate food for all.[48]

A South African Food Justice Theology will require collaboration with a wide variety of voices and perspectives. Christianity's social mission of charitable giving cannot be a substitute for adequate social participation by the Church to effectively deal with the historic, structural and systemic nature of food insecurity as we experience it today. The post-apartheid theological discourse in South Africa, argues theologian Clint Le Bruyns, "may not necessarily be as appropriate and responsive as we would like for the kind of public impact and critical participation the times demand. Emphasis must be placed on contextuality, criticality and change in order to make a meaningful impact towards transformation".[49] The development of expertise in other disciplines of knowledge must accompany a commitment to engage in conversations and programmes that transcend ecclesial and theological discourses. Those in positions of power and influence and those whose participation is limited must be engaged equally from a theological perspective with the aim of meaningful participation, transformation and change. Moreover, theological engagement must draw its resources and what informs it, from the African soil in its quest to overcome dehumanisation and oppression.

For a Christian response to food insecurity to be relevant, biblical and theological engagement must address what dominates policy and practice in the nation's food systems and how this affects the lives of the poor and food insecure. Biblical and theological engagement must conduct social analysis of what perpetuates existing structures of power and privilege and what reinforces structural and systemic racial inequality. A critical issue that requires theological engagement is reparations and redistribution. The forceful dispossession of black people's land under colonialism and apartheid robbed them of a means of livelihood, survival and sustenance. The theological task should therefore be working towards land restoration. Theologically, the failure to meaningfully engage the land issue should be regarded

---

47 See Alkon AH and Agyeman J (eds). 2011. *Cultivating Food Justice: Race, Class, and Sustainability*. Cambridge: MIT Press.

48 Alkon and Agyeman, *Cultivating Food Justice: Race, Class, and Sustainability*.

49 Le Bruyns, "The rebirth of Kairos Theology and its implications for Public Theology and Citizenship in South Africa".

as justice denied. From this perspective, restorative justice should be advocated for through continued dialogue with the aim of achieving socio-economic progress and food security for all.[50] The Church and theological engagement must advocate for the basic right to food for all people living in South Africa and conduct focused analysis of how violations of such rights intersect with systemic racism and structural inequalities.

CONCLUSION

The need for economic accessibility to food, employment, skills development and liveable wages, as well as addressing racial and gender disparity in the workforce, must be engaged theologically in the context of food insecurity. The important issue of how land dispossession systematically oppressed and exploited people, as well as reparations and redistribution, must be approached from the perspective of justice and equity. Access to proper housing, infrastructure and adequate health care must be advocated through theological engagement with all stakeholders in the food security landscape. Within the framework of a holistic theological response to food security, the Church must enter into dialogue, debate and meaningful action that challenges the status quo and calls for the realisation of freedom from economic oppression and food security for all.

In an effort to demonstrate the need for government, the Christian Church and all other stakeholders to rethink and revaluate the manner in which they address the food insecurity crisis in South Africa, I lift up an excerpt from sociologist Janet Poppendieck's book, *Sweet Charity: Emergency Food and the End of Entitlement*, which highlights the long-term ineffectiveness of current ecclesial interventions:

> In a quaint village situated on a river, a villager one day sees a baby floating down the river. She rushes into the water and saves the baby. Her neighbours help her find clothes, a crib, a blanket and food for the baby, making sure it is warm and fed. The next day two babies are rescued and the day after that, several more. Soon, babies are being rescued in large numbers as a regular feature of life in the village. Finally, after much consternation over the source of the babies landing up in the river, one of the villagers suggests that they make an expedition upstream to determine how the babies are getting into the water in the first place. The villagers however are too afraid to take time and energy away from the immediate rescue project, fearing that the babies will drown if there was no one there to save them.[51]

As one of the most unequal countries in the world, economic justice is an important measure of redress. However, for the South African context, charity and justice cannot be viewed as opposing ideals. Both are needed in order to address the dire

---

50 Resane K. 2015. "Naboth's Vineyard: Theological Lessons for the South African Land Issue", *Acta Theologica* 35(1):174-188.

51 Poppendieck J. 1998. *Sweet Charity: Emergency Food and the End of Entitlement*. New York: Viking.

state of food insecurity in the country – charity cannot replace justice and justice cannot replace charity. Out of necessity, these two aspects must exist side by side.

In this chapter, I discussed critical issues such as structural and systemic oppression and race and class disparity as it intersects with food insecurity. I demonstrated how the embedded political and economic power imbalances entrench food insecurity and the need for restructuring the current food system to include all stakeholders, inclusive of food insecure communities and the cultural religious sectors. With focus on Christianity,[52] I maintain that there is an urgent need for a contextually based South African Food Justice Theology that will comprehensively address South Africa's broken food system.

---

52 While the focus of this chapter is a Christian response to food insecurity, it must be stated that the Jewish, Muslim, Hindu and other faith-based charitable organisations and communities in South Africa are actively involved in providing humanitarian support and food to vulnerable communities on a regular basis. Moreover, I wish to categorically state that when I speak of the involvement of the religious sector, I include all cultural and religious sectors of society.

28 THE ROLES OF LAW, RELIGION AND THE COVID-19 PANDEMIC IN SOUTH AFRICAN CHURCH ARCHITECTURE

Yolanda van der Vyver[1]

INTRODUCTION

During the Covid-19 pandemic large gatherings, including church services, were prohibited by law, and once these were allowed again, churches could only comply with the rigorous requirements of social distancing by leaving empty seats between congregants. Covid regulations led to a resurgence of authoritarianism, as civil rights, including freedom of religion and belief, were suspended in reaction to the global pandemic. In South Africa, some religious groups continued to conduct services and hold religious gatherings in defiance of lockdown regulations, and church ministers and congregation members became lawbreakers, attracting criminal records. Some religious groups saw the ban on faith-based gatherings as an attack on religion and challenged what they called irrational and arbitrary regulations in court. But many churches and faith leaders actively concurred or passively accepted these restrictions. As denominations moved to online or virtual services that streamed sermons and messages of health and healing to a wider, global audience, questions on how the pandemic is changing the religious landscape arose.

During the pandemic, many South Africans were forced to reconsider how and where they worship, but as restrictions were lifted, public health protocols often remained, and although churches attempted to return to a new normal, services continued to be livestreamed and in-person attendance remained optional. The trend of substituting in-person services with online services is concerning when one considers the future of traditional church architecture. A historical investigation of the evolution of Christian church-building through the ages, reveals five important elements of its architecture. First, Christianity is a congregational religion, focused on the sense of community through worship *in which concepts of ecclesia*[2] *and koinonia*[3]

---

[1] PhD in Architecture, University of the Free State; Founding member of Y and K Architects; 2021 inaugural Emory University–Halle Institute Fulbright South Africa Distinguished Chair at the Center for the Study of Law and Religion.

[2] The word *ecclesia* was originally used to describe Christian assembly and refers to the congregation or community of believers. *Ecclesia* derives from the Greek for "called together". The church consists of those that are called together by God. Gaum F, Boesak A and Botha W (ed). 2008. *Christelike Kernensiklopedie* [Christian Core Encyclopedia]. Wellington: Lux Verbi: Bybelmedia, 286.

[3] *Koinonia* is a Greek word that means Christian fellowship, joint participation and communion with God, or more commonly, with fellow Christians. See Roth LM. 1993. *Understanding*

are especially important: Second, Christian churches have a religious function and are designed to include liturgy and rituals of worship that represent the communal response to and participation in the sacred. Third, Christian religious structures containing sacred space have through the millennia been regarded as the pinnacle of architecture for their ability to transcend the physical world and to create a sense of God. Fourth, church architecture has a spiritual dimension that is not limited to its religious function. Buildings designed specifically for spiritual activities have experiential qualities that play a role in spiritual healing. Finally, although church architecture symbolises the unified intent of a congregation and its expression of faith, its pastoral care function of charitable giving extends beyond the limits of its architecture and is performed outside the boundaries of the physical structure of brick and mortar. These statements address both the functional and the spiritual requirements of church architecture.

The five points above can be summarised as assembly and community, liturgy and ritual, sacred space, spiritual healing and pastoral care. This chapter argues that the prohibition by law of faith-based gatherings during the Covid-19 pandemic seriously disrupted these important functions of Christian worship. Although online services have become a valuable part of the ministry of the church, they cannot replace what is contained in its architecture: the congregation of a religious community that actively participates in its rituals in the sacred space of a church building. There are, however, functions that will always be performed in the outside world, beyond the confines of church-building. When the pandemic disrupted pastoral care, it was proved to be an essential service that could not be done through the virtual medium of cyberspace.

COVID-19, THE LAW AND THE CHURCH

On 15 March 2020, Dr Nkosazana Dlamini Zuma, South Africa's Minister of Cooperative Governance and Traditional Affairs,[4] declared a national state of disaster, due to the magnitude and severity of the Covid-19 outbreak, which had been declared a global pandemic by the World Health Organization (WHO). On 18 March 2020, Dlamini Zuma issued regulations aimed at preventing an escalation of the disaster, and alleviating, containing and minimising its effects. On 23 March 2020, President Cyril Ramaphosa announced an initial 21-day lockdown. Community gatherings

---

Architecture: Its elements, history and meaning. New York: Herbert Press, 243; Koorts J. 1974. *Beginsels van Gereformeerde Kerkbou* [Principles of Reformed Church-building]. Bloemfontein: Sacum Beperk, 1.

4   The Minister of Cooperative Governance and Traditional Affairs (COGTA), as designated under Section 3 of the Disaster Management Act, 2002 (Act No. 57 of 2002, *Government Gazette* Vol 451 No 24252), through the Disaster Management Act of 18 March 2020 (*Government Gazette* Vol 657 No 43107) and the Regulations to address, prevent and combat the spread of Coronavirus Covid-19 of 25 March 2020 [the last, hereinafter Covid Regulations]. The National State of Disaster was only lifted on 5 April 2022, nearly two years after it was introduced.

other than funerals were stopped immediately and wedding receptions and celebrations had to be cancelled.

Between 26 March 2020 and 1 October 2021, the country's alert levels fluctuated between Levels 5 and 1. This risk-adjusted approach was guided by several criteria, including the level of infections and rate of transmission, the capacity of health facilities, the extent of the implementation of public health interventions and the economic and social impact of continued restrictions.[5] The aim was to "flatten the curve" of infections and deaths related to Covid-19. Under Alert Levels 5 and 4, only fifty people or less were allowed to attend funerals, provided that not more than 50% of the venue capacity was used, with persons observing a distance of at least one and a half metres from each other. Travel between different metropolitan areas was forbidden, but since funerals were deemed essential services, attendees were allowed to travel. However, this was only under the condition that a permit was obtained from the nearest magistrate's office or police station upon submission of a death certificate. The duration of a funeral was restricted to two hours,[6] and attendees had to adhere to health protocols, including the wearing of masks.[7] Faith-based gatherings were prohibited, and church services with live congregations came to a halt completely.

Under Level 3, faith-based or religious gatherings were allowed, but attendance was limited to fifty persons or less for indoor venues and a hundred persons or less for outdoor venues, provided that not more than 50% of the venue capacity was used and with persons observing a distance of at least one and a half metres from each other.[8] According to modern building standards and ergonomic requirements for church buildings, the space required in a Protestant church is 0.4-0.5 m² per person.[9] Social distancing meant that the minimum of 2.25 m² per person as required by law could only be obtained by leaving empty seats between congregants. As alert levels decreased, more people were allowed at indoor and outdoor faith-based or religious gatherings, as well as at funerals, but health protocols remained in place.

The regulations determined that a convener of faith-based or religious gatherings had to ensure compliance with the limitation on the number of attendees, failing which the convener was committing an offence and was liable, upon conviction, to a fine or imprisonment for a period not exceeding six months or to both a fine and imprisonment.[10] Also, a person who attended a faith-based or religious gathering and who knew or ought reasonably to have known or suspected that the number of

---

5   South Africa. 2022. "About Covid-19. About Alert System". Online at: https://www.gov.za/Covid-19/about/about-alert-system
6   Covid Regulation 35(5).
7   The wearing of face masks in public space was compulsory under Regulation 67(a).
8   Covid Regulation (36)(4)(i).
9   Neufert E. 1970. *Architects' Data*. London: Crosby Lockwood and Son Ltd, 334. Protestant churches do not require kneelers with hassocks as do Anglican and Catholic churches.
10 Covid Regulation 36(6).

persons exceeded the limitation provided for in the Covid regulations, was committing an offence and was subject to the same potential penalties.[11]

Where a gathering was in contravention of the regulations, an enforcement officer had to order the persons to disperse and, if they refused, take appropriate action which might, subject to the Criminal Procedure Act,[12] include the arrest and detention of any person at the gathering.[13] These regulations had the potential to make lawbreakers or criminals out of church ministers and congregation members, which is exactly what happened.

CRIMINALISING CHURCH ATTENDANCE AND CHALLENGING THE LAW

During the Covid-19 pandemic, over 400 000 South Africans spent time behind bars for failing to adhere to Covid lockdown regulations.[14] Congregants who defied these regulations by gathering to worship were dispersed by police, who often fired rubber bullets and tear gas at them. Churchgoers became lawbreakers, were arrested and given the option of admission of guilt fines, which enabled a person to admit guilt in advance to avoid having to appear in court on a minor criminal charge. But these fines had long-term consequences. Section 56(1) of the Criminal Procedure Act clearly states that the payment of an admission of guilt fine will be the same as being convicted and sentenced in court. Traffic offenses do not lead to criminal records, but contraventions of lockdown regulations often did. If a criminal record arises from paying an admission of guilt fine, the criminal record will be valid for ten years, which naturally has serious implications, especially when seeking employment in future.[15]

The Covid-19 pandemic had many consequences, and one of most notable was that it further exposed existing fault lines in society, which in South Africa means the extremes of inequality between rich and poor.[16] Rich people, who could afford lawyers, were advised to not pay admission of guilt fines and could therefore avoid attracting criminal records for curfew violations, but poor people who do not have access to lawyers, were advised by arresting officers to pay these fines without knowing that they would have a criminal record, which can take up to ten years to expunge.[17] Ultimately, lockdown regulations did not affect the rich as much as they

---

11 Covid Regulation 7.
12 Criminal Procedure Act No. 51 of 1977, s 56(1).
13 Covid Regulation 16(a) and (b).
14 "Over 400,000 people have been arrested for breaking South Africa's Covid-19 rules", *BusinessTech*, 8 April 2021.
15 "The consequence of paying an admission of guilt fine", *LegalWiseZA*, May 2020.
16 York G, "Covid-19 exposes the fault lines of equality across South Africa", *Globe and Mail*, 5 July 2020.
17 "Covid-19: Eased lockdown and rule of law webinar", *Mail & Guardian*, 25 May 2020.

did the poor. Townships are densely populated, and stay-at-home orders presented a challenge when ten people or more lived together in a single shack.[18]

Critics of the regulations said that law enforcement was using a sledgehammer to kill a fly and that the crime did not fit the punishment,[19] but the Department of Justice stated that regulations were there to curb a wave of infections. Initially, we did not understand the virus, and the rules were harsh. Police were accused of trying to reach a target in terms of number of arrests. People were angry, because police focused on soft targets such as surfers on a beach,[20] or congregants in a church.[21] Police Minister Bheki Cele was accused of diverting attention away from real criminals, or those responsible for state capture.[22] Furthermore, if the aim was to lessen infection, it made no sense to arrest people and force them into a crowded holding cell with 20 to 25 people sharing the same space, where the danger of getting infected was greater than staying out past curfew by a few minutes.

When the pastor and several congregants were arrested during a church service in Sebokeng for defying lockdown regulations under Level 3, even though the service was conducted outdoors and worshippers were wearing facemasks,[23] many religious groups saw the Disaster Management Act of 18 March 2020 and the Covid Regulations of 25 March 2020 as an attack on religion. Congregants insisted that the government had no power over them and that they were not consulted when these regulations were made, since they were not members of the South African Council of Churches.[24]

---

18   Harrisburg K. 2020. "Coronavirus exposes 'brutal inequality' of South Africa's townships", *Reuters*, 12 June. See also Fisher DA et al. 2022. "Locked Down: Economic and Health Effects of Covid-19 Response on Residents of a South African Township", *Global Social Welfare*, 3 August. Townships are urban living areas that were historically created under South Africa's apartheid regime for exclusive occupation by people classified as non-white, i.e., black, coloured or Indian. Although these segregated areas have undergone transformation since the end of apartheid, they are still mainly occupied by lower socioeconomic groups. See Donaldson R. "South African Township Transformation", in Michalos AC (ed). 2014. *Encyclopedia of Quality of Life and Well-Being Research*. Dordrecht: Springer.

19   Broadbent A and Smart BTH. 2020. "Why a one-size-fits-all approach to Covid-19 could have legal consequences", *The Conversation*, 24 March; Muller SM. 2020. "Covid-19 in South Africa: A critical assessment of the first 90 days", *The Conversation*, 7 December.

20   Taylor K. 2020. "South Africa's lockdown exposes inequalities", *Pavement Pieces*, 14 May.

21   Sangotsa V. 2020. "Eastern Cape villagers arrested over lockdown church service", *Sunday Times*, 11 April.

22   Trippe K. 2022. "Pandemic policing: South Africa's most vulnerable face a sharp increase in police related brutality", *Africa Source* (blog), The Atlantic Council, 24 June. So far, prosecution of state capture is slow and former president Jacob Zuma, under whose watch it happened, still manages to avoid persecution. See Republic of South Africa, "Judicial Commission Inquiry into State Capture Report, Part III, vol. 2, BOSASA.

23   "SAPS breaks up Sebokeng church gathering", *eNCA/YouTube*, 10 January 2021.

24   Ramaphosa held a conference with religious leaders, but churches outside the Council of Churches say they did not agree anything with the president. See "Sebokeng Church says they were brutalized by the police", *South African Breaking News*, 2020.

This attack on religion did not remain unchallenged. The South African National Christian Forum (SANCF) filed urgent papers in the Gauteng High Court in Johannesburg to challenge the lockdown regulations that resulted in churches being closed. The decision to ban religious gatherings was heard in a virtual sitting of the court. Senior Council Advocate Margaretha Engelbrecht argued on behalf of the SANCF and Solidariteit Helpende Hand:[25] "Let me make it clear: what is being challenged is not [the] government's response to the pandemic. What is being challenged is the irrational and arbitrary decision of the minister to prohibit faith-based gatherings whilst she allowed at the same time, a variety of social gatherings in restaurants."[26] The case, however, was removed from the urgent court roll in February following the announcement by President Cyril Ramaphosa lifting the ban, with places of worship being permitted to resume their services with a maximum amount of fifty people indoors and a hundred people outdoors.[27] But Engelbrecht continued that, while the ban had been lifted, the country was moving towards the December period, and a real possibility existed that the Cooperative Governance and Traditional Affairs Minister Dlamini Zuma might ban faith-based gatherings once more, while keeping open restaurants, gyms, and casinos. Engelbrecht questioned banning faith-based gatherings, when people in restaurants, casinos and other public places could not keep a distance of 1.5 metres.[28]

EXPOSING AUTHORITARIANISM

The recent "Partygate" debacle in the United Kingdom, where former Prime Minister Boris Johnson was fined for contravening the lockdown regulations by hosting a birthday party at 10 Downing Street, is not unique to that country. In South Africa, similar double standards came to light when officials were spotted attending funerals and other gatherings without wearing face masks.[29] It must be said that the South African government is notoriously corrupt,[30] and many government officials were linked to tender fraud in the provision of personal protective equipment (PPE)

---

25 Solidariteit Helpende Hand is an affiliate of Solidarity trade union that promotes social issues in the Afrikaner community. The name means "Helping Hand". Online at: https://helpendehand.co.za

26 Maphanga C. 2021. "Lockdown advocate tells court curb on religious gatherings was 'irrational and arbitrary'", *News 24*, 22 November.

27 Maphanga C. 2021. "Lockdown: Issue of curb on religious gatherings still relevant as state of emergency continues, court hears", *News 24*, 24 November.

28 Maphanga, "Lockdown advocate tells court curb on religious gatherings was 'irrational and arbitrary'".

29 Magome M. "South African cops investigate official for not wearing a mask", *Associated Press*, 25 January.

30 See Lodge T. 1998. "Political corruption in South Africa", *African Affairs* 97(387):157-187; Gumede W. 2019. "Why corruption killed dreams of a better South Africa", *University of the Witwatersrand News*, 19 September; Southall R. 2019. A democracy or a kleptocracy? How South Africa stacks up", *The Conversation*, 6 February.

and communication services to the government.³¹ Millions of rand from Covid funds meant for the poor, disappeared or cannot be accounted for. Covid has made more visible, or has exposed, the dysfunctional aspects that already existed, including unemployment, poverty, government inefficiency and corruption.

Law and religion scholar Mark Hill writes in the introduction to the *Routledge Handbook on Freedom of Religion or Belief* that:

> [The Covid-19 pandemic] has led to a resurgence of authoritarianism, particularly in Western democracies, with towns, cities and entire countries being placed into lockdown and places of worship closed, with the active concurrence, or passive acceptance, of faith leaders. Civil rights, including freedom to manifest religion and belief, have effectively been suspended in consequence of a global health emergency. Severe limitations on personal and associational autonomy – unthinkable in normal times – have been imposed, in circumstances in which most major faith groups have been complicit and supportive. It will be interesting to see how the landscape will have changed after the current public health emergency has passed.³²

Although one can debate whether South Africa is a Western democracy,³³ this statement is equally applicable, and asking how the religious landscape has changed and what the reaction of the church was in South Africa, is relevant to this argument.

VIRTUAL SERVICES: A NEW FORM OF WORSHIP

As mentioned above, some religious groups continued to conduct services and hold religious gatherings in defiance of lockdown regulations, but many churches and faith leaders actively concurred or passively accepted these restrictions. Churches that could, replaced their traditional services with online or virtual services, and

---

31 Health Minister Dr Zweli Mkhize has close links to the communications company *Digital Vibes* that colluded in the tender awarded by the national health department. See Singh O. 2021. "SIU prob into R82m tender related the Zwele Mkhize's associates 'at an early stage'", *The Sunday Times*, 25 February. There are many more examples. "An estimated R500 billion Covid-19 budget allocation is alleged to have been whipped away in just three months in tender fraud schemes to members of the ruling African National Congress and senior government administrators, their family members and even diseased members of the public"; Mbandlwa C and Netswera F. 2021. "The effect government supply chain processes have on the procurement of Covid-19 personal protective equipment", *Ilkogretim Online-Elementary Education Online* 20(4):1782-1790.

32 Hill M. 2020. "Locating the right to freedom of religion or belief across time and territory", in Ferrari S, Hill M, Jamal AA and Bottoni R (eds). *Routledge Handbook on Freedom of Religion or Belief*. London: Routledge.

33 South Africa is a constitutional democracy with a three-tiered system of government and an independent judiciary. The president is the head of the government and is elected by parliament. See Republic of South Africa. Structure and Functions of the South African Government. Online at: https://www.gov.za/about-government/government-system/structure-and-functions-south-african-government

those with access to the internet could tune in. But others without internet access could not attend church services at all. I would like to use my own church as an example: before the pandemic, the Nederduitsch Hervormde Kerk Menlyn Maine, Pretoria created a nickname *"die Kerk"* (the Church), with a Facebook page and a logo resembling the universal WiFi symbol. The credo was "extend the reach of the church, increase our bandwidth and strengthen your signal".[34] The church's reach was compared to internet connectivity, with the aim of reaching as many Afrikaans-speaking people as possible. Every morning from Monday to Friday, our ministers took turns to present a daily reflection that was made available on YouTube. Every weekday had a different theme, the most unusual being our youth minister, who filmed his messages with a selfie stick while skating, on a skateboard, through the suburbs near the church. The message was clear: "Please like and share this video, and if you can, make a payment, because we are wholly dependent on contributions for the sustainability of our ministry." The church's banking details, and a SnapScan QR Code was provided at the end of each video.[35] Once restaurants were allowed to open, pop-up Sunday church services were held at different restaurants with tremendous success, and the short service was livestreamed via Facebook, which meant that anyone with access could tune in. The Facebook page states that: "Our dream for *die Kerk* is to create a space not only for the growth of the Hervormde Kerk, but also for the church and Christianity overall." When church services were allowed to resume under Level 3, there were still restrictions on the number of worshippers that were allowed to attend, so services continued to be livestreamed. Even after all restrictions were lifted, in-person attendance became optional.

In general, virtual services have increased the church's ecumenical reach and extended its influence beyond the physical brick and mortar structure of the church building, but that does not mean that the church building and in-person church attendance will have no place in a post-pandemic world. To substantiate this statement, one must consider the reasons for the historic advent of Christian religious architecture, which is centred on the community of believers.

SEEKING SHELTER
FOR THE ASSEMBLY OF BELIEVERS

Christianity is a congregational religion, not built around the individual, but rather focused on the sense of community through worship or *koinonia*. As architectural historian Leland M. Roth states in *Understanding Architecture: Its elements, history and*

---

[34] die Kerk. 2021. "Oordenking | Deel Dit Donderdag | Op Die Board Deel 39 | Nog 'n koue front". Online at: https://www.youtube.com/watch?v=xT9rQ1SWwuQ [Accessed 18 December 2022].

[35] SnapScan is a South African contactless mobile payment solution. A QR code™ is a pattern of black and white squares that contains information, often a web address, that can be read by the camera of a smartphone. It is the abbreviation for "quick response code". "QR Code", *Oxford Learner's Dictionary*.

meaning,[36] the church refers not to the building but the assembly of believers. There is no rule that a church service has to be in a specific type of building or space. It could be in the veld[37] or under a tree, or in a tent or a school hall. Matthew 18:20 makes it clear that the act of gathering is central to worship: "For where two or three are gathered together in My name, there I am among them."[38] Even though a community can use a private living room, hall, or temporary structure for many years, it will through time develop the need for a space specifically designed for the purpose of assembly. Architecture then becomes the facilitator of the gathering of people. A building provides shelter, and a level of privacy to concentrate on the service. In the early days of Christianity there was no need for specialised buildings. Early Christians gathered where space was available and adapted their worship to the space. When they faced persecution, their worship spaces where the sacraments of mass and baptism were administered, needed to be concealed from public view.[39] But when it became an accepted mainstream religious movement, Christianity outgrew the private house and dedicated buildings for Christianity emerged. Worship space changed from private to public spaces. The movement grew and by the fourth century, it had moved past the stage of repression.[40] With the conversion of Emperor Constantine and the Edict of Milan in 313 CE, Christianity became the official religion, and the problem of devising a building type, one that would be suitable in terms of function and symbolism for public worship, arose. Christianity differed from older religions in which individuals made private offerings. It was focused on the gathering of the faithful which required a large, enclosed space with good acoustics so that congregants could hear the sermon and in which choir singing could be projected. The development of buildings that could accommodate large groups and that had the appropriate symbolism were architectural considerations that continued into modern times.[41] Roman basilicas that fell out of use were famously adapted for early Christian purposes.[42] The basilica had characteristics that fitted the needs of the worshippers. These buildings were originally designed for public gathering and the symbolic connotation with justice was a bonus.[43]

But as religion scholar Mona Siddiqui so eloquently explains, "in traditional, sacramental, or quasi-sacramental understandings of what constitutes the church as church, a more balanced dialectic moves back and forth between local congregation

---

36 Roth, *Understanding Architecture*, 241.
37 Open, uncultivated country or grassland characteristic of parts of Southern Africa (https://www.merriam-webster.com/dictionary/veld).
38 English Standard Version of the Bible.
39 Roth, *Understanding Architecture*, 241.
40 Kostof S. 1995. *A History of Architecture: Settings and Rituals*. Second Edition. London: Oxford University Press, 248.
41 Roth, *Understanding Architecture*, 243.
42 Kostof, *A History of Architecture*, 248.
43 Roth, *Understanding Architecture*, 243.

and universal *ecclesia*. Every church polity gives an account of the congregation's relationship with the whole church that shows itself in analogies to modern democratic thought and political forms."[44]

DESIGNING CHURCH BUILDINGS FOR RITUAL AND SYMBOLISM

Basilicas were more desirable than the temples of other religions that already had their own embedded symbolism. By taking over the plan of the basilica, patterns of activity and symbolism that were associated with that building type were incorporated into the rituals of Christian worship. Christian rituals, on the other hand, were well-suited to the space provided by the nave and the linear plan of the basilica. The light from the clerestory windows served the symbolism of salvation, divinity and reverence. Two principal divisions marked the basilica: the great rectangular hall, destined for the laity, and the apse, used by the clergy.

Architecture is thus more than shelter. Although religious architecture provides basic function and shelter, closely linked to its rituals, the need for symbolic and aesthetic representation of the congregation's communal values and beliefs is equally important.[45] Buildings are informed by both use and aesthetics and in spaces with a religious function, the need for symbolic representation is closely linked to the ritual.[46] Architect and community planner Tara Johnson sums it up: "Beyond the pragmatic, churches are monuments to community cohesion and physical markers of a sense of place in a city. The building not only symbolises the unified intent of a congregation … it is also an expression of faith."[47]

Journalist Charles C. Mann suggested in a 2011 *National Geographic* cover story on Göbekli Tepe that it was the urge to worship that sparked civilisation, rather than the rise of agriculture, as we used to think. He added that "[t]he human sense of the sacred and the love of a good spectacle, may have given rise to civilisation itself."[48] Rory Olcayto, an architect and award-winning journalist and critic, explained: "We chose to design and build places of worship before any other kind of building, perhaps even before house and home. We used to think agriculture gave rise to cities and later to writing, art, and religion. Now the world's oldest temple implies the urge to worship sparked the idea of a civilised world no longer bound by

---

44 Siddiqui M. 2022. "Martyrs, Minorities, Faith and Fidelity" (online course), *Canopy Forum*.
45 Roth, *Understanding Architecture*, 5.
46 Verster W. 2013. *A Study of the Life-cycle, Re-use and Adaptation of Places of Worship in Bloemfontein from 1948 to the Present, with Specific Reference to the Afrikaans Reformed Churches*. Master's of Architecture Thesis, University of the Free State, 13.
47 Johnson TA. 2004. *Socio-economic and political issues in the successful adaptive reuse of churches*. Cincinnati, OH: University of Cincinnati, 1.
48 Göbekli Tepe ("potbelly hill" in Turkish) are ruins on a hill in Southern Turkey, consisting of broken limestone slabs dotting the site. German archaeologist Klaus Schmidt claimed it is the world's oldest temple, dating back 11 600 years. See Kabil A. 2018. "Did the Urge to Worship Lead to Civilization?", *Long Now/Medium.com*, 1 February.

hunting and gathering."⁴⁹ He concluded that the buildings created for these rituals reveal the intimate relationship between religion and architecture.

Similarly, in Christian church-building, new building types developed to provide space for religious worship, suited to its rituals. Church architecture grew to became more than just utilitarian. Added to its primary function of accommodating large congregations, the church also represented the symbolic: its spires, cross or centralised plan types, the use of daylight and the placing of pulpits, all strengthened, facilitated and enhanced symbolism and ritualistic events. Christian rituals include baptism, communion (Eucharist), the ministry of the word or church service (ceremony) from the pulpit, weddings and funerals, but the importance placed on these rituals differed between the various denominations. For instance, in the early medieval Roman Catholic Church, the focus fell on the liturgical centre, with altar in the east, but with the Reformation in 1517, the church service itself became the focus of the interior layout, and the pulpit became the essence of the liturgical space, as it symbolises *sola scriptura*.⁵⁰ Church design revealed the importance of the rituals embedded in the daily lives of the congregation. The medieval cross churches no longer fitted the needs of the Reformed Protestant service, especially since the lines of sight in these buildings did not allow for a clear view of the pulpit.⁵¹ Church design thus changed to follow a specific Reformed ritual. A church building is generated from the plan form, which in turn is determined by the dominant activities or rituals. The distribution of the main elements of a church plan reflects the hierarchy of activities taking place in the assembly, and by extension it also reflects the theological doctrines that determine these rituals. South African churches followed specific European-historical form language elements, revealing a close art-historical bond between the Nederduits-Gereformeerde Kerk in South Africa and the churches in the Netherlands and England. Protestant churches mostly took over old church forms. Luther maintained the division of the interior into a main nave and choir, and the two areas were used for preaching and communion respectively.⁵²

---

49   Olcayto R. 2012. "Sacred Space", *The Architects Journal: Places of Worship* 235(14):35.

50   *Sola scriptura* is Latin for "word alone", which is the Reformed Protestant Church's theological focus. Liturgy is the customary public worship performed by a religious group, especially by a Christian group. As a religious phenomenon, liturgy represents a communal response to and participation in the sacred through activities reflecting praise, thanksgiving, remembrance, supplication or repentance.

51   Kesting DP. 1978. *Afrikaans-Protestantse Kerkbou Erfenis en Uitdaging: 'n Ondersoek na Kerkbou met besondere verwysing na die gebruik en inrigting van die drie Afrikaanse (moeder) kerke, te wete die Nederduitse Gereformeerde Kerk, die Nederduitsch Hervormde Kerk van Afrika en die Gereformeerde Kerk in Suid-Afrika* [Afrikaans-Protestant Church-building Heritage and Challenge: An investigation into church-building with particular reference to the utilisation and furnishing of the three Afrikaans (mother) churches, namely the Dutch Reformed Church, the Dutch Reformed Church in Africa and the Reformed Church in South Africa]. Unpublished PhD Thesis, University of Port Elizabeth, 109.

52   De Waal LM. 1978. *Europees-Historiese Vormtaalelemente in Nederduits-Gereformeerde Kerkargitektuur van die Groot-Karoo* [European-Historical Form Language Elements in Dutch

But the Dutch Reformed tradition to use the choir as a vestry originated in the Netherlands, as Protestants took over Roman-Catholic churches.[53] The rectangular church hall with liturgical centre in the middle of the congregation was ideal for Protestant worship. Traditionally, the entrance was west and a long, narrow main nave with a passage in the middle led to the pulpit with dignified, stiff, formal wooden benches on each side of the passage along the entire width of the nave. The pulpit, baptismal font and communion table were centrally placed in the east with the vestry behind it, separated from the rest of the church by a dividing wall. The pulpit could be reached directly from the vestry and an external door on the east provided a separate entrance to the vestry for clergymen. Decoration was sparse.[54]

Although guidelines by the Dutch Reformed Church in South Africa, stipulating the appearance of interior spaces, were not published until the middle of the twentieth century, church buildings had a simple rectangular form and a horizontal liturgical axis in common. The pulpit was invariably the liturgical centre and focus point to where sight lines without visual disturbances were directed.[55] Architects such as Johan de Ridder claimed the form was a result of Reformed principles. The auditorium, or modified Greek cross with Romanesque influences, became popular from the early to mid-twentieth century, due to the influence of Gerard Moerdijk (1890-1958).[56] South African churches with their spires are particularly iconographic. They are significant landmarks in the landscape that remind us of the religious institutions that they house. Urban theorist Kevin Lynch states that "a church in a city is a landmark: an external point of orientation, usually an easily identifiable physical object in the urban landscape".[57] Seen as God's house on earth, church buildings and the ministry of the Word were combined with other means of reaching people, which included education, physical health and spiritual healing.

CREATING SACRED SPACE FOR THE BODY OF CHRIST

Creating sacred space has through the millennia been regarded as the pinnacle of architecture. Religious structures, such as Gothic cathedrals, have the ability to transcend the physical world and to create a sense of God. St. Augustine saw light as the

---

Reformed Church Architecture of the Great Karoo]. Unpublished MA Thesis, University of the Free State, 53.

53 De Waal, *Europees-Historiese Vormtaalelemente*, 79.

54 De Waal, *Europees-Historiese Vormtaalelemente*, 53-54.

55 Le Roux SW. 2008. "Die soeke van drie argitekte na 'n planvorm vir Afrikaanse Gereformeerde kerkbou [The search by three architects for appropriate plans for Afrikaans Reformed church-building]", *Tydskrif vir Kultuurgeskiedenis* [Journal of Cultural History] 22(2):20-21.

56 Verster, *A Study of the Life-cycle, Re-use and Adaptation*, 29.

57 Lynch K. 1960. *The Image of the City*. Cambridge, MA: MIT Press.

symbol of divine illumination,[58] and thus devices such as light, scale, materiality, procession and verticality were used in the design of these ecclesiastic spaces to evoke the divine, and cause wonder and a spiritual experience that goes beyond the boundaries of the church. After the Reformation, transcendence became less important, because believers had direct access to God and did not need the power of the church, but even Protestant churches have an ephemeral quality and are different from other building types in that they remained places of mysterious presence.[59] Physical needs are often placed on the forefront of the pursuit of human betterment, often to the detriment of spiritual needs,[60] but as architecture and communications theorist Julio Bermudez argues: "transcending architecture considers the mysterious, profound, and real power of designed environments to address the spiritual dimension of our humanity."[61]

HEALTH AND HEALING

The healing quality of architecture is usually associated with health care and hospital design and addresses the body, but when used in a spiritual context, church architecture also has a healing dimension, which is broader than religiosity. Publications on the subject are rare, as architect and theologian Bert Daelemans points out,[62] but the buildings designed specifically for spiritual activities play a role in spiritual healing. Daelemans describes the multisensory and synaesthetic (spiritual) dimension of church architecture that engages the body and all the senses, as a highly personal experience, one of being in the world, that cannot be replicated by virtual space. Synaesthetic means a specific atmosphere or *genius loci* that comes to the fore when a human is in or moves through a space. He describes healing as a process that implies motion. It is more than just the absence of disease: it incorporates sustenance of emotions. He adds that synaesthetic atmosphere is an essential element often overlooked in the design of modern church buildings, which are criticised for being cold and soulless. A church building has the ability to address the body and therefore the soul. It has the ability to slow us down and heighten our perception. The healing dimension of space reminds us of our wholeness, and that we are embodied and spiritual beings.

---

58 See Goodyear D. 2019. "180. St. Augustine and Divine Illumination", *Philosophical Eggs*, 11 June.

59 Verster, *A Study of the Life-cycle, Re-use and Adaptation*, 17.

60 Ripley E. 2020. *Transcendent Architecture: Faith Inspired through Sacred Design*. Bachelor of Architecture Thesis, Ball State University, 9 May.

61 Bermudez JC. *Transcending architecture: Contemporary views on sacred space*. Washington DC: CUA Press. Professor Julio Bermudez directs the Sacred Space and Cultural Studies graduate concentration programme at the Catholic University of America's School of Architecture and Planning.

62 Daelemans B. 2020. "Healing Space: The Synaesthetic Quality of Church Architecture", *Religions* 11(12):635.

Healthy buildings provide a quiet atmosphere that reduces stress, good ventilation, fresh air and natural light that improves mood, health and the immune system. A healthy building also engages with nature. Finnish architect Juhani Pallasmaa likens walking through a cathedral with a forest of columns to walking through a forest in nature, which makes one aware of the eternal natural cycle of the world.[63]

The American architect Steven Holl stressed the importance of authentic physical and sensory experience, what he called "the silent intensities of architecture", that cannot be assumed, reproduced or substituted by words, photographs or even films.[64] It can only be found in a certain place, here and now. As Holl puts it, "Only the architecture itself offers the tactile sensations of textured stone surfaces and polished wooden pews, the experience of light changing with movement, the smell and resonant sounds of space, the bodily relations of scale and proportion."[65] All these different, particular sense experiences converge in one synaesthetic event.

French philosopher and founding father of spatial theory, Henri Lefebvre, devised the triad *perceived*, *conceived* and *lived* space in his book *The Production of Space*.[66] His spatial theory can be successfully applied to the argument relating to the experiential quality of in-person Christian worship facilitated by church architecture in the here and now, as opposed to virtual services. Church attendance of a body in architectural space is a social (*lived*) practice. The spiritual and healing experience of being in a sacred space (*perceived* space), can only come about when the body is in the social or *lived* space.[67] Cyberspace is like Lefebvre's *conceived* space. It is not real space, but only a representation of space. Pallasmaa talks about the inhumanity of being pushed out of space to become a mere spectator and pleads for the return of the healing role of architecture that can reconcile us with the world. He adds that the actual religious space stimulates the acoustical and tactile, more than the visual and allows for materiality and the *chiaroscuro* of light and shadows.[68]

CHRISTIANITY OUTSIDE THE CONFINES OF ARCHITECTURE

This chapter argues for the preservation of church architecture, emphasising the important role that the church building plays in continuing Christian worship in a post-pandemic world, but is also presents the counter argument that paradoxically claims that religion can be served just as well outside of the building. Mona Siddiqui presents another paradox when discussing the value of in-person and virtual

---

63 Pallasmaa J. 1996. *The Eyes of the Skin: Architecture and the Senses*. London: Academy.
64 Holl S. 1994. "Questions of perception: Phenomenology of architecture", in Holl S, Juhani Pallasmaa J and Alberto Pérez-Gómez A (eds). *Questions of Perception: Phenomenology of Architecture*. Tokyo: A+U, 39-120.
65 Holl, "Questions of perception", 41.
66 Lefebvre H. 1991. *The Production of Space*. Translated by D. Nicholson-Smith. London: Blackwell Publishing.
67 Daelemans, "Healing Space", 6.
68 Pallasmaa, *The Eyes of the Skin*, 34.

rituals, as opposed to charitable work. She explains that the internet enabled many rituals online during the pandemic, which have made congregants feel as if they were still part of a ritual and at least they were seeing other people and interacting with them. But she warns that a continuation of online prayers, services and church meetings will further disembody believers from the wider community. Rituals are about physical and mental effort, focusing on something in a group, and online rituals demand less physical exertion. She then adds to the argument that there is no moral value in ritual but that helping others is a moral act.[69]

The answer to this paradox lies in the belief that the church is more than just a building. According to Ephesians 1:22-23, God placed all things under the authority of Christ, appointing Him head over everything for the church, which is His body. Biblically speaking, the church is the entire group of Christians, and the Eucharist sacramentally associates both the individual with the local community and the universal church through the body of Christ. It also fulfils an important pastoral care function outside the church. During the pandemic access to patients and health care workers were limited by law until spiritual care to these individuals was deemed an essential service. Charitable giving is not something that can be done in a virtual environment.

CONCLUSION

During the Covid-19 pandemic, large gatherings, including church services, were prohibited by law. Once gatherings were allowed again, the rigorous requirements of social distancing affected religious congregations. The regulations have forced many South Africans to reconsider how and where they worship, and whether their faith is best expressed in a house of worship or whether it can be equally expressed at home through a virtual YouTube or Facebook transmissions.

Many denominations moved to online or virtual services that streamed sermons and messages of health and healing to a wider, global audience. Modern digital technology has made it possible for Christian churches to extend their reach and influence, and church members strove to find a new normal in the ongoing negotiation with public health protocols to curtail infection rates, by taking up social distancing and forging a greater reliance on technology to bridge the gaps between themselves and others.

But the idea of social distancing, as required in the Covid-19 regulations, runs completely counter to the concept of assembly by a congregation in religious or sacred space. The pandemic has blurred the lines between secular and sacred space, and where the boundaries between these spaces were once clearly defined by walls of brick and mortar or stone, these spaces are now blended into cyberspace. One has to question whether the infiltration of secular space (home) into religious or sacred space (church) through the medium cyberspace (the internet) has changed the face of religious worship forever.

---

69 Siddiqui, "Martyrs, Minorities, Faith, and Fidelity".

INDEX

A

Abacha, Sani, 56, 79, 80

African Charter on Human and Peoples' Rights (ACHPR, Banjul Charter), 55, 56, 258

African Initiated Churches (AICs) (also African Indigenous Churches, African Independent Churches, African Instituted Churches [see also CITAM Ngong Church; Johanne Marange Apostolic Church; Nomiya Church]), ii, ii, vi, viii, 4, 6, 7-8, 9, 20, 35, 36, 37, 46-48, 50-51, 300, 317, 318-319, 325, 326, 336-337, 343, 344-347, 351, 352-353, 355, 363, 366, 397, 398

    Apostolic traditions of (see also Johanne Morange Apostolic Church), iii, 4, 6, 7, 10, 11, 12, 13n41, 36, 37, 46-48, 50, 51, 330, 341

    syncretism as a healing method in, 336, 337, 340-342, 346-347

    Zionist traditions of, iii, 4, 6, 7, 9, 11, 395n5

African Traditional Medicine (ATM) (see also Benin; Botswana), vii, viii, 19, 193, 282, 285, 289, 315, 317, 319, 320, 321, 322, 323, 325, 326, 328, 330-334, 335-347, 351, 353

    and colonial era, 319, 320-321, 323, 324, 332, 333

    Covid popularisation of, 317, 318, 325-333

    decolonial perspective on, viii, 319, 332, 333

    dilemma for Christianity, 325-333

    plant-based and herbal remedies in, ii, viii, 19, 156, 159, 170n23, 176-177, 191, 192, 193, 195, 279, 285, 298, 309, 320, 341, 342, 346

    water and steam-based remedies in (see water)

    Western and Christian views of (see Western culture)

    World Health Organization (WHO) and, 321-323

African Traditional Religions (ATR) (see also customary law; Obatala traditional religion), 36, 54, 62, 75, 177, 179, 299, 319, 321, 338, 341, 345, 350, 353, 395, 397

African Union (see also "Agenda 2063"), ii, iii, 73, 82, 176

"Agenda 2063", ii, iii, iv, 73, 75, 80, 81-82, 83, 84

    aspirations of, 73, 81

    religion and, 73, 81-82, 83, 83, 84, 85

Akufo-Addo, Nana, 15, 16, 21, 24, 25, 27, 59

Algeria, iv, 87-97

    authoritarianism in, iv, 87

    constitutional law of, 88-90, 92, 93

    Covid-19 regulations and measures in, 87-88, 91 92, 93-96

    freedom of religion in, 87, 88, 89-90, 92, 93, 94, 96, 97

    Islam in, 88, 89, 90, 91, 92, 95-96

    lockdown in, 87, 91, 92, 93, 94

    Ministry of Religious Affairs in, 89, 92, 95, 96

    non-Muslim religions in, 89-90

    popular protests in (see also Hirak), 91-92, 97

    sociopolitical context of Covid pandemic, 87, 91-92

almajirai (see Islam)

Amanze, James, 338, 339, 343

Andrews, Christian Kwabena (Osofo Kyiri Abosom), 30-31

Anglicans, 119n45, 120, 121n55, 124, 152, 180, 303, 367, 388n29, 395n5, 429n9

antiretroviral treatment (see HIV/AIDS)

apartheid, 81, 417, 419n31, 420-421, 422, 424, 431n18

Apostolic Faith Mission in Zimbabwe (AFMZ) (see also Pentecostal Christianity), 35-36, 37, 42-46, 49-50, 52, 326, 330, 341

architecture (see also South Africa), ix, 427-441

and Covid ban on religious gathering, 427, 428-429, 430, 432, 433, 435, 436-437, 441
ecclesia and, 427, 436
and five elements of Christian architecture, 439
and freedoms of assembly and religion, 427, 433
and health and healing, 427, 438, 439-440
koinonia and, 427, 434
and ritual and symbolic design of church buildings, 428, 435, 436, 437, 438, 439, 440-441
and sacred space, ix, 428, 436, 438-439, 440, 441
and virtual worship, 427, 428, 432, 433-434, 439, 440-441
artemisia, 176, 193, 349
authoritarianism, iv, 87, 427, 432-433
Awolowo, Obafemi, 79, 80

B

Baha'i, 395n5
Battersby, Jane, 417, 418, 420, 421, 422
Benedict XVI, Pope, 148, 150
Benin, vi, 144, 187-197
    cultural drivers of vaccine hesitancy in, 188, 189, 190-193, 194-197
    Covid-19 regulations in, 187, 188, 194-195
    media and social networks in, 187, 191, 195, 197
    plant-based and herbal medicine in, 191, 192, 193, 195
    traditional medicine in, 188, 189, 192, 193, 196
    traditional religion in, 188, 189, 190, 195
    vaccine hesitancy in, 187-197
    Waaba people of, 187-197
bereavement (see also death; funerals), vi, viii, ix, 78, 276 354, 355, 357, 361, 365, 366, 369, 371, 372, 374-378, 390
Bible (see also Mozambique, scriptural messaging in the pandemic in), vi, viii, 6, 25, 38, 64, 102n17, 119n44, 122, 158, 163, 168, 170-171, 201-215, 292, 296, 321, 338, 339, 340, 341, 343, 358, 360, 361, 396, 406-409, 420-421, 422, 424, 441
    human dignity and, 209, 210, 213-215
    laws on sex and sexuality in, 201, 202, 203, 204, 205, 206, 208, 209, 210, 211, 215
    sex and gender-based violence (SGBV), vi, in, 201, 205, 209, 213
    women's sexuality in, vi, 201-215
Botswana, viii, 242, 335-347
    African Independent Churches (AICs) in, 335-347
    African traditional medicine in, 335-347
    African traditional religions in, 338, 341, 345
    impact of Covid-19 on churches in, 336, 342-347
    missionaries in, 336, 337, 338, 339, 340
    plant-based medicine in, viii, 341, 342, 346
    syncretism healing atonement motif in, 335-347
Britain, 4, 5n10, 56, 64, 75, 77, 79, 83, 133, 173, 249, 278, 311, 344, 361, 432, 437
Buddhism, 303
burial (see funerals)
Burkina Faso, 99, 188n6, 190

C

Cameroon, 148
Castells, Manuel, 366, 370, 374, 377
Catholicism (see also Côte d'Ivoire and Niger), v, viii, 28-29, 61, 102, 103, 122, 123, 141n5, 142-145, 146, 148, 150, 158, 178, 180, 191, 193, 270, 303, 325, 326, 330, 337, 353, 367, 388n29, 395, 397, 408, 429n9, 437, 438, 439n61
    Holy Week of, v, 142, 145, 147
    Lenten holiday of, 142-143, 144, 145
    liturgical practices of, v, 142, 143, 144, 145, 146-147, 150
    magisterium of, 148, 150
    Paschal triduum of, 143, 144, 146
    and the Second Vatican Council, 148, 150
    theological foundations of media in, 145, 147-148

theology of, 141, 142, 145, 147-148, 149
Cavender, Tony, 320, 323
charismatic Christianity (see also Pentecostal-charismatic Christianity), 19, 26, 27, 28, 46, 61, 118, 338, 345, 401, 422
children, 12, 13n41, 21, 33, 39, 48, 50, 100, 123 171, 172, 203, 212, 214, 215, 242, 247, 252, 253, 256, 262, 265, 269, 279, 271, 274, 280, 281, 283, 284, 285, 290, 291, 292, 293, 295, 300, 303, 305, 310, 311, 320, 332, 354, 355, 367, 369, 374, 375, 386, 403, 415, 416n16, 417-419
China, i, 112, 125, 127, 157, 174, 187, 196, 239, 325, 327, 335, 402
Chitando, Ezra, 49, 251
Christianity (see also African Initiated Churches; Anglicans; Catholicism; charismatic Christianity; Lutherans; Pentecostal Christianity; Protestantism), iii, iv, v, ix, 4n6, 6, 7, 9, 19, 20, 25, 27, 29, 35, 37, 38, 39, 49, 51, 54, 60, 62, 67, 71, 73, 77, 103, 104, 105, 109, 111, 113, 115, 118-125, 127, 129, 134, 141, 142, 143, 144, 145, 147, 149, 150, 154, 155, 156, 168, 170, 177, 179, 180, 190, 208, 210, 270, 272, 275, 280, 282, 290, 291, 299, 303, 317, 318, 320, 321, 325-333, 337, 338, 339, 340, 342, 346, 347, 351, 352, 353, 361, 367, 380, 385, 387-388, 395, 397, 401, 403, 406, 407, 409, 411, 412, 413-414, 420, 422-425, 426, 427-428, 432, 434-441
Church of Jesus Christ of Latter-day Saints, 122n57
CITAM Ngong Church (see also Pentecostal Christianity), viii, 379-391 435, 436
  Covid-19 response of, 380, 384, 388-390
  digital ethnography at, viii, 379, 381, 382-390
  effects of Covid on, 379, 380, 381, 383, 384-385, 387, 388-391
  networked theology at, 370, 385-391
  participant observation of, 382, 383, 384, 385, 388
  virtual communities in, 379, 381, 382-383, 386-391
civil society, 91, 94, 108-109, 159, 161, 413, 421, 422

colonialism (also pre-colonial and postcolonial) (see also decolonial theory), 8, 20, 56, 75, 76, 77, 133, 223, 227n79, 320-321, 323-325, 332, 367, 395, 397-398, 424
communality, African value of (see also *Ubuntu*), 83, 299, 352, 354, 360, 362, 365-378, 436
  relational theory and, 371-373, 378
  and worship, 44, 354-355, 405, 428
conspiracy theories on Covid-19 (see also Covid-19 pandemic, misinformation and disinformation on), i, ii, v-vi, ix, 24, 30, 39, 61, 112, 116, 123, 133, 149, 167-186, 195, 326, 349
  5G radiation transmission conspiracy, 61, 170n23, 172-173
  disease of others conspiracy, 118, 133, 174-175
  legal measures against, 167, 168, 170, 173
  Mark of the Beast 666 conspiracy, 168, 170-171, 179, 182-183, 184, 185, 186
  religious debunking of, 178-180, 185
  religious propagation of, 168, 170-171, 173, 175, 177
  staged health crisis conspiracy, 170n23, 173-174
  vaccine-related conspiracies, 167, 171-172
corruption, 84, 171, 172, 205, 245
  moral, 68, 157
  political, 109, 113, 128, 133, 245, 432, 433
  sexual, 221
Côte d'Ivoire, v, ix, 141-150
  Catholic Church in, v, 141n5, 142, 143, 144, 145, 146, 148, 150
  constitutional law of, 150
  Covid-19 regulations and measures in, 144, 145, 150
  digitalised cults in, v, 141, 142, 143, 145, 146-147, 149-150
  lockdown in, 141, 142, 143, 145, 146, 147, 148, 149
  religious media in, 142, 145, 146, 147-148, 149, 150

445

Covid-19 pandemic
- African emergence of, i, 15, 34, 59, 91, 101, 106, 112, 130, 144, 156-157, 167, 187, 230-231, 237, 249, 269, 287, 326, 335, 349, 379, 396, 402
- Chinese origins of (see China)
- conspiracy theories on (see conspiracy theories on Covid-19)
- criminal penalties and policing of regulations against, 9, 10, 11, 12, 13, 16, 22, 23, 30, 47, 53, 62, 92, 93, 106-107, 108-109, 118, 137, 173, 186, 207, 218, 228, 229, 230, 231, 232, 241, 246-247, 253-254, 258, 261, 264, 265, 272, 274, 280, 427, 429, 430-432
- curfews in, 10, 59, 91, 102, 103, 106, 107, 108, 144, 201, 207, 218, 230, 232, 233, 234, 250, 349, 357, 369, 430, 431
- "double religiosity" in, 42, 49
- economic effects of, i, vi, 23, 24, 81, 91, 99, 100, 108, 113, 127, 128, 130, 131, 174, 175, 196-197, 238, 241, 243-244, 247, 271, 276, 277, 284, 305, 307, 313, 314, 359, 362, 360, 419, 429
- "flattening the curve" of, i, ix, 112, 118, 128, 131, 132, 136, 306, 429
- and flouting of regulations against, 6, 10, 12, 23, 30, 44, 47, 53, 62, 74, 95, 114, 118, 127, 128, 133, 135, 137, 175, 180, 218-219, 229, 230, 241, 266, 407, 427, 430, 432
- government regulations and measures against (see individual countries)
- herbal remedies against (see also African Traditional Medicine; Benin; Botswana), ii, 193, 279, 298, 309, 327, 328, 330, 332-333
- hygiene and, 27, 60, 102, 103, 109, 125, 273, 277, 280, 284, 285, 373
- lockdown in, 10, 11, 12, 13n41, 14, 16, 22, 23, 31, 33, 34, 39, 42, 43, 52, 53, 54, 58, 59, 60, 61, 62, 63, 64, 69, 72, 73, 74, 87, 91, 92, 93, 94, 99, 112, 117, 118, 119, 120, 121, 122, 123, 124 , 127, 130-134, 141, 142, 143, 145, 146, 147, 148, 149, 153, 167, 169, 180, 182, 201, 207, 208, 219, 228, 230, 233, 237-247, 249-255, 259-267, 270, 272, 276, 278-281, 284, 285, 287, 289, 290, 292, 294-301, 305-306, 307, 308, 309, 310, 314, 326, 327, 330, 335, 342, 343, 349, 351, 353, 355, 357, 358, 359, 369, 379, 387, 388, 390, 396, 398, 403-406, 407, 412, 419, 427, 428, 430, 431, 432, 433
- mask-wearing and, 27, 119, 121, 180, 218, 219, 230-231, 232, 233, 234, 313
- misinformation and disinformation on (see also conspiracy theories on Covid-19), 113, 134, 167-168, 169-170, 175-178, 179, 181, 182, 183, 184, 185, 186
  - Covid-19 prophecies, 170n23, 176, 177-178
  - supernatural powers, 170n23, 177, 339
  - traditional herbs and alternative medicine, 170n23, 176-177
- religious opposition to measures against, 12, 29-30, 43-44, 48, 50-51, 54, 61-62, 95, 96, 106-109, 133, 427, 433
- religious support for measures against, ii, iv, v, 8, 12, 27, 39, 40-42, 43, 44, 46, 49-50, 52, 60, 64, 68, 69, 87, 103-104, 105, 106-109, 120, 125, 180, 427, 433
- school closures during, ii, 16, 34, 51, 91, 100, 101, 130, 144, 217, 242, 265, 287, 343, 349, 420
- social distancing and, i, vi, ix, 9, 34, 35, 38, 40, 41, 44, 46, 47, 48, 51, 52, 60, 64, 93, 95-96, 102, 104, 112, 113, 116, 128, 135, 169, 180, 218, 219, 228, 229, 230, 231, 232, 233, 242, 287, 301, 307, 329, 343, 349, 351, 353, 354-355, 357, 358, 362, 366, 397, 398, 399, 410, 427, 429, 441
- spiritual interpretations of, 40, 42, 52
  - as end times, iv, 119, 380
  - as punishment of sin, iv, viii, 107, 108, 115-116, 117, 118, 155, 157, 396, 397, 401, 402, 403, 406, 408, 409, 410, 412
- religious responses to (see individual countries)
- vaccination against (see vaccination)
  - customary law, 75-76, 83, 208, 210

D

death, viii, 45, 48, 52, 53, 64, 74, 143, 190, 191, 194, 197, 203, 212, 243, 249, 259, 261, 276, 307n37, 318, 327, 337, 341, 342, 361, 362, 365, 396, 397, 406, 412, 420, 423, 429

decolonial theory, viii, 319, 333

Deka-Zulu, Bernadette, 270, 278, 280-281

deliverance, 296, 297-298, 300, 349, 351, 353, 354, 355-358, 362, 363

Democratic Republic of Congo, 337, 395

Devil (see Satan)

Dholuo (see Kenya)

digital ethnography (see also CITAM Ngong Church), 142

digital religion, v, 51, 141-150, 361, 365-378, 379-391

as expression of popular crisis religiosity, v, 142, 143-144, 149-150

and liturgical and spiritual resilience and, v, 141, 142 144, 145, 146-147, 150

disinformation Covid-19 (see conspiracy theories on Covid-19; Covid-19 pandemic, misinformation and disinformation on)

divorce, 102n17, 223, 300, 303

domestic violence (see also gender-based violence), i, vii, 262, 287-301

Covid-19 pandemic effects on, 287, 288, 289, 290, 292, 293, 294-296, 297, 298, 299-301

Muslim perspective on, vii, 289, 290, 291, 292, 293-294, 294-295, 296, 297, 298, 299

Obatala traditional religious perspective on, vii

Pentecostal perspective on, vii, 289, 290, 291, 292, 293, 294, 295, 296, 297, 298, 299

religious responses to, 288, 289-299, 300, 301

Dunamis International Gospel Centre (DIGC), 61, 180

Dutch Reformed Church, 35, 437n51, 438

E

Ebola, 109, 130

ecclesia, viii, ix, 421, 424, 425, 427, 436, 439

economy (see also Zimbabwe, informal economy), i, 20, 26, 67, 81, 99n2, 174, 201, 204, 213, 238, 244, 247, 256, 257, 262, 270, 350, 368, 405, 416, 417, 420, 421n39, 422, 423, 424, 425, 426, 431n18

Covid-19 effects on (see Covid-19 pandemic, economic effects of)

informal, i, vi, vii, 6, 8, 131, 237-248, 421

religious organisations and, 9, 14, 83, 94, 144, 343, 404

women's participation in, 204, 208, 213, 227, 276, 278-279, 285

Ecumenical HIV and AIDS Initiatives and Advocacy (EHAIA), 152

education, ii, iv, vi, 35, 57-58, 71n5, 72n5, 78, 83n59, 82, 84, 100, 114, 118n37, 124, 125, 129, 131, 137, 152, 160, 162-164, 180, 186, 225, 226-227, 234, 237, 291, 305, 310, 322, 336, 352, 357, 366, 380, 410, 415, 416, 435, 458

Covid-19 disruption of (see Covid-19 pandemic, school closures during)

women workers in, 152, 278, 284

Egypt, 64, 176

elders, 29, 38-39, 43, 123, 124n70, 274, 275, 352, 377, 380, 384

executive powers, 13, 14, 16, 21, 22, 29, 58, 67, 79, 89, 93, 94

exorcism, 352, 352, 357-358

emergency powers, iv, 4, 13n41, 14, 15, 18, 21-22, 23, 182, 398-399, 407, 433

Europe, 55, 67, 88, 106n33, 112, 123, 157, 174, 188, 196, 305, 312, 313, 338, 397, 437

F

Facebook, 9, 38, 43, 119, 122, 142, 146, 148, 149, 170, 181, 184, 266, 279, 284, 342, 354, 356, 358, 361, 366, 370, 373, 374, 388, 389, 409, 434

faith healing, viii, 7, 36, 46, 48, 49, 50, 155, 317, 325, 330, 331, 333, 346

Fani-Kayode, Femi, 181-182

fatwas (see Islamic law, *fatwas* in)

feminism, 213, 219, 221, 228, 270, 271, 272, 280, 383

Ferkous, Mohamed Ali, 95

food (see also food insecurity; water), 22, 73, 103n17, 131, 178, 206, 233, 238, 241, 242, 243, 250, 266, 277, 279, 281, 284, 298-299, 305, 359-360, 374, 375
   right to food, vii, 5, 14, 238, 241, 251n12, 256-257, 262, 415, 417, 418, 425
food insecurity, ii, ix, 131, 241, 243, 257, 284, 288n8, 299, 359, 413-426
   Christian engagement with, 413-414, 420, 422-426
   and Food Justice Theology, 423-424, 426
   kairos response to, 419-421, 422-423
   religious responses to, 22, 73, 103n7, 131
   in South Africa, 413-426
      strategies and interventions against, 414, 415, 416, 417, 421-422, 423, 425
      structural and systemic nature of, 413, 417-419, 421, 422, 424, 425, 426
      theological responses to, 414, 420-426
France, 88, 141, 143, 47, 269, 312, 412, 440
freedom of religion (see also individual countries), i, ii, iii, iv, v, vii, 3, 4, 8-12, 14, 33, 34, 35, 37, 42, 41, 43, 51-52, 53, 54, 55-60, 63, 64, 68, 69, 71n5, 74, 87, 88, 89, 90-93, 96, 97, 127, 128, 130-134, 136, 144, 150, 224, 234, 235, 258-259, 298, 398, 427, 433
   and the *forum externum/internum*, v, 127, 132, 136
funerals, xvii, 16, 60, 124-125, 178, 233, 269, 275, 276, 277, 282, 284, 327, 355, 361, 366, 367, 370, 374, 375, 377, 429, 432, 437

G

Gates, Bill (see also conspiracy theories on Covid-19, vaccine-related conspiracies), 171, 172, 178, 181
gathering
   bans on, 259, 260, 263, 273, 275
   religious, 259, 260, 274,
   social, 217, 218, 263, 276
gender, ii, vi, vii, 5, 114, 163, 201, 213, 271, 283, 250, 264, 285, 294, 309, 385, 410
   and bias in law, 202, 215
   and equality, 82, 211, 214, 227, 250, 270, 380, 425
   and sexuality, 162, 201-215
   and vulnerability, vi
gender-based violence (GBV) (see also Bible, sex-and gender-based violence in), vi, 201-215, 225, 250, 260, 262, 276, 280-281, 285, 359
Ghana, iii, 15-31, 53-54, 55, 57-58, 59-60, 62-64, 66-69, 158, 182, 310, 322
   constitutional law of, iii, 15, 17, 18, 22, 23, 24, 54, 55, 57, 58, 62, 63, 66, 68
   Covid-19 regulations and measures in, iii, 16, 21-24, 27, 29, 30, 31, 53, 54, 58, 60-65, 68, 69
   Electronic Communications System Instrument, 2020 (EI 63), 24
   freedom of religion in, 16, 18, 30, 53, 54, 55-60, 69
   Imposition of Restrictions Act, 2020 (Act 1012) in, 21-24
   lockdown in, 16, 22, 23, 31, 54, 58, 62, 63, 64, 69
   public health law of (see also Act 1012 and EI 63), iii, 17-20, 23, 59-60
   religion and public health in, 20-21
   religious responses to Covid-19 pandemic in, 27-31, 31
   secularism in, iii, 17, 19, 31, 65, 66
Gnonzion, Célestin, v, ix, 141n1
grief (see bereavement)
Gutteres, António, 167, 283

H

hadith (see Islamic law)
hadj/hajj, 89, 116
hijab (see also Kenya, *hijabi* women in), ii, vi, 57, 71n5, 72n5, 217-235
   Covid-19 moment law and experience of, 219, 220, 223, 228-232, 234
   discrimination against, 219, 224, 225, 227, 233, 234
   education and, 225, 226-227, 234
   employment and, 224, 225, 226-227, 231
   five rules of, 219, 222, 234, 235

and freedoms of movement and
association, 229, 234
and freedom of religion or belief (FoRB),
223, 224, 234
and *hijabi* women, ii, 220-228, 232, 233,
234-235
Islamic requirement of, 220, 221, 235
and *jilbab*, 219, 223, 223, 231, 233, 235
post-Covid-19 law and experience of,
223, 232, 235
pre-Covid-19 law and experience of,
219, 220, 223-228, 232, 234
and *purdah*, 115, 223
scholarly debate over, 221, 222
social distancing and, 218, 219, 228-231,
232, 233, 234
Hinduism, 179, 230, 303, 356, 395, 426n52
Hirak, iv, 91, 92
HIV/AIDS, ii, vii, 109, 151, 152, 153-156,
162, 163, 164, 165, 178, 205, 207, 249-267,
340, 415
access to antiretroviral drugs for, 253-254,
265-266
access to healthcare facilities, 254
Covid-19 pandemic effects on, 249, 250,
254, 257, 262, 263, 264-265
faith- and science-based messaging on,
153-156
and freedom of religion, 258-260
human rights and, 249, 250, 251-266
and right to food, 250, 256-257, 262, 266
and right to privacy, 257-258, 264
and right to water, 254-256, 262-263, 266
women living with, 249-267
human rights (see also freedom of religion;
HIV/AIDS), iv, vii, 4, 8, 14, 17, 18, 21, 23,
26, 34, 37, 51-52, 53, 54, 55, 56, 57, 82,
127, 131, 136, 201, 213, 224, 225, 237, 250,
251, 252, 303, 350, 413n3

I

immunisation (see vaccination)
incest, 202, 207
indigenous peoples (see Waaba; see also
African Indigenous Churches; African
Traditional Medicine; African Traditional
Religions), 75-76, 253, 325, 336, 351,
368, 371
inequality, 3n3, 206, 214, 227, 257, 380, 423,
424, 425, 430
infertility (see also Nigeria), ii, vii, 303-314
assisted reproductive technologies/
treatment (ART) and, 303, 304, 305,
306, 308, 309, 310, 311, 312-313
definition and causes of, 303-306
Covid-19 effects on treatment of, 304,
305, 306-310, 311, 313, 214
legal regulation of, 310, 311, 312, 313, 314
medical ethical dimensions of, 310, 311
religious views of, 314
stigma regarding, 303, 311
influenza, and comparison of Covid-19 to,
20, 48, 174, 192, 193328, 329, 335, 344,
347, 349
informal economy, i, vi, vii, 6, 8, 131,
237-248, 421
Covid lockdown effects on, 238, 239, 240,
241, 242, 243, 244-246, 247
legalist theory of, 239, 241, 243, 244, 245,
246, 247
men and, vi
strategies for Covid survival in, 244-246
trade sector of, vi, 238, 239, 240, 241,
244-245, 247
transportation sector of, vi, 238, 239,
240-241, 242, 243-244, 245-246
women and, vi
International Covenant on Civil and
Political Rights (ICCPR), 55, 132, 136,
257n50
International Covenant on Economic, Social
and Cultural Rights (IESCR), 252, 256
International Labour Organization, 238
Islam (see also Islamic law; Muslims; Quran)
almajirai in, 103n17, 131-132
Jumu'ah and *salaat* prayers in, 64, 91, 92,
116, 180
ulema (Islamic scholars) in, 103, 104, 106
women in (see *hijab*)

Islamic law, 75, 76-77, 83, 95, 96, 104, 113, 115n24, 116, 117, 121, 219, 221, 408
fatwas in, iv, 89, 92, 95-96
Issoufou, Mahamadou, 102, 103, 109n41

J

Johanne Marange Apostolic Church (see also African Initiated Churches; Zimbabwe) 6, 10-11, 12-13, 36, 37, 46-48, 50-51, 326, 330
Jehovah's Witnesses, 179-180, 326, 330
John Paul II, Pope, 148, 150
Joshua, T.B., 61, 156, 177
Judaism, 206, 303, 426n52

K

kairos, viii, 419-422
Kairos Document, 420, 423
Kaunda, Chammah, 276, 280
Kealotswe, Obed, 339, 341-342, 346
Kenya, viii, 217-235, 349-363, 365-378, 379-391
    African Initiated Churches in (see CITAM Ngong Church; Nomiya Church, Eastleigh)
    constitutional law of, 220, 223-225, 228, 230-231, 232, 234, 235
    CITAM Ngong Church in (see also CITAM Ngong Church), viii, 379-391
    Covid-19 regulations and measures in, 211, 217-220, 228-234, 235, 349, 351, 353, 354, 355, 358, 362, 365, 369, 374, 375, 378, 388
    Dholuo language and people in, 355, 367
    freedom of religion in, 224, 234, 235
    hijabi women in (see *hijab*)
    lockdown in, 349, 351, 353, 355, 357, 358, 359, 369, 379, 387, 388, 390
    Luo people of, 355, 366, 374, 377
    National Emergency Response Committee on Coronavirus (NERCC) in, 217, 228
    Nomiya Church in (see also Nomiya Church, Eastleigh), 349-363, 365-378
    patriarchal society in, 201, 202, 205, 206, 207, 209-210, 211, 213, 214

    religious responses to Covid-19 in (see CITAM Ngong Church; Kenya, *hijabi* women in; Nomiya Church, Eastleigh)
    sex and gender-based violence in, 201, 204, 205, 206, 207, 208, 210, 211, 213, 214, 215
    women in, 201-215, 217-235, 359, 367, 374, 375, 384

L

land (including borders and property), 29, 83, 95, 101, 112, 116n24, 144, 187, 190, 242, 262, 409, 416, 417, 418, 423-425
Lesotho, 156-157
Libaert, Thierry, 143-144
Libya, 99
Living Faith Church Worldwide (Winners Chapel International) (see also charismatic Christianity), 124, 134, 180
Lompo, Djalwana Laurent, 103, 104
Lungu, Edgar, 273, 274, 275
Lutherans, 156, 437

M

malaria, 176, 189n105, 192, 195
Mali, 99
Mandela, Nelson, 420n32, 422
marriage (see also weddings), 8, 113, 203, 211, 212, 213, 220, 223, 233, 292, 296, 297, 310
medicine (see African Traditional Medicine; Western culture)
mental health (see also domestic violence), 35, 204, 222, 251n12, 262, 287-290, 295-296, 297, 298, 299, 300, 301
Metz, Thaddeus, 371-373, 376
misinformation (see also Covid-19 pandemic, misinformation on)
missionaries (see also Botswana), iii, 4, 21, 35, 39, 290, 318, 321, 323, 336, 337, 338, 339, 340, 366, 367, 388, 397-398, 405
Mohammed, Prophet, 64, 95, 102, 104, 105, 116, 118, 180, 219, 221n33, 222
Mozambique, viii, 395-412
    Catholics in, viii, 396, 397, 408
    constitutional law of, 397-393, 399

Covid-19 regulations and measures in, viiii, 396, 397, 398-401, 407, 408, 412

interpretations of Covid-19 origins in, 401-403

lockdown in, 396, 398, 403-406, 407, 412

lockdown spirituality in, 403-406

missionaries in, 397-398

Muslims in, viii, 397, 407, 409

Pentecostals in, viii, 396, 397, 401, 409

Protestants in, 396, 397, 399, 404

prosperity gospel in, 396, 404

scriptural messaging in the pandemic in, viii, 396, 397, 405, 406-411

Mukuka, Bridget, 270, 275, 280

Musa, Ibrahim A., 112, 120

Muslims (See also *hijab*; Kenya, *hijabi* women in; Islamic law; Nigeria, Muslims in), ii, iv, v, vi, 7, 12, 20, 25, 27, 57, 62, 64, 67, 71n5, 72n5, 73, 76, 90, 93, 95, 104, 105, 106, 107, 108, 110, 111, 112, 113, 115-118, 120-125, 127, 129, 132-133, 179, 180, 217-235 280, 290, 291, 294-295, 296, 297, 298, 303-304, 397, 407, 408-409, 412, 426n52

Mutemwa, David, 281-282

Mutendi, Nehemiah, 9, 11-12

Mwale, Nelly, 270, 274

N

networked theology (see CITAM Ngong Church)

Niger, iv, 99-110

acceptance and rejection of pandemic measures in, 106-109

armed conflict and terrorism in, 99, 107, 109

Catholics in, 102, 103, 122

Covid-19 regulations and measures in, 100-102, 103, 104, 106-109

Muslims in, 104, 105, 106, 107, 108, 110

public freedoms in, 99, 107, 108

religious authorities in, 102-103

religious and violent extremism in, 99, 100

religious holidays under Covid in, 105-106

religious support for house of worship closure in, 102-104

security threats and insecurity in, 99, 100, 108, 109

Nigeria, iii, iv, v, vi, vii, 4, 53-69, 71-84, 99, 101, 102, 111-125, 127-137, 156, 158, 167-186, 188, 190n15, 287-301, 303-314

Association for Fertility and Reproductive Health (AFRH) in, 310, 314

Bauchi state in, v, 127, 129, 131, 133, 136

Christian responses to Covid in, iv-v, 111, 113, 115, 118-125, 127

Christians in, iv, 54, 60, 62, 67, 71, 73, 77, 111, 113, 115, 118-125, 127, 129, 134, 141, 290, 291, 299, 203

constitutional law of, 53, 54, 55-56, 58, 62-63, 64, 66, 68, 69, 73, 76-77, 78-80, 83, 132, 135, 137, 182

Covid-19 conspiracies in, 167, 168, 171-172, 173-174, 176, 177, 179, 181, 182, 184-185

Covid-19 regulations and in, 53, 54, 58, 59-65, 112, 113, 114, 116, 117, 120, 121, 122, 125, 127-137, 306

customary law in, 75-76, 83

domestic violence in, 287-301

English law in, 75-77-78, 83

freedom of religion in, 53, 54, 55-60, 63, 64, 68, 69, 71n5, 74, 127, 128, 130-134, 136, 298

Federal Capital Territory (Abuja) in, 54n9, 59, 112, 135

infertility treatment in (see also infertility), 287-301

Islamic law in, 75, 76-77, 83

Kaduna State in, 59, 68, 67, 133

Lagos State in, 57, 59124n70, 130, 156, 182. 301, 313

lockdown in, 53, 54, 58, 59, 60, 61, 63, 69, 72, 73, 74, 112, 117, 118, 119, 120, 121, 122, 123, 124, 127, 130-134, 167, 169, 180, 182, 287, 289, 290, 292, 294-301, 305-306, 307, 308, 309, 310, 314

mental health in, 287-301

mobile/virtual courts in, v, 135, 137

451

Muslim responses to Covid in, iv-v, 112-113, 115-118, 120-125

Muslims in, 57, 60, 62, 64, 67, 71n5, 72n5, 73, 76, 127, 129, 132-133, 179, 180, 280, 290, 291, 294-295, 296, 297, 298, 303-304

National Health Act, 2014, in, 310-311

Nigeria Centre for Disease Control and Prevention (NCDC) in, 58-59, 112, 130, 174, 182-183, 184

Nigerian Supreme Council for Islamic Affairs (NSCIA), 60, 64, 180

northern regions of, 75, 76, 77, 83, 127, 128, 129, 131, 132, 133, 136, 174

Ogun State in, 59, 112, 118 122, 130, 182

Plateau State in, v, 127, 129, 133, 136

Presidential Task Force (PTF) in, 112, 120, 123, 129, 136

Quarantine Act, 1926 in, 130, 182, 306

religion-state relation in, 53, 54, 66-69, 74

religious authorities and leaders in, 127, 128, 134, 136-137, 175, 177, 178, 179

religious conflict in, 73, 77, 78, 82, 83, 129

religious and violent extremism in, 82, 132, 133-134, 184-185

secularism in, 65, 66, 79-80, 84, 114, 132

vaccination resistance in, 118. 123, 158, 167, 181

Yoruba people/land of, 114, 289n17

Nomiya Church, Eastleigh (see also Kenya)

African value of communality in, 265-378

bereavement communities in, 354, 355, 357, 361, 365, 366, 369, 371, 372, 374-378

death rituals in, 361, 362, 365

healing and deliverance in Covid in, 351, 354, 355-358, 362, 363

impact of social distancing and worship ban on, 349, 351, 353, 354-355, 357, 358, 362, 365, 366, 375

material support groups in, 353, 358-360, 362, 375, 377

relational theory of, 351, 371-373

virtual communities and worship in, 360, 361, 366, 368-370, 371, 371, 374-378

WhatsApp communities in, 355, 359, 361, 365-378

North Africa (see also Algeria), 87, 88, 94

Nyashanu, Mathew, 253, 258, 266, 270, 281, 283

Nyika, Aceme, 168, 170, 172, 173

O

Obatala traditional religion (see also domestic violence), vii, 289, 290, 291, 292, 293, 294, 298, 299, 300

Onayeikan, John Olorunfemi, 80

Organisation of African Unity (OAU), 81

Oyakhilome, Chris, 30, 61, 173

P

patriarchy, 7, 201, 202, 204, 205, 206, 207, 209, 210, 213, 214, 215, 250, 367

Pentecostal-charismatic Christianity, 19, 26, 46, 401

Pentecostal Christianity (see also Pentecostal-charismatic Christianity), iii, vii, 4n6, 10, 19, 26-27, 28, 35-36, 37, 38, 42-46, 49, 51, 61, 62, 68, 119, 122, 142, 149, 152, 158, 173, 177, 178, 289, 291, 293, 294, 295, 296, 297, 298, 299, 325, 326, 330, 345, 381, 387, 396, 397

Pink, Sarah, 382, 387

poverty, ii, ix, 3, 9, 14, 18, 19, 22, 109, 113, 119, 129, 175, 182, 205, 238, 241, 245, 247, 257, 262, 269, 276, 358, 359, 413, 416, 420, 421n39, 422, 424, 431, 433

pregnancy (see also infertility), 214, 303, 304, 305, 306, 307, 313, 314, 418

prosperity gospel, 36, 49, 396, 404

Protestantism, iii, vii, viii, 35, 37, 38-42, 49, 69, 142, 269, 325, 337, 397, 404, 429, 437-439

public health, i, iii, v, 3, 4, 9, 15, 16, 17, 20-21, 22, 23, 27, 30, 31, 33, 34, 36, 49, 50, 51, 52, 53, 59, 62, 64, 88, 92, 101, 107, 109n41, 120, 127, 130, 131, 133, 134, 136, 137, 151-165, 169, 178, 179, 180, 182, 183, 185, 197, 217, 219, 223, 224, 228, 229, 231, 232, 237, 258, 264, 266, 273-274, 314, 323, 332, 335, 380, 407, 427, 429, 433, 441

and public-health messaging, 151-165

and conflict between faith and science messages
  on Covid-19, 153-155, 156-159
  on HIV/AIDS, 153-156
and strategies for harmonising faith- and science-based messages, 159-164
and studying faith- and science-based messages, 152-153

Q

Quran, 89, 103, 116, 117, 219, 220-222, 291, 396, 407

R

Ramaphosa, Cyril, 428, 432
rape (see also gender-based violence)
Redeemed Christian Church of God (RCCG) (see also Pentecostal Christianity), 122n57, 180
religious freedom and religious liberty (see freedom of religion)
reproductive health, 152, 207, 308, 310, 311, 313, 314, 414
resilience, v, ix, 10, 129, 142-144, 145, 146-147, 150, 181, 202, 366, 367, 374, 378
Rheingold, Howard, 370, 376
Roman Catholicism (see Catholicism)
rural, 7, 119, 134, 137, 188, 237, 261, 305, 415, 416, 417, 418

S

Salafism, 90, 95
Satan, 61, 145, 149, 158, 172, 181, 321, 325, 332, 336, 342, 358, 397, 402, 407
secular/secularism (see Ghana, secularism in; Nigeria, secularism in)
Senegal, 196
sex and gender-based violence (SBGV) (see domestic violence; gender-based violence)
sharia (see Islamic law)
social justice, 71, 72, 322, 423
social media (see Côte d'Ivoire, digitalised cults in; Facebook; Twitter; virtual world; WhatsApp; YouTube) i, v, 6, 9, 27, 30, 118, 122-123, 142, 145, 169, 170, 173, 181, 182, 183, 184, 185, 244, 284, 309, 332, 372, 373, 375, 378, 379, 386, 387, 388, 411, 419

South Africa (see also architecture; food insecurity), xi, 4, 35, 63, 81, 158, 168, 173, 182, 242, 245, 249, 252, 258, 259, 310, 339, 341, 371, 405, 413-426, 427-441
  architecture of churches in, ix, 427-441
  authoritarianism in, 427, 432-433
  constitutional law of, 413, 414-416, 422, 423, 433n33
  Covid-19 regulations and measures in, 427, 428, 429, 430-432, 433, 441
  criminalisation of church attendance in, 427, 430-432
  die Kerk in, 434
  food insecurity in, 413-426
  freedom of religion in, 427, 433
  Integrated Food Security Strategy (IFSS) in, 414
  Integrated Nutrition Programme in, 515
  National Policy on Food and Nutrition Security in, 416
  National School Nutrition Programme in, 415
  poverty in, 413, 416, 420, 421n39, 422, 424, 431, 433
  Reconstruction and Development Programme (RDP) in, 414, 417
  Reformed Church in, 406, 437-438
South Sudan, 5n10
sub-Saharan Africa, 151, 153, 154, 156, 167, 276
Sultan of Sokoto, 64, 180
Sustainable Development Goals (SDGs), 211, 247
sunnah (See Islamic law)
The Synagogue, Church of All Nations (SCOAN), 156, 177
syncretism (see also Botswana, syncretism healing atonement motif in), viii, 142, 336, 337, 340-342, 346-347, 395

T

Tanzania, 152, 156, 158, 172, 175, 176, 196
Togarasei, Lovemore, 35, 339, 363
Tutu, Desmond, 371
Twitter, 119, 170, 181, 184, 373, 388

U

Ubuntu, 371, 372, 378
Uganda, v, 152, 157
Ulema (see Islam)
unemployment, 14, 169, 238, 2412, 247, 256n41, 359, 416, 418, 419, 422, 424, 433
United Church of Zambia (UCZ) (see Zambia, UCZ in), vii, 269-285
  communication in, 280, 283-284
  Covid response of, 275-276, 284
  five golden rules against Covid, 273, 274, 275, 276
  self-reliance and self-sustenance in, 282-283
  suspension of sacraments and traditions in, 275, 279, 282
  women in, vii, 269-285
    economic experiences of, 278-279, 285
    social experiences of, 277-278, 285
    spiritual experiences of, 279-280, 285
    use of African traditional medicine by, 281-282, 285
United Kingdom (see Britain)
United States, 67, 125, 179, 196, 379, 242
Universal Declaration of Human Rights (UDHR), 55, 56, 136, 251n12, 256n41, 350
urban areas, iv, 7, 37, 39, 42, 44, 119, 178, 182, 237, 239, 240, 244, 247, 261, 269n6, 317, 359, 361, 367, 379, 381, 415, 416, 417, 418, 421n39, 431n18, 438

V

vaccination (see also Kenya; South Africa), i, 12, 13n41, 43, 50, 110, 157-158, 175-176, 179, 193, 203, 309, 314, 329
  conspiracy theories about (see conspiracy theories on Covid-19)
  government requirement of, 6, 8n27, 11-12, 34, 43, 44, 45, 192
  hesitancy and resistance to, i, vi, 5n10, 50-51, 157-158, 168, 184, 188-197, 329
  religious discrimination over, vi, 167-169, 170
  religious perspectives on, 6 12, 39, 40, 41, 43, 44, 45, 46, 47, 157-158, 168, 191, 342-343
virginity, 202, 206, 207, 210
virtual courts (see Nigeria, mobile and virtual courts in)
virtual world (see also digital ethnography; digital religion), v, vii, ix, 148, 150
  and communication, vii, 145, 295
  and community, vii, 145, 146, 147, 150, 360-362, 368-378, 379-371
  and worship, 9, 64, 72n8, 147, 360-362, 379-371
vulnerability, i, vi, vii, 14, 19, 22, 119, 120, 131, 136, 137, 168, 170, 199, 201, 238, 241, 245, 246, 247, 250, 252, 253, 266, 269, 275, 275, 279, 280, 282, 283, 285, 310, 360, 418, 420, 426n52

W

Waaba (see Benin, Waaba people of)
water, 22, 117, 159, 193, 231, 247, 256, 262, 263, 266, 282, 352, 360, 418, 425
  holy or healing water, 48, 61, 120, 156, 177, 325, 328, 341, 358
  right to water, vii, 5, 14, 238, 254-256, 262, 414
  and sanitation, 27, 180, 181n5, 247, 274, 369, 373
  and steaming remedies, 175, 181n45, 281-282, 328, 329, 345, 349
  theologies of, viii, 345
weddings, vii, 102n17, 105, 108, 269, 275, 277, 284, 374, 437
Western culture, 49, 84, 88, 116, 133, 187, 196, 312, 321, 339, 342, 349, 433
  and medical, healthcare and healing methods and systems, iii, viii, 8, 12, 46, 83n59, 312, 313, 318, 319, 321, 325, 337, 339, 344, 347, 351, 352
  and perceptions of African traditional medicine, 317, 319, 321
WhatsApp, 266, 279, 283, 284, 343, 355, 359, 361, 365-378, 388, 389
widows, 121n55, 256n41, 262
witchcraft, 320, 321, 330, 333, 340, 341, 353

women, i, ii-vii, 26, 41, 45, 99n2, 100, 115, 116, 163, 189, 201-215, 217-235, 237-248, 249-267, 269-285, 287, 291-292, 293, 294, 295-296, 303, 304, 307, 310, 313, 314, 339, 367, 374, 375-376, 384, 396

    access to technology of, 283-284

    and domestic violence, 287-301

    domestic work of, 265

    economic activity of, 204, 208, 213, 227, 276, 278-279, 285

    living with HIV, 249-267

    mental health of, 287-301

    and Muslim *hijab*, 217-235

    and sexual dignity of, 201-215

    in the United Church of Zambia, 269-285

World Health Organization (WHO), i, 15, 112, 120, 128, 153, 168, 187, 237, 249, 252, 287, 321-323, 335, 349, 350, 428

Y

YouTube, 9, 170, 181, 363, 370, 388, 409, 434, 441

Z

Zambia, vii, 269-285

    access to communications and technology in, vii, 283-284, 285

    Christians in (see also United Church of Zambia), 270, 272, 275, 280, 282

    Covid-19 regulations and measures in, 269, 270, 271, 272, 273-274, 275, 276, 277, 279, 280, 281, 282, 284, 285

    gender-based violence in, 276, 280-281, 285

    lockdown and curfew in, 270, 272, 276, 278-281, 284, 285

    United Church of Zambia (UCZ) in (see also United Church of Zambia (UCZ), vii, 269-285

    women in, vii, 269-285

Zimbabwe, iii, vii-viii, 3-14, 33-52, 177, 237-248, 249-267, 317-334, 339

    African indigenous churches in, iii, 4, 6, 7-8, 9, 35, 36, 37, 46-48, 50-51, 325, 326

    African traditional medicine in, vii-viii, 317, 319, 320, 321, 322, 323, 330-334

    Christians in, 4n6, 6, 7, 9, 35, 37, 38, 39, 49, 51, 54, 317, 318, 320, 321, 325-333

    constitutional law of, 3, 4-5, 8, 11, 12, 13, 14, 33-34, 35, 39, 41, 42, 43, 51, 52, 241, 250, 251, 252n21, 255, 256, 257, 258, 259, 350

    Covid-19 regulations and measures in, 3, 4, 6, 8, 9-10, 11, 13, 14, 33-34, 36, 37, 39, 40, 41, 42, 43, 45, 46, 47, 48, 51, 52, 237, 238, 239, 240, 241, 242, 243, 244, 245, 246, 247, 249, 250, 253, 254, 258, 259, 260, 261, 265, 327, 335

    freedom of religion in, iii, 3, 4, 5, 11, 12, 13, 14, 33, 34, 35, 37, 42, 41, 43, 51-52, 234, 235, 258-259

    informal labour and economic sectors in, vi, 237-248

    Johanne Marange Apostolic Church in, 6, 10-11, 12-13, 36, 37, 46-48, 50-51, 326, 330

    Johanne Masowe Church in, 10

    lockdown and curfew in, 10, 11, 12, 13n41, 14, 33, 34, 39, 42, 43, 52, 237-247, 249-255, 259-267, 326, 327, 330

    Reformed Church in Zimbabwe (RCZ), 38-42, 49, 51

    women living with HIV in, vii, 249-267

Zimbabwe United Passenger Company (ZUPCO), 240-241, 261